James Petigru
BOYCE

AMERICAN REFORMED BIOGRAPHIES

D. G. HART AND SEAN MICHAEL LUCAS
Series Editors

Robert Lewis Dabney: A Southern Presbyterian Life
John Williamson Nevin: High Church Calvinist
Cornelius Van Til: Reformed Apologist and Churchman

James Petigru
BOYCE

A Southern Baptist Statesman

THOMAS J. NETTLES

PUBLISHING

P.O. BOX 817 • PHILLIPSBURG • NEW JERSEY 08865-0817

Page design by Lakeside Design Plus

Printed in the United States of America

Library of Congress Cataloging-in-Publication Data

Nettles, Tom J.
  James Petigru Boyce : a Southern Baptist statesman / Thomas J. Nettles.
      p. cm.
  Includes bibliographical references and index.
  ISBN 978-0-87552-664-5 (cloth)
  1. Boyce, James Petigru, d. 1888. 2. Southern Baptist Theological Seminary—
History. I. Title.
  BV4070.L759B7 2009
  286'.1092—dc22
  [B]
                                    2009005804

To the late Ernest C. Reisinger,

*through whose vision and generosity
a generation of Southern Baptist pastors
was introduced to the theology of
James Petigru Boyce*

Contents

Series Preface

"All history is biography," Ralph Waldo Emerson once remarked. Emerson's aphorism still contains a good deal of truth. History is the memory and record of past human lives, thus making biography the most basic form of historical knowledge. To understand any event, period, or text from the past, some acquaintance with specific persons is crucial.

The popularity of biography among contemporary book buyers in America supports this insight. Recent biographies of John Adams and Ben Franklin have encouraged many—who fear for America's historical amnesia—to believe that a keen and formidable interest in history still exists among the nation's reading public. To be sure, the source of this interest could be the stature and influence of the subjects themselves—the founding fathers of the United States. Still, the accessibility of biography—its concrete subject matter, intimate scope, and obvious relevance—suggests that the reason for the recent success of these biographies is in the genre of writing itself.

American Reformed Biographies, coedited by D. G. Hart and Sean Michael Lucas, seeks to nurture this general interest in biography as a way of learning about and from the past. The titles in this series feature American Reformed leaders who were important representatives or interpreters of Reformed Christianity in the United States and who continue to be influential through writings and arguments still pertinent to the self-understanding of Presbyterian and Reformed theologians, pastors, and church members. The aim is to provide learned treatments of men and women that will be accessible to readers from a wide variety of backgrounds—biography that is both sufficiently scholarly to be of service to academics and those with proficiency in American church history and adequately accessible to engage the nonspecialist. Consequently, these books are more introductory than definitive, with the aim of giving an overview of a figure's thought and contribution, along with suggestions for further study.

The editors have sought authors who are sympathetic to Reformed Christianity and to their subjects, who regard biography not merely as a celebration of past accomplishments but also as a chance to ask difficult questions of both the past and the present in order to gain greater insight into Christian faith and practice. As such, American Reformed Biographies is designed to make available the best kind of historical writing—one that yields both knowledge and wisdom.

Acknowledgments

Bringing to culmination this project would have been impossible without the help of some people who are very good at what they do. I thank the editors, Darryl Hart and Sean Lucas, for including me in this publishing project. I thank Presbyterian and Reformed Publishers for willingness to include a Baptist theologian, J. P. Boyce, in the series.

Several people have helped me gain access to material. Foremost has been the staff of the archives at the J. P. Boyce Memorial Library at the Southern Baptist Theological Seminary. Jason Fowler and Chris Dewease in particular have been immediately responsive to every request that I have had for archival material concerning Boyce or others with whom his life intertwined. One of the coeditors of this series, Sean Lucas, was archivist in this library for several years and, while there, helped put together a most valuable source for research on Boyce. Sean and Jason Fowler transcribed and printed most of the correspondence between Boyce and his intimate friend John A. Broadus from the years 1857–88. The reader will quickly learn that I have used that source in full and with increasing appreciation with every quote. The Southern Baptist Library and Archives in Nashville, Tennessee, where Bill Sumner is archivist also gave excellent help at one critical juncture of putting together some missing pieces of Boyce's financial responsibility. Also Carol Jones at the Charleston Library Society sent me a catalogue of

11

the books that were available to Boyce during his childhood as well as some other bits of information about the Boyces in Charleston. John Aloisi, my teaching assistant, provided editorial aid.

Greg Wills, colleague par excellence, worked on the 150th anniversary history of Southern Seminary at the same time I was laboring on Boyce. He provided encouragement, provocative questions, and hints about source material on some issues. R. Albert Mohler Jr. and Russell Moore, president and academic vice-president of the seminary that Boyce founded, have provided encouragement, scholarly example, and opportunity for academic labors through a generous sabbatical leave program.

The most courageous and selfless encourager I have had has been my soul mate, wife, and friend Margaret. She has urged me forward when I felt overwhelmed, read chapters and offered helpful advice, kept up with family and social items, and prayed earnestly. I would not have finished this without her.

Introduction

*J*ames Petigru Boyce fits well into Brooks Holifield's category of Gentlemen Theologians. In the list of Baptists that he included in this category we find Boyce along with two of the teachers that partnered with Boyce on the first faculty at the Southern Baptist Theological Seminary, John A. Broadus and Basil Manly Jr. William Williams, the fourth member of that first faculty, also could have fit the announced criteria of Holifield. In addition, Holifield lists the pastors under whom Boyce sat for his first eighteen years of life, Basil Manly Sr. and William T. Brantly Sr.[1]

Boyce certainly was a gentleman. Reared in a gentleman's home, he found the developing culture of the cities of the South much to his liking. Far from being in the middle class of most of the men Holifield discussed, Boyce fit into the category of the wealthy, having real estate in 1860 worth over $120,000 and a personal estate worth over $330,000. Raised as a South Carolinian in Little London, Charleston, he gladly embraced the taste for exquisite culture fostered carefully by his predecessors. His daughters bore testimony to his love of fashion, beautiful textiles, elegant book bindings, art, music, punctuality, and his delight in trees, glaciers, flowers, quaint houses, social grace, and impeccable manners. They were quite amused and amazed that "carpets, curtains, table linen, furniture, china and silver were purchased by him with no advice

13

or assistance on the part of his family." These tasks gave him the "greatest pleasure."

In considering how to please others, Boyce "always showed a remarkable faculty in the choice of beautiful and unique presents." Giving culture to his children was a personal project, joining them in lessons in French and German, buying them "quantities of beautiful and expensive books and magazines to enhance the pleasure of the studies and give [them] every opportunity possible to the acquisition of the language." He built a large library prior to the Civil War but had to diminish his indulgence in book buying under the more straitened conditions after the war. "I have heard him say," one of his daughters related, "that it caused him positive pain to see beautifully bound or illustrated books and not possess them." A trip to California and a horse ride into Yosemite Valley produced exactly the effect on his daughters and wife that Boyce reveled in: "It seemed to us impossible how that anything could be more beautiful—the snowy cliffs bathed in the last gleams of the sun, the atmosphere of shimmering blue, the magnificent trees, the cascades, the ever-changing vistas all combined to make a scene that brought to our minds the description of the mountains from which Bunyan's Pilgrim was said to look on the beautiful land of Beulah."

Though he had no personal talent for painting or drawing, he developed "excellent judgment, and great critical ability fully appreciating good drawing" along with "an excellent eye for color. He cultivated his taste in this direction by constant visits to art exhibitions." Boyce ordered flowers for the garden in Greenville and taught the Latin names to his eldest daughter. She recalled, "These flowers were called by their botanical terms and very learned it sounded to my childish ears and much it astonished me to hear the tremendous Latin names with which even the tiniest flowers were named. I learned many of them and it was a source of amusement to Father and Mother to hear me use them."

Music was a part of every well-rounded gentleman's life, and Boyce made it a point to be learned on the subject. When on trips to New York, Boyce attended symphony concerts and oratorios, and made sure to hear every great singer. He went from Greenville to Charleston to hear Carlotta Patti and told his daughters many times "of the exquisite pleasure he had in hearing Jenny Lind sing 'I Know That My Redeemer Liveth' at Covent Garden." His daughters also were sure that if any young man or young lady wanted to know how to conduct oneself in public, one should take their father's lessons in etiquette.[2]

Boyce shared the intellectual outlook of his Gentlemen Theologian peers. He affirmed, contrary to Thomas Paine and Thomas Jefferson, the authenticity of Scripture, its defensibility as revelation using rational arguments, the competence of the mind in engaging evidence, and the integrity of subject/object relationships as defined in Thomas Reid's commonsense philosophy. Reid's understanding of corporate experience and rational discourse built on such experience was important in Boyce's argument for the Bible as a deposit of revelation. Boyce joined the conservatives, and resisted the liberals, in affirming that each individual doctrine of Scripture, such as the Trinity, does not have to pass muster before the sentinel of reason as an autonomous authority, once the authority that affirms the doctrine, that is, the Bible, has been authenticated as revelation.

Boyce believed in the unity of truth since the creator also was the upholder and redeemer. He accepted the traditional arguments for the existence of God as compelling, eschewing David Hume's skepticism. Unlike some of his peers he found the ontological argument the most intrinsically powerful but admitted that the a posteriori argument seemed more plausible to most people. He believed in the convincing power of Christian evidences and studied *Elements of Moral Science* under the quintessential ethicist in mid–nineteenth-century America, Francis Wayland. Boyce, however, went beyond the normal categories of moral science in his discussion of ethics and saw the Christian standard as embodied in the voluntary character of God manifest in the incarnation and sacrifice of Christ.

Boyce also shared the Southern political commitment to the sovereignty of the states and the potential greatness of the South through the wise execution of the institution of slavery. Boyce, nevertheless, believed that the Union of the states had great advantages for all, and he was pleased that his father had opposed nullification in 1832 when Boyce was five, and Boyce himself opposed secession in 1860.

He wanted to see the South make a proposal of conditions for operation together on the basis of perfect equality, a proposal surely to be rejected by the North, but putting the North entirely in the wrong through their rejection of these Southern overtures for compromise. Then the North, and not the South, would be responsible for separation. His views on nullification and secession, however, did not diminish his strong sense of states' rights or his commitment to the Confederacy once secession had occurred. He worked for the financial stability of the Confederate government in the South Carolina legislature and served as a chaplain in the Confederate Army and as aide-de-camp to Governor Magrath, holding the rank of lieutenant colonel. Subsequent to the war he explained the situation to a young nephew:

> While you are in Virginia you will hear a great deal about the war, and see many men who have been in battle. Suppose you keep a little book, and whenever you hear any matter of interest write it down in your book, being particular to keep the dates and names of persons perfectly correct, and to state the events as fully as you can recollect them. Always be accurate, only putting down what you know was said, and also the name of the narrator. . . . Whatever else may be the verdict of history,—let its writers be so befogged as to believe that the North fought to free the slaves, and not for its own selfish interests of gain, and that the South fought to defend slavery, and not the constitutional rights of the States,—one thing is sure, that history must accord to the Confederate army in Virginia, under Generals Lee, Jackson, and others, the exhibition of fortitude, bravery, chivalric courtesy, and knightly courage never surpassed in any nation or period of time. Try then to hear of these things, and remember.[3]

Boyce knew that the South must change after the war, and he worked to contribute positively to that change and to restore relations with Baptist brethren in the North, but he did not want it forgotten that the South had been noble and its leadership great.

Boyce accepted with full confidence the task described by Jon Butler as the "African Spiritual Holocaust," the conversion of the slaves to Christianity. Butler argues that "slavery's destruction of

African religious systems in America constituted not only wholesale cultural robbery but cultural robbery of a quite vicious sort." Butler makes his case through studying the systematic breakdown of African native religion among the colonial slaves, a "holocaust that destroyed collective African religious practice in colonial America," to be replaced by Christianization in antebellum, postrevolutionary America. According to Butler, the "systems" that gave coherence, meaning, beauty, security, and hope to Africans were destroyed but individual practices survived. Religious practices according to system were reorganized to be consistent with the dominant religious persuasion of their captors and a crippling system of affectionate regard known as "paternalism." The original culturally appropriate and helpful religious systems of native Africans "collapsed in the shattering cultural destructiveness of British slaveholding."[4] Butler's analysis of this process reveals much about the systematic deconstruction of the societal humanity of Africans who had come from a wide variety of backgrounds and the complicity of Christian ministers in this process. His argument also reveals his tenaciously held commitment to the cultural origins of all religion, including Christianity.

Boyce inherited a mature system of paternalism and embraced its definitions of the relation between slave and master fully. Boyce, in addition, testified to a transcendent concern for his slaves and the entire population of African slaves. Along with others in his social and religious position, he believed that God had committed a special stewardship to Christians, especially Baptists, of the South in preaching and teaching the gospel to the slaves entrusted to their care. While it is difficult to grasp how a conscientious Christian could be convictionally sympathetic to the arguments for slavery, one must concede that after the perspective of one hundred fifty years, the resultant social changes induced by the Civil War, and several cultural revolutions, including a major conflict in the civil rights movement, the context of our reception to arguments is quite different from Boyce's. He, like his peers, found the exegetical argument sound, and that trumped every other concern.

The peculiar obligations resting on Southern Christians were taken too lightly, Boyce believed, and part of the divine retribution for not evangelizing with sufficient love and zeal was the removal of slavery. However slavery may have been defined culturally, politically, and economically, Boyce knew that the religious dimension had infinitely greater importance than any of those transient and temporal matters. Hopefully, he would have changed his mind about slavery as an honorable arrangement for melding a "degraded" race into a society dominated by the economic concerns of the Americanized Anglo-Europeans of the South. In time he would have conceded that the slave system was insensitive cultural brutality and racial superiority a myth. He would have approved the justness in the observation that some religions in particular and much about religion in general, even Christianity, were socially constructed. Boyce would see that as intrinsic to humanity's rebellion against God. But that the message of Christ's incarnation and atoning work and the operations of the Holy Spirit to bring about repentance from sin and faith in Jesus Christ—his commitment to the doctrines of grace and justification by faith—were only the results of social forces he did not and would never embrace. These, Boyce remained convinced, are revealed from the mind and purpose of God by the Holy Spirit and will never change from one generation to another nor from one culture to another.

Central to everything in his life was his commitment to the gospel of Jesus Christ. His particular gift in service of the gospel was the teaching of theology. This was present in his mind from the earliest days of his remembrance when he heard from the family pew the theologically driven pastoral messages of Basil Manly Sr. and then William T. Brantly Sr. His study at Brown under Francis Wayland reinforced this, and his conversion under the preaching of Richard Fuller showed him the transforming power of coherent doctrine fervently proclaimed and applied. His experience as an editor of a denominational newspaper steeled his spirit for a life of theological controversy, and his education at Princeton provided an elongated demonstration of the clarity and transsectarian applicability of the great doctrinal truths of Reformed Christianity. His preaching experience at Columbia, South Carolina, followed by his teaching theology at Furman gave him an invincible conviction affirming the usefulness of theology, Calvinistic theology, in the churches.

However much Boyce's background might have predisposed him to elitism, his theological conviction and his zeal for the strength and purity of Baptist churches drove him to an unrelenting advocacy of theological education for Baptist preachers from every level of social standing, economic condition, and educational preparation, that is, among white Southerners. The recurring chorus of every public message, the driving theme of every promotional speech, the intensified focus of every explanation of the seminary's goal had the theological curriculum, with systematic theology as the centerpiece, as its theme. Every preacher should get theological education in some way. Such study helps clarify and strengthen the necessary activity of biblical exegesis, it gives power and coherence to preaching, Boyce argued, and it keeps God-in-Christ at the center of life and ministry. Find an older and capable preacher to study with, get a few good books and master them, or go to seminary—but do it somehow, and the best way is the seminary.

Boyce lived and breathed theological education. For the preacher it greatly transcended classical education in importance. If one must choose between them, choose theology. He used his influence to begin the school, he sought to stabilize Confederate currency to salvage the endowment of the school, he used his personal finances as collateral to support the school, he ruined his health in moving the school to a more secure environment, and he drove himself to death in assuring both the financial and theological stability of the school. When he died, the last audible utterance from his lips concerned the seminary and his friends, the professors. As he lay dying in Pau, France,

> he was out of his head a great deal and in his wanderings his talk was mainly always of the Seminary. We would constantly catch the names of the different professors. The day before he died he was conscious for several hours but could not talk as his tongue was much swollen. He recognized us and pressed our hands and returned our kisses but did not attempt to talk. The English clergyman whom we called on to visit him, saw him for a few moments that morning and

prayed and talked with him. Father said a good deal to him but it was impossible to understand what he was saying. He soon became unconscious remaining so until the end.[5]

Boyce distinguished between the permanent and the transient. He treasured much that was transient but was willing to accept, and even to effect, change when he saw it to be necessary. The permanent, however, he would never surrender. To those projects designed to promote the eternal, to prepare a gospel ministry, to elevate divine truth, to these he gave his time, his energy, his money, and finally his life.

The First Two Decades

t. Paul wrote with deepest solemnity, "Moreover it is required in stewards, that a man be found faithful."[1] Born on 11 January 1827, James Petigru Boyce, the first child of his father's second marriage, had more than his share of responsibility. Named after a brilliant and distinguished lawyer, reared in the cultured city of Charleston, shaped mentally in the home of the most astute and successful businessman of Charleston and perhaps all of South Carolina, trained spiritually in his mother's church, the first and leading Baptist church of the South, served by the most able and theologically sound and clear pastors of the Baptist denomination, and granted every advantage that culture and education could afford a son of the South in the first half of the nineteenth century, Boyce's life would be a testimony to a stewardship embraced and well executed. Given an opportunity to live his days in benign leisure, Boyce chose a course that presented a most arduous and unrelenting challenge to his time, energy, wealth, health, and faith, and inspired others to follow in his train.

First Baptist Church, Charleston

In 1682, the First Baptist Church of Boston, Massachusetts, by means of a committee sent for the purpose, recognized that a congregation in

Kittery, Maine, had a "Competent Number" and held the "same faith with us." The congregation had "given themselves up to ye Lord & too one Another in A Solemn Covenant," had chosen their officers, and had already suffered for their Baptist cause. The committee helped the congregation set aside their officers by ordination, and upon their recommendation, the Boston church, "in ye name of ye Lord Jesus & by the Appointmtt of his church" recognized them "to be a Church of Christ in ye faith and order of ye Gospel."[2] Their recognition as a church by the sponsoring body took place on 25 September 1682.

The "faith" that Boston and Kittery held in common had only recently been given a succinct formulated expression when in 1677 the Particular Baptists of London adopted a confession of faith much like that of the Presbyterians in 1646 and the Independents in 1658 in the Westminster Confession of Faith and the Savoy Declaration respectively. The Boston committee examined the Kittery group on that very point and found them orthodox. The covenant mentioned probably is the earliest example of a Baptist covenant in America. They promised to "walk with God & one with another In A dew and faithful observance of all his most holy & blessed commandm.tts Ordinances Institutions or Appointments, revealed to us in his sacred word of ye ould & new Testament and according to ye grace of God & light att presently through his grace given us." It was signed by ten men and seven women.[3]

Fourteen years later, after a brief time of opposition in Kittery, followed by several years of toleration due to a changing political situation that saw William Screven the pastor participating in the civil affairs of the town, the church moved from Maine to Charleston, South Carolina. A more favorable situation for shipbuilding, the presence of other dissenters and Baptists in Charleston, and the appointment of Joseph Blake as governor all possibly played their part in the move.[4] Whatever else might have been determining factors, the thirty persons that accompanied Screven on the difficult and long journey in 1696 engaged it as a religious pilgrimage and became the first Baptist church in the South. Eventually other Baptists united with the church.[5]

The First Baptist Church of Boston asked Screven, then seventy-eight years old, to come serve as their pastor in 1707. He could not do it for, as he explained, "our minister who came from England is dead, and I can by no means be spared," but he suggested that they "improve the gifts you have in the church." This they did and Screven wrote again: "I have been brought very low by sickness; but I bless God I was helped to preach and administer the communion last Lord's day, but I am still weak. Our society are for the most part in health, and I hope thriving in grace. We are about ninety in all. I rest your affectionate brother and fellow laborer, in the best of services, for the best reward."[6] Upon his stepping down as pastor, Screven urged the church in procuring a pastor to "take care that the person be orthodox in faith, and of blameless life, and does own the confession of faith put forth by our brethren in London in 1689."[7]

Screven's counsel proved insightful, for the failure of the church scrupulously to heed it led to severe difficulties. During the next thirty-five years, dissension within the church between the General Baptist faction and the Particular Baptist majority almost brought the church to nothing until it rebounded around 1747 through the influence of a great revival in Charleston under the preaching of George Whitefield. The stability of the church was secured by the coming of Oliver Hart in 1750. He was succeeded by Richard Furman from 1787 to 1825. Then came Basil Manly Sr., who served from 1826 through 1837, followed by William T. Brantley Sr. from 1837 to 1845. The scrupulous adherence to confessional Calvinism promoted by Screven made its way through the generations to James Petigru Boyce and formed the foundation of his lifework.

Charleston, South Carolina

The city in which the church settled was barely over twenty-five years old. It was part of a land grant given by the restored monarchy in England subsequent to the Cromwellian interlude. In two separate grants, 20 March 1663 and 30 June 1665, the entrepreneurial John Colleton and his friend Lord Ashley Cooper along with six men who had the confidence of the crown received appointment as lords proprietor of a tract of land from 29 degrees latitude to 36 degrees 30 minutes latitude. This included land from the very edge of Spanish Florida in the south to the border of Virginia in the north. Two earlier attempts at populating the vast lands south of Virginia had produced only slight results, but Colleton, a high official in Barbados, sought this site as an opportunity to expand the profitable, but geographically straitened, sugar economy of Barbados. One exploratory venture into the land came upon a chief of the Kiawah tribe who reported that a deep and broad harbor existed in a fertile land further south. Among the allurements publicized in seeking people willing to settle this promising but undeveloped southern climate was the proposal that its people, like those that lived in Barbados, "shall have the freedom of Trade, Immunity of Customes, and Liberty of Conscience." A later tract promised among the many advantages of settlement in Carolina "full and free Liberty of Conscience granted to all, so that no man is to be molested or called in question for matters of Religious Concern."[8]

Precisely during the time of these guarantees, religious intolerance, through the increasingly harsh and unreasonable constrictions of the Clarendon Code, had gripped the throat of church life in England with a stranglehold that threatened to suffocate the very life from all English dissent. Developments in the settlement gave even greater appearance of advantage in a movement to Carolina. The original settlement was of ninety-two persons from England and sixty from Barbados. They eventually slid twenty-five miles south of their original site, Bulls Bay, into a place on the western bank of the Ashley River that they named Charles Town. By 1672, because of the rapid increase in immigration to the promising new venture, three colonies were formed, the original Charles Town with James Town and Oyster Point added. Oyster Point became the most pleasant and economically promising of these because of its location at the confluence of the Ashley and Cooper rivers, originally called by their Indian names Etiwah and Kiawah. Lots for houses were granted there from 1677. This was the place of the deep harbor so celebrated by the Kiawah chief ten years before and became what presently is known as Charleston.

The first settlers from Barbados brought slaves with them to work the rich fields. The slave population hovered as a small minority throughout the last third of the seventeenth century but by 1720, in the Low Country where Charleston was located, the percentage shifted to 65 percent slave and 35 percent free, corresponding almost completely as black to white. By 1740, out of a population of 60,000 in the entire colony, 20,000 were white and 40,000 were black. Some free blacks also employed black slave labor. Increase of commerce called for expansion of agricultural enterprise and the corresponding importation of 42,000 more slaves from 1760 through 1774. Almost all of these came to the Low Country. Charleston became party to a centuries-long slave trade that had begun in sub-Sahara Islamic empires and had involved the transporting of African slaves to Islamic communities from Spain to India. In the early sixteenth century, Europeans dipped into this vast reservoir of human merchandise and continued the practice with only gradual and late abatements until beyond the middle of the nineteenth century. Of the 10,000,000 men, women, and children that were transported from their homes along the western coast of Africa to various destinies, including Spanish America, Brazil, the British Caribbean, the French Caribbean, a variety of locations in Dutch America, British North America, and after 1776 the United States, about 160,000 of these arrived in Charleston.[9]

In July of 1736, Charles Wesley, leaving Georgia and its traumatic difficulties to return to England, stopped in Charleston on his way out. He observed some of the worst horrors of slavery as an eyewitness and heard other accounts that he believed to be authentic regarding the relations of master to slave. His *Journal* recorded the horrific realities encouraged by the private ownership of human property.

> I had observed much, and heard more, of the cruelty of masters towards their negroes, but I received an authentic account of some horrid instances thereof at Charleston before I set out on my return voyage to England. . . . The giving a child a slave of its own to tyrannize, to beat and abuse out of sport, was, I myself saw, a common practice. Nor is it strange, being thus trained up in cruelty, they should afterwards arrive at so great perfection in it; that Mr. Star, a gentleman I often met at Mr. Lassere's, should as he himself informed Lassere, first nail up a negro by the ears, then order him to be whipped in the severest manner, and then to have scalding water thrown over him, so that the poor creature could not stir for four months after.[10]

Wesley also remarked that the government practically countenanced such cruelty and underwrote the murder of slaves by its policy of levying a fine of only seven pounds for the killing of a slave, "half of which is usually saved by the criminal's informing against himself."[11] When this anecdote from the journal of Wesley became a part of abolitionist fodder in their attack on the slave system, Southerners cast aspersions on the credibility of Wesley and impugned the sensationalism of abolitionist methodology. E. T. Winkler, editor of the *Southern Baptist*, wrote in 1852 that no such rejection of Wesley's credibility was necessary, particularly since knowledge of his character would make such a dismissal itself incredible. Nor could present polemics "remove this stigma from our forefathers." Instead, he opined, "We believe that slavery, like every other lawful institution, is susceptible of abuse." Many abuses, as a result of wise legislation, had been removed in the intervening decades. "By shaking off evils that once drew upon it the unqualified reprobation of philanthropists," Winkler surmised, "it has demonstrated an existence independent of these evils." More, however, remained to be done, especially in the area of religious instruction.[12] Boyce, sharing Winkler's confidence in the biblical legitimacy of slavery, also knew that its former abuses had left a residue of bitterness virtually impossible to erase; and its present form, one hundred twenty-five years subsequent to Wesley, retained injustices, at both the personal and the political level, that led Boyce to lament, "I believe I see in all this the end of slavery. I believe we are cutting its throat, curtailing its domain. . . . I feel that our sins as to this institution have cursed us."[13]

Though religious liberty eventually molded the character of the colony, its first settlers had few deeply religious concerns. Erskine Clarke notes that "these early settlers were an aggressive, ambitious lot, often unscrupulous, certainly with only a minimum of concern for the common good of the colony."[14] Other early observers made equally unflattering notes: "Bold adventurers," according to the Presbyterian pastor Alexander Hewat, "who improved every hour for advancing their interest, and could bear no restraints which had the least tendency to defeat their favorite views and designs." An Anglican minister, speaking of the group that Robert Weir described as "pirates ashore," expressed with unoptimistic candor, "The people here, generally speaking, are the vilest race of men upon the earth."[15]

The colony's proprietors, however, wanted the colony to be more than a haven for land-bound privateers, and began to make overtures to stable and sturdy folk with deep-seated religious convictions. New England Puritans found the opportunity for economic advantage attractive and the policy of religious freedom not at all onerous. Small Reformed communities asked successfully for pastoral provision from Massachusetts.[16] Soon persons came from places where religious persecution was most intense, including English dissenters from the west of England suffering from the intolerant provisions of the Clarendon Code, Scottish covenanters in danger of losing their Presbyterianism because of the repressive and murderous religious policies of Charles II and James II, and Calvinists from France, increasingly under repression culminating in the revocation of the Edict of Nantes in 1685. Huguenots surged into the cities of Europe escaping the ravages of French Catholic intolerance, and some settled among the Scots who had emigrated to the northeast part of Ireland. From there both sides of James Boyce's family came to America.

The Boyces

James P. Boyce and James R. Boise, of Brown University, corresponded about their names and found no fewer than twenty forms of it in six languages. John Broadus judged, "There is some reason to believe that all were primarily of Huguenot origin, their ancestors having emigrated, when banished from France, to the north of Ireland, where they found Protestant sympathy."[17] "Boyces" of various spellings settled in Virginia, North Carolina, and South Carolina, as well as in New England.

J. P. Boyce's grandfather, John Boyce, was born in Ireland and moved to North America in 1765. He fought for American freedom in the Revolutionary War after having married Elizabeth Miller in 1777. He fought in the company of his brother, Captain Alexander Boyce, and performed consistently with acts of bravery and daring, and "lived long after the war, enjoying the rich blessings of the glorious liberty for which he had periled so much."[18] When his wife died in 1797 she left him with seven sons and a daughter, Robert, John, David, Alexander, Ker, James, Andrew, and Mary. John Boyce served as an elder in the Presbyterian congregation in Newberry, South Carolina, more than 120 miles from Charleston, and reared his children in the nurture and admonition of the Lord and with keen wit and a penchant for tireless industry.

His son Ker, born 8 April 1787, established himself as a merchant in Newberry. Through shrewd business practices, good humor, and relentless energy, Ker Boyce began to establish the practices, contacts, and capital base that led to his acquisition of great wealth by the mid-nineteenth century. In 1815 he married Nancy Johnston, daughter of a Scotch-Irish family, devoted Presbyterians. Boyce moved to Charleston in 1817 and entered into business partnership with his brother-in-law Samuel Johnston. They engaged in a variety of business initiatives including an immensely lucrative enterprise as cotton factors, supplying both capital and supplies for cotton planters for repayment with interest. Sometimes the legal arrangement involved a lien on the crop. Boyce and his wife lost a child, David, in December 1821, and held the funeral at their home at 382 King Street on December 24.[19] Very soon after that, his business partner Johnston died in 1822.

Subsequent to Johnston's death, Ker Boyce formed partnerships with two other men, Henry and Walter. Boyce's wife died in 1823. The financial panic of 1825 had the potential to ruin the small fortune that Boyce had amassed, but his business skill, determination, and trustworthiness observed by the president of Planters' and Mechanics' Bank enabled him to remain solvent.[20] Later that year, in October, he sought to form a marriage with his deceased wife's nineteen-year-old sister, Amanda Jane Caroline Johnston. The Presbyterians refused to solemnize the marriage, and Boyce, therefore, resorted to the Baptists, who found no reason not to oblige his desire. He developed great sympathy for the Baptist work though he never became a member of the church. Like her sister, the new Mrs. Boyce was a sturdy Presbyterian from the same Scotch-Irish geographical background as the family of Ker Boyce. She bore five children to Ker after he had had three by his first wife, her sister. These five were James, Nancy, Rebecca, Ker, and

Elizabeth. H. A. Tupper, who married Nancy, described Mrs. Boyce
in amiable terms:

> A more gentle and lovelier Christian woman never lived. Her person
> had the frail beauty of the lily; her character, the rich fragrance of
> the rose. The writer, as a little boy, knew her well and admired her
> greatly. Tristram Shandy says a man's history begins before his birth.
> The almost womanly gentleness and amiability of James P. Boyce may
> be clearly traced to his mother,—just as his hard common-sense, great
> executive ability, and deep vein of humor may be with equal readiness
> traced to his father and his paternal grandfather.[21]

Early Preparation of Mind and Heart

J. P. Boyce was reared in one of the richest homes in South Carolina. He was named after his father's close and trusted friend, James L.
Petigru. Broadus described Petigru as "a highly distinguished lawyer of
Charleston, a man of brilliant wit and other attractive qualities." He
and Ker Boyce had moved to Charleston at the same time. He opposed
the nullification movement in 1830 and later opposed secession.[22] His
mother, with Ker Boyce's blessings, having begun to attend the ministry
of the Baptist church, came to faith in Christ under the ministry of
Basil Manly Sr. in 1830. She dismissed herself from the Presbyterian
to be a part of the Baptist congregation.

This change came as a result of Manly's sermon preached at the
funeral of his young son John Waldo. On November 3, the child became
seriously ill, and because his malady was "very violent" Manly believed
it "would probably terminate in death." A meeting of the Charleston
Association, however, depended on his being there. "Waiting would
only make it more difficult for me ultimately to depart," he recorded in
his diary, and if he stayed he knew that he "could not be of service to
the child." Moreover, he had confidence that "my dear wife w[ould] be
supported in any event." He resolved to attend the meeting and "trust
him to take care of mine." John Waldo died on November 6 while
Manly was away, "but the Lord took care of [his] wife, and strengthened her to close the eyes of the dear child with a quiet resignation."
On his return home, Manly was met with the news of the death. He

recorded, "I was dumb; I opened not my mouth, because *Thou* didst it. . . . I trust I can say with Jacob—If I am bereaved of my children, I am bereaved." He preached on that text at the child's funeral.

Manly and his wife had lost another child, Zebulon Rudolph, the year before. When Mrs. Boyce called for Manly to visit her, she mentioned in particular "a sermon of mine occasioned by the death of my dear little Rudolph." The Manlys' spirit of submission to the divine prerogative had drawn her to a saving encounter with the living God. "We see here," Manly wrote, "part of the means by which the Lord carries on this great work. The death of my child may have been an answer to my own prayers. What a lesson for resignation!"[23]

Manly's ministry at Charleston came during the sesquicentennial celebration of the church's founding in Kittery, Maine. He was commissioned by the church to write its history, the final product appearing both in pulpit and print.[24] Its printing, however, was of his own doing five years later as the church failed to follow through and have it published. Manly believed that this failure immediately to publish showed some lack of appreciation for his hard and long labors on the project and, at the same time, resulted in a lost opportunity for the enhancement of his reputation in the cultured circles of the city.[25] His labors on the manuscript also had given Manly an opportunity to interpret himself in light of three former pastors of the church—William Screven, Oliver Hart, and Richard Furman. Their quests for freedom from political and religious oppression solidified Manly's convictions concerning the Baptist quest for religious liberty and, what he considered its concomitant, the political powers of the state vis-à-vis the federal government. Manly, though as a minister he sought to keep his politics private, sympathized with the nullification proclivities of many South Carolinians. His vote for that party became public in 1832 when "one of the managers at the polling place recognized Manly's handwriting, and soon the word that the Baptist preacher had voted States' Rights was all over town."[26]

Manly also accepted the social orthodoxy of owning slaves and disciplining them. Such, he believed, were the natural and necessary conditions of a well-organized society. Manly, according to the 1830 census, owned seven slaves. By 1837 he owned another. They should be treated kindly, given religious advantages, protected, allowed the full range of church privileges, but disciplined when necessary that they might be more useful and develop a character consistent with their status and to the optimum advantage of the society in which they function as an integral part. In June, Manly sent "my man Larrey" to James Lamb "on trial for a month." Manly wanted it understood that Lamb could "enact discipline" and "chastise him if necessary." Manly knew that Larrey was a capable worker so if "his business is not done as you direct, it may be well early to teach him the necessity of tractable & obedient habits."

On 5 July 1831, Manly recorded in his diary, "I sent my boy Claiborne to the work house to be put on the treadmill and kept in solitary confinement." Claiborne's repeated misconduct had led to this measure, and though Manly felt it a "great trial" to himself, he viewed it as "indispensable to preserve him from ruin." Claiborne, it seems, had "contracted habits of evil company and gambling and was fast getting into their attendants lying and stealing." The past Sunday he had been involved in an activity that officials adjudged worthy of five lashes. "Upon this slight sentence being enacted upon him, he gave evident tokens of despising all authority and although I had determined never to send a servant to such a place, I saw it was necessary now to let him have his fill of the place." On July 6, Manly retrieved a penitent servant with promises of submissive behavior.[27]

Manly knew that the South had violated the proper relationship of slave and master and could well be punished by God for this abuse. In spite of abuses, regulations prescribed by Scripture, when followed with pious intentions, produced benefits for both slave and master and had potential for the development of an idyllic society. Manly's sermon "Duties of Masters and Servants" outlined the relation as described throughout the Bible and painted the picture of a balanced, stable, happy society filled with more pleasures than pain. Though slaves in their assigned role must be disciplined, they also must be seen as potential heirs of the same kingdom of heaven as their Christian masters. Conversions among properly instructed slaves, Manly observed, were remarkable and testimonies were evangelical. They responded particularly positively to the Baptist way of preaching and organizing church. Manly even brushed against the edge of the law in granting equal privileges to slave church members in many aspects of church discipline, government, and manifestation of gifts of preaching and exhortation. A. James Fuller observed, "As an evangelical minister, a concerned master, and a moderate, he was willing to approach the bounds of acceptability, but as a Southern gentleman and slaveholder, he also stood ready to defend those boundaries against transgressors."[28] But conversion was no transgression of the biblical standard for slavery. Manly believed that slave Christianity gave a warmth and experience-based aspect to Southern Christianity that made its overall effect superior to the religion of the North. Participating in a prayer meeting among the "Negros" would always break the iciness of a purely cerebral religion.

Warmth and orthodoxy in religion characterized Manly's ministry at Charleston more than any other single thing. His oldest son, Basil Manly Jr., born in 1825, felt keenly the loss of two brothers in a little over a year. He came to his father in September 1831 and asked him to compose a prayer for him that he might "pray for his father and mother and anybody that is anything to him." Manly was greatly pleased with the six-year-old's "knowledge of the truths of the gospel" and was convinced that the boy was impressed in some degree with their force. Manly wrote a prayer that young Basil could use in his childlike intercessions and at the same time uttered in ink a prayer for the child: "O may the Lord smile upon the child—early lead to saving knowledge of Jesus Christ and employ him in Thy service. My own desire is that he may early become a child of God by faith in Jesus Christ and may live to the glory of Him who loved us and gave Himself for us." The prayer he composed for Basil Jr. is a summary of his own experiential orthodoxy:

> O Almighty God, who art a Spirit, grant me thy Holy Spirit that I may worship thee in Spirit and in truth. Forgive all my sins through the merits of thy dear Son, Jesus Christ; who is my only Saviour. For his sake, grant me a new heart, make me thy child, and keep me from all evil: and do thou so guide my mind and ways, that I may serve and please thee all the days of my life. Have mercy, O Lord, on my Father, my Mother, and all my dear relations—my teachers, and all

my friends: keep them in life, in health, and in thy fear continually; and when our mortal lives are ended, may we all meet in thy Kingdom above, to love and praise thee forever.

These blessings, with all other good things which thou seest I need, I humbly ask for the sake of Jesus Christ, who is worthy, with the Father and the Holy Spirit, to receive all the praise and glory, both now and forever. Amen.[29]

H. A. Tupper, Boyce's brother-in-law, was born in Charleston during the ministry of Manly. "I thank God," he wrote, "that I was born under the ministry of one whom I always regarded the holiest man I ever knew." As a worthy successor to the sainted and loved Richard Furman, Tupper observed that Manly was "imbued, at least in some degree with his earnest, wise and evangelical spirit." Under Manly, "year after year of revivals blessed the church; the children were carefully catechised; candidates for baptism were required to relate, before the church, an experience of grace; the membership were regularly reminded of their solemn covenant; the measures adopted for benevolent and denominational enterprise were substantially those most approved in our day."[30]

Manly's preaching, pastoral kindness, and probably catechizing made a lasting impression on the young Boyce. He memorialized Manly in the funeral sermon preached on 22 December 1868 with an earnestness that shows an uncontrived and deeply felt affection. Boyce compared Manly favorably with the highly revered Richard Furman, who had only recently died when Manly came to the pulpit in Charleston. Manly "made himself accessible to all, manifested deep interest in their welfare, readily advised them according to his best judgment, and above all showed a cordial sympathy with their joys and sorrows." Boyce recalled an abundance of occasions when Manly had the right word, whether in the presence of joy and mirth or sorrow and lamentation. "Would that I could venture to speak more at large about his life in this respect," Boyce pined, "or to state personal recollections which crowd upon me as to that part of his ministry." After more than thirty years, Boyce recalled "the weight of his hand, resting in gentleness and love upon my head." He recalled the "fatherly tenderness" of his counsel, his visible form in study in the pastor's house on King Street, and the place where "the bands, which he was then accustomed to wear with his gown, were laid on a certain Thanksgiving day, on which he dined with us." He recalled conversations Manly had with Boyce's mother and "the words of sympathy, which he spake, while he wept with her family over her dead body, and ministered to them as it was laid in the grave."[31] Boyce's mother died when he was ten years old, the last year of Manly's time at First Baptist Church, Charleston.

The impression of Manly as preacher also stayed with Boyce, particularly as a preacher of the gospel. Though deeply intelligent and filled with knowledge, "he spoke with eminent spirituality from the depths of his inner nature." Manly had, according to Boyce's recollection, "beyond any other man I ever heard, a pathos which enabled him in a moment to melt a vast audience to tears." This could happen instantaneously as witnessed by "almost innumerable" instances. Though his sermons were "full of instruction," to his parishioners "they were chiefly remarkable for their pathetic power."[32]

This observation does not minimize the importance of doctrinal content for Manly. Boyce knew it was important to remind the mourners on the day of his funeral that "in his doctrinal sentiments, Dr. Manly was a decided Calvinist." A survey of Manly's preaching confirms Boyce's impression. Manly's sermons, as Boyce's would be, were filled with theological reasoning and showed a comprehensive grasp of the full range of systematic theology from a historically Calvinistic perspective.[33] The church to which he ministered, Boyce's home church, "maintained the doctrines of the 'Century Confession,' which accords, on all points except peculiar Baptist doctrines, with the well known Confession of the Westminster Divines." Manly gave his "cordial consent" to these doctrines, and they were joyously advocated and maintained by him. Boyce pointed to them as "the doctrines by which he lived, and by which he died" and, notably, that "were the subject matter of his preaching." Boyce made the important personal observation that "holding these doctrines of grace has been thought by many inconsistent with the preaching of the gospel to all men," but "Dr. Manly felt no such inconsistency." "No one," Boyce continued, "could preach the gospel more freely than he," or "ever urged sinners more earnestly and successfully to believe in Christ as their Saviour."[34]

Manly left in 1837 to become the president of the University of Alabama. After eighteen years he returned to Charleston, in 1855, to serve for four years as pastor of the Wentworth Street Baptist Church, a church that had been founded in 1844 by former members of First Baptist. His ministry there succeeded greatly in comprehensive ways: building, financial contributions, and membership increased, and his status in the state convention surpassed what it had been during his first tenure in Charleston. In 1859, Manly returned to Alabama to do itinerant work as a missionary and evangelist. He served as pastor in Montgomery for two years before moving to Tuscaloosa to live with his son Charles. He suffered a stroke in 1864 and in 1867 moved back to South Carolina to live in Greenville with Basil Jr. He died just after the noon hour on 21 December 1868. His contributions to the rise of the Southern Baptist Theological Seminary will be noted later.

John A. Broadus, using material gathered from personal interviews and letters written to him immediately subsequent to the death of Boyce, filled in J. P. Boyce's boyhood with many interesting anecdotes. H. A. Tupper provided him with much of this material in a packet of letters sent on 24 May 1889. "Dear Doctor," he began; "I send by today's Express three files of Dr. Boyce's letters, I retain a large number filed with other papers of a business nature.... I cannot say how serviceable or unserviceable they may be. Wishing you all success in your labor of love, I am yours affectionately, H. A. Tupper."[35] The letters were highly serviceable and provide charming glances of Boyce's early life and characteristic traits.

Though strong physically, in size and shape Boyce was ill suited for many of the boyhood games enjoyed by his peers such as running, swimming, rowing, sailing, horseback riding, gunning, boxing, fencing, or fighting. He relished archery and began an archery club that used the "spacious grounds about his home in George Street" for practice. His lack of participation in so many of the other activities did not come from a morose, unsocial, or shy personality for "he was the quintessence of fun and jollity." He also found pleasure in billiards and chess. He attended dancing school, and one of the young ladies that also attended recounted to Broadus that she was always pleased when the instructor paired her with "Jimmy Boyce" because he was "so springy and strong, and they went whirling." This kind of instruction obviously contributed to his remarkable grace, courtesy, and gentlemanly deference toward ladies in all social situations in later life. "A friend of about the same age who knew him well," Broadus recorded, "adds the testimony that he was scrupulously temperate, and that the most searching scrutiny of memory does not recall a single act which stained his youth or young manhood with the slightest dishonor."[36]

Boyce read incessantly, pillaging the local library for all that it had. His father helped maintain the library by his membership in the Charleston Library Society.[37] The boy's appetite for books only increased throughout life, and "the number and variety of books that he read . . . was a marvel to his family and intimate friends."[38] By 1845 the library had 1,383 separate titles, many of them multivolume. In addition it held 527 pamphlets on a wide variety of subjects. It included books on antiquities and fine arts, geography, astronomy, agriculture, botany, husbandry, biography (132 volumes), encyclopedias, dictionaries, grammars, catalogues of books in other libraries, foreign and classical language volumes, moral philosophy, law, politics, military and naval tactics, mathematics, mechanics, medicine, surgery, chemistry, natural philosophy, natural history, novels and romances (354 titles), poetry, trade and commerce, and theology (65 titles).[39]

Boyce's early love for a variety of books bore fruit in the richly developed personal library he acquired throughout his life. This interest in such a wide variety of ideas led him to start, in addition to his archery society, a debating club that met regularly in a room above his father's carriage house. From his mother, who died when James was ten, he learned gentleness, tenderness, orderliness, and scrupulous truthfulness. From his interaction with seven siblings, he maintained a spirit of fair play, generosity, deep gratitude, and earnest solicitude for the well-being of his friends and close associates, all blended with a playfulness and winsome sense of humor. All of these traits were writ large in Boyce's relationships in the future.

Boyce's practice of reading according to his own interests transcended his application to the tasks of his school assignments so that he did not perform up to the potential his instructors envisioned. He learned his lessons "with wonderful rapidity" and then went about his chosen authors in which he took such great pleasure, never, however, according to Broadus, of "evil or doubtful character." His pastor, William T. Brantly Sr., called the attention of his father, Ker Boyce, to this lack of intense application. Mr. Boyce knew just the solution to this academic foible. Broadus recounted the anecdote:

> James was taken from school and put in the wholesale drygoods store of Wiley, Banks, & Co., in which his father was a partner. This new life would give excellent training of a certain kind until he grew old enough for college. James himself once told the writer [Broadus] in later years how his father gave express directions, both to him and to the men in the store, that he was to perform his full share of all the roughest and hardest work done by other boys of the same age. He must rise at six in the morning, go down and help to sweep out the establishment, and at any time be ready to help bring out the heaviest boxes, and in general must stand back for nothing. All this exactly suited his energetic temperament. . . . However, six months of it sufficed for the lad's wishes, and he was quite willing to return to school.[40]

Charleston surrounded Boyce with educational advantages that molded him for his future usefulness. The advanced literary culture of Charleston fostered the publication of the *Southern Review* described by John A. Broadus as "brilliant and powerful." The library had a collection of all the volumes from 1828 to 1832, a total of eight volumes. Boyce read these later in life but presently came under the influence of teachers and writers whose tastes and scholarship were molded by the "gifted and eminent men who had contributed to it essays seldom equaled in even the great English Quarterlies."[41] William Gilmore Simms (1806–70), a famous poet, novelist, and historian of the nineteenth century, lived and wrote in Charleston during Boyce's childhood. His stories of the military heroics of South Carolinians as well as a variety of other works appeared while Boyce was in Charleston and doubtless constituted part of his zealous reading. William E. Bailey, one of Boyce's first teachers upon returning to school, loved Boyce and put great confidence in him as shown by the gift of over thirteen hundred volumes from his library to the seminary on its founding in 1859. This included many elaborately bound classical works as well as a full run of the novels of Simms. At Charleston High School, Boyce studied with many capable teachers and received a silver medal at commencement for the correct solution to an original problem in algebra. His propensity for finding just the right word in his written manuscripts for oral presentation probably found its origin in the influence of Andrew Flynn Dickson, who was especially "zealous about distinguishing between words." In this school context Boyce was surrounded by persons who came from families of publicly acclaimed accomplishments or who would soon themselves be recognized in the culture as distinguished teachers, lawyers, scholars, and literary artists.

One of the Sunday school teachers at First Baptist Church, Charles Lanneau, made such a profound impression on his students that from his class came a number of highly effective ministers among Baptists in the mid-nineteenth century. J. L. Reynolds, a graduate of Charleston College and Newton Theological Seminary who served as pastor at Columbia and Richmond, as professor at Furman, Mercer, and South Carolina College, and as president at Georgetown, and stood as a champion of Baptist orthodoxy against tides of change, preceded Boyce by a few years. Basil Manly Jr., just one year and three weeks older than Boyce, who served on the first faculty with Boyce at the seminary, also served several churches as pastor including First Baptist of Richmond, Virginia, and was president of Georgetown in Kentucky from 1871 to 1879. William Royall, three and one-half years older than Boyce, achieved great usefulness as a preacher, professor, and school administrator, and served at Furman University during the same years, 1855–59, that Boyce occupied the chair of theology. Another Sunday school teacher Boyce enjoyed was Henry Holcomb Tucker, who became a distinguished educator and editor. Tucker served four separate terms as editor of the *Christian Index* in Georgia, supported the seminary enthusiastically, and maintained a close and mutually edifying friendship with Boyce.[42]

When Manly left in 1837, W. T. Brantly Sr. became pastor until his death in 1845. Robert A. Baker suggests that Manly influenced the church to call Brantly. He recounts the long-term relation between the church, Brantly, and Manly:

Brantly was well known to the Charleston church, having been pastor at Beaufort, South Carolina, for eight years and at Augusta, Georgia, for seven years, and had gained national distinction as pastor of the First Baptist Church, Philadelphia, for eleven years. He had preached the funeral sermon for Richard Furman in 1825, and evidently had appeared before the church on other occasions while his protégé, Basil Manly, was pastor. H. A. Tupper hinted that perhaps Richard Fuller . . . had a part in the coming of Brantly to Charleston. It is likely, however, that Basil Manly was the chief human instrument for suggesting Brantly to this church as pastor. . . . [Brantly] became the key link that brought Basil Manly to South Carolina and helped mold the life of Richard Fuller and perhaps that of James P. Boyce by his teaching.[43]

Brantly had enjoyed a useful and distinguished career as a minister and educator and supporter of benevolent activities for the denomination when he arrived in Charleston. Robert Snyder, employing the terminology of Daniel Walker Howe, characterizes Brantly, though a Baptist, as an "insider." An "outsider" evangelical was content to let holiness develop in a society through separation, distinctiveness, and individual piety. An "insider," those that Howe names "Whig evangelicals," were seeking to "create the functional equivalent of an established church, within which evangelicals would take the lead in reforming society as a whole along their own moral lines."[44] As Baker chronicles, Brantly had served as pastor in Beaufort, South Carolina, founded the Baptist church in Augusta, Georgia, and spent the past eleven years as pastor of the First Baptist Church of Philadelphia. Brantly also had been instrumental in moving the *Columbian Star* from Washington, D.C. to Philadelphia in 1827 where he became its editor for five years. In 1832 he encouraged Jesse Mercer to buy the paper and move it to Georgia where it could serve the Baptist cause in the Southern states, having been renamed the *Christian Index*. Because of his many writings and his zealous service in Baptist benevolent institutions, Brown University awarded him the doctor of divinity degree in 1831.[45] Brantly also was outspoken for the cause of ministerial education. He was married twice, having four children by his first wife and ten by his second. The first son of each marriage went into the ministry. William T. Brantly Jr. served as pastor of First Baptist Augusta, a church established by his father. Brantly Jr. was serving that church when a consultative convention met there in 1845 to form the Southern Baptist Convention.

Brantly's preaching ministry surely had an impact on Boyce. From the time he was ten until eighteen, Boyce attended the preaching of Brantly week by week. Both Basil Manly and Richard Fuller provided personal perspectives on Brantly for William Sprague's volume on the Baptists in the *Annals of the American Pulpit.*[46] Manly, fully confident in the "sincerity and vigour of his piety," noted that Brantly's prayers were "always plain, yet not commonplace; comprehensive, yet brief." Though he came directly to the prayer meeting from a harried and bustling atmosphere of the classroom or academic administrative responsibilities, he was never disinclined or unfit for devotion, but he attended with "alacrity and delight" seemingly having come "as if fresh from the closet, and from communion with his Saviour,—as though his devotion had been mellowed and enriched amid hours spent by the still waters of prayerful seclusion."[47]

Brantly's greatest strength in his preaching, besides his native, yet cultured, eloquence, was "the readiness with which he could turn the whole vigour of his thoughts on any subject at will, together with his power of comprehension and analysis." Manly recalled,

> Being often in his study when he was preparing for the pulpit, he has seemed to me to make a sermon, complete, in a time not much longer than it has required to write this paragraph. I have then gone with him to church, and heard him preach those sermons, the skeletons of which I took down, and have preserved to this time; and, on every review of them, they surprise me by the justness of their distributions, and the rich veins of well elaborated thought to which they lead. Imagery and illustration he had very aptly at command. . . . But, whatever was the haste of his composition of a sermon, or the suddenness with which an illustration or argument was suggested, his audience could not be aware of it by any seeming want of familiarity or comprehension. On one occasion, when preparing a sermon for the afternoon, the bell struck, denoting the hour of service. "Ah," said he, smiling, as he rose from his paper

on which he had hastily dashed off a dozen lines in large misshapen letters,—"my sermon is like a half formed insect on the banks of the Nile,—part out, part in." I walked with him to the house of worship, and never heard him more fully in command of his subject, or of the minds and feelings of his audience. The secret of this was, he elaborated ideas, not particular sermons. . . . Certain it is that, both then and since, I must regard him as the most uniformly engaging, instructive, inspiring, preacher that it has ever been my good fortune to hear. . . . I do not remember that I ever heard a remark fall from him, which I considered commonplace, or feeble, or said merely to fill out the time.[48]

The words of Richard Fuller about Brantly boiled with even more passion and superlatives than those of Basil Manly. Brantly had been his teacher since childhood; Fuller had profited from his loving and faithful counsel. He found him filled with warmth, wisdom, generosity, and hospitality. Unlike many others that knew only his public figure, Fuller knew his childlike simplicity of heart and the deep spiritual passion of his soul. Describing his preaching, Fuller referred to "the sacred knowledge flowing from his lips, making the pulpit a throne of light." That which struck Fuller most, he recalled, was "the grandeur of his conceptions, and his earnest love of truth. No one," he remarked, "could have sat under his ministry without recalling sermons, in which his mind seemed to soar quite beyond the verge of time, and, in high and rapt communion, to mingle with eternity."[49] A young man as attentive and alert as Boyce could hardly have failed to be deeply impressed with the importance of genuine spiritual life and the necessity of preparation to meet God through Christ.

Manly and Fuller both emphasized the deep spirituality and genuine emotion shown by Brantly as well as the earnestness that supported his preaching because a significant contingent in Charleston failed to recognize that part of his pastoral make-up. Even with such perceived excellencies, Fuller believed that the church in Charleston did not come to know Brantly as "a pastor and a man." He regretted the "circumstances which rendered his removal there a misfortune to him, and retrenched his influence in that city."[50] Some of the detachment could have been prompted by Brantly's penchant for practical change. Brantly made several changes in pastoral style, style of worship, preaching, and ministry that disturbed some of the members of the church. Tupper characterized Brantly's seven years as "the innovation pastorate." Tupper pointed to the church's sharing Brantly with the college, the consequent limitation on strictly pastoral duties, eliminating the sounding board above the pulpit, moving the Sunday school class to a lecture room, and making several physical changes in the sanctuary.[51] His sermons were more rhetorical than impassioned, he visited little if any because of the pressure of the college administration and instruction, and he made some structural changes in the church sanctuary, suggested but wisely abandoned by Manly. The time seemed propitious for establishing a second church of the denomination in the city, started by members of First Baptist Church. In 1841 the Wentworth Street Baptist Church officially organized, and First Baptist dismissed perhaps ninety-two persons to initiate the new venture.

In addition to the superlative demonstration of pulpit power and profound instruction in biblical matters in church, Brantly provided for aspiring young men an opportunity for some individual instruction. He began a Greek class for them and eventually turned it over to B. C. Pressley, an eminent lawyer in Charleston. The class included Boyce along with his longtime friend and future brother-in-law H. A. Tupper, who also served as corresponding secretary for the Foreign Mission Board of the Southern Baptist Convention. Also James Mendenhall and R. Furman Whilden, both of whom became gospel preachers, received instruction in this unusual class. At fifteen years of age, Boyce heard the great J. H. Thornwell preach. He had gone to the Presbyterian church to see a girl in whom he had developed an interest. From the gallery he could command a view of the entire lower floor and certainly would be able to see the young lady and her family. He became so entranced with the preacher and his message, however, that he gave his initial purpose not another thought. Broadus remarked that the preacher "probably never received a higher tribute to his powers."[52]

Upon finishing Charleston High School, Boyce enrolled in Charleston College. Dr. Brantly, the pastor of First Baptist Church, also served as president of the college. Boyce increased in his scholarly discipline while in the college but still enjoyed humor and innocent fun. Once in the middle of a practical joke Boyce hid behind a tree, but could not be concealed; Brantly, seeing the prank develop from a window above the lawn, remarked to a colleague, "There is Boyce, who will be a great man, if he does not become a devil."[53] In spite of his penchant for fun, Boyce rose to the top in academic matters and gained the respect of his peers for fairness and courage in matters of principle. One of his classmates, Francis Miles, a native of Charleston, became a noted physician in Baltimore. When he heard of Boyce's death in 1888, he wrote a letter to H. A. Tupper, testifying to his "strong and affectionate remembrance of him" during the college days in Charleston:

> He was conspicuous among his class and the students of the college by his talents and the strong, rapid grasp of mind, which not only enabled him to master with ease the studies of the curriculum, but caused him to push his reading, though, and inquiry quite beyond the circle of required recitations. But it is not only as the clear, original thinker, the quick, cogent reasoner, that I remember him. I recall him as the genial, amiable, affectionate companion, who was never tempted (how rare a quality among young men!) to give pain or annoyance by a jest, nor, standing as he did on the high ground of a very pure morality, to scorn or animadvert upon those on an inferior level.

Miles believed that Boyce's subsequent life "was the bright day of this clear Dawn."[54]

Brantly suffered a stroke on 13 July 1844 as the culmination of several years of declining health and strength. He had been a man noted for his great reverence for Scripture, his infectious spirituality, his riveting eloquence, and his tireless zeal for the unity of Christians in benevolent concerns, and was particularly active for Baptist denominational unity in the South.[55] He moved to Augusta in February 1845 and died there on March 28. Richard Fuller preached the funeral discourse at the church in Charleston. "He loved the Bible," Fuller asserted, "and studied the Bible, and preached the Bible,—preached it as it is,—neither seeking to be wise nor orthodox above what is written."[56]

Witnessing the Birth of a Denomination

These were years of intense denominational tension among the Baptists of America. After great suffering in the strife caused by the anti–mission-society movement, the issue of slavery and its implications for the morality of union in missionary labors between slaveholders and nonslaveholders now rocked the unity of the missionary Baptists participating in the General Missionary Convention. One Southern observer wrote, "For several years past the abolition excitement had been rising and spreading in the North." Its effect on Baptist meetings was to turn them into "seasons of painful solicitude and exciting controversy." He likened the atmosphere to "standing on the heaving sides of a volcano. The hoarse rumbling, and clouds of smoke, not unmingled with sparks, were portentous of an approaching eruption."[57] Increasing pressure on the North from the abolitionist movement had prompted the development of an American Baptist Anti-Slavery Convention in 1840. They had written in an open letter to the South, that if they remained deaf to their entreaties to do all in their power to give freedom to the slaves, "we cannot and we dare not recognize you as consistent brethren in Christ . . . and we cannot, at the Lord's table, cordially take that as a brother's hand, which plies the scourge on woman's naked flesh,—which thrusts a gag into the mouth of a man." Their convention was composed of Baptists who were not slaveholders and who believed that "slavery, under all circumstances, is sin, and treat[ed] it accordingly."[58]

After more years of increasing tension, Basil Manly Sr., now in Alabama, came to believe that the North looked on Baptists in the South with a condescending sense of moral superiority. He began to sense in conscience that a clear understanding between "parties" was necessary, that is, "to settle the question of social equality, and principles of future union." Would the South be considered equal in the various associations of benevolent work or be looked upon as "mere aids and vassals"?[59] He spoke for many when he wrote his son Basil Jr.

at Newton Theological Seminary, in Newton Center, Massachusetts, about the developing tensions. On 22 November 1844, three days prior to official action on the part of Alabama Baptists, but subsequent to the meeting in which the fatal resolutions were adopted, Manly opened the floodgates of frustration and concern prompted by the reality that soon many long-cherished friendships and denominational relations would be torn apart.

> The resolution of the Boston Association has had a very great effect at the South, whatever may have been its purpose. We are in no condition to hear that subject tampered with. . . . That resolution & the management of the Georgia case have [stirred?] up a spirit which it will be difficult to allay: and which have had the effect to lock up every dollar of funds sent up to our convention (some several hundred dollars) until complete satisfaction is obtained. We will not beg any set of men to allow us to remain in their society. If we can be admitted on equal terms, & can avoid impeachment & annoyance, we shall be pleased to remain in the fellowship of well-doing. If not, we must be content to labor and suffer alone. We are not unwilling to be told our faults, so long as that act of faithfulness & friendship can be useful. But as to slavery; we have examined that matter, & come to the deliberate conclusion that it is not wrong to hold property in our slaves. We have told our brethren so, and given them our reasons. Here we mean to stand. Now, it is for them to say, whether, with this understanding, they are willing to work with us on equal terms, acknowledge us as brethren—& let us alone. This last, as to the subject of slavery, is a *sine qua non*. We are tired of having to sustain all manner of contumely, invective, & reproach, whenever we go up to meet them in our labor of love.[60]

Manly told his son of the action of the Alabama Baptists, summarized the resolutions, and told him that he had written the resolutions. They were adopted by a standing vote unanimously. "We have now told our brethren how we feel, and where we stand," Manly continued; "if they like, they can have us for associates & fellow laborers. If not, Be it so: The consequences be upon their own heads." On November 25, the Alabama Baptist State Convention formalized the action by sending a letter under the name of Jesse Hartwell to the acting board of the General Missionary Convention demanding "the distinct, explicit, avowal that slaveholders are eligible, and entitled equally with non-slaveholders, to all the privileges and immunities of their several unions." Among Baptists in the North, such an action was desired by some, regretted by a few, but expected by all.

At the twenty-fifth anniversary of the Southern Baptist Convention in 1872, William Williams reflected on these events and astutely observed, "Among the Northern churches, so prevalent was becoming the opposition to Christian fellowship and co-operation with Southern churches that there would have been a disastrous rupture among themselves if a separation of the Southern churches had not taken place, even without its being forced upon them by the infringement of their rights and the denial of their moral equality." He referred to the antislavery mission society that had been established upon the explicit provision of "non-co-operation with Southern churches." It was growing in popularity and threatened to divide the North. "If there must be a rupture," Williams continued, "it was very naturally preferred by the North that it should be between the North and the South, and not between themselves."[61]

Accordingly, the board of the General Missionary Convention, meeting in Boston, responded that "if anyone should offer himself as a Missionary, having slaves, and should insist on retaining them as his property, we could not appoint him." Baptists in the South responded by meeting in Augusta, Georgia, in May 1845 "to confer on the best means of promoting the Foreign Mission cause, and other interests of the Baptist Denomination in the South."[62] Though he was not a church member at this time, James Boyce attended this meeting in Augusta and observed the proceedings which led to the formation of the Southern Baptist Convention.

Wayland, Brown, and Conversion

With the death of Brantly, Ker Boyce decided that his son should leave Charleston to complete his education. He sent him to Brown University to enter the junior class of 1845–46 where he hoped he would prepare for a career in law and politics and would be able to care for the extensive estate that he and his siblings would inherit. Brown was named after Nicholas Brown, a seventh generation descendant of Chad Brown, who came to Rhode Island as friend and fellow pioneer of the colony with Roger Williams. Each generation of the Providence Browns contributed positively to the well-being, government, education, and religious interests of Providence and Rhode Island. Nicholas Brown inherited both capital and business that he used to good advantage and, along with his brother-in-law Thomas P. Ives, became not only wealthy but highly reputable for trustworthiness, generosity, and zeal for American excellence. He gave a valuable collection of law books, land, equipment, and money to the college, beginning four years after his graduation and continuing through his death. In 1804, the college, founded in 1765 in Warren and moved to Providence in 1770, changed its name from Rhode Island College to Brown in recognition of Nicholas Brown's unusual generosity.[63]

Francis Wayland had already served for eighteen years as president at Brown when Boyce entered. The first president had been James Manning who served from 1765 to 1791. Jonathan Maxcy succeeded him until 1802. Asa Messer took the position in 1804 until 1826. Francis Wayland was elected as president in 1827. Wayland was born in 1796, the son of a Baptist preacher, also named Francis Wayland, who had come from England in 1793. The senior Wayland in 1807 left a thriving business to become pastor at Poughkeepsie and later served as pastor at Albany, Troy, and Saratoga Springs. He was among the first promoters of the temperance movement, and he died in 1849. He gave himself to Bible study tirelessly and savored every opportunity for growth in his knowledge of truth. "My father's associates seemed to me," Wayland recalled, "to have been far better acquainted with the Scriptures and with the doctrines of the gospel, and more thoroughly religious, than we commonly find professing Christians at the present." He also felt the impression of their discussion as they often quoted from Abraham Booth, John Gill, Andrew Fuller, William Romaine, Augustus Toplady, and John Newton.[64]

Wayland graduated from Union College in Schenectady when he was seventeen years old and then went on to a three-year study of medicine in the offices of two prominent physicians, during the third year of which he was converted and united with a Baptist church. His conversion released him from a lengthy and severe struggle of soul that had prompted him to write his mother on one occasion, "I think I can say that God would be just, were he to send me to hell; but I know that he alone can save me."[65] He studied theology for one year at Andover and returned to Union as a tutor, gaining experience in a wide variety of college studies. In 1821, Wayland was called to serve the First Baptist Church of Boston as pastor when it was in a dangerously low condition. After five years he returned to Union as professor, but soon, in February 1827, Brown University asked him to come as president.

Wayland sought to bring about reform in the manner as well as the subject matter of the college education, emphasizing the student's need for close personal enquiry and analysis. He prepared new lectures on each subject that he taught because he disliked the textbooks that were then in use. As a result he published in 1835 *Elements of Moral Science* (a copy of which was in the library in Charleston), in 1837 *Elements of Political Economy*, and in 1854 *Elements of Intellectual Philosophy*. In 1850 he achieved a thorough reorganization of the university, increasing its offerings in science, economics, and modern languages, and expanding the elective system of courses. While pastor, Wayland showed his fervent commitment to the recently embraced foreign mission movement among Baptists by preaching "The Moral Dignity of the Missionary Enterprise." The sermon eventually was published as an apologetic for expanding commitment on the part of evangelicals to worldwide missionary efforts.[66] When Adoniram Judson, the quintessential missionary and alumnus of Brown, died, Wayland published a two-volume *Memoir of the Life and Labors of the Rev. Adoniram Judson*.[67] His knowledge and practical wisdom in Baptist life flowed with delightful ease throughout his 1857 work *Notes on the Principles and Practices of Baptist Churches*.[68] The overall intellectual, spiritual, and denominational outlook of Wayland informed Boyce's outlook on education in general and the demands of theological education for Baptists in particular.

Boyce retained clear perceptions of Wayland as president. Wayland "stamped his mind" upon his pupils, exerting enormous influence "over the intellectual nature." Dr. Wayland's mental vision, according to Boyce, was telescopic, "reaching a long distance, and bringing objects near, which to other men were distant." Boyce believed that analytical power "was more remarkable in him than in any man America has ever produced." He found it difficult, however, to move to a broader perspective after having so finely isolated an idea and, as a result, "his observations were left unmodified by the information given by other objects or through the other senses."

Though Boyce's perception might have been true in the way Wayland actually operated, Wayland's intellectual outlook as described in *The Elements of Intellectual Philosophy* showed not only a keen commitment to analysis but broad and applicatory comprehension. This book was not published until 1854, but according to Broadus, "Dr. Wayland was already giving a full course of original lectures on Intellectual Philosophy."[69] In describing the "separate acts that form the process of abstraction," Wayland discussed three necessary disciplines: "acuteness of observation," that is, "analysis," the "power of generalization," and the "power of combination." In the integration of these powers one discovers intellectual maturity and advancement in true and original knowledge. On analysis Wayland noted, "He who is the best able to analyze the constituent elements of the objects to which his attention is directed, whether in the world within or the world without, is the most richly provided with the materials for accurate judgment." The provision of valuable materials must be supplemented by the philosophical discipline of generalization so that from one fact or several the thinker may trace out a cause or enunciate a law that leads to important and useful changes. Beyond the ability to trace out these laws and causes is the power of combination, to suggest an internal operation by which they can be tested and further generalized. "As the laws of nature and her modes of operation are better understood," Wayland surmised, "we form conceptions more and more analogous to truth." That is, "we learn to think more and more in harmony with the ideas of the Creator; and, from a larger and more accurate acquaintance with the known, we are the better able to unravel the mysteries of the unknown."[70] Wayland, at least in theory, found the entire process of intelligent

49

investigation invigorating, but Boyce found his powers of analysis more astute and memorable.

The intellect sometimes hid another quality in Wayland that Boyce recognized. "Under the powerful frame and massive intellectuality, and commanding, oftentimes stern aspect of Wayland, there was the most childlike spirit that I ever knew in man—the most sympathizing heart, the most fatherly affection."[71] The concern that Wayland had for the spiritual condition of the students prompted him to work for campus revival, encourage prayer, and seek the conversion of students. This atmosphere of urgency increased Boyce's seriousness about his eternal state.

Broadus recognized the massive impact that Wayland had on Boyce and attributed this to the great similarity in temperament and overall character. Boyce found someone with whom he identified naturally and whose personal and professional demeanor he could emulate. Broadus made the comparison:

> For we can perceive that each possessed sound practical judgment, combined with love of abstract thinking, and intense but quiet religious fervor; each showed great force of will and personal dignity, united with humility, considerateness, and benevolence; each was eminently truth-loving in studious inquiry and in statement, promptly indignant at any exhibition of insincerity or dishonesty, and yet forbearing, and in all personal matters ready to forgive; each was cheerful and sometimes merry, yet full of serious aims and purposes. In style also, both men were clear in explanation and strong in argument, and used excellent English. These similarities may help to account for the profound and permanent impression made by Dr. Wayland upon this pupil, who throughout his life delighted in every grateful expression of obligation, and in supporting his own views by reference to any similar opinion of the great college president.[72]

During Boyce's first year at Brown, the justly famous and revered missionary Adoniram Judson came to Brown and spent some time as guest of Dr. Wayland. Judson's sacrificial and single-minded devotion to the glory of God in emulating Christ's humiliation filled the minds and prayers of all missionary Baptists in the mid-nineteenth century. A. J. Holt recalled "having heard Dr. Boyce relate the circumstances of a visit made by the great Adoniram Judson to his Alma Mater and how the very pressure of the hand of this world renowned missionary sent a thrill into the soul of young Boyce that in effect never afterwards departed."[73]

Wayland, from the beginning of the missionary movement, had been one of its most outspoken and vigorous promoters and apologists. Preaching on 26 October 1823, while he was pastor at First Baptist Church of Boston, Wayland affirmed that the missionary enterprise far surpassed any other human endeavor in greatness, first, because of "the grandeur of the object," that is "radically to affect the temporal and eternal interest of the whole race of man." It would bestow everything that intellectual and moral cultivation can bestow and also rescue man from eternal wrath and indignation.[74] Second, it calls into action "the noblest energies of man" and will aggravate the deepest opposition of the basest, most vile, and inveterately evil propensities of fallen man. Such a purpose must engage consummate wisdom, perseverance of character, "self-denial of the highest and holiest character," courage, and deep-seated faith. Third, its dignity and greatness heighten when one considers that all this is to be done by the "preaching of Jesus Christ and him crucified."[75] "The preaching of the cross," Wayland affirmed, "is a remedy for the miseries of the fall, which has been tried by the experience of eighteen hundred years, and has never in a single instance failed." This enterprise, moreover, most certainly will succeed "until this whole world has been redeemed from the effects of man's first disobedience." Given this, Wayland called for all his hearers, and readers, to reflect:

> Reflect upon the dignity of its object; the high moral and intellectual powers which are to be called forth in its execution; the simplicity, benevolence, and efficacy of the means by which it is to be achieved; and we ask you, Does not every other enterprise, to which man ever put forth his strength, dwindle into insignificance before that of preaching Christ crucified to a lost and perishing world?[76]

This same passion for world evangelization Wayland transferred to his concern for his students. Broadus records, "It is known that Dr.

Wayland earnestly longed and labored for the conversion of all his students, and often greatly impressed them by private conversations as well as public addresses and sermons."[77] Reuben Guild, a classmate of Boyce, wrote a series of articles for *The Watchman* tracing out the remarkable history of revivals at Brown University. He included a testimony from Silas Bailey of Wayland's method of interviewing students:

> Often, when an undergraduate entered the doctor's study, he was invited to be seated. Then followed a conversation of great tenderness, rich in gospel truth, and prolific in motives, urging him to the salvation of his soul. He was entreated to read his Bible daily; he was shown its treasures, and its influence upon his character and his destiny. He was called upon to consider his standing in the sight of God. He was affectionately urged to suffer no delay, to peril no longer interests so momentous, but to commence at once a life of piety. The interview was closed with prayer—a prayer so humble, sincere and affectionate that the young man felt convinced, as he rose from his knees, that at least one soul, second to none in greatness, believed his moral danger to be real and imminent, and yearned for his salvation.[78]

William T. Brantly Jr., according to Guild's recollection, was saved during one of the periodic revivals that occurred during Wayland's administration. He gave the date as Thursday, 22 February 1838.[79] H. M. Dexter, the notable Congregational pastor, historian, theologian, confessionalist, and polemicist, was converted during this revival and recorded Wayland's manner of dealing with him:

> I arose and went into the presence of Dr. Wayland. He was in his study, reading his old, well-worn copy of the Sacred Word. He received me kindly, and I at once made known to him the anguish of my soul. I felt and said, "My sins are so great and so many that God cannot pardon me." Fixing his keen black eyes, beaming with tenderness, on me, this good man said,—and never till my dying day can I forget the earnest solemnity, the eloquence of the tone,—"When he was a great way off, his father saw him and had compassion on him, and ran, and fell on his neck, and kissed him." I felt that the

case was mine, and hope, reviving hope, came to me. Dr. Wayland then knelt down and prayed with me and for me; and on leaving him, he lent me his well-thumbed copy of Bishop Wilson's *Sacra Privata*, advising me to read that, and the life of Brainerd, instead of Byron. . . . I never knew till then the full meaning of that great word, friendliness. I never knew Jesus Christ.[80]

The same article records a revival in 1841 in which E. T. Winkler, of the class of 1843, was converted. Winkler eventually would become a friend of Boyce as well as serve as editor of the *Southern Baptist* and pastor of the First Baptist Church of Charleston. Number 8 in the series records the connections of the revival atmosphere at Brown to the conversion of Boyce and his subsequent contribution to one of the revivals. Guild narrates:

The revival of 1847 commenced with my class, the greater part of whom were professors of religion. The same was true of the class of 1846, but not of the two lower classes. This was a source of anxiety to Dr. Wayland, who in his familiar talks to us, frequently alluded to the subject, and urged upon Christians the importance of earnest prayer and special effort in behalf of the impenitent. Meetings for prayer and conference were for a time held every evening and there were several conversions. In September, 1845 James Petigru Boyce, whose recent death is so deeply deplored, especially throughout the South, entered the class as a student from Charleston College. He was a fine scholar, very popular in his ways, and the heir presumptive to large wealth, his father being the richest man in Charleston. His classmates at once became deeply interested in his spiritual welfare, and made him a subject of special prayer, that his wealth and gifts and graces might all be consecrated to the Master's use. Several of the class who were thus interested, had "power in prayer." . . . The usual College Fast, for the last Thursday in February, was a day of great solemnity, and was attended by the students generally, including Boyce, who appeared deeply interested. The meeting in the morning was conducted by Dr. Wayland, who made the opening prayer. He was followed by Dr. Caswell, who spoke upon the necessity of religion in college, and dwelt upon the influence exerted by pious students. Prof. Gammell enlarged upon the importance of cultivating our spiritual

natures as well as improving our intellectual faculties. In the afternoon
Dr. Wayland preached an eloquent and practical discourse addressed
mainly to the impenitent. Shortly after this occurred the spring vacation for 1846. The Rev. Dr. Richard Fuller, of Beaufort, S. C. was
then holding a series of meetings in Charleston. Under the influence
of his powerful preaching, and in answer doubtless to the prayers of
his pious classmates, Boyce was hopefully converted, and on the 22d
of April he was publicly baptized. He returned to college a changed
man. He at once joined the Religious Society, and with characteristic
energy and zeal engaged in efforts to promote a revival, of which his
conversion may be regarded as the beginning.[81]

As indicated by Guild, during the spring vacation from Brown
University in 1846, Boyce showed signs of deep conviction about
his sin and the undeniable truth of biblical Christianity. Boyce and
his friend James Mendenhall took a steamer from New York to
Charleston where they would spend the break. Boyce kept to his
stateroom a good deal of the time reading his Bible. Eventually his
talks with Mendenhall showed the power of this conviction. On
arriving in Charleston, they found that Richard Fuller, the great
preacher from Beaufort, South Carolina, held forth each evening at
the First Baptist Church. A friend, H. A. Tupper, had been converted
and received into membership in the church. He spoke earnestly
to Boyce. In the words of John A. Broadus, Boyce "felt himself a
ruined sinner, and like the rest, had to look to the merits of Christ
alone for salvation."[82] He was baptized on April 22 while the meeting was in progress.

Richard Fuller (1804–76) was from a wealthy family in Beaufort,
South Carolina. He had entered Harvard University when sixteen years
of age but left in 1823 before he finished due to a severe respiratory
difficulty that caused a hemorrhage of the lungs. Because of the quality of his work the university awarded him his degree though he had
not finished the course. In Beaufort, he became a lawyer, well known
for the care he put into the cases he tried and for his rapier-like preci-
sion in dismantling any argument of his opponents built on a faulty
assumption or logic. He had been immersed as an Episcopalian, but
after his conversion in 1831 he believed that he should be baptized as

a believer. He was ordained in 1832 and became pastor of the Baptist church in Beaufort. J. H. Cuthbert described the meeting in which Boyce professed conversion:

> In the spring of 1846 Dr. Fuller and Rev. Mr. Wyer visited Charleston to hold a meeting with the two churches,—the old First, and its daughter, the dear Wentworth-street. The First Church was then under the pastoral care of the excellent Crawford. Dr. Curtis, one of the best Bible expositors in the land, had recently resigned the pastorate of the Second Church. The meetings were conducted by Dr. Fuller and Mr. Wyer, with the advice of Dr. Crawford. For more than a week there seemed to be no impression either in the churches or in the community. "For nearly a whole night," said Dr. Fuller, speaking of this discouragement, "Wyer and I walked the market . . . anxious and prayerful." . . . Multitudes began to throng the services, the meetings being held alternately in the two churches.
>
> The order of exercises was, a meeting for inquirers at sunrise, and the usual service at night. This was carried on, with little or no intermission, for over a month. The work of preaching was done mainly by Dr. Fuller, besides his constant interviews and conversations with the people,—a work often more exhausting than preaching. But with unflagging energy he ceased not day and night to warn the people with tears, declaring unto them the whole counsel of God. . . . It was what James W. Alexander . . . calls "logic on fire,"—truth in earnest. . . . The vast audience was held by some strong argument (where the training of the lawyer shows itself in the manner and method of the preacher); then moved with a ripple of pleasurable surprise at some pointed exposure of error; then melted to tears, if not loud sobs, under some outburst of overflowing tenderness. Wonderful enchanter with the wand of truth! . . .
>
> As a result of this meeting, the two churches were brought closer together, their memberships revived, and between one hundred and two hundred souls added to their roll. . . . The Rev. Dr. Boyce, President of the Southern Baptist Convention, Rev. Dr. Tupper, successor of the beloved Taylor in the foreign-mission office in Richmond, and many more, useful in the ministry and other departments of the church are the living witnesses of the grace and power of that meeting.[83]

On returning to Brown, Boyce immediately began Christian service in earnest as he taught a Sunday school class at First Church in Providence, began reading devotional and theological literature, and presented a witness to his fellow students. In one case, Boyce convinced a Unitarian classmate of the deity of Christ and the need for an atonement. Upon hearing a lecture by J. L. Shuck, the first Baptist missionary to China (1835) appointed by the General Missionary Convention and the first missionary appointed by the newly established Foreign Mission Board of the Southern Baptist Convention, Boyce, impressed with the presentation, drew some conclusions about the nature of gospel work in the world. The combination of high culture, education, scientific sophistication, and literary heritage with "degradation in morals" demonstrated the vanity of placing education before Christianity as a means of uplifting civilization. "I only wish," Boyce urged, "there were more to go to carry the news of salvation to the ends of the world."[84]

Boyce's reading regimen during his last year in college was very impressive, demonstrating an increasing zeal for Christian theology and apologetics, including Bishop Butler's famous *Analogy of Religion*. The impact of Wayland during this year was substantial, particularly in moral philosophy and intellectual analysis, as Wayland liked to take advantage of the final year to imprint the students with both zeal and method for future learning. Boyce's letters home showed that his intellectual growth was matched by his interest in spiritual experience and revival. He asked James Mendenhall's sister to pray for the salvation of one of his family members. He also let her know about the pizzazz with which the senior class had passed the scrutiny of the examining council for their fall courses. "Symptoms of gratification ever and anon broke forth from the examining committee and strangers present while we proceeded in stately dignity to enlighten their ideas, and teach their withering minds to blossom with new vigor." He intended to expand his knowledge over the winter break by laying out about four-thousand pages of reading including Plato, Wayland, Bunyan, Milton, and Mill.

In the spring of Boyce's final year, 1847, a spiritual renewal for which he had prayed began on the campus. It yielded many conversions and brought about radical change in the tone of the college. Boyce remarked that the revival did not involve "a particle of excitement." Not a single person to his knowledge had been "converted under excitement" but rather through reading works of the evidences of Christianity with a "determination to learn the truth." In this way they were "convicted of their sins, and taught to cry out, 'What shall I do to be saved?'" The urgency of such matters pressed on Boyce's conscience. He resolved, with the help of God's Spirit, "to continue this work during the next term, and not to rest until not a soul can be found here who has not felt and known the pardoning grace of God." The importance of this work seemed to transcend even the accomplishment of having completed successfully his college course. "Never have I felt until this revival," Boyce revealed, "what a blessed privilege it is to save a soul." Giving a foretaste then of his future calling, Boyce remarked, "May my prayer evermore be to God that he may make me instrumental in his hands in the salvation of many! It is indeed a glorious and blessed privilege to labor in the vineyard of my Master."[85]

During the spring vacation, Boyce went to Massachusetts to visit with one of his college classmates and wrote his fellow Charlestonian, H. A. Tupper, "I believe I have never told you my intention to study for the ministry." In a follow-up letter two weeks later he continued, "As to my profession, I think at present that I shall study for the ministry. That seems to me the only subject in which I could have any interest; and it seems to me a theme so glorious, and one so much needed by mankind, that I should love to proclaim it." When his father learned of Boyce's intentions, he thought a visit home over the summer would help cool his ardor for that future and renew the course he had planned for his talented son. He learned, however, that James's resolve had deep roots and seemed unshakeable.

2

A Time of Theological and Denominational Refinement

*B*oyce, along with his friend and future brother-in-law, H. Allen Tupper, was licensed to gospel ministry on 14 November 1847. John Broadus recorded that Ker Boyce, "while strictly a moral man, and a generous supporter of the church he attended, . . . had no great sympathy with the claims of the ministry."[1] He, along with many of his associates in business, believed that his talented son would throw away his great gifts as a "parson." Boyce, convinced of the will of God, went to New York with the intention of enrolling in the theological department of Madison University in Hamilton, New York. Madison was opened as a school in 1820. It eventually absorbed the resources of Hamilton Theological Institution and by 1846 was chartered as a university. Boyce's acceptance into the theological program depended on his mastering a certain level of competence in Hebrew within a three-week period. Though Tupper completed the rigorous requirement and entered, Boyce discovered in preparation for entering that his eyes could not withstand the strain of study and received advice from a doctor that he should abandon the idea of a life given to such labor. With obvious stress of conscience, Boyce resigned himself to return to Charleston, leaving behind his pursuit of the gospel ministry. On the voyage home, however, as Broadus reported with Victorian delicacy, bad weather prolonged and aggravated the trip "and through the consequent nautical experiences he was relieved of extreme biliousness, and this contributed to the cure of his eyes."[2] Soon Boyce returned to full health and began to preach in a variety of villages in the area, including Washington, Georgia, a place in which he had an interest beyond the glories of the pulpit.

A Marriage Made in Washington

Boyce married on 20 December 1848. One year earlier he had been an attendant at the wedding of a college mate, Milton Robert, in Washington, Georgia. While at the wedding Boyce had been smitten with the many appealing traits of Lizzie Llewellyn Ficklen, a friend of the bride and the daughter of a prominent physician and planter of Washington, Fielding Ficklen. So overcome was Boyce with Miss Ficklen that he proposed to her one evening during the marriage festivities. She had deep roots of education, culture, and Christian character on both sides of her family and, according to Broadus, "to these advantages of family and education were added rare personal attractions, great kindness of heart, and extraordinary brilliancy in conversation." Sensibly, she refused his overture of matrimony and made him work with greater perseverance for so dear a prize. After several months of entreaties, rejections, renewals of proposal, visits, letters filled with "outpourings of a lover's wretchedness when rejected," finally a positive agreement was reached in May. Given the character of the lady in question, Broadus judged that "our young collegian, with all his ardor, may be defended as not having lost his head when he so quickly lost his heart."[3] The last issue of the *Southern Baptist* for 1848, December 27, carried the notice, "Married at

Washington, Georgia, on Wednesday, Dec. 20th, by the Rev. L. J. Robert, James P. Boyce, of this city, to Elizabeth Llewellyn, eldest daughter of Dr. F. Ficklen, of Washington."[4]

Editor of the *Southern Baptist*

It is no accident that the notice was carried in the Charleston paper that focused on items of interest to Baptists in South Carolina. A month before his marriage, Boyce had accepted the position as editor of the *Southern Baptist*. On the day of his marriage, December 20, an article written by Boyce entitled "I Blot Out a Day" appeared in the paper. While Boyce and Miss Ficklen shared the joy of uniting in marriage, the subscribers were reading something about the profound earnestness with which Boyce understood the stewardship of each moment of life.

The article was typical of much that Boyce wrote during his months as editor—devotional, reflective, pious, and hortatory. Boyce mused on the spiritual relevance of his daily practice of crossing out a day on the calendar when its time was done. What had become of it? "Then an opportunity for improvement is gone." The day was a gift of God sent on "an errand of kindness" to offer momentary opportunities for a "longer probation or an opportunity to do something more for my own eternal welfare, something more for the eternal good of others." Blotting out the day on the calendar can never blot out its significance as a day of history. It stands as a "part of the active, busy, responsible existence of my soul." No action can be leveled to nonexistence, and all its facts stand "whatever I may wish or attempt to do about them."

Also the day had its influence. A day used rightly increases "the moral power of spending another day as well or better." One ill-spent day "weakens the power of principle, and increases the probability of another" such day. Sins project themselves "forward to throw their baneful influence" on the next day. The "bands of iniquity" increase in strength; likewise, "the active holiness of one day prepares the golden thread of that girdle by which the saint binds his soul to more devoted and eminent consecration to God." None can arrest the influence that one day lends to another. When a day is gone, blotted out, its moral power remains.

As he wrote his last paragraph, the day of his marriage was close at hand. He was aware that people would read it even as he made vows before God to his beloved Lizzie. The vows of that day would project their influence into all that he did for the rest of his life. Perhaps he bore this in mind as he closed his article:

> I pause to say, I have just read a prayer that a day might perish. I think that a dreadful prayer, [even] if so good a man as Job did utter it. In the pressure of his sorrows, he must have lost his balance just at that moment. I will venture so great a variance with him as to say, "Let the day live." I will try so to improve it, that it shall live—shall live in my happy recollections—shall live in the life and power it shall give my spiritual being in its appropriate work—shall live and come and meet me at the judgment, and give a joyful account of the manner in which it was improved.[5]

Through the years, correspondence to Boyce included greetings of great fondness and appreciation to his wife. He knew that 20 December 1848 was well spent.

A similar concern Boyce expressed in the December 27 article, the day on which his announcement of marriage appeared. As he felt the close of the year edging nearer at rapid pace, Boyce asked himself and his readers, "How much has it assisted us and you to prepare for Heaven?" He continued with a series of questions along the same line, seeking to enforce the truth of the preciousness of time well spent in preparation for eternity through "serious meditation" and "constant prayer." The Christian, or anyone who would seek to improve the present for the sake of eternity, must use it "not for the acquisition of wealth, not for the pursuit of pleasure, not for the gratification of ambition, but to prepare for Heaven, to enable us to assimilate ourselves to Christ, and to enforce upon us the fulfillment of our obligations to our Heavenly Father."[6]

These kinds of admonishing articles constituted the simple execution of the editor's task as Boyce saw it. He had pledged this from the beginning. The paper announced on 22 November 1848 that the editorial management of the paper was committed to the Rev. James P. Boyce. The article described Boyce as "a graduate of Brown University, a licentiate of the first Baptist Church in Charleston," and noted that he possessed "qualities of mind and heart, which give promise of distinction and usefulness in the new field of labor he has entered."[7] During that week a friend of the paper wrote with congratulations that "their paper at last rejoices in the care and management of a responsible head." He implied no slur on the past management, but conceded the tremendous burden it must have been to attempt such a project when their full attention was required elsewhere. J. R. Kendrick, the pastor of First Baptist Church, James Tupper, a lawyer and leading Baptist layman, along with other devoted Baptists had served as the committee responsible for publication. "But a newspaper needs the individual attention of at least *one* suitable person" because of the diversity of material to be sorted through and the "mere writing of Editorials, requires no small amount of labor." The writer, who dubbed himself "Amicus," congratulated Boyce for having "stepped forward to assume the useful toils and share the honorable rewards incident to your present position."[8]

The twenty-one-year-old Boyce had zeal for the responsibility he had undertaken, but he might not have been ready for the intense scrutiny that he would endure. He viewed himself as serving the Lord by encouraging Baptists to unity and doctrinal purity. That the denomination would not always share his viewpoint as to what constituted its unity and purity he was not quite ready to absorb.

In his salutatory editorial, Boyce acknowledged that it was "no little thing to write for three thousand families—to have one's thoughts spread throughout the length and breadth of our State, to be perused by many whose minds are susceptible to the faintest impressions." Spiritual edification must, therefore, be uppermost. Included in this Boyce perceived that it would be necessary also to argue for a doctrinal standard to mark the Baptist witness statewide. He therefore staked a claim to the task of theological watchman: "We are as editor of the *Baptist* as much a Watchman on the Walls of Zion as he who sounds the alarm from the sacred desk. May God strengthen me to perform

His work." He asked the readers to provide material for inclusion such as missionary intelligence and notices of revivals. His recent experiences at Brown had made both these items of special concern to Boyce. Along with all the denominational information, he promised to include pertinent secular news to keep the reader informed appropriately.

As he believed the paper to be worthy of the patronage of the Baptists of South Carolina, Boyce asked his subscribers to do all they could to enroll new paying subscribers and to be conscientious to pay up themselves. Their confident support combined with "the zeal, the industry, and untiring perseverance" he was prepared to give should make the *Southern Baptist* "worthy of the efforts" expended and of their patronage. He pledged with the pregnant sentiments of a lover of truth: "But if an earnest desire for the furtherance of the principles of our denomination, and a full belief in their scriptural truth, accompanied by a determination to labor earnestly, industriously and prayerfully, be any index of success, we have that index."[9]

In furthering the principles of the denomination, Boyce regularly included reports of the associational meetings, revival meetings, and articles about missions. He discussed "Missions among the Southern Slaves" with the assurance that the writer/evangelist among the slaves was "no encourager of anything in the shape of abolitionism, but at the same time he recognizes the duties which the South owes to the negro population."[10] "The Practicability of the Missionary Work" was the title of a circular letter from the Charleston Association that addressed the question as to whether missionary expectations were "extravagant and fanciful, or are they authorized and reasonable?" The article showed that such labors were authorized by Scripture and well within the possibility of accomplishment by a wise, devoted, and persevering strategy on the part of the church. Though money is not the "sinews" of missionary work, "it is indispensable to its successful prosecution." To send missionaries, furnish them with necessities, print Bibles and other literature all require "no inconsiderable outlay of money. But this the church has, as well as the men." In an appeal that would be existentially vital for Boyce, J. R. Kendrick, the author of the letter, wrote, "If the mantles of Cobb and Mercer rested upon the great mass of Christians, famishing schemes of benevolence would no longer be compelled to go knocking and begging at the doors of our Churches, but, amply furnished with all requisite assistance, would exhaust their energies in their legitimate toils."[11]

When he published a notice about spring collections for the Foreign Mission Board, Boyce prefaced the report with remarks of his own. "It is a matter of great importance that the different boards under the charge of the Southern Baptists should have the support which will enable them to work effectually," Boyce urged. "Nothing is so disadvantageous as to be cramped for want of payments," he continued in anticipation by twenty years of a refrain that would become the recurring chorus of the hymn of his life. "Besides, Brethren," he continued, "we are not acting with fairness to our brethren who have gone abroad if we do not at least give them that support which we gave them reason to believe they would receive before they left us." None would like to be in their situation surrounded by enemies of our faith and unable to pay for necessaries of life. Southern Baptists should pay the "mite and the mass" and replenish the low treasury. "Lend as much as we may we are yet debtors. Ponder the extracts and *do something*."[12]

Boyce sought the edification of his readership. His first editorial, entitled "Purity of Heart," focused on the purity of Christ, a theme that he would revisit often as a profound theological motif, as a prod for his disciples "to look upon purity of heart as one of the most desirable of attainments," enabling them to see God. "How delightful the pleasure, how ennobling the honor," to "live in his presence, ever near him." Unlike the impure that are shut off from this beatific vision, the pure in heart find that "there is sacred pleasure, as well as a holy fear, in beholding God. God is to him the image after which he would be formed."[13]

In the same train of thought on the Beatitudes, Boyce wrote "The Blessedness of Affliction" on the concept of the blessings that come for God's children in the context of mourning. While they may at first blush "feel a disposition to murmur against the dispensations of Providence," when they begin to reap the benefits of removal from the world, "so soon do we cease to murmur at our calamity." When God's providence visits his people with the affliction of sickness or death, "the king of Terrors," and takes away a counselor, friend, or family member, "the providences of God may appear to us mysterious and mournful, but we know him who hath sent them and therefore we cannot murmur." In light of God's goodness and wisdom, we learn to arrive at a degree of submission characteristic of the full submission of Christ, and then we may be said truly to "have profited from our calamity." Boyce noted a church that had lost three highly useful members to death and others to change of residence. Even in this, the church must see the hand of God, for "what can be done but to rely upon the arm of the Lord." Soon she will rejoice, for another will emerge "to supply the place of the departed worthy" who will "labor as if God had appointed him to that work, and as though he was looked to for its due performance."[14]

In "The Love of the Spirit," Boyce reflected on the ministerial neglect of attention in preaching to the work of the Spirit. Given the reality of the Trinity, and that God is love, why do we withhold praise to the Spirit for his love? If we praise the Son for his condescension in the incarnation, "why do we withhold praise from the Spirit, who conceived the Son, and thus became the means of his incarnation?" If we praise the Son for his death for the "redemption of the multitude of saints, why do we neglect to praise that Spirit by whom Christ is made known and enforced upon our unwilling hearts until we are convicted, converted, and sanctified as his followers?" Is such neglect not an egregious failure in worship? In preaching about Christ and the cross from the word, do we forget that the Spirit inspired the Scriptures and does himself testify of Christ? "Be entreated, brethren," Boyce boldly admonished his elders, "duly to weigh this subject, and see if it be not worthy a place in your regular ministrations."[15]

Boyce included a section each week entitled "Our Book Table." In that column he would recommend new books and periodicals. Often these had to do with denominational items but sometimes they were of a broader and even secular perspective. He gave a summary of the contents of *Blackwood's Magazine*, a digest of recent literature published in Edinburgh. Boyce freely recommended some reviews as worthy of further notice and just as freely criticized those that he thought unworthy of time. An article on the Caxtons "takes away much from the merit of the magazine." Another on "The Dodo and

Its Kindred" "would hardly be interesting to any, except those well versed in Natural History, and especially ornithology." An article on the White Nile, however, is "exceedingly interesting," and one on art and artists in Spain is "well written in easy flowing style, and will amply repay the time spent in its perusal." On the *Memoirs of Sir William Kirkaldy of Grange*, Boyce closed his remarks with the quip, "To the lover of Scottish history, and who is not? This cannot fail to prove of interest."[16]

Boyce's review of the "Centennial Oration before the Charleston Library Society" composed by his father's good friend and the man for whom he was named, James L. Petigru, must have given him special pleasure. "Every Charlestonian loves her Library," Boyce claimed, with obvious pride in the culture that it represented and the many hours of joy that it had afforded him. He continued, "and every lover of literature will be delighted with this address." After several commendatory observations of the style of binding, printing, and paper, which prophesied of his continuing disposition for finely executed literature, Boyce declared, "In fine clear type, on thick and beautiful paper, it affords a proof that as good printing can be done in Charleston as in any other city of the United States. We are proud of the pamphlet, and proud to say that it was printed at the office of the Southern Baptist."[17]

One periodical Boyce listed came from Madison University, the school to which he had sought entrance but found his health prohibitive. "We rejoiced to learn that it is in so flourishing a condition," he wrote, and as he listed the numbers of students indicated, "Of these there are four southern students, two from Virginia, and two from this State—one of the latter in the theological department," a reference to his friend and future brother-in-law, H. A. Tupper.

Boyce listed pamphlets of a religious nature, especially after he was appointed depository agent for the Southern Baptist Publication Society by A. M. Poindexter on March 7. Poindexter, one of the most astute theologians, eloquent preachers, and effective denominational statesmen among Baptists in the South, took a special interest in Boyce and encouraged him in accurate and clear theological thinking.[18] Prominent Southern Baptist thinkers such as J. L. Reynolds of Richmond, William Carey Crane of Mississippi, R. B. C. Howell of Tennessee, and Joseph

S. Baker of Georgia, often entered the lists of those that contributed pamphlets. Two items, in light of Boyce's future work, deserve to be mentioned. J. L. Reynolds produced a pamphlet on the "Importance of the Study of Systematic Theology." Reynolds had already contributed to the paper several articles on justification by faith that Boyce deemed important. Also, R. B. C. Howell wrote "A Great Southern Theological Seminary" about which Boyce commented, "This article will in all probability be laid before the readers of the Southern Baptist, and be judged by each one of them for himself. We like it much."[19]

Boyce's voluminous reading of substantial theological works and his zeal for orthodoxy stood in the background of all that he wrote but rarely came to the surface. He had begun gathering an impressive theological library during and immediately after his final year at Brown and had scheduled an arduous and aggressive reading program. Broadus attested to his "burning ambition for profound scholarship" as indicated by the "character as well as the number of the books he began at once to procure, at large cost."[20] The most ambitious theological undertaking during the few months that Boyce edited the paper consisted of his publication of a lengthy defense of the doctrine of imputation in a series of eight articles. Concurrent with these articles, Boyce included seven articles by W. B. Johnson that defended a scheme of redemption that did not involve the imputation of the righteousness of Christ to the believer. Broadus did not attribute any of these articles to Boyce but said, "His own penchant for theology, even at this early period, appears in his allowing the paper to be for many weeks weighted down by two distinguished brethren with long and elaborate articles on the doctrine of 'Imputation,' in which comparatively few of the readers could be expected to take much interest." Broadus perhaps underestimated the readership of the paper as well as the importance of the articles at that time, but his awareness of their symbolic importance to Boyce is well stated. Not only did they express Boyce's "penchant," they helped form his own concept of theological polemics.

The target of these articles probably was the professor at Furman University whose place years later Boyce was to fill, J. S. Mims, currently the treasurer of the South Carolina Education Society. Mims rejected the doctrine of imputation and had made caustic remarks on the issue in 1848 in an address entitled "Orthodoxy." Mims considered the doctrine of Christ's federal headship and said, "The imputation of Adam's sin, *in this sense*, I grant may be true. But I deny that it is *explicitly scriptural*. It is not revealed in the Bible. I am, therefore, not bound to receive it as *divine truth*." He rejected imputation as a prior fact that explained the corruption of human nature. Second, he rejected the "imputation of Christ's righteousness to believers." He contended that neither Christ nor the apostles spoke of "Christ's active obedience as being vicarious." To the theologians who argue that "the justice of God demands perfect obedience, and hence Christ's perfect obedience must be imputed to us," Mims responded, "I reply, no!" If guilt is removed by the death of Christ, no imputation of righteousness is necessary.[21]

William B. Johnson, president of the South Carolina Baptist Convention and the Southern Baptist Convention, represented the position of Mims. Johnson was chair of the trustees at Furman when Mims made the presentation and headed the committee that requested its publication. Deep earnestness and serious-mindedness about issues of doctrinal truth permeate the entire series. In his announcement of the series Boyce wrote, "Opposed as we are to controversies generally, we can never refuse our columns to contributions such as these." He could not object to a "temperate discussion of any theological question" because "controversy is apt to elicit the truth."[22]

Greg Wills has made a strong case for J. L. Reynolds as the author of the eight articles defending imputation.[23] Reynolds's maturity as a doctrinal thinker and his energetic interest in the issue make him a prime candidate. Mims was probably referring to Reynolds when he wrote, "I stand charged, though not by a member of your body, with heterodoxy."[24] Reynolds's inaugural discourse given before the trustees when he began teaching at Furman (1839) was published in 1842. He set before the trustees a clear picture of his vision for training ministers in theological discipline. He gave an exposition of exegetical theology, systematic theology, historical theology, and practical theology. He strongly advocated a knowledge of biblical languages as the key to the treasure chest of Scripture as the foundation to every activity dependent on revealed truth. Systematic theology must not serve the ends of humanly constructed documents posing as a brutal Procrustes, but should represent the full synthesis of biblical truth arranged by topics relevant to the purpose of biblical revelation and discussed in such a way as to intersect with knowledge, or speculative ideas, derived from other disciplines. Historical theology helps locate the ways in which error has been introduced and traces its development. At the same time this discipline helps isolate distinct formulations of truth important to all Christians. Practical theology, particularly the discipline of rhetorical theory in its relation to preaching, is important for the clear proclamation of the gospel.[25]

At the very time of the writing of these articles, Reynolds was seeing through the press an American edition of Benjamin Beddome's *A Scriptural Exposition of the Baptist Catechism*.[26] In the introduction, Reynolds expressed his hope for a return to sound doctrinal instruction in the churches, an influence that would bring about early and sound piety among the young people and would preserve biblical orthodoxy in the churches. Pointing out that the lack of catechetical instruction was behind the decline in orthodoxy among the churches of New England, he quoted the *Christian Review*: "The orthodoxy of New England failed, more than a quarter of a century since, doubtless, as the result, in part, of a defection in the habit of parental religious teaching." He wanted to destroy the mistaken notion that "for parents to teach their children a system of doctrinal truth" constituted an "infringement of mental liberty." Reynolds clearly favored rigorous instruction in biblical doctrine, found the *Baptist Catechism* suitable for the task and sound theologically, and wanted Baptists to avoid the same decline that had overtaken New England.[27]

Reynolds considered the New Divinity the particular theological culprit in the New England decline, viewed it as a road to heresy, and felt the necessity of warning Baptists against its heterodoxy. Even though out of the state from 1845 to 1851, and presently serving as pastor of Second Baptist in Richmond, he had deep concerns about the past influence of Jonathan Maxcy, who had served as president of South Carolina College in Columbia for sixteen years prior to his death in 1820, and the similar influence of J. S. Mims at Furman College. All of these concerns of Reynolds make their way into the articles on imputation.

Given the probable authorship of Reynolds, some evidence, however, favors the direct involvement of Boyce, not only as having editorial responsibility for the articles' publication, but perhaps in contributing to their content. That this particular subject intrigued him can be seen in his editorial written during his first week on the job and appearing on 29 November 1848. Entitled "Purity of Heart," the article set forth the absolute purity of Christ as the goal of purity, earnestness in seeking purity as an evidence of saving faith, and the grace of God as providing a right standing for the earnest seeker. Those who feel themselves "actuated in all things by the propelling influences of God's grace" may feel confident in the status of being "pure in heart" and may comfort themselves "with the promise in the enjoyment of which the pure are called blessed." How does this comfort come? "Christ is made your righteousness. He imputes unto you the purity of his own pure life and ensures unto you the blessings which that purity gives."[28]

In addition to this clear commitment to the theology of imputation, the manner in which the articles appear shows Boyce's predisposition to affirm the positive presentation. He allowed them to appear unsigned, without initials or pseudonym. Also the style of argumentation looks very much like that which Boyce eventually developed. That was later, however, after much more education in theological reasoning and polemics and a more comprehensive exposure to the Reformed literature than he had at this time. Both the style and content and the breadth of familiarity with historical literature would have been more characteristic of Reynolds. Reynolds certainly had reasons to use the pages of the *Southern Baptist* to draw attention to this doctrine.

Boyce admitted such a lengthy discussion on this subject, therefore, because it was a matter of current concern to him. Even though only twenty-one, Boyce's immediate and intimate acquaintance with the catechisms and confession used in the First Baptist Church of Charleston along with his frequent references to Dr. Furman and great sympathy for Basil Manly shows someone who had a heart for the Charleston influence, which was also true of Reynolds. Books that are quoted are books that for the most part had come out in the past two or three years, some of which Boyce had just purchased for his library. The commentaries of Haldane and Hodge on Romans,

Turretin, and Butler's *Analogy* are all cited in the article. Boyce had just finished a detailed study of Butler's work. Also Boyce had made marks in these books just in the places that are quoted in the articles. For example, one long quote from Hodge in the first article has a mark by it in Boyce's copy. Even more notable is a side note written in pencil, an uncommon practice of Boyce, in Hodge's commentary, a note that appears substantially in the article. Written in pencil is this comment about Paul's discussion of faith: "Rem[ember] that while the apostle uses *pistis* [written in Greek characters] with all other prepositions speaking of justification he never uses it with *dia*, 'on account of.'" In article 7 defending imputation, the author has a long discussion on that issue and says, "We are said to be saved by or through faith, but never *on account of* it."

Books by Jonathan Edwards and Andrew Fuller, also quoted in the articles, do not appear to have been in Boyce's library until after the writing of the articles. There is good reason, therefore, to conceive of Boyce as receiving articles from Reynolds with license to add to them arguments and other material that he saw as fitting for the occasion. This might particularly be true as some articles appearing in the same week interact with each other point for point. At any rate, it is clear that Boyce approved the articles that endorsed imputation of the righteousness of Christ.

Johnson sought to defend a view of justification in which the sinner is justified apart from the works of the law—that is, apart from anyone's works of the law. Of sovereign grace, God grants a changed nature which gives rise to faith. That faith, though void of works, by divine mercy is imputed as righteousness, when one confesses with his mouth that Jesus is Lord. Only in this way can we truly be said to be justified apart from works but according to mercy. "I am aware," Johnson wrote, "that not a few of God's dear children believe that the righteousness without works, which God imputes, is the righteousness of Christ. . . . But I submit, with all Christian courtesy," he continued, "whether the righteousness of Christ—be it His active and passive obedience, or His active obedience alone—does not consist of *works the most pure and noble*." If this is true that Christ's works are of the most pure sort, then it further follows that "this righteousness" as the believer's "whole and sole righteousness" is most surely a "righteousness with works," though it is not wrought by the believer himself. On the other hand, if the believer's faith is imputed for righteousness, then this surely is an "imputation of righteousness without works."[29]

Johnson went through columns of reasoning on a variety of Scripture passages to draw this conclusion on several occasions: "But here I see not the doctrine of the imputation of Christ's righteousness for justification."[30] No positive expression of perfect obedience is needed at all, Johnson posited, but merely freedom from the verdict of condemnation—a freedom that comes by gratuitous forgiveness on the basis of repentance, confession, and belief. Along the way Johnson quoted Andrew Fuller and Jonathan Edwards as ostensibly in support of his position. He also questioned the validity of an appeal to historic confessions "as standards of Faith and Practice, or as tests of orthodoxy," for the use of such in theological discussion amounts to an unfair restraint on the conscience by the works and words of men. He desired to "bow only to the teachings of God the Spirit in His holy word."[31]

Reynolds began by creating a presumption in favor of the imputation of Christ's righteousness by showing that this view was present in the most important Protestant confessions, including Baptist confessions, most notably the Charleston Confession of Faith. He then argued through biblical exposition of texts such as Romans 5:12–21 the relations between imputation, original sin, corruption, and justification. He argued against the imputation of faith itself or infused righteousness, and included a survey of Baptist theologians on the issue. Reynolds contended that biblically it is impossible for faith to be identified as the righteousness by which we are justified. He aligned the view that Johnson defended with Socinianism as well as with the New Divinity theologians of New England. "The advocates of the New Divinity," he attested, "are laying the foundations broad and deep, of a new phase of philosophical infidelity . . . which pretends reverence while it really insults—which, like Judas, betrays the Son of Man by a kiss."[32] He also objected to Johnson's use of Fuller and Edwards by quoting their arguments in context and concluding, "This is what Edwards and Fuller mean, when their writings are fully quoted, and not partially, for the purpose of recommending, under the sanction of their names, a portentous error, which they expressly and repeatedly condemned."

When Johnson asserted that only forgiveness, and not positive righteousness, was all that was intended by justification, Reynolds responded that pardon "delivers him [the sinner] from the curse of the law, but it gives him no title to eternal life." That blessing is the "reward promised to obedience." In addition to forgiveness, the sinner needs "a positive righteousness, which will bring him within the legitimate scope of the divine government and entitle him to happiness."[33]

To argue against imputation as a model in accordance with which God operates on account of its apparent unfairness is to argue against the Bible itself as well as the unanimous verdict of Baptist confessions. A sense of honest stewardship demands that faithfulness to a confessional standard be maintained. A simple agreement that the Bible is inspired while "exploding" its distinctive doctrines does little to protect the substance of the Christian faith. A confession of faith protects the denominational witness to full-orbed truth and must be set forth as the documentation of unity. If Baptists tolerate the "explosion" of such doctrines as the deity of Christ, total depravity, and the imputation of Christ's righteousness, "unless the churches interpose, it is difficult to predict what explosions are to follow." Should other explosions begin to occur, however, "the final explosion," so Reynolds asserted, "will rend the denomination in twain." If such a division may be avoided "only by conniving at pernicious errors, and standing silently by, while the landmarks of our fathers are one after another stricken down, I for one say—Let it come."[34]

Though Boyce had great respect for Johnson, a respect that he demonstrated in years to come, his agreement lay with Reynolds in this interchange. He agreed with Reynolds's evaluation of the importance of justification by imputed righteousness and later would express his own mature views clearly on that issue. In the opening paragraph to his discussion of justification in the *Abstract of Systematic Theology* he affirmed his evaluation of the centrality of that doctrine when he wrote, "No doctrine of Scripture is more important than that of justification. It involves the whole method of the salvation of sinners. It is vitally connected with all other fundamental doctrines. A correct conception of it cannot exist when other truths are ignored, or only partially received. The opinions held upon this point control in great part the theological views in general of all Christian individuals and parties." Further in the discussion, he affirmed another major part of Reynolds's emphasis: "But justification confers righteousness as well as pardon. Not only are sins remitted but men are made partakers of the righteousness procured by Christ which is imputed to them."[35]

A bit more than halfway through the series of articles, one of the subscribers to the *Southern Baptist* wrote Boyce asking that he publish a sermon by Samuel Stillman entitled "Imputed Righteousness, One of the Glories of the Gospel."[36] He assumed that Boyce had heard of Stillman and knew of the sermon, but, if such was not the case, the subscriber promised to provide it. Boyce wrote that he did not know of the sermon and could not promise to print it until he had seen it. The anonymous subscriber responded that given such a response it would probably be fruitless to provide the sermon, for to him it seemed clear that Boyce had embraced the views on imputation that were put forth by W. B. Johnson. Since Stillman's views were opposite, and would be rejected, the subscriber concluded, "This evidently proves your paper to be a one-sided, party paper" on the important issue of imputation. "And . . . I do not wish to read one side of the question of this great subject," the correspondent continued, "particularly that side that I do not and never can in time believe." He then promised that when his subscription terminated, he would no longer be "a subscriber."

Boyce responded with vinegar. He rejected the accusation that he edited a "party paper" and expressed amazement that the subscriber could have drawn the inference that he did about Boyce's theological position. In addition, the impertinence of his request for the publication of an alternative view surpassed credibility. Did he not see that one holding Dr. Stillman's position led off the interchange? Was he unaware that the two viewpoints had run virtually side by side? He wondered how "a subscriber" could "reconcile it to his conscience to have made the charge of partizanship [*sic*] against us." Then for good measure, Boyce indicated that he felt more than willing to terminate the correspondent's subscription. "If he will but forward his name, it shall be immediately stricken from the list. We would not for ten times the sum of his subscription be again subjected to so much impertinence and injustice."[37]

Boyce found himself in the middle of another misunderstanding over the interstate discussion concerning a central theological institution. The *Alabama Baptist Advocate* of March 9 carried a summary of a meeting held in Georgia about a Southern theological school. Georgia was suggested as a possible location. Boyce carried the Alabama summary in his March 21 paper. On March 28 he expressed his views on the subject. Boyce's quotation of the summary from Alabama was taken by some Georgia brethren as Boyce's own summary, which they found entirely misleading. They called the young editor to account, provided a more accurate presentation of the report in question, and concluded, "We consider that justice to the committee requires that there should be a correction of the impression calculated to be made by the publication in the Southern Baptist." Boyce presented the reason for the misunderstanding along with the correspondence from Georgia and stated frankly, "And yet, we are not to blame."

In the same issue, April 11, Boyce had to answer another objection written under the pseudonym "Countryman." His objections concerned Boyce's own remarks about a meeting called by W. B. Johnson to discuss the same issue of theological education. The meeting proposed by Johnson would convene in time to move the matter to the Southern Baptist Convention meeting in Nashville. Boyce doubted the wisdom of calling such a meeting at that time, and for expressing this he was soundly reprimanded. Boyce gave a further explanation for opposing the meeting because of the obvious deleterious impression it would make on the rest of the Baptists in the South. He favored the proposed theological institution; he opposed the proposed meeting of South Carolina Baptists at Aiken, South Carolina. Countryman drew some unwarranted inferences from Boyce's article and expressed these inferences in language to which Boyce took strong exception. "We said no such thing," Boyce retorted, "and how a man of common sense and common honesty can assert it we know not." Is this the language of Southern courtesy? "This may seem strong language," Boyce continued, "but we desire to use it. It is enough to irritate any man to have his language perverted in this way—or rather not to have it perverted, but to have expressions put in which he never used and never thought of."[38]

Two weeks earlier, March 28, Boyce had expressed his views concerning a "Central Theological Institution." The proposed meeting in Aiken, the discussion in Georgia, and the response from Alabama all were placed in context in the opening paragraph. He included analysis of an editorial in the *Religious Herald* of Virginia that had sounded a pessimistic note concerning the theoretical school. Boyce felt that the discussion was moving in the wrong direction. He wrote, "We regret this the more since we have long wished for so happy a consummation, and until the present period have been pretty sanguine of its success." Pessimism and reticence in the Southern states with a large Baptist population made Boyce confess, "The aspect of affairs is exceedingly dark, yet we cannot but hope, even though it be against hope, that brighter prospects may yet cheer us, and that the object may be accomplished."

Boyce deftly set aside a variety of objections raised in each of the respective states concerning trustees, funding, faculty, and realistic hopes of success. He proposed a simple model for the relation between trustees, faculty, and school operation; he suggested that using funds set aside for such education in the respective states could easily be managed legally. That simple action would provide an abundant source so that "there need be no excuse arising from want of means for procuring a thorough theological education." Faculty would be no difficulty when the entire corpus of Baptists in the South provided the legitimate field from which they would be selected. "No longer would our theological students be compelled to study theology as they best may," Boyce remarked, clearly with a substantial list of Baptist ministers past and present in mind as he so wrote, "but men of experience and talent, men of piety and intellect, could be easily secured, and our young men supplied with the requisite means, and educated under these teachers would themselves be mighty in the scriptures, conversant with the doctrines of the Bible, and able expositors of its sacred truths." Then, under the assumption that such an institution is not only feasible, but eminently desirable, he dreamed, "Our institution will occupy a deservedly high position, able to compete with all in its means for instruction and working out such results for the cause of Christ, as shall tend soon to spread his kingdom throughout the world." Boyce had argued the merits of the institution and proposed a means through which "the first talent of the country" could be procured to establish "a college of high standing throughout the country." Will Southern Baptists have such an institution? This would not be the last time that Boyce would propose such an arrangement for theological education.[39]

On 2 May 1849 Boyce resigned his position as editor with the announcement, "Our own connexion with the paper is to close with the present number." Its number of subscribers had expanded but it still stood a few hundred dollars in debt. The next week, an editorial appeared that stated, "During five months the paper has been gratuitously and efficiently edited by Rev. James P. Boyce." It also mentioned that editors sometimes have "their motives misapprehended and rudely impugned, their honest opinions perverted and unkindly assailed." Broadus commented, "This goes to show that the young editor had keenly felt the injustice done him, especially by the writers he had replied to on April 11." Broadus went on to note, "The close of the paper's third year was a convenient time for ending his connection with it, and the recent assaults perhaps made him impatient to throw the task aside without delay."[40] This convenient ending, along with the restored health of his eyes, and his ever heightening zeal for theological education made this a perfect season for renewing his pursuit of formal theological study.

Princeton

Boyce briefly considered returning to Hamilton, where his friend Tupper neared the end of his study. His boyhood friend Basil Manly Jr. had attended one year at Newton and then had transferred to Princeton where he graduated in 1847. Manly Jr. reminisced in 1891 on these events. Under the advice of John L. Dagg, Manly, when he had decided to devote himself to the ministry, went to Newton Theological Institution. After one year, however, circumstances dictated another plan.

When the disruption of 1845 occurred between Northern and Southern Baptists, in their voluntary missionary organizations,—for the
division extended only to these, and never to the actual relations of
the churches,—it led to the withdrawal from Newton of the four
Southern students who were there—S. C. Clopton, E. T. Winkler,
J. W. M. Williams, and myself. The other three went directly into
ministerial work, while I determined, as I was younger, to prosecute
further preparatory study, and went, under the advice of my father,
of Dr. Dagg, of Dr. Francis Wayland, and other friends, to Princeton
Theological Seminary. On the same grounds a few years after, my early
friend, and late colleague, James P. Boyce, went to Princeton also.[41]

The feelings that characterized the Baptists in the North and the
South did not develop as quickly among Presbyterians, especially at
Princeton. Given the love that Archibald Alexander had for Virginia,
the hospitality extended to Southern students made them immediately
feel accepted. Boyce concluded that Princeton held the greatest opportunity for him. David Calhoun records that "J. W. Alexander described
some of the new seminary students: 'Of Scots and Hibernians we
have about a dozen, several being Glasgow graduates; also a Baptist
preacher, and wife, from Charleston. Last year there were five or six
Baptists, all most promising young men.'"[42] The Baptist preacher from
Charleston was J. P. Boyce.

Boyce came to Princeton at a propitious time when the first gen-
erational change was palpable. The atmosphere of the school had
been established by its first two professors, Archibald Alexander
(1772–1851) and Samuel Miller (1769–1850). Alexander had been
elected the first professor in 1812 as the culmination of a desire to
provide for theological instruction for ministers in a school separate
from Princeton College. Ashbel Green had led the way since 1800 for a
theological seminary and found great support in his effort from Samuel
Miller and Archibald Alexander. Miller, after a stirring speech made
by Green to the 1805 General Assembly of the Presbyterian Church,
wrote to Green, pastor of Second Presbyterian in Philadelphia, that "if
it be desired to have the divinity school uncontaminated by the college,
to have its government unfettered, and its orthodoxy and purity perpetual, it appears to me that a separate establishment will be on many

accounts desirable." At the meeting of the General Assembly in 1808 Alexander, pastor of Third Presbyterian in Philadelphia, stirred the delegates with his call for presbyteries or synods to found theological seminaries to provide a future ministry for the church. By 1810 the General Assembly had decided to establish a single theological seminary. The Assembly pledged "to make it, under the blessing of God, a nursery of vital piety as well as of sound theological learning, and to train up persons for the ministry who shall be lovers of religion, and a blessing to the church of God."[43]

When Alexander was elected to the position of first professor of the new school, he brought with him the experience of education under William Graham, several months in itinerant evangelism, serving as pastor of several smaller congregations in Virginia including a church composed of slaves "eminent for piety," the presidency of Hamden-Sydney, a wide range of firsthand experience in the dizzying theological options in American evangelicalism, serving a large congregation in a large urban center, the personal knowledge of mature Christians who were converted during the First Great Awakening, and an advanced and advancing knowledge of the entire corpus of theological literature in Western culture. He was perfectly fitted to fulfill the plan of creating a school that would "unite, in those who shall sustain the ministerial office, religion and literature; that piety of the heart which is the fruit only of the renewing and sanctifying grace of God, with solid learning."[44]

When Boyce entered, Alexander was seventy-seven years old and taught pastoral and polemic theology. Boyce, according to Broadus, was amused as well as edified by the demeanor of Alexander, who seemed to take to himself some of the prerogatives of advanced age during Boyce's time there. Boyce, at twenty-three, judged that Alexander, in his declining years, was not "as gifted as his sons, but has a clear logical mind." Boyce reminisced also about Alexander's correction of the young students in their preaching that led Broadus to remark, "His general kindness and sympathetic appreciation gave keener edge to the caustic remarks which sometimes appeared needful." One student who pressed his rhetorical gifts to their limits in describing God's creation of light evoked the brief remark from Alexander, "You're a very smart young man, but you can't beat Moses."[45]

Alexander, however, had provided much more than the material of anecdotes to the experience of Boyce. He infused a commitment to historical doctrinal standards, a sound commitment to Christian evidences, a spirit of fervent Christian experience founded upon a sound theology of conversion, a consuming zeal for missions through pedagogy, prayer, inquiry, and active recruitment, a support of revivals rightly conceived combined with a sustained criticism of the "new measures" revivalism of Finney and his associates, and fervent, Bible-centered, Christ-centered preaching. His works on Christian evidences (*A Brief Outline of the Evidences of the Christian Religion*, 1825), Christian experience (*Religious Experience*), and Christian doctrine (*A Brief Compend of Bible Truth*, 1846) show the blending of mind and heart that Alexander desired to be the hallmark of Princeton. In addition, he wielded a greater influence on Charles Hodge, Boyce's favorite professor, than did any other factor or combination of factors. Hodge testified that he was "moulded more by the character and instructions of Dr. Archibald Alexander, than by all other external influences combined."[46]

Alexander, like Boyce subsequently, used Francis Turretin's *Institutes of Elenctic Theology* as a text, and, like Boyce subsequently, required his students to recite their way through its twenty loci and subdivided questions.[47] Like Boyce he added his own lectures at certain points by way of correction or expansion, these personal comments growing until they formed a sizable portion of the course. He also divided polemic theology from systematic theology, a curricular idea also followed by Boyce.

In 1854, Francis Wayland read the *Life of Archibald Alexander* written by his son J. W. Alexander. He commented:

> I have just completed your admirable biography of your father—now with God. A more charming biography I have never read. While you write as a son, it is as a son of Archibald Alexander. There is nothing filial that is not admirable, and not a word that could not be attested even more strongly by a host of witnesses. A more beautiful or noble specimen of Christian character can hardly be conceived. His gifts were great and abundant beyond the common lot of humanity; and God placed them where they shone with a radiance that illumined the whole church of Christ.[48]

They certainly illuminated Princeton Seminary and glowed within the very fabric of the school as they insinuated themselves into the lives of every other professor until the last quarter of the nineteenth century. Alexander died on 22 October 1851, several months after Boyce had left the seminary.

Samuel Miller perfectly complemented Alexander. For one year Alexander carried the teaching load himself, but knew quickly that another professor was needed if a serious three-year program was to be fulfilled. Miller, coming from the Wall Street Presbyterian Church in New York City, took the position of professor of ecclesiastical history and church government on 29 September 1813. When Boyce arrived at the seminary, it had become clear that Miller no longer could meet his classes. He died during Boyce's first year, on 7 January 1850. Evidently he presented periodic lectures attended by Boyce, for in a biographical questionnaire completed by Boyce in 1872 he noted, "At Princeton Theological Seminary, I studied under Drs. Archibald Alexander, Samuel Miller," and others.

Though Miller's time was short after Boyce arrived, Miller had invested enormous energy in creating an ethos conducive to serious pastoral training in a confessional context. He had been active with Ashbel Green since about 1800 in the push to establish a seminary independent of the college and probably had aided Green in developing the "Plan" for the seminary that was adopted in 1811. The "Plan," containing eight sections of descriptive expectations for every facet of seminary life, called for every student to subscribe the following statement:

> Deeply impressed with a sense of the importance of improving in knowledge, prudence, and piety, in my preparation for the Gospel Ministry, I solemnly promise, in a reliance on divine grace, that I will faithfully and diligently attend on all the instructions of this Seminary, and that I will conscientiously and vigilantly observe all the rules and regulations specified for its instruction and government, so far as the same relate to the students; and that I will obey all the lawful requisitions, and readily yield to all the wholesome admonitions of the professors and directors of the Seminary, while I shall continue a member of it.[49]

That pledge, however, by no means constituted the only mark of Miller on Boyce's experience at Princeton. Miller helped establish an atmosphere of intensity about the study of divinity. In 1827 Miller published *Letters on Clerical Manners and Habits, Addressed to a Student in the Theological Seminary at Princeton, N. J.*, which consisted of a number of addresses and talks given to the students at Princeton. Letter 8 entitled "Habits in the Study," listed thirty separate bits of advice about study. The first was, "Cherish a deep sense of the great extent, and the infinite importance of theological science." The student should approach his studies every day "under the deep impression, that what you have to do, demands your best powers, and your utmost diligence." Miller also contended that none would ever study theology to advantage unless he cherished "a peculiar and devoted attachment to the office." Miller encouraged a passion for sanctified knowledge in observing, "If you have not learned, my young friend, the precious art of pursuing your professional studies, not only with a deep sense of their importance; but as the Italians say, *con amore*: if they do not form the pursuit in which your heart delights, for its own sake, and more especially for the sake of its blessed end; your attainments will be tardy and imperfect."[50] Miller never spoke words that were more fully embraced. Boyce studied *con amore*, expected his students to do so, and constantly emphasized the "infinite importance of theological science."

Miller also presented an energetic and highly convicted defense of creeds and confessions. He gave seven positive reasons for their implementation, dealt with five prominent objections, and drew six practical inferences. He affirmed that such not only were expedient but "indispensably necessary to the harmony and purity of the visible church." Without them biblical unity cannot be maintained but will necessarily give way to "all the evils of discord and corruption." A written creed arms a church to be a depository, guardian, and witness of the truth. It does no good to say that one believes the Bible when at the same time one "really den[ies] all its essential doctrines." A church must extract certain articles of faith from the Scriptures and compare "these articles with the professed belief of those whom she supposes to be heretics." A creed fulfills the necessity of truth and candor and is friendly to the "study of Christian doctrine and . . . to the prevalence of Christian knowledge." All ages have found them "indispensably necessary" for their witness to truth in light of the heretical challenges that have developed in each age. They do not replace, but highlight, the Bible; they are not repressive of freedom of conscience but express it; they do not restrict free inquiry but give voice to the views that years of pious and vigorous inquiry have produced. They do retard the development of heresy when conscientiously administered and do not produce discord but protect the church from it. Miller believed that any conscientious minister with a love for truth, for the glory of God, for the peace and edification of the church, with a desire for her protection from destructive error will hold forth the standards of truth symbolized in the Westminster Standards.[51] Boyce would project this same view of the function of a creed into his call for the establishing of a theological seminary for Baptists.

Boyce studied with two sons of Archibald Alexander. From J. W. Alexander (1804–59) he took the course on the composition and delivery of sermons. This great man taught only two years at Princeton, the two years that Boyce attended, and then served as pastor of Fifth Avenue Presbyterian Church in New York. Jeremiah Calvin Lanphier attended this church and went from there to serve as a missionary of the North Reformed Protestant Dutch Church. His missionary labors eventually led to the establishment of a midday prayer meeting that became the impetus for the nationwide revival of 1858. J. W. Alexander was active in leading prayer meetings, preaching on occasions, and writing tracts that were widely used in this movement of the Spirit of God. Alexander became seriously ill, took a trip to Virginia in an effort to recover, and died in July 1859. While he taught at Princeton, his wife, who found the Baptist students very cordial, was especially drawn to students from the South, and, along with her daughter Janetta, paid special attention to the wife of James P. Boyce.[52]

The third son of Archibald Alexander, Joseph Addison Alexander (1809–60), taught Oriental and biblical literature. He died on 28 January 1860, not quite six months after the death of James Waddel Alexander, his quickly declining health aggravated by the shock of having lost his brother. All those who observed his habit of life concluded that he did as little as any educated man they knew for his physical health, worked and read incessantly with no attention to physical exercise or proper diet. He was recognized as one of the most brilliant linguistic minds in America. "He learned languages himself with marvelous facility," Broadus remarked, "and could not sympathize with, or patiently endure, the slow mental movements of the ordinary students."[53] He had been teaching since he was twenty-four years of age in 1833. His brilliance did not subvert his utter simplicity of faith in the inspiration of Scripture or his fierce loyalty to its thorough consistency. Broadus was impressed with the power and clarity with which he would wrestle with knotty issues of interpretation and other difficulties that often confront the serious interpreter of Scripture, and would then emerge with a startling conversion of "objections to truth into arguments for its support."[54]

On January 29, the day after the brilliant scholar's death, Charles Hodge spoke to the student body on "The Lord reigneth, let the earth rejoice." He closed with a eulogy for Alexander, noting, among other excellencies, "his sincere devotion to truth," in particular, "his faith in the infallible authority of the gospel, and his reverence for the word of God, and his thorough orthodoxy notwithstanding his familiarity with all forms of modern, historical, and doctrinal scepticism."[55] That presupposition lay beneath all of his exegesis and led Charles Hodge to say before the General Assembly of 1860, "His thorough orthodoxy, his fervent piety, humility, faithfulness in the discharge of his duties, and reverence for the Word of God, consecrated all his other gifts. . . . He glorified the Word of God in the sight of his pupils beyond what any man I ever saw had the power of doing."[56]

Charles Hodge (1797–1878) was the third professor at Princeton Seminary. For two years, 1820–22, Hodge taught biblical languages as an instructor and was elected in 1822 as Professor of Oriental and biblical literature. When Boyce attended, Hodge had become professor of exegetical and didactic theology, an assignment he held from 1840 to 1854, at which time he added polemic theology. This professor, having deferentially waited his time, now rose to a place of prominence ("at the height of his powers," as Broadus expressed it), and captured the admiration of Boyce. Hodge had edited the *Biblical Repertory and*

Princeton Review since its beginning in 1824 with the exception of two years that he spent studying in France and Germany. When there, Hodge studied closely with Wilhelm Gesenius, the premier Hebrew scholar and Old Testament critic, became friends with the leaders of German evangelicalism such as Tholuck, with whom he developed the strongest friendship, Neander, and Hengstenberg, and heard Schleiermacher preach. His colleagues at Princeton kept up correspondence with consistent warnings against being deadened by German criticism and philosophy while he benefited from the rigorous study of the biblical text.[57] He returned in September 1828, invigorated intellectually but unmoved theologically, having found his faith in Christ and his commitment to infallible biblical truth sufficient to withstand the subtle allurement of the romantic Christianity of the evangelicals and the withering blasts of destructive criticism.

He also was broadened culturally and manifested an attractive catholic spirit that made its way into his rigorous theological discussions. The combination of clear affirmation of truth, vigorous criticism of error, but openness to the transcendent nature of Christian experience surely stamped Boyce with the same commitment to broad sympathies. He also saw living proof that study in Germany did not conclusively lead to infidelity. Hodge viewed Schleiermacher as the source of "German speculative principles" and a theological method that infected many varieties of thought that differed "only in the length to which they carry their common principles in modifying or overthrowing the faith of the Church." This perception included the Mercersburg theologians Philip Schaff and John Nevin. Hodge, nevertheless, told a story about his experience in Berlin that affected his conception of the relation between theology and experience. This story is a footnote in a section in which he criticized the implicit pantheism of Schleiermacher's system as well as his acceptance of Bible-destroying higher criticism.

> When in Berlin the writer often attended Schleiermacher's church. The hymns to be sung were printed on slips of paper and distributed at the doors. They were always evangelical and spiritual in an eminent degree, filled with praise and gratitude to our Redeemer. Tholuck said that Schleiermacher, when sitting in the evening with his family, would

often say, "Hush, children; let us sing a hymn of praise to Christ."
Can we doubt that he is singing those praises now? To whomsoever
Christ is God, St. John assures us, Christ is a Saviour.[58]

This brave confidence in the power of the Spirit of God to transcend the crippled intellectual apparatus of mystical theologians peppered Hodge's theology. In concluding a section on the person and
work of Christ, Hodge remarked, "After all, apart from the Bible,
the best antidote to all these false theories of the person and work
of Christ, is such a book as Doctor Schaff's 'Christ in Song.'" The
hymns come from all the churches through the Christian era and set
forth Christ as truly God, truly man, as the expiation for sin, as the
object of worship, love, and adoration and "as the ultimate ground
of confidence." Hodge asked for no better theology and no better
religion than contained in those hymns. "They were indited by the
Holy Spirit," he claimed, "in the sense that the thoughts and feelings which they express, are due to his operations on the hearts of
his people."[59]

By 1849 Hodge had published two volumes of essays extracted
from the *Theological Review* and two editions of his commentary
on Romans. Though his *Systematic Theology* did not appear until
1871, the notes for it were well developed by this time, and Hodge
filled the students' minds as well as their notepads with the massive discussions that eventually crystalized into the textbooks. Basil
Manly, who had graduated in 1847, recalled that the students said,
"His thoughts move in rows." Broadus reported, "James Boyce was
more powerfully impressed by Dr. Hodge than by any other teacher
except President Wayland." Then, in an expression of his own opinion as well as what he had observed in Boyce through their years of
collegiality, Broadus wrote, "It was a great privilege to be directed
and upborne by such a teacher in studying that exalted system of
Pauline truth which is technically called Calvinism, which compels
an earnest student to profound thinking, and, when pursued with
a combination of systematic thought and fervent experience, makes
him at home among the most inspiring and ennobling views of God
and of the universe he has made."[60]

While the schedule might not have been the same for a married student, Boyce probably participated in student life in a normal way. Calhoun outlined a typical day in the life of a student at Princeton in 1850.

> They rose early, usually about 4:30 in the morning, and in cold weather built fires in their stoves. Some took short walks before the 6:45 a. m. prayer meeting. Breakfast was in the refectory—a separate building constructed in 1842. The fare was plain but abundant. Many of the students formed themselves into "little clubs" and studied the Shorter Catechism during mealtimes. There were classes to attend in the morning and afternoon and daily chapel. Most students took a walk before supper. There were meetings nearly every night in the week, then there was study until bedtime.[61]

Broadus recorded a portion of a letter that Boyce wrote soon after his arrival at Princeton. It shows a student intent on gaining all he could from the opportunity of study. He wrote of his "full course of reading in Mental Philosophy" as well as attending lectures on that subject from the Greeks down to the present day. In addition he pursued "Hebrew exegesis in Genesis, and Greek in Romans" and had designed a personal reading course of biographies "of the great and the good who have shed luster upon the Christian name."[62] The latter pursuit was not in a lecture course but a personal study that the faculty encouraged each student to develop. Boyce found J. W. Alexander "the most delightful lecturer I have ever heard." While Addison was the most gifted, he was not, because of an acerbic temper, the most admired. Hodge rose above all, however, as "one of the most excellent of men; so modest and yet so wise, so kind and fatherly in his manner, and yet of so giant an intellect, he is a man who deserves a world of praise."[63]

During this first year, two of Boyce's sisters got married in Charleston, one to H. A. Tupper. Boyce regularly informed Tupper of the activities at Princeton and encouraged Tupper in the pastoral charge that he had undertaken in Graniteville, South Carolina. Boyce himself began regular preaching at Penn's Neck Baptist Church a short distance from Princeton. One of his classmates, Casper Wistar Hodge, remembered Boyce's "high reputation for eloquence and strength in the pulpit." He probably developed many of his propensities in preaching through the constant contact with Princeton sermons during the Sunday afternoon weekly conferences. He would have heard in regular rotation all three Alexanders and Charles Hodge.

In the last conference of the session, 4 May 1850, Charles Hodge spoke on 2 Corinthians 5:14, "The love of Christ constraineth us." Hodge emphasized that "no man becomes great or successful, who has not one object, and one constraining motive." He set forth "the love of Christ as the constraining motive, and the glory of Christ as the one object." These two ideas Hodge developed with fullness, employing both theological detail and motives to true piety. The love of Christ consists of his manifestation in the flesh, its particularity, its sovereignty apart from merit reaching us when we were enemies and ungodly, its infinite scope in procuring our salvation by the death of the Son of God, its immutability, and its tender sympathy. In this way the love of Christ "takes possession of us, of all our faculties, of our thoughts, affections and powers." His dying love "satisfies justice, frees from the penalty of the law, honors God, and promotes the good of the universe." By the power of his death we renounce sin and become free from its power. We glorify Christ by making that purpose the definite object of our lives, by entire subjection to his will, by adherence to his truth and by "striving to bring men to know, to love, to worship, and to obey Christ." By living in the consciousness of his love and to his glory "you will be blessed, and a blessing, go where you will, and suffer what you may."[64]

During the summer following that first year, Boyce and his wife spent four months in Virginia visiting her relatives, traveling through the beautiful Piedmont area of Virginia country, with his being called on to preach on all but three Sundays. Broadus described a sermon on John 3:16 as including "perhaps too much of theological discussion about the divine nature and purposes, and the relations of the Father to the Son, for a discourse meant to be thoroughly practical."[65] Boyce never fully recovered from this theological tendency in his sermons, and, in his own view, considered it rather a strength than a weakness.

In the *Memoir*, Broadus, when context suggests too big a temptation, lards his narrative with extended words of counsel, personal observation about theological education, the nature of pastoral ministry, the value and dynamics of friendship, and a variety of pithy exhortations that an unusually astute sixty-six-year-old preacher/educator would want to say. Many of these remarks are in praise of the subject of the *Memoir* while a few acknowledge, with words of kindest explanation, shortcomings. Broadus's description of the summer of 1850 contains two of those extended encomiums on the natural gifts of Boyce. "Few men so promptly win and so permanently hold the confidence and affection of others as did James P. Boyce," Broadus opined with more than thirty years of friendship giving credibility to his observation. "Highly cordial in manner and manifestly sincere," Broadus continued his eulogy of Boyce, "big-hearted and considerate, overflowing with vitality, and yet full of gentle courtesy and abounding in delicate tact, he seemed perfectly at ease, and made all around feel at ease, alike in the palaces of the rich and the cottages of the poor." Even the sermon that Broadus considered too influenced by the "lecture-room" has its profound charm when delivered under the power of Boyce's personality. "The sermon is earnest," Broadus affirmed, "and aims at practical results; and it can hardly have failed to have been heard with great interest, when read in the sonorous and musical tones, and with the impressive and engaging aspect, of the young preacher."[66]

In Boyce's second year at Princeton, he decided to include the senior year of work in addition to the second. The load was heavy but Boyce's health and endurance were up to the task. Besides, he already had begun to lay out his options for the next summer. Would he return to South Carolina in pursuit of pastoral ministry, or, remembering the energizing scenes of his college days, would he find a ministry opportunity in Providence? St. Louis presented one possibility. Wherever his future lay, he was sobered by the gravity of his calling and engaged in self-examination on the genuineness of his call to ministry. These thoughts he shared with his friend and brother-in-law Tupper. Boyce congratulated his ministerial peer in his determination to preach to the slaves as well as hired free men. He encouraged him to teach them as well as preach to them. He himself would relish such an opportunity, for, as Tupper would remember, "I have long thought that for such congregations there should be given a great deal of exposition, such as is suitable to explain and cause them to remember the sacred text. I should delight to preach to them myself."[67]

Finding a Place to Serve

At the end of formal lectures, Boyce left Princeton without completing his series of examinations. The rules called for an examination after three years on the subjects of study with the intent that this examination, if passed, led to the candidates' receiving a certificate of recommendation "to their several presbyteries, to be disposed of as such presbyteries shall direct."[68] As Boyce needed no such certificate, he left before the examinations and thus did not receive his certificate. He spent several months in New York, visiting with his sister, Mrs. William Lane, and reviewing his theological studies. From there, it appears that he went to Washington, Georgia, to visit his wife's parents and relatives and received a contact from the First Baptist Church of Columbia, South Carolina. By August 9, he had responded positively to their invitation and he would be initiating his duties as pastor by October 1.

In late November, Boyce was ordained to the gospel ministry. The examining council, or presbytery, met on Saturday, November 29, and consisted of Thomas Curtis, John Culpepper, and J. R. Kendrick. News of the event was carried in the 10 December 1851 publication of the *Southern Baptist*. The paper reported that "Rev. Dr. Curtis was chosen moderator" and Kendrick served as clerk. Boyce gave an account of his "Christian experience, his call to ministry, and his views of doctrine." The presbytery, being fully satisfied, recommended compliance with the request of the church for Boyce's ordination.

The next morning, Sunday morning, Kendrick preached the sermon, J. M. Timmons led the ordaining prayer, and Curtis gave the charge to the candidate. Curtis's charge, so the editor of the paper observed, was "a much more elaborate performance than is customary on such occasions." It was "replete with sound advice, and presented some very striking views of the minister's work." Culpepper's charge to the church "was to the point, practical and excellent." Boyce closed with prayer. The paper reported that "the weather on this interesting occasion was exceedingly unfavorable, and the congregation gathered to witness and unite in the solemnity was, by reason of this fact, quite small." Several Baptists from the legislature as well as some visitors from out of town attended in addition to the small number of church members. The *Southern Baptist* looked with pleasure on the return of its former editor to South Carolina, and especially to a place with such a small Baptist witness but with need for a large one.

> Bro. Boyce enters upon the work of the ministry under encouraging circumstances. While he gives pleasing evidences of possessing those spiritual qualifications without which all others are vain, he has been favored with more than ordinary opportunities for mental culture. He is a graduate of Brown University, and has spent about ten [*sic*; two] years at the Princeton Theological Seminary. It is an occasion for general congratulation, that we are permitted to record the accession of this promising brother to the rising ministry of our State. The Church with which he has associated himself, is small and has passed through trying vicissitudes. Its members receive their new pastor with great cordiality and affection, and seem disposed to rally to his support. That this union may be blessed, will be the prayer of many a pious heart throughout our State.[69]

The same paper that announced Boyce's ordination mentioned two other items that could not escape the notice of and promised future pleasure for Boyce. Dr. J. H. Thornwell, the great Presbyterian preacher and theologian who had captured the young Boyce's rapt attention in Charleston ten years before, was coming to Columbia as president of South Carolina College. At the same time J. L. Reynolds, the former pastor of the Columbia church, president of Georgetown College, pastor of Second Baptist in Richmond, and writer of the articles on imputation came to South Carolina College as professor of belles lettres. All the influences of Boyce's life to this point seemed to converge when he answered one of the questions asked him during the meeting of the ordaining presbytery: "Do you propose to make a life-long matter of preaching?" Curtis asked. "Yes," Boyce responded, "provided I do not become a professor of theology."[70]

3

From Preacher to Professor

*T*he Baptist church in Columbia, South Carolina, was established on 1 October 1809 from five newly baptized converts and eight other members. The young minister that had just performed the baptisms was William B. Johnson.[1] The president of South Carolina College, Jonathan Maxcy, had preached intermittently in the college chapel on Sunday beginning in January 1805, but continued only a few months. In 1808 William T. Brantly Sr. began preaching, and he was succeeded by Johnson in January 1809. Several preachers had kept the meeting alive for the next few decades; it gradually increased in numbers, mainly through the conversion of slaves. The *Southern Baptist* reported in 1851 that the church was "small and has passed through trying vicissitudes."[2] Among the vicissitudes was the absence of a pastor for three years after the resignation of William Curtis in 1845. H. A. Duncan served the church effectively from June 1848 through July 1850 but left because he could not survive on the salary. Then for another fifteen months there was no pastor. Though the church had 465 members in 1849, over four hundred were slaves, making the financial abilities of the church extremely diminished.

Meeting the Challenge of Columbia

The city of Columbia, having a population of seven thousand, was quite impressive. Not only did it have the legislature during its season, but it was home to South Carolina College. John A. Broadus, well acquainted with the attractive elements of the South Carolina capital, described the allurement of its situation.

> Columbia was already quite a handsome Southern town. The spacious streets were well shaded, some of them having not only trees along the sidewalks, but a double row along the centre, with a walk between, as in Augusta, Savannah, and other Southern cities, and in Commonwealth Avenue, Boston. There were many handsome residences, built in the Southern style, with large rooms and ample windows, and with broad porticos or verandas, sometimes on all four sides of the house, and even repeated for the second story. The principal dwellings were surrounded by extensive grounds filled with trees, shrubbery, and flowers. It is difficult for one who has not seen them to imagine the delightsomeness of these Southern abodes, found often in the country as well as in the town. From the blazing sun you passed into an atmosphere of delicious coolness, delicately perfumed by the odor of growing flowers that entered at every window. The family were often highly educated, and always had in a high degree the charming manners of an aristocratic society. The hospitality seemed perfect. The memory of even brief visits to those noble Southern homes bears now a touch of romance.[3]

Such elegance presented a contrast to the diminutive influence and lack of attractiveness of the Baptist congregation. J. R. Kendrick, pastor of the First Baptist Church in Charleston and a frequent writer of editorials for the *Southern Baptist*, lamented that in Columbia the "Baptist interest should be so depressed and languishing." A state legislator, a Baptist, in the absence of a pastor in the Baptist church worshiped with other congregations until one Sunday late in the session Duncan came to preach. The legislator found "a contracted, old-fashioned building . . . scarcely large enough for a lecture room." The congregation consisted of fifty. What inducements, he wondered, did such a situation present? "No stated ministry—an uncomfortable house, presenting exteriorly more the appearance of a prison house than one of praise!" Does this not make an observer think that "the Baptists are a poor, cripple set, that they lack energy and zeal and that pride which I maintain is essential to the success of any Christian enterprise?"[4]

The congregation at Columbia felt the sting of these public representations. On 2 March 1851, at a church conference in which six men were present the following resolution was crafted:

> Whereas, the attention of this Church having been called to two editorial articles and one communication recently published in the "Southern Baptist," making a proposition in relation to building a new Baptist meeting house in the town of Columbia,
>
> Resolved, That this church with great pleasure accepts of those propositions, and do hereby pledge itself to respond to the utmost of its abilities, in raising an amount sufficient to build a house of worship, such as may be deemed suited to the circumstances and location.[5]

James Lyles, the church clerk, felt that the resolution should be followed by a letter. On March 11 he wrote, with some sense of betrayal and discouragement, but with resolve to test the sincerity of the Baptists of South Carolina about their corporate desire for a more attractive presence in Columbia. Should they respond with help commensurate with their criticism, "it will speak loud in their praise, and redound greatly to their benefit." Lyles noted the denominational interest in "an able and stated ministry at this place," but pointed out that "it can not be maintained under existing circumstances." The house of worship was "unsightly," there was no pastor, and thus no "regular ministration of the ordinances of God's house." Baptism in its "true and impressive mode" was not "exhibited before the eyes of the people" and thus was in danger of passing from their minds. "I might almost say," he lamented, "that the seeds of decay are so apparent that our ultimate dissolution as a Church is inevitable, unless speedy and efficient help is derived from abroad."

Though the church's contributions came from willing and generous hearts, considering their destitute condition, and with zeal for the causes of the denomination, they found themselves helpless, overpowered, and with all the influences against them. They felt their weakness and mourned it "with deep mortification and regret." Is it their fault? "I will acknowledge the sin," Lyles confessed, "but still the difficulty is not removed; we are still weak and overpowered." Should the contemplated help from the denomination materialize, it would be an important step toward boosting the morale of the congregation and aiding it to "procure, support and maintain a talented ministry." Such a rallying of help would encourage both the congregation and the soon-to-come pastor. Under such encouragements, "things, with God's blessings, may surely be expected to improve." The willingness of the church to receive aid now being made public, Lyles challenged the conscience of the criticizers: "You can dispose of these proceedings in whatever way you think will most promote the objects in view."[6]

Ironically, two columns removed from the letter from Lyles, J. R. Kendrick described a more agreeable ministry, and public impression, at the church in Graniteville. H. A. Tupper, Boyce's friend and brother-in-law and frequent correspondent, was pastor. "At the hour for religious service we were at Graniteville," Kendrick recounted, "a village which has been so often described in our paper, that we must resist a very strong inclination to launch into a fresh laudation of its beauties." The factory bell rang at the appointed hour for worship, and "multitudes of happy-looking people came hurrying on to the Sanctuary, until the handsome Gothic House was nearly filled." Kendrick had enjoyed the experience of preaching and remarked, "To a more attentive and interesting audience, it has not often been our pleasure to deliver the word." Afterward, Tupper led the congregation "to the adjacent water's side" and baptized two young ladies. The week before, Tupper had "baptized several persons" with others waiting to be immersed. "The Graniteville church," so Kendrick concluded, "has been greatly prospered since its beginning two years earlier with thirteen members." It numbered over one hundred with twenty of those added by baptism.

Would it be possible for the church in Columbia to be such an ornament on the Baptist name and thus bring an end to the obvious embarrassment Kendrick and others found it impossible to hide? On 9 August 1851, the church received a letter from "Bro. J. P. Boyce accepting its pastoral charge," to take effect on the first of October. In addition to acceptance, Boyce "asked & received one month's vacation each year of his pastorate."[7] On October 11, Boyce moved his membership from First Baptist Church in Charleston and was installed as pastor. As he was not ordained, a council was called for the first Sunday in December. W. C. Lindsay remarked, "No further information on this point is given, this not even stated whether said Council ever convened!"[8] The *Southern Baptist*, however, recorded the proceedings.

After the ordination of Boyce, J. R. Kendrick noted, "The question of building a new house of worship, or greatly changing and improving the present one, is now agitated by the Columbia Church. In our opinion this is an indispensable measure. If determined upon, we bespeak for it the cordial and liberal assistance of our readers in all sections of the State."[9] With Boyce's personal financial condition being substantial, thus not feeling the financial oppression of a small salary, and his influence potentially great, due to his father's business contacts (his father owned stock in a bank in Columbia) and his own friendships in the Charleston Association, Boyce seemed the perfect man to effect a change in Columbia. The church records state, "May 23, 1852, Dr. Boyce was granted three months, or longer if necessary, to visit other churches in the State to solicit contributions for the new church building which had been decided on the year before he took charge."[10]

Broadus made the inauspicious, but true, remark, "These early years of ministry present, as frequently happens, but little to record."[11] W. C. Lindsay, having searched through the minutes at Broadus's request, observed, "I have carefully examined our Ch. Records for the information you desire, & am sorry they furnish so little of interest. Important matters are omitted & trifles relative to discipline of negro members fill about five-sixths of the ch. book." Membership went from 477 to 393 during the first year due to discipline and removing from the church rolls those members whose whereabouts were unknown. Though these deletions of various sorts occurred, Boyce baptized twenty during his first year of ministry, and membership gradually rose to 428 by the time of Boyce's resignation in 1855.[12] One inducement was his making the music in the church more attractive through the purchase of a melodeon in 1853 and hiring a "chorister" in 1854 for $100 per year.[13]

In 1853 Boyce purchased, furnished, and selected appropriate appointments for a home in which he and his wife lived for two years. Broadus, drawing on his acquaintance with Boyce and years of observation and conversation, surmised that he was busy reading theology, preparing sermons with a deep sense of stewardship, reading in the library at the college, making acquaintance with every segment of society including the legislators and other leading men of the town, and visiting in the homes of both the wealthy and influential and the modest and humble. He had a special zeal for preaching to the slave population and saw many of them converted during his ministry. Lindsay recalled, "Under his charge the church greatly developed in the grace of liberality, & large numbers were added especially of negros (for whom he seemed to have had special consideration)." Broadus, having at his disposal sermon notes of Boyce from the Columbia days, made an observation about Boyce's preaching:

> From this ministry of four years there remain notes of several sermons, and a good many sermons written in full. He usually prepared by making a rather extended sketch,—what lawyers call a "brief,"—which he kept before him when speaking. Most of these were allowed to perish in the course of years. From the outset we find him grasping with decided vigor the thought or several thoughts of the text, explaining and strongly vindicating the great doctrines of Scripture, applying the truth to his hearers with direct and fervid exhortation. There is still not much of illustration, but now and then an expanded figure that shows imaginative powers worthy to be oftener employed. The style is sometimes negligent, but rarely fails to be lucid and vigorous. Above all, the sermons show a man very anxious to do good; they belong to "an earnest ministry."[14]

Boyce immediately became active in the work of the Charleston Association and soon became clerk. In March of 1852 we find him requesting from all the churches in the Association a list of the ministers who were members of those churches. The list should include any that served as "Missionaries, Teachers, Colporteurs, Agents" along with their addresses. This was for the American Baptist Publication Society that desired "some statistics with reference to our Association." From some church clerks (he listed the ones), he requested they forward information to him that had not been reported during the year to the association.[15] In October 1852 Boyce served on a presbytery for the ordination of James K. Mendenhall to the gospel ministry at Camden Baptist Church in Camden, South Carolina. He served as clerk of that presbytery and during the service led in the introductory portion and presented the Bible to his boyhood and college friend. Just a few months earlier, Mendenhall had supplied the pulpit at Columbia while Boyce went on his first money-raising tour.

Boyce asked for a second leave of absence in April 1854. Lindsay reported, "April 8, 1854, Dr. Boyce asked for & obtained leave of absence from pastoral duties until Oct. 'at which time he hoped to be able to resume them.' His salary to be used in securing a supply."[16] While he might have been involved in some attempts to raise money for the church building during this absence, its main object was probably related to the new duties that had fallen on him as executor of his father's large and complicated estate. When he resumed his pastoral duties in the fall, he was elected to serve as moderator of the Charleston Baptist Association. This put him in contact with another young and aggressive Baptist theologian, E. T. Winkler, the new pastor of First Baptist Church, Charleston. Winkler had been corresponding secretary for the Southern Baptist Publication Society and editor of the *Southern Baptist*. He had carried on an aggressive editorial policy of dealing with profound theological ideas, pertinent biblical exegesis, and gentlemanly but straightforward polemical engagement with other denominations. In 1858, he would be elected as a professor at the Southern Baptist Theological Seminary, but would refuse the invitation.[17]

Boyce made time to write articles designed for the exhortation and encouragement of the churches. On 18 February 1852 he published

"Church Discipline—Its Importance." Evidently he looked into this historic Baptist ordinance with existential interest. "Anyone who will make a careful examination of the state of our churches," he began, "will be astonished at the low degree of spirituality which they manifest." He believed this arose primarily from the leniency of the churches toward corrective discipline, a practice that he had revived in Columbia. Apart from some who denied the church's right to such power, Boyce pinpointed the main reasons for this laxity as worldliness and fear, or an "unwillingness to blame others when we ourselves are liable to error." The abandonment of discipline, however, soon would result in "the utter ruin of the church." He cited three reasons for the importance of consistency on this issue:

First, "it is necessary for the purification of the visible church." Christ himself purifies the invisible church by the calling and sanctifying operations of his Spirit. But the visible church is given standards to which its members are required to conform in exercising oversight of its purity. The church is not in such an untarnished condition that it has no need of the exercise of excommunication. Its purity is under challenge and should be maintained, for "a church of inconsistent members is the laughing stock of the world." An inconsistent membership gives no evidence "of the transforming power of the Spirit" or of the "blessedness of obedience to the precepts of Christ."

Second, "the exercise of discipline leads to the advancement of personal piety among the members of the church." Christians need every inducement possible for the increase of holiness. Discipline sets a high standard and helps establish a habit that tends toward holiness and mortification of sin rather than laxness and indulgence. Those churches that are most strict "are universally filled with the most vital piety." Discipline lets the members know their duty and helps destroy evil habits. "By that course of conduct, therefore, by which we may destroy evil habits and form good ones," Boyce argued, "we are constantly led to increased holiness; and the church discipline which prevents sin, in so doing tends to holiness. By furnishing a restraint from the one, it gives an assistant towards the other." Exercise of discipline removes the dead branches and provides the necessary pruning of those branches that need the knife.

Third, only by discipline can the church "be led to perform the glorious work of evangelizing the world." Boyce argued for this proposition in one long sentence:

> Not only is it true that to none but a holy church will the Holy Spirit be given as an assistant, and as a consequence of this, it could have no success; but the want of obedience to Christ's will in minor matters, and of conformity to his example in ordinary life, will prevent obedience to him with respect to those commands which require the exercise of self-denial, and the putting forth of earnest and continued effort, and conformity to an example so far above that which man can attain, without divine assistance, as to give of itself sufficient proof of the discipleship of him who thus conforms.

In other words, God will not bless an unholy church with the fruit of conversion; nor will an undisciplined church embrace the self-denial needed for evangelistic success. Strict discipline will restore the spiritual vitality of former days and produce efficiency in its "present and future efforts for Christ."[18] Boyce sought to implement this kind of discipline at Columbia.

Corrective discipline must be complemented in the life of the church by formative discipline, that is, continuous instruction in life-transforming truth. Boyce published an article the very next week entitled "Preaching Plain Truths." Piety suffered greatly, not from neglect of preaching on practical issues, but from passing by the simplest facts and doctrines of Scripture. He issued a challenge to the preacher-reader to "talk with the most ignorant or the most indifferent of his hearers." He will find that their ignorance and indifference arises from inattention to the plain and obvious in the Bible. "It would astonish those who have not thus conversed," Boyce coaxed, "to find how ignorant even men of enlightened views are upon such matters." Ignorance on these matters lies at the base of their "constant indifference" to other elements of divine truth. Boyce himself made trial of this with a person that had a long-time habit of church attendance. In another agonizingly long sentence, Boyce gave the results of his inquiry:

It is not long since a very intelligent merchant—one who has always been a constant attendant at church during at least forty years, and having during that time enjoyed the ministry of many most able minds—manifested this very ignorance to the writer of this article, and the examination of his state of mind proved conclusively that the indifference which he has thus far manifested towards divine things, has been owing to a great extent to the obstacles which this ignorance of plain truths presents to the truths to labored arguments, in proof of which he constantly listens.

Deep theological truths and astute polemical arguments simply pass over the heads of those that have no grasp of "plain truths." Boyce believed that plainness and simple truths would make ministers more useful and be pleasing to Christ. Even at the risk of dullness, ministers should "determine to be plain, neglecting not to make ourselves level to the comprehension even of the most ignorant." Conviction in the hearts of many intelligent persons, now utterly indifferent, could well be the result.[19]

On 29 April 1855, Boyce, through J. C. Phelps, tendered his resignation to take effect October the first. The church "resolved not to accept it until they could communicate with him and express 'the reluctance of the church to have him dissolve his relations with it.'"[20] On May 6 his resignation was accepted. The church instructed the clerk to express to him their "sincere and profound regret," as well as their gratitude for the "deep interest and aid he still proffers to the church." That "deep interest and aid" amounted to a pledge of $500 per year toward the $1,200 dollar salary of the new pastor, G. D. Boardman.

Though Boyce was unable to collect enough during his leaves of absence for a new building, he stirred interest and collected enough for the people to continue their quest. In 1856, Boyce himself pledged $10,000 toward the construction if the church would raise another $15,000. At the South Carolina Baptist Convention that year, the pastor, John T. Zealy, made an appeal on behalf of the church in Columbia. A resolution was adopted to raise $6,000 of additional funds to complete the amount needed. "Rev. James P. Boyce, having pledged $10,000, on condition that $15,000 more shall be raised by a given time," a report on the convention noted, "about $5,000 is now pledged in Columbia, about $4,000 elsewhere in the State, leaving $6,000 to be secured and paid in cash by January 1, 1858, otherwise the munificent donation of Prof. Boyce is to be forfeited."[21] Zealy led in the ceremony when the cornerstone was laid in June 1857.[22] Lindsay noted with irony, "It is strange that there is no record of his munificent gift of $10,000 to the new building. The records from 1857 to 1865 were burnt by the union Army, & it is quite probable that they contained a notice of it." When the completed building was dedicated in September 1859, Boyce returned to preach the dedication sermon, entitled "The Uses and Doctrine of the Sanctuary."[23]

Inheriting Another Lifetime Responsibility

Boyce was able to deal so generously with the church in Columbia because in 1854 he had become heir to a fortune at the death of his father, and at the same time became executor of the estate. *The Courier* of Charleston carried the story on 21 March 1854. "Death of the Hon. Ker Boyce: With deep and sincere regret, we discharge the melancholy duty of recording the death of the Hon. Ker Boyce, after a brief illness, at Columbia, in this State, at 12 o'clock on Sunday night last, in the 68th year of his age. The disease which terminated his earthly career was, we learn, an affection of the heart." The article went on to give some of the details of Ker Boyce's career:

> Mr. Boyce was a native of Newberry District, but for nearly his whole adult life, he made Charleston his home, and the theatre of his enterprise and usefulness. He devoted himself to mercantile pursuits, and as both factor and merchant, manifested a capacity, skill and integrity, which crowned his labors with golden rewards. Although without the advantages of early education, he was naturally strong minded and sagacious, and wisdom and prudence marked his whole career. He was a man of eminently practical talent; and was public spirited and charitable in the use of his great wealth, contributing liberally to rail road and other public improvements, and dispensing friendly or generous aid to numerous individuals. In public station, he was active, energetic and useful, for several years filling the posts of Representative and Senator in our state Legislature, with credit to

himself, and presiding with efficiency, over that great monied institution, the Bank of Charleston. In the domestic and private relations of life, he was exemplary, as husband, father, and friend, faithfully filling up the measure of duty. During the late movement in favor of separate secession, he threw the weight of his influence against the current. Having become a millionaire, he had retired, for many years, from active engagements in business, to a beautiful country seat of villa, called Kalmia, near Graniteville, in this State, where he enjoyed the repose requisite for the comfort of waning years. His obsequies took place yesterday afternoon, in this city, at the Second Presbyterian Church, in the cemetery of which, after an appropriate, eloquent and affecting funeral service by the Rev. James H. Cuthbert, Pastor of the Wentworth Street Baptist Church, and a prayer by the Rev. Dr. Smyth, his mortal remains were deposited beneath the green sod, amidst a concourse of mourning relatives and friends.[24]

This same notice significantly was carried in the *Southern Baptist* on 29 March 1854.

Ker Boyce had gone to visit his preacher son James at Columbia when he was stricken with an apparent heart attack. He lingered for ten days. All his children had time to come to Columbia and were with him at his death. He had lived for a few years with his daughter Nancy, Mrs. H. A. Tupper, until she and her husband moved in 1853 to Washington, Georgia, where he served as pastor for almost twenty years. Tupper reported that during the time Ker Boyce was with them in Kalmia, "he showed great love of the Bible, and special interest in the family worship." According to a source reported by Broadus, the children expected him to recover, but "he was persuaded of his approaching death, and in view thereof he spoke calmly and with resignation, expressing his hope and trust in the mercy of Christ."[25]

The death of his father affected James Boyce far beyond the immediate sense of loss. As the executor chiefly responsible for the management of the massive estate, he inherited not only wealth, but a responsibility that could have been a full-time occupation. The will of Ker Boyce showed the complexity and heaviness of carrying out this duty. Each of the seven children was to receive a designated portion of the estate in cash as well as a yearly payment of dividends on investments. Ker

Boyce received a gold watch, Samuel Boyce received a gold-headed cane, and James P. Boyce received the "other gold-headed cane." The "issue" of each child were provided for in the current legal vocabulary in case of the death of the parent. The children of his deceased son John Johnson Boyce, who had died in April 1849, received $5,000 each, a sum considered by Ker Boyce satisfactory in light of the "handsome advances made to my son in his lifetime." These advances came in the form of a plantation in Florida that he purchased for him, hoping that the Florida climate would help heal him of consumption.

The language of the will reflects some of the massive holdings of Boyce as well as the complexity of administering them:

> In trust, for the following uses, that is to say, as to all my South Carolina Property with the exception hereinafter mentioned. In trust to sell the same as soon after my decease as conveniently may be done for one-fifth cash and the residue on a credit of from one to five years with interest payable annually and as to my lands in Texas to sell the same as soon after my decease and on such terms as they may think fit, and as to my lands in Mississippi, Georgia, Tennessee and Alabama, in trust to preserve the same by paying the taxes assessments and necessary expenses for protecting the title until my youngest child shall attain the age of Twenty-one years or be married unless they should deem an earlier sale of the whole or any part thereof more advantageous. . . .

Other properties were to be disposed of by the executors in the most advantageous way to the heirs. The shares of all the children were to be equalized "by taking into account all the advancements which I may have made, or hereafter may make to them severally" as recorded in his books. Boyce set forth a scheme of selling "if advantageous," and reinvesting "the shares of my children severally in lands, Negroes, or stock or other good estate excepting bank or insurance stock." The income from rental properties was to be divided appropriately, certain shares to the sons and others to the daughters. Samuel J. Boyce was to be assigned the "hotel at the corner of King and Society streets . . . for a part of his share at its cash value," the trustees being responsible to manage the trust "to permit him to take the income for his own use and maintenance." More than a full page was given to eventualities concerning that property.

The disposal of the capital included an initial payment of $100,000 to each child after which $50,000 was given in trust to the Orphan House of Charleston and $25,000 to the College of Charleston. Any remaining residue of capital would be divided between the children. A subsequent codicil changed the distribution of money given to the Orphan House and the College and added "the sum of ten thousand dollars to the Corporation of the Graniteville Manufacturing Company to found a free school at Graniteville for the instruction of the children of the operatives in said factory in the branches of a plain English education."[26]

An inventory and appraisal of the estate of Boyce's properties was completed on 26 March 1853. It included a list of the stock holdings of Boyce, outstanding loans from which he was receiving income, and properties in Charleston in which he had part ownership. Among the companies in which he held stock were the Exchange Bank of Columbia, Farmers and Exchange Bank of Charleston, E. T. I. W. Manufacturing Company (stock worth $80,000), Lauren's Rail Road, South Carolina Paper Manufacturing Company (stock worth $15,000), Washington and New Orleans Telegraph Company, Bank of Milledgeville, Graniteville Company (stock worth $50,000), Commercial Insurance Company, Fireman's Insurance Company, Macon and Western Railroad, Georgia Rail Road and Brokerage Company, Camden Branch of South Carolina Rail Road, South West Rail Road Bank and Rail Road, Memphis and Charleston Rail Road, Bank of Charleston, and others. In some business arrangement the inventory showed that he had a balance due from L. M. Wiley and Co. of $493,821. From Wiley Banks and Company (where J. P. Boyce had worked during a six-month trial in order to reinvigorate his interest in academics) he had over $74,000 due and over $88,000 due from William Gelane. Properties in town and the Boyce wharf were valued at $84,300.

In 1886, James Boyce published a detailed account of the "Division of the Assets of the Principal of the Estate of Ker Boyce, Deceased, Among the Legatees." He figured dividends periodically for thirty-two years and also calculated the cumulative interest of each dividend from the time of its initial assignment to the several heirs forward to 1886. For example, for 19 March 1854, property shares worth $112,019 were distributed which gained over the next thirty-two years $250,923.0080. (The amounts of interest were always figured to four decimal places.) By 31 January 1856 interest from his property had been distributed to the amount of $613,975 and accumulated over the next thirty-two years to $1,340,521.2883. During 1860, three distributions totaled just a few dollars below $169,000 and bore an interest of $307,000. Comparatively small distributions came during the next six years, probably because of both the difficulty and the great caution exercised by Boyce during what was clearly a tumultuous time financially. The financial crisis of 1873 was pictured in the diminutive nature of the distribution during that year. Distributions continued until 1882 with interest from each respective investment figured to 1886 beside the record of the distribution. Boyce did not record any distributions of investments or interest-bearing property after 1882. The cumulative interest from the property for the thirty-two years was $2,319,691. Boyce himself had received investment property of various sorts worth $164,743, the cumulative interest from which was $314,473. Though three other men, Arthur G. Rose, J. B. O'Neall, and James A. Whiteside, were appointed by Ker Boyce as trustees and executors, they left the lion's share of the work to James P. Boyce. In the future this would take large portions of his time and provide a constant challenge for his financial acumen.

Professor of Theology at Furman

Immediately after his resignation from the church in Columbia, Boyce attended the Southern Baptist Convention that met in Montgomery, Alabama. On the trip to Montgomery, Boyce met the young pastor of the Baptist Church in Charlottesville, Virginia, John A. Broadus. Broadus recalled how eager J. B. Taylor and A. M. Poindexter were to greet Boyce when he stepped onto the train and how insistent Poindexter was that the two young Southern Baptists meet. "Yonder is a man I want you to know," he recalled Poindexter saying. "He is a minister of ability and thorough education, and full of noble qualities. His father was a man of great wealth, and he is now very generous in his gifts." Then as if uttering a prophetic word, Poindexter continued, "He is going to be one of the most influential of all Southern Baptists. I want you to know him."[27]

Boyce seemed to thrive in the social atmosphere of the convention. He took an active role in the convention procedures, making motions and presenting the report of a special committee concerning the relation of the Foreign Mission Board to one of its missionaries, I. J. Roberts.[28] He also participated in a special meeting called "the friends of theological education," which had been initiated by the General Association of Baptists in Virginia. J. L. Burrows served as chair. Burrows had been pastor of First Baptist Church, Richmond, for about one year at this time, and continued in that service for twenty years. He was a graduate of Union College in Schenectady and Andover Theological Seminary. Basil Manly Jr. served as secretary of the meeting. He had served First Baptist Church of Richmond from 1850 to 1854 and currently served as president of Richmond Female Institute.

The Montgomery meeting resulted in the adoption of several resolutions proposed by A. M. Poindexter: "that it is demanded by the interests of the cause of truth that the Baptists of the South and Southwest unite in establishing a Theological Institution of high grade." Another suggested that "a Committee of Correspondence be appointed to call the attention of the denomination to this subject." This committee included J. P. Boyce along with J. B. Jeter and five other brethren. A third called for a "Convention . . . of those favorable to this object to meet at Augusta, Georgia, on the Wednesday after the fourth Sabbath in April, 1856," and included the suggestion that the appointed committee should "take measures to secure, if possible, the attendance of representatives for our various Colleges, Education Societies, and Conventions."[29] J. B. Jeter and J. P. Boyce were made responsible for the practical work of the Committee of Correspondence. The work that followed this meeting soon will be discussed, but presently, the career of Boyce must be allowed to mature a bit more. Soon, Boyce was put into a position that he felt could result in the desired institution.

Furman University was just one of several Baptist colleges in the South that had theological departments. The school had moved to

Greenville from Winnsboro, South Carolina, in 1851. It had opened in 1827 but had struggled to survive. By 1839, attempts at a manual labor school combined with a classical and English school had failed, and all that remained was a theological institute. It functioned in that capacity for nine years, until 1848. In 1843, J. C. Furman joined the recently acquired James S. Mims, an 1842 graduate of Newton who also had been a private student of Furman for eighteen months. In 1846 they were joined by P. C. Edwards, a graduate of South Carolina College and Newton Theological Institute who also had studied at Union Theological Seminary in New York. He came as professor of biblical literature and exegesis. They desired to expand the curriculum and the programs taught at the school. With hopes of success in this expansion, the school made its move to Greenville. The name was changed to Furman University, and J. C. Furman became president. Edwards became professor of ancient languages in the newly formed collegiate department, and Mims retained the position of professor of theology.

Mims came under pressure for his theological views in 1848 and published a defense in an address entitled "Orthodoxy." At the request of the trustees, it was printed in 1848.[30] This prompted the articles on imputation Boyce carried in the *Southern Baptist*. Mims became ill in the early part of 1855, and it soon became clear that he would not recover. On 22 August 1855, the *Southern Baptist* carried a notice of Boyce's election to the position of professor of theology at Furman University. "We are happy to state that the late election of Rev. J. P. Boyce, to the professorship of Theology in Furman University, made vacant by the death of Prof. Mims, has been accepted by him." The article related that Boyce already had made his arrangements to begin his work at the opening of the theological session, on the first Monday of September. Steps had been taken by the trustees "to adopt additional measures for the greater efficiency of the Theological department." That was doubtless their consent to Boyce's acceptance on the condition that he have assistance. The article projected great growth for the future of the theological department, expecting "an increase of students for the ministry, somewhat in proportion to the growing numbers of the college proper."[31]

Perhaps with an instinct that Furman would provide the "Theological Institution of high grade" called for by the friends of theological education, Boyce wrote H. A. Tupper, while Tupper was on a trip to Europe, to consider taking the position of professor of biblical studies. He refused because of his love for the pastorate and for the particular work at Washington, Georgia. Boyce, therefore, toiled alone during his first year, teaching five to six hours per day in as many as five different subjects. This experience showed him the difficulty of building a comprehensive theological program in such a provincial and limited sphere. In his funeral sermon for Basil Manly Sr., Boyce reflected on the development of this conviction, one that Manly had reached much earlier. "During that period," Boyce recited, "the different Baptist State Colleges had been making decided progress in general education. But they had accomplished only a partial work for the theological education of the rising ministry." With an obvious reference to the state of his own convictions during these Furman days, Boyce went on, "The necessity of concentration became apparent. It was evident that separate efforts must be failures."[32]

Unlike previous professors in this position, Boyce felt more at home in systematic theology than the other subjects. One of his students, John G. Williams, recalled the experience of learning from Boyce:

> Dr. Boyce taught us Systematic Theology (using Dick's Theology as a text-book), Church History, Greek New Testament exegesis, and Hebrew. It was easy to see then that Theology was his strong point, and had already taken a strong hold on him. . . . Dr. Boyce impressed me as being a very hard student, and one who had found his true calling as a theological professor. It was a calling that stirred his enthusiasm and brought out his real power, thus proving that this was to be his life-work. Dr. Boyce was always interesting, thorough, and patient as a teacher. He took great interest in us, and we felt that he was our friend. We went to his recitation-room, which was in his own house, with the feeling that we were not only going there to be taught, but to have a good time with a warm-hearted, sympathizing friend and brother.[33]

During the final days of his first year of instruction, Boyce attended the meeting of the Educational Convention in Augusta. It began on "Wednesday after the fourth Sabbath in April, 1856." Basil Manly Sr. chaired the meeting and was elected as president with I. T. Tichenor as secretary. Boyce was appointed to a committee of fifteen to present a report of all the proceedings. The report, as its first item, suggested "that another meeting of the same kind be held in the city of Louisville, Ky., during the two days before the next session of the Southern Baptist Convention."[34] A committee consisting of Basil Manly Sr., A. M. Poindexter, and J. B. Jeter was appointed to ascertain many practical matters such as the conditions under which funds already marked for theological purposes in the various colleges would be available. The committee also inquired as to "what efforts would be made" by any group with special interest in securing a location and "what pecuniary subscriptions or pledges will be given as a nucleus, in case such location should be selected for the common institution." The report appeared under the name of Basil Manly Sr., but in the words of John A. Broadus, "it is clear that this report to the Augusta meeting was written by James P. Boyce."[35]

The report proceeded with a characteristically energetic defense of the idea of a single common theological school for the South. The efforts of the colleges to provide this showed the universal desire and need for theological training. Their failure to provide it, however, at a creditable level, showed the need for a new approach. "The cause why the colleges have taken direction to literature and science, exclusive of theology, and why the schools exclusively theological have been but feebly sustained, belong to an enquiry into which the committee do not now enter," Boyce wrote for the committee. "It is sufficient," he confirmed, "for our present purpose, to observe the fact that, while every effort has moved off in that direction, no one of them nor have all together, yet produced a single Baptist theological school for the south, well furnished for its purposes and commanding united patronage."[36]

Soon after this meeting, the South Carolina Convention met in July. The convention heard a report from E. T. Winkler, appointed by the Augusta Convention for this purpose, "on the recent Convention for forming a Union Theological Seminary for the Baptists of the South and Southwest." After his report, a special committee was appointed to report on the subject the next day and "to nominate a delegation to the Theological Convention, to be held in Louisville" the next April.[37] When the committee reported the next day, acting on the suggestions of Professor Boyce, it recommended that $100,000 be given as the endowment of a general theological seminary upon the following conditions: "That the Institution shall be located at Greenville, S. C.; that the said Institution shall be further endowed with an additional sum of one hundred thousand dollars; and that should such an Institution thus endowed not be located at that place, the funds given . . . shall inure to the Furman University for theological purposes in South Carolina."[38] The state already had $30,000 toward the endowment and would need to raise another $70,000. The committee also appointed five men as delegates to the Louisville Convention: I. L. Brookes, J. C. Furman, J. P. Boyce, J. G. Landrum, and J. A. Lawson. Boyce had entered heartily into all these proceedings in Montgomery and Augusta, and fully concurred in the decision of the South Carolina Baptist Convention. He was now primed to deliver his most detailed and impassioned call for this kind of institution.

On the day following the convention, Furman University held its commencement exercises. J. P. Justin editorialized, "The most noticeable feature, considered by itself, of the performances at this Anniversary, was the Inaugural address, by Prof. James P. Boyce, of the Theological Department." He delivered an address entitled "Three Changes in Theological Institutions."[39] Justin went on to remark, "It will be received, we have no doubt, with a wide diversity of opinion, as to its positions."[40] Boyce had surveyed, and experienced, a variety of proposals for theological education. His views of what was needed specifically for Baptist life had matured. They crystalized on a form consistent with many of the ideas that had preceded him and served as a gentle corrective to others. At some points he stood in stark opposition to the views that others had expressed. Before investigating the changes he suggested, we must look at the views that preceded him.

How to Develop an Educated Ministry

In 1722, the Philadelphia Association proposed that the churches "make inquiry among themselves, if they have any young person hopeful of ministry, and inclinable for learning." Should any be found, the churches were to notify Abel Morgan so that he might recommend them to "the Academy" at the expense of Mr. Hollis.[41] In 1795 Jonathan Maxcy wrote to Richard Furman from Rhode Island College. He envisioned a school of training for ministers connected with the curriculum of the college and urged its desirability. "Why cannot the funding system for educating pious young men be carried into effect in all our churches?" he asked. Should the churches in general become persuaded of its importance, the Baptists could establish "a College of Divinity under the direction of a Committee appointed by all the Baptist Associations in America." The candidates for ministry would pursue an education in the college first, that is, "in the languages, arts and sciences." Subsequently, they would "spend two years in the other in the study of the Scriptures, attending lectures of the professors, writing sermons, and preaching." Maxcy challenged Furman to think of anything more promising to the prosperity of the denomination than "to be yearly supplied with 20 or 30 pious, learned ministers."[42]

Two years later, in 1797, Furman composed a circular letter for the Charleston Association. It was written in response to a question "respecting the obligations of churches, to make provision for the instruction and improvement of the persons they call to the ministry." Furman wanted a thorough education both in preparatory subjects and subjects related directly to essential knowledge of the faith. The one would include "solid, rational, and useful knowledge" that "comprehends an acquaintance with the construction, force, and beauty of language; the right exercise of reason and judgment; and with the laws and powers of nature, of the material world, as established by the Great Creator." The other would include a theology of God and other rational beings—"just views of God himself, his perfections and government; the nature, properties, and powers of created spiritual beings, their relations to God, and to each other; their dependence, duties, and obligations." He envisioned church history as useful—

112

"the history of events, in which the providence of God, the interest of the church, and the truth of religion, have been, and are deeply concerned." This would be in the service of understanding the doctrine of the gospel—"a clear and well digested acquaintance with the doctrines of revelation, concerning our gracious Redeemer and his glorious salvation."

Churches need learned men, not only to help God's people understand the Word of God much better, but to counteract the destructive influence of aggressive hostility to Christian truth. When controversies "on intricate and delicate subjects arise; when men of genius and learning appear in opposition to the truth, and labour to subvert the faith," some need to be prepared to stand in defense of truth lest the cause of God suffer. "The infidel, or Deist, denies the authority of the scriptures, and with pretentions [sic] to learning, confidently asserts, for the encouragement of his associates, and the grief and embarrassment of the uninformed Christian, that Christianity is an imposture." Deists deny the necessity and power of divine revelation, and learned critics destroy the credibility of the biblical text. Universalists deny the reality and terror of divine judgment in its eternal proportions. Socinians use proud reason in their attacks on the Trinity and in their bold attempt "to degrade our Redeemer, and sap the great pillar of our hope, the divine atonement, by similar criticism." The church assuredly has a stewardship in its love and worship of God to contend, and to be able to contend, earnestly for the faith and to prepare some for this worthy task.[43]

If churches have the scriptural duty to discern between those truly called and others merely presumptuous, they also must make every exertion to help those they set apart to obtain "all necessary and useful qualifications." The training of natural gifts does not diminish the spirituality of the call or the necessity of divine blessing. Even the disciples who had the promise of extraordinary influences of the Spirit and the office of speaking under the influence of divine revelation and inspiration, were taught with great intensity by Christ himself. Human learning, it is true, is only a "handmaid to grace," and many have attained high degrees of usefulness with no formal learning. Learning without the gracious operations of the Spirit is "rendered impotent," but that fact in itself "furnishes no just reason for its being despised or neglected."

Some because of personal circumstance cannot take time to attain "what is commonly called a liberal education." No matter how many obstacles, however, "where the duty is faithfully attended to, some useful improvement may be arrived at: by the help of proper books, which may be obtained without great expence; and by the occasional assistance of those who have themselves obtained some advantages." Obstacles arise in the churches from "low contracted sentiments and an avaricious disposition." The same keeps ministers unpaid and "houses created for the worship of God" mean and contemptible. Properly rebuked by Scripture for such a covetous spirit and thoroughly convinced that scriptural example and mandate justify it, "churches should combine their strength, and bring their contributions to a point of common interest and usefulness" since a "subject of such vast importance should be the object of united efforts." Just before his final series of exhortations Furman summarized his argument and enforced the urgency of his conclusion:

> If, therefore, it is enjoined, by divine command, that we render our best services to God, and be zealous for the honour of his sacred cause—if in this view we are taught to pray that his kingdom may come, and that he may send forth labourers into his harvest—if our obligations to our Redeemer are infinite, and the reasons for our gratitude without number—if we have by solemn, covenant transactions, surrendered ourselves to God, and engaged all we are and have to be laid out, ordered and disposed of by him, for his own glory—and, if this plan of preparing candidates for the ministry, by a previous course of study and improvement, is a measure evidently calculated to answer the noblest purposes in religion, and is supported by scripture, reason and experience;—Then, surely, we may conclude in the most decided manner, that the churches of Christ are under real and great obligation, to reduce it to practice; and that the obligation extends to the best improvement of their ability and opportunities.[44]

Twenty years later, in 1817, when Richard Furman served as president of the newly formed General Missionary Convention, he wrote the "Address of the Convention" to the constituent churches, societies, and associations that composed it. This address dealt with many aspects—most thoroughly with the missionary efforts and aspirations of the union—but included a statement of desire for the education of ministers. The General Missionary Convention, also known as the Triennial Convention, had organized in 1814 under the impetus of Luther Rice. Rice, along with Adoniram Judson and Ann Judson, had converted to Baptist views after having been sent into foreign missions by Congregationalists under the auspices of the American Board of Commissioners. Furman expressed the joy of the convention in the providential arrangement of that circumstance and that the "support necessary to carry their objects into full effect, has increased with each succeeding year." Funds in fact beyond the most optimistic expectation "have poured into our treasury."

Furman included many other aspects of ministry such as the British Baptist work in India under Carey, the British and Foreign Bible Society, the work of other evangelicals in missions, the zeal of female societies eliciting mission workers and money to support them, and the sending of Baptist missionaries to enforce the work of the Judsons. Furman urged the adoption of Sunday schools for the training of church youth in the truths of the Bible. He announced a "Western Mission" of two young men whose "pulpit talents are in a high degree respectable." St. Louis became the base for their labors "with the approbation and encouragement of the Board." In his postmillennial exuberance, Furman, on behalf of the convention, could hardly "suppress its joy" in observing many evidences that the "Head of the church is preparing to effect some glorious result," even the defeat of the strategies of hell and the casting out of "the prince of this world."[45]

Central to such a strategy as providence has initiated is "the subject of education." The convention reminded its constituents of its importance, "particularly in relation to such pious young men, as shall possess talents which promise usefulness in the Word." Furman duly addressed the important, and constantly recurring, theme of the requirement of "grace in the heart, a sacred necessity compelling to the work." Only the Lord "can make able ministers of the New Testament." But how plainly anyone can observe "the advantages which those servants of the church enjoy who can read the lively oracles in their original languages." This combined with the "rapidly improving state of society in which the grammar of the English language is generally taught," and the "zeal which other Christian societies are exercising on this subject, and the advantages which it secures them" makes them "solicit your bounty and influence." When the theme favoring education was introduced, "the Convention were unanimous as to the importance of the subject, and left it in charge with the Board to give it that maturity and publicity which they shall approve. It is hoped that something on this point will be speedily and vigorously attempted." With all the objections that have been raised in the past, "the difficulties on this subject felt by pious brethren, are like vapours of the morning, vanishing."[46]

This interest led to the establishing of Columbian College in Washington, D.C., in 1821, and contributed to the founding of many Baptist colleges in Southern states. These colleges began, for the most part, as an effort to train students for the ministry. In addition to Furman, Mississippi College began in 1826 as Hampstead Academy with an emphasis on ministerial education. When it became Mississippi College in 1830, it was authorized to "confer such degrees in the arts, sciences and languages as are usually conferred in the most respectable colleges in the United States." Wake Forest in North Carolina was begun by Samuel Wait, a graduate of Columbian College, in 1834. The college focused on liberal arts education and did not initially develop a specifically theological department but proposed only the "education of young men called of God to the ministry." Mercer Institute, founded in 1833, provided both literary and theological instruction for students preparing for ministry, and for several years limited enrollment to that class of student. In 1837, the executive committee of the Georgia Baptist Convention (organized 1822) elevated the Mercer Institute to Mercer University. In 1839, Adiel Sherwood, who had written the resolution that led to the formation of the state convention, also organized the theological department at the new university.

Alabama Baptists, under the impulse provided by the General Missionary Convention, discussed education for ministers and failed in an attempt at a theological and manual labor school before establishing

Howard College in Marion in 1842 with both literary and theological departments. Basil Manly Sr., president of the University of Alabama, provided both encouragement and educational expertise in this successful venture. Virginia, led by Robert Ryland, started Virginia Baptist Seminary in 1832 to educate ministerial students. It became Richmond College in 1840 and gradually placed more emphasis on the liberal arts part of the curriculum than on the theological, reasoning that "the preference should be to the former as a basis for theological studies which should be continued through out life."

Kentucky provided another clear example of the impetus provided by the educational emphasis of the General Missionary Convention when, influenced by the preaching and presence of Luther Rice, it founded a college in Georgetown in 1829. Consistent with this influence was its election of William Staughton as its president. Staughton had been active in the Philadelphia Association, giving it a deep missionary consciousness. First president of Columbian College and first corresponding secretary of the General Missionary Convention, Staughton as a young student in England had been present when Carey, Fuller, Ryland, Sutcliff, and others formed the Particular Baptist Missionary Society. But he died en route to Kentucky and thus never officially served at Georgetown College. An initial gift by Issachar Pawling was to be administered for the education of Baptist preachers.[47]

One year after the founding of Mercer Institute, Jesse Mercer presented before the Baptist Convention of Georgia an impassioned defense of education as a requisite qualification for Baptist ministers. In a message entitled "Knowledge Indispensable to a Minister of God," Mercer argued that knowledge, wisdom, and understanding, all necessary to be a shepherd of God's people, had inextricable connections with each other.[48] This knowledge, for the minister, was indispensable. Arguing from Proverbs and Hosea, Mercer insisted that "a minister of God, to approve himself, as a wise man, must have a share of learning, and be ardently desirous of, and assiduously seeking for, increased attainments in wisdom and knowledge. Otherwise he will be cast among the companions of fools; who despise wisdom and instruction, and hate knowledge." An aptness to teach requires knowledge, for "the minister of God is a teacher of the deep things of God; but how shall he approve himself, as such, while he is destitute of a literal knowledge of those things in which he professes to give instruction?"

Mercer did not detract from the necessity of "spiritual endowments" when he insisted that "a literary qualification [was] necessary to render [the minister] able to teach his fellow men. For this he cannot expect divine revelation but must gain it in the ordinary way of its attainment, and without which he cannot be able to afford instruction." Any steward's task involves "an intimate knowledge of the will and designs of the parties concerned." The steward of God "must be instructed into the nature and perfection of Him, for whom he ministers—must be acquainted with his mysteries, or the treasuries of his Grace, of which he is a steward—must know his purposes in the use to be made of them." This he learns through a thorough knowledge of the works and words of God.

No branch of knowledge, therefore, can be seen as inconsequential for the preacher. "For we know of no truth," Mercer contended, "the knowledge of which, would be unimportant to a minister of God. We know of no truth which is not in Christ Jesus." A thorough knowledge of God in "his natural and moral perfections" fills the minister "with a holy reverence" and guards him "against fanciful constructions of scripture, and the forming of false systems in Theology. The standard of truth is in the God of Truth. The most fruitful source of error is ignorance, or vague notions of God."[49]

Such requisite knowledge is attained only by "a close application to the study of the works of God." Though the Lord gives wisdom, we learn throughout Scripture, from Solomon, Moses, Daniel, and Saul of Tarsus, that "God, besides those inward and spiritual endowments he affords, will have men qualified, by such literary attainments, as are necessary to discharge the duties of those stations he intends them to fill."[50] One should not reason that since these were educated prior to their call as servants of God, we therefore have no responsibility to educate. Their circumstances prohibited the possibility of a purposed educational opportunity. One might as well argue that because God fed "his prophet Elijah by ravens, now if God wants his ministers supported, he can send ravens to feed them. But who will dare to indulge in such a thought!" Instead, since a minister must have knowledge and "must acquire it by the study of the works of God," it is "wise to have places of learning." In this way, the best books can be gathered with the least expense, the best faculty can be maintained for the largest number of students, and young men will learn better in the group than when alone.[51]

This learning should be comprehensive, and though garnered through human instrumentality must not be caricatured by the misnomer "human learning." Geography, geology, chemistry, history, astronomy, philosophy and theology, all imply the study "of the works of God, in creation, and providence, and grace." Mercer defended the study of each of these as part of our necessary knowledge of God and his works. History, for example, traces "the rise and downfall of nations and Kingdoms, together with a minute account of those facts which have transpired under the providence of God, in the successive generations of earth; so indispensable to a right understanding of scripture." Philosophy "teaches the nature and reason of things and clarifies the context of cause and effect relationships." It explores the mind "both human and divine, with all its natural properties and moral powers," and examines and exhibits "its dignity, beauty and moral excellence." Theology teaches divine things through a critical examination into the language of the Bible. One must discern how its language employs "the modes and figures of speech [and] the manners and customs of the times in which it was written—and the best rules of construction, in order to come at the truth, taught in that sacred volume."[52]

A school cannot make a minister. The historic commitment of Baptists to a divine calling and equipping for ministry consistently had to be given priority when discussing education. Mercer echoed that concern in stating that "the Convention believes that no man ought to attempt, or be encouraged to preach the gospel, until he has a full satisfaction in his own conscience, that God requires it of him, and can afford his brethren the same satisfaction in regard to it." A prerequisite in accepting a person to ministerial education is that he "must be licensed to preach by the church, of which he is a member, and be approved by surrounding churches—so that if the Convention should unfortunately contribute to raise up a set of graceless ministers, the churches shall share in the first blame."[53] Considering all these facts and relationships, Mercer enjoined on his convention congregation the acquisition of knowledge as a chief way to "approve yourselves as the ministers of God."

The next year, 1835, Basil Manly Sr. discussed the issue of "Theological Education in the Southern States."[54] As he surveyed the attempts at theological education in the South, he lamented. He was not at all impressed with the results. In his opinion the Southern states had failed to do what needed to be done, but if a lesson was learned, then true progress had been made. "It is perhaps incident to every great undertaking, that its commencement should exhibit the mistakes of inexperience, and the consequent waste of time and strength—and indeed, it seems to be a part of the plan of Divine Providence, that every good institution should grow up amid solicitudes and disappointments, and attain its usefulness by the nurture of prayers and tears and anxious labors."

Ministerial students cannot pay sufficient amounts to support a school entirely dedicated to theological instruction. They are too poor, the number is too small, and the subject matter is too diverse. The method of annual subscriptions for support is too precarious, and on such a basis no creditable and stable faculty can be funded. Nor can a theological school be successfully merged with a college. This results in unequal comparisons between the types of students to the embarrassment of the preachers; it results in too little time devoted to theological students; success of the school in general, that is, larger numbers of paying nontheological students, means the suppression of the theological department. "Is it not true," Manly asked with candor, "that the money given by Baptists and their friends to provide liberal facilities for the benefit of young ministers, must needs be diverted in the mixed institution, from its principal design?" The sons of gentlemen benefit from it, "who are much better able to form schools for themselves, than the Baptists are for them." This plan is defective and will have to be abandoned.

Manly did not denigrate the benefits of providing a liberal arts education. "In contributing to found schools for common education under religious auspices," he conceded, "we not only provide a rich inheritance for our children, but place ourselves among the benefactors of mankind." This project must proceed, however, in such a way as not to destroy the more vital goal of providing theological instruction in a comprehensive way. Manly believed Baptists needed separate institutions for these two very different goals.

Theological education needs to be established so that ministerial students receive the full devotion of both time and curriculum and are thus enabled to have a program designed for peculiar individual needs. Manly envisioned both the semiliterate and the college graduate in the same classes with special attention being given according to needs. The preachers need this kind of instruction, but if put in a school where that kind of remedial work is concentrated on, then it will occupy the bulk of the time and energy and the distinctive theological work will be minimized. "They have no time to spend in waiting for instruction at the occasional and ill adapted lessons of ordinary schools. They are wanted in their Master's service with the least possible delay of preparation. . . . How is it possible that this can be done in an institution, where this class of students is necessarily subordinate, and reduced by uncontrollable circumstance to a fragment of their teacher's time!"

Each Southern state could even now endow one chair in their respective schools. This would be something. But the situation calls for the combined strengths of the states in one institution. Manly proposed, for example, that South Carolina, North Carolina, and Georgia should "adopt a common site, and a name for the Institution, suitable to them all—should establish a board of trustees, consisting of an equal number from each State, to administer the affairs of the Institution—which, being thus furnished with three well endowed Professors, would be reputable and adequate to all the demands of the Denomination in the Southern States." Endowments would allow churches to focus on supporting and encouraging students by their gifts and also contribute to the growing needs of the institution's physical facilities. Manly also included the idea of "manual labor, as a necessary part of the plan of education." In short, Manly triumphed, "we have here sketched the outline of a plan for a great Southern Baptist Institution, which would grow and expand itself under the divine blessing into an importance and usefulness of which we cannot now conceive." More than twenty years would pass before this vision would find fulfillment.

121

Almost a decade later, in 1844, after Manly had moved to Alabama to serve as president of the University of Alabama, he received an invitation to become president of Mercer. He wrote his friend J. L. Reynolds at Furman Theological Institute about this. The time approached when his son Basil Jr. would leave home for further education. This put the senior Manly in a reflective mood again about theological education. "Basil is staying at home this year for the purpose of hardening and strengthening his body by work on the farm, and other athletic exercises," Manly wrote, showing his enduring commitment to physical labor. "After that, he will commence a theological course." Manly considered sending him to Furman to study with Reynolds and thence to Newton, spending an equal time in both places. "His mind is worth cultivating with the amplest means in our power." Manly then revisited his idea of theological education set forth almost a decade before: "A serious notion has been all along cherished by me for uniting our states on Georgia, as a center in educational interests. I have already a plan and picture of the whole thing as it would be in the event of union." Georgia Baptists wanted to give Manly a chance to try his idea and therefore "in the summer they made me the President of the Mercer University." At that time, he immediately refused the position. "Lately," he continued, "they have renewed the appointment and insist that I have heretofore said that, could a union of the three states be effected, I would be willing to devote to the common cause the energies of my life." He confessed that he still felt that way, and he could think of "no object so important, so worthy to be cherished & sought by the Baptists at the South, as some great literary & theological centre."

Such a rallying point would give Baptists in the South sufficient strength to be strongly influential. "The single, divided & meager efforts of each state" could never accomplish this. If the three states, the Carolinas and Georgia, unite, "we should have at once three or four well-sustained Professors, and an institution of sufficient force & completeness to attract all our first rate young men." Even if some local funds were forfeited, the amount gained by union would more than compensate. "Georgia," he had come to believe, "is more favorable for a rallying point on many accounts." Not only is their number greater, so are their wealth, zeal, and determination. Having the site in Georgia would also draw in Alabama, he was convinced. Now the question— "Would it favour the object of union, if it should be understood that I would take the head of the Mercer University in case of a union? The theological schools might be taken up and moved, bodily, as they are." On top of that, "Bro. Dagg, now created a D. D. is made Prof. of Theology at Penfield. It is probable, though not certain, that he will accept."[55] Thus, in Manly's vision the central theological institution could soon materialize with Reynolds, Dagg, and possibly himself as its first professors.

That specific vision for establishing a single theological institution for the South would soon fail, for the tensions between Baptists of the North and South increased, demanding that energies be put into the formation, not of a theological school, but of an entire denomination. Brief discussions of the need for a school were held at the consultative convention in Augusta in 1845. More pressing issues pushed aside the completion of that discussion until later. In Nashville at the Southern Baptist Convention in 1849 little could be done because of very slight attendance in view of rumors of a possible cholera epidemic. Two men destined to be intense antagonists in later years, R. B. C. Howell and J. R. Graves, felt that the time had come for a theological school particularly for Southern Baptists. That convention dismissed to Charleston, and several men spoke there about the need for a central theological institution, including W. B. Johnson and Basil Manly Jr. Manly made two major points in his presentation—such an institution is desirable and such an institution is practicable. Under both these heads, Manly made the point that centralization would be economical and efficient for concentration of funds, usefulness and retention of professors, the cultural growth of students, the gathering of a library, and construction of buildings. He suggested that the most workable plan would be the establishment of a new institution, with a new board of trustees selected from every state represented in the Southern Baptist Convention.[56] The 1855 Montgomery Convention had started the movement that finalized the vision. Now in 1856 J. P. Boyce would articulate a theory and a structure that would bring to fruition desires more than a century old.

A Seminary for Southern Baptists

Boyce, energized by the progress made in the number of ad hoc meetings organized to discuss forming a theological seminary, now felt that the time had come for his putting before the public an elaborate discussion of the issue. His address before the trustees at Furman University on 31 July 1856 was "two hours in the delivery, and certainly made a marked impression."[57] Boyce distilled the best ideas that had emerged hitherto in the discussion about theological education, fed off the energy generated at the state convention, and set the stage for the discussion that would take place the next year in Louisville. He could not have kept himself from a deeply fixed excitement about the decision of the South Carolina Convention to offer $100,000 for the endowment of such a school. Boyce felt sure that his suggestions would finally give concrete reality to the desires that had been expressed for decades, would avoid the pitfalls of other schemes, be consistent with a Baptist view of ministry, and flesh out the biblical requirements for gospel ministry.

The three ideas around which he built his address were the need for an abundant ministry, a learned teaching ministry, and an orthodox ministry. The first goal concerned the many ministers set apart in Baptist churches who, though destitute of much foundational education of a classic nature, may nevertheless become apt and capable of rightly dividing the word of truth. In producing a learned ministry, Baptists must develop an ability to train their own scholars to engage the larger culture and theological world without dependence upon institutions that have declined from historic orthodoxy. In order to guarantee the confidence of the Baptist people and discourage the tendency to apostasy that plagues many institutions of learning, the professors must sign a creedal statement. This requirement should safeguard the school by guaranteeing an orthodox confessional ministry whose doctrinal ideas are set firmly within the framework of biblical theology as expressed in the historic orthodox settlements of disputed doctrinal issues.

Theological institutions have failed to "call forth an abundant Ministry for the Churches." This reality sadly marked Furman University, so Boyce believed, in spite of the ideas, dreams, intentions, and prayers of its original founders and nurturers.[58] An abundant ministry is vitally needed for the world as well as for the expanding number of churches, but whatever growth in the ministry has occurred, it has not been due to the work of the theological seminary. The cry for help is not met largely because Baptists have failed to follow the principles plainly laid out in the Word of God. "And does he not now chastise us by suffering our schemes to work out their natural results, that we, being left to ourselves, may see our folly and return to Him and to His way as the only means of strength!"[59]

Boyce acknowledged clearly his confidence in the "sovereignty of God working His own will and calling forth" those he chose to build his church. Nor did he omit the place of the churches and the pastors in calling out the gifted, thus producing an increase of laborers. In theological education itself, however, the difficulty has been the requirement that "the student should have passed through a regular college course or made attainments equivalent thereto." This plan has prevented many from entering the ministry, being without prospects for help, and has hindered the development of an educational plan adapted for such as cannot attain the general education of a full college course. Echoing the concern Manly expressed twelve years earlier, Boyce proposed that a school of theological training should make it possible to "obtain that adequate knowledge of the truths of the Scriptures systematically arranged and of the laws which govern the interpretation of the text in the English version, which constitutes all that is actually necessary to enable them to preach the gospel, to build up the churches on their most holy faith, and to instruct them in the practice of the duties incumbent upon them."[60]

Like Mercer over two decades earlier, Boyce defended the idea that "scriptural qualifications of the ministry do, indeed, involve the idea of knowledge." He seemed to reflect on Mercer's view, however, with a spirit of careful correction as he noted, "but that knowledge is not of the sciences nor of philosophy nor of the languages, but of God and of His plan of salvation." One who knows this, though he be not learned in the subjects of the schools, but knows this, not superficially, "not merely in those plain and simple declarations known to every believing reader, but in its power, as revealed in its precious and sanctifying doctrines, is fitted to bring forth out of his treasure things new and old, and is a workman that needeth not to be ashamed, although he may speak to his hearers in uncouth words or in manifest ignorance of all the sciences."[61]

John Bunyan served as an example of a formally unlearned man who nevertheless had power in the knowledge of God, truth, and the gospel. On the other hand, Theodore Parker was held forth as an example of a formally learned man with great natural gifts pleasing to the carnal intellectual instincts of cultured unbelievers. Parker commended his poison with a rhetorical ease and a storehouse of knowledge unmatched by any of his contemporaries. With such desirable gifts, however, he was

> so destitute of the knowledge of true Christianity and of a genuine experience of the influences of the Holy Ghost, that he denies the plainest doctrines of the Bible, saps the very foundation of all revealed truth, and manifests so profound an ignorance of the Book he undertakes to expound and the religion of which he calls himself a Minister that the humblest Christian among our very servants shall rise up in condemnation against him in the great day of accounts.[62]

Boyce readily conceded the usefulness of the numerous faithful who both loved the truth and possessed the knowledge of the schools. They stood forth as the most prominent and efficient workmen for the cause of Christ in their respective ages. At the same time, he concluded that God "will work out the greater proportion of His purposes by men of no previous training and educated only in the mysteries of that truth which is in Christ Jesus." Baptists should never forget this, for they have benefited more than any other Christian denomination from these zealous men of God who had "no collegiate education, of no learning or rhetorical eloquence, of no instruction even in schools of theology." Though lacking these, however, they did train themselves through a voluntary and joyous thralldom to the Bible and one or two commentaries and works of divinity with which they became intimately familiar. "And if," Boyce reasoned, "by any course of training, substantially of the same kind, our Theological schools can restore to us such a mass Ministry as was then enjoyed, the days of our progress and prosperity will be realized to have but just begun."[63]

For these laborers in truth Baptist theological education must be devised if it is to prepare an abundant ministry. Boyce believed that Baptists had bypassed this obviously biblical principle in training men for ministry. "Let such a change be made in the theological department," Boyce said speaking specifically of Furman University, "as shall provide an English course of study for those who have only been able to attain a plain English education." The course should include the evidence of Christianity, systematic and polemic theology, the rules of interpretation applied to the English version. He included practical studies such as knowledge of the rules of rhetoric, sermon preparation, and pastoral ministry. He wanted a course of study to "train the mind to habits of reflection and analysis, to awaken it to conceptions of the truths of Scripture, to fill it with arguments from the word of God in support of its doctrines, and to give it facility in constructing and presenting such arguments." This course would take perhaps two years, but with an unusual discipline of concentration could be finished in one year. This class of men, zealous for the glory of God and for the souls of men, now consigned to endless frustration because they "soon find themselves exhausted of their materials, forced to repeat the same topics in the same way, and finally to aim at nothing but continuous exhortation, bearing constantly upon the same point, or as is oftentimes the case, destitute of any point at all," would soon improve themselves to "occupy positions of greater respectability and usefulness."[64]

Boyce described with pathos the dilemma in which a mature man without college education finds himself in his pursuit of some way to maximize his knowledge and effectiveness for the cause of the gospel. He is called to teach, and has a mind capable of qualification, but without requisite knowledge cannot be considered apt to do so. Boyce described a scenario with which he must have been familiar in reality: "Let one of them take up the Scriptures, and he finds himself embarrassed in the midst of statements which the Church, for centuries after the Apostles, had not fully harmonized—statements which constitute the facts of Theology, from which, in like manner with other sciences, by processes of induction and comparison, the absolute truth must be established." He turns to books and finds technical terms which he has an equal incapacity to understand. No formal training can he receive without impoverishing his family or spending essentially useless years just qualifying himself to enroll in a theological course. His usefulness in an appropriate sphere of service is lost. Boyce considered that this situation could be remedied if the trustees would adopt the changes he proposed.[65]

Boyce also argued that many in the ministry who had a college education, but had neither time nor financial means to go further, would have spent their time better in a theological course than a liberal arts course. The college-trained man was in a better position for service than the man with no formal education, but he still lacked that training that is most valuable and, to use Boyce's word, "essential." In their preaching they fear to touch upon many doctrines vital to the spiritual health and growth of their members; they have not tasted strong meat and find themselves unable to feed it to others. They motivate their churches through principles of fraternal cooperation but are unable to feed with the sound doctrine that the most holy faith generates for both corporate and personal holiness. No less than the one with no training, the college-trained man without theological education finds himself intimidated by the task of teaching doctrine. "The disturbances felt about unsettled doctrines, the inability experienced to declare the whole counsel of God, the doctrinal mistakes realized as frequently committed, have long since convinced them that all of their other education is of but little value, compared with that knowledge of Theology which they have lost in its acquisition."[66]

For some the choice must be between a "thorough literary and a thorough Theological course." Boyce did not hesitate one moment in declaring that the theological far surpassed in importance for the gospel minister the merely literary course. If both are possible for some few, that would be the most desirable; but for the four-fifths that will give the churches and the world the abundant ministry so needed and required by scriptural principles, Boyce's plan was requisite. "And we look with confidence for the blessing of God upon this plan, not because we believe that He favors an ignorant Ministry, but because, knowing that He requires that His Ministry be instructed, and that by His word and His providence He has pointed out the nature of the learning He demands, we believe that the plan proposed is based upon these indications."[67]

The second change Boyce proposed, he dealt with more briefly than the first but not with less intensity. He called for the development of a course of study that would prepare men for a life of superior scholarship. This could be developed parallel with the provision he already had discussed. Dependence on Germany for all the "learned investigations in biblical criticism and exegesis" and in other areas of study such as history and history of theology, has introduced "much of error mingled with truth." In fact, American theological studies in general have suffered from this dependence. The rising ministry "should be trained under the scholarship of the Anglo Saxon mind, which from its nature, as well as from the circumstances which surround it, is eminently fitted to weigh evidence, and to decide as to its appropriateness and its proper limitations."[68]

Baptists urgently need such an infusion of scholarship. The broader world of scholarship has "overlooked, ridiculed, and defamed" Baptists and has classed them historically "among fanatics and heretics." This situation must change; Baptists owe it to themselves to demonstrate that they have not made the gross errors imputed to them. They owe it to Christ "whose truth we hold so distinctively as to separate us from all others of His believing people" and to have thrust Baptists into the pathway of banishment, imprisonment, martyrdom, scorn, and reproach, not only from the world but from "those who love our Lord Jesus Christ."[69]

Boyce envisioned the development of a library that would include the "lore of the past," the means of annual increase of books, "rare and costly" volumes for research that would lead to the possibility of scholarly work beyond the normal theological course. Boyce envisioned graduates from theological studies spending one or two more years doing theses of exegetical research, comparative theological studies, and learning methods of original research, thus producing a "band of scholars" from whom original and valuable contributions could be expected to "our Theological literature." This number would be comparatively small and would require only "two additional recitations a week for each of three or four professors." The language studies involved would also be available to missionaries in their evangelistic work among those that speak Arabic; but the ability to train native preachers in theological studies and translate substantial theological works into their language would be perhaps an even greater benefit. Not only would theological instruction on the mission field be forthcoming, but from those that devoted this extra time to scholarly work "our institutions at home would chiefly look for their Professors." This suggested change in theological education means that "learning will abound among us. The world will be subdued to Christ. The principles dear to our hearts will universally prevail."[70]

Boyce's last change was "the adoption of a declaration of doctrine to be required of those who assume the various professorships." Boyce had seen the dangers in the exchange over imputation in the *Southern Baptist*. He had read J. L. Reynolds's careful but compelling use of Baptist confessional history in his articles and showed a detailed grasp of J. S. Mims's attack on confessions in the treatise "Orthodoxy."[71] He had seen the benefits of a confessionally based education during his years at Princeton. The subtlety with which both Campbellism and Arminianism had infected segments of Baptist life led Boyce to believe that "a crisis in Baptist doctrine is evidently approaching." Those that held to the "doctrines which formerly distinguished us" must not slack in their duty but contend for that same faith.[72]

Every doctrine of Scripture must be "determined and expressed," and those responsible for calling and ordaining ministers must ascertain that they are orthodox. Nothing could have been more reprehensible to Mims than this proposal of Boyce. Mims argued that orthodoxy is an attempt to "lord it over" others. "In all countries, and at all times, there has existed a class of men who," Mims snarled, "if we may judge from their conduct, decided the question, by teaching that he is the greatest who contends most earnestly for conformity to some standard of orthodoxy."[73]

Confessional faithfulness, nevertheless, in Boyce's perception of Christian truth, should apply to every segment of Baptist life, although with different expectations of understanding and knowledgeable conformity. He set forth his view of expectations for church members, for ministers, and most stringently, for theological professors. He spoke of the "peculiar obligations" that rested on those invested with the teaching ministry to be preserved from corrupting the Word of God by "the crime of teaching a single error, however unimportant." Likewise, those that had authority over these professors, the boards of trustees, required "faithfulness to the trusts devolved upon them, that false doctrine, however trifling, may receive no countenance."[74]

Mims, however, had argued that the use of a confession to investigate orthodoxy was not a protection of the Word of God but amounted to a denial of the Bible. "If they undertake," he said in speaking of the enforcers of confessional orthodoxy, "the grateful task of investigating the orthodoxy of any supposed heretic, they never appeal to the Bible, but only to their Standard." Biblical truth never changes, Mims reminded his hearers, but "orthodoxy is as various as times and places are different from each other. Truth is always the same, and knows no standard but the Bible."[75]

Boyce wanted to remind his hearers, however, that Alexander Campbell flew under the banner of "no creed but the Bible," and at the same time had drawn thousands of members of Baptist churches away from some of the fundamental truths that Baptists profess to be biblical. Had he been in a theological seminary and influenced the men that went to the leading pulpits of the denomination, the devastation could have been greater than it was. The power of a single individual in teaching a single error has had enormous destructive power in the past, and the recurrence of such a situation with no means of checking it and setting it right could "influence all our churches, and the fair fabric of our faith may be entirely demolished."[76]

In order to reinforce this point for those that read the address, Boyce added a footnote in the published version that made it even more strongly. For those who "teach the Ministry," through whom the fountain of truth will flow to the students, "no difference, however slight, no peculiar sentiment, however speculative, is here allowable." A teacher's "agreement with the standard should be exact. His declaration of it should be based upon no mental reservation, upon no private understanding with those who immediately invest him into office." Before consenting to teach and signing a confession, he should be convinced that its position is "an exact summary of the truth" contained in the Bible. Under no circumstances should a principle be adopted that a professor may "sign any abstract of doctrine with which he does not agree, and in accordance with which he does not intend to teach," or that he is "at liberty to modify the truth, which he has been placed there to inculcate." A theological institution cannot tolerate erroneous tendencies in its professors, and "hence his opinions must be expressly affirmed to be upon every point in accordance with the truth we believe to be taught in the Scriptures."[77]

Boyce assumed, also, that he knew the most logical selection for such a confessional standard. The one that "had almost universal prevalence in this State at the time of the foundation of the Institution" was the confession of faith "then acknowledged in the Charleston Baptist Association."[78] Again, Mims ridiculed the idea that associational confessions had functioned as standards of orthodoxy at any time. When he considered the suggestion that the Philadelphia Association, or the Charleston, adopted confessions precisely to instruct their member churches, and discipline them if necessary, as well as to investigate the orthodoxy of newly applying churches, he fumed in resentment and resistance. "Who gave them this authority?" he queried. "Certainly Christ did not, and no one else could."

Then he asked a series of rhetorical questions to which the true answers would have been far different than Mims implied by his asking them. "What is the evidence of so great degeneracy in our American churches, in having so widely departed from the spirit and practice of their elder brethren of the other hemisphere? How many ministers of those Associations ever instruct or convince the members of their flocks out of the Confession? How many of them *could tell you what its Theology on any given point is*? How many even possess copies of it? How many have perused it with any attention, if at all?"[79]

The fact is, however, that the associations had used the confessions precisely in the way Mims implied they had not. Boyce knew this. The Charleston Confession not only had been the confession of his childhood and youth, but, in its original Presbyterian form as the Westminster Confession of Faith, governed the theological education at Princeton, and had been implicitly already functioning as a safeguard at Furman. The board had required that all texts used in the institute pass muster theologically and assumed the unanimity of doctrine among the churches. The introduction of more lectures in the school and more diversity of sentiment in the denomination now demanded a clearly stated confession to govern theological studies.

When Mims had appeared before the board of trustees in 1848 to answer for his theology of imputation, he protested against his accuser's method by proclaiming, "I shall now attempt to evince by unquestionable historical evidence, the truth of this proposition: that GOD'S WORD, AND NOT CONFESSIONS, HAS ALWAYS BEEN THE ACKNOWLEDGED STANDARD OF ORTHODOXY AMONG BAPTISTS."[80] Boyce knew that he must overcome Mims's historical argument against the regulative use of confession. He made the claim, therefore, that such a confessional test had been common in Baptist life. Though he knew some would object, he pointed out that a theological institution, because it is not a scriptural institution, must meet only the criterion of not contradicting Scripture. It must conform to the most expedient rules that human wisdom can devise to "carry out the laudable designs of its founders." The confessional standard, therefore, guarantees that the doctrine taught will reflect the consensus of those who established the school in order to press forward the faith of their churches.[81]

Even in local churches, however, Boyce argued that Scripture abounds with exhortations about the faith that assume the church's commitment to a body of clearly enunciated doctrines and its obligation to preserve, propagate, and protect it. Baptists, so Boyce argued, had used confessions in a twofold way: (1) the declaration of faith, and (2) the "testing of its existence in others." Boyce demonstrated that such a confession of truth operated during the ministry of Jesus; it was expanded and required as a test of faith under the apostles as they delivered the gospel in its fullness in establishing churches. Following the apostolic model, churches continued evaluating their teachers in light of the rule of faith for the next three centuries. Baptists of all ages also have used creeds in this twofold way.

Some have mistaken the Baptist commitment to liberty of conscience as a rejection of a creedal test in the church. Mims made this mistake. He applied the Baptist rejection of creeds as an instrument of civil repression as reason to reject their use as instruments of doctrinal purity in the church. Early in Mims's presentation, he set the tone for his discussion by reminding the trustees, "For it is an indisputable fact of history, that many who could reason soundly against the traditions of the Elders, according to the logic of the Bible, have yet been utterly confounded and silenced by the irrefragable argument of 'bonds, imprisonment,' and appeals to confessions."[82] So the Church of England had done. As well as the Congregationalists, the Presbyterians, and that great mother of persecution Roman Catholicism. The subtle rhetorical connection of creeds with the oppression of civil authorities bolstered Mims's argument throughout his speech. Boyce broke the connection by agreeing that Baptists have refused to use creeds to enforce civil punishment or disability. The spirituality of the church demanded this civil freedom; at the same time, the church's spirituality has "impressed upon us the necessity of excluding those who have violated the simplicity which is in Christ," and thus the necessity of a doctrinal standard.[83]

Boyce closed his discussion of the third change with an intensified recommendation of the justness of such a provision. The adoption of a test of doctrine, Boyce considered as perfectly consistent "with the position of Baptists, as well as of Bible Christians." In correction of Mims, Boyce saw this as "based upon principles and practices sanctioned by the authority of Scripture, and by the usage of our people." Requiring subscription, Boyce contended, "will infringe the rights of no man," and will secure the rights of those that expect a sound ministry to emerge from the educational experience.

Mims had expressed with exclamation points his resistance to being judged by a confession of faith. In his closing remarks in 1848, he had declared, "In conclusion, brethren, undismayed by the efforts made to intimidate me, and to excite prejudices against me, I appeal from the tribunal of Confessions to that of Bible truth." He demanded to be tried "not by the stale and vapid canons of Confessions, but by the sober truth of the Bible." To argument and appeal to God's Word he would gladly reply, but to "a hostile array of human authorities" he would only show disdain.[84]

Boyce believed that all this rhetoric of truth and courage missed the point. "It is no hardship to those who teach here, to be called upon to sign the declaration of their principles," he reminded his audience, "for there are fields of usefulness open elsewhere to every man, and none need accept your call who cannot conscientiously sign your formulary." He reminded the trustees that a confession was no enemy of biblical truth but would help "to distinguish truth from error, and to embrace the former," and would enforce "the same precious truths of the Bible which were so dear to the hearts of its founders."[85]

These changes Boyce proposed implied "gathering all our students into a single Institution." With its success, eventually many such institutions would be called for, but, for the present, the greatest advantage would be secured by one. Sectional jealousies would gradually vanish, suspicions and prejudices would be subjected to the light of personal friendship and common scholarship, and appreciation for a variety of gifts would foster mutual love.[86] Boyce's vision of Camelot would soon be put to the test.

4

The Dream Fulfilled

he Education Convention of 1857 in Louisville met intermittently during the Southern Baptist Convention. As in the previous educational convention in Augusta, Basil Manly Sr. served as president in Louisville. Other prominent Southern Baptists helped with official duties as J. B. Jeter served as vice president and I. T. Tichenor, secretary. The convention met on May 7 in Walnut Street Baptist Church. Delegates from Virginia (26 including John A. Broadus), Maryland (6), South Carolina (7), Furman University (3), North Carolina (3), Georgia (5, all trustees of Mercer), Kentucky (10), trustees of Western Baptist Theological Institute (2), Tennessee (8, all trustees of Union University including J. R. Graves, A. C. Dayton, and J. M. Pendleton), Mississippi (2 from the state convention and 4 from Semple-Broaddus College), Alabama (6), Louisiana (2), and Arkansas (1), initially heard the report of the committee appointed at Augusta.[1]

The Accomplishments and Aftermath of Louisville, 1857

At the close of the enrollment of delegates J. P. Boyce offered a resolution that the report with its accompanying documents together with any other pertinent material from the participating delegates "be referred to a committee of fifteen to be appointed by the chair, which committee shall prepare the business for our subsequent action."[2] The committee of fifteen included Boyce who was elected as secretary of the committee. On Friday at 11:00, after the morning session of the Southern Baptist Convention, the committee on business presented its report "through Bro. Boyce, their secretary." Boyce reported that the committee saw no point in debating whether such an institution was wanted or needed, for that fact had abundant verification. The duty, therefore, of the present moment was to make provisions for a central theological institution. The attainment of this end through existing institutions would take many years of "protracted labor" and "we have providentially no need to wait so long a period." The offer of South Carolina to produce an immediate endowment of $100,000, "the only one distinctly before us," made available a central and easily accessible location "upon such a pecuniary basis as renders success almost certain."[3]

The committee proposed a series of resolutions accepting the South Carolina offer with some additional considerations. The South Carolina money was to be raised by 1 May 1858 "ready to be placed in the hands of the Trustees then to be appointed over this Institution." For three years the trustees were to be permitted to use interest from that amount to pay faculty, buy $500 in books annually, and hire agents to raise $100,000 outside of South Carolina. They were to look for recitation and lecture rooms free of rent. If at the end of three years, the rest of the endowment was not secured, South Carolina's portion would revert to that state to be used there for theological purposes and the rest to the respective donors.

The committee also called for another convention to assemble in Greenville in May 1858 to hear reports from several committees to be appointed consisting of five persons each. The committees would bring reports and recommendations concerning the plan of organization, the nomination of professors, the plan of agency, the securing of a charter, and the preparation of an address to Southern Baptists. On Saturday afternoon at 3:30, the "Friends of Theological Education" convened again to discuss the recommendations. After energetic discussion, the report passed unanimously. Basil Manly Jr. recalled that "the whole subject was earnestly discussed, and it was concluded with great unanimity and cordiality to accept the South Carolina offer."[4]

In a subsequent article, Manly summarized other aspects of that Louisville conference. The Georgia delegation arrived late, contemplated making a proposal, but "nobly joined in urging the acceptance of this offer from South Carolina." He also noted that the harmony as well as the driving purpose of this meeting were due "mainly to the personal influence and the patient and persevering labors of one man. That man was James P. Boyce—young, comparatively inexperienced, but already a leader for his brethren in thought and action."[5]

When the committee recommendations were accepted so enthusiastically, the convention, under the motion of J. B. Jeter, "united with the President in thanksgiving to God for the harmony and good feeling which has prevailed during our deliberations."[6] Boyce recalled,

> The proposition was made, that Dr. Manly should lead in a prayer of thanksgiving for the unanimity which had been attained. Bowing himself upon the platform of the pulpit, he led the hosts of his brethren in acknowledgement of the Divine hand in all that had been done, and in thanks for the attainment of what he had hardly hoped his eyes would see. The great desire of his lifetime was secured. He saw that God was with His people, and he lost all apprehension as to the future result. The whole assembly was moved to tears. The gushings of his own heart stopped the utterances of his lips, and for a time the supplication of the Spirit was indeed made with tears and groans that could not be uttered.[7]

The committee to nominate professors consisted of A. M. Poindexter, D. R. Campbell, H. Talbird, and J. H. Eaton with Dr. Manly serving as chairman. The committee to procure a charter included J. P. Boyce, B. D. Pressley, James Trapper, and C. J. Elford along with Basil Manly Sr. The committee on the plan of organization had five young men, all potential candidates for professors: J. P. Boyce, J. A. Broadus, Basil Manly Jr., E. T. Winkler, and William Williams. Boyce also was made agent for securing the South Carolina pledge of $100,000.

In July, Boyce resigned his professorship at Furman and, according to Broadus, "spent a considerable part of the next eight months in traveling through the State to raise an endowment for the projected theological seminary."[8] In August, Mercer University elected him as president. He refused the position, "not because he does not appreciate the honor, nor because he has not a high regard for the brethren of Georgia; but because the acceptance appears to him, at present, to militate against cherished plans, long since formed—labored for during many years—and apparently now within his reach."[9] A. C. Dayton, the corresponding secretary of the Bible Board, wrote Boyce about a donation to the Bible Board and asked, "Do you accept the presidency of Mercer? I almost hope not, for you will be needed in the new Theological School at Greenville. But the Lord will guide you."[10]

Boyce called for the committee of the plan of organization to meet in August 1857 at the Richmond home of Basil Manly Jr., at that time president of the Richmond Female Institute. The group of young scholars, having already formed subcommittees to handle the variety of arrangements given to their charge, discussed their progress. Basil Manly Jr. had the assignment to draw up a "creed." Boyce pursued legal arrangements and practical arrangements for trustees, finances, professors, and the relation of the seminary to the Southern Baptist Convention. John A. Broadus was assigned the task of sketching a plan of instruction. Broadus recalled that "the difficult matter of uniting all grades of theological students in the same institution, could be effected through a plan adapted from that of the University of Virginia." Manly and Boyce were able to make "valuable emendation to the plan of elective education" through their experiences as students at Newton and Princeton.[11] E. T. Winkler and William Williams were unable to be at this Richmond meeting but had contributed by correspondence to the discussion.

In the meantime, Boyce became the personal confidant of J. L. Reynolds and his wife. Reynolds's career had come to a crisis at South Carolina College, to which he had returned in 1851. Reynolds wrote Boyce, thanking him for mentioning him as a possible candidate for president of Furman. Difficult circumstances had created a forced resignation, what Reynolds called a "wanton abuse of power." Reynolds's wife also wrote to Boyce, explaining, "By the late action of the Board of Trustees of the S. C. College my husband has been dismissed from office (for the circumstances are equivalent to a dismission)." Her family would be compelled to leave under a cloud. She lamented the probable necessity of leaving family, home, and native state in addition to the "pecuniary embarrassment" this would cause. They had anticipated the position as permanent and had gathered around them "the comforts of home, and his sudden removal will necessarily compel an entire breaking up of our happy household." She begged Boyce to exert his influence with members of the board "to have my husband re-placed, and by that act restored to public favor."[12] Evidently someone was able to influence the board, for Reynolds continued to teach there until, under the Reconstruction government, he was fired to make room for teachers more acceptable to their purpose.[13]

In the winter and spring of 1858, Boyce and his committee worked on their respective parts of the recommendation. Basil Manly invited Broadus to come on February 22 and visit with him for a week. "If you will come down, we can have a chat about our work committed to us—that creed, schedule of theological studies, etc." Manly admitted that the project suffered from the ill manners of rudely urgent things—"pressing, knocking at the door, pleading, 'let me in now,' 'attend to me'; and so the quiet visitor, who can be put off is postponed indefinitely." If Broadus would come, however, this would put "a fire coal on my back," they could spend the time pleasantly, and "do our work besides."

On April 9, Boyce wrote Broadus, "As I am forwarding your portion of the report, I also send mine. Please get Bro. Manly's and then send all to Williams of Georgia, begging him not to keep them over a day, and send them to Winkler. Let him forward to me. I must have them by the 25th of April." He included the information that he had almost finished raising the South Carolina portion of the endowment. Three days later it occurred to Boyce that Williams would not be present at the Georgia Baptist Convention. This would delay the reports, so he wrote Broadus with an amended plan. "We may be put in the unpleasant predicament of having no report to present. I think therefore you had best return the Reports forthwith, as soon as Manly can add his. Let me have them printed and send a copy each to Williams and Winkler." They could suggest amendments if they desired, and the report would go on record as "that of those who met."[14]

Manly wrote, suggesting arrangements about a possible reduction of fare to attend the meeting and informing Boyce about the progress of the doctrinal statement. "I thought I should have had the 'Creed' done by this time," Manly wrote, "but I must take 2 or 3 days longer. I will send a copy to you next week and one to Bro. Broadus, for consultation when we meet." He also passed on the disturbing news that William C. Buck had come out against "centralization" in theological education. Buck had attended the 1857 Louisville Convention, apparently had participated positively in the proceedings, but had since changed his mind. He was highly educated, but all of it gained through personal grit and application without the benefit of formal instruction.[15]

The committee met in Boyce's home to finalize the report just prior to the Greenville theological education meeting. Manly recalled,

> In due time, this Committee met at the residence of Dr. Boyce in Greenville, and I remember that, as Dr. A. M. Poindexter was there, he was invited by the Committee to be present and assist them in their labors. Every sentence and word of what had been prepared by the sub-committees was subjected to a careful examination and revision. Then, at the suggestion of Dr. Boyce, and at his expense I think, the report as a whole was set up in type at Elford's printing office, and copies struck off for further revision before it should be presented to the Convention. If I mistake not, as many as three or four corrected and revised proofs of the report, as it was enlarged or altered by the private discussions, were obtained until it was thought to be as nearly perfect as the Committee could make it.[16]

Prior to the meeting, Boyce received letters giving clues about the uncertain path that the supporters of the seminary must walk before it became settled in fact, and especially about the affections of Southern Baptists at large. John Landrum, an agent for circulating bonds in South Carolina, informed Boyce that protracted meetings had occupied his time, but he was now ready to canvass the association for support for the seminary. One venerable minister, "Old Bro. Drummond,"

Landrum noted, "has got in a good humor with me [and] has spent two nights at my house since the association. He will give nothing to the Seminary—He knows already more than fifty theological Teachers could teach him."[17] Elias Dodson wanted to come to the theological convention but could not get appointed. "I shall therefore be absent," he noted, "but I will send a short speech and $100 in 3 equal annual installments of $33 1/3 each. I hope this enterprise will succeed."[18] George Dargan declined to accept Boyce's invitation to support "so good an enterprise." "If I was out of debt," he confessed, "it is probable that I would make a contribution" but not because it was a Baptist institution. No sectarian name could summon him to support any scheme that could not otherwise claim his attention. If he were going to be anything, it would be Baptist, but he considered himself "catholic (in the original sense of the word)."[19]

From Americus, Georgia, Sam Cross wrote that the Georgia Baptist Convention appointed "Professor Williams and Rev. Bro. Ryerson to represent them in our Convention." He suggested to C. D. Mallary and J. H. De Votie that a larger delegation should be sent. "But the fact cannot be concealed [underlining his] that if there is not a direct opposition," he revealed, "there is at least a disposition on the part of many leading Brethren in this state, to give your enterprise the 'cold shoulder.' They are fearful I think that it will conflict with their own 'Cherished Mercer.'" He expressed the hope that time would eliminate that feeling and "that the Brethren will at last cooperate freely and cordially with their Brethren of S.C." Cross affirmed this new idea as "worthy the age in which we live and the noble and generous South of which it is intended to be the representation." He prayed that it would not prove abortive, but would "live and grow and flourish; and prove the nursing mother to many noble sons whom God may raise up in our midst to withstand the mighty flood of infidelity now rolling over our country—attracting in its wake many a noble, yet unsuspecting youth."[20]

Greenville, 1858

When the Education Convention met in Greenville, Boyce had a more mature and ever-developing idea of the nature of the positive desires as well as the subtle difficulties that were posed by the attempt to build a central seminary for all Southern Baptists. The convention opened on 30 April 1858 and continued through May 4. The prayer revival of 1858–59 was exerting an influence throughout the South so that many pastors who had intended to attend were so involved in the pastoral demands of the spiritual awakening that they could not break away. Notes of support were received from many of them.

The convention voted to spend one hour in "devotional exercises" and spent over one and a half hours praying, singing, reading the Bible, exhorting, and giving addresses. Basil Manly Sr. was elected president, and G. W. Samson secretary. Attending were delegates from Maryland, Virginia, North Carolina, South Carolina, Georgia, and Louisiana. Out of 44 participants, 6 were from Virginia and 33 were from South Carolina. In light of this, Boyce, always eager to make sure that no impression of heavy-handed provincialism could be imputed to the proceedings, offered the following preamble and resolution that was unanimously adopted:

> Whereas this Convention is designed to secure the co-operation of the Baptists of all the Southern and Southwestern States in a Theological Seminary adapted to the wants of our denomination; and Whereas, of the States here represented, the number of Delegates is very irregular: Therefore, Resolved, That on the motion of any member of this body, the vote of all questions involving the organization of the Institution shall be taken by States—each State represented to have one vote, to be cast by the majority of her delegates.[21]

In the afternoon, Boyce presented the report on the "Plan of Organization, Plan of Instruction, Abstract of Principles." The discussion of these matters was then scheduled for the next day at 10:00 A.M. Four more committees were appointed by Manly: on the endowment provided by South Carolina, on the completion of the general endowment, on nomination of the board of trustees, and on a site for the seminary. Boyce served on the committees for the general endowment and for nomination of the board of trustees. An evening sermon was preached by A. M. Poindexter.

On the next day the convention discussed the plan of organization and adopted "sundry articles" as they passed muster or underwent slight amendment to the satisfaction of the entire group. Although a committee had been appointed in Louisville to nominate a faculty, only two, Manly Sr. and Poindexter, of that committee were present. Manly, therefore, appointed others: Samson, Toby, Williams, Jeter, and Curtis. William Williams preached before a large audience that evening. On Sunday the various churches of Greenville invited members of the convention to their pulpits to preach. J. B. Hartwell was set aside for missionary labors in Shanghai, China.[22] John A. Broadus preached at the evening service in the Baptist church after which twenty-one persons were baptized. His pulpit abilities made a remarkable impression on the editor of a Greenville paper, and his obvious pulpit power and charm became one of the most persuasive commendations of the seminary immediately and for decades thereafter. Basil Manly Sr. preached in the Presbyterian church. On Monday, the entire day was spent in discussion of the Plan of Organization and the Abstract of Principles.

The next day, Tuesday, the fifth day of the meeting, "in the course of the forenoon, the remaining articles of the Abstract of Principles were adopted, with the modifications submitted by committees to whom sundry articles had been referred." Broadus recalled, "Drs. Poindexter and Samson were particularly earnest, various others also taking part, in discussing the Abstract of Principles; and Dr. Samson remembers the special interest that was taken in the article about the Doctrine of Imputation, which nine years before had been discussed in two long series of articles in the *Southern Baptist* when young Boyce was its editor."[23]

Basil Manly Jr. also wrote his reminiscences of that convention:

> Those were memorable days to some at least of those who engaged in them. In the freedom of brotherly discussion, in the warmth occasioned by the contact and collision of the ideas of the younger and the older, the brethren from different sections of the country, and who had enjoyed different kinds of training and different associations, there was keen stimulus to thought. Every great topic in theology was handled earnestly, freely and yet reverently. The learning of the past was not ignored. The various forms of expression in which the

faith had been declared in our own and other denominations of Christians were carefully compared and consulted; the safe-guards which had been thrown around other Seminaries, both as to doctrine and as to funds, were thoughtfully considered; the different methods of instruction, by curriculum, by free election, by courses more or less flexible, were passed in review. The result was almost unanimously approved by the Convention after somewhat elaborate explanation and debate, and has remained practically without modification to the present day.[24]

The initial proposal in the report stated, "The name of the Common Seminary at Greenville, S.C., shall be *The Southern Baptist Theological Seminary.*" It then listed eleven fundamental laws, seven regulations not considered fundamental, and a plan of instruction. The "Fundamental Laws" gave regulations for trustees, such as, they must be a member of a "regular Baptist Church," eleven trustees would serve from South Carolina and one from each of thirteen other states if they contributed $5,000 to the endowment. Provisions for the addition of trustees depended on increased contributions in increments of $5,000 to $10,000. No professor could be a member of the board of trustees.

Article 3 became very important sixteen years later during a crisis concerning the "ownership" of the seminary. Although the board was described as "self-perpetuating," the election of replacements, or additional trustees, "shall be from a nomination to be made by the Southern Baptist Convention, at the session of that body next ensuing," with the provision that should the Convention fail to nominate, "the Board may proceed to an election without such nomination." From this article, Boyce was able to show that the seminary belonged to Southern Baptists, and the Convention was given as much control over the seminary as could be devised under the exigencies of the situation.

Article 9 stated the important and formative provision concerning professors: "Every Professor of the Institution shall be a member of a regular Baptist Church; and all persons accepting Professorships in this Seminary, shall be considered, by such acceptance, as engaging to teach in accordance with, and not contrary to, the Abstract of Principles hereinafter laid down, a departure from which principles, on his part, shall be considered ground for his resignation or removal by the Trustees." One hears in this requirement the statement of Boyce two years earlier to the trustees at Furman, "It is no hardship to those who teach here, to be called upon to sign the declaration of their principles, for there are fields of usefulness open elsewhere to every man, and none need accept your call who cannot conscientiously sign your formulary."

The twenty-article "Abstract of Principles" followed. It contained articles on the Scriptures, God, the Trinity, providence, election, the fall of man, the Mediator, regeneration, repentance, faith, justification, sanctification, perseverance of the saints, the church, baptism, the Lord's Supper, the Lord's day, liberty of conscience, the resurrection, and judgment. The doctrine of election was defined as "God's eternal choice of some persons unto everlasting life, not because of foreseen merit in them, but of His mere mercy in Christ; in consequence of which choice, they are called, justified and glorified." The article on the church contains an affirmation of the church as universal and timeless as well as local and temporal:

> The Lord Jesus is the head of the Church, which is composed of all his true disciples, and in him is invested supremely all power for its government. According to his commandment, Christians are to associate themselves into particular societies or churches; and to each of these churches he hath given needful authority for administering that order, discipline and worship which he hath appointed. The regular officers of a Church are Bishops or Elders, and Deacons.

The articles reflected the wording and order of the Charleston Confession of Faith that had been suggested by Boyce in his address on "Three Changes."

The Plan of Instruction called for implementing Boyce's view of providing an abundant ministry. Its clearly stated objective was the preparation of students "for the effective service as preachers of the Gospel." Thorough scholarship would be pursued; instruction would be adapted to the best qualified students, but "Provision must be made for selection of certain subjects, or pursuing them only to a certain extent, in the case of those whose time, preparation, taste, etc. might not admit of their doing more." In addition, both types of students should pursue the same subjects and study them together.

To attain this goal, the convention approved the committee's recommendation of eight distinct departments of instruction. The first, Biblical Introduction, would include the study of biblical criticism, the canon of Scripture, inspiration, biblical archaeology, and a special introduction to each book of the Scripture. The second department, or school, was Old Testament Interpretation, including both an English class and a Hebrew class. The third school was Interpretation of the New Testament, which included both English and Greek. Fourth was Systematic Theology, which had a regular course in English and a second course in Latin. This latter was designed for those well equipped in the Latin language. The fifth school dealt with Polemic Theology and Apologetics. Sixth, every student was to have the opportunity to take Homiletics, or Preparation and Delivery of Sermons. The seventh school was Ecclesiastical History, and the eighth, Church Government and Pastoral Theology. Diplomas would be awarded in each of the schools, and a general diploma for students who received diplomas in all eight schools. This arrangement allowed for a concentration on classical orthodoxy and the doctrines of grace in a focused manner apart from having to make time for ecclesiological discussion. At the same time a greater emphasis could be given to the distinctives of Baptist ecclesiology, by its discrete treatment in the course on Church Government and Pastoral Theology.

This plan called for four professors. The committee that had been appointed for the selection of the professors therefore submitted four names, suggesting that one professor be responsible for two departments. J. P. Boyce was elected professor of Systematic Theology and Polemic Theology; John A. Broadus was assigned Interpretation of the New Testament and Preparation and Delivery of Sermons. Basil Manly Jr. was elected to teach Biblical Introduction and Interpretation of the Old Testament. E. T. Winkler was asked to take the departments of Church History and Church Government and Pastoral Theology. A committee to nominate a board of trustees reported, and the list they presented was duly elected.

After it was ascertained that the South Carolina funds for endowment were secured, a provisional committee to whom the care of the seminary was given until the trustees could be legally organized was appointed; that committee included J. P. Boyce. Poindexter was appointed to oversee completion of the general endowment with the resolution "that Prof. Boyce be requested to lend whatever aid may be in his power to the General Agent now appointed." The elected professors were requested to give their answer as soon as practicable. The reporter for the *Southern Baptist*, J. P. Tustin, said that "the spirit and incidents of the meeting deserve special mention, but we can only say in a word, that the impression of the whole was so encouraging, that some of the oldest and most experienced ministers said that they had never before been so able to look hopefully into the future."

Tustin also felt that an explanation of the adopted "Abstract of Principles" was in order. It was adopted as a "test for the Faculty," he explained, "and not as binding upon Baptist Churches." The statement would be a guarantee of the integrity of the endowment funds, protecting them against "future perversion from their original intent." He also explained the method used by the committee of five in forming the confession from a comparison of "the principal Ancient and Modern Symbols, both of our own and of other denominations," but particularly the family of confessions related to Charleston. It was condensed as far as seemed "practicable, without obscurity or weakness."[25]

A Dangerous and Unexpected Delay

G. W. Samson, the member of the committee from Maryland, talked with Broadus, Manly, and Winkler and wrote Boyce that he believed they would accept the positions at the new seminary. He especially urged on them a matter he considered preeminently important: "no faculty could be expected to be gathered which would be a unit, one in intellectual completeness and one in heart, should they decline." If men could be found to take their present positions, he was sure they would consent.[26]

This decision was no small matter. Manly wrote Broadus discussing with utmost seriousness all the implications of their uprooting themselves from their present vital ministries to go to a place that might have no students and an unfulfilled endowment, and soon perish. Virginians all over the state objected to the idea that Virginia would be robbed of two of her most promising and prominent young leaders for the sake of South Carolina. For this reason, Poindexter's general agency took on more than ordinary importance. Not only was he trusted as a faithful preacher of the gospel, his advocacy of a cause of general interest to Baptists went far toward securing its success. "The real decision rests with you," Manly insisted, and "If you decline, I think Poindexter will." If they declined, he certainly would, and Winkler would, under those circumstances, be unwilling to leave his church. "Shall it fail," Manly Jr. asked, "and shall the disappointment in this instance serve as a lasting discouragement, a decisive and unanswerable objection to all similar attempts?" Boyce will be left alone in need of finding other candidates of like mind, that is, of "more self-sacrifice." Then he corrected himself with an analysis that made the entire possibility of their rejecting this opportunity appear ludicrous: "What I should have said is, men of more deep convictions of the comparative importance of such a seminary." Where would Boyce find such? "He too must give up the ship, a grand *finale* indeed, after all that has been said and done." Through great turmoil, with many compelling reasons to stay in Virginia, and though he delayed his decision until after Broadus's, Manly finally convinced himself that the path of duty lay in accepting the position.[27]

John A. Broadus, as Manly's letter indicated, "carried the matter home as a great burden, because Poindexter and others were pressing it upon him."[28] Broadus wrote Boyce and explained. On his return to Charlottesville, he "spent some days in hearing the leading brethren of the Church, and consulting a few judicious friends." This did not settle him so he "left home on Tuesday, and went to see other friends in Alexandria, Fredericksburg, and Richmond." He felt deeply the burden for the responsibility of this decision, considered the question carefully, and sought to exercise his best judgment. "After more anxiety and difficulty than I ever before experienced," he continued,

"I have at length decided, that I cannot leave here." Only an option like the seminary would even make him consider leaving, but finally he decided, "I could not dare to go away." He promised to help all he could in getting the Virginia endowment, and encouraging young men to attend the seminary. Since they had agreed that none should give a public answer before notifying the others, he wished the matter settled quickly for "my people here are in great perturbation." He regretted that he would miss "that association with you which would in many ways be so pleasant."[29]

Upon learning of Broadus's decision, Manly wrote, "I think your declinature, under the circumstances, is the death blow to it" and would probably mean that Manly himself would refuse. He didn't. Winkler, however, found Broadus's decision the turning point for him. At the time he received correspondence from Broadus regarding his refusal, "I was inclined to believe that duty required me to leave my present field." That news, however, pressed him toward the opposite conclusion. The distress of his church, First Baptist in Charleston, had been so extreme, "I might also say so extravagant, as to excite my unfeigned astonishment." Winkler expressed regret that the seminary would not have the efficiency and scholarship of Broadus and would also miss the necessary patronage from Virginia that Broadus would bring. For his part, however, he thought that in justice to his church, "I ought not to go." Speaking of Broadus, and legitimating himself by his observation, Winkler wrote, "I cannot blame any pastor who is cultivating his special field of labor successfully, when he declines, for any cause whatever, to leave it. The luxury of such a vocation is legitimate."[30]

In addition to the refusal of Broadus and Winkler, Poindexter decided to turn down the appointment as general agent. These refusals meant that the seminary could not open in the fall of 1858, but they gave extra time and money for a more intense and broader canvass of the other states in the South for completing their portion of the endowment. Boyce, who had been requested to aid Poindexter, carried the lion's share of this burden. In spite of this apparent failure, he worked intensely and brilliantly for the eventual success of his highest earthly desideratum. In June he was in Virginia speaking at churches and associational meetings presenting the cause of theological education and the urgent need for Baptists to unite in its support. He wrote Broadus that he would be in Charlottesville and asked him to "judge best as to the advantage of a public meeting," and informed Broadus of a meeting in Richmond, urging him that "the brethren say you must be here, if possible, and make a speech."[31] Meanwhile Boyce took advantage of each opportunity to sell the seminary hard to his hearers. The Hampton Association requested the publication of the speech he made at their meeting.

After Boyce reviewed the history of the theological conventions, he spoke of the encouragement he had, as agent of the South Carolina Baptist Convention, in knowing of the "cooperation of the brethren of other States, which was given at Louisville." In particular, however, because of the enthusiastic nature of their participation in this effort, he looked to Virginia to lead the way. "It was because of these things also," Boyce related, "that I have believed that the first efforts outside of South Carolina should be made among your constituents. Let Virginia speak out and the work is accomplished." He urged them not to consider the possibility of failure. Since so much had been done, "it would be a waste of Christian energy to allow it to be for naught."

Boyce showed sincere and intense commitment to divine providence that kept him operative throughout his life when he opined, "So marked have been the providences by which it has been brought to its present position, that the work is seen to be of God, and he will not let it fail." Now the time has come, Boyce argued, that Baptists can set in motion a school fully consistent with their historic principles and views of truth. In order for personal theological idiosyncrasies not to foul the process, "We have guarded our institution by an abstract of principles, to prevent any one holding erroneous views from being among its instructors." The theological ideas will be taught in submission to the knowledge of Scripture. Each student will be encouraged to "study the word of God to see if this be not the truth. May God deliver us from any other kind of teachers." If any other manner of teaching should be pursued "in this institution, I would be the first man to lift the hand for its destruction."

Prior to this opportunity, students from the South had no option other than to go to the Northern Baptists or to the pedobaptists, north and south, for theological education. The number in such institutions was five times the number in all the theological departments of the Baptist colleges in the South. The situation had unsavory elements. On the one hand, they would have to listen, however incredulously, "to false views of the church and of its ordinances." On the other, the students had to be willing to accept "charity from those from whose fellowship we are cut off, from whom in all matters we are separated, and whose opinions upon the subject of our internal institutions are such as, if imbibed by our young ministers, will render them unfit to labor successfully in our midst." Boyce believed that the position a professor took on slavery was important for the training of ministers for Southern churches.[32]

Boyce believed the curriculum proposed was perfect for Baptists. Its summary intent was to give "a student a thorough knowledge of the word of God." Hardly any object to the idea of teaching the languages to this end, but what of the other subjects? The teaching of systematic theology was to place before the student "a map of Christian truth." Boyce expressed thankfulness that Scripture "can be systematized" for it "does not teach any two truths which are opposed to each other." Who, however, is sufficient on his own to handle this idea and "balance the statements of different doctrines"? Systematic theology books, good ones, distill the wisdom of the church in all its conflicts and struggles through the centuries in showing the harmony of all parts of Scripture. "With the helps now in use, every passage which bears upon a given doctrine may be gathered in a few hours; a few more will enable us to arrange them and to compare them with the statement made." None need fear that the minds of students will not be sufficiently independent and personally responsive to the Word of God. The real danger is that "in the absence of a thorough knowledge of the truth, the great doctrines of the Bible are never developed, their relation to the Christian life never made known, and the ministry itself, which should be apt to teach, thoroughly instructed in every good word and work, are found acknowledging their ignorance, and excusing it upon the ground that these truths are not frequently to be proclaimed." Tragic it would be should any doctrine be ignored, for every truth has its place and is to be proclaimed. Every truth must be given the importance that the Word of God assigns it, and "systematic theology best enables us to do this."[33]

The study of church history gives aid to the theological task by setting error in context. Our propensity to error thus is checked when we see its grounds and its implications exemplified. Ignorance of this "leads to more frequent mistakes." Boyce provided an illustration of a current writer, highly respected, who made an error that was "exploded fifteen hundred years ago." He mentioned the current interest in "church government" and the immediate relevance of it in dealing with many important matters, a likely reference to the growing uneasiness, particularly in Virginia, with the energy and agitation flowing out of Tennessee and its Landmark contingent.

Boyce expressed the concern he knew filled the minds of many who were nervous about this new venture when he spoke of securing a "more practical ministry." The location of the seminary in the "midst of an extensive rural population" where preaching opportunities among the common people will be extensive, and where in the four months of vacation "they can labor as colporters, carrying books from house to house, speaking to the people about their spiritual interests," should be just the factor that will give a blending of piety and learning to the young ministers. Virginia Baptists should feel keenly the call to support this effort. Boyce urged them for the sake of the church and "for our most earnest young men, who desire it that they may learn more of Christ, whose hearts, burning to tell his love, and to feed his sheep, feel sadly the deficiencies of our present provision for them." Surely Virginia Baptists will not refuse to take their place in this great enterprise![34]

By March 1859, Boyce began seeking to settle the matter of completing the selections for the faculty. As a member of the provisional committee, Boyce stated their conviction that only Broadus and Winkler would do. He seemed desperate, in fact, to secure the name and talents of Broadus. "We are assured," he wrote Broadus, "that we cannot make any other nominations that would be acceptable." He begged

Broadus to consider this and asked, probing his judgment, "Have not circumstances so changed since your refusal last year as clearly to point this out as duty now?" Though he wanted to write at length, trying to convince him, he knew that "this is a question for your own decision." If Broadus believed that under no circumstances could he accept, he should say so before the report is made. If he will accept, also say so, for his decision in the affirmative will secure Winkler, "who hangs off still."[35]

Broadus wrote back within the week, "Your letter is before me, before me continually. Providence permitting, you shall receive my final answer before the 25th inst. Meantime, do not let it be known that I am considering the matter."[36] One week later, Boyce gave greater urgency to Broadus's decision by sending him an extract from a letter of Basil Manly Sr. "The prospects of the theological school have been shaded, at least," Manly confided, "by failing to obtain the officers we sought and to commence business last fall." Then, in a mingling of both hope and apocalyptic sobriety, "The trustees are to hold their first meeting in Richmond at the time of the approaching anniversaries. Make another failure and you will see what will come of it."[37]

Boyce asked Broadus to consider committing to the seminary "in order to inaugurate the matter" even if he did not feel that he could commit a lifetime to it. Broadus's name would be a "tower of strength," and he could "preach Christ daily to the most attentive hearers" and also reach into every quarter of the globe. Boyce believed that the seminary would help alleviate several problems that yet plagued Baptist life—the lack of educated men to help form public sentiment, radicalism and "demagogism" in the country—and Broadus was key to this needed transformation. "Ought you not to make the sacrifice?" Boyce queried; "Are you not called by God to enter upon this work?" Then in a statement of desperation similar to many that would punctuate his labors for the success of the seminary, Boyce closed, "If you fail me and Winkler fail me, I must give up, and I fear Winkler will go. My chief hope of getting him now is that he looks to you and your coming may move him."[38]

Broadus began to see Boyce's vision. The larger call weighed heavily on him, and he consented "with much difficulty, and much distress." He trembled at deciding either way, but, while hesitating to write words "which must be irrevocable," he penned, "if elected, I am willing to go," while praying that if he had erred in judgment God would overrule the error "to the glory of his name." After the paragraph of trembling, Broadus gave a paragraph of assurance. "Do not fear that I shall change my mind," he consoled, and added, "And my dear Boyce, suffer me to say, that few personal considerations about the matter are so attractive to me, as the prospect of being associated with you." He rejoiced in the present warm friendship and believed that they would learn to love each other as brothers. Broadus urged Boyce to come to Richmond (where the first trustee meeting would be held, an event it cannot be imagined that Boyce would have missed!) where they could discuss several items concerning the seminary and plot to overturn a scheme to keep Basil Manly Jr. from leaving Richmond to teach in the seminary. For good measure Broadus also wrote to Manly that he had accepted. He wrote Winkler with the same information, encouraging him to do likewise. "I heard it whispered in Richmond," he informed Manly, "that a plan was on foot for keeping you there." He begged him to resist their plea. "You have been regarded as identified with the Seminary; don't forsake it now."[39]

Boyce wrote Broadus with expressions of exuberant joy and positive expectations for the future. "I have ever esteemed it one of the most pleasant things connected with the election last year that if it should be the one finally made, it will bring together four of us who can feel like brothers indeed toward each other. What a power we have here!" Winkler still had not committed.[40]

Richmond, 1859

When the trustees met in Richmond in May 1859, their first item of business was to accept the charter that had been enacted on 21 December 1858 by the legislature of South Carolina. The provisional committee then reported the state of the seminary. "They regret to say," the report noted, "that owing to events not within their control, such progress as was expected has not been made."

155

The general agent refused his appointment and none could be found to take his place. Winkler and Broadus had refused their professorships. These events "destroyed so certainly the probability of success that the Committee felt compelled not to attempt to open the Institution to students at the time appointed."

They were glad to report, however, that W. F. Broaddus, John A. Broadus's uncle, had accepted the agency to Virginia alone and already had begun to succeed in collections. In addition, the "Chairman of the Committee," that is, Boyce, was occupied in South Carolina in securing the balance for the South Carolina pledge, and reported that as of 1 January 1859 the amount "exceeded one hundred thousand dollars, with interest from the first of May, 1858." He was also able to report that North Carolina had pledged $15,000 and Virginia had pledged $25,000. That of course meant that agents must be employed actually to sell bonds and gather the money. Boyce provided the details for the money in hand from South Carolina and noted, optimistically, "In addition to the above it is to be borne in mind that of the $7,000 of interest naturally accruing to this fund from 1st May, 1858, we have expended less than $1,000, and that $2,000 more will accrue before September, subject only to the deduction of the salary of Brother W. F. Broaddus, or any other agents who may be put in the field."[41]

Boyce reported that the committee had secured a lease on the old Baptist church building for ten years at a nominal fee for classroom space and a library. The theological works from the Furman library had been donated, about two thousand volumes, but according to Boyce "by no means so valuable as had been supposed, although it has many rare and valuable books." He viewed it as deficient in modern works "such as will at once be needed in the departments of instruction." The committee recommended, and the trustees approved, $500 for immediate purchases on recommendation of the faculty.

Boyce then recommended for the provisional committee that the board reelect Broadus and Winkler, "believing that the call thus extended to them a second time will come with such force as can not be resisted." At least the board must not dismiss until the matter of faculty is resolved, for "so far as the committee can see, another failure to open the Seminary will be disastrous." When the trustees considered this recommendation, "Bro. Boyce expressed for himself and Bro. Manly a strong desire that the Board should re-elect said brethren to the Professorships heretofore declined by them."

As expected and promised, Broadus accepted, but Winkler again declined as Boyce had suspected he might. The committee immediately elected William Williams of Georgia by unanimous vote and wrote him to that effect. A moving expense of $250 was voted for all professors not residing in Greenville. The beginning date for the first session was set as the "first Monday in October annually and [there was to] be an annual vacation of four months commencing on the first Monday in June." Boyce was elected unanimously as "Chairman of the Faculty." An amendment to one of the "Regulations Not Fundamental," which called for an executive committee composed of three members of the board of trustees, called for an executive committee of "five members, at least two of whom shall be from its own body." Under that change, Boyce was elected to the executive committee. He also served as treasurer for the trustees.[42]

Basil Manly Sr. gave a postconvention report that summarized the proceedings and presented an apologetic for all the details regarding the seminary—its place, the time of its session, its faculty, its finances, its usefulness to the convention. He called on Southern Baptists to complete the endowment and, presently most pressing, send students. Do not let the bold enterprise have the chill of a slow and hesitating start. Though God does not need our learning, much less does he value our ignorance and ill manners. Earnest devotion to truth and duty is far more valuable than "great and shining talents." An abundant ministry is needed, and the prayer to send forth more laborers into the harvest must be accompanied by determination to do what we can. Others have sown in tears, desiring a means for fitting a ministry for the task to which God has called; now we may reap where others have sown.

By May 30, William Williams had decided he would accept.

Selling the Faculty, Pushing the Seminary

The call for students and the commendation of the faculty seemed to be two issues immediately necessary leading up to the opening of the school in October. In one sense the former depended on the latter. Broadus wrote Boyce, jesting about his newly minted D.D. bestowed by Columbian College, and mentioned both these issues. "What has become of you, that you haven't yet appeared in print about the Seminary?" he quizzed; "Has the weight of Columbian College honors crushed you?" Or perhaps he had worn himself out with the highly congratulatory article about the new professors that had appeared in the *Religious Herald* reprinted from the Greenville-based *Patriot and Mountaineer*. It was a piece of "most extraordinary puff, of the four new wonders of the world." Then with a playful familiarity that characterized the next thirty years, Broadus suggested, "The most satisfactory hypothesis, perhaps, as to the origin of that most laudatory eulogium, is that one of the four, in a paroxysm of self-esteem, wrote his opinion of himself, and then praised the others to keep up appearances; as you are near the paper, the suspicion lies at your door." Publish something that will give the seminary a more definite shape in the eyes of the people, Broadus urged, "or else, I am considerably afraid, there will be four Doctors of Divinity met together on the 1ˢᵗ of October to teach—each other, which operation might be serviceable enough, if it should not prove too much like the opposite sides of an empty stomach digesting each other."[43]

Baptist colleges had "amiably recognized their destitution of all titles of dignity" and in the May and June commencements had bestowed the degree D.D. on all four of the professors.[44] Broadus commented, "What a formidable array of D. D.'s it makes! I do wish the good friends had held up their honors for a few years at least. We are of course obliged to print them, out of respect for the donors of the dignity, and yet for a parcel of young men on their first legs, it cannot but look slightly ridiculous. It is no doubt well, however, that we have so many real and serious troubles in life as to leave little time for fretting over such minor annoyances."[45]

Boyce wrote his bits of publicity, sent them to Broadus, who approved heartily, and submitted them to the Baptist papers. Broadus proposed to write three articles reinforcing Boyce's advertisements for the *Religious Herald*. The bit of "puff" about which Broadus exclaimed gave the necessary facts about each of the professors larded with an abundance of exuberant praise. The South was clearly proud of its sons and of the new endeavor in education. The trustees showed wisdom in their selection of faculty, choosing "young men inspired with the energy, zeal and confidence necessary for the arduous task of starting a new institution of learning." Their youth, however, is infused with "moral and intellectual worth" of the type that would "reflect honor upon much older men." These selections will surely "command for the Seminary the affection and confidence of the Baptist public throughout the South."

William Williams, professor of systematic theology at Mercer University, whose acceptance of a position made the faculty complete, "has achieved for himself a very high reputation for learning and ability." His addition to the faculty is "one which adds another to the numerous indications of its future usefulness and success." Manly's "talents and attainments generally, but especially as a Hebrew scholar and Linguist, fit him peculiarly for the occupancy of this chair." The positions that he formerly held were of "great responsibility and dignity." First Baptist Church in Richmond and Richmond Baptist Female College, both institutions of great importance, better as a result of the "signal" honor with which he served, must give way to his acceptance of a position "more congenial with his habits of thought and study, and with his views of duty as a minister of the Gospel." Broadus, "though quite a young man, . . . is the most distinguished Baptist minister in Virginia." Not only is he "remarkably gifted as a pulpit orator," he combines "uncommon intellectual powers and attainments" with a "degree of modesty and meekness that gives ample proof of the higher attainments which he has made as a Christian." Broadus had spent eight years in Charlottesville serving as university chaplain, tutor in Latin and Greek, and pastor of the Baptist Church. The writer, probably Boyce's friend G. E. Elford, continued, "It is a phenomenon to meet a man so rarely gifted, and yet so seemingly unconscious of his superiority."

Boyce, so claimed the laudatory writer, though barely thirty, "is deservedly the most influential man in his denomination in the South." Boyce possessed a combination of qualities—"talents, learning and piety," along with "remarkable practical and executive faculties"— that fitted him "peculiarly to the honorable and responsible position he occupies as Chairman of the Faculty, and presiding officer of the Seminary." The seminary, the writer correctly observed, "owes its existence and establishment to his untiring and judicious efforts, and his election to its highest office is at once an appropriate tribute to his labors in its behalf and the guarantee of its success in the future."[46]

One writer, George Boardman Eager, commenting later about the influence of William Williams, applied an observation about him to the entire faculty: "What it cost him and his colleagues to turn aside in the prime of their splendid young manhood, from the inviting careers and sunlit prospects that beckoned them in other directions, to launch out on untried and threatening seas in this new and then problematic enterprise, we can never fully know."[47]

Boyce began his advertisements the first week in August. They first appeared in the *Religious Herald* on August 4. Broadus started his series on August 18. The advertisements blended description, promotion, exhortation, encouragement, and delicate public relations into a half column article. He explained how easily accessible Greenville was from all points in the South through a combination of railroads and stages. He explained the relation of the different schools to each other and how a student could take courses in as many or as few as he liked. It is a Baptist school built on Baptist principles. If one wants to complete the entire course and receive the general diploma, one should plan to stay for three years, though "some students of superior abilities and preparation may complete it in two years." The special feature of accessibility for those "that had not enjoyed the advantages of Collegiate Study" was strongly emphasized. "Taken in connection with the special Courses which have been added in the Departments of Exegesis, Homiletics and Theology, opportunity is thus afforded to those who have been limited merely to a good English education, to obtain facilities heretofore never afforded for preparation for the Gospel Ministry."[48]

Boyce, showing he had no intention of destroying the efforts on the part of each state to provide some kind of theological training, encouraged the existing theological department in the colleges to work for this kind of student also, for "there are students enough of this class, in each State, to give full employment to one or two Professors."

Boyce's observations came from personal experience in receiving letters from this needy class of Baptist preachers. For example, one year later, John S. Gilliam wrote Boyce saying that as a small boy he was left as an orphan, had few resources, and had "found it a hard matter by my own exertions to get an English education." Nevertheless he had been teaching school "in this village for the last two years." He also had "commenced trying to preach" but felt "the great want of the knowledge which the Southern Baptist Theological Seminary proposes to assist me in obtaining." Mr. Gilliam requested a catalogue.[49]

Boyce explained that just one session of eight months allows the students to spend the summer months in distribution of literature and work in protracted meetings—good not only for ministry and experience but "to add something to their means of support." Practicality is the emphasis of the school, for "each of the faculty is deeply impressed with the greater importance of the office of the preacher than that of the mere scholar." Students should be licensed to ministry by their churches or give a letter of approval for their desire to prepare for gospel ministry. No charge is made for tuition; "board, including fuel, but not lights nor washing, can be obtained in private families at twelve dollars a month." A list of the eight schools as found in the minutes of the 1857 theological meeting completed the article.[50]

Broadus's first article offered a commentary on the advertisement with some attractive plain talk. It is a Baptist school built to accommodate Baptist ideas as well as Baptist theology. No one can compel a Baptist preacher to get a specific amount of education, but the provision of it is a good thing. One may take at this school what he wants and leave alone what he suspects. "If it is feared that the study of the Preparation and Delivery of Sermons may alter his genius, or Systematic Theology cramp his opinions, these can be abjured, and other subjects chosen which are thought more useful and less dangerous." If one so chooses he may take classes in every school, and only in three will there be an extra course designed peculiarly for those with a classic collegiate education—Old Testament, New Testament, and Systematic Theology. Broadus did not think that the advantages set forth in the advertisement were exaggerated. Many a brother would benefit by improved preaching and more disciplined mental life by taking at least one session—October through May—at Greenville. "A brother told me," Broadus argued anecdotally, "that, having been perhaps a little too precipitate in getting married, so as to interrupt his studies, he thought even to deny himself his wife's society, in order to spend a session at the Seminary." Broadus did not envy the separation, but many a man has endured it to study medicine.[51]

Broadus's second article again emphasized the unique "Baptistness" of the seminary. Some faults in the existing systems of theological education come from "methods conformed as they are to Presbyterian models and not sufficiently suited to Baptist ideas and wants."[52] These faults are corrected for Baptist purposes. This idea perhaps had been suggested to him by W. M. Wingate, president of Wake Forest, who said in a letter to Broadus, "I like much the feature suggested in your letter. I saw it elaborated to some extent in Doctor Boyce's address some three years ago. Our theological seminaries have been based too much upon Presbyterian theories of preaching, and they have on that account been of very little use to Baptists."[53]

The particular difficulty Broadus wanted to relieve was the nervousness some felt over the idea of a Baptist institution governed by a "Creed." All Baptists, including the seminary professors, want no uninspired statement imposed on a young minister, or any Christian. In such an institution, however, where the trust of a broad body of churches is required, "it was thought possible that a man might some day be elected professor, who, without the knowledge of the trustees held some very objectionable doctrinal opinion; or that some professor might in the course of years come to entertain seriously erroneous notions." In such a case, a short and carefully worded confession like those used in Baptist associations and many Baptist churches, affirming "those great doctrinal views about which Baptists are in general agreed," would be useful. By his coming to teach, any professor agrees "he shall not teach contrary to these doctrines." If a professor begins to entertain, as occasionally happens with a Baptist, "opinions that are essentially Campbellitish, or Arminian, or Open Communionist," he cannot teach.

The student, however, will have nothing to do with the document. Any man recommended by a Baptist church may come and believe what he wants when he comes, while he is here, and when he leaves.

"We shall teach," Broadus affirmed, "what we believe to be truth; and brethren have warrant that these teachings will not be contrary to the doctrine they love." But no student will be asked to accept the professor's views as his own. All the students will be "expressly and repeatedly encouraged and urged to examine everything for themselves." This is not because personal peculiarity defines wisdom, but because one is not truly a man unless he thinks for himself. "Every preacher is individually accountable for what he believes and teaches." No one either plans or wishes "to interfere with Baptist independence."[54]

In article 3, Broadus felt it necessary, before the fact, to give two caveats about seminary education so as to anticipate future criticism apart from its possible invidious application to any known student. One, the seminary must not be expected to turn out finished preachers. If they do not come with gifts, they will not leave with gifts. The unspoken, but oppressively felt, expectation for great display has often injured both preacher and hearers. The native genius of one like Spurgeon is so rare that it usually takes years of practice before the benefits of thorough training can appear. Broadus believed the greatest observation that could be made of a student would be, "This is a modest and intelligent young brother, without airs or oddities. He preaches sensible sermons, practical and earnest; and I think he is going to make quite a good preacher." Two, some students may leave offended and disappointed that extraordinary attention was not given to them in accordance with their own estimation of worthiness. They may complain in places where none are present with a more sensible and accurate understanding. Brethren should test the credibility of such judgments before attributing the fault to the seminary. "But I hope," Broadus anticipated, "that no one who reads this paragraph may ever have occasion to recall it."

In order to alleviate the murkiness of this mention of unsavory situations, Broadus assured the readers of the deep satisfaction he had in contemplating the exalted purpose and potential relations intended in such a school. "With hearts full of affection for the beloved young brethren, and the purpose to work faithfully for them, and with them, we shall have their good will, even if we cannot deserve their good opinion." Though possible difficulties must be considered, in principle "it must certainly prove a great pleasure, to be for many months intimately associated, in public instruction and private intercourse, with a number of young men preparing for the ministry." The thought of what is sought evoked the earnest prayer, "O! That an atmosphere of devotion may continually surround us—that love to the souls of men, and to him who died to save them, may ever burn in our hearts!"[55]

Broadus ended this final article with an assurance that in going to Greenville to teach he had not ceased to be a Virginian, nor would he and Manly allow students from Virginia to lose their fervor for the Old Dominion State. Each, with the full consent and help of their colleagues, would be returned "safe and sound, without damage to his Virginia patriotism, pride, or principles." Finally, send students, and don't fail to help with the endowment.[56]

Opposition Arises

In addition to endowment and attracting students, the seminary would face another challenge—opposition. Broadus mentioned this in a letter to Boyce in July 1859. "As to pleasing everybody, I suppose it must be our lot, the balance of our lives," Broadus prognosticated, "to have various persons all the time finding fault with us. There are people in abundance who don't mean to be pleased with anything we can do." But his enthusiasm suffered no dampening on that account, for "if the Lord spare and bless us, for a few years, I am sure it will appear, even to many who now doubt, that we are doing a great work." Broadus mentioned the "severe sacrifices" the move placed on him, but added, "they are nothing compared with the self-denying labor you have bestowed on it." It was the Lord's work and their labor was not in vain, but "no doubt, we have far more remaining to bear as well as to do."[57]

The steadiest and most widespread opposition to the well-being of the seminary came from the influence of J. R. Graves and the Landmark contingent in Southern Baptist life. Graves (1820–93), born into poverty in Vermont, had attained by dint of personal zeal a great deal of knowledge. He taught briefly in Ohio and Kentucky. In 1845 he moved to Nashville, Tennessee, virtually penniless, and soon became assistant editor of the *Tennessee Baptist*, a paper formerly owned by R. B. C.

Howell but given to Tennessee Baptists. Graves "soon commenced agitating the question of the validity of alien immersions, and the propriety of Baptists recognizing, by any act, ecclesiastical or ministerial, Pedobaptist societies or preachers as *churches* and ministers of Christ."[58] Graves became editor in 1848. In 1849 at the Southern Baptist Convention in Nashville that was cut short by the cholera threat, he attended a meeting of the "Friends of Theological Education." Basil Manly Jr. recalled that "Brother Graves was especially earnest in this conviction," that is, that the time had come for a central seminary. "I remember," he recounted, "when I, a young horse-back preacher from Alabama, without any pastoral charge, in rather frail health, ventured to express a doubt whether matters were ripe for what I agreed was a desirable purpose, Brother Graves, who was already a skilled and renowned debater, challenged me to a discussion then and there, each to take a half an hour of time, and fight the question out."[59] Manly declined the opportunity.

Subsequent events cooled Graves's ardor for the school. In 1851 he issued a call to Baptist ministers "willing to accept the teachings of Christ and his Apostles" regarding the local church to convene at Cotton Grove, Tennessee. Five questions that led to resolutions were discussed at the Cotton Grove conference. The first question set the stage for the other four and had the answer to all implied in the way it was framed: "Can Baptists, consistently with their principles or the Scriptures, recognize those societies not organized according to the pattern of the Jerusalem Church, but possessing different governments, different officers, a different class of members, different ordinances, doctrines and practices, as churches of Christ?"[60] Once the first question was answered with a "No," the following questions rejected the title "church" for non-Baptist religious societies, rejected the ministerial status of their preachers, rejected any possibility that they could be invited into Baptist pulpits, and even questioned that the members of such societies could be addressed as "brethren."

In 1854, Graves requested that J. M. Pendleton write on the question of "pulpit affiliation," building on the question "Ought Baptists to recognize Pedobaptist preachers as gospel ministers?" Since infant baptism is not baptism, Pendleton argued, religious societies that baptize infants are not churches. The action, sprinkling, is wrong, and the subject, unbelievers, is wrong. They therefore are not churches and their ministers not gospel ministers. If that is true, Baptist ministers must not invite them to preach or exchange pulpits with them.[61]

In 1855, the Landmarkers challenged the usual resolution in the Southern Baptist Convention of inviting, as a matter of fraternal courtesy, non-Baptist ministers to "sit with us and participate in our deliberations." After much discussion, the resolution was withdrawn by its supporters in order "to concede thus much to the views of their brethren who objected so strongly."[62] In 1857, Howell returned to Nashville from Virginia, and a bitter dispute broke out between him and Graves over Graves's proposal of a Southern Baptist Sunday School Union. Graves wanted to give greater influence to his publishing house and to the Landmark sympathizers throughout the convention. Howell opposed this move for the sake of the Southern Baptist Publication Society. The ensuing controversy led to the excommunication of Graves from the First Baptist Church, the dismissal of A. C. Dayton from his position on the Bible Board, and a controversy that spilled over into the entire convention.

In 1859 Graves confronted the annual gathering of the convention with an effort to defeat Howell as president, to destroy the Bible Board for its handling of Dayton, and not to recognize the First Baptist Church of Nashville as the "true" First Baptist Church. On 28 May 1859, he mentioned by name thirty-seven men who "were distinguished for their bitter hostility to the Southern Baptist Sunday School Union." Among those named were W. T. Brantly Jr., Richard Fuller, J. B. Taylor, J. B. Jeter, Richard Furman, R. B. C. Howell, P. H. Mell, John A. Broadus, and J. P. Boyce. Whereas eight years earlier Graves had been an energetic, vocal, and ardent supporter of centralized theological education, he had come into controversy with virtually every person that was connected intimately with the newly approved theological school. This generated much antagonism and created stressful personal difficulties for the agents commissioned to collect the endowment for the seminary.[63]

The Difficult Work of Agency

While the endowment from South Carolina was essentially secured through the work of Boyce, the good will of the South Carolina trustees, and the encouragement of Manly Sr., a great challenge lay in collecting the designated endowment from the other states. Manly wrote Boyce in December with a contribution and a prayer: "Enclosed is a check for my contribution toward the fund of the seminary Viz—$60 with one years interest from the first of Jany 1858 in all $64.20. This together with my former contribution is a little seed, which I plant with the prayer that God will concentrate all the efforts of His people, and bless this enterprise."[64] The work to be done in the other states, however, needed to be consummated quickly. Various state conventions had endorsed the plan of raising money in their state, but this had no binding effect on any association or church. It simply represented a gesture of good will from some of the leaders of the Baptists, but the actual collection still had to be done by agents hired by the seminary.

J. H. De Votie refused the agency for Georgia because the revival in his church had so occupied him that he could not leave it in good conscience. He informed Boyce that in the last two years he "had the pleasure of baptizing 123 white persons for which God be praised. We are about to build a new house of worship."[65] W. F. Broaddus had consented to do the work in Virginia after the refusal of R. H. Bagby and appeared at churches and meetings of associations to advocate the claims of the Greenville school. He had heard, so he stated in one association, that thirteen men from Virginia were going there, and he "wanted that money as well as men should be given." Putting practical work to his desires, "Elder Broaddus spoke at length and with much force of the desirableness of such an institution and procured some $500."[66]

Broaddus worked with alacrity and wisdom, giving Boyce advice about the best way to appeal to the Baptists of Virginia. He advised Boyce against the use of bonds for another form of subscription. He believed that the $25,000 could be raised in Virginia "especially if the subscriptions be made payable as I have stated above, in three annual installments." Later he continued this theme, informing Boyce about "an almost universal unwillingness in this state, to pay interest on voluntary bonds, especially interest dating back." The method chosen by the committee would "seriously prejudice the effort to get subscriptions, without a modification of the terms proposed by the committee."

Broaddus knew they must be precise legally but also amenable to the propensities of the people of the state.

Broaddus also visited the Chowan Association in North Carolina and recommended appointing an agent there. He thought of men who would be effective as agents for Mississippi, Alabama, and Georgia. Encouragement was often abbreviated by recognition of opposition in general but also in particular from the followers of J. R. Graves. By December 1859, Broaddus could write with an encouraging perspective, "My impression is that I can get the balance of $25,000 before Oct. 1860" in Virginia. Other places have greater resistance, still Baltimore and Washington should be canvassed. "I have had a hard year of it. Opposition to 'Theological Schools' has met me at every step," he admitted. Nevertheless, "I hope some good has been done, in the way of removing prejudices. Hereafter, I think there will be a better feeling, especially if you do your work well."[67] The agency would succeed, he thought, as real confidence grew in the effectiveness of the school.

For a brief period, I. T. Tichenor served as an agent and worked steadily at the task, offering observations, encouragement, and advice along the way. After his first month he wrote, "When I entered it I did not anticipate being able to do much for the institution. The political commotion, the stagnation of business, the failure of crops all forewarned me that the work would be difficult, laborious and slow." He was surprised, however, that he had "succeeded beyond my expectations—I have within the four weeks of labor raised in cash and bonds $2430. This amount has been raised in sums varying from $10 to 300."

The political climate had made all men, particularly men dependent on business, cautious. They must "see whether the present storm will leave them a shelter for their families," so the more wealthy have the greater hesitance to help. The brethren and churches in the country and amidst the sparse population do better. Tichenor hoped, however, that "the sale of the cotton crop and the brightening of the political horizon before the spring will enable me to do something in the commercial centers." He recommended a couple of strategies for reaching the largest sections of Alabama and Georgia. "I must not forget to say," he informed Boyce, "that I am very much indebted to Bro C. D. Mallary for his assistance in this part of the state. He has entered into the work with a degree of zeal that has shown him the first friend of the Institution. There is no better friend to it in Georgia." This was good news, for Boyce had heard by innuendo that Mallary was cool toward the seminary. Then with a happy expectation of political changes that would occur in the next few months Tichenor closed, "Hoping to be able in my next to address you as a citizen of the independent state of Alabama."[68]

Perhaps the most aggravating and yet indispensable work as agent was done by J. F. B. Mays. When Mays was a student during Boyce's second year of teaching at Furman, Boyce had loaned him money to help keep him in school. Mays had imbibed Boyce's love for theology and wanted Boyce to respond to questions about complex theological issues—issues in Hebrew exegesis, the theology of the Holy Spirit, theology of decrees, atonement, and the priesthood of Christ. He mentioned several books that he borrowed and was seeking to return. He shared with Boyce all the difficulties, and joys, of his life and looked to Boyce for calming answers and consummate wisdom. If Boyce did not seem to be forthcoming with the most compelling advice in a timely fashion, he felt dejected and betrayed. But he worked hard, and talked a lot about it; and he endured resistance, and talked a lot about it; and pressed on through hardship, and talked a lot about it.

In December 1857 Mays wrote Boyce a letter about his pecuniary embarrassment, "If my churches would have treated me even as a band of infidels would treat their leader," Mays complained, "I would not have been so much trouble to you. I feel that my demands have been like those of the horse leech." Boyce, out of compassion for his situation, appointed him agent for North Carolina. When he began, he bought a horse and buggy for $200 and wrote Boyce about his first encounter. "I hope you will pray for my success. The magnanimity of the enterprise increases in my mind. I've succeeded in making others feel as I feel. One man gave me $250 with tears in his eyes." He asked Boyce to write ahead to a pastor, Mason by name, in Yancyville to encourage him to raise a thousand, or perhaps two, before he got there, but especially to recommend him as a good catch for a husband. "He is the pastor of a certain little ewe lamb that I want." He assured

Boyce that his "family is spotless as to character. So you need not be afraid to say all you want to for me." And by the way, "One pastor said he thought the seminary worse than a penitentiary and a curse, but when I was done with him & his church he gave me $10 and his church $100."

In the Tar River Association Mays encountered "Hardshells" and had some choice words to say about them. He would not allow them to defeat him in his purpose. "Many of the old fogies especially the preachers are opposed to the enterprise, some bitterly." But not to worry, for "I am perfectly willing to make any and every sacrifice necessary for the accomplishment of my ends. My full determination is to raise it anyhow." Later he wrote, "I've just reached here to day weary and dusty, and very anxious as I am in a money country, but hard to get thro because of hills. Steep ones too." In this report he listed gifts of $1,900. He was disappointed that Boyce did not write to Yancyville as he requested, but Mays got his amount anyway. Though the "ewe lamb" issue was personally important, he assured Boyce, "I do not think hard of you at all."

On October 1, Mays wrote "with extremely melancholy feelings." He had worked hard enough to raise $20,000 but all he had to show for it was $5 from a mechanic and a buggy almost broken to pieces. He had encountered stinginess, deceit, opposition, and caricature. Fayetteville he considered "the habitation of devils." He was soured and embittered, but strove "to live as near the cross as possible. But when all my soul is absorbed in an enterprise of this sort," and wealthy Baptists with no heirs lie and give poor excuses for their greed, "I think of the boundless love of God in sparing such poor miserable creatures." He gave one association a "rasping," and they responded with $700. Opposition to the seminary, however, was rampant. They feared that "Greenville would decide the faith and practice of Baptists" and would elevate "the preachers above the masses." The seminary would produce "stiff straight-jacket reading men instead of preaching."

In the middle of November Mays had continued the pattern of rejection, some success, overpriced fare, an almost dead horse, and devastating hardship, yet "I feel it is glorious to suffer for so great a cause." He cautioned Boyce, "Look out for wise work against yourself from certain quarters." He would come home as soon as possible, "but must have my amt."[69]

In December, the editor of the *Biblical Recorder* wrote Boyce, "I presume ere this you have received my second note stating that Bro. Mays has secured the amt. adjudged to this state for the Theological Seminary. I intended making an editorial in connection with the letter announcing the fact published in this weeks paper, but was taken violently ill on Monday and have been unable since to write."

By January, Mays had a new appointment, Mississippi. He had been married in the meantime, and he wanted Boyce to know that not only did he "feel as much concerned as possible for the Seminary," but "all of the friends of my wife and myself seem to think we are perfectly matched, which I feel to be the greatest compliment ever paid me, as she is all that any man could wish physically, mentally, and morally." As in his agency in North Carolina, Mays wrote frequently with news at a personal level but also reflecting his perceptions of the larger conditions in the South and especially among Baptists. Several references to J. R. Graves and the growing sympathy for his Landmark views wend their way into numerous letters. Mays warned Boyce against what he perceived as deceitfulness and believed part of the resistance was due to R. B. C. Howell's presence on the board of trustees and the use of Dagg's *Manual of Theology* as a text.[70]

Mays wanted Boyce to write along the way to help him gain credibility and entrée in proper places to collect funds. He feared that the convention would abolish the seminary if it did not come up with the $200,000. He found Mississippi a hard place to get money, especially in light of the growing political excitement and financial uncertainty, and the rich who he thought would help him only teased him and eventually gave nothing. J. L. Pettigrew had left Mississippi College to attend the seminary, but Mays felt he had been sent as a spy for Graves.[71] Pettigrew had been "petted, probably spoiled," in Mississippi. Boyce might turn it to his good, however, if he could "give him his freedom on the Landmark foolery if I may so speak, then get him to write an article in the Miss Baptist" and find some places for him to preach.

In November, Mays left Mississippi briefly and found his wife "now under medical treatment." He felt "very badly for staying away from

171

her so long." He had stayed in Mississippi until he felt it was folly to stay any longer, "for the very men that I expected to do something handsome gave me nothing." They told him it was "madness" to ask any thinking man to commit to the future in the way demanded by the bonds. The bonds read:

> I do hereby bind myself, my heirs, executors, administrators and assigns to pay to The southern Baptist theological Seminary, located at Greenville S. C., the sum of [Nine] dollars, payable in three equal annual Installments; the first on the first day of January, 1862, the second on the first day January, 1863; and the third on the first day of January 1864.
>
> Witness my hand and seal, this __ day of _____ 1860

Later in the month Boyce requested Mays to return and seek to complete the agency; Mays complied. In December he wrote from Canton, "I am on the eve now of finishing Mississippi as its agent." He reminded Boyce of the faithfulness of his labors and of his loyalty to the seminary as an agent. "God knows that there is no living man that would or that has made the sacrifices I have, for the school." Boyce and the seminary had a claim on him to such a degree that he had turned down lucrative offers from churches, other agencies, and administrative positions in schools. "I mention this to show you that you were not mistaken in your man." He always wanted to be of service and was mindful of the kindness of Boyce.

In March of 1861, from Tuskegee, Alabama, Mays reported that he had "$9,815 in bonds" and "6 or 7 hundred in cash." He thought more could be gained from Mississippi when the times got better. At the same time he was bogged down in a business deal, perhaps on the verge of financial disaster, and thoroughly frustrated: "I want a pastorate that will pay me or else a situation in a female college if I can get my matters all arranged to suit me." He was deceived by his partner, manipulated by his wife's family, and now pleading with Boyce to rescue him. "Now I want you to pull me out of this scrape if you can by July. . . . Now if you please keep this to yourself, & do what you can for me."

In June, Mays demonstrated in a more breathtaking way his possessiveness toward Boyce's good will and a startling presumptuousness of spirit. Again from Tuskegee, he reminded Boyce that some time ago he had informed him of his losses and had been treated badly by his partner. Others had come to his aid, including Dr. Manly, for which he expressed deep appreciation. "I'm greatly attached to him," he said. He then began an assault on Boyce for his inattentiveness to his call for help. "Why is it I get no answer from you, when I make a call in distress? Have I directly or indirectly forfeited any claim I ever had upon your confidence or affection?" Then in a revelation of his unwarranted presumption, he added, "I used to think, you were absolutely the very best friend I had on earth. I think you had the very best proof, of its reciprocity. I wrote you that I was out of money, and had been thrown in the midst of the year out of employment, and shamefully cheated by a man." Laconically he lamented, "I wrote, and got no reply." Having vented his hurt he closed, "I hope you are all well & that you have sustained no loss in this war."[72]

In order to assure the success of the endowment, on 30 April 1861 Boyce signed two bonds for $50,000, each pledging to pay the sum lacking in raising the endowment. One was for the states of Maryland, Tennessee, Texas, Kentucky, and Louisiana, each to raise $5,000 within ten years for the endowment. Another was for $50,000, the "amount still remaining to be raised" of the second $100,000 of the endowment fund of the said seminary.

The First Seminary Session, 1859–60

The week before the seminary opened, Boyce went to Columbia for the dedication exercises for the new Baptist church in his former pastorate.[73] The service opened at 10:30 on 25 September 1859 on a bright, clear day with a new auditorium completely filled, the bottom floor almost exclusively female, the galleries crowded, and many standing along the walls. Singing hymns, reading psalms, prayer, and preaching constituted the service. J. O. B. Dargan prayed, a lengthy and eloquent prayer filled with words of adoration, praise, and deep gratitude for the gift of Christ. Boyce then preached from Psalm 26:8:

"Lord, I have loved the habitation of thy house, and the place where thine honour dwelleth." His commitment to theologically informed exposition permeated his presentation on this day so auspicious in its witness to the providence of God.

Boyce used the text as indicating that God's designation of places of worship should inspire his people to deeper worship, knowledge of divine truth, and genuine piety. While some have regarded religious places as having sacramental power in themselves, Baptists have often engaged in the other extreme and treated their places of worship in a "sacrilegious" manner. "It is time," Boyce preached, "for the sake of religious taste and the sacredness of Christian worship, that the voices of the Churches should be raised against this desecration of the objects for which their houses of worship have been built, and of the religious associations with which they are connected."[74] The fact that the Word of God will be preached, that the Holy Spirit "will here be poured forth on the individual and upon the assembly," that it is the home of a Christian church, and "especially the home of a Baptist church," should be enough to evoke reverence. Those who worship in this "new, handsome edifice" have come together in the "firm conviction of the truth of the distinctive doctrines and practices of that people, and are earnestly desirous so to exhibit these peculiarities as to commend the simple truth in Jesus to their fellowmen."

Beyond those obvious and immediate considerations that should provide sufficient motive for reverential conduct, Boyce pointed to the "doctrine of the Sanctuary." The house itself should evoke appropriate feelings of worship and remind us of the deepest truths of redemption. We are reminded of the gracious presence of God among his people, not isolated to one place, in Jerusalem, but over the whole world. Particularly, however, as the church comes together in obedience to the Lord's ordinances, he has promised he is in the midst of them. A house of worship, moreover, should draw us to see the dwelling of God in man, particularly in the person of Christ in his mysterious incarnation. Jesus himself referred to his body as the temple. Even his enemies drew the conclusion that his statements about the temple meant that he claimed to be the Son of God. Our houses of worship should remind us that that "type of the temple" found fulfillment "in the antitype, the incarnate

Son of God." And certainly those who would meditate with proper sobriety and awareness on the temple and its continuous sacrifices must have learned that "the Deity would dwell in humanity, attaching to it His own glory, as did the Shekinah in the temple, and securing an inestimable value for its acts of obedience and suffering."

Even more mysterious, although to some degree explicable on the basis of Christ's atonement and imputed righteousness, is the immediate contact that God has condescended to have with man in the gift of the Spirit to indwell his people, sanctifying them, fitting them for more pure praise above. Finally, the house of worship typifies the reality that God himself forms his people into a sanctuary of praise to himself out of people from every tongue and tribe and nation. So, Boyce concluded, "Let us dedicate it indeed, to the worship of God, to the promulgation of His word, to the administration of His ordinances. Let it be sacred as His chosen dwelling place among his people. Let it tell of Him who was made flesh, and dwelt among us. Let it remind you of the sacred presence of the Spirit in the individual believer. Let it ever bring to view that glorious temple which shall be truly fitted to speak forth the praises of God."[75]

The next week on Monday the long-awaited day arrived. The seminary held opening exercises. W. B. Johnson was present, led in prayer and gave a message appropriate to the occasion, "in an impressive and interesting manner." He compared the rich opportunity that lay before these students with the sparseness of educational advantages just fifty years ago. "He expressed his high appreciation of the Faculty, and congratulated the Students on the favorable opportunity furnished them by the 'school of the prophets,' for instruction in knowledge and duties pertaining to their high calling; admonishing them, however, that the Bible alone was the religion of Christians." He rejoiced in the "auspicious commencement" of an institution that had been the object of the prayers and labors of so many good men.

The students presented credentials from their churches and registered their names in a book prepared for that purpose. The professors each described their courses in a "brief and lucid manner." The writer of the article in the *Southern Baptist* commented, "I do not think I speak in a spirit of partiality in saying, that with this Faculty may be found an amount of talents, genius and learning not surpassed by any other, of equal number, in the United States." He was certain that no school would have better models for preachers.[76] All four faculty members— Boyce, Broadus, Manly, and Williams—had distinguished themselves as earnest, accurate, attractive, and powerful pulpiteers.

The first catalogue, published subsequent to the first academic year, listed the names of twenty-four students who took classes, although Broadus claimed that there were twenty-six. William Ballard, from Greenville District, South Carolina, was forty-five years old when he came. Described as a "plain country pastor," and also "a deeply pious man and a deeply earnest student," he stayed for one session, and on his resuming his pastoral labors, the churches that heard him preach remarked at the substantial improvement. J. A. Chambliss from Alabama completed the entire course in two sessions, becoming the seminary's first full graduate. He served churches in Richmond, Charleston, and East Orange, New Jersey. C. H. Toy from Norfolk, Virginia, went one session and completed all the Old Testament, both English and Hebrew, all the New Testament, both English and Greek, all the Systematic Theology, English and Latin, and Ecclesiastical History. He thus studied with all four professors during that year. Later he studied in Germany and came in 1869 to be the fifth teacher at the Seminary.[77]

The catalogue described the benefits of the seminary's location in Greenville, defended the design of its course work, which made it accessible, with the exception of three courses, to "those acquainted merely with the English language," and showed the advantage of having every course structured in such a way that each separately could be completed in one session. It listed the eight schools of the seminary and gave a description of each course taught. Having come subsequent to the first year's teaching, the catalogue accurately portrayed what each professor actually taught in the respective courses during the first year. Boyce's description of Systematic Theology showed his concern for the peculiar advantages of the school:

> It is intended to bring the instruction of the English department of the School of Systematic Theology within the reach of all who have acquired a good English education. On this account all references to

176

other languages are dispensed with, so far as practicable, and when made, are made in such a way as to be understood by this class of students. It is attempted to teach all points of Theology in a Biblical point of view, reference being made to the opinions of men only so far as may tend to elucidate the Scriptural presentation of a doctrine. A text book is used as being adapted to convey thorough instruction, and as furnishing the means, by thorough analysis and study of its contents, to train the mind to habits of systematic thinking and close application. In order, however, that the instruction may not be confined to the subjects or method of treatment of any one author, lectures are given by the Professor, and the students are required to read additionally upon the topics of the text-books and lectures in other treatises of Theology to which they may be directed.

The textbook was Dagg's *Manual of Theology*. The second year's catalogue contained the same description but with some amendments only for the sake of a better style. An additional textbook also was listed, Dick's *Lectures on Theology*.[78]

The second course in Systematic Theology showed that provision was made for advanced study for those who were qualified beyond the level of a plain English education. The student should be "well acquainted with the Latin language." Original texts in Latin would be studied as well as a textbook that for "more than one hundred and fifty years occupied the highest rank as a full and complete treatise upon Theology." This course complemented both the English course and the course in polemics. The text as listed was Francis Turretin, *Institutio Theologiae Elencticae*.[79]

The most elaborate description of the entire catalogue was Boyce's Polemic Theology and Apologetics. Again it showed the high expectations Boyce had for theological astuteness among the students. Mastery of the issues involved in the confrontation of truth with error was no small matter for Boyce, but constituted one of the noblest responsibilities and delightful acts of a servant of the God of truth. He revealed the ambitious nature of his teaching.

> The design of the School is the examination of the various forms of error, and the refutation of objections brought against the truth. The

subjects which come under consideration are, therefore, extensive; for there is no truth which has not been opposed, no form which error can take which has not presented itself. A few of the subjects treated may serve to show more fully the character of this School. After introductory lectures upon various topics, the following, among other subjects, are discussed:

The different phases of infidelity—as Atheism, Pantheism, Deism, &c.; the various forms of Heathenism, and especially those now to be encountered in Brahminism, Buddhism, &c.; Systems of false religion, as Mohammedanism and Mormonism; Erroneous systems of Christianity; Socinianism, Arianism, Pelagianism, and Arminianism. These are considered with especial reference to their modern forms, as, for instance, the latter in connection with the English, Methodist, and Lutheran Churches. The system of Romanism receives the attention due the influence of that sect in this country and abroad, and the extent of its controversies. The subjects treated under that head, however, are those only peculiar to the system. In the Anglican Church, in connection with Tractarianism, are treated Sacramental Efficacy, the authority of Tradition as to Usages and Ceremonies; the value of the Fathers, Apostolical Succession and External Unity. Subsequent to this are discussed several sects which cannot well be classed, as Quakers, Campbellites, Universalists, &c.

The modifications of Calvinism, especially by the New England divines, are also considered, and various other questions involving controversies with persons more or less closely approaching the truths of the Bible as taught by Baptists. Especial attention is paid to the controversies upon Baptism, both as to the mode and the subjects. In the discussion of topics an examination is made of every theory on the subject that has had any prominence; the differences that have arisen in them from philosophical, denominational or other peculiarities, are indicated, and the various points of attack and defence relative to each opinion are shown.

This is necessarily but an imperfect list of the numerous topics which are discussed. The lectures on Infidelity, for example, are not confined to the topics mentioned, but embrace every form of it, ancient and modern, secret and avowed and the same is true of almost every subject indicated. The topics mentioned are not intended to give an idea of the extent, but of the character of subjects discussed.

The course is pursued entirely by lectures, references being made to such books on each subject as may give additional information.[80]

Near the end of the first session, the seminary received a visit from J. B. Taylor, corresponding secretary of the Foreign Mission Board. He had not participated in the educational conventions, but his son G. B. Taylor had. He was impressed with what he observed, particularly in the attitudes of the Virginia students. He assured the readers of the *Religious Herald* that the seminary posed no threat to the full college courses offered by Richmond College, but instead could enhance the desire of students "to obtain the intellectual discipline furnished by the academy or college, ere they shall enter upon a theological course." The facilities of the seminary were plain but pleasant and an appropriate reminder of the task to which they had been called. "The old Baptist house of worship, whose walls have often resounded with the proclamation of the gospel, has been so modified, as to make three convenient recitation and library rooms." Classes met in the two recitation rooms from early morning until afternoon "in conference with their godly and gifted teachers." One of the Virginia students, "with his young wife and his little child, all domiciled in a small, plain cottage, living without a servant, and on plain fare, was bending all his energies to those investigations, which would prepare him to become a workman needing not to be ashamed." Taylor, whose second son, James B. Taylor Jr., would attend the next session of the seminary, proclaimed the school "a decided success," and accompanied his verdict with a prayer "that God may preside over it and abundantly prosper it."[81]

Boyce had enjoyed great health during the year and had been untrammeled by significant financial worries for the seminary. The extra $100,000 outside of South Carolina had been pledged and the prospects for the seminary, given its splendid start, were encouraging. He often had students in his home in groups for meals and encouraged their informal visits also. He loaned means of transportation to students and faculty alike who had preaching engagements in places several miles away.

Broadus became sick during the first year from the strain of overwork and had to miss more than three months in the middle of the session. In a letter to Miss Cornelia Taliaferro in February 1860, Broadus described the difficulty: "For nearly three months I have been unable to meet my classes, though never violently ill." The problem began as "indigestion" but had "settled down into confirmed and obstinate dyspepsia." He had overworked himself, was imprudent in eating, and "after resting a few days went to work again too soon and too hard, and in a week more was laid up."[82] The other three professors took Broadus's load during those months. "They did it so ably, and with such cheerful kindness," Broadus recalled, "such unfailing and delicate efforts to prevent their colleague from being pained by the situation, that, now when they have all passed away, the matter is remembered with unspeakable gratitude and affection."[83]

During Broadus's illness, Boyce invited him to go on a trip with him and his family to Charleston where he would visit family and care for some of the issues related to his duties as executor of his father's estate. The trip took twenty hours by carriage, and when they reached Charleston, Boyce carried Broadus, wrapped in an elegant and warm coat, "in his own arms from the carriage into his room at the hotel. He seemed strong like a giant, and he was tender as a woman."[84]

The first commencement closed the academic year with the promise of great advances in the future sessions. "Observer," writing for the *Religious Herald*, commented, "The large number of students in attendance, the very high character of the instruction given, the ardent love for the institution felt by all its students, and the growing interest which Southern Baptists are taking in it, all give assurance of its future success and usefulness."[85] The events began on Saturday evening, May 26, with an address by J. A. Chambliss before the Andrew Fuller Society. The "fair daughters of Greenville" had decorated the hall tastefully and the choir of the Baptist church sang anthems. On Sunday, I. T. Tichenor preached before the seminary, and in the evening G. W. Samson preached before the Society for Missionary Inquiry. On Monday, May 28, the first annual commencement of the seminary was held. The program consisted of music, prayer, more music, an address by Basil Manly Sr., the chair of the trustees, music, conferring of diplomas, the seminary hymn, an address by James P. Boyce, more music, and the benediction. The hymn was written by Basil Manly Jr., and has been sung at every commencement.

> Soldiers of Christ in truth arrayed,
> A world in ruins needs your aid;
> A world by sin destroyed and dead;
> A world for which the Saviour bled.

Forth to the realms of darkness go,
Where, like a river's ceaseless flow,
A tide of souls is drifting down,
Blasted beneath th'Almighty's frown.

No human skill nor power can stay
That flood upon its gloomy way;
But God's own love devised the plan
To save the ruined creature man.

His gospel to the lost proclaim;
Good news for all, in Jesus' name;
Let light upon the darkness break,
That sinners from their death may wake.

Morning and evening sow the seed,
God's grace the effort shall succeed;
Seed times of tears have oft been found
With sheaves of joy and plenty crown'd.

We meet to part, but part to meet,
When earthly labors are complete,
To join in yet more blest employ,
In an eternal world of joy.

In reporting the address of Boyce, the writer described it as one "appropriate to the occasion." "Eyes unused to weeping were filled with tears during its delivery." Boyce opened his "hospitable mansion" to the students, trustees, faculty, and friends of the seminary.

The first session had objectified the vision. Soon events, both personal and national, would challenge its viability and the commitment of Boyce and his colleagues to its continuance and give cause to wonder if the seminary itself had been "Blasted beneath th'Almighty's frown."

5

The Devastation of War

*T*he summer after the first session proved prelude to increasing difficulties and a lifetime of mounting pressure for Boyce. It began with Broadus still in slow convalescence. He was able to preach an ordination for four students, Toy, Johnson, Jones, and Taylor Jr., which he hoped "did much good." In addition he made a positive report on a speech and sermon Boyce had made at Staunton, Virginia, "which were frequently mentioned in my hearing, and with high praise." He had evoked a lively interest in the seminary.[1] Looking forward to the fall, Broadus wrote Boyce about several possible texts for an extra class in Greek he had decided to teach and informed him that a Latin section of the book could do well for his Latin Theology class if he "cannot do better." He then expressed his concerns for his health in a humorous vein. The effort at the ordination exhausted him. He had "disconcerted some of the folks here considerably by complaining of the climate, water, etc., saying that I was improving rapidly till I came here, that I had some thoughts of gathering up my family and going back home for my health." Some of his Virginia friends believed that Greenville water was so bad "that we had to send three miles for all the water we drank—and it was that that was making me sick." The South is a "homogenous swamp in vulgar estimation."[2]

The Situation Deteriorates

Broadus's illness concerned Boyce, and in addition, the unexpected death of student James Witt within a month of the commencement was very painful. When several months later Boyce delivered the commencement address of 1861, he noted the mystery of divine providence in the taking of Witt. "Yea, even our parting of last year, in better circumstances, was scarcely over before the hand of death was upon one of the most beloved of our men," Boyce lamented. "With his manly form and frank and noble countenance, he mingled with us in the last commencement," having as sure a prospect of long life as any. Within a month, however, "all that was left of him was the blessed memory of that pure and genial presence, which will remain ever green and fragrant until all that knew him will rejoin him above." Even though Witt had laid out plans of labor and study for years to come, "it pleased the Allwise Disposer of events to remove him from the earthly to the heavenly schools, and to employ him in the labors of the eternal rest."[3]

Boyce managed, however, to write with a spirit of buoyancy, humor, and delight as he surveyed the scenes before him. He did not want to use the book Broadus suggested for Latin Theology, for it is impossible to read "save under heavy passion. Have you seen the type and paper?" he asked. He would not risk his eyes on it but would "rather lug a folio each day to the Seminary." Evidently he still was wary of the eye difficulties that almost drove him from the ministry more than a decade earlier.

The church that Boyce served was "having a gracious revival" and had added more than twenty since it began. Upon return in the fall he wanted Broadus to preach "that sermon on the ministry you are preparing this summer." And on the subject of preaching, Boyce himself had had quite a triumph recently. So well did he do, in fact, that he had the gratification "to report the criticism of my boy William" that "my sermon had even beaten Mr. Broadus' efforts." Neither, however, had done quite as well as one of the students, Samuel N. Whiston, in William's opinion. "Your laurels are gone, my friend," Boyce triumphed; "or rather we now stand Broadus! Boyce!! Whitson!!! Ad infinitum."

Some of the students had provided entertainment. Caspari had picked up palmistry for the amusement of Boyce's wife and sister Mary. Whiston, the impressive preacher, learned to grow watermelons. "Lo and behold," Boyce exclaimed, "before anyone else had the article the great divine, the shining light, appeared on Main Street with a big wheel barrow full of the dark green shining fruit and he wheeled it, that he did, down to Steen's and then sold them out at about forty cents a piece. Imagine the man, the barrow, the fruits, and the admiring crowd." On the succeeding Sunday Whiston preached the "powerful sermon." It was especially composed for "the negroes that day *by special request on Baptism.* The Methodist darkies who, not knowing the subject, had been lured in by the praises sounded forth of the great preacher were astounded, angered and then put to flight. They left him in possession of the field. It was a splendid effusion, so the darkies say—so convincing, so scriptural, so confident, so learned. Not a doubt had he upon any point. It was the plainest sailing imaginable." Boyce asked if Broadus were responsible for Whiston's Greek and if Manly would stand sponsor for the Hebrew. Boyce disclaimed any credit for the New Testament English, for Whiston was not in the class. Boyce thought that the effort might see publication, for "from the enthusiasm among the blacks" he was convinced that a sufficient sum could readily be raised.

Water was scarce, making the price of corn high. Boyce was part of an initiative to start a gas company in Greenville. "We will have the town lighted with it in November," Boyce wrote and also informed Broadus that it would pass near his house. He was going north in August or September and asked, "Can I get anything for you, anything for your house, or otherwise?" A postscript said, "I receive every week one or two applications for catalogues—our prospects next session I think are good."[4]

Broadus returned sad news. His daughter Maria had died of diphtheria on July 15. Maria was about four years old and was the youngest daughter of Broadus's first wife, who had died on 21 October 1857. He marveled at the providence that took two such diverse prospects as "James Witt, and that laughing little girl. O my daughter! But the will of the Lord be done. I have stood by the deathbed and the grave of father and mother and sister, of wife and child; I am confident that they are all safe in heaven; God help those who are left, to follow them there." He had gained weight and felt stronger. Commenting on the antics of Whiston, Broadus said, "Pity that the recent occupation of Bro. Whiston could not be generally known, as showing that the Seminary does not inevitably, at least not in one session, make *every* student 'bookish' and 'puffed up with ministerial dignity.'"[5]

Broadus reported by August 31 that his health was almost back to normal, as indicated by his ability to preach for an hour in the open air "with about as much boisterousness as I ever reached." Although he knew he would never have vigorous health, he could stand work tolerably well with sensible exercise and diet. Concerning the latter, he found himself able to "digest a respectable amount of bread and meat without any brandy or whiskey, and have lately been eating peaches without any indication of injury." Also a more broad-based sympathy for the seminary was developing in Virginia. Sadly, with the possibility of Lincoln's victory in the coming election, the talk of secession dominated the political discussion, energetically so in South Carolina. If South Carolina secedes alone, "we'll be in a sweet fix."[6]

By late September, problems had arisen concerning some investments of the Boyce estate. Boyce had to go to New York to take care of them. This difficulty eventually had devastating results for Boyce as its implications extended into financial issues beyond the Civil War. He telegraphed that he would be home by October 21 at the earliest. He did not anticipate a great loss but had to be "on the ground" to secure himself. Also he wanted to save his brother and brother-in-law from serious loss. He asked that the faculty do whatever they thought expedient about his English Theology class for the entire session. Even when he did return, concerns about the seminary endowment would cause great interruptions. After January 1 he would have to be gone entirely on seminary business. "If anyone could simply take my class through Dagg," he suggested, "it will do with what total comments could be made extempore." He suggested Williams. "You who know my feeling for the Seminary need no assurance that I will be back as soon as possible."[7] Faculty schedules made Manly the best choice, Broadus informed him, and Boyce should take care of everything required of him without any fear that the seminary would be crippled, though they all missed him greatly.

The second session eventually enrolled thirty-six students.[8] On November 6, Abraham Lincoln was elected president of the United States of America with 180 electoral votes. Three other candidates, Douglas, Breckenridge, and Bell garnered a total of 123 electoral votes. The next day, November 7, Charleston, South Carolina, raised the Palmetto Flag. On November 10 the South Carolina legislature called for a special session to meet on December 17 to discuss secession. On hearing this news, C. H. Toy wrote Broadus, "I suppose you are a secessionist . . . inclined to snub us in Virginia, hardly willing that we should enter the Southern Confederacy." Broadus's brother, also fearing the consequences of secession, wrote, "Are you willing to be alienated from Virginia? Are you willing when you come to Virginia to be considered a foreigner?"[9]

Boyce became a candidate for the legislature in opposition to secession, but was defeated convincingly. His resistance to secession indicated no sympathy at all for even the mildest Northern argument against slavery. The action, he believed, was precipitous, because it put the South in the position of having dissolved the Union, and having done so without a plan in place for Southern cooperation. The complex, difficult, and inflammatory tensions of these days gave Boyce visions of a number of conflicting scenarios. Boyce favored resistance to Northern ideology by demanding "first new guarantees, and if these were not granted, then forming a Southern Confederacy." He wanted to see the North put "entirely in the wrong, by making them dissolve the Union" by refusing to grant Southern conditions.

Even after secession, however, Boyce, reminiscing about the loyalty of his grandfather and father to the Union, stated, "Nor do I yet despair; I believe that ere many months have gone by we shall all be safe again under the folds of the glorious Stars and Stripes of our own United States." He wanted if possible to preserve the Union, but he would consent to it only as a "pro-slavery man." But the substance supporting that conviction soon would dissolve, he prophesied. "I believe I see in this," he wrote his brother-in-law Tupper, "the end of slavery." We are cutting its throat and curtailing its domain. Boyce viewed himself as "an ultra pro-slavery man," yet he bowed to what God would do. "I feel that our sins as to this institution have cursed us,—that the negroes have not been cared for in their marital and religious relations as they should be; and I fear God is going to sweep it away, after having left it thus long to show us how great we might be were we to act as we ought in this matter." Boyce believed it possible that some propositions, some arrangement, some ultimatum could be presented that the North would accept, or if not, on their part press the South into leaving without sanguinary consequences. If this could not be arranged, however, and the "fire-eaters" of the South had their way, "We shall have to go through a long and bloody war."[10] In losing slavery, an exalted and idyllic culture would be crushed.

Slavery among Baptists in the South

The depth of the Southern Baptist conviction about the identity of the South with slavery may be inferred from a strange attack on J. R. Graves in the *Southern Baptist* in May 1858 that had appeared in the *Southwestern Baptist* about two weeks earlier. Graves had sought to discredit the Baptist orthodoxy of the Southern Baptist Publication Society located in Charleston in an effort to bolster support for his Sunday School Union. His motto for this campaign was "Let Southern Baptists now be true to those who have been true to them." But true to Southern Baptists Graves had not been, according to the writer. Instead he had cast suspicion on and caused significantly diminished support for the "great benevolent enterprises of Southern Baptists." He must be dealt with as a "public enemy."

And what more than anything showed his disloyalty to the South and thus Baptist causes? His "unreliability and quondam opposition . . . to the God ordained institution of African slavery." The editor spent fourteen columns and two full pages to prove that J. R. Graves "animadverted severely on the institution of slavery in the presence of an eminent Baptist minister now deceased, and that he left Kentucky because of his opposition to Slavery." Around 1844, Graves had closed a school in Kentucky in which he was teaching and moved to Ohio on account of his opposition to slavery. He told John Waller the reason for his move. Those who became privy to the story considered Graves "unsound on the slavery question" and thus in no position to claim loyalty from Southern Baptists for his personal enterprises. "We know the adroitness of Mr. Graves," the editor warned, and "his effort will be to waive the issue that he has made." But can he say that "he was opposed to slavery, and denounce it at one time, but is a great friend now to the South?" Should he do so, it will not relieve him from the proven fact that "he has been opposed to Southern institutions—that he did express his opposition to slavery to an eminent Baptist minister of Kentucky." What confidence can be placed in one when "it is shown that in the hour of her extremity, he turns his back upon her and seeks an asylum from her institutions among her bitterest enemies"?[11]

It comes as no surprise that *The Baptist* carried a defense of Graves's loyalty to the South by denying that he ever said any such thing as reported by Waller and that he was not "unsound on the Slavery question." To seal the question as to Graves's soundness on this issue, the guest editor, J. M. Pendleton, published a letter recently received when the accusation became public. The correspondent wrote that he knew Graves as well as any person alive, and he knew him to be "as much opposed to abolition sentiments as if he had been born and raised upon the largest cotton farm in the patriotic State of South Carolina."[12] Loyalty to the South, and any of her institutions, including denominational ones, meant loyalty to slavery.

About the time Graves left the South, in supposed deference to his conscience on slavery, P. H. Mell, a thirty-year-old professor of ancient languages at Mercer and eventually a leading voice in the Southern Baptist Convention, produced a piece that shaped the tone of Southern discourse on this subject and helped create a new Baptist orthodoxy of the South on slavery.[13] Some loyal Southerners, beaten down by the moral outrage of the abolitionist rhetoric, had begun to capitulate and consider slavery "a burden and a curse." It was something that "gladly would she get rid of" if she could do so "without inflicting greater mischiefs than those which she would attempt to remove."[14] In opposing this state of affairs, Mell resurrected a manner of argument presented by Richard Furman twenty-two years earlier.[15]

Mell, following closely the reasoning of Furman, believed concession on this issue intrinsically erroneous, morally and methodologically. Furman had warned against it, saying, "To pious minds it has given pain to hear men, respectable for intelligence and morals, sometimes say, that holding slaves is indeed indefensible, but that to us it is necessary, and must be supported." Such policy would never do and should be unacceptable to any Christian. Nothing intrinsically immoral— theft, falsehood, adultery, murder—can be negotiated as temporarily necessary. "Had the holding of slaves been a moral evil," Furman had reasoned, "it cannot be supposed that the inspired Apostles, who feared not the faces of men, and were ready to lay down their lives in the cause of their God, would have tolerated it, for a moment, in the Christian church."[16]

Mell regretted the spirit of capitulation on the part of Southern political and religious leaders to the idea that slavery was intrinsically evil, a burden and a curse to be dropped as soon as possible, and seethed against the air of moral superiority promoted by Northern abolitionism decrying slavery as an awful crime and its perpetrators as "ruffians unworthy the countenance of God or man."[17] Mell proclaimed that the time had come to confront antislavery declamations with rational argument in defense of the proposition that "slavery is neither a moral, political, nor social evil." He invoked the scriptural regulations on slavery as proof that slavery was not immoral in itself. Slavery is recognized, sanctioned, regulated, and neither directly nor indirectly forbidden. It does not have an immoral tendency. He was willing to be found in company with the patriarchs and the apostles when standing before the adjudication of the Lord on this issue.[18]

Interacting mainly with the arguments of Francis Wayland, Mell countered accusations that slavery tended toward selfishness, pride, anger, cruelty, and licentiousness.[19] None of these vices is the product of slavery per se any more than they are the product of any legitimate social relationship. "If the mere possession of authority has this influence, how proud must parents and teachers be." "To my poor apprehension, it would seem that slavery has a tendency to counteract rather than cultivate selfishness." "If it is asserted that there is gross and beastly licentiousness to be found in the slaveholding States, I admit it; but if the charge be that there is more than in the non-slaveholding, I deny it, and defy any one to prove it."[20]

As a political evil, slavery tended to prevent the accumulation of national wealth, opposed the supremacy of the laws, and hindered the increase of public intelligence, so Wayland cast the argument.[21] Mell objected strongly, summarizing Wayland's objections along with other Northern arguments as contradictory and equally repugnant to the factory system of Northern cities. Rather than being politically disadvantageous, slavery "tends to promote public order" and there is no evidence that its presence diminishes the public intelligence. While Rhode Island, Philadelphia, and Massachusetts have had to call in the militia to control the Whiskey Rebellion, Shays' Rebellion, and riots in Philadelphia, there is little social disturbance in the communities of the South.[22] As far as the social influence of slavery is concerned, it produces a society that is more friendly, dignified, frank, openhearted, polished, and hospitable. Slavery, therefore, not only is not an evil, but is a positive good.[23]

The time has come, Mell believed, for "the southern people to maintain the system of domestic servitude by argument as well as by other means." It is advantageous "both to the white and the colored race; and, until it becomes a pecuniary evil, so long as we have the Bible, our reason, and our independence, we expect to maintain it."[24] Not only did Mell believe that slavery was neither a moral, political, nor social evil, he believed that "slavery has not been an evil to the negroes themselves." In their moral, intellectual, and physical condition they far outstrip the condition of their race in Africa. In addition, the slaves of the slaveholding states are in a condition far superior to that of the freedmen of the emancipated British possessions or of the workers in the "mines, workshops, factories, farms and palaces of 'The Fast-anchored Isle.'" Also, the slave is better off "than are his brethren in the non-slaveholding States of this confederacy." He is better off in his religious advantages—"There is not one of our three millions of slaves but what enjoys the same sanctuary privileges that his master does"; in political condition—"Let me be a slave a thousand times over, rather than *such* a freeman as the New England Negro"; in pecuniary advantage—in the squalor of the living conditions of blacks in the North "we have completed a picture wretched beyond anything that has been imagined by the most 'downtrodden slave' in our midst."[25] Mell thus not only defended slavery as a just system but celebrated its advantages for the African who had been placed in an Anglo society.

In 1852, E. T. Winkler, who would be invited to the first faculty of the Southern Baptist Theological Seminary, wrote an editorial for the *Southern Baptist* expressing the same viewpoint promulgated by Mell. In spite of, or perhaps because of, the existence of slavery, the South, rather than being degraded morally, had attained a laudable moral high ground and had seen wonderfully demonstrated the transforming power of the gospel. The system had been abused early in its history as the relation of capital to labor, adventurous colonists forcing the labor of "idolatrous savage captives." Its development, however, has shown the "power of Christian civilization." The African slave has been brought immeasurably above his progenitors, light has come into his beclouded mind, he has learned art and the skill to practice it, and "while his native tribes are still votaries of Fetishism, it has imparted to him the priceless gift of true religion." Slavery has a self-correcting and recuperative power, and the people of the South must move on to "perfect their own institution."[26]

Those who have taken the time to study the situation as it is, rather than believe the fantastic reports of the outdated and uninformed, conclude that "the slave population had reached a higher degree of comfort, progress, and religious welfare, than any other race of equal numbers, so recently brought from savagism."[27] They are more honest and law-abiding than any comparable group of "the servile classes of white people" in any country. More divorces occur in Rhode Island than either voluntary or forced separations in any three Southern states among the slaves over a comparable period of time. Should the reality be reduced to the science of statistics, "there would be found to be more real poverty, vice, unattended sickness, and heartrending misery in its manifold forms, in the four large cities of Boston, New York, Philadelphia, and Baltimore, than in all the fifteen slaveholding States."[28]

The virtues of slavery, its evangelistic success, and the superior moral condition of the South continued to be a major theme of the Southern self-evaluation. Sooner or later the "abolitionist excitement will spend itself from its very vanity." Though they fancy themselves as heroes and liberators, by their invidious agitations, they are the real enemy of the slave. "The real friends of the black race are the people of the South." So prejudiced and ruled by passion, however, are the minds of the abolitionists that they deny their own heritage of high development of the powers of observation and the philosophy of human understanding. The South clearly transcends the North in this power, for they have cultivated their understanding by reading solid literature and are temperamentally less excitable, less impulsive, less susceptible to the machinations of the mass meeting.

"We can see nothing of good, and only evil," a Southern spokesman wrote, "coming from this persistent, gratuitous and offensive aggression on the South." The South resents it. The theology of antislavery has ruined the pure gospel of the evangelicals who have too long taken their cue from the humanitarian gospel of the Socinians.[29] Mell also viewed abolitionism as a harbinger of theological decline. He insisted that "more than one thousand Baptist churches are more engaged in denouncing the 'sin of slavery' than in preaching 'Christ and him crucified.'" In like manner, they emulate the "Neologists of Germany" who "apply the knife to the sacred scriptures, with a freedom limited only by their inclinations." The newly enlightened moralist feels justified in declaring obsolete biblical passages unpalatable to his advanced ethical standard and also in declaring "what should be engrafted upon the remainder to supply the deficiencies of bible morality."[30]

The professors of the seminary accepted this defense as normative. Slavery proved the most adaptable means to achieve an equitable arrangement for the greatest happiness of both races. Slavery served as a discipline necessary for the stability of society while allowing ample opportunity for the civilizing powers of the gospel to permeate an uncivilized sector of society. The faculty believed the abolitionist spirit was misguided and misinformed at best and insurrectionary and heretical at worst. Like their contemporaries who offered analyses of slavery in the Baptist papers, they believed the abolitionists had no eyes to see and no ears to hear the truth. In the census of 1860, all four faculty members are listed as owners of slaves. John A. Broadus owned two, ages sixty-five and seventeen, both mulatto, one male and one female. Basil Manly owned seven, ranging in ages from three to thirty-seven, all black. It appears that this was one family with the youngest being three-year-old female twins. William Williams owned five. Four, a man, woman, and two children, were listed as mulatto, and one, a one-year-old, as black. James P. Boyce owned twenty-three slaves and seven slave houses. There were nine females and fourteen males, eleven mulatto and twelve black ranging in ages from two months to forty-seven years.

The unanimous observation of Boyce's treatment of his slaves is that he was not only kind but solicitous of their welfare. His daughter Lizzie recorded for Broadus an intriguing account of Boyce's responsiveness to the needs of his servants. "My Father was always exceedingly kind to his servants," Miss Boyce wrote, and "never failed to greet them when returning home after an absence on some trip. His manner towards them was always considerate and kindly." She recalled how he helped them, even after emancipation, with many matters of personal and domestic interest such as balancing their bankbooks and giving advice as to how to save their earnings. One servant "had been my mother's maid, being a gift from her father on the eve of her marriage." Miss Boyce described her as "a handsome mulatto about twenty years of age at the time." She fell in love with a servant on a neighboring plantation, a man who had been trained by his master as an expert builder. Marriage was out of the question "unless father would purchase the bridegroom. The price for the man was $3,500 and father had not the least need for him." To gratify his female slave, however, he paid the purchase price for the young man, and, in addition, he "bought a large box of most expensive tools." The couple moved to Memphis after the war and worked diligently to give their children an excellent education. When Boyce and Manly went to Memphis for a convention meeting, they "were visited by this woman, who invited them to take dinner with her. They accepted and she received them with pride and joy, seated them at a well ladened [sic] table and waited on them herself."[31] Boyce found deep satisfaction in continuing relationships, even friendships, with his former slaves.

Slaves were property obtained or inherited legitimately, and were to be listed as taxable capital along with bank stock, railroad stock, horses and cattle, pianos, gold watches, gold and silver plate, and pleasure carriages. In 1863, according to the War Tax Assessment, the total worth of slaves in nine of the Confederate states, excluding Tennessee and Alabama, was $1,247,536,541. Boyce and his colleagues, however, believed they were worth much more; they were sinful men and women, in need of redemption, and Christ had died for them. They endorsed John L. Dagg's reasoning that the "benevolent design of Providence in bringing the sons of Africa into bondage in the United States" should be regarded "as a stupendous missionary movement, accomplishing more in the evangelizing of the heathen than all the missionary operations of Christian churches throughout the world."[32]

Broadus fully concurred that "Providence has brought millions of heathens to our doors, and to a very great extent prepared them to our hand." God should be thanked for such an opportunity, and the South must not fail in this stewardship. None can doubt the necessity of this task and the "obligation to provide religious instruction for those who form so important and so sadly neglected a portion of the community." It can be "easily and effectively performed." It certainly provides no greater challenge than the apostle had in preaching to and instructing the Corinthians. They must be treated firmly but gently as children, be given information from the story sections of Scripture rather than the didactic, and must be engaged with unusual fervency in order to indulge their "enthusiastic nature as well as their ignorance." Personal sacrifice and conscientious attention to this opportunity "for others' good, will hardly diminish the benefit these exercises afford."[33]

When Boyce edited the *Southern Baptist*, he carried a series of articles encouraging missions among the slaves. Boyce assured his readers that the writer of the articles was "no encourager of anything in the shape of abolitionism" and that the matter of instruction to the slaves was "no longer a problem." The First Baptist Church had established a school for "the colored portion of the congregation" and as a result "genuine and intelligent conversions are taking place among the scholars." Among the children there is much religious interest and "the Spirit of God plainly manifests his presence both in his convicting and converting power." In light of this success, "who can deny the importance of providing means for religious instruction to the slaves?" No planter should rest until this has been arranged for "his negroes." No one can estimate the value of even a partial acquaintance with the Bible. "Who knows what effect for eternity the knowledge of the plan of salvation may have? A soul saved is worth all the labor, all the toil, all the expense, which is now expended for the whole South in missions among the blacks. Of how much more value is the salvation of thousands."[34]

Secession Brings Seminary Cessation

On the day that the South Carolina legislature opened its meeting, December 17, J. W. Jones wrote Broadus that the Foreign Mission Board had decided not to send out any new missionaries under appointment, which included him and Toy. He added, "I suppose you will be in a foreign land in a few days." On December 20, after three days of discussion, by a unanimous vote the South Carolina legislature dissolved the union between South Carolina and the other states of the United States. By December 30 South Carolina troops had seized all federal military property—Fort Moultrie, Castle Pinckney, and Fort Johnson, each of which was located on an island in Charleston harbor—with the exception of Fort Sumter at the entrance to Charleston harbor. Broadus summarized the feeling that pervaded the seminary as well as the state:

> The presidential election occurred when the session was but a month old. Then promptly arose the great Secession excitement in South Carolina, and we went about our daily tasks beneath dark and stormy skies. . . . The students almost all remained throughout the session, and they and their instructors strove to study faithfully. But you could hear nothing on the streets, or in the homes where the students boarded, save excited political discussion. Well might it be so, for the times were big with destiny.[35]

On the issue of secession the faculty was divided. Boyce strongly opposed secession, and Broadus at least equally so. Williams strongly supported secession, and Manly mildly so. "Neither that nor anything else," Broadus reported, "has ever caused the slightest jar among us."[36] For a brief time, even after the precipitous action by South Carolina, hope remained that some compromise could be arranged, recognizing the sovereignty of the states on the issue of slavery. Such hope receded into hopelessness as secessions continued with Mississippi leaving the Union on January 9, soon to be followed by Florida, Alabama, Georgia, and Louisiana. On 4 February 1861 in Montgomery, Alabama, the six seceding states established the Confederate States of America with Jefferson Davis elected as provisional president. Texas immediately followed in approving by popular vote an action taken earlier by the legislature.

On 4 March 1861, Abraham Lincoln was inaugurated as the sixteenth president of the United States. Within two weeks he decided to send relief and subsistence supplies to Fort Sumter and notified South Carolina Governor Francis Pickens. The Confederate secretary of war instructed General Beauregard to demand the evacuation of Fort Sumter. Brigadier General Pierre G. T. Beauregard, who had studied artillery under the tutelage of Robert Anderson at West Point, now informed his former instructor that he would began firing on the fort at 4:30 A.M. on April 12. On April 14, Major Anderson and his garrison left the fort and boarded a ship for New York. This led to Lincoln's declaration of a "state of insurrection" and the call for a militia of seventy-five thousand men to subdue it.

Hesitant Virginia now responded on April 17 and seceded from the Union by a vote of 88 to 55. This vote showed a state deeply divided on the issue and made the pro-Union faction hopeful that secession could be resisted. The northwestern counties organized in favor of the Union, and by 20 April 1863 Lincoln had announced that a new state, West Virginia, was to be formed out of those counties. On 20 June 1863, West Virginia became the thirty-fifth state in the Union with Wheeling as the capital. The tensions and divisions in Virginia gave rise to feelings of fear, resentment, deep confusion, and readiness for battle on both sides. Broadus's brother, J. M. Broadus, wrote him about his perception of the situation on 27 April 1861:

I am not a secessionist—the word angers me now—but I am a Virginian. Virginia in the Union, if men were wise enough, unselfish enough, virtuous enough to appreciate and preserve a union, is my favorite idea—but if Virginia cannot belong to the Union without servile degradation from the Northern aggression and domination, then I am for Virginia and nothing else at present. . . . We are wild with the idea that Lincoln has insulted—threats of vengeance for our offers of peace; and we may be called fully united in a determination to see him through. And before the New York "Tribune" has the pleasure of apportioning the beautiful lands of Virginia among the wretches to whom he has promised them there will be such a carnage as the world has never seen. . . . I must try to bear the humiliation of belonging to the Southern Confederacy under the force put upon me by the North. We cannot stay with them, therefore we turn the other way.[37]

The Confederate Congress declared on 6 May 1861 that a state of war existed with the United States. Boyce and Broadus went together to the Southern Baptist Convention, 10–13 May 1861, at Savannah. They visited Fort Sumter on the way down and other sites made famous by the recent conflict, and on ship from Morris Island to the mainland encountered a violent storm that Boyce quite enjoyed because of his love for water and his skill as a swimmer. Broadus was terrified and bargained with the black boatman to save him if the boat capsized. "Enough must be promised," Broadus explained, "and yet not too much, or the boat might be helped in going over."[38]

At the convention, a resolution was passed that a "committee be appointed to recommend such vital changes in the Constitution and minutes as may be necessary, growing out of the recent formation of the Southern Confederacy."[39] J. P. Boyce presented the report of the Foreign Mission Board; Broadus was supposed to preach the convention sermon, but was too ill and was replaced by J. H. McIntosh. Robert A. Baker noted, "The Southern Baptist Convention meeting in Savannah in 1861 issued a strong declaration justifying the formation of the Confederate States of America."[40] The president, Richard Fuller, appointed a committee to bring a report "On the State of the Country."

After a discussion that placed the blame squarely on the Union States for the looming bath of tears and blood, and lamented the spectacle of churches and pastors in the North "breathing out slaughter, and clamoring for sanguinary hostilities with a fierceness which we would have supposed impossible among the disciples of the Prince of Peace," the report called the convention to "utter its voice distinctly, decidedly, emphatically" in the adoption of ten resolutions. Resolution 2 stated the cordial approval of "the formation of the government of the Confederate States of America." Resolution 4 stated, "We most cordially tender to the President of the Confederate States, to his cabinet, and the members of the Congress now convened at Montgomery, the assurances of our sympathy and entire confidence. With them are our hearts and our hearty cooperation." Other resolutions blamed the North, invoked divine direction, justified the "good work of repelling an invasion designed to destroy whatever is dear in our heroic traditions, . . . sweet in our domestic hopes and enjoyments, . . . essential to our institutions and our very manhood; whatever is worth living for or dying for," pledged prayer for the Southern army, prayer for the enemies that God would grant them a "more politic, a more considerate and a more Christian mind," recommended days of fasting and prayer for the aversion of "calamities due to our sins as a people," and recommended that "these resolutions be communicated to the Congress of the 'Confederate States,' at Montgomery, with the signatures of the President and Secretaries of the Convention."[41]

Broadus knew Boyce's convictions on the nature of the church: "Dr. Boyce discouraged anything of the kind, and through life he always strongly opposed the interference of religious bodies, as such, with political affairs."[42] Boyce had such a view of the spirituality of the church that he felt any professions of a peculiar political alignment by churches or those organizations that were a direct expression of their mission violated the biblical standard of the church's mission. Neither the body, nor the place it met, should be put to uses other than those that God has ordained—"separate them from all other purposes than those for which they are designed." The church is for the worship of God, to unite in prayer and praise, where "the penitent shall draw nigh confessing his guilt" and the pardoned "will here give utterance to his exceeding joy." God shall be worshiped, by the power of the Spirit, in spirit and truth through the proclamation of the gospel of

Jesus Christ. In this context the sanctifying of God's people occurs, and the final abode of God among his people is constructed. "Each stone is fitted for its place by the workmanship of the Spirit, the messengers of God are daily gathering them to their places. The time approaches when the work will be completed and the King of Zion shall enter to take up his perpetual abode." The church thus transcends all national interests, and the endorsement of a particular political strategy has no warrant from Christ's instructions to his church.[43]

Boyce was not averse to participation in patriotic duties as a private citizen, however, and did all that lay in his power to seal the success of the attempt to establish a new nation. He showed his spiritual concern for the Confederacy by encouraging the chaplaincy. J. William Jones wrote him on 23 May 1861 thanking him for the "kind letters and for the very material aid you rendered me in my application for the chaplaincy." Jones knew the "life of a chaplain will be a toilsome, and dangerous one" but had accustomed himself "to be unmoved by hardships when they beset the path of duty." He would enter on his duties "with a firm reliance upon God's promised help and a firm determination not to be carried away by the excitement incident to the camp, but to preach the Gospel." He mentioned the confusion in Virginia concerning the vote to ratify the vote of the Legislature: "It seems to be the general impression that V[irgini]a will be invaded at several points with a view to defeat the vote on the secession ordinance but our people are determined to vote if they have to pull trigger with one hand and deposit their ballots with the other. And if an Abolition army does invade our soil every man capable of bearing arms will at once take the field."[44]

Boyce sought to absorb the implications that a state of war would have for the future of the seminary in general and for his students in particular. The immediate implication would be the opportunity for ministry. "The field of labor is increased," he told them. "The threatening circumstances of war have occasioned this. Multitudes are away from home in immediate peril of life. These require the faithful warnings of such as would wean them from the temptations of the camp, and teach them the way to that home to which alone perhaps shall they ever go."

In light of the encroaching likelihood of death for many in the immediate future, Boyce encouraged his students to go to the army as distributors of books. Perhaps others might even find opportunities as chaplains. Others could preach in churches that were in need as a result of their pastors' entering the army or following their sense of duty to preach to the troops.

The war presented the minister of the gospel with the opportunity to remind the new nation of the necessity of reliance on God; perhaps an awakening of massive proportions would accompany the birth pains of the new Confederate States of America. "The people that rest on Him will not be disappointed," Boyce reminded the seminarians. "This reliance upon God you may aid to inspire, and thus in a humble, perhaps an entirely unknown sphere, may be doing more than a mighty army to secure final success." The advances in their own piety would be enormous as they felt the presence of God's blessings on their sacrificial labors and as they felt more keenly than ever the proper motivation for such labors—the glory of God in the salvation of souls. They must not forget, however, that the change in labor from continuous study to arduous activity would be only temporary, for they must return to their studies in the fall to complete the course to which God's call had obligated them.[45]

From Georgetown, Kentucky, Andrew Broaddus wrote Boyce that so much confusion reigned in Virginia that he hesitated to take his family there. But the same circumstances prevailed in Kentucky. Kentucky was less likely to become a battleground than Virginia, but the situation was volatile nevertheless. The Union partisans received "arms from Lincoln, with which, as they say, to prevent any set of men from precipitating the State out of the Union." Southwestern Kentucky talked of seceding and joining Tennessee, but the Unionists say they will have to "fight their way out." Both North and South would join the fray and Kentucky despite her pretensions to neutrality "would be deeply involved in the fight." Broaddus believed that Lincoln would duplicate his action in Maryland and Missouri and "station men at different points." "I am anxious to get out of the State," Broaddus confessed, "that I may mingle with a people who show sentiments more congenial with my own. But scarcely know what to do."[46]

Trying to make progress with all the confidence he could muster, Boyce sent a letter to the trustees on 25 November 1861. The trustee meeting in May had not gathered a quorum but decided to do business anyway and then ask for approval by mail. The letter asked for the approval of new trustees for several states. In addition, the letter asked for confirmation of an action "to appoint the Faculty of the Seminary with the members of the Executive Committee to locate the place for the future building and to purchase the lot. Also to prepare plans for the buildings."

Most of the trustees wrote approving all the actions, but W. B. Johnson saw one problem. He disapproved of the appointment of the faculty as members of the executive committee to locate the place for the future building, and to purchase the lot. Disagreements of opinion on the board concerning location convinced him that the board should form a majority of the committee appointed to fix the location. In addition, "The state of things in our country in May last . . . nearly six months since differs very materially from the present; & forbids the attempt to fix the location of the Seminary & purchase the lot now." Also, the "diminution of the students in number does not now call for the measure." In recognition of these facts and his own inability to speak with certainty "of the state of the funds of the seminary in cash" and their sufficiency "to meet all the expenses of the Seminary" as well as purchase the lot, he believed that providence dictated a rejection of this action. Johnson's foresight proved prophetic.[47]

Though Boyce needed no information about the feelings in South Carolina, he was flooded with letters verifying his understanding of South Carolina independency. A seminary trustee, Iveson L. Brookes, wrote Boyce affirming the trustees' suggestions but clearly more eager to vent his disgust with the arrogance of the North. On a visit to Charleston, he "found the city in a state of much excitement from the threatened attack of the Yankee marauders." The Yankees plan to capture Georgetown, Charleston, and Savannah without much resistance, but Brookes prayed that "God will frustrate their nefarious designs against us." South Carolina, however, cannot expect divine blessing "if we do not develop the energetic resistance which the means God has given us may enable us to make." The enemies, "relentless and heartless," had given plenty of warning but the people were not sufficiently pre-pared. Even the governor was not awake to the danger. Most of the sixty thousand fighting men had gone to Virginia and "those at home seem all to want office!" He feared defeat and, as a result, especially severe measures since the enemy viewed South Carolina as the heart of the rebellion. "Christians should be importunate at the throne of grace for the interposition of divine protection at the approaching juncture of our struggle," Brookes insisted. He believed that the North-ern invaders, "those myrmidons of Satan," intended "to execute the insurrectionary commotion of our domestics against us" as the most likely, but nonetheless cowardly, way to subjugate the South. "I trust our people will prefer extermination rather than be subjugated by the ruthless dynasty of Yankee fanatics & infidels whose object long has been to degrade us below the status of our slaves."[48]

By November 1861 Boyce had decided that the seminary could function for a while without his presence. Only twenty students had enrolled for the session. All courses could be taught by the remain-ing three faculty members. His friend C. J. Elford had urged him to become chaplain of a new regiment of volunteers from the Greenville District, and he felt it his duty to comply. Boyce's movements would be strictly in South Carolina so he could maintain contact with the seminary. In December he wrote about his deep feelings of tenderness as he contemplated their imminent movement to the "brunt of the battle." "You cannot know how tenderly my heart yearns over them," he wrote, especially considering how many "must go unprepared into the presence of God." He felt like preaching all the time if he thought he could accomplish more that way, "but alas for the unwillingness of men to hear the gospel." One senses his own feeling of urgency when he wrote, "Oh, that God might aid me and help me in what I can do! It would be enough to bring multitudes to him. But I often wonder as I look at the indifference of men." One of the "half-witted" soldiers said in jest that they all should get converted before going to battle. "How fearfully true it is," Boyce commented.[49]

Frequently Boyce called on Broadus to send items to him by mail, by express, with other individuals coming to join the regiment, or with one of Boyce's servants. The instructions were given in great detail and involved a good bit of time, physical activity, and arrangement by Broadus. In addition to serving as chaplain, Boyce still had to maintain his guard over the finances of the seminary, his personal financial matters, and the work as executor of the Boyce estate. He also kept up with events in the churches and the convention, offering advice and seeking to affect decisions and movement when he believed it advantageous.

Following is a substantial sample of the detail in Boyce's instructions to Broadus: "Send down for me my horse. . . . Please send me also my two saddles and bridles. I am going to try to use him. . . . If Roberts cannot bring them send them by the cars to come through to Charleston without stopping and write me (the mail that leaves with the horse will do) care of Hayden and Whilden." "[A. E.] Dickinson sent me a box of tracts, etc. which my servants will get for you from out of the Bathing Room. . . . If you can put that atlas in a box with the tracts, etc., send the box to me. . . . But if not send the Atlas separately and send the box as it is. Put the Atlas in strong paper and send it by express as well as the box." "Again I have to trouble you. I wish you to send me a tin box which you will find in the left hand side of my iron safe. Take the key out and send it to me by mail. Then take the tin box and pack it inside of a small wooden box and send it down to me. I wish you to send my servant boy John down having it in charge. Tell him not to let it go out of his sight." "Let him bring with him one suit of clothes but two pair of pantaloons and two sets of underclothes. He need not buy anything which he has not already except a pair of thick shoes." "Stupid fellow [speaking of himself]. I neglected to say that you will have to get Sherman to open Elford's safe and get my duplicate key from the drawer inside. Then take the key and put it in the lock with the handle horizontal, the numbers of the key underneath as it then stands. Then with the thumb of the right hand press the left side of the key downward until you bring the handle perpendicular. . . . The door will then simply need to be pulled open. Leave the key in the lock until you have gotten out the box and then work the door to and simply bring the key back to the original position." "The lock of this trunk is somewhat curious. Before you turn the key you put the hasp in the hole by pushing down the little brass cover that hangs over the key hole, this fastens the hasp and then the turning of the key fastens it a second time. As to the safe key there are only eight ways in which you can attempt to put it in and it will go in only in one way. When you find it in then you can turn it only one way." "Should there be a fire and you have time *carefully* to take out all the papers and remove them do so, but if not if possible throw the safe out the banisters of the east piazza and have it pulled as far as the garden fence." "I would not give you so much trouble about this box but it contains many of my most valuable papers belonging to James and Ker Boyce which I daily find must be in Charleston and I am afraid to trust them to ordinary carriage." "The funds you have and those Manly has . . . please send to me. . . . I desire to invest them as fast as I can." "John has arrived safely with the trunk and contents. Many thanks." "Was laid up with lameness and on another occasion with an agonized jaw having had a tooth broken in it. . . . We had twenty five men with measles and no place. We succeeded in arranging for them. I suppose you have heard of the poor fellow who fell dead of apoplexy on dress parade two weeks ago. Though very dissipated before he had much improved in camp yet was still not such a man as to leave us any hope. Since then we have lost five others and I think I may say of them all that they had hope in their death. . . . My great trouble is my inability to see our men every day." "I would suggest that William T. Brantly is not our man," he advised concerning the need for a pastor in Greenville. In all candor, however, he opined, "Winkler would like a temporary position so would Kendrick, but I would prefer at once to call a pastor and take William D. Thomas. I do not think we could get Brantly. My only objection to Winkler is that he is as bad a pastor as Furman and if anything worse." "I send you on the next page an order for dividend on my gas stock. Send that also with the rest in a draft."[50] Broadus did his best to comply with all these instructions.

By March, the seminary was seeking a clearly stated exemption of ministerial students from conscription. Broadus informed Boyce, "We are in much anxiety about the application to the Governor and Council of which Manly wrote you. . . . If the students are not exempted from the draft, all that are now here, eight will leave Tuesday morning."[51] Boyce responded that in light of the situation commencement should be suspended and the session should end on May 1. George Hyde, the second full graduate, must wait "till the war is over" for his diploma. An announcement should be made, however, that the next session will begin on September 1. Boyce thanked the faculty for the kindness to him during his absence and especially to William Williams for teaching Boyce's class. "I shall have the comfort of knowing," Boyce reflected, "that at least one class ought to understand theology." He commented on Williams's extraordinary teaching gifts by saying, "What would I not give for his wonderful power to put things clearly before those he addresses."[52]

At the close of the session, with little prospects of opening in the next fall, Manly and Williams took their servants and moved to Abbeville District a hundred miles removed from Greenville where they rented plantations, produced crops, served churches as pastors, and sought to remain studious in their areas of instruction. Broadus remained in Greenville and began to preach in churches in the area. Boyce asked each to maintain his official capacity with the seminary and to be ready to begin whenever providence allowed. Boyce bought several years' provision of groceries for Broadus because of his accurate fear that the war would last years, not months, and staple goods would become scarce and, therefore, expensive. Boyce's foresight greatly aided the Broadus family in the difficult days ahead.

Efforts to Salvage the Confederacy

By May the demands of managing the estate had become so complex that Boyce had to resign his chaplaincy. James McCullough, who replaced Elford as colonel of the regiment, described Boyce's work as chaplain:

> Dr. Boyce served with us as chaplain while in this State, on the coast, in the winter of 1861–1862, at Charleston, Adams Run, Johns Island, and elsewhere. He was always found at his post of duty, and was highly esteemed and much loved by the entire regiment. They all had absolute confidence in his Christian integrity and manhood. He used to preach us some very able and feeling sermons. My mind recurs to one especially, where he had almost the entire regiment in tears. . . . I love Dr. Boyce very much, and

so did my men; and I believe the influence of his godly life was
felt by more than one.[53]

Before the scheduled opening of the fourth session in September
1862, Boyce wrote to G. W. Randolph, the secretary of war for the
Confederacy in Richmond, inquiring if the clause in the Conscription
Act excluding ministers of the gospel "does not also by fair construction exempt students of theology preparing for the Christian ministry."
He argued that it should be so, for if not, the theological seminaries
of all denominations would have to close and "the supply of educated
ministers to their respective denominations be entirely cut off." To
destroy such a supply "will be disastrous to the moral and religious
condition of the country. To continue it will scarcely weaken at all the
army of the Confederate States." The exclusion was not granted, and
the seminary could not open for the 1862 fall session.[54]

In spite of Boyce's conviction that the church should not position
itself according to the political systems of the world, he felt perfectly
justified as a private citizen in the deepest patriotism. His work as
chaplain had been one manifestation of this, but he now concluded
that more immediate involvement in the details of government and
finance was necessary. Accordingly he worked for the viability of the
Confederacy by an effort to secure its financial stability and even
worked for its ascendancy over the North, its enemy, in matters of
military strategy.

On the first count, Boyce ran and was elected to the House of
Representatives of the State of South Carolina in 1862. He devised a
scheme for the purpose of giving stability and credibility to Confederate finances. He proposed a bill and served as chair of the committee
that recommended the bill for adoption to guarantee the validity of
Confederate bonds through state endorsement. Boyce, in this bill,
sought a remedy to the large and increasing circulation of Confederate treasury notes that was creating rampant inflation. The attempt of
the treasury to reduce the amount in circulation by funding portions
of it in Confederate bonds had failed in large part. "The object of this
endorsement would be," Boyce advised, "to give the Government all
the advantages to be obtained by uniting State security to that offered

by the General Government." These securities would be offered to the entire country by "public advertisement to the highest bidder" with South Carolinians given preference at equal bids. The state endorsement would greatly increase the value of and confidence in Confederate bonds. "Our government," Boyce admitted, "is still looked upon as an experiment, which may prove a failure." How could it not be liable to such a suspicion when composed of states that had so recently broken with the United States? The individual states, however, "are regarded as permanent, and their existence, under all circumstances, considered as certain." Boyce then specified the amount of guaranteed funds that would be most advantageous to the Confederacy to help absorb the excess, or redundant, treasury notes still in circulation.[55]

One week later he wrote his wife that he had met Mr. Semmes of Louisiana, a senator in the Confederate Congress. As chairman of the committee of finance in the Senate he was "very much pleased with our bill on Endorsement and spoke very kindly to me on the subject."[56] The bill was passed by the South Carolina legislature on December 18 but had too many instructions as to how the sale of the bonds would be arranged. It passed again in a different form in January 1863.

> Sec. 1. Be it enacted by the Senate and House of Representatives, now met and sitting in General Assembly, and by the authority of the same, That the Governor for the time being, whenever application for such guaranty shall be made to him by the government of the Confederate States of America, be, and he is hereby, authorized and directed to endorse the guaranty of the State of South Carolina upon the Bonds of the Confederate States of America [to be hereafter issued] according to a plan to be adopted by Congress, to the amount of thirty-four millions four hundred and eighty-two thousand seven hundred and fifty-eight dollars, sixty-two and two-twenty-ninth cents, being the proportionate share of the sum of five hundred millions of dollars, according to the representation of South Carolina in the House of Representatives of the Confederate Congress, the representation of the States of Missouri and Kentucky being omitted in the calculation.[57]

Boyce also informed his wife, whom he addressed as Lizzie, that he had taken stock in the old *Nashville*, renamed the *Rattlesnake*, a boat to be used in the war effort against the Union. It had been designed "to go out as a privateer after California steamers. We expect to do a great deal of harm to the Yankees," he continued, "and also to make a great deal of money." Certainly they would run very great risks, "but the steamer is very swift and will do a great deal of damage before she can be caught." Not only would the partners in this enterprise get one half from the Confederate government of all that they captured, "we will make a good deal in catching gold on the way from California."[58]

At the same time Boyce wrote his wife of success and future strategies, Broadus read the news about the passing of the bill and penned his congratulations and compliments to Boyce with an urgent warning. "If eloquence consists in speaking so as to carry your point," Broadus remarked, "you must have been eloquent." It is plain that Boyce had "at one majestic step risen to a position of the highest honor" and was now reputed as the leading man of the House. Broadus also was pleased "not merely as your friend, but as a minister," and for the sake of the seminary. A preacher can show practical wisdom when he puts his mind to it, and Boyce's accomplishments, when peace comes, will "put the Seminary clearly ahead of the others." "You have doubtless been told already," Broadus continued, "that such capacities for public usefulness ought to be permanently devoted to the public good." Broadus wanted to remind Boyce of his true calling and value, so exhorted, "My dear fellow, don't listen to it." Boyce had a call to "bring theological science into practical relation to this busy world." If he is spared and peace returns, "this Seminary which was founded by your labors shall yet shine in conspicuous usefulness."[59]

During the war years, Boyce along with the faculty worked to keep some degree of vibrancy in denominational life among Southern Baptists. The Foreign Mission Board had found any forward action virtually impossible. When Union troops occupied Nashville in 1862, the Bible Board became inoperable. At the Southern Baptist Convention in 1863, Boyce served on a committee that recommended the abolition of the Bible Board, since the city had fallen into the hand of the enemy. Funds intended for that benevolence should be distributed to the Foreign Mission Board and the Domestic Mission Board.

Actions of the Union Army toward ministers of the gospel and church property steeled the commitment of Southern Baptists to the Confederacy. A committee on the "State of the Country" reported that recent experience had "only strengthened our opposition to a reunion with the United States on any terms whatever." Sharing the views of the South in general, the committee declared, "We have no thought of yielding, but will ever render hearty support to the Confederate Government in all constitutional measures to secure our independence." Several resolutions followed, the seventh of which acknowledged sad news: "we have just heard with unutterable grief of the death of that noble Christian warrior, Lieut. Gen. T. J. Jackson; . . . we thank God for the good he has achieved, and the glorious example he has left us, and pray that we may all learn to trust, as he trusted, in the Lord alone."[60]

On the demise of the Bible Board, the convention endorsed the founding of the Sunday School Board. Robert A. Baker recorded that "Basil Manly, Jr., introduced a resolution calling for a committee to look into the need for a board to promote Sunday Schools," and wrote "in most eloquent language" (employing the rhetoric of war training) the first argument for the Sunday school movement among Southern Baptists.

> All of us have felt that the Sunday School is the nursery of the Church, the camp instruction for her young soldiers, the great missionary to the future. While our other benevolent agencies relate primarily to the present, this goes to meet and bless the generation that is coming, to win them from ignorance and sin, to train future laborers, when our places shall know us no more.[61]

Manly argued that all accepted the idea of Sunday school as good, that such a project fit well within the constitution of the convention, that one board for the denomination would be far more efficient than individual Sunday school societies in the states, and that Baptists should do it and not wait on other denominations to join. Manly urged "now" as the most propitious time and appealed to the future stability of the Confederacy as dependent on their immediate actions. "There are more orphans and destitute. There are more ignorant and neglected. These must grow up to vice and ruin—must poison the very fountains of our young confederacy—must infect the moral atmosphere in which we and our children shall live, unless [we take] early and vigorous efforts." After the war will be too late to act. The battle rages not just on the fields of war, but in the homes and souls of those left behind.

> It will be a thing worthy for our children to remember, that in the crisis of this great revolution, in the very blood of our birth as a Confederacy, we are careful to think of and provide for the religious nurture of the children that are growing up; and that while thousands from our Churches were swelling the army of independence, their children at home, and the fatherless and destitute, were not left neglected, but that a noble and generous plan had been set on foot, for taking our part fully in training in knowledge and piety, the future citizens of our land.[62]

Manly recommended, therefore, that the convention establish a board of the usual number of members to be called the Board of Sunday Schools of the Southern Baptist Convention. The board would be charged with making all the necessary arrangements for the ongoing ministry of benevolence. To facilitate this immediately, a committee of one from each state was appointed to recommend a suitable location and nominate the board.

Manly became first president of the Sunday School Board with its headquarters in Greenville, South Carolina. Broadus came alongside him in the work as corresponding secretary in the fall, and together they engineered a marvel of efficiency and productivity in generating a great variety of literature for Southern Baptist churches. One production was a monthly periodical entitled *Kind Words for the Sunday School Children*. This endured for the ten years of the Sunday School Board, became the foundation for a larger series of educational materials during the time the Home Mission Board managed Sunday school work (1873–91), and continued under the new Sunday School Board until 1929.

For the summer months, before he became connected with the Sunday School Board, Broadus served as a chaplain to the Thirteenth

Virginia Infantry. Revival began to take place during those months, and Broadus preached frequently and effectively until his throat gave way in the middle of September.[63] He also worked on his commentary on Matthew. On May 28 he wrote Manly about the work of the Sunday School Board with the information that "Boyce's catechism is in the printer's hands." A report from the Sunday School Board in 1864 lists Boyce's catechism as one of its publications. The notice summarized the vital information: "*A Brief Catechism of Bible Doctrine*, by J. P. Boyce contains twenty lessons, suited to children of ten or twelve years, and upwards. It brings out the 'doctrines of grace' and the views of Baptists. Of this, 2,500 were issued in June, 1864, and 7,500 more in September, of which about 2,000 remain." Ten thousand of these catechisms were in print within a four-month period in 1864.[64]

Boyce, participating as he could in those denominational concerns, at the same time continued his efforts to stabilize Confederate finances. A fall of the Confederacy would crush Southern Baptist benevolent enterprises. He entered into correspondence with C. C. Memminger, secretary of the treasury for the Confederacy. "I have read with much interest your letter of December 26," Memminger responded to Boyce, "and find that our views do not differ so much as you seem to think." Memminger proceeded to explain his strategy in stabilizing the Confederate economy, part of which involved the "sales of State guaranteed bonds" to enable the government "to call in any redundancy." He promised to send Boyce a printed copy of the report that he would present to Congress. He asked for Boyce's aid in getting the states to agree to guarantee to "purchase up and hold the whole war debt." Along with Boyce he believed this financial policy had great advantages. "I will be much obliged to you for your views at any time," he told Boyce, and informed him, "I received and read your speech with much pleasure." He was "much rejoiced" that God had raised up "another helper in this most difficult and laborious department."[65]

In compliance with Memminger's request, Boyce appeared on 1 April 1863 before the legislature in Georgia to explain the financial concept of the several states securing the Confederate debt. He explained in detail, much as he had explained in South Carolina, how the scheme proposed would remedy the radically insecure situation of Confederate finances. The attitude of other countries, particularly Europe, toward the States is fundamentally different than toward the Confederacy: the former are seen as stable and permanent, the latter as not yet secured and intrinsically transient. The Confederacy cannot stabilize its finances apart from state endorsement of bonds, and without stabilizing its finances it cannot survive. Families left at home will be unable to afford food, clothing, and shelter, and the soldiers will leave the armies in order to care for hearth and heart. But with state endorsement, the worth of the Confederate currency can even approach par, that is, be virtually equal to the amount of gold and silver (specie) that would constitute the same face value, stabilize the entire financial infrastructure, and thus keep the armies in the field.

Boyce answered seven objections normally proposed to this theory: the bonds would be sold to a few favored individuals; the scheme would centralize power in the Confederate government; Congress would fail to arrange for the debt, leaving it to the states; there is not enough capital in the country to retire a $500,000,000 debt; bonds must be sold at a depreciation in sales abroad; state credit will be hurt; and the measure "will alienate capital from allegiance to the Confederacy, and lead them to desire reconstruction." From each of these objections Boyce removed the substance, but particularly emphasized the emptiness of the last: exactly the opposite was the case. The traitor does not want to see the debt secured. The scenario Boyce envisioned occurred exactly as he said, when, as Lee attempted to defend Richmond, the ranks of the army were depleted by soldiers returning home to care for families on the verge of starvation.[66]

> The spirit of our people is such that the States will be worth nothing after the war, if we do not succeed. We will be ruined rather than fail. Those who will be in the States after such an event will be the Yankee hordes who will occupy the soil on which we have perished. This debt would be repudiated by them. But let our finances be ruined—let food and clothing continue to advance, until our soldiers find their families are starving and naked—they will return to attend to that first of all duties, to provide for their own households. Then will demagogues arise to counsel reconstruction. Until then, never, never; and we can avert that period; only selfish, traitorous capitalists

will wish it. Patriots will in wisdom try to prevent its coming, with its fearful array of famine, desolation and destruction.[67]

Within the week, Boyce received correspondence from Memminger thanking him for the "able and satisfactory manner in which you have discharged the trust confided to you." He also informed Boyce of some details concerning the Currency Act about which Boyce had asked. To Boyce's enquiry about other financial activities, Memminger responded on April 15 that a cotton arrangement with a French firm had gone much better than anticipated. He explained that he and "the committee" felt that five-year bonds at 8 percent were sound at home, but also included the concession, "But as to six per cent bonds to be negotiated abroad, your views are undoubtedly correct, and I will endeavor to carry them out." He also referred to a political reality that signaled the failure of this attempt at stabilization. "I look upon the concession of our friends in Georgia to refer the matter to the people as equivalent to an acknowledgement that the guaranty cannot be had from the Legislature. So that we shall have to leave Georgia for a future effort." As a matter of policy, therefore, Memminger continued, "I do not propose to act upon the guaranty of any one state until the others concur—or until after a refusal to concur a state may still be willing to act, an alternative which I cannot reasonably expect."[68]

Perhaps because of the greatly distressing events of late spring and early summer 1863, these matters were dropped and the state guarantee of Confederate bonds failed. Lee lost at Gettysburg, Vicksburg failed, control of the Mississippi River was lost, European interest diminished severely and rapidly. Memminger wrote Boyce on 31 March 1864 expressing his concurrence with a viewpoint that Boyce had expressed about some puzzling financial decisions of the Congress. "I have been embarrassed," he confided, "during my whole term in office by being obliged to administer plans which I neither originated nor approved." He had endeavored to pursue measures to "prevent a redundant currency." He reviewed a series of decisions that had violated his understanding of sound financial policy, including one about which he concluded, "Its flagrant injustice would provoke severe criticism in quiet times." He disclaimed responsibility for any of these measures, but, at the same time, did not "feel at liberty to abandon the post which I providentially occupy, so long as I think I can be of service."[69]

Meanwhile, in August 1863, Boyce had run for the Confederate Congress, obviously hoping to promote there the financial viewpoints that he thought would salvage the Confederacy. His opponent was an experienced campaigner and politician, Colonel James Farrow of Spartanburg, South Carolina. Broadus, in a letter rich with information about troop movement, injuries, and his efforts at preaching, reported that some of the South Carolina troops "spoke warmly of their desire for your election, and said the soldiers would vote for you, certain." Some ministerial brethren expressed regrets at Boyce's entering politics, "but have withdrawn them after my explanations." Broadus assured them and others that Boyce would be perfectly fit for entry back into the work of the seminary subsequent to the extraordinary demands of the current conflict.

Boyce responded to some of the concerns Broadus expressed about the defense of Charleston, and also wrote about the political campaign, "I am deep in it, have appointments to speak daily from Tuesday next until the first Monday in October." The legislature had to make provision for the election and that would not occur until after the next session in November. "The fact that I am a preacher is run against me hard—one is doing his most to defeat me and has done me great injury." He still believed his chances good, and probably would soon meet his opponent in a debate. "I do not think he will do much at it as I do not feel inclined to let him dodge and the *facts* are *facts*." He knew Farrow to be experienced at this sort of interchange and he was inexperienced at it. "I confess to you," Boyce wrote, "that I am not much pleased at the idea of an excited contest. I have chosen however to speak to the paper as the best means of enlightening them on the progress of our money matters and Farrow has chosen to reply." Farrow and his friends had been very active, but Boyce seemed content to say, "If beaten I will have done my duty. If elected I will stick to do it but I fear the success more than the failure."[70]

Boyce was defeated in the election. He eventually continued his political involvement, however, as aide-de-camp to Governor A. G. Magrath and held the rank of lieutenant colonel. He served as a member of the Council of State, was consulted by the governor, and was acting provost marshal in Columbia at the time Sherman captured and burned it. Sherman claimed that it was burned by retreating Confederates when they set on fire an abundance of cotton piled in the streets. Boyce, however, claimed to have been the last confederate to leave the city as the invaders entered. The cotton had not been fired when he left on 17 February 1865. On the next day Charleston fell into the hands of the Union.

Boyce made his way with the governor to Charlotte and from there, mostly by foot, to Greenville.[71] Soon after he arrived there, federal troops in pursuit of Jefferson Davis encamped at Greenville and took advantage of the time to disarm the city and to enrich their take of spoils from a soon-to-be-defeated enemy. The Boyce house offered a strong temptation. The census of 1860 had listed the value of his real estate at $123,000 and the value of his personal estate at $330,000. The Boyce dwelling, ample in its yards and impressive in its stateliness, soon attracted a group of soldiers in search of jewelry and money. They burst open closets, rifled through wardrobes and trunks, stole the horses and plundered the house, "flinging everything about, in the wild search for precious things." Looking for jewelry and silver that they had been told were there, and unable to find any, they held a gun to Boyce's head and demanded, under threat of death, the location of the treasures. Boyce replied that he had sent them all away the day before with his brother and could not tell them where they were because he did not know. He instructed his brother simply to leave with the treasures and not tell him where he went. After many threats, they finally were convinced. They left, taking everything they could, including "the wonderful warm overcoat in which Boyce had so carefully wrapped his invalid friend five years before." Another group found the bank, discovered a brick wall behind which specie was hidden, destroyed the wall, and stole the specie. Broadus remarked, "Ah, they were old hands. Walt Whitman ought to have written a so-called poem in their praise."[72]

After a series of surrenders from April 9 to May 4 and the capture of Jefferson Davis on May 10, the armed conflict was at an end, the Confederate government existed no longer. Lincoln was assassinated on April 14, and Whitman did write a poem in his praise. The Union was saved, but its preserver was lost.

> O Captain! My Captain!
>   Our fearful trip is done,
> The ship has weather'd every rack,
>   the prize we sought is won,
> The port is near, the bells I hear,
>   the people all exulting,
> While follow eyes the steady keel,
>   the vessel grim and daring;
> But O Heart! Heart! Heart!
>   O the bleeding drops of red,
> Where on the deck my Captain lies,
>   Fallen cold and dead.[73]

The question now for Boyce was, would the seminary fall cold and dead?

6

The Struggles
of a Phoenix

*T*he endowment for the seminary, so promising in 1859, had itself fallen cold and dead. Confederate money invested in Confederate bonds—gone with the wind. Unpaid subscriptions were worthless for no one had any money to pay. Antebellum investments could not possibly be collected because businesses were bankrupt. The situation was desperate.

Getting a New Start

Included in the overall discussion among the faculty members at this time had been the possibility that Boyce would go into business and support the seminary from his profits, "paying the faculty salaries." Initially, Boyce would lend money to each professor to be repaid when the seminary was once again able to give the professors their salaries. Manly considered this proposal from the vantage point of every imaginable contingency, given the overall horror of the Southern economy and infrastructure. The important point, however, even with some intrinsic dangers was that the seminary's "prompt reestablishment secures the institution for the churches of the country with all its boundless possibilities for good. And we are committed and pledged to it, not only by being its representatives before the public, its active officers, but also by having received our salaries during the war." Even with all the hazards involved for them all, "In short, if there is a reasonable probability that Boyce's generous advance can be refunded by the Seminary, in a reasonable time, we ought to try it, otherwise not."[1]

Other factors involved stock held by the seminary that still had value and Boyce's volunteering a contribution of $1,000 though still uncertain as to the value of his own estate. The stock, $5,000 worth of Georgia Railroad stock given by H. A. Tupper, brought $3,878 and probably saved the seminary's existence at this point. With little possibility of money, and the likelihood of few students, the faculty met in the summer of 1865 and surveyed the unpromising situation. Broadus described the poignancy of the meeting:

> He [Boyce] pointed out that our Seminary, which after years of effort made so hopeful a beginning, had no small hold of confidence and affection of the Baptist people in several states, and so might possibly keep alive; while if it were abandoned, a whole generation or more must elapse, and we be all in our graves, before brethren would have the heart to attempt again the establishment of a Common Theological School. We had prayed over the question, again and again. Presently some one [Broadus], said "Suppose we quietly agree that the Seminary may die, but we'll die first." All heads were silently bowed, and the matter was decided.[2]

Boyce knew that the cause was not lost. God still called men to preach, and they still needed theological education. Prophetically, in November 1864, he had received a letter from J. B. Richardson. Richardson requested a catalogue of the Greenville Theological Seminary and asked, "Is the Seminary in operation at present and is it probable that it will continue?" He wondered if a regularly ordained Baptist minister could be a student with no liability to conscription. Richardson, a single twenty-five-year-old man, had graduated from Wake Forest in 1861. He served as pastor of four churches and in two of them had baptized sixty-eight persons. He was indigent, nevertheless, and needed aid if possible. Most of all, "I am anxious to take a theological course." He believed that was essential for his future usefulness in light of the "magnitude of the glorious work, and the great demand for faithful and efficient Baptist ministers, who can advocate Christ's cause, and will dare maintain it." Presently he felt inefficient. Boyce could hardly turn a deaf ear to that kind of voluntary testimony.[3]

With little ability to advertise and few papers operating to carry notices, the seminary opened in October 1865, eventually reaching the number of seven students for the session. By January, one of Broadus's two students in homiletics, Mr. Getsinger, had to return home under financial constraints, leaving only Mr. Lunn, a blind student, who could gain no advantage from the reading of texts. Broadus's lectures, therefore, were more full and detailed than would normally have been the case. "Really," he wrote his wife, "it is right dull to deliver my most elaborate lectures in homiletics to one man, and that a blind man." From the lectures in that session came the foundation of the book that would appear five years later, *On the Preparation and Delivery of Sermons.*[4]

George Hyde, a full graduate of the seminary just before its close for the war, wrote Boyce with an accurate analysis of the difficulties Boyce faced in beginning the school again. He also referred to the general declaration of amnesty and pardon for Confederates issued by Andrew Johnson in May 1865. A Methodist friend had informed Hyde that the seminary was again in operation, and he had also seen recent notices in the *Religious Herald.* "Please allow an old student and steadfast friend to congratulate you upon the recommencement of your blessed labors," Hyde wrote, and so shortly after "the collapse of our government and finances." The entire denomination should be grateful. "But I saw an omen of this," Hyde continued, "when you were 'pardoned' by his excellency Pres. Johnson." In asking about the endowment he surmised, "I greatly fear that you have lost it all in common with our other schools & colleges." Hyde had lost his health with bronchitis and could not preach, but even if he could, the new state constitution as a provision of reconstruction "forbids southern men preaching. Many of our brethren stand indicted for this grave offence, & others have been imprisoned."[5]

Boyce wrote a series of letters in the spring of 1866 to his friend H. H. Tucker to be published in the *Christian Index*. He analyzed the economic conditions and, in spite of the widespread devastation and debilitating poverty, he noted several items indicating the first vibrant signs of a recovering economy. He believed that the political situation would improve under Johnson and was convinced that the radicals would be defeated in the upcoming elections. "During the interval that has elapsed since I came North," he wrote in March, "I have had some time to look around at the political prospects of the day. One thing I think may be set down as certain. The President's policy will prevail. The radicals will be defeated."[6] Both predictions failed.

In April Boyce described the conditions of several South Carolina towns including Greenville, Columbia, and Charleston. In light of Sherman's attempts to exculpate himself from the burning of Columbia, Boyce gave an extended narrative of his personal knowledge of the events surrounding the "firing" of the city. In spite of distressing conditions Boyce saw the churches as doing good work to restore the spiritual as well as the material stability of the people. "I think upon the whole, that the Baptist cause in Charleston is quite prosperous," Boyce pointed out. Other denominations also worked energetically, and "it is cheering to see, while our people have begun to repair the material desolation around them, that they are also laboring with equal zeal to build up the walls of Zion."[7]

Boyce was appointed by President Johnson to serve on a committee to write a provision in the new state constitution for South Carolina abolishing slavery. His version of the provision was adopted. Some friends urged him to seek election to the United States Congress but he refused. Creditors connected with the New York business, from which Boyce had withdrawn before the war, found within a legal technicality a way to make him responsible for the entire debt. "I am at present lying *perdu* at this point," he informed Broadus. "The truth is that some of my creditors are very violent and I have begun to lose all hope of a settlement with them." He could prognosticate the final result, but knew that some misperception of both his debt and his holdings in

Greenville led them "to suppose that I have property which I have not."
He had plans he hoped would alleviate the issues, but could not be back
to resume classes until "Monday after the 4th Sunday in November."[8]
Through his business expertise and awareness of another legal aspect
of the contract, Boyce managed to arrange for payment of one-third of
the debt. Broadus commented, "The considerable sum which he agreed
to pay occupied much of his attention for several years, and drew heavily upon what remained of his estate."[9] Other parts of his estate Boyce
used as collateral to obtain loans for salaries for the professors. This
hindered his using collateral for himself to stabilize his estate.

The constant challenge that faced Boyce now was putting the seminary
on a solid ground financially. He faced not only the anti-institutional,
anti–formal training bias of many in the Baptist constituency, not only
the Landmark zeal against the seminary, but the very real financial devastation of a South under Civil War destitution and Reconstruction
privation. He felt little hope for substantial aid from brethren in the
North, though he maintained good friendships with a number of individuals. Overall their attitude was oppressive and manifested a sense
of superiority. They did not trust the South to be able to deal with "the
negroes," and in their clumsy attempts at raising the spiritual prospects
of the former slaves gave a mission field to Unitarians and Universalists,
folks most unwelcome in the southern Zion. Boyce observed with some
energy and perhaps a bit of outrage:

> The whole South is occupied as a vast missionary field, by Unitarians,
> Universalists, &c, and others of that kind whose hearts never rose to
> the mission work, before, and have seen men perishing around them
> and yet have done naught. Is it mission zeal in these, or is it political
> feeling, or worse, is it actual hatred of the South? Those who come
> to spread the gospel, and not these heresies, are more welcome, but
> let them well consider what manner of spirit they are of. If Christ be
> preached, though it be of contention, we shall rejoice; but we fear,
> nay our certain conviction is, either that Christ will not be preached
> at all, or if preached, it will be so mixed with political evil, that the
> good that is done will be completely overshadowed by the evil.[10]

The present was dark and the future formidable.

Real consideration was given to closing the seminary after the session in the spring of 1866. All depended on the advice given and the response to the needs of the seminary at the Southern Baptist Convention in Russellville, Kentucky. Broadus wrote his wife, visiting in Charlottesville, "See Uncle William and say that I earnestly hope he will find it practicable to go," for the fate of the seminary will be decided there. "The enterprise must fail," he confessed, "unless there is a vigorous effort on the part of its special friends." One week later he mused, "Made my last lecture in homiletics today. Quite possibly it will be the *last* indeed."[11]

In Russellville, Boyce's appeal was able to procure over $1,200 in cash and over $10,000 in subscriptions to be paid in five annual installments (much of which was never paid). Boyce wrote to Tucker at the *Christian Index*, "It was one of the most delightful meetings I ever attended. It was an exceedingly able body—as much so probably as has ever gathered together at the South. Every thing was pleasantly conducted, and the liberality of the brethren exceeded all expectations. Over ten thousand dollars was raised in bonds for the Southern Baptist Theological Seminary, and one-half of this was from the States which have suffered severely by the war."[12] This removed the cloud of certain failure from the seminary, secured it for the immediate future, and, at least in Broadus's estimation, "insured the success of the institution."[13] Boyce wrote, "There is no longer any doubt that this Institution is to be sustained with its full corps of four Professors." The convention had provided many words of encouragement, and the "liberal contributions" there and at the General Association of Virginia soon following "show that the brethren are fully resolved to make the Seminary go."[14]

Boyce began, therefore, to argue his case again in the Baptist papers. Through the *Biblical Recorder*, the state paper of North Carolina Baptists, Boyce sought students. Many young men who have found their life calling to be the ministry, Boyce believed, "would have their lifetime usefulness greatly increased by spending some time at the Seminary." Their knowledge of Scripture would increase, and they would be "saved from solemnly declaring a passage of God's word to mean something which in after years they find it does not mean at all." Tools for proper interpretation are given at the seminary. At the beginning of one's ministry one should gain a knowledge of the whole field of revealed truth so as not to push one truth to an extreme in conflict with another truth. What is more important than gaining a clear view of "those great doctrines of Scripture which form the subject matter of all our preaching?" Sermon preparation and pastoral duties can be greatly enhanced with experienced guidance. Some men do not know of this opportunity, and others do not have the finances. The brethren and the sisters, therefore, must look around for these men and "encourage them to come to Greenville."[15]

James D. Hufham, the editor of the *Biblical Recorder*, had received a secondhand report that Boyce stated in Virginia that the seminary "brings forth the laborers who are to teach the Gospel throughout the land." He felt this was absurd and questioned the fitness of the seminary as a legitimate place of training for Baptist ministers. Boyce immediately wrote him and asked for space to deny the charge and explain what he did say. Hufham returned an answer: "Your communication which has just been received, will appear in next week's Recorder accompanied by editorial remarks to remove any injurious impressions which might otherwise result from the article in a previous issue of the paper." He acknowledged that he did not think Boyce could have made so absurd a statement "as the reporter attributed to you but it appeared in the Richmond Dispatch and again in the Herald, I think, and I was quite sure it would damage you and the seminary in the estimation of many excellent brethren." He assured Boyce of his esteem for the seminary and of his desire to "aid it to the full extent of my ability." He was in favor of all institutions that would save the South "from Yankee subjugation, moral, intellectual, and spiritual."[16]

Boyce's response corrected the false impression with playfulness but straightforward clarity. "So you think me a heretic on the subject of theological education," Boyce opened his article. "Well you might had I uttered the language imputed to me." Hufham seemed a bit defensive at Boyce's approach, wondered why he had not bothered to correct the false attribution before Hufham published it, and felt Boyce should be grateful for the "opportunity and occasion to set himself right before the denomination." In order to set himself right, Boyce explained what he said, set it in context, and affirmed that only the Spirit of God makes ministers and only the church sets them aside. He added his appeal for taking advantage of the opportunity for training in the doctrines of God's Word and affirmed the duty of "every man to seek all means by which he can preach Christ better." The seminary, he believed, offered the most effective and efficient means to this worthy end. He was sure no one could attend the seminary for just one session without "great advantage to himself" and to the interests of missions and the churches. Having cleared himself of heresy on the point in question, Boyce encouraged his readers to "stir up the churches to send called men," as the professors were very anxious to have plenty of students, and "to do as much good in this way as we can."[17]

Boyce also began to publicize the school as environmentally healthy, easily accessible, and stable socially. An article in the *Western Recorder*, written by invitation, described the location of the school by latitude and longitude and gave a thorough analysis of how easily accessible it was from any point in the South. Also, contrary to some impressions about South Carolina, it was very healthy, not in a swamp at all, but in a mountainous region "surrounded by three fourths of a circle formed by the Blue Ridge Mountains, which are about thirty miles distant." It is diversified in its production, not at all dominated by cotton, and has "a large number of manufactories." There are a "small negro population" and a large white population, an abundance of churches, especially Baptist churches, and several other "institutions of learning." The Baptist church, by far the largest congregation in Greenville, was served by W. D. Thomas, who had been "eminently successful, and has secured the love and affection of his people for his devotedness and Christian simplicity." The church itself had just passed through a season of revival. The environment, therefore, in the seminary culture was in every way salubrious.[18]

A second article renewed Boyce's defense of theological education, especially the kind provided at Greenville. Sufficiently chastened, however, in the exchange with Hufham, he was careful to note that education could be gained in ways other than seminary enrollment. Boyce gave a brief history of education for ministry among Baptists from the Philadelphia Association to Columbian College. Much that

Baptists did, however, in giving education to ministers made them less effective than the Baptist ministry had been fifty years before. This is explained by the type of literary education given—"it was not perceived that the education mainly desirable was education in the Word of God"—and this type of education, because of its high literary expectation, excluded from the ministry many who had no capacity or opportunity for that kind of collegiate course. The grand error, therefore, of previous attempts at training was the omission of theology. "The true theory," Boyce believed, "in accordance with the scripture and with the history of our pulpit, is rather that which seeks after instruction in theology as first of all in importance."

This theory of education presupposes and exalts, "first of all, the feelings and devotion of the heart—not only piety—but a piety that longs to speak of Jesus, and to win souls to Him." This is the "most effective power." Second is "a proper knowledge of God's Word." All other knowledge is subservient to this, the increase of knowledge of divine truth and the ability to communicate it. If this is primary, the evils that have hindered ministerial education will be eliminated. "The founders of the Southern Baptist Theological Seminary have proceeded upon this theory." Those with and those without formal literary training are taught in the same classes, creating an edifying atmosphere of mutual respect between the two types of students and giving fullness to the preparation of both—personal warmth of affection and zeal for God in league with disciplined attention to the biblical text and its doctrinal importance. A man should get all the education that providence will allow him, but none should forgo a thorough knowledge of the Word of God and its important doctrinal connections. "How many errors, how many schisms, how many weak Churches, how many lost souls, are due to an imperfect knowledge of the Word of God by him who is set forth to teach it!" With the conviction and passion that led Boyce to forsake worldly wealth and position for the sake of the seminary he wrote:

> You will see, therefore, that I am a strong believer in Theological Education. I am convinced that every preacher should have it; either by himself from the Bible and good books, or through the aid of

225

some brother minister, or at a theological school. It is not hard to say which of these is best. The latter furnishes several ministers with different subjects, divided out for special study and instruction; and, it is to be presumed that, at least, on the majority of subjects taught, the best instruction can be obtained at the Seminary.

For those who cannot spend time in college but have one, or perhaps two years for preparation and "whose hearts are fired with a desire to labor for Christ, I earnestly urge that they study theology." If possible, "Come to our Seminary, . . . and spend one, two, or three years." If you cannot come, then get some willing brother to help you; if that is not available, then do it yourself as our fathers did. "They familiarized themselves with the Bible, and Gill and Andrew Fuller, and they made good and effective preachers."[19]

Bonds, Agents, and Begging

Boyce continued his relentless work for both immediate support and long-term endowment. He traveled to Baltimore, Richmond, Missouri, Kentucky, taking so much of the work on himself because of the expense of hiring agents. He maintained the unshakeable conviction that the seminary was right and would be a key to the revitalization of churches, as well as the culture, of the South. The periodic indications that others shared his conviction tantalized Boyce just enough to drive him forward. Rufus Burleson, president of a Baptist college in Texas, wrote to Boyce about a young man of "rare talents for preaching" whom the people called "Spurgeon." What would it cost "to sustain him at Greenville one year?" He mentioned "another of equal promise we await to send you as soon as we drill him more in the rudiments of education." The faculty had moved "from Independence to the city of Waco five years ago. We have every prospect of a great central Baptist College for Texas."[20]

From Pine Bluff, Arkansas, W. M. Lea wrote that the area needed preachers, for the war had made most move away. He wanted men of "godly morals and piety," intelligent and of "social disposition," preferably single, who would come to "this great missionary field" that once had wealth but now had little hope even of pay. "Talk not of Foreign fields while there is so great destitution here." Remember, he must be a real "Baptist, no milk and cider about it. The time has come when Baptists should be consistent with their profession."[21] Boyce's disposition exactly.

Though he had great sympathy from many people with affirmations of the necessity of the seminary, few could help monetarily. George Lorimer emerged in Kentucky as a supporter. He requested Boyce to preach regularly in Louisville on his trips there and promised to canvass the membership to find possible donors. Andrew Broaddus believed in the sincerity of Lorimer, noting that he "affirms his deep interest in theological education and says he wishes that he had had such opportunity." Broaddus, however, was sick and would be delayed in getting started back on his agency. J. W. Jones refused an agency because he was in such demand for protracted meetings. He loved the seminary and "would most gladly do anything in my power to promote its interests." He was the only Baptist preacher "within 30 miles of here in two directions, within 60 miles in another and within 100 miles in another direction." If Boyce failed to get an agent, Jones gladly promised to "represent you at the Albemarle, Goshen and Valley Ass[ociati]ons and will work for you as hard as though I were a paid agent."[22]

Boyce also asked the noble and erudite A. M. Poindexter to serve as an agent. Poindexter had been energetic and insistent in his support of the seminary and even had been elected to the faculty in the initial stages of formation. His estate had been obliterated in the war and two sons had been killed, one by an "accidental discharge of his own pistol, and the other at the head of his company, by a bullet of the enemy." Poindexter had to refuse as he must stay with his farm and also comfort his wife in the "loss of our dear boys." He was happy that the seminary had reopened and that Boyce had "so far preserved your means as to be able to assist the brethren, your colleagues."[23] Poindexter still managed to attend the Southern Baptist Convention.

Strangely, J. F. B. Mays emerged from the shadows of the war with the same indomitably presumptuous spirit that had driven him earlier. "I have labored here in N. C. as a missionary until I am sick of it &

finding the climate does my wife no good," was the first line in a letter to Boyce. He continued with talk about theology books, his intent to write a tract on the call to ministry, the need to sell or swap for his farm in Alabama, and a request: "Will you give me a string to pull at to get away from here?" For emphasis he rephrased his meaning later, "Will you simply give me your best thots, as to the best course to pursue for the sake of usefulness, Self-culture & financial gain?" Nine months later he made himself available to Boyce as an agent for the seminary. "I will in the ordinary Providence of God be able to go to work for the Seminary by Xstmas probably before; as my wife's condition now seems to warrant the hope that I can leave here by that time." He informed Boyce, probably in answer to an earlier query, "I suppose with great care and warm dressing I can go safely into Ky. You know my feelings for the cause." And then as a P.S., "I write this in the event you still need me."[24]

Mays went to Kentucky for the seminary. In November 1866, he wrote Boyce that he would be ready by the first of January, when he would be able to board his wife and children.[25] In January 1867, George Lorimer wrote Boyce, and informed him about the delicacies of the agency in Louisville, saying, "Bro Mays visited a few brethren, but was unsuccessful they pleading the hardness of the times, and the gloomy prospects ahead." Mays was perplexed and asked Lorimer for advice.[26] From Washington in March, G. W. Samson wrote, "Bro. Mays* [*Is that his name?] came to my house one night, supped & slept, & disappeared next morning before breakfast. He said he was on his way from N. Car. to meet you in Louisville. He was absorbed in inquiries about Hamilton's Metaphysics."[27] Three days later Mays wrote, "I transmit with crushed feelings 37 dollars after expenses, salary etc. . . . The high water and unheard of weather explains why I've done so little traveling, but if ever on this earth I've exerted myself, it has been in Ky. My determination is only greater than before if possible. . . . I feel deeply for you for I know that this report is chilling your hopes. I still feel I will succeed. Are you all praying for my success?"[28]

In April Mays informed Boyce who were friends and who were enemies in Kentucky, mentioning the continuing labors of J. R. Graves against the seminary as well as those of N. M. Crawford, the recently installed president of Georgetown College, who had served as pastor of First Baptist Church, Charleston, at the time Boyce was baptized. "The secret harm Dr. C. & G are doing to the cause is known to God only," Mays related, as they "are hunting up all the rich places" in Kentucky for "the strongest Landmark preaching." He described the multiplicity of machinations devised against the seminary by these men and gave the warning also that "Lorimer at heart opposed to us too." Others he called "pretenders."[29]

About the time this less than exhilarating news reached Boyce, he was preparing for the spring 1867 commencement. W. D. Thomas, the pastor of the Greenville Baptist Church, reported the event. Boyce's message reflected something of the desperation of the moment as well as resignation to the possible vanity of all his efforts. He reviewed the history of the founding of Southern, its initial promise, the decline of hope to gloom in the recent war, and ventured the surmise that "but for the war, the Seminary would be now enjoying the highest prosperity and usefulness." Should the present extraordinary circumstances cause its failure now, "enough had been done to show how in ordinary times its principles would successfully operate."

Boyce proceeded with material that he had used often and would draw upon several times in the future, giving biblical rationale for education even for those called and prepared by God. History from the first century to the present, including Baptist history, approved education for the called and also showed the errors and pitfalls of certain types of education. Boyce, clearly needing the widespread approval of Baptists, noted that "the hearts of the pious had always been in unison with" the principles established at the seminary. Secular learning had been "subordinated to theological," and different grades and varieties of instruction had been offered so as to exclude none that were earnest in their desire for improvement of knowledge in the Scripture. Earnest and pious people always had found a way to improve their gifts and calling. With both logical power and deep feeling, Boyce set forth "piety as of all qualifications the most indispensable and the most valuable for the minister" and urged the graduates to cultivate it throughout their ministry.

The observer of this message "could not help wishing that very many of our brethren from the different states had been present to hear it." Then in a word that was bound to have been more encouraging than Mays's correspondence, the writer noted, "If I had been indifferent to the Seminary, I should have been converted into a warm friend to it by what I saw and heard on these occasions. May God give the Institution an abiding place in the affections of our people."[30]

Mays stuck it out in Kentucky, for on June 8 the *Recorder* announced, "Bro. Mays, as agent of the Southern Baptist Theological Seminary is now making an effort to enlist the sympathies of our brethren in behalf of this object, and secure their pledges; and I hope he may receive such a response as its merits deserve." The writer, George Hunt, believed that this work was not of secondary character "but one with which our best interests are intimately associated."[31] The unsolicited article pointed to the need for theological education among the Baptists done in a Baptist way and commended the seminary as well adapted for that purpose. Hunt briefly reviewed the founding of the school, commended its faculty, and urged his fellow Kentuckians to support it wholeheartedly. He reported on trustworthy authority that "Brother Boyce, who is regarded as one of the finest financiers in the South, has been offered within the last two years, two positions, which he declined, either of which would have been worth $30,000 a year." Before the war he was wealthy, and contributed "to different objects of benevolence not less than $200,000."[32] He would personally give the seminary a firm basis now if he could.

He could not. By April 1867, in view of the solemn correspondence from Mays, Boyce saw clearly that the bonds of 1866 were not producing the needed income. Payments were tardy or utterly delinquent. Boyce advertised that he would have the bonds at the Southern Baptist Convention meeting in Memphis and informed people how they could pay. "Punctual payments," he reminded, "are earnestly requested as we are sadly in need of the money."

This diminishing hope for income led Boyce to make another sort of appeal to the Baptists of the South. On 1 July 1867, he sent out requests for contributions. Using a mailing list provided, at least in part, by J. J. Toon, proprietor of the *Christian Index and Southwest-*

ern Baptist, he sent one appeal designed for the ladies and one for the men. Boyce, always sympathetic to a woman's disposition, appealed to the ladies' instincts of compassion in describing the needs that the professors had for food and clothing for their families. He explained that the endowment "was either paid to us in confederate money or is still due by parties not able to pay us." Boyce had raised $50,000 payable in five-year bonds, but the professors' needs were immediate. They had refused larger salaries, paid punctually, to remain at their present posts.[33]

To the men, he pointed out that the South needed a self-supporting institution to train Southern men for Southern pulpits. He described all the inviting features of the school: its curriculum, the content of its courses, and its teachers. "The truth is," he urged, "as has been universally acknowledged we have just exactly the school needed by our churches for the best training of the ministry. And we have but this one and it must be sustained." He explained the loss of the former endowment, the present situation with the bonds, and stated frankly, "I have concluded therefore, to write to each of our more liberal brethren and ask a small sum for this present emergency. We must have ten thousand dollars by 1st of September or our professors must suffer."[34]

As returns began to arrive, Broadus wrote Boyce, "The returns do not strike me as highly encouraging." Broadus believed that some refusals from the North came because "they are afraid of being considered southern sympathizers." Many of the refusals came with words of sympathy and encouragement and an explanation that nothing was available for donation. Broadus acknowledged each one who sent a donation, a writing task that took from two to four hours per day. Boyce and Broadus learned about conditions and attitudes all over the South in the responses to this request. An old friend, J. R. Kendrick, sent a donation with the word of hope, "The present crops of the South will put a different aspect, I fondly hope, on all your affairs."[35] Thomas Porter expressed happiness at being able to support "truth and a pure gospel" but feared the rule of the tyrant over South Carolina as well as "the humiliation and danger of being placed under the control and government of the Negro."[36] Another, D. B. Deland, gave $50 from himself and two others, with regrets that he could not do more. He deprecated "most sincerely the mad & wicked fanaticism that is now ruling & ruining our once prosperous and happy land."[37]

J. William Jones, Adiel Sherwood, and Joseph Baker expressed their desire for the well-being of the school and sent what money they could. Jones forwarded a gift from Susan Parks, one of the poorest members of his church, who "supports herself and an aged father by her needle—and yet she always has something to give to every good work."[38] Sherwood, highly regarded in antebellum Georgia as a major contributor to the growth of denominational benevolences, told Boyce that St. Louis was "too much anti-South to subscribe to them in this city." He wanted a copy of Broadus's "highly extolled speech," and also asked, because he had conflicting reports from Northern men, what would happen to the Baptist meeting houses "taken possession of during the war."[39] Joseph Baker, former editor of the *Christian Index*, reminded Boyce of Baker's long-term editorial support of, even when other prominent men opposed, the idea of a common theological seminary, but he regretted that "so far from being able to afford the pecuniary aid you seek & need, I am as dependent upon a merciful creator for my daily bread as are the ravens." The war left him destitute, and now at seventy years of age he hoped "hereafter if life be spared, to be able to support my family by the labor of my own hands."[40]

M. S. Forsyth wondered where Boyce had obtained his name and how he knew that he was not "a persecutor of Baptists like a great many of the Northern people are." He was, in fact, "a Baptist and will forever defend their cause, and do all I can to break down the strongholds of infidelity and skepticism and build up our beloved Zion." Another, Cordelia Mansfield, sent a contribution with the plea, "We greatly need faithful ministry here, and seldom have Baptist preaching in our neighborhood."[41] D. Bartley wrote of his great sympathy for the cause of the South but also that he was "opposed (you will think wrongly) to theological schools for preparing young men, or others, for the ministry," and thus could not conscientiously contribute.[42] Another, however, who had only seven dollars, sent five and also, if God so willed in the present season of blessing in their church to call his five sons to gospel ministry, would "commit them to your charge with inexpressible pleasure."[43]

Thomas J. Truman sent the requested five dollars because "Your school is the only one I am willing to recognize as a legitimate work for our churches as churches." He lamented the lavish waste of money on the so-called Baptist Colleges, where "we can conveniently secularize our educated ministerial talent and thus deprive the world of their labors for Christ." Going beyond the preparation of training for preaching the gospel, Truman opined, is "getting wiser than our master," a haughty labor that "brings evil, and only evil, and that continually." He did not approve of such education, but did of the seminary because he believed in "the power of the preached word, to spread the Gospel—and meet and crush all the isms—from Romanism to Campbellism."[44] Though a bias against theological education still survived, and money was distressingly unavailable, Boyce must have been encouraged that so many of the feelings expressed by the poverty-stricken Baptists of the oppressed South coincided with his own.

Seeking Stability during Transition

On 23 April 1868, Broadus wrote Boyce with a proposal suggested by C. C. Bitting, the corresponding secretary of the Sunday School Board. He mentioned the possibility of moving the seminary to Lynchburg, Virginia. A college building was vacant there on the edge of town. "Lynchburg is nearer to every part of our field, except South Carolina and lower Georgia," Broadus argued, "and would *feel much* nearer to Alabama and Mississippi because on the through line to New York." Other geographical advantages existed. This would give connection to "a strong Baptist population," and the seminary could become part of an expansive educational culture including the "University of Virginia, Washington College, and Virginia Military Institute, and with Richmond and Columbian College." Since Lynchburg was not Richmond, it would not seem clearly identified with Virginia interests exclusively, and the whole region of Virginia "is not strongly committed to any other denominational institutional." The town could provide work, literary advantages, and it is "white man's country." There was also a rich Baptist who had given some, but not nearly enough for Baptist causes. Bitting would visit with him soon to convince him that the time was propitious for him to "do a grand thing." Given certain other conditions about buildings and finances, Broadus indicated, "I should be in favor of going there. Think it over."[45]

At the Southern Baptist Convention of 1868 in Baltimore, several special meetings concerned the future of the seminary. Broadus said that new plans were discussed and great feeling exhibited, but he told the meeting frankly that "reliable arrangements must be made or I must resign this very summer." The next morning, May 9, the convention session was given over to the seminary. Broadus supposed that "we shall be sustained, but it is not absolutely certain." His hopes for a return to Virginia had been dashed, however, as he confided, "It is certain we shall not, for some years to come, remove the Seminary from Greenville." Verbal pugilism broke out between Poindexter, who had lost two sons in the war, and a Northern Baptist named B. T. Welch. Broadus remarked, "These old men are rather hotheaded and I fear some of the young men may catch the contagion."[46] When Welch left on the afternoon of May 11, the minutes record with no hint of the previous failure of decorum, "The convention was addressed in a Christian farewell by our venerable brother, B. T. Welch, of New York, who was about to leave for his home."[47]

The Sunday School Board, now five years old, faced a crisis, but in the meanwhile had abundantly demonstrated its usefulness to the churches of the convention as "indispensable to the completeness and the success of its work." A committee recommended its removal to Memphis, Tennessee. Broadus summarized, "Sunday School Board moved to Memphis after somewhat hot debate, Boyce and Graves." The minutes show a lengthy debate over this recommendation that lasted through the morning of May 11 and well into the afternoon. Jeter, Manly, Connor, Mills, Troughton, Burrows, Boyce, Mansfield, Jones, and Dodson all spoke in the morning. The afternoon saw a renewal of the debate with Mills offering a substitute motion and the issue then being engaged by Cuthbert, Broadus, Samson, T. G. Jones, Poindexter, Renfroe, Williams, Winkler, J. R. Graves, and others. The debate was suspended for the farewell speech of Welch. Upon its resumption Boyce submitted an amendment to the substitute motion, and, according to the minutes, "enforced it with an argument." The previous question was ordered and "the original report of the committee was adopted."[48]

One month prior to the meeting of the convention, R. B. C. Howell had died. Howell had served seven years at Cumberland Street Baptist Church in Norfolk, Virginia. In 1834, he moved to Nashville, where he revived First Baptist after a devastating Campbellite split. He labored there for sixteen years until 1850. For seven years he then served the Second Baptist Church in Richmond and returned in 1857 to Nashville. He had fought the anti–mission-society Baptists and the aspirations for dominance of the Landmark Baptists, particularly J. R. Graves, and Alexander Campbell and his followers. He was an early advocate and perennial friend of theological education and thus the seminary, and was listed as one of its trustees in the Act of Incorporation for the seminary when it was chartered by the legislature of South Carolina in 1858. For four two-year terms he had been president of the Southern Baptist Convention. In 1862 with the fall of Nashville he had been imprisoned by the military governor, Andrew Johnson, for his refusal to take the oath of allegiance to the United States federal government. James P. Boyce read the memorial to Howell at the convention, noting that "his biography is identified with the history of this body in all its trials, conflicts, joys and sorrows." Boyce said that Howell was "calm, logical and persuasive" as an author, and "evangelical, tender, and mighty in the Scriptures" as a preacher. He gloried in the "Cross as his only theme and chiefest delight." It was a privilege to be a fellow laborer in the cause of Christ.[49]

Howell was not the only faithful supporter of the seminary to fall in 1868. Basil Manly Sr., Boyce's first pastor, the first president of the trustees, and the father of one of the original faculty members, died in Greenville on 21 December 1868. Since July of 1867, he had lived in Greenville with his son. Boyce delivered a memorial discourse on December 22 entitled "Life and Death the Christian's Portion." He took advantage of the occasion to apply a comprehensive theological idea to the life and ministry of one saint.

The first half of the discourse consisted of a theological exposition of 1 Corinthians 3:21–22: "For all things are yours; whether Paul, or Apollos, or Cephas, or the world, or life, or death, or things present, or things to come; all are yours." Boyce explained why this life should be considered a blessing. Though it presently presses us down and we find the promise of joy attached only to self-denial, it still is a gift. It is a blessing because God enables the Christian to pass through it. With some exceptions, the pilgrimage seems to be essential. Many beneficent providences as yet unseen will be seen as ineluctable blessings. "Yet as in the Resurrection body the elements, however scattered, will be gathered together to consciously full identity, in like manner when God shall make plain all His works from the beginning to the end, the Christian will perceive the now unseen influences which have bound to this life of his all that has been, is, and shall be."[50]

Life is a blessing also in the content of its excellence in that we are moral and spiritual beings who can make God the chief end of our being. We are sanctified and drawn out into new moral dispositions by God and, incomprehensibly, our future is made to depend on our own actions here. "It is by this glorious co-working that in this life the Christian is enabled to live as becomes an immortal and moral being." None but God can thus control all things and still leave our development to us, uncontrolled. God's purposes "extend to every act, and word, and thought," and yet "every act, and word, and thought, is consciously the result" of man's own will as well as "of his previous acts." How we differ in degree from others we cannot discern here. But God marks every step with his own grace and takes account of every step as a point at which he will be able to say, or not say, "Well done, good and faithful servant."

Life also is the Christian's in that "he carries it with him in all its entireness into the eternal world. Not a particle is left behind." Every item of this life will furnish "the food for the contemplation and joy of God throughout eternity." On the one hand we confess we are nothing, but on the other we know that we are "fearfully and wonderfully made," and that all our days were determined by God, before any of them existed, to be the material for wonder and praise in eternity.[51]

For the Christian, death has been so transformed by grace that "the dread of death is dissipated" not throughout life, but "most frequently at the hour of death." The Christian possesses death in that it "draws the soul away from this world, and ripens it for heaven." "Its sting has been removed in the removal of sin," and because "it is the portal to Eternal life." While it is not permitted all Christians to testify to Christ's sustaining grace through martyrdom, all may testify of him in death, even the weakest and most unimpressive. The testimony of dying grace will be universal.

> Let the scoffing world account for the universality of such testimony. Were it seen only in the best, it might be thought the result of virtue. Were it only in the wisest, it might be attributed to philosophy. Were it only in the bravest, it might be ascribed to courage. Were it only in the strongest, it might be said to be endurance. Were it only in the most faithful, it might be said to be innocence. Were it only in the unlearned, it might be said to be ignorance; but, to go no further into such particulars, which might be greatly increased, when it is seen in those without any of these advantages, but afflicted with their very contraries, to what can it be ascribed but to grace, the grace given by Christ, through whose strengthening the weakest can do all things?[52]

The second half of the message spoke of the life of Manly, his labors as a preacher, pastor, and consummate educator. Boyce recalled his personal kindnesses, his preaching excellence, his social affability and skill, his quietly triumphant death, and moments of important influence on his own life as a child. Manly's life as a denominational statesman, like Howell's, was aligned with the history of the Southern Baptist Convention from its beginning to the present moment. His value to the seminary could not be calculated, in Boyce's opinion, and in one passage he traced the lines of Manly's involvement with the school. After describing the emotion Manly exhibited when the school finally was affirmed by the 1857 educational convention, Boyce observed:

> The child of such desires, the offspring of such prayers, guided by such Providences, aiming at such purposes for the glory of God, that institution remains to this day, stronger than ever, more endeared to its supporters, and giving renewed evidences daily of its efficiency to advance the cause of Christ, through its instructions to the rising ministry. To its support Dr. Manly contributed, not only from his

pecuniary means, but also by his counsels; and from the number of his sons, it has received as one of its instructors the one who bears his father's name. Dr. Manly became the first President of the Board of Trustees, an office only vacated by his removal from the State for which he had been appointed. Upon the occurrence of a vacancy in the State to which he had removed, his counsel was again sought, and from that time until his death, he continued one of its Board. During that period, his confidence in the protection of God over it was confirmed by the fearful darkness through which it passed, and the manifest blessing God worked out through that darkness. The losses suffered by the war, and the depressed condition in which it was left, have but endeared it the more, and given it a wider influence than ever. Dr. Manly lived to see it thus outstrip even the remarkable progress it had attained before the day of trial came.[53]

Boyce knew, however, that more dark days lay ahead, and the security of the seminary was yet in a most precarious state. Relief from the interminable pressure of mammoth academic toil, the continued constriction on operating expenses, not the least of which was a livable salary for professors, from month to month and session to session, and the ever-looming perennial issue of endowment was far from view. He must do what he could, find the wisdom and energy to take the next step, in order to give transgenerational longevity to the institution that he increasingly saw as vital to the interests of Baptists in the South and the cause of Christ in the world.

Gain and Joy amidst Loss and Sorrow

Pressures seemed insurmountable. The loss of a culture, the loss of endowment, the loss of a supportive economy, the unstable status of Boyce's personal estate, the responsibility for the estates of his siblings, the loss of those denominational statesmen so vital to the initial well-being of the seminary all amounted to an emotional and physical load crushing in its weight. Boyce's respite in this circumstance, as one element of his profound trust in the sovereignty of God, was the delight he found in his family. By 1868 he and his wife had three daughters. Elizabeth, called Lizzie, had been born in 1855. Frances, called Fannie, had been born in 1859. Lucia, called Lucy, had been born in 1865. Boyce was extraordinarily attentive to his wife and his daughters. He seemed to revel in his home life.

His children remembered his love of reading aloud to them. "One of my earliest recollections of my Father was his reading to us Pickwick Papers and his fruitless efforts to control his laughter," Lizzie recalled. "Tears would roll down his cheeks and his voice would fail him as he tried to take us through the trials and scrapes of Mr. Pickwick." He could read for hours, controlled and pleasant, "with easy rapidity and much expression" and without any apparent fatigue.

Lizzie could not recall her father ever being cross or scolding. "Sometimes," she said, "when he found it necessary to admonish us, it was always done with so much tenderness that we loved him more than ever and were more than anxious to atone for anything that did not meet with his approval." He cared for them when they were sick, and "no mother could have been more tender in her devotion or more wise in her ministration" than her father. She considered him the "ideal father" filled with "supreme tenderness, mingled with great firmness, utter self sacrifice and tireless care and love towards his children." He studied their every need, and proof was never lacking that his "thoughts were centered in our childish interests."

Particularly at Christmas this showed itself. Boyce entered into the season of Christmas with the delight of a child. "Christmas was always a time of great enjoyment in our home and to my Father a time dearer than any other part of the year I think." He showed this in his insistence on selecting gifts for each member of the family. "In the selection of gifts for us at Christmas," Lizzie reminisced, "he took the keenest pleasure never allowing any one to take this matter off his hands, and he always showed a remarkable faculty in the choice of beautiful and unique presents." Dolls, games, or books—all were selected with special purpose by Boyce, showing that "amidst all his duties these little things that he need never have troubled himself about he claimed as his special pleasure."[54]

He also loved to make sure that his ladies were dressed appropriately. Boyce felt genuine pleasure in "pretty dressing" and encouraged them to purchase the best material, never objecting to the size of the bills. "In early married life, he bought nearly everything worn by his wife," often spending time on his trips to New York to purchase "dresses and bonnets, laces and jewelry for her." He showed excellent taste, Lizzie thought, but, because he was a man, was extravagant. He stayed current with the latest in fashion and knew all the jargon of the dressmakers. If his girls purchased something of inferior quality, he objected because he did not consider it "sufficiently handsome and would tell us that he could buy better things." Had his wife not given severe injunctions against it, he would have purchased his wife "many a costly jewel."[55]

Ladylike behavior should be the natural concomitant of Christian character, Boyce believed. He was "most fastidious in his notions about the deportment of women," insisting that "they should always have themselves under perfect control no matter how awkward the situation or how amusing the circumstances." If the situation was inappropriate for lightness, a true lady "should be able to be greatly dignified." He could never be convinced that a lady could do anything "out of the way," but he believed all that they said and was "always deferential to any woman." Even young girls were treated with marked respect. And "his own daughters received many a courtesy from him which many men would never think of showing their home people."[56]

Boyce also loved flowers and often relaxed by helping tend the garden in Greenville. The climate and soil provided a rich context for cultivating a large variety. "Mother's devotion to them amounted to a craze," Lizzie recorded, "and she was ably upheld by my Father." He often spent winter evenings reading catalogues and involved the family in long and earnest discussion about what would be best to order for spring planting. After ordering they waited eagerly for delivery, and "when the boxes would arrive from the North with all the newest plants beautifully packed in them, we all had a holiday and father would put his books away and lay aside his pen for a trowel and would follow Mother around with the watering pot glad to do his share toward the planting." Each plant received the greatest care with great anticipation for the "first sign of leaf or flower." Mrs. Boyce had developed a collection of over four hundred potted plants when she left Greenville for

Kentucky. Her zeal for this inspired a contest in Greenville among the ladies as to who could cultivate the greatest variety or discover a new plant. Boyce's visits to Kentucky had made him love the rich bluegrass of the state and, consequently, he sought to have his lawn in Greenville covered with bluegrass. "He spent a great deal of time and money, had the lawn ploughed and enriched but was unsuccessful in obtaining any steady growth."[57] He soon would have abundant opportunity to see the bluegrass grow in its native environment.

Preserving and Promoting the Faculty

In 1869, with increasing pressure on the health of Broadus and the time and energies of Boyce, the faculty urged the trustees at their spring meeting to consider the hire of a fifth faculty member. They presented a detailed case for their request.

Dear Brothers,

The faculty of the Seminary, encouraged by your kind confidence, & readiness, on all occasions, to consider their suggestions, would respectfully ask your attention to the importance of appointing an additional Professor. The obvious & natural objection on the score of inadequate means will be considered after stating the reasons in favor of such an addition. These reasons are two.

1. Two of the Professors find their work burdensome beyond their powers of endurance. Professor Boyce, whose course of instruction, in Systematic Theology and Polemics, is more extensive than in most seminaries, and involves a much larger number of recitations and lectures, has besides to manage the finances of the Institution. This task has already involved an immense amount of labor, and its burdens will be increased by the contemplated arrangements & efforts looking to permanent endowments. He cannot properly perform all the work of the two schools now taught by him, & also give constant & close attention to the finances. His health has already suffered, without his being able to discharge either department of his duties in a manner satisfactory to himself. The necessity that Bro. Boyce should personally superintend the financial operations of the Seminary seems to be

generally recognized, & he cannot do so unless somewhat relieved in his work as Professor.

In teaching New Testament Greek, with which it is so important that some of our ministers should be thoroughly acquainted, Professor Broadus finds it necessary to make much use of written exercises, in both the Junior & the Senior Class. The labor of correcting these increases with the number of students. But the same Professor teaches homiletics, in which the written exercises, viz. numerous sketches of sermons & several sermons written in full, are exceedingly important, and should be corrected very carefully, & the written corrections accompanied by frequent private interviews with the students, for further explanations and suggestions. This task, which also increases with the number of students, is so heavy that in many Seminaries a professor devotes his whole time to Homiletics, with the addition, in some cases of lectures in Pastoral duties; and in none of them is the class studying Homiletics larger than it is likely to be here during the next session. The addition in our Seminary of exercises in Homiletics to exercises in Greek has already become a sore burden to the Professor, whose health is known to be feeble, and with the increased number of students which we have reason to expect another year, it will be simply more than he can bear.

2. Our number of students is passing beyond all the Baptist Theological Seminaries, & in a year or two more bids fair to mount up to the number attending the great Pedobaptist seminaries. Now these leading institutions are not content with the four Professors usually found in smaller (including all Baptist) seminaries, but have a larger number. Princeton has five professors, Union (New School Presbyterian in New York) five, and Andover seven. Moreover, in consequence of our peculiar plans, adapted to all classes of the ministry, the course at this Seminary is decidedly more extensive, & much more laborious to the professors than in any other Seminary of the country.

With five professors, and the increased attendance to be expected next fall, our Southern Baptist Seminary will be working on a much larger scale than any other Baptist Seminary, & be in a position to rival in magnitude & in all respects, the great Pedobaptist institutions mentioned. In most of our operations at the South we are compelled to accept acknowledged inferiority to others. Our missionary operations, which we all dearly love & feel determined to sustain, must inevitably look small when compared with what Northern Baptists, as other denominations, are doing. But in this one respect, of theological education, it is possible for Southern Baptists now to have an Institution unquestionably superior, in working force & in the number attending, to all that Northern Baptists have been able to achieve, & bidding fair in a very few years to become the largest theological school in America, while it will continue to have the advantage of being carefully & thoroughly adapted to the wants of our Baptist ministry.

Will not this idea enkindle a just spirit of emulation in many of our brethren, including some who are wealthy, making them more willing to help an institution which will stand forth so prominently, & promise so large & rapidly growing results? Will it not be just as easy to secure support at present, & speedy permanent endowment, with five professors as it would be with four? Much as the faculty need that increase of salary which has been contemplated from the beginning, & several times referred to by the Board, they are satisfied that the prospect of its becoming practicable to make such increase would not be at all diminished by the addition of another Professor; & meanwhile they would rather see the enlargement of the capacity of the institution for good, than the enlargement of their own means of support.

The faculty was unanimous and hopeful in submitting the request, feeling that they had justified the proposed addition, particularly with regard to the relief of Boyce and Broadus. Whatever reassignment of course this addition involved could be managed amicably by the faculty. By the fall, C. H. Toy, a former student in the first session and present faculty member at Furman University, had been added to the faculty as an instructor of Old Testament.

Broadus's health had been precarious since before the war and had improved little, sometimes declined, since the seminary resumed in 1865. Stabilizing his health became a major priority for Boyce. After the accession of Toy, Boyce again considered going into business for the sake of the seminary, an option he considered each year since the war, but again decided to remain as professor. Thus, with four faculty members present, Boyce arranged for Broadus to travel for one year to Europe. Broadus's wife consented, and even insisted, and Broadus felt it the right thing to do. He now felt renewed urgency to complete a textbook on preaching that he had been working on since the past summer, *Treatise on the Preparation and Delivery of Sermons*.

Through the spring and into June he labored, and finally, with the help of pertinent suggestions by Basil Manly, the book was ready for publication. Broadus financed the first edition himself and believed it should be out by August 15. The faculty promised to do all they could to promote it. He committed to Manly all the financial matters, knowing all that Boyce had to do.[58] He wrote Boyce from Harrogate in England, unable to make gratifying statements about his health (in fact some vivid descriptions could not have stirred anything other than concern in Boyce's mind), but with a request, "I should be glad if anybody would cut out and send me notices of my book—or just send a newspaper, postage 2 cents."[59] This Boyce was glad to do.

Boyce, in fact, strategized mightily to see that Broadus's work was noticed in every prominent place possible. This, after all, was the first scholarly work to appear in print from the faculty of the Southern Baptist Theological Seminary. He wrote Broadus a long and jocular letter in which he included information about the book. "The best notice as yet, and indeed the only worthy one," he judged, "has been in the Herald." He included also two notices that he had written, "one for the Phoenix and the other for the Courier, both of which were admitted." He begged a friend to get a notice into the *New York World*, which did appear on 5 November 1870. He explained that the "notices are too brief to do justice but had to be brief to secure the insertion. My object in writing them was to make them sell the book." Boyce told Broadus how he would advertise it, "not only differently, but more extensively." "Repeated advertisements," he observed, "and especially by pointed statements," would lead to increased sales. "A brief paragraph—sensational advertisement—in each religious paper in the United States would pay," Boyce believed, but even now, because of its real value and its fine appearance, "I am more sure of its sale than ever. You ought to sell five thousand copies in two years if you will have the matter well managed."[60]

The notices sent by Boyce expressed confidence in the superior quality and usefulness of the book. With regard to the New York readers of *The World*, Boyce intended to gain a hearing both for Broadus and the seminary. He informed them that though the author was from the "far South," he was quite active among all scholarly circles. The American Baptist Publication Society in Philadelphia had engaged him to prepare a commentary on Matthew, and he was presently engaged with the "translation and editing of the famous commentary of Dr. Lange, now publishing under the supervision of Dr. Schaff." Various preaching and speaking opportunities had made deeply edifying impressions on the Baptist clergy of the North. These opportunities "secured for him here the reputation he had long possessed at the South of one of the first preachers of the day." As one would expect in a work of erudition, the book is "full of the evidences of thorough scholarship applied with conscientious care to the development of the subject." His massive bibliographical knowledge allows him to gather "from the Greek and Roman classics, from the fathers and writers of later ages, and from the best writers of modern days in Germany, France, England, and America." The whole field of homiletics, Boyce found, "has been carefully surveyed," the materials "thoroughly digested" and subjected to "the patient thinking of an independent and vigorous mind, guided by an unusually suggestive experience." Among its most potent contributions, Broadus's *Preparation* teaches how one may speak extemporaneously "with all the power of unfettered and living oratory." Broadus's own success in this mode combined with "his wide-spread opportunities of analyzing the powers of others, and especially his ten years' experience in teaching large classes in the largest Baptist theological seminary of America, make his suggestion worthy of the most careful examination." To assure its widespread advantages to many classes of people, the volume "is exceedingly readable, and charmingly written."[61]

Crafting his review for the Charleston *Courier*, Boyce called Broadus "one of the best scholars of the age," whose reputation is fully sustained in this book. One peculiarity that "renders it eminently suitable to this section of the country" is its concentration "on the art of speaking more than on that of writing." He readily understands and communicates "those points of difference between the orator and the author, which give the speech of the former an efficiency beyond the printed page of the latter." This makes the book valuable not only for the preacher, but for the lawyer and others who must make an impression and bring conviction to minds by the medium of the spoken word.[62] The same material appeared in the *Phoenix* at Columbia, South Carolina, artfully rearranged.

While Broadus was gone, Boyce made another widespread appeal for support. A letter sent to the pastors of Southern Baptist churches gave eleven reasons why they should do all they could to secure the stability of theological education for the South by taking up a collection in February or March. He needed $15,000 by April. "Will you not share that anxiety, and beg," he said with shameless frankness, "earnestly beg your people to help us at once." He had no fear about the survival of the seminary but wanted it "carried through these years of trial and poverty at the South without being too much crippled." Just a little from everyone would do; even a trifling sum from each member would be ample for the necessary relief.[63]

The Resignation of Manly

In July 1871 the trustees of Georgetown College in Kentucky asked Basil Manly to be its president. He refused. They telegraphed that they desired a personal interview and would pay expenses. He interviewed in August and after a severe struggle decided to accept the position. Manly had not enjoyed the curriculum change that placed him in the position of professor of Homiletics. The toil of correcting written sermons brought tedium, not fulfillment. He believed his departure would be best for the seminary, and relieve some of the awkwardness about the curriculum, allow Toy to continue in Old Testament and restore Homiletics to Broadus. The salary was higher, his sons could be educated partly under his tutelage and totally under his authority. He himself had attended the University of Alabama when his father was president, and he knew the advantages of such an arrangement. His colleagues expressed with furious earnestness their opposition to his leaving. "I entreat you to be very slow to think it your duty to change," Broadus warned, but also acknowledged, "I have much more confidence in your own judgment than my own."[64] The faculty was back to four. The leaving of Manly had shown just how damaging the Spartan financial situation was. None of the faculty could continue long with such relentless pressure. A change had to be effected.

7

The Move to Louisville

he tellers in the election of a President, reported, that
Bro. Jas. P. Boyce, of S. C., had been elected to fill that
position." So read the minutes for the Southern Baptist
Convention on 9 May 1872. After Boyce made a few appropriate
remarks in accepting the elected position, John A. Broadus presented to the convention for use by the president a mallet brought
from Jerusalem.

> Its handle is made of the balsam tree which grows by the river Jordan,
> forming a large part of that beautiful fringe of green trees which has
> always marked the banks of the sacred river, and beneath whose shade
> the multitudes looked on as the Saviour was baptized. The head is
> of olive wood, reminding us of the Mount of Olives, from which
> He ascended to Heaven. This simple mallet thus suggests to us the
> beginning and the end of our Lord's public work on earth.[1]

That evening, Broadus set aside time to write his wife. "Doctor Boyce
was elected president on first ballot, by a considerable majority," he

informed her. "He made a good address on taking the chair." And then, of course his part in the event would be of interest to her: "I presented Boyce the mallet, with a few words, and it was quite unexpected to find it exciting much interest."[2] Broadus believed that presiding over a Baptist convention posed many peculiar difficulties as every Baptist "feels himself perfectly free, and wishes to be personally uncontrolled, and yet all desire that the president shall maintain perfect order." He characterized Boyce as a master of such situations in maintaining "perfect courtesy and fairness to all" while recognizing every speaker with "glowing cordiality and vivid sympathy."[3]

Closely connected with the meeting of the convention, the seminary trustees met and elected William Heth Whitsitt professor of Biblical Introduction and Polemic Theology and assistant professor of New Testament Greek. Whitsitt had studied at the University of Virginia, the seminary for two years, and two years in Germany. At the time he was called to the seminary, he had been pastor of a church in Albany, Georgia, for only a few months. He was to become the third president of the seminary in 1896. In 1899 he would resign under pressure from the Landmark contingent in the convention over his views of Baptist origins.

Whitsitt's coming allowed Broadus to resume his class in Homiletics. In order to remove some of the pressure of controversy from the shoulders of William Williams, Boyce took over the course in Church Government. His views on baptism accorded with those who had raised a storm of protest about Williams's view on "alien immersion." Boyce also agreed to teach Church History to leave Williams free to teach Systematic Theology, his true love and delight. The real motive behind this change was hidden from Williams, and he probably would not have consented to it had he known. Boyce soon had to leave, however, for Louisville, leaving Williams with a double load of teaching, a task that rapidly compromised his health.

On May 7, Broadus wrote his wife concerning the proposed move of the seminary: "It is more and more clear to my mind that the board cannot decide, and will have to appoint a large committee to meet, . . . and let Louisville in the meantime be canvassed. The question is pretty clearly between Chattanooga and Louisville." In fact, the trustees had heard appeals from Nashville, Russellville (Kentucky), Chattanooga, Memphis, Atlanta, and Louisville. Broadus summarized the method of the trustees:

> The Board resolved that it was expedient to remove, but that it was proper to avoid all complications with existing or proposed institutions of learning, and that this would restrict them (among the places to which the Seminary had been invited) to Louisville, Nashville, Chattanooga, or Atlanta. They further resolved that at least three hundred thousand dollars ought to be secured in the city and State where the Seminary should be placed, with the expectation that two hundred thousand more would be raised elsewhere. They appointed a committee of seven to visit proposed places, examine proposed sites, etc and inquire into the amount and validity of the subscriptions. . . . Nearly all of this committee, with Dr. Boyce, shortly after visited the several cities suggested, and reached the conclusion that it was best to remove to Louisville so soon as the requisite amount for endowment should be subscribed in the city and the State.[4]

That "so soon" was to stretch into a more extensive period of frustration than any anticipated.

A Slow, Sobering Start

In June 1872, Boyce spoke in Philadelphia at the American Baptist Educational Convention. A conflict with Edward Bright, editor of the *Examiner and Chronicle*, gave opportunity for Boyce, before his speech, to extend a grand gesture of kindness to Bright, who had been selected to chair the meeting in which Boyce spoke. "Bright took it well," Boyce reported, "and all that soreness is healed." In addition the speech went well, and the entire crowd was so impressed with Boyce, both his speaking and his magnanimity, that the "crowd jumped to their feet, raised their handkerchiefs in the air, and hurrahed lustily." Overall, Boyce felt that the experience had done the South much good in the eyes of the Northern brethren.[5] Broadus concurred, as he wrote to his daughter, "I learn, as coming from Professor Harris and Professor Winston, that the Philadelphia breakfast was a delightful affair, and that among all the amusing and taking speeches, Doctor Boyce quite carried off the palm. He made a fine impression throughout the Convention."[6]

In September, Whitsitt made a good impression with his inaugural address, "The Position of Baptists in the History of American Culture." He positioned Baptists firmly within Reformed evangelicalism, which stresses the principle of *sola scriptura*. In investigating the tendency of the thought of Schleiermacher, Whitsitt emphasized, "There is nothing against which they [Baptists] interpose a more energetic protest than that species of subjectivity which in self-sufficient pietism emancipates itself from the authority of the Holy Scriptures, and which, in its ultimate analysis, is a form of infidelity."[7]

In a closely argued presentation of his historical thesis, Whitsitt placed Baptists at the forefront of the development of many axiomatic American values as based upon the application of this principle:

> In its broadest generalization this principle is enounced by the declaration that the church of Christ is, in the highest possible sense, a spiritual organization; or to employ more exact language, the Baptist would so explain the second note of the Council of Constantinople— that concerning the sanctity of the church—as to deny the right of membership to all except true believers in Christ, or such as make a credible profession of faith.[8]

Piety as essential to church involvement, individualism, independent thinking, resistance to sacramentalism and denial of superstitions, the rights of conscience, the separation of church and state, and the removal of the clergy from the realm of political power—a healthy desecularizing of the clergy—all these tenets of American Christianity stem from the Baptist principle. This overall approach to life gave the Baptists "a foremost position among the iconoclasts of their day, being unappeasable opposers of imposition and sham in every range of thought and action." This philosophy produced characters full of "vigor, business capacity, and practical unadorned simplicity." The Baptist image is "stamped ineffaceably upon the American people."[9] Whitsitt was satisfied to be a Baptist, and the seminary was satisfied with Whitsitt's beginning.

The beginnings of Boyce's work in Louisville did not satisfy him quite as much. Dr. Arthur Peter had responded quickly with a subscription of $20,000 in bonds. Others who were needed, however, failed to come through. Included in a letter that contained checks to pay the faculty, Boyce commented on the status of his early efforts at fundraising in Louisville: "Progressing slowly." The fund-raising efforts for other causes meant that "things are working in some respects badly." A prominent member of Walnut Street Baptist Church and world-renowned scientist, J. Lawrence Smith, "has refused me utterly," while another man of considerable wealth, Dr. Caldwell, "will do little if anything." Boyce was not discouraged, however, for the feeling in the state was favorable toward the proposed move of the school. Yet he did not believe that he could raise over "$150,000 from Louisville," though he had hoped for $200,000.[10]

In the meantime Boyce wanted Broadus to secure the good will of the Baptist Convention of South Carolina. The decision to move must not work to sour the support structure secured through careful and faithful work in years past. Broadus must go to the convention and secure resolutions in four areas: the value of the seminary to South Carolina; grief at its loss; commendation of its professors and students; enthusiastic cooperation in raising endowment and sending students.[11] In a subsequent letter Boyce suggested several names to Broadus as likely candidates to present the resolutions and remarked, "Eason would do it best of all."

The resolutions, presented by F. W. Eason, followed Boyce's guidelines point by point. First, "it is our conviction that the Theological Seminary at Greenville, has been of great value to the cause of Christ in this State," through its professors, students, and especially those students that settled in the state and are among the "most useful and devoted pastors." Second, though the loss of endowment has made removal necessary, "most reluctantly and sadly we consent to see this noble institution remove to another State." Third, "We most heartily commend our beloved brethren, the President and Faculty of the said Institution," to the cordial reception of "the State to which it is about to remove" with a reiteration of grief at the loss to South Carolina. Fourth, "we will exert ourselves to the utmost to see to it that South

Carolina" will not be lacking in efforts to obtain the new endowment. Fifth (Eason added this on his own initiative), should the efforts to remove it fail to achieve the necessary goals, "the brethren of the Southern Baptist Convention [are requested] to allow it to remain with us."[12] Broadus wrote that the resolutions had been successfully executed but that "Eason's resolutions are very badly written. . . . I had no idea that Eason would write such bad English."[13] J. C. Furman, president of Furman University as well as president of the State Convention, spoke words of real encouragement and assured the constituency that the presence of the seminary had not hurt the university at all, but rather had helped. These words could be useful for those who feared that Kentucky colleges would be hurt by the seminary.

Days of discouragement, faint praise, misconstrual, and opposition began to show in the outlook of Boyce. "I find Nimrod Long so much in my way that I think I shall go down and try my best to conciliate him." "E. T. Winkler's speech is ruinous to me." "I may be obliged to ask you to come here and make a speech and spend a week in December or January. . . . But I may have to have you, Curry, and Fuller in order to get out the people, or some trio of you at least, I cannot get them out to hear me." "Things are fearfully gloomy. I fear Kentucky, at least Louisville, will fail."[14] Winkler, originally elected to the first faculty, claimed that with the move to Louisville the seminary would lose its distinctively Southern character. Such statements, Boyce feared, would further wound the seminary's chances of accumulating the necessary enthusiasm for long-term support.

Even more strenuous efforts brought only slightly improved response. A significant bequest was promised from a Dr. Wise, but it would not help currently as its proceeds were not to be distributed until the death of Wise and his wife. With regard to other possibilities, Boyce cautioned, "All things are so uncertain that you must keep this strictly within ourselves." All of this difficulty pushed Boyce to rest on a more fundamental confidence.

> I have had some blessed experience in this work of mine. I fear I came in too great self-confidence and conviction that so good a cause must commend itself. The Lord has taught me that all hope

in man is vain and as I have been able to look to Him alone I have some wonderful evidences of His aid. Do you wonder then that in the moment of real disdain, and when all felt that nothing could be done, I was enabled to rise and say all is right? I shall succeed. I have no fears. And I feel confident, though human flesh sometimes fails and I fear. My experience was like that of David in the cave (Ps. 142). Even the temptation was put before me to destroy my enemies, and I was graciously enabled by my publications of minutes to show what I could have done. And I believe God has blessed my peaceful intentions and answered my prayers and accepted my trust. Or shall I not rather say others' prayers, for all of you have been praying for me—or rather none of ours but only those of Christ whose Spirit has taught us what to ask for and who has himself asked that the prayers be granted. All the glory be to God. The work is succeeding I am sure. Yet I have no more subscriptions yet to report, but my plans are working.[15]

The Dismal Prospects of 1873

Boyce traveled back to Greenville in January for personal business and upon his return to Louisville found that Mrs. Ficklen, his wife's mother, had died in Washington, Georgia. He was glad that she had been "for many, many years, perhaps 30 to 50, a pious and consistent member of the Baptist Church here, and one whose religious character was marked and outspoken." Mrs. Boyce was overwhelmed with grief.

Back in Louisville, Boyce found the opposition mounting and circumstances creating greater difficulties. Two new churches were to be built, and others planned fund-raising campaigns for the expansion of their buildings. The orphans' home needed to add a wing at $35,000. "These efforts are all intended to throw me off." Collections for the seminary must be motivated by avarice, so one fearful opponent claimed, and "everything wrong is at once put to the account of the Seminary." His supporters, including Arthur Peter, said that it was not a good idea to move before an endowment of $250–300,000 was raised. The students must be told that Greenville would be home for another year.

Most egregiously did Dr. Lawrence Smith cause problems. Boyce felt compelled to give some of the details.

I am told Dr. Lawrence Smith is actively arguing against me, which I could hardly believe for he told me he would not. I have heard however of talks he has had with Burton, Peter, Helm, Coleman, Wharton and have heard of his going to see others but with what intention I do not know nor what he said. But to the ones named he has undoubtedly argued against it and by some of the most foolish and narrow arguments I have heard. He urged upon Wharton that the ministers here were very foolish to encourage our coming, that before the learned professors they would not be able to preach half as well as usual, that he had found that [to be] the effect produced upon him when learned men attended his lectures. Burton, to whom he said the same thing, said "yes, you know <u>we</u> are all of us now here a very ignorant set, and so for the sake of comfort we will continue steeped in our ignorance." He also said to Wharton that if we were here, we, and the students, would do all the work and the church members would remain undeveloped. These are samples. He told Coleman that we would drive Kentuckians out of office and that our influence would override that of the native preachers. He is now dreadfully afraid that I am seeking to make the churches invite me, as if they would be bound any more by that than they are already. Yet withal this he is a liberal man. Something that I cannot find out has been stirring him up. Wharton thinks he does not like to be pointed at when we come as the one who did nothing; others say that he does not like to be beaten.[16]

Boyce did find eventually that Smith was a "very liberal man" but suffered great perplexity from him in the meantime.

Arthur Peter, in light of increasing difficulties, increased his estimate of the amount of endowment that would be needed. Not only must the Kentucky amount of $300,000 be met, but the $200,000 from other states should also be secured. Boyce knew this meant even more delay and more difficulty in raising annual expenses while the school remained in Greenville, "but I suppose," he conceded, "that we shall have to adopt that policy." Knowing that the bulk of the agency work would again fall on him, he compared his present rate of success with future expectations and gazed at what seemed an untraversable ocean of pleading and fruitless appeal. "And I almost feel ready to give up and resign rather than attempt it," he confessed. In addition, a couple of humiliating experiences in two leading churches led Boyce to confide another lament to Broadus:

> I can say to anyone who thinks I am having or have been this winter having a nice time what the deacon said after trying to preach. Let him try it. I begin to fear lest I am not the man for this work. It requires more personal power of impressing oneself and more persistence and harsh treatment of others than I can feel to be gentlemanly. Still, where can I get any one to do it?[17]

Broadus felt compelled to respond almost point by point. The stakes were mounting both for the seminary and for the well-being of his friend Boyce. Broadus agreed with Peter about the Kentucky endowment but not for the other states. A delayed move would strangle the school and its resources, while a move sooner rather than later would stimulate everything. Delay also would engage Boyce even longer in the other states, forfeit the aid that the move would provide, and keep him from the classroom for "five to eight years" after Kentucky was secured. "I protest," he insisted, "against any plan which is to cut you off from your study and lecture room longer than one year more." And then the exhortation:

> I do not wonder that you sometimes feel discouraged, painfully. The task is difficult, and the kind of opposition encountered is very depressing. But life is always a battle. My dear Fellow, nobody but you can do this thing. I believe you can do it, and it will be, all things considered, one of the great achievements of our time. To have carried it through will be a comfort and a pleasure to you through life, a matter of joy and pride to many who love and honor you, an occasion of thanksgiving through all eternity. Opposition—every good thing encounters opposition. Think of Paul, of Jesus! Nay, Nay, no such word as fail. Somehow, somehow, you are bound to succeed.[18]

He added, "The Seminary is a necessity. Our best brethren want it. God has blessed it thus far. It is your own offspring. You have kept it alive since the war—fed it with almost your own heart's blood. It must succeed, somehow, and you are the man that must make it succeed."[19]

Plugging away, living in the "Louisville Hotel," Boyce kept working with both the unwilling and the resistant. "I am bringing things to a point," he noted as part of a developing strategy; "have a mass meeting on Sunday afternoon." He felt certain of obtaining $80,000 on the amount of $100,000, which would virtually guarantee success, "for I have still a large number who yet promise to help and I have not gone outside among the citizens." He believed that the insistence on the sum of $500,000 before moving was right and strategically advantageous: "Since I have declared that I have begun to conquer. The opposition in the state is dying out."

Still many contingencies flurried through his mind and the possibility of utter failure always loomed near. He still had been unable to get any response from "the Smith, Caldwell, or Long party" and only $14,000 from Broadway Baptist Church with more offered on certain conditions. Other money was promised on other conditions and conditions upon conditions. He believed nevertheless that he could "safely count on finishing this Kentucky subscription in one year from September next [1874]." Other propositions involved a request that "the North" give $200,000 for "a union offering commemorative of the Baptists' influence on the American Government." If they complied, the cornerstone for the building could be laid on 4 July 1876. Boyce felt that the raising of the endowment was so urgent that if he had to get the entire faculty involved and even suspend the operations in Greenville, it would be worth it. The "suspension" arose, as we shall observe, more than once and was not met with enthusiasm by the faculty.

Boyce explained to Broadus his method of working both for current expenses and the endowment. "I am making my bonds (Kentucky) payable with interest from 1st October last. Said interest to be used first for expenses of agency work in this state and then to the annual expenses of the Seminary." He thought that only a few would object to the interest, and when they did, he would "cut that out." The same scheme he believed would operate in the other states. Boyce conferred with Basil Manly Jr. at Georgetown about using that location as a fail-safe. "I am glad to have that to fall back upon," he averred, but then admitted that "It is a good scarecrow, if no more." That possibility probably seemed contrary to the purpose of the move from South Carolina in the mind of Broadus, and Boyce quickly added, "But have no fears. Trust my judgment. With God's help we shall come to Louisville."[20]

Should Louisville not succeed, Boyce considered Memphis, and perhaps Chattanooga. He preferred Memphis, for Chattanooga held too many lurking dangers in light of the many investments his father's estate held there. J. R. Graves would like nothing better than to find reason to assault Boyce for pursuing his personal advancement under the guise of helping the Southern Baptist Convention. "Set a rogue to catch a rogue," Boyce proverbialized; "Personal benefit as at least some if not all of my friends will believe has never entered into my head."[21] Throughout the letters concerning the fund-raising, the need to tiptoe around the landmine of Landmarkism projects itself. Boyce considered sending William Williams to Mississippi to confront the issue in that state: "If they should treat him badly I shall be sorry on his account and theirs, but it will help us. Soul liberty is worth more than alien immersion, even with Landmarkers."[22] His heart, though he had now begun to experience debilitating physical pain, was in the work of effecting the move of the seminary, and on that account he would have to miss the spring commencement in Greenville.

In May 1873, Boyce again won election as president of the convention. S. L. Helm presented in behalf of the trustees the decision "to remove that institution from Greenville, S. C., to Louisville, Ky., after a certain endowment shall have been secured." The convention went into a "Committee of the Whole" to discuss the issue. Boyce stepped aside and I. T. Tichenor of Alabama took the chair. After two such sessions the following resolutions were presented:

> *Resolved*, That this Convention cordially approves the action of the Board of Trustees in locating the Southern Baptist Theological Seminary at Louisville, Ky., when a sufficient endowment of at least $500,000 shall be raised.
>
> *Resolved*, That the Baptists of the other Southern States are earnestly recommended to contribute liberally to raise the amount of $200,000 for its permanent endowment.
>
> *Resolved*, That the Convention recommends to the Board to raise the money outside of Kentucky, on the condition that if the sum of $300,000 shall not be raised in Kentucky, the Board shall have the

right to use the amount thus contributed outside of Kentucky for a location at Greenville, S. C., or at some other place chosen by the Board, said location, however, to be approved by the Convention.[23]

Largely due to an hour-long speech made by Boyce, the resolutions passed with only one nay. Broadus recalled:

> Dr. Boyce took the floor at a time he had not expected, and spoke a whole hour. He reviewed the history of the Seminary, the terrible losses by the war, the noble generosity of the brethren in South Carolina and elsewhere in gifts for current support; he then showed the necessity of permanent endowment, and the impossibility of obtaining this save in a State where the Baptists had much greater financial strength than was then true of the State he himself loved so well. But this statement, or any statement must be unjust to an address full of fact and argument and passionate appeal. It was a lifetime concentrating itself upon one point; a great mind and a great heart surcharged with thought and feeling; a man of noble nature appealing to all that was noblest in his hearers; a Christian speaking in Christ's name to his brethren.[24]

If post–Civil War distress, Landmark contrariness, and institutional suspicion did not give enough difficulty in raising money, the financial failure of Jay Cooke on 18 September 1873 that plunged the nation into a financial panic and then prolonged financial crisis, certainly cemented the task in virtual impossibility. On October 2, Boyce had to write, "I feel very badly in having no comfort to give all of you about money matters." Receipts were less than one-fourth of what was needed, and Boyce paid the July salaries by selling some of his own stock. "I fear this financial crisis is going still further to shorten my collections and make it still more difficult to borrow money." Should the banks in Greenville need their loan money, Boyce feared that he would have to sell the Greenville property. Though "great enthusiasm is awakening" for the seminary cause, the Louisville banks suspended operations and Boyce now found his task "heavier than I had feared." "It may be that terrible times are ahead which may engulf everything," Boyce conjectured. His confidence in God's purpose remained firm; "Thank God *all* things work together for *us*, for His cause, and I believe shall work for His Seminary."[25] The faculty responded with appreciation for "your great exertions and sacrifices for our common work, which would have perished a dozen times, but for you." They also assured him that they expected he would not be able to raise anything for their salary, and though "it will be hard for us to get along, . . . we will do our best, and work ahead."[26]

With little hope of accomplishing anything in the city, Boyce began going out to the rural areas. They were affected less by the panic than were the businessmen of the city, and his presence in their churches and associations would build good relations and slay the specters of fear and misunderstanding. His sojourns produced good feelings but little money. By December, Boyce had become so frustrated with the slowness of the work that he refused to employ another agent, remarking, "Our affairs look to me more like stopping everything than entering into new expenses." He believed that to gain some kind of cooperation and bring the brethren to their senses about the seriousness of the situation he would have to resign his place.[27] Broadus wrote with news about his paying faculty members with money received from Baltimore and sought to console Boyce, while reminding him that all depended on him, and no one else.

> I sympathize with your annoyance that the people respond so slowly. But I am satisfied that if you were to *resign*, it would do harm rather than good. It is true the people have come to think you can accomplish impossibilities, and so they are disposed to stand by and let you run the machine by your financial skill and influence, but if you resigned, they would say, "Well, if Boyce has given up, there is no hope." Our people have suffered so many losses that they are too ready to give things up as lost. I am sure this is the effect which your resigning would produce. . . .
>
> Cheer up, my dear brother. "Through much tribulation." But God has been with us in six troubles, at least.[28]

The Critical Challenge of 1874

1874 was the darkest year for the seminary since the war. Dr. Boyce and Dr. Broadus thought the institution would have to die. Broadus said, "Let us die first." Broadus went to the convention. Texas hadn't been heard from. A collection was taken, but not enough. Broadus had been preaching several summers for the Colgates in New York. He got ten minutes before the Northern Baptist Anniversary to present the need of $10,000. The feeling between the North and the South was hard. He got the money, and the Northern Baptists saved the seminary. We are here today because of that. Things were not so beautiful then as now. Paul was doing this thing here. We thought a great deal more of the Northern Baptists after that.[29]

That recollection from A. T. Robertson came in his comments on Paul's determination to go to Jerusalem in Acts 21. He wanted to deliver the collection for the Jewish saints from the Gentiles. That summary of 1874 tells a story that is true, but misses the most trying and heroic episodes.

Both in Louisville and beyond, Boyce's zeal for garnering broad-based financial support of the seminary generated suspicion and opposition. On February 4, he wrote Broadus, "I find that I have been well abused here, and much disaffection, if Helm is to be relied on. But he is sensational and after all there may be but few complaining. I shall see. If I have been subjected to any insolence I shall not keep my mouth shut or rather keep my pen quiet, but will put an article in the Recorder. But I am very quiet as yet, and shall cautiously inquire before I act."[30]

Editorials in *The Baptist* by J. R. Graves, however, began to turn up more pressure on the seminary by implying its unreliability to provide a satisfactory ministry for Baptist churches. In "The Influence of Unsound Theological Professors," Graves pointed out that the professors in English schools were of "the open communion order" and turned out students of like mind. This was destroying the churches. "If open communion professors exert this pernicious influence in England," Graves pointedly asked, "have we not reason to believe that they will do it in America?" He went on to suggest, "Is it not a sad and serious fact that every professor of ecclesiastical history and church polity in our theological chairs and schools in America, hold and teach the validity of alien immersions?" This unsoundness doubtless explains why the "grand theological schools are being regarded with less and less favor by the masses of our people."[31]

On February 28, *The Baptist* included a doubly threatening tandem of attack implying the seminary's unsoundness as a provider of preachers for Southern Baptists. Graves again went after the increasing discord among English Baptists because of open communion practices generated by "the tutors of every Baptist theological institution in England." He again inserted questions with unquestionable implications: "Is it not a startling fact that every Professor in our theological seminaries, North and South, do today hold and teach such sentiments that do inevitably lead to open communion? Do they not deny the regular succession of Baptist churches? Do they not endorse the validity of immersion by Pedobaptists, Campbellites and Mormon ministers?" The natural follow-up to such a line of questions was, "Can our churches long expect to get ministers from our theological seminaries holding like sentiments with our churches?" Expecting an answer in the negative, Graves then asserted, "As our seminaries are now organized the churches can not displace a Professor however heterodox he may be. Is this right?"[32]

The same issue drove this point home more deeply by moving from the general to the specific. The "Mississippi Department" contained an article of vital importance to the seminary's struggle for survival. A. V. Rowe, a Mississippi student enrolled in the seminary, reported to his home state about a meeting of students in which enthusiasm for the support of the seminary ran high. The young men present apparently pledged themselves to serve no church as pastor that would not contribute annually to the seminary. When the ministerial students at Mississippi College, a Baptist school in Clinton, Mississippi, heard of the report, they called the pledge "contrary to Bible, and therefore, contrary to Baptist doctrine, and . . . Popish in its very nature." While they desired the prosperity of the seminary, they believed the principle implied in such action would hurt the seminary eventually. Rowe and another student who took the pledge wrote the protesters at Mississippi College and gave a satisfactory explanation of their meaning, but, as the editor coyly reminded his readers, "private explanations do not reach the public."[33]

Another correspondent hearing of the action observed that "there are good and liberal men who will not support the Seminary because they cannot conscientiously aid in supporting an institution with which our vital interests, our future purity of faith and soundness of practice are so intimately connected, unless the institution were under the control of the denomination." That correspondent believed that the seminary students acted under "the influence of enthusiasm," not considering what they were doing; they should by some means correct the impression they had made.[34]

Another correspondent had heard Boyce speak of the "desperate conditions of that institution" and concluded that "things must take a turn and that right soon, or we will have no Southern Baptist Seminary." While he had never been "a zealous advocate for such institutions," the character of the men from Greenville had strongly inclined him toward it. Naturally, caveats followed.

> There are, however, two things connected with this school which must of necessity greatly injure it. 1. It is a close corporation managed by a self-perpetuating Board of Trustees, and neither owned nor controlled by the denomination. There are thousands of honest Baptists who will never build up an institution of this sort, and I think not without just reason. 2. There are doctrines taught in the Seminary against which some four or five State Conventions have earnestly protested. Now I do not know whether these States are expected to contribute to the support of the Greenville school or not, but I presume they are. If so, it is one of the strangest things to think of, that people should be expected to support men to teach what they not only do not believe, but believe to be ruinous to the truth. I fear the Seminary, on account of the two reasons just named, is too far removed from the people to ever recover from its embarrassments.[35]

Boyce knew only too well the "embarrassments" clinging to the seminary. He also knew that he must respond to the "two reasons just named." Without undue delay, the response must be informed, measured, and issued in light of a variety of circumstances and needs. On March 24, Boyce, just a bit downcast, wrote to Broadus, citing a combination of developments that did not bode well for the seminary. Pledges for operating expenses looked very slim and, if he had to report by April 15 or May 1, he noted, "I think we are going to fail." He had been unable to raise over $20,000 for that purpose, which amounted to only about $6,000 per year. Because of such slow response Boyce decided "to publish next week an appeal, stating the grounds of my statement to you, appending your letter to me, calling upon all to whom I have written to reply, and asking others to send for bond." If Broadus thought that course unwise, he was to let Boyce know soon; otherwise, he would proceed for "I think this will chink the nail. If it does not, all is up."[36]

Before surrender, however, he must strategize to meet the crises of both perception and finances. They were not unrelated. Boyce believed that in order to settle the ire raised in Mississippi, both he and Broadus should show up at the Mississippi Convention: "Yes, somebody must go to the Mississippi Convention and that must be you or I, perhaps both, but we will have that to be developed at Frankfort. Oh for the power of multiplying ourselves. There is ten fold as much work for each as we can do."[37] At the same time, Boyce began preparation of several articles to put the plight of the seminary before the public as well as address the objections that had been stated.

His first line of response appeared on April 4 in the *Western Recorder*. In this initial article, he highlighted the pressing need of completing the seminary's endowment along with the reality that even annual expenses were not being met. Addressing "the Baptists of Kentucky," Boyce poured forth his heart in an effort to avoid what seemed inevitable—the suspension of the operations of the seminary. Though the strategy focused on getting the endowment from Kentucky and the annual expenses from other states, Boyce now pleaded with Kentucky Baptists to give money for the annual operations. The failure to pledge the endowment had the effect of increasing annual expenses because of lost interest and continuing costs in Kentucky. "I trust," Boyce declared, "that I may also say to Kentucky, without offense or risk of misconstruction, that had the Seminary endowment, pledged by the Baptists of this State, been subscribed as readily and as liberally as the Board had reason to believe it would be, the present difficulty could not have occurred." For that reason Boyce now called on them to give money for the annual operations as well as the continuance of the expenses of canvassing Kentucky. "I need money," he stated plainly, "in order that I may bring my colleagues here, and also that I may employ other agencies, and that traveling expenses, and printing, and other necessaries may be met. And I am forced to say plainly that I have not the means of my own to pay them."[38]

The second part of his article was titled "A Question for Every Baptist." Boyce explained the financial impossibility of maintaining the school at the present rate of response to the appeals to give and to subscribe five-year bonds. He proposed, therefore, to his Greenville colleagues a suspension of the seminary's operations or, even more drastic, "to close the Seminary altogether, at the end of this session." Financial calamity accompanied even this solution because, as he wrote, "I am not willing, in closing up the Seminary, to have to appeal to the denomination to pay up its past debts. It will be hard enough," he continued, "to have to ask brethren to pay the bonds which they have heretofore given; still, this will be just, for had they paid them when they fell due, our expenses would have been met and we would have been saved the payment of heavy interest."[39]

Boyce shared with the public that the faculty had urged him to try again with a series of five-year bonds of $500 and others for $250 and $100. He did that and included in these requests, sent to particularly selected individuals, the letter of deep concern his faculty colleagues had sent him. Even at that, the failure rate was more than 50 percent, and the money raised would not sustain the most austere and minimal projections of seminary expenses year by year. For that reason he published this general appeal to "thousands of Baptists throughout the South, readers of the press, with whose names even I am not acquainted." He felt an obligation to the denomination to "inform them of this imminent danger, nay almost certain suspension of the Seminary."[40] After a final appeal to all of those to whom he had formerly written, he appended the letter sent to him by the seminary faculty:

> You say, as Chairman of the Executive Committee, that in your judgment the Committee will be compelled to recommend to the Trustees that they *close the Seminary* at the end of this session, until such time as the permanent endowment can be secured. Your reasons are, that the receipts for the last two years have been very small, notwithstand-

ing earnest and varied appeals; that, to save the Professors from suffering, you have borrowed money to an amount somewhat beyond the value of the real estate in Greenville, and it is neither possible nor right to borrow further; and that, upon the whole, you see no prospect of obtaining the large sum necessary for salaries and other expenses during the two or three years it will probably require to complete the proposed endowment. So you think it will be necessary to suspend the exercises, and employ all the Professors as agents to obtain the endowment.

But the idea of suspending is to us inexpressibly painful. Our number of students is greater this session than ever before, notwithstanding the panic which has lessened the attendance at so many institutions. Very many of the young brethren are expecting to return for one, two, or three years more, so as to complete their proposed course of study. For a large proportion of these, suspension will ruin their plans, sadly mutilate their preparation, and greatly damage their usefulness for life. The very thought of such a thing alarms and distresses them. We have already a number of letters from other brethren wishing to enter next session. The desire for theological education is rapidly growing among our rising Southern ministry; must there be this sudden interruption—this painful shock? Even if we get the endowment after some years, think what a difference the suspension will make in our number of students! If we go on, we can begin at Louisville with at least a hundred, very likely more; if we have suspended, the number will at first be comparatively small, and the ground we have gained in this respect in the trying years since the war will be mainly lost. Besides, will not suspension affect very injuriously the effort to endow? People who would give freely to endow a living Seminary, more largely attended every year, would in many cases hesitate when it seems to them practically dead. Moreover, if the teaching be kept up, the long vacation of four months will enable us to help not a little in agency work, with no cost save for travelling expenses.

But it is impossible adequately to express our strong convictions as to the great evil which would result from suspending the instruction. We ask, with unspeakable anxiety, cannot something be done to prevent it? Have there not been many and growing proofs, during all these years, that the Seminary is warmly loved by very many of our best brethren everywhere? True it is very disheartening to see how slender the contributions have recently been; and when we learn of the few responses to your earnest appeals, and the meager contributions in some cases when you were present, we are sometimes tempted to despair. But a few churches and individuals have done nobly. Is it not likely that many others, oppressed with the almost universal losses and financial difficulties, and struggling to support *literary* institutions in their respective States, have contented themselves with the hope that brethren elsewhere, more favorably situated, would help us—and have not really been lacking in hearty affection for the Seminary? Has not the general and well-known popularity of the Seminary misled its friends each thinking there would surely be plenty of churches and brethren to help it without them? And if our beloved brethren can only be made to understand the situation, will they not rally nobly and say, "The Seminary's work must not be interrupted and its future imperilled—we will help, at all hazards."

They cannot forget that the Seminary is the only place in the whole vast South where a full course of instruction in Theology is given by Baptists; that at the same time it offers opportunity of studying the English Scriptures for those who do not learn Hebrew and Greek, and a full course in other branches of Theological study; and by its flexible plan allows each student to form such a course for himself as suits his gifts, preparation and circumstances. They know it encourages the students to be decided Baptists, and aims to prepare them for meeting various forms of errors, and that the constant effort is to make them practical preachers and working pastors, which we are sure has been the usual result.

Six or seven years ago, the existence of the Seminary was in peril. But by the movement begun in the S. B. Convention in Baltimore, bonds were given to pay $100 a year for five years. These kept us going, and the Seminary has already done a work for which many in every Southern State are thankful, and awakened the hope of a bright and noble future. Will not churches and brethren make some similar arrangement now? We know you had hoped it would never again be necessary to ask this. We know it will require great exertions and sacrifices on the part of some brethren—that most people will never do their share of anything good, and a few have to do much more than their share if good enterprises are to succeed. But we *do* believe, we will believe, that there are brethren who will not hesitate at difficulties and sacrifices when the continued usefulness, the whole destiny of the Seminary from which they expect so much is in question.

So then Dear Brother Boyce, try again. Do not appeal in the papers to the general public—that amounts to but little. Write to a few private brethren who have means and liberal views, and a few pastors who have superior intelligence and large hearts. Tell them what we say, we who have gone on with the teaching while you have been toiling for the endowment. Tell them we are sure the Seminary will, ere many years, be doing a wide and blessed work, which will rejoice their hearts, if they will keep it alive now. Tell them we believe in them, we look to them with trembling fear for our cherished enterprise, but with confidence in their devotions and generosity. Tell them it will not do to wait for others—that the very life of the Seminary depends on them. And O! they will not deny us,—they cannot disappoint us. By the dear love of Christian hearts we know they will not refuse. We are working for Christ—they know we are—and for Christ's sake they will help us.

Brother Boyce, the Seminary must not stop its work, must not risk its future. Never mind now what you and we have done and suffered in its behalf. But remember the fathers who lived for it through weary years; who rejoiced unspeakably when they saw it established; who died believing it would live to do the great work for which they had hoped. Taylor, and Howell and Johnson, Mallory and Dawson—why Basil Manly the elder, were he living today how would he weep and lament!—and Poindexter would cry aloud in agony; no, no, this child of prayer, and hope, and promise must not perish. With many other things we loved, it seemed likely to go down in the vortex of the war; but we have struggled all these years to save it—friends have helped us before, and they will help us now.

So make out your list—you know the brethren right well—and whatever you write and ask each one to do, we shall pray God it may come to his heart as a very call of Providence, to which he will cheerfully and even gladly respond. Most affectionately yours,

John A. Broadus
Wm. Williams
C. H. Toy
W. H. Whitsitt

267

Having exposed the seminary's financial distress with as much transparency and poignancy as discretion allowed, Boyce now turned to address the objections, including the problem of skewed perception. In the meantime, however, this problem had increased in complexity. J. R. Graves had targeted George Dana Boardman, whose father had been a faithful missionary to Burma and whose stepfather was the famous Adoniram Judson, for his open declaration of himself as an "open communionist."[41] Graves identified Boardman's theological training in the North as responsible for this fall from Baptist principles. Precisely these non-Baptist principles "are strenuously taught all our young ministers at Greenville."

Graves isolated three deleterious principles in particular. One error harbored in the seminary was "that there has been no succession of scriptural churches from the days of the apostles." A second in Graves's syllabus of errors was that "all Protestant and Reformed societies [are] evangelical or Christian churches." The third error involved the acceptance of their ministers as true Christian ministers. Graves knew for a fact that "not a few who went to Greenville one year ago strict communionists in all things, have already become quite 'liberal' in sentiment and practice."[42]

On April 7, in view of this attack Boyce contacted Broadus for information necessary for concluding the series of articles. After making suggestions about strategies for raising money in the various Southern states, he asked a series of questions. "You have seen my article, 'A Question for Every Baptist,'" that had just appeared that week. "I have also sent answer to two objections . . . in 3 articles[;] a copy of the first I enclose and will send advance copy of 2nd in three days to you." After mentioning "Graves' attack as to Boardman," he requested information he needed for completion of his argument in light of the persistently agitated Landmark question. This could be provided quickly by a simple survey of the faculty. Broadus was to take responsibility for getting the faculty response on record.

Because Boyce did not have all the facts about the "objections," he was seeking more precise information but foreknew that it had something to do with William Williams's views on baptism. He personally did not distrust Williams and did not try to hide him from the convention.

He considered sending Williams to Georgia, one of the trouble spots, although he and "G. F. Cooper, pastor at Americus, would not have a pleasant time together." This could be beneficial, for if Williams "can go and succeed, it would be a great triumph on him." He also considered Williams the only one who could do canvassing in Texas and would do much good if he could "spend some time there in meetings."

Given this, Boyce needed to be shrewd as a serpent in his discussion. "Now I wish to ask this question," Boyce requested, "which please ask each one and let me know." First, "Does any professor teach that there has been no succession of Baptist churches from the apostles?" In the second question he implied a nuance to the first question by asking, "Does anyone believe this?" and then proposing, "This is a different thing from teaching that it cannot be proved." The third question reiterates the same issue in only slightly different terminology: "Does anyone doubt that there have been churches in all ages holding distinctively the principles which are held by Baptist churches?" The Landmarkers, led by J. R. Graves, contended with incessant perseverance that the kingdom of Christ consisted of *true* local churches (Baptist churches) and that that kingdom had existed with unbroken perpetuity and continuity since Christ established it. The purpose of those connected with Graves in this denominational contingent was "to preserve and perpetuate the doctrine of the divine origin and sanctity of the churches of Christ, and the unbroken continuity of Christ's kingdom, 'from the days of John the Baptist until now,' according to the express words of Christ."[43]

Boyce asked Broadus to copy each answer from each professor "or let Williams set forth his views, etc., and let the others assent." Boyce included resolutions on the issue from different state conventions and asked William Williams "to state to me his views about them—not argument but points of assent and dissent." In addition, any "declaration of Baptists upon alien immersions in any of our creeds, etc.—also any action that any one is aware of taken by Baptists until within the last few years. Don't be alarmed," he assured; "I am going to make no attack, but to show that the Seminary is Seminary of no parts, but of the whole denomination, and as such does not (I will not say ought not) make any responsible for views upon mooted points."[44]

The next week, on April 11, Boyce began a series of five articles in answer to the articles by J. R. Graves that had appeared in *The Baptist*, February through April. Boyce felt that the objections stated represented widespread misconceptions that should be corrected. These objections would offer Boyce an opportunity to express his unstinting commitment to theological education in general, and the seminary in particular, as an undiluted good for Southern Baptists.

The first objection said the seminary was "neither owned nor controlled by the denomination." Or as Graves had worded the concern, "As our seminaries are now organized the churches cannot displace a Professor, however heterodox he may be." Boyce answered energetically and exhaustively.[45] Boyce used a rhetorical repetition of the idea of ownership, seeking to answer a question he proposed, "To whom then does it belong?" When some suggested that he owned it, Boyce shoved this aside by demonstrating how carefully he had avoided exerting any pressure on the board of trustees: "Even at the meetings of the Board," he pointed out, "when required by them to be in attendance, I have remained alone in an adjoining room within call, so that the body should be perfectly untrammelled by my presence." In the process of clarifying the issue, Boyce gave a rare glimpse of the emotional collateral he had invested in the school.

> If to have longed for the existence of such an institution from before the time of my ordination to the ministry, if to have prayed and labored for it, for the past nineteen years, if to have urged it upon unwilling hearts, and to have argued for it with those who found objections to it in other theological seminaries which had no application here, if to have succeeded in developing a plan which had never before been adopted of combining all classes of our ministry in one institution without detriment to any, if to have sacrificed for it the ease and comfort which might otherwise easily have been mine, if to have spent days and years of humiliation in begging for it, stooping to do for this institution what I would not do for bread to eat if I were starving, if to have foregone numberless opportunities of bettering my pecuniary condition, and to have oftentimes incurred embarrassments that its credit might be sustained and its faculty paid, if to have subjected my

family to deprivations which have caused my nearest friends to accuse me of injustice to them, if to have spent sleepless nights and to have more than once endangered my health and even my life, if to have done these things makes the Seminary mine—and in what other sense is it so?—then may I not say?—I accept it as such to make all that it is and all its glorious possibilities a free gift to the Baptist denomination of the South.

He then pursued an equally emotion-filled answer to the rhetorically proposed suggestion that the seminary belonged to the faculty. Precisely in the same way it belonged to him, Boyce answered. To them it owes its existence, and they have asked nothing in return but the "privilege of serving the churches and their Saviour in that sphere of labor which they most love—not for self-ease or gratification, though its work is a blessed privilege—but because of its usefulness to the cause of Jesus." To this faculty the seminary owes its "extended and well-deserved reputation." The seminary would cease to exist without "their pre-eminent ability, their breadth of scholarship, their love of the truth, their brotherly affection for their students, their high character, their preferring one another in honor, their steadfast sacrifices, their willingness to forego all things for the sake of doing this work, their constant holding up of my hands, their singleness of desire to see the ministry of the land growing up in the knowledge and love of the truth in Jesus."[46] Not to Boyce nor to the faculty does the seminary belong, but to the denomination at large.

Having asserted, therefore, in article I that the denomination owned the seminary and controlled it through trustees, he proposed the topic for his second article, "The Baptists of the South through the Southern Baptist Convention, their only general representative body, have full power over the board in the election of every Trustee."[47] Article II explored the history of the vexed question concerning the control of the seminary. Boyce explained the dangers of putting its control on a "money basis" in which those who, as it were, bought stock controlled the school. It would not long remain Baptist or serve the interests of Baptists at large. Should the state conventions control it through their election of the respective trustees as their representatives? Boyce showed the inconveniences created by the differing times of the meetings of the

271

state conventions as well as the "insuperable difficulties" of such an arrangement because of the variety of divisions within several states. The Southern Baptist Convention itself was not prepared to take control of the appointment of trustees, so the Educational Convention that proposed the establishment of the seminary seemed "shut up to the plan of a self perpetuating Board." Boyce opposed this option resolutely, for he felt that such a board could not be controlled "should it depart from the faith." In such a dilemma, how could the dangers of a self-perpetuating board be avoided, a position of courtesy and dignity and justice be maintained toward the Southern Baptist Convention, which had not indicated a willingness to embrace such a responsibility, and yet "the Board of Trustees [be put] under the supervision, and control of the Southern Baptist Convention?"[48]

Article III explained in detail the policy of trustee selection and all the eventualities surrounding the simple and clearly stated policy.

> The Board shall be self-perpetuating, filling any vacancies that may occur in its number, and appointing additional members. . . . But the election shall be from a nomination of not less than three persons for each vacancy to be filled, or new appointments to be made—said nomination to be made by the Southern Baptist Convention, at the session of that body next ensuing after such vacancy shall take place, or new appointment shall be required; provided, that, should the Convention fail to nominate, as above, then the Board may proceed to an election without such nomination.[49]

The Educational Convention of 1858 publicized this policy as widely as possible through the arms of communication available. Only once, however, had the Southern Baptist Convention ever acted upon the prerogative of appointment. That came in 1868 in light of the large number of trustees that needed to be replaced. Because of the wording, the board could maintain the perpetuity of the seminary through its own appointing power, thus securing the seminary apart from the disinterest manifest by the convention. At any time, however, that increased ownership of the process was desired, the Southern Baptist Convention could exert its appointive power. Boyce considered this arrangement the wisest of all possible courses in light of the situation prevailing at the time. He appealed for greater interest, greater cooperation, lowliness of mind, and submission to the common judgment. If one cannot cooperate conscientiously, "let each one follow his own views without let or hindrance, without bickering, or strife, and especially without vituperation, and blame."[50]

As the students learned more of the unstable condition of the seminary's finances and the possible suspension of the school, they expressed their dismay at the possibility. Broadus wrote Boyce on April 21 after the appeal to Baptists and the first two articles on "Objections" had appeared. "The students are constantly inquiring with the deepest concern, whether the Seminary is likely to be suspended, or will go on next session," Broadus reported. "I tell them I hope it will go on—that I don't know how we are to manage—but I hope and pray that God may put it into the hearts of the brethren to help manfully and immediately." Boyce would attend the Georgia Convention as a barometer of how the various states would respond to the necessities of the seminary. "We shall look with great anxiety for the results of your visit to the Georgia Convention," Broadus confided, hoping that "our dear brethren may have a heart given them to rise up to the demands of the hour." Could they but "set an example of heroic determination and cheerful sacrifice," it would "be a keynote for all the Conventions of the year, and will prove to all the land how much it means to be a Baptist." Broadus believed, and well he knew that Boyce agreed, "that ours is the most thoroughly Baptist Theological Seminary in the country. My heart leaps up at the thought of the good it will do, if it can be kept alive now."[51] Bright hope and dark despair often curiously coalesced.

The students wanted to do their part to keep the seminary alive. At a meeting on 27 April 1874, they adopted the following resolution:

> Whereas, we have heard with deep pain of the possible suspension of our Seminary; and, whereas the experience of one, two, and three years has satisfied us of its unsurpassed advantages and great importance to ourselves and the denomination at large; and whereas we believe its suspension would materially affect its future prospects, and result disastrously to the best interests of our churches in thus interrupting the work of ministerial education among us, so nobly begun and so

273

faithfully prosecuted; and whereas, we cannot believe that it is the purpose of our brethren to permit all the sacrifices made by the professors to go for naught, all the hopes with which the Seminary has inspired our people utterly fail of accomplishment, and all its capabilities of good be lost to us; therefore Resolved, that while we disclaim all right to dictate or give advice to our brethren, yet as those who feel a profound interest in the Seminary, by reason of our special relations to it, an interest which constrains us to express ourselves in this crisis of its history, we do most earnestly entreat our brethren throughout this South not to allow the threatened suspension.[52]

At the same time, Boyce kept strategizing as many plans and schemes as he could to gain the right kind of attention for the seminary. Broadus had provided the necessary material from the professors in answer to the questions but had remained silent, along with the other faculty members, about Boyce's public appeal to all Baptists. "You have kept an ominous silence about my public appeal," Boyce noted, "and I fear you all disapprove of it." But that was behind, and they must press on with other plans. Boyce even proposed that he recommend to the board a minimum amount that must be collected to avoid suspension. They would disagree with establishing that kind of ultimatum, and then Boyce would fight their reluctance to be decisive. That certainly would draw the attention of the convention to the plight and get the board to press the matter to take up the subscription.[53]

Boyce gave elaborate suggestions about the summer work: the faculty members should disperse into different states in the South.[54] He suggested as a matter of the utmost secrecy that all five faculty pursue a goal of $25,000 which would complete "the greater part if not the whole of the permanent endowments of the states outside of Kentucky." Boyce would then "come down with a swoop" and close up the Southern states. Then he could handle Kentucky "without gloves, and close up here the next summer at latest." Strict secrecy about this approach Boyce felt necessary for "if we let them know, anyone, that we are aiming for more than this subscription we shall not succeed, and yet if we do not aim for more we shall fail to get even that."[55]

Beyond the schemes for collections, political prominence might pay important dividends for the success of the school. Boyce had been elected president of the Southern Baptist Convention in 1872 in Raleigh, North Carolina, and again in 1873 in Mobile, Alabama. He was in fact to continue to be elected to that post through 1879 in Atlanta, Georgia. In light of the strength of Landmarkism in the southwest, Boyce felt that his election to the same post in 1874 at the meeting in Jefferson, Texas, would give good visibility to the seminary's usefulness. He believed that he would be elected president again, but was "apprehensive knowing with what men or rather man and satellites we have to deal that an effort will be made to oust me." Though such a scheme probably would not come to fruition, Boyce knew that sentiment against him prevailed in those parts. Perhaps the opposition would "run Graves." Probably, however, "they will be too wise to make that issue, lest at the very next Convention he be defeated." They could resort to the ploy of convincing some that "the brethren do not want me, and thus get Burleson or Crane,[56] or some other man to allow his name to be used."

> Don't breathe this suspicion unless you see prospects of such work as you are going there. For the very suggestion may lead to the act which may not yet have entered into their heads. I say this confidentially to be kept within our little quintet with much care. But I think you will see some signs that they would do this if they find it possible. I am of the opinion, however, that unless managed more shrewdly than they can, any attempt of the sort will be defeated.[57]

Before the convention, more strategy and work had to come to fruition. Boyce's mind still whirled with all of the possible scenarios for obtaining the needed endowment and operating expenses while continuing his work on the articles in answer to the two objections. He had filled three articles in answering completely the objection concerning the ownership of the seminary. Now he worked toward completion of the fourth and fifth articles that would take up the second objection. He sent copies to the faculty in Greenville, in very rough shape, and asked for any input they thought could be vital, especially if they judged anything in them to be harmful to William Williams. Boyce himself felt that he had "avoided all evil," had done nothing to advance the purpose of those "who have put me on the stand," and had "used their thunder skilfully" for his purpose.

And that is precisely what he did. Searching the minutes of three state conventions, Mississippi, Georgia, and West Tennessee, he found that the only reported objection to the doctrine of the seminary was that one of the five professors believed alien immersion was acceptable. On that issue "four of the five professors at Greenville are opposed to the reception of alien immersions." Boyce quoted the pertinent parts of the respective minutes and found that even though they protested against the reported views of one professor, they nevertheless recommended earnestly that their young ministerial students receive their theological education at Greenville. One state, Georgia, even desired that the school be located in its bounds. If such be the case, "the correspondent of *The Baptist* is therefore not justified in thinking it strange, that, in the face of this action, we should expect contributions for the Seminary from these States." Rather, if they recommend it as a place of study, "it is reasonably to be presumed that they would be willing that they themselves and their constituents should contribute their just proportion."[58]

In this entire discussion, Boyce argued only as if the conventions under question believed the report to be true, but not as if it really were true. He neither admitted nor denied the truth of the charge. Boyce believed that Williams "has in many respects been misunderstood." Why apparent theological diversity on that point was not seen as improper Boyce would explain in the next, and last, article.

That must wait. The convention approached and the seminary must be well represented. It would be necessary to request an opportunity to appeal for operating funds. The convention again elected Boyce as president, and the entire experience turned out to be quite a triumph for the seminary group. Broadus, Boyce, and Williams all participated in an ordination service on Sunday night. Broadus preached on 1 Timothy 1:12. His full outline was given in newspaper reports on the event with one correspondent expressing, "This was one of the most impressive discourses we have ever listened to, and will long be remembered by the hundreds who heard it."[59] Boyce participated in the laying on of hands along with Broadus and Williams and others, and Williams offered the ordination prayer.

Another breakthrough was more immediately important. The earlier appeal for funds through five-year bonds produced pledges of $40,000. Another $30,000 was needed for the support of faculty and agents for five years. Seminary trustees requested that Boyce be given time to address the convention on the history, design, and needs of the seminary. "The noble brethren," to use the words of Broadus, "though just rallying from the financial collapse of the year before, gave him the pledges he asked for, $30,000."[60] This amount would provide the need, with no margin for any lapse, a condition as yet unattainable.

Over six weeks passed between the fourth and fifth articles. When Boyce turned his attention back to the articles, the issue of theological integrity had to be addressed. His opening sentence stated, "The most perplexing of all the questions before the Educational Convention at Greenville, was, how to secure the perpetuity of sound doctrine in the chairs of the Seminary."[61]

Given the necessity of teaching sound doctrine, the question of securing its perpetuity demanded careful attention. Boyce already had stated its necessity in 1856 in his famous inaugural address: "Three Changes in Theological Institutions." At that time he suggested that the Charleston Association Confession most admirably suited that purpose. He recalled the difficulty some brethren had in accepting the idea of a "creed." At the time the seminary was founded many, perhaps most, had great sympathy for the Philadelphia Confession of Faith. The brethren in the West, however, disliked some portions of it. Others preferred the New Hampshire Confession while others found it objectionable. The decision, therefore, to write a new doctrinal platform met with approval.

As many Baptist confessions of faith as could be gathered entered the lists as candidates for consultation. As was described in an earlier chapter, Basil Manly Jr. did most of the compiling, editing, and writing. The entire educational committee joined in discussion of the articles. Finally, a twenty-article platform, distilled mainly from the Charleston Association Confession (like the Philadelphia Confession of Faith it related almost verbatim to the Second London Confession), was adopted and entitled the "Abstract of Principles." Boyce highlighted three principles that governed the final articulation of the text. "1. A complete exhibition of the fundamental doctrines of grace, so that in no essential particular should they speak dubiously; 2. They should speak out clearly and distinctly as to the practices universally prevalent among us; 3. Upon no point, upon which the denomination is divided should the Convention [that is, the Educational Convention convened for this purpose], and through it the Seminary, take any position."[62]

Boyce believed that each of these three principles found full expression in the "Abstract." He would have abandoned the project, in fact, had that not been the case. The doctrines of grace "are therefore distinctly brought out in the abstract of principles" as well as Baptist practices on baptism and the Lord's Supper. Just as important, however, was adherence to the principle that "upon those questions upon which there was still a difference of opinion among Southern Baptists, the Seminary articles should not bind the institution." Profoundly germane to Boyce's point of discussion, the doctrinal division to which he referred as operative in 1859 differed not one whit from that currently creating suspicion—alien immersion. Although the "Abstract" contained strong articles on baptism and the Lord's Supper, it affirmed neither a specifically pro- nor anti-Landmark position on those practices. Boyce showed that this policy was reasonable and purposeful. It was developed in the interest of unity and justice toward the large Landmark contingent in the convention, though the brethren present could have inserted "an article which would forever have prevented anyone holding such views from even being a professor in the Seminary."[63]

Shrewdly, Boyce quoted A. C. Dayton to the effect that both North and South were divided on this issue prior to the Civil War just at the time that the seminary organized. "It is to be hoped," Boyce mused, "that the time will come when all Baptists shall see eye to eye upon all points." On a matter such as this, not one of vital orthodoxy or the doctrines of grace, "mutual forbearance and instruction" under the guidance of God's Spirit should make for a discussion filled with "love for each other and a desire to bring others to the truth."[64]

Even with the call for forbearance, Boyce identified himself unmistakably with those that did not accept "alien immersion." To the advantage of those who agreed with him, the proportion of seminary professors that agreed with him exceeded the proportion in the

Southern Baptist Convention at large. No division ought to occur on this issue, however, as the opinion at the time of the founding of the seminary focused on mutual forbearance. Boyce quoted A. C. Dayton, "We perfectly agree . . . that differences of opinion upon this subject should cause no estrangement between brethren of the same faith and order. We hope and trust it will be no cause of non-fellowship between brethren of churches."[65]

With hopes that the objections might fall as a result of the benevolent blows he had dealt them, Boyce closed the articles with the reminder to the reader that these answers were prepared "amid perplexing cares and deep anxieties, in time snatched from labors twice as great as I have had to perform in any like period of my life." This closed the mild uprising of controversy as far as Boyce had concern in it. There was work to be done.

Spirits were somewhat revived by the time of the fifth article, for, immediately following the convention, Broadus made the trip to the anniversary meeting of the Northern Baptists. The American Baptist Publication Society was now fifty years old and the General Missionary Convention celebrated its sixtieth year. Broadus described how with the help of S. S. Cutting and Samuel Colgate he took the floor for ten minutes to plead for the seminary. Because of the "overwhelming applause"[66] he spoke only "5 or 6 minutes"[67] and "felt all that he ever learned and thought focused" in that speech.[68] Colgate rose in the aisle and proposed an effort to get pledges of $2,500 per year for five years. "In fifteen minutes they pledged $2,100 a year," and his friends in Orange, New York, said that the $2,500 would be made up. "I am the more pleased at all this, as it was not at all my doing (and I said so, very distinctly)," Broadus continued to Boyce, "and because I have said no word in any speech that looked like yielding our convention, or truckling to or fawning upon the North." Broadus stood convinced that neither his wife, his brother, nor Boyce would condemn anything that he had said.[69] To his wife he wrote, "They are great and bitter sacrifices that you and I have to make, dear wife, for this Seminary enterprise; will you not rejoice with me at this unexpected help which Providence has raised up for us?"[70] That amount provided what was needed for the margin of error endemic to five-year bonds. "They paid it, too," Broadus recalled, "scarcely a dollar ever failing,—it is a way they have, to pay the pledges they make in public meetings."[71]

The following summer Boyce traveled throughout central Kentucky with his good friend Broadus for a prearranged tour of forty days. They preached every evening except Saturday and twice on Sunday. Their activities kept them up until after midnight but with the necessity of an early train the next day. Boyce prospered in health on this tour, according to Broadus, who needed an afternoon nap. Broadus observed that Boyce "was habitually a small eater" and "even Kentucky hospitality did not tempt him beyond a decided moderation."[72] His large frame and the attacks of gout had led people to believe otherwise, but it was never so throughout his life. The tour provided a contact with Nimrod Long of Russellville that proved fruitful several years later. When Boyce asked for a similar investment of time and energy from Broadus two summers later, Broadus recoiled. "I am really ashamed to say I can't come to Kentucky in August," he wrote Boyce. "I have a positive terror of summer work there. That tour of 2 years ago I feel in every nerve today." He then recalled the entire context of pressure: "Coming just after our long agony about the 5 year bonds, after Jefferson [the Southern Baptist Convention] and Washington [the Northern Baptist anniversaries], it almost killed me."[73]

Though it almost killed him, it gave Broadus a keen look at the operation of Boyce. His respect for Boyce's labors greatly increased, and his realization of the personal sacrifice involved moved him sincerely. With another three years of similar labor yet to be done before the seminary could move to Louisville, Broadus summarized these years of work for his friend:

> Numerous journeys had to be made into all parts of Kentucky, not only to associations and churches, but again and again to the home of some man who was able and possibly might be willing to help largely. Little by little brethren were brought to understand the nature and the aims of the Seminary, and what he considered its unrivalled adaptation to the wants of the Baptist ministry in general. Slowly one and another man came to believe that it was really worth while to have such an institution in Kentucky, and worth his while to help. More and more the excellent Baptist men and women of the city and State

came to know Dr. Boyce personally, to appreciate the strength and nobleness of his character, the breadth of his good sense and beauty of his gentlemanly bearing, the sincerity and devotion of his personal piety. In fact, a large proportion of people, even among those of considerable intelligence, can seldom be brought to take lively interest in something still future and distant, in some enterprise of which they have no personal experience, until they come to know and love its living representative. . . . Many began to help Dr. Boyce because they loved him and sympathized with his intense desire; others because they saw he would never give up, would keep at it till he succeeded, and would politely keep after them till they yielded. Oh, the long, sore struggle for the high-toned gentleman, the ambitious student cut off from the studies he loved, the man who had devoted himself to teaching, and now, year after year, could not teach at all![74]

Not only could he not teach, he found that Kentuckians had a lower opinion of preachers than he had been accustomed to further east. While, therefore, Boyce worked for money, he worked as well for respect and for ministers sympathetic to the seminary in well-placed pulpits. He achieved one major victory at Broadway Baptist Church in Louisville. When J. B. Hawthorne, thirty-seven years old, resigned from that congregation to go to New York, Boyce worked for their calling J. Lansing Burrows from Richmond to that pulpit. "I worked Hawthorne into Tabernacle [Baptist Church]," Boyce informed Broadus, "and Burrows here, and I think I have made two good moves for the Seminary." He added, to assure Broadus that he was able to maintain a larger scope of concern than just the seminary, "I did not in either case, however, work for that but for the good of all parties."[75]

Under Hawthorne, Broadway, though deeply involved in their own building project, had provided substantial pledges prior to the 1873 financial panic. Under Burrows, Boyce believed, they would mature in their commitment to see the seminary in Louisville. Burrows, pastor of the First Baptist Church of Richmond since 1854, had chaired the 1855 meeting of "friends of theological education" in Montgomery, Alabama. Hawthorne, who had built a $100,000 edifice at Broadway debt-free, thrived spiritually in New York but failed rapidly physically, and in later 1875 moved to First Baptist Church, Montgomery. Four years later, in the fall of 1879, he went to First Baptist Church, Richmond, where he stayed until 1884, when he moved to First Baptist Church in Atlanta.

Boyce also had heard that First Baptist Church of Augusta needed a pastor; he was anxious to recommend the right person. In the space of two letters, Boyce mentioned the names of fourteen persons that might be considered. For one the "work would be too heavy," and he had too many relatives in the church, and another, T. T. Eaton, Boyce considered "too hifalutin."[76] Though by his own estimate some ministers simply would not fit in certain pulpits, he believed that the overall status of ministers in Kentucky was shockingly low. "Kentucky has no station for preachers," he lamented. For entrance into society, Boyce complained, since a minister cannot dance, "a preacher here to be popular must be a horse jockey and not above that level." He was sure the seminary would change all that, but in the meantime, their status was shaky. "In Virginia they worship their preachers," one church member quipped and another answered, "Well, I hope never to see that down in Kentucky." Boyce, chagrined at the conversation he overheard, remarked, "Now he knew what the word worship meant. I see hotelkeepers, women who started life as cooks, men who were once errand boys or slave blacks worshipped here—not for their moral or intellectual worth." Boyce had no desire to pose as an aristocrat but despised the kind of preference and respect given to people simply because of wealth. "Yet men thank God that ministers are not worshipped, who surely ought to have some claim as men of intelligence and virtue to public regard."[77]

In spite of this downside to ministry, the opportunity to preach in the churches still presented the best opportunity for influence. When asked in November to supply the pulpit at Walnut Street Baptist Church, Boyce wrote Broadus about the opportunity, confessing, "I have done this not merely to accommodate them, but in order to get in that congregation and influence for my work, and also a position before the community in Louisville. From that standpoint I hope to be able to do much for the Seminary."[78] Broadus responded enthusiastically, encouraging Boyce to make the absolute most of this entire opportunity.

> I think your Walnut Street arrangement is very judicious. I should say, throw yourself into the preaching, with all your might, so as to do them all possible good, and to do yourself justice, and make them feel your *power*. There are men who excel you in clearness and sweetness, but very few men make sermons of nearly such strength and weight. Make most of your sermons <u>short</u>, but when you have a great *and attractive* subject, make it long, shortening the other services. Use your rare taste in poetry, for the careful selection of hymns. Take great pains to make the entire *worship* attractive and impressive.
>
> And informally *visit* a good deal, as temporary pastor. That will give you a great hold upon *families*, the ladies and the young folks.
>
> These hints as they occur to me, only on the principle that two heads are better than one, if one is a cabbage head.[79]

Boyce's presence at the church evidently produced a positive effect. In March of 1875 Boyce reported that he had been "strongly pressed to take Walnut Street, but have put my foot on the proposition every time suggested." Arthur assured Boyce, even in the face of issuing a call to another, that he could assure Boyce of "a unanimous vote."[80] On 31 December 1874, he received from Mrs. J. Laurence Smith, a member of the church, the donation of $15,000 worth of land with the stipulation that it not be sold for fifteen years. She believed that it would be worth much more at that time. Lest this cause too much optimism for Broadus, Boyce let him know that she had given this gift with the clear assertion that she still opposed the removal of the seminary to Louisville.[81] Later, Boyce warned Broadus not to ask Mr. Smith for any aid for the student fund, for one of the "great arguments that he has pressed . . . has been that we will throw on the Baptists of Kentucky a number of 'pauper' students which they will be obliged to support."[82] Care not to offend must take many forms.

Testimony to the weightiness of Boyce's obligations appeared in the *Western Recorder* in November 1874. A student from Kentucky, Z. A. Owens, reported on the beginning of the fall term in Greenville with an expression of deep gratitude for the privilege of such study and a testimony that time had been of "inestimable advantage." He was disturbed, however, by reports of the slowness of the financial support from Kentucky Baptists. He had heard one respected brother say that the money would in due time be raised, "but Dr. Boyce will be worn out first, and perhaps four or five more men." Kentucky Baptists must not let such a tragedy befall them and the denomination. Did they have even "half a conception" of the value of the seminary, then "the Seminary would be in Louisville next September, and Dr. Boyce would be relieved of the four or five years predicted."[83]

Though the prediction of four or five years was too long, another three would pass before the Southern Baptist Theological Seminary could be located in Louisville. Other challenges and heartaches still lay ahead.

8

Finalizing the Move to Louisville

*T*he year 1875 received only two brief mentions in Broadus's memoir of Boyce.[1] Boyce stayed occupied with travel, correspondence, canvassing the Louisville folk, and devising new schemes for raising money. One such attempt concerned commemorating the coming celebration of one hundred years of nationhood with the "Dollar Roll." As he began preparing it, he had an engraver make likenesses of each professor and even included Basil Manly Jr., now for several years the president of Georgetown, and sent a specimen to the faculty. The engraver, Boyce quipped, made an improvement on their faces, making Whitsitt's appear twenty years older than he was so as "to put him upon an equal footing with Williams." Boyce also assured his faculty that he himself "was regarded too handsome for my company taken *au natural* and so he has taken off some of my good looks."[2] The others were truer likenesses and he was well pleased with the overall effect. In the text of the "roll" Boyce took full advantage of the part Baptists had played in fashioning the ideals of the Revolutionary War:

Baptists of the United States, Including Members of their Churches, and of their Congregations, their families, and persons ancestrally or otherwise connected with the denomination, in commemoration of American Independence, of the triumph thereunder of their Historical Principles of Religious Liberty, and of the Growth, Prosperity and Influence, vouchsafed to them by the Grace of God during One Hundred Years, in connection with other efforts in behalf of higher education unite in a simultaneous and uniform contribution for the endowment of THE SOUTHERN BAPTIST THEOLOGICAL SEMINARY, alike as a thank-offering for the century past, and as a preparation for the century to come.[3]

In January, Boyce approved the discipline and stripping of the ordination of H. M. Wharton, a seminary student and brother of the former pastor of Walnut Street for being a "slave to intoxicating liquor."[4] Boyce also supported a protracted meeting under a union arrangement among the churches. They invited D. W. Whittle and P. P. Bliss, "two laymen who have been at work at Detroit and Pittsburgh with great success." Boyce said they "entered into a prepared field" and took charge of what he described as a "delightful session of meetings" that involved all denominations.[5]

At the same time, Boyce began to send whiskey regularly to Greenville at the request of Broadus. On February 16, Broadus asked Boyce to "direct some reliable house to send me by Express 2 gallons first-rate Whiskey." He wanted "first-rate" because "my wife can't bear any that is not mild and pure—and I have been getting Scotch Whiskey in New York, at a high price $6 and $7 and $8."[6] He looked forward to "a really good article in Louisville, cheaper than that." These orders continued through the months, and on 18 July 1876 Broadus requested, "Please order sent to my address 4 gallons Whiskey, such as heretofore. Mamma needs it constantly now, besides the general family use."[7] The nature of the correspondence in the Broadus family at this time indicates that not only "Mamma," but Broadus's wife Lottie and children had a variety of ailments that called for whiskey as the base for a tonic or medicinal solution.[8] In addition to that for Broadus, Boyce sent whiskey frequently to William Williams, seemingly to aid him in his fight against an increasingly potent respiratory disorder.[9]

Boyce made trips to Texas and Mississippi, places where Landmark influence was high and the seminary's approval was surrounded with great reservations. He called his visits a "fine time" and felt that he had made some friends. The Texas brethren were "particularly cordial" as demonstrated by the patriarch Z. N. Morrell's[10] gesture of initiating a handshaking ceremony accompanied by the hymn "How Firm a Foundation." Boyce made a "centennial speech" in Texas and heard B. H. Carroll, who demonstrated his "fine powers as a speaker" and did "remarkably well." His contacts in Mississippi pleased him equally as well where he spoke for an hour and a half, evoking testimony that he had "converted unbelievers, confirmed doubters, and enthused the faithful." Boyce believed he had made special friends with J. A. Hackett and John Lewis Pettigrew, both prominent and productive Mississippi pastors whose writing ministries greatly influenced denominational opinion.[11] These Texas and Mississippi relations would soon be strained.

In September 1875, Broadus wrote Boyce about a proposal that the seminary award degrees for completion of work in the several subjects and not just for the full graduate. "Our present full graduate is too difficult to be our only degree," Broadus reasoned, "considering that imperfect preparation and general haste of our Southern youth, and the fact that at all other Theological Seminaries of the United States graduation is a matter of course."[12] The possibilities, in fact, for anyone to graduate that academic year looked slim. The faculty proposed three degrees, English graduate, eclectic graduate, and full graduate. Boyce responded:

> Your letter as to the action of the faculty received. I am fully in accord with you. You will remember I told you I fear the result of our rigid course. Let me suggest. Could we not graduate in full over all the course except Latin Theology, Senior Greek and Senior Hebrew— and then give a degree of (B.D.) Bachelor of Divinity for those who will complete that course. I make the suggestion again could we not arrange for those not taking this latter course to return and upon certain examinations receive that degree "out of course," not exactly honorary. Besides if we should confer it could we not also give it as an honorary degree to certain of our own or other students whose

subsequent attainments or usefulness would authorize it. And could we not thus make it more honorable than the D. D. of the colleges. These are only suggestions.[13]

When the board of trustees met in Richmond in May, they approved one further degree, that of English graduate. This was awarded to those students who had studied in every class with the exception of the Hebrew and Greek and the class in Latin Theology. In 1890 the degree of eclectic graduate was added.

Tests of the Seminary's Freedom

A Merge with Crozer?

In the beginning of 1876, a multiplicity of pressures mounted. The condition of William Williams had worsened, Boyce still had to maintain the agency in Louisville, Whitsitt had great limitations on what he could be prepared to teach, Broadus was "so overwhelmed and worn," fighting bronchitis, that he feared to undertake new courses. In addition, "Toy still has seven chapters of Lange on Samuel, which will push him to 1st May, and we shall be disgraced if we don't have it out by next fall—they will say that Southerners can't be relied on, etc."[14] Boyce had to apologize for meeting only about half the salary for the first quarter of 1876, and Broadus reported that "our Northern subscribers are right slow."[15]

For the sake of the Baptist colleges North Carolina asked Boyce to withdraw his agents. Alabama came close to making the same request. Boyce felt the dilemma keenly: "If I assent, we shall never get a dime, for the colleges have been trying for ten years and we have kept out of the way, and they will be struggling for ten more. If we refuse them we shall be charged with want of liberality, and we shall have to make a fight which is very unpleasant." Broadus said that he must not withdraw, for that would be "yielding the point that they have a prior claim." They would find a way to continue the delaying tactics and then other states would join them. The only safe course, Broadus encouraged, is to "push right on." He felt no harm would come to the colleges "half so much as we help them. And if the college men are blind and don't see it, we mustn't stop for them."[16]

With a potentially fiery and still uncertain future, a great temptation for a quick solution came Boyce's way in April of 1876 just as he struggled to use the Centennial celebration as a means of raising capital. With a flurry of convention, union, commission, and associational meetings close at hand and the necessity of some seminary presence at each of these, Boyce was confronted with two major decisions. First, William F. Norton began to insist that the seminary move to Louisville in the fall. Boyce believed such a move would be a financial disaster while Norton believed that a failure to move would prove to be a financial mistake. Perhaps a move would create a greater sense of responsibility and "render necessary other subscriptions hereafter because we start with insufficient amount." But he confessed transparently, "What is best I know not."[17]

Second, J. B. Jeter proposed, with the real possibility of success, that the seminary unite with Crozer, move to Washington, and make a national seminary in service of all Baptists. Crozer, which began in 1868 with a $275,000 endowment from the wealth of Samuel A. Crozer, was located in Upland, Pennsylvania. Henry G. Weston was president. Benjamin Griffith, brother-in-law to Crozer and son-in-law of the John Price Crozer who had originally garnered the fortune, believed that the Crozer family would "like it in that they know they could only make a local Seminary at Upland, but that at Washington would be national." Many in the South might be repelled at such an idea, but with work and with the presence of Southern men on the faculty that could be overcome.

The possibility of an extra $500,000 from the Crozers and perhaps as much as $2,000,000 in endowment when combined with what others would be energized to give made the possibility even more attractive. The Southern plan would die but, "on the other hand," Boyce contemplated, "I am sure if we left the name of Crozer we could get the modeling of the Seminary according to our model and open the way for a grand success in this respect north and south. I confess this charms me. It almost blinds me to the evils." And just think, with that kind of foundation and the administrative personnel to help, "Why should we not have a Seminary with a dozen professionals who could teach without being drudges, and teach thoroughly because not compelled to limit their course, or the time for any one topic. Why can we not have a Seminary like Germany with professors whose reputation shall be like theirs?"[18] If they would come to the South, Boyce could drop all objections, and "If they would but come to Louisville, that would be the very thing." He was willing that they "have the name and the glory and all they wish that we could grant" for Louisville and "half the professors."

Broadus and Toy must be certain but Boyce could "gladly give way." He cared nothing for his place but only for the "success and usefulness" of the seminary, "as much as I love to be with all of you and love its work." Boyce believed that he had no selfishness in this matter and would gladly die "any day to secure its success with my death." Because of the probability that the Crozers would not consent to "some Southern point" ("Oh that the Crozers, or some one else would only give us the foundation without the Washington City part") he felt "1/10 in favor and 9/10 against." Boyce swore Broadus to the "most positive secrecy"; it must not "go beyond our charmed circle."[19]

Jeter went beyond the stage of discussion within a small circle and published his desire for amalgamation as an editorial in the *Religious Herald*. He entitled his editorial "A Singular Dream." In this dream, Jeter saw the old campus of Columbian University in Washington in a splendid condition with lovely buildings and engaging landscaping. He asked what had happened. "Have you not heard that the Crozer Seminary and the Southern Baptist Theological Seminary have united," answered Dr. James Welling, president of the university, "and erected these convenient edifices in connection with the Columbian University?" Dr. Welling then took Jeter into a public meeting, and there to his surprise he saw "the professors of both Seminaries mingled together, as teachers in a common school with the utmost cordiality and pleasure, surrounded by more than one hundred fifty students drawn from all parts of the country." He also saw S. S. Cutting, a prominent Northern Baptist and secretary of the American Baptist Education Commission, who "expatiated most eloquently on the great advantages of the union of the two Seminaries," calling it "the most important arrangement for promoting theological learning, as it is received among Baptists, that has ever been adopted in this country, or even in the world." He had hopes that both Rochester and Hamilton would relinquish their charters and merge their funds in the endowment of Crozer, the name of the mega-seminary now adjunct to Columbian. Another visitor who had heard of the newly crafted fame of Crozer declared that "it bade fair to be the finest theological institution in the world."

But what dream of such a nature would be complete without the appearance of Boyce? And there he was in another idyllic scene. Boyce, "seemed to have grown more fat and chubby since I last saw him, and his countenance was uncommonly serene." Boyce asked Jeter if he admired the grounds. How could one not admire such a splendid surrounding, but how did the Kentucky folk consent to such a thing? "Oh," said Boyce, "when it was proposed that they should unite in founding a Seminary in Washington, the plan seemed so reasonable, so promising, and so grand, that every subscriber consented that his money should be transferred to the new Seminary, and many of them doubled their subscriptions." Then Jeter saw, in his dream, the immortal dreamer himself, Luther Rice. Rice shone splendidly and brought a message from many of now departed Baptist brethren regarding their extreme pleasure that "the noble Crozer and the promising Southern Theological Seminary were united and placed on College Hill, in connections with the University." Now, said Rice, "our prayers were answered, our toils rewarded, and our anxious wishes fulfilled in a way that we had not expected." From their heavenly perspective, they believed a "brilliant future" lay ahead for Baptists.[20]

When Baptists in Kentucky heard of this "singular dream," they thought that it might give the Atlantic states a "brilliant" future, but would leave the Southwest destitute. Kentucky Baptists must "see our opportunity and complete our portion of the endowment without further delay."[21] Boyce, having had time to digest the suggestion and sort out its disadvantages from its supposed advantages, answered swiftly and succinctly:

1. Let me say that this project has received no favor from any of the professors of our seminary and only two or perhaps three of the members of the Board.
2. I have reason to believe that it would not be favored by the gentleman of all others at Crozer, whose favor is most important.
3. As soon as mentioned to Dr. Broadus and myself we stated that the objections are insuperable.
4. It was at first thought of by Dr. Jeter when he supposed that our endowment scheme would be a failure, and he acknowledged to me, that if we could succeed it would be best to carry out our original plan.
5. I have no reason to doubt our final success in establishing the Seminary at Louisville. If we should fail I believe it will be best simply to fail and not to attempt such a union to save failure.
6. Our Seminary at Washington City, could never reach the field to which our work is especially important, namely the Southwest and West.[22]

Oppression by Landmarkism?

The seminary through Boyce had asserted the necessity of its independence from other institutions. But the arduous task of securing the endowment continued. At the same time, the seminary had to endure another strong attack from J. R. Graves and his Landmark friends in the South and Southwest. Always looking for some way to embarrass the seminary and discredit its usefulness to Southern Baptists, Graves found sufficient fodder to satisfy his hunger for controversy when a pseudonymous "Pike" began a series of articles in the *Religious Herald*. Broadus allowed his name to appear as an associate editor for the paper. "These fellows," as Boyce surmised, "only want another chance at another professor to try and deal ruin out to us."[23]

Pike argued that the "reimmersionist brethren," a term he used for the Landmarkers, sawed the limb from under themselves and, by their doctrine of what constituted a "regular" Baptist church, eliminated the possibility of any such body. We must say, he argued, "that, if there be a true act of baptism and a proper subject, the baptism is valid no matter who the administrator is."[24] Pike's position, endorsed by J. B. Jeter, the editor of the paper, evoked several responses, contrary viewpoints, and questions. Pike answered in another article entitled "Concerning the Landmark Doctrine." He used J. M. Pendleton's assertion that "authority to preach the gospel [and of course to baptize] emanates under God from a [Baptist] church." Using that principle Pike suggested, "And now I see nothing in this why the stiffest old landmarker could not consistently vote to receive a person into a Baptist church on an immersion by a Methodist preacher" or even the devil himself.[25] Pendleton responded with more than a bit of outrage at Pike's reasoning and what Pendleton considered most irreverent language. "Enough, and more than enough of such language," Pendleton wrote after quoting a peculiarly offensive section of Pike. "I beg the reader's pardon for quoting words so offensive to all refined Christian sensibilities. I have had much to do with the baptismal controversy in the course of my ministry, but I think 'Pike' is the first man so irreverent as to refer to the devil as an administrator of baptism!"[26]

All of this would make quite informative and even entertaining fare had not accusations against the seminary emerged in the middle of it. Graves republished Pendleton's *Herald* article and at the same time suggested that Pike was a "professor at Greenville Seminary"![27] "If this is the ripened fruit of the Seminary," Graves inferred, "better its doors were at once closed, and *forever*." R. C. Buckner in the *Texas Baptist* reported Graves's surmise and added, "Now we begin to fear and tremble." None excelled Buckner in "love for the Seminary," Buckner testified, and went on to suggest that "if 'Pike' is one of the faculty he should be removed, and the doors kept open now 'and forever.'" If that cannot be done, "We had better have no Theological Seminary."[28] Buckner's further comments brought Broadus into the picture and resulted in eventual accusations that Broadus indeed was "Pike."

> The *Religious Herald* is being denounced all over North Texas, at least, and perhaps in Southern Texas also, because of lending its influence, editorially and otherwise, so decidedly to "Pike's" views;

and many of the best friends and former students of the Seminary deplore the fact that one of its most prominent professors is on the editorial staff of the *Herald*. The waters are troubled; what the result will be we cannot divine. We must have the Seminary; but our people will not swallow "Pike" nor the *Herald*.[29]

Broadus already had been criticized by some "brethren in Mississippi"[30] for perceived opposition to Landmarkers in his seminary classes and in his capacity on seminary committees. In explanation he wrote a letter of some 1,550 words to Boyce. Broadus was incredulous that any could understand him in such a manner. He had not opposed issuing Graves an invitation to preach a missionary sermon, but "thought it inexpedient to elect any brother a *second time*, when so many noble brethren in every state have never been invited." In a Homiletics class he had illustrated the use of syllogisms and, among other examples, referred to a Landmark syllogism concerning the authority to preach being granted only by a church. Because it was misunderstood, Broadus decided to omit the syllogism entirely since it had "no substantive importance in that school." "I have been," Broadus assured, "and am, heartily desirous of respecting not only the opinions, but the most sensitive feelings, of all brethren throughout the South. As to Landmarkism, many of my cherished friends hold those views, and I, while not accepting them, feel no call whatever in my position to antagonize them."[31]

Broadus also cleared up two observations that he had made in New Testament class, one concerning Matthew 16. He pointed out that "the gates of hell shall not prevail against it" seemed too ambiguous and obscure an expression to build a doctrine of the perpetuity of regular Baptist churches on it. "I welcome sharp observation of what we say and do in the Seminary," Broadus affirmed, and went on to defend the right and obligation to do this. "Only I could wish that when any brother hears of my saying or doing what he thinks unfair or improper he would sit right down and frankly write to me about it." Perhaps he could relieve the brother's mind immediately, but certainly he could learn how he was misunderstood and be on guard for the future.

Broadus was astonished at the suggestion that Landmarkers were "socially" neglected in Greenville. He had never dreamed of such a thing. "Whether I have been injudicious, or simply misunderstood," Broadus noted, "I shall take due note of the way it strikes esteemed brethren. And I repeat, I shall always welcome criticism, asking only that it be made immediately upon hearing of supposed improper conduct on my part, shall be made directly to me, and with perfect frankness." He asked Boyce to use the letter as he saw fit to answer any questions that might arise concerning his attitudes toward the Landmark viewpoint and its adherents.

Broadus was not through with the "Mississippi outburst," however, and felt that he needed to warn Boyce about giving away too much in deference to the Landmark gentlemen, particularly M. P. Lowry and J. A. Hackett. Under pressure from their accusation that Boyce had not shown sympathy toward their viewpoints, he revealed that the transfer of Williams from Church History to Theology in 1872 had been done with sensitivity for their alarm at his ecclesiology. "But Williams will infallibly hear it, and will be cut to the quick," Broadus warned. "He would never have consented to the change on that supposition. He questioned me very narrowly at the time. I tried simply to *conceal* that part of your purpose, but I fear from what he told Hackett that I may have unintentionally deceived him." Boyce must not give the wrong impression in his desire to maintain friendships. "In standing up straight," Broadus advised, "don't lean backwards. You are not a Landmark man, as their extremists hold it—don't say you are." Don't give in too much on the issue of church succession "in your large-hearted desire to be magnanimous and conciliatory." Above all, "don't say you agree with Graves, for you don't, as they will understand it."[32]

More sniping at the seminary in letters and newspaper articles continued to perplex Boyce. "Has any institution such malignant enemies as ours?" he asked. "What can be the cause? It is personal, not a matter of principle; yet what have any of us done to arouse such feelings?"[33] Broadus responded that such treatment is the penalty of greatness. Besides, a newspaperman must have something riveting to write about. If he can attack a person or institution of importance on plausible grounds, he will gain a reputation for astuteness and spiciness.[34] J. A. Hackett, the editor of the *Baptist Record* of Mississippi, wrote Boyce that Broadus had admitted to the charge of a supposed prejudice against Landmarkers. Commented Boyce, "The letter is as mean as it can be."[35]

The Pike issue soon would come with all its subtle fury on Broadus. When Graves suggested that the author was from the seminary, Boyce noted that Buckner had copied "Graves's lie about the authorship of Pike." He wrote a denial to Graves and Buckner and asked Graves for the name of his supposed informant. "It is very hard," he moaned, "that one cannot avoid their lies and rascalities. But people will always seek to do harm."[36] The denial said simply, "Dear Bro.—Will you be kind enough to deny upon my authority that any professor at Greenville or elsewhere, in any way connected with the Southern Baptist Theological Seminary, is the author of the articles signed, 'Pike,' which have appeared in the *Religious Herald*."[37] When some of his readers cautioned Buckner that he had been too quick to raise the alarm on the authority of Graves, Buckner defended himself by pointing out that he had used the word "if" and that his article had prompted Boyce to send "an official statement that will silence the aspersion forever" and give "satisfaction on this point to all the true friends of our beloved school of the prophets."[38]

Buckner also printed an article by "One Who Knows" that pointed to Norman Fox, once professor at William Jewell College, as the writer. "One Who Knows" asserted with utmost confidence, "The Seminary is no more responsible for Pike than your self, brother editor, or brother Graves." He also chided Texas Baptists for being so quick to "fall out with Dr. Broadus, because he is one of the associate editors of the *Herald*." Broadus no more endorses the ecclesiology of Jeter than does J. M. Pendleton, "who almost as frequently writes for the *Herald*." When denouncing the *Herald*, the people of Texas should not "strike at random, lest they injure some of the grandest, truest and most useful men whom the Spirit of God ever made Baptists."

Boyce received Buckner's actions as an indication of his kindliness and his love for the seminary. The *Herald*, however, continued to play into Graves's hands by stirring the pot of controversy and publishing Pike. Graves continued to hold Broadus responsible for the articles and called him to disclaim the views published in the *Herald*. Boyce wrote to Broadus that "it would be wise to separate from the Editorship, and then write so far as you please."[39] He also continued to press Graves for information concerning his informant and reiterated, "The fact is I believe he lied."[40] Broadus, responding to Boyce's letter of October 21, wrote Jeter and Dickinson at the *Herald* that he "wished to cease to be called an editor."[41] But Boyce changed his mind concerning Broadus and the *Herald*, noting, "I am decidedly of the opinion that you had best retain your editorial connection with the Herald, because we must not ruin ourselves with our real and tried friends everywhere to avoid a little attack now and then." Perhaps as a matter of policy, editorial connections should be avoided, but when separation is demanded, "the demand should not be yielded to." Boyce had decided "not to yield an inch more, but to take a firm stand."[42]

Boyce's change of mind came at a propitious time, for when Boyce penned his note to Broadus, Broadus sent a feisty letter to Boyce with every indication that Graves had pushed him too far. He would not yield one more inch.

> I had much rather, personally, my name were dropped from the Herald, and I have been inclining to insist on that, notwithstanding what I wrote in sending you Dickinson's letter the other day. But really this letter from Graves seems to make it nearly impossible that I should draw off. How can I submit to such dictation? I do not wish to be foolish, but a man must have some self-respect. If I choose to write for the paper published in my native state, as I have been doing for 10 years, what business has J. R. Graves to forbid it, under pain of his opposing a general denominational enterprise with which I am connected. Compare this. I am rather afraid that if I draw off now, it will cool Dickinson, and strengthen somewhat the current that is flowing towards Crozer; but if Dickinson were in the slightest way to intimate a threat of that, I'd drop him in a minute, and give him a piece of my mind to boot. How can I subject to act under such a threat from Graves?
>
> Besides. Is there really any use in trying to satisfy Graves? Give an inch and he asks a mile. First he conjures me to say whether I am responsible for everything in the Herald. I answer, and the very next week he begins demanding, virtually, that I shall retire altogether. If

I did that, if I should measure the lines, and write exactly as much for his paper as for the Herald, he would soon begin to claim that a Seminary professor should not write at all for a paper so unsound and hurtful, etc.

You try to put the Seminary in a neutral position. But neutrality will not satisfy him. Four professors may substantially agree with him on a point as to which the denomination is divided, and still he tells you if you don't restrain the fifth from saying a word to the contrary he will thunder. Don't you see it plainly? Have we long known that every man whom Graves cannot make his *subject* he regards as his enemy? Why delude yourself with the notion that he is your friend, or that you can manage him?

You see now, it is not enough that I should cease to be called associate editor of the Herald; I must not even write for it unless I will write just as much for him. Now, my dear fellow, there are many things I would do to please you or to serve the Seminary; but to become a contributor to Graves' paper is a thing I cannot and will not do, without a great change of present feelings and purposes. I can write for Gambrell without hesitation; but to write regular for the other, once a month, or once an anything, no. When my father died, he thought he was leaving his son a scholar and a gentleman.[43]

Boyce smiled, even laughed heartily at such spunk from his dear, gentle-spirited, accommodating friend. Broadus had asked Boyce to burn the letter, but Boyce said that it was too good to consign it to the flames. As far as he was concerned, the issue was at an end. "I propose we strike now for independence," he resolved in the spirit of the Centennial, and "let Graves make his issue upon your writing for the Herald." Boyce was confident that Graves could not sustain himself in his attacks. "I am now anxious for matters to remain as they are, don't yield one inch."[44] The taste of freedom was sweet.

The Death of William Williams

In January 1877, John A. Broadus wrote George Boardman Taylor, a Southern Baptist missionary to Italy. Among other items of mutual interest he reported on the state of health of William Williams. "Doctor Williams went down last spring with incipient consumption. At

Asheville, N. C., he got better during the summer, and he is wintering at Aiken." Broadus knew that his getting better was only temporary and feared that "he will never teach again." He described Williams as "a noble man, of great abilities, and is the finest lecturer I have ever known. His lectures on Systematic Theology, the last two or three years, were something wonderful for clearness, terseness, power."[45] Broadus simply acknowledged what Boyce had said in 1862, "What would I not give for his wonderful power to put things clearly before those he addresses."[46]

Since 1872 Williams had been teaching Systematic Theology, Church History, and Church Government and Pastoral Duties. This overload combined with regular preaching in country churches, little exercise, a less than vigorous constitution, and intense mental strain "wore him out more seriously" than any of his colleagues were aware. Probably in late fall or early winter of 1875, he slept in a small room that had a window from which a pane of glass was missing. He caught cold and progressively became worse but would not stop his work.

In January Boyce and Broadus began including reports on Williams in their correspondence. "Dr. Trescot told me today that Dr. Williams is seriously sick—feverish, night-sweats, cough—for some time," Broadus reported. The doctor did not think it advisable that Williams teach. Broadus made several suggestions as to how the classes could be handled. Boyce was upset. "I fear Dr. Trescot is right. I have been uneasy about Williams for some time." He saw little merit in most of Broadus's suggestions and proposed that Williams's courses be handled by assigning textbook reading for private study with an examination at year's end. "I do not think any of you should burden yourselves to take these subjects and especially to lecture upon them." Soon, Broadus responded with an arrangement for teaching that avoided Boyce's objections for the most part and incorporated efforts to help Williams.

> We have a pretty good arrangement about Williams' classes. Whitsitt did study Church History and takes that. Toy will hear recitations in Dick. They will send for Pond's Patristic Theology. Dargan and Ebeltoft will read Augustine's Confessions without a teacher. Trescot begged Williams to go for 6 weeks to Florida. Williams finally told him

no money. Werne offered to furnish it, $125, but Williams hesitated to receive. Through Toy I have this afternoon arranged, that *Seminary* pays Williams' expenses, $125, and Werne, of his own accord, will refund the money to Seminary. I have sent Williams a check for that amount, and hope he'll go. Trescot thinks he can return (from Madison, Fla.) by 1st April, able to lecture that month. Lungs slight affected, and change of climate will probably stop it.[47]

Williams went to Florida but found that he was sicker than he knew. He wrote Broadus on March 23 that he should remain longer and should not attempt to teach or hold examinations. He also needed fifty dollars. By April he reported that he was considerably better and would be home by the twenty-second. On April 26, Broadus reported to Boyce that Williams was not better but worse, he never expected him to lecture again, and believed he might live a year. Special financial arrangements, as well as whiskey, were provided from month to month.

In July Williams reported to Boyce that he was getting stronger and hoped yet to do service. By August, Williams had practically abandoned hope of recovery. Broadus commented, "This shows that he cannot last long, and also that he is like to be very sad, till so near his end as to rest exclusively in religious hopes." In addition to many special arrangements for money Broadus said, "We must do something, for our dear friend is evidently in very trying circumstances."[48] Broadus saw him again in September and observed that his appearance was "wonderfully improved. I never saw him look better." Well, who would not with such a radically changed life style—He "quit tobacco and nearly quit coffee, quit work, rode morning and afternoon, also walked, played croquet a great deal (very fond of it), and slept all night." Both his appetite and digestion proved excellent, his weight had increased, and his doctor said his lungs were better. Though Williams was confident of recovery Broadus wrote, "*Between you and me* it is a melancholy delusion. He coughs now every minute, slightly. I don't for a moment believe he will ever be able to work again." Broadus made complicated financial arrangements to help Williams and his family settle in Aiken on the doctor's orders. Boyce was glad to hear of the improvement, but, like Broadus, feared the cough.[49]

By January, Williams clearly had no chance of teaching again or of recovery to health. Boyce was grieved to have his "fears confirmed" and sought merciful arrangements for him. He favored the trustees "making him Emeritus Professor, and paying salary, for life, or for one year." He wanted this to be a policy for others—"It is what other institutions do." His only doubt was whether they would give full salary, but he was firm that they "put Williams beyond reach of dependence upon others."[50] On February 9 Boyce wrote again, concerned about the impending move to Louisville and how that would affect the new trustee arrangement. How many faculty members would the trustees feel obliged to provide for? Maybe only three—Broadus, Toy, and Boyce. Could they find Whitsitt a church to pastor? "The only trouble is Williams," he lamented; "We must have some provision for him."[51]

This letter also included an allusion to an event that offered some brief and exhilarating diversion from the soberness of the issues pressing them both. Broadus had been preparing for months for lectures on preaching to be delivered at Rochester Theological Seminary. These were to begin on February 12. Boyce desired one meeting with him while he was in Rochester to talk about some details of the move, but also said, "I should like to hear one lecture while there."[52] Such an auspicious presence among the rich Baptists of New York State could only benefit the reputation of Baptists in the South and perhaps facilitate a more healthy endowment.

Broadus lectured each evening, Monday through Friday. A. H. Strong had been president of the institution since 1872. It had begun in 1850 and accepted only college graduates into its programs. A. T. Robertson described the lectures as "free talks on the general subject of preaching, made from carefully prepared notes."[53] During the week, Broadus wrote his wife with comments on each evening's events. He called the third lecture "highly successful." "There are supreme moments," he observed, "in which all the energies and experiences of a man are concentrated with the highest intensity upon focal points, and it is curious how things blaze." The fourth lecture, though Broadus "felt flat," many considered the best, "containing many fresh thoughts about the preacher's private life." The fifth lecture, in light of the increasing diversity of the audience and the presence of many ministers of other denominations, seemed risky—in fact, his wife earlier had advised against using it. It dealt with the duties of a Baptist minister to oppose the errors in other groups while being able to distinguish sharply "between the sacrifice of principle and the exercise of courtesy." One attendee reported that "it was acceptable to all who heard it, both Baptists and Pedobaptists." Broadus mentioned to his wife that pedobaptist ministers came up afterwards "to say pleasant things."

A time of question and answer followed each lecture and, according to Broadus, "we had a great time." A student observer reported that Broadus "submitted to be interrogated at the close of each." This interchange "elicited many not only amusing, but interesting and important points." When the five nights were over, he reported, "Professors Strong, Wilkinson, and Kendrick expressed themselves in singularly strong and gratifying terms about the lectures, the former thinking I had done the students and the Seminary important service. So I may well be thankful."[54]

A student from Kentucky enrolled at Rochester Seminary attended the lectures and concurred with that evaluation. He reported the lectures for the *Western Recorder*. As a young minister himself, he felt that the discussion could be particularly relevant for other young ministers. Though Broadus's reputation, according to the reporter, was not known to many of the citizens of Rochester, "he left an impression on many minds which will not be obliterated soon." After giving a synopsis of the highlights of each of the five lectures, the young reporter said, "His lectures caused in my heart a desire to return to my native and beloved Kentucky, that I may hear again some good old-fashioned gospel preaching."[55] This is an impression that could hardly hurt the seminary as it made its plans to move to Louisville.

Four days after the lectures at Rochester closed, William Williams died. William A. Mueller summarized, "Though the trustees granted him a leave of absence in 1876, the ravages of tuberculosis laid him low at last, and on 20 February 1877, Professor William Williams died at Aiken, South Carolina, at less than fifty-six years of age."[56] Broadus, who observed that he never "knew a man more completely genuine, more thoroughly sincere, more conscientious in all his doings," called the fatal illness "the fell ravages of consumption."[57] Boyce came from Louisville to Greenville, where the funeral was held, to take part, and Broadus preached from a prearranged text, "My Times Are in His Hands." On February 23 the faculty wrote an expression of appreciation, placed it in the minutes, and had it printed in newspapers and denominational journals of the South.

> The Faculty of the Southern Baptist Theological Seminary desire to place on record an expression of their sentiments in regard to the death of their friend and colleague, the Reverend William Williams, which took place on Tuesday, the 20th inst. at Aiken, S. C.
>
> He was of the number that were present at the foundation of the Institution, and was chosen almost at the start as a member of the corps of instructors. After nearly eighteen years of unremitted toil he has fallen just at the period when his powers and usefulness had attained their completest development. During all these years so full of vicissitudes for our Seminary, we have enjoyed abundant opportunities of learning his worth.
>
> The sweetness and openness of his temper, his abundance and genuineness of his sympathy, and the transparency and solidness of his character rendered him always a charming and most desirable friend.
>
> It is extremely gratifying to our feeling to be able to record the fact that during eighteen years of almost daily intercourse in which we were called on to discuss and decide innumerable questions, frequently of great importance and difficulty, the cordiality of our relations was never for a moment disturbed.
>
> He possessed great fitness for and achieved great usefulness in the position he occupied as Theological instructor. The breadth and clearness of his views, the terseness of his expression, his probity, his force, the depth and fervour of his piety were acknowledged and valued by all his pupils. Few men could have been more successful in acquiring their admiration and affection, and in impressing them for good.
>
> As a preacher, though he was seldom equal to himself on distinguished occasions, and always shrank from them, those who enjoyed his ordinary pulpit ministrations cannot lose the impression of his massive power and engaging clearness and simplicity.[58]

Difficulties and Despondency

Providing for Williams at the time of the move to Louisville was, therefore, not a concern Boyce would have to deal with. Others, however, continued to press on his mind and brought him to the edge of surrender. One concerned the replacement of Williams. Boyce mentioned several individuals with caveats concerning each, including E. T. Winkler, about whom he said, "I fear for selfishness and besides he must be ruler." "We can get Manly," he confided, "if we are able to give full salary." He also envisioned having "partial professorships," with Louisville pastors, "not the present ones," taking a special study upon which they could make themselves expert "and thus make a more effective faculty." If, however, the new Kentucky trustees desired a more abstemious budget, talk of such addition was entirely moot. Suppose they wanted only three professors—some graceful way of disposing of Whitsitt would be necessary, perhaps at Oxford, Mississippi, or Second Baptist Church in St. Louis.[59]

Williams's death had left some debt to be settled, which perhaps could be handled through a compromise arrangement. The ongoing finances of the seminary still presented virtually insuperable difficulties. Boyce could manage the April salaries himself through some money that his sister owed him, but the long-term prospects seemed impossible.

> The average collections for the past year, from April to April, have not been $8,000, while our expenses have been for salaries alone $12,400. The money that should protect me in the advances made (from property at Greenville) will not now one half suffice. I really fear that it would be prudent to stop the seminary, let you go to Eutaw Place for a couple of years, and then reopen here. I am in great perplexity. The brethren will not and some cannot pay. W. D. Thomas has never paid on his bond or the 2nd draft bond given by Toy's father. We received little just last year and nothing this. E. H. Graham writes me from Waco that the brethren there are talking of repudiating their pledges (bonds taken by Williams and at Jefferson) and others make no talk about it but just do it. May God guide us for I am blind and can see no longer.[60]

The great Texas victory some years earlier had fizzled. Friends of the seminary could not or would not pay. Boyce was quickly losing his own solvency. Prudence demanded quitting; perplexity overwhelmed him; and he could see no way out. Broadus responded quickly and with compelling reasoning. Though the brethren are negligent, the situation is discouraging, and prospects look gloomy, suspension promises disaster. First, the interim would provide even less funds, for the brethren would conclude "we had broken down." Second, students would either scatter to "Northern seminaries" or go to work, and the entire process would have to start over. Third, the professors might get into living situations that would make it difficult if not impossible to leave, so "you might not get your professors back, such as you wanted."[61]

Boyce responded with thanks and new resolve. Broadus was the only person to whom he could reveal his moments of despair and weakness. "With you I feel like a wife to a husband not ashamed to show my weakness." Boyce was having to make arrangements for his brother-in-law C. L. Burckmeyer to be taken to Charleston where he was expected soon to die. Boyce had been able to arrange for the April salaries, and they would soon be delivered. He took to heart Broadus's arguments against suspension and noted, "I fully appreciate and shall push forward keeping up Seminary for one year longer, hoping we may work through without any suspension." Now Broadus must increase his contacts in New York with lists of desirable men.[62]

The annual meeting of the Southern Baptist Convention approached. Boyce had served as president for five years and felt that was enough, except for the advantage his position as president could be for the seminary. P. H. Mell, perennially president prior to his sickness when Boyce began to hold the elected position, now was regaining health, presiding in Georgia again, and perhaps would make a try for the presidency. Broadus thought not, for he had seen him at the Georgia convention, and though Mell would like to show he was able to preside, he feared another attack on his health and had excused himself from the Sunday morning preaching on that account. It seemed, therefore, that in New Orleans, Boyce would reign again.

A New Opening of the Seminary in 1877

A Hard Decision to Make

Boyce again presided at the Southern Baptist Convention in 1877, beginning May 10, held at Coliseum Place Baptist Church in New Orleans, Louisiana. P. H. Mell's book on parliamentary practice was adopted as the official rules of the convention; Edmonia Moon, the sister of Lottie Moon, had left China and returned to America for health reasons; seminary professor William Williams had died, W. F. Broaddus had died, and the great Richard Fuller had died. Boyce rose to the occasion in inimitable style and, "on taking the chair, made remarks that affected many present to tears." When he mentioned the death of Richard Fuller, he recalled, "'Twas Fuller that led me to see my sins, then pointed me to Christ, and then baptized me." Boyce felt the occasion presented enormous challenge. "We all mourn the loss of these. *We* now have *their* works to do, and ours too. Yes, *a greater work than they ever did* devolves on us," Boyce emphasized, possibly referring to the necessity of solidifying the common theological school. "In the hand of Saladin any sword was made powerful, and in the hand of *King Jesus* even the '*weakest earthen vessel*' will be made to accomplish a glorious triumph."[63] Perhaps that weak earthen vessel was Boyce himself.

During the convention, the board of trustees met to consider the immediate removal of the seminary to Louisville, even though the proposed endowment had not been reached and annual operating funds fell significantly short each year. Boyce suggested a more deliberate approach that would make the issue of endowment a matter of more conscientious concern for the Baptists of Kentucky. Broadus could not attend the convention, so Boyce recounted the important decisions in a letter.

> Your telegram was not received at New Orleans. It must have been sent after Monday. Toy just telegraphed that you could not be at Virginia association. I wished to have a faculty meeting there. . . . Just back from General association of Kentucky. Our board at New Orleans authorized the Faculty and Executive Committee (now located here) to act upon any proposition from KY General Association and to modify and annul any fast action of the Board relative to removal to

Louisville. The Board was willing to remove at once, but I preferred the action to come from the general association here. I enclose copy of their action. The Committee met this afternoon and fully endorsed action of association, and Toy and Whitsitt agree to removal. Unless you object we shall therefore open next session here.[64]

A. T. Robertson summarized the mutual sense of loss involved in this move. "It was a painful uprooting to leave South Carolina. It was the Seminary's home and the ties of friendship were very tender. The State had done nobly by the institution and the people loved it with whole-heartedness." If they had been able, they would have sustained it and given it every advantage available, but the "State was prostrate still from the war and the reconstruction period."[65]

The news of the trustee action reached Greenville more quickly than the General Association of Kentucky could act. "The question of the removal of the Southern Baptist Theological Seminary from Greenville, S. C., to Louisville, Ky., is finally settled . . . and the city of Greenville will be the loser in many ways." So began an article in the *Greenville News.* Lost to the city would be James P. Boyce, "the Christian gentleman, the profound theologian, and the practical business man." Gone also John A. Broadus, "the distinguished author, the unsurpassed pulpit speaker, the learned and ever ready controversialist, the delightful companion, and altogether lovable man." Williams already had died, known as one unequaled for "clear, concise and convincing logic in the pulpit" and a man "as pure in his life as his speech was in the pulpit." Dr. Toy, on the highway to "distinction as a scholar," already brandished superior attainments yet still worked as an "indefatigable student, mastering the Oriental languages and all that bears on Biblical history." Whitsitt, the youngest of the professors, possessed remarkable intellect, showed a German-like tenacity to scholarship, and gave the promise of "ever-developing" expertise in his "chosen fields of labor."

After quoting the article, "M.G.H." in the *Working Christian* of 21 June 1877 wrote that the extract shows "what even the secular press considers the loss to this place and the State at large by the removal of the Seminary." The removal is "like a widowed mother parting with her only daughter in marriage." It will be better for her but she loves her nonetheless. "Born and reared on her soil—the child of her affections—her love will go out to it, though transplanted to another State, and her fervent prayers ascend that God will greatly increase its usefulness, and may it be the 'Alma Mater' of thousands who shall go forth to proclaim the glad tidings of salvation to the lost."[66]

The same paper carried a notice written by Broadus that students may ship their books with those of the seminary and thus at no cost to them. In addition, they may sell their Greenville furniture, for Dr. Boyce, according to Broadus, proposed "to furnish the rooms with bedstead and mattress, bureau, table and chairs." Boyce responded, "I fear your notice to students may mislead. I am not sure we can bring their books free or do anything that will make us responsible." At the same time he noted the first wave of the greatest disturbance he would ever experience when articles appeared in the *Working Christian* in South Carolina that he surmised were "some of the fruits of Toy's teaching."[67] He thought that he had secured the goodwill of Kentucky Baptists in bringing F. H. Kerfoot, a Kentucky pastor, to the faculty.[68] Instead Kerfoot went to Eutaw Place Baptist Church in Baltimore and would not come to the seminary until 1886.[69]

Boyce had to arrange for the classrooms, the cafeteria, the dormitory, and the furnishings for the rooms as well as think about houses for the professors and the distance they would be from the school. In seeking to arrange residential facilities, Boyce had to deal with Louisville businessmen, such as William Norton, and defer to their opinions on some seminary matters. "I tell you it is very pleasant as in the past to do just as I please," he groused, "or upon consultation with my faculty who know as much as I do about what we need."[70]

Broadus sympathized with him completely. "I grieve over giving you trouble about hunting my house. Boarding house, ½ fare, what not," he commiserated, "but I shall not apologize every time I feel like it."[71] Later, as Boyce continued to relate to him the variety of facilities for possible seminary location, and to describe the advantages and disadvantages of each, Broadus responded, "It is evidently a hard question about a Hall," and assured Boyce that he would make the best of anything that he decided. "At the same time I can appreciate the bother of having it all to decide alone" with the distraction of being "bothered with suggestions from excellent brethren who don't understand the inside working of the machine." He pledged his willingness to offer any advice he could give, however, and proceeded to give several reasons why one possibility suggested, the smallpox hospital, did not seem promising at all.[72]

Boyce had taken a good bit of time to investigate that particular property and seemed intrigued by it. He felt he should describe its possibilities in detail to Broadus.

> I am no nearer arrangements about hall than when I wrote before. There is a building that would suit us admirably, but it is half a mile from short line railroad and nearly a mile from nearest streetcar. I think it would do for us permanently. Were it ours for that purpose we could have streetcars extended to it. It was built for a small pox hospital, cost the city fifty thousand dollars—has thirty rooms, about 22 feet square besides splendid basement, is entirely new, substantially built, as good a building as needed, can be added to, has never been used, except since June 21 for a temporary lying in hospital for women. It is about a mile and a half from the heart of the city, as near as we will probably get— has a fine road from one direction and will have from another. Two more stories added would make it most conspicuous and it will bear them. It is said we can buy it for $15,000, and for thirty thousand more we should have all the building we want. This is 1/3 my estimate. The distance to the city can easily be reached by the students. I do not see why the professors could not live in the city and even now. There are not a dozen days when it would be unpleasant in winter. It is about twice as far from me as Furman University when I was there. Then those who like to live a little out from town would find a good place nearby.
>
> The objections are, beside distance, that there are but five acres. We should need more. But even that can be remedied. I am inclined, therefore, to look carefully into this. At times I feel inclined to take it temporarily for one year and see how it will do. This would test too the matter of distance from city. But if so, you and I still have to ride and drive out there, from any place near where I am now, or walk ¾ a mile from head of streetcars.
>
> This place is in the direction above Bear Grass Creek in which McFerran wishes us to go, though not exactly what he desires. The

309

walk from head of streetcars is no greater than from my Greenville home to University, and I went that often. The building is new and strong, thick walls, stone basement, brick three stories above, two bathrooms and water closets on each floor. No gas or water in building, but all the pipes for purpose laid, and a magnificent engine house to pump water up by hydraulic elevator in building. You are there too as free from dirt and smoke, etc., as if you were in Greenville.[73]

When Broadus responded, he spoke of the practical difficulties of the location and the types of arrangements each person would have to make to negotiate life. He mixed a bit of humor with his analysis.

The idea of the Small Pox Hospital is very tempting—good building and all that. But I think it must be taken in permanence, or not at all. We can't work it without running out street-car, at once. The students might walk to church in town, etc., but it would greatly hamper all plans for their taking trains regularly to go off and preach. When very muddy or deep snow, and a man must have at least a small bag to be decent, how can they get to the L&N Depot, with a mile before reaching the present street-cars? And for ourselves, I can't give 2 lectures in succession. So I must take out books for 2nd lecture when I go to 1st. Therefore I can't well walk. I should have to keep a horse and carriage, and if Sam stays in Greenville should have to keep a manservant to attend to the horse—all very pleasant for the poor wife if I could afford it. If I attempted to live nearer the building, the family must have the carriage to get to church. Without going further into details, it seems to me that you can't *try the experiment* for one year with the Small Pox building. You must take it permanently or not at all. So it looks to me now.[74]

One particularly intriguing offer came when Boyce considered purchasing the Galt House for the seminary:

No result as yet as to hall. I feel today the powerlessness of poverty. I am offered the Galt House, which cost two million, for $200,000. Small amount cash, balance in ten years at six percent. But I cannot spare $12,000 per annum. I have sometimes felt tempted to offer

$150,000, if they will give me the refusal at that for six months, and make a raid upon our Northern brethren, getting the amount in cash—150, to give 1000 (churches and persons). That would make necessary to get $1000 each day. But what is to become of my teaching meantime? The Galt House could give us residences for all faculty, lecture rooms, library room, and accommodation for six hundred to one thousand students. Our buildings to accommodate 200 will cost us all of that. It is the place upon which I have set my heart for some time. If I had the money to risk it I would buy it and trust to raising it. But I cannot risk the loss of anything to the Seminary as I would to myself, yes even to my wife and children. This is the grandest opportunity for success I have ever seen.[75]

To this suggestion, Broadus, spending some weeks in New York preaching, gave a quick and unambiguous response: "Don't think of the Galt House. You couldn't raise 10 thousand dollars in all the North now. Whew! They feel so poor here. Galt House too big a sum, and too big a place—a caravansary, no home life."[76] He offered clear opinions on other venues described by Boyce.

Boyce and Broadus corresponded often and lengthily during June, July, and August and traveled extensively. In this correspondence, Boyce's spirit seems rejuvenated as he contemplated reunion with the faculty and time in the classroom. He enjoyed writing about textbooks, teaching methods, and getting supply-preaching opportunities for the students. "I have hopes of doing well with Systematic Theology English, and of getting along so well that I have been thinking of taking Latin Theology also." He hoped to use van Oosterzee because "I can use all my old lectures and all my familiarity with Dick and Turretin to supplement and also Hodge."[77] He proposed a peculiarly innovative way of teaching Parliamentary Practice that would involve theological thinking also. "Let a topic of theology assigned by me be put up for consideration" such as might be found in the doctrinal creeds. It would be "partially correct" and the class would suggest amendments, substitutes, strike-outs, and promote debate on the issue for the best wording. Boyce would allow five-minute speeches. He seemed quite pleased with the multiple advantages of such an approach.

Broadus felt the significance of the coming change also. "We must both try and keep alive, till, if it please God, we can see the Seminary strong, and as safe as such things can be made. How I should rejoice some day to shake hands with you over such a result." And to make the venture more personal, he added, "You don't know how glad I am that we are to be close together again. I feel that I know you better than my own brother, and love you almost as well." Surely Boyce would not be offended at these words of brotherly affection: "Does it need to ask pardon for saying this, because we are both getting gray?"[78]

By August 1, Boyce had secured both living quarters for the students and lecture halls for the classes. Elliott House, at the corner of Second and Jefferson, provided the former and Library Hall provided the latter. By request of the executive committee, the opening lecture would be August 31. In the meantime, Boyce would need to make trips to Chattanooga and New York.

Students were asked to arrive in Louisville on August 27 or any day thereafter. They would go directly from the railroad depot to the Elliott House on the corner of Second and Jefferson where they would board. On the evening of August 31 the opening lecture would be held at the Public Library Hall with a reception to follow given by the citizens of Louisville.[79] Boyce intended to present to Louisville and the Southern Baptists a formidable apologia both for the move to Louisville and for the necessity of the kind of theological education provided by the Southern Baptist Theological Seminary.

Introducing the Seminary to Louisville

Boyce needed to engage the citizens of Louisville firmly with an account of the establishment of the seminary, the pressing need for just such a school as this proposed to be, and the theory that gave rise to the particular curriculum offered. He did not propose to give a history of the school itself, for that "should come from one less intimately associated with it than I." When such a history is done, Boyce requested, let it "tell only of the toils and trial and sacrifices and wisdom and prudence and foresight and prayers and tears and faith of the people of God, to whom it will have owed its existence and its possibilities of blessing."[80]

Boyce's purpose was to show how the seminary provided a solution to the problem of how to "provide suitable theological training and education for the Baptists of the South." The initial problem faced was a lack of "deep and widespread interest in theological education." Early days saw this interest confined to a "few of the leading men." The vision of Richard Furman and Jesse Mercer for full theological training was sacrificed as a number of literary institutions provided only partial training. Boyce discussed the influence of R. B. C. Howell beginning in 1845 and the eventual work of the several educational conventions culminating in the establishing of the seminary in Greenville in 1859. An endowment quickly gained was even more quickly ruined by the Civil War. That event, providentially, had the effect of expanding sympathy for the school and its purpose so that "it has become what it was intended to be, the common Seminary of the Baptists of the South." The efforts to secure a "much larger endowment" have given opportunity for correcting misinformation and winning over much of the opposition so that "no enterprise of Southern Baptists lies nearer to their hearts, or is more liberally contributed to of their means, than this." Boyce took special pains to communicate optimism while indicating that the work of endowment was not complete.

The second issue, beyond securing interest, was securing the most advantageous location. For several reasons Greenville had seemed ideal, but several disadvantages emerged in the subsequent years. Apart from the loss of the initial endowment and the inability of South Carolina to reinvest, the number of places for practical work for the students did not compare with the massive expanse of opportunity in Louisville. Not only were the number and size of the churches greater, the access provided to surrounding areas by the railroad was far superior to that in Greenville. The territory of the Southern Baptist Convention from Maryland to Missouri to Texas to Florida and back up the East Coast embraced 13,000 churches, 7,000 ministers, 1,100,000 members and 5,500,000 associated persons. "From these," Boyce believed, "we must expect large numbers. I have been accustomed to estimate the possibility of five hundred annual attendants after the lapse of some years. I see no reason why this should not be so." This central location provides the greatest opportunity for large attendance from all

313

the states involved at the most reasonable cost, and with the increasing tendency to abandon theological departments in the colleges for the sake of secular and literary studies, necessarily concentrates "within this Seminary all the theological institutions of the South."

Interest and location, however, were minor problems compared to the third—"the varied degrees of cultivation and knowledge possessed by our ministry." Both in educational background and gifts, such diversity existed as would seem to many a glaring weakness in Baptist ministry. But Boyce reveled in it and saw the glory of the challenge of providing a fit theological education for just such a ministry.

> That God has blessed the ministry of various classes with which they are associated we can not doubt, as we remember the abundant fruits it has brought forth. And standing here tonight amid the cultivation and scholarship of the ministers of this favored city, and among some doubters who disagree with the opinions I express, I freely state my own personal conviction that it is the kind of ministry which God has ordained for the conversion of the world and the edification of His people. . . . The laborer in one field may not at all be fitted for another. But he who sends forth the laborer secures his fitness and preparation for the field which has been ordained for him and in which he can do effectual work for the Master.[81]

So the problem is endemic to the peculiarities of Baptist ecclesiology. Shall separate schools be established for the variety of possible students, or "shall we combine in one common seminary instruction for them all?" Boyce believed he had found the "true solution" in the way the curriculum of the seminary was constructed. All levels of students could attend classes together with the exception of those courses that required knowledge of classical languages. For example, two of the three courses in systematic theology, English Systematic Theology and Polemic Theology, may be taken by all students with only Latin Systematic Theology dependent on classical learning.

Exegetical courses in both Testaments also have a substantial component of English-only instruction. Boyce argued strongly that much may be accomplished in exegesis without any reference to other than English works. Historical and circumstantial backgrounds, harmonization and discussion of apparent discrepancies, the relation of each passage to the "whole Word of God," rules of interpretation that pertain to literature in any language, all these may be studied profitably in English.

> But there is another and one still more important. I refer to the mastery of the scope of the arguments and the perception of the force of the reasoning of the sacred writer secured by reading the writing as a consecutive book divested of chapters and verses. It is astonishing what a flood of light is thus thrown upon the meaning of some of the Epistles, indeed upon even the parables and discourses in the Gospels and the Acts. Yet such reading can scarcely ever be done except in the English Version. . . . In the pursuit of this plan, with three recitations each week, a Professor can in one session teach the Harmony of the Gospels, the History of Christian Organization in the Acts, with an account of the labours of the Apostle Paul, can present an analysis of each of his Epistles as well as of the other books of the New Testament, and may still have time for particular comment and thorough study in English of any two of the Epistles.[82]

Both types of students participate in these classes. The language courses are adapted well to the schedule so that no obstacle stands in the way of full participation in the entire range of courses by any student. This works well not only in theory but "has been reduced to successful practice." Such success "calls upon all who love the ministry and desire it to be effective to use every effort to carry it forward to even greater measures of success."

The solution thus provided for theological education for Baptists in the South invites another important possibility—theological study for "pious Christian members who have no thought of the ministry." The curriculum thus arranged gives that opportunity, and "the theological schools of the country owe the privilege of such access to the membership of the churches." Boyce thus invited the community of Louisville to take advantage of the riches newly planted among them, while he challenged the trustees to "arrange some form of endowment for this class of students." Also he reminded his hearers that if the seminary is to be "adequately equipped for the work before it" the endowment must be completed and "increased to four-fold its present attempted limits." If ample provision is made, the seminary will glorify the city of Louisville, will elevate the denomination that established it, will aid in the diffusion of Christianity until the day of its "universally prevailing sway." No special favors did Boyce court, but the common affection that Louisville residents bore to its several educational institutions. "But we confidently believe," he spoke in closing, "that in breaking the cherished ties which have bound it to its former location, and in turning away from the friends who weep its departure there because they know its worth, we have come among those of equal kindliness of spirit and capacity of appreciation."[83] The city, particularly its Baptists, would show that Boyce's confidence was not ill placed.

Finalizing the Shift

The trustee meeting of 1878 made arrangements for the final disposition of the property in Greenville for the closing of outstanding debts. Those members of the trustees who constituted the "South Carolina Board" voted "to recommend such disposition of the assets of the Seminary as may liquidate as far as possible the present liabilities resting on the institution." When the Kentucky board met, Boyce was authorized to secure the purchase of the Greenville property and assets with existing money so that no permanent injury would come to the seminary as constituted in Kentucky. The loss of that property would not be nearly as devastating as the loss of confidence that threatened the seminary upon the theological defection of its star scholar and teacher, Crawford Howell Toy.

The Toy Affair

To this point the seminary had endured several blows that threatened its existence, but still it hobbled forward with hope of attaining vigorous stability. At the opening of the session for 1878–79, two issues that concerned Boyce were what text to use in Systematic Theology and the threat of a yellow fever epidemic coming up from Memphis by way of the river. He wrote Broadus, "I am very anxious about the opening. I fear some one may come who may have in him the seeds of yellow fever and a case break out at the Hall." He gave detailed instructions as to how such an eventuality should be handled including moving the patient "to the hospital where he can be well cared for," but with the provision that this be done "in a carriage, and so as not to aggravate the disease." "Spare no expense in this matter," Boyce wrote, even pay "an exorbitant rate rather than send anyone in a wagon exposed to the sun." Whitewash the walls with disinfectant and use carbolic acid in the privies in all locations used by the students. In fact, Boyce thought, "if the young men would only stand the smell a little carbolic in each room would be useful." Boyce would do this at his own house. Also he settled on Alvah Hovey's new theology as a text for his students.

A Sickness unto Death

The yellow fever did make it to Louisville, causing several deaths, but did not affect the seminary. A greater difficulty than yellow fever, however, came to head in the next few months. It found expression in the lamentable words:

> It having lately become apparent to me that my views of Inspiration differ considerably from those of the body of my brethren, I ask leave to lay my opinions on that subject before you and submit to your judgment. . . . And now in conclusion I wish to say distinctly and strongly that I consider the view above-given to be not only lawful for me to teach as Professor in the Seminary, but one that will bring aid and firm standing ground to many a perplexed mind, and establish the truth of God on a surer foundation.[1]

When C. H. Toy opened and closed his resignation letter with those words, he implied a challenge to the theory of theological education proposed by Boyce at every level. Broadus, who knew Boyce's intensity on this point more clearly than any other colleague, reminisced, "Dr. Boyce was not only himself opposed, most squarely and strongly, to all such views, but he well knew that nothing of that kind could be taught in the Seminary without doing violence to its aims and objects, and giving gravest offence to its supporters in general."[2] Could defection on such a fundamental issue ever encourage the churches that seminary education could help provide an "abundance of able, sound, and faithful men to proclaim the gospel of Christ?"[3] Could a learned ministry, fully conversant with the books and research techniques commended by Boyce, be provided for Baptist churches without embracing destructive ideas of inspiration and revelation? What does this divergence from the brethren on the view of inspiration say about the integrity of the confessional commitment of the school? Especially when Boyce had declared that "no difference, however slight, no peculiar sentiments, however speculative, is here allowable. His agreement with the standard should be exact."[4]

Precisely at this point Toy protested his innocence of any real violation of the expected standard. "I fully accept," Toy declared, "the First Article of the 'Fundamental Principles' of the seminary" affirming the inspiration of Scripture and its standing as the "only sufficient certain and authoritative rule of all saving knowledge, faith and obedience." Toy affirmed that he had always taught in accordance with and not contrary to it. On the details of that idea, nevertheless, Toy had perceived, as had his colleagues, a growing divergence from "the prevailing views of the Denomination."[5]

The Early Symptoms

This indeed had also been perceived by his colleagues. It was impossible to miss. Throughout his tenure at Greenville, Toy's intellectual curiosity and his drive to reconcile biblical descriptions with the "assured results of physical science" led Broadus to devote a very long paragraph to a description of Toy's efforts.[6] Geology and astronomy and eventually Darwinism prompted the changes in Toy's views. His acceptance of Darwin's views of biological evolution opened him to the evolutionary reconstruction of Israel's history and the Old Testament documents promoted by Kuenen and Wellhausen.

Broadus recalled, "Near the end of the Seminary's first session at Louisville it became known to his colleagues that Professor Toy had been teaching some views in conflict with the full inspiration and accuracy of the Old Testament writings."[7] The problem with Toy and the attendant complexity of the relation of the seminary's confession to the theology of the denomination prompted a letter from Broadus to Boyce. Toy's deviation on this point had been raised in public by a pseudonymous writer in the *Religious Herald*, E. T. R., though not attached to Toy's name. She wrote of "at least two professors in Baptist theological institutes" that were unsound in doctrine. "One does not believe in the inspiration of Moses," she reported, "nor indeed, of various other parts of Scripture." He must regard himself as either infallible or inspired in order to "decide what part to receive and what to reject." Seemingly he saw himself as superior to Christ, "for he does not consider David as inspired . . . and Christ did, for Christ declared that David 'spoke by the Holy Ghost.'"[8] Broadus had learned that the writer was a woman, the former Miss Josephine Eaton. She was

319

the sister of Thomas Treadwell Eaton, who was soon to be a major figure among Baptists in Louisville as pastor of Walnut Street Baptist Church. Broadus proposed a strategy for dealing carefully but forthrightly with the difficulty.

Broadus referred to E. T. R. as *Religious Herald* editor A. E. Dickinson's "pet sensation." Confessing to be "somewhat in doubt as to what is best," he suggested silence. Given the eventuality of "an outburst of inquiries," some publication from Toy might be necessary rather than seek to answer the writer directly, "for she is not only unfair, but impudent and foolish." Impudent she might have been, but she had uncovered a major difficulty. In light of that, Broadus saw the future clearly. "I fear Toy will be obliged to go before the Board in May," he speculated, "and state what he holds and what he teaches." Recognizing the dilemma created by a peculiar technicality, Broadus observed, "The point is not covered by our Articles of Belief, but his views differ widely from what is common among us," and, therefore, "it may be best, probably will be, that he should tell the Board so, and tender his resignation." Should Toy not be able to convince the board that his views were safe and in accord with the "Abstract of Principles," "he ought not to retain the position." If he could, then "we need not care for E. T. R. and Co." Perhaps the present tension could be relieved if Boyce would write a note to J. B. Jeter, the editor of the *Religious Herald*. "I think you ought to talk it frankly over with Toy at once," Broadus suggested to Boyce, because "the question is a very difficult one, . . . and we need perfect unreserve among ourselves" in light of such "perfect confidence as we all have in each other's character and spirit."[9]

Again in January, E. T. R. made reference to this issue in an oblique way. Writing about a young minister who stirred up a commotion in his church by making "too much of the Old Testament," E. T. R. remarked:

> I submit that any man who exalts the Old Testament, in these days when it is fashionable to sneer at Moses, should be silenced from preaching. To be sure, Christ had a great reverence for the words of Moses and David, and Paul was continually quoting the Old Testa-

ment (I'll defy a preacher to "make more" of it than he did), but Christ and Paul lived before the days of scientific discovery; and moreover, they evidently believed in verbal inspiration—which our theological professors of this generation are too enlightened to do.[10]

Awareness of Toy's divergence, however, according to correspondence between Boyce and Broadus, was quite fixed well before the first session in Louisville. More than two years before E. T. R. shed public light on the issue, Boyce began to give heightened attention to biblical inspiration vis-à-vis seminary instruction. Particularly onerous was the awkward reality that divergence on inspiration emerged as a threat through the influence of graduates of the seminary.

In February 1876, Broadus wrote Boyce outlining the great difficulties confronting the faculty's division of labor due to Boyce's absence in Louisville and the grave sickness of William Williams. Among the many suggestions he made to try to cover all courses was the use of Abraham Jaeger. The Jaeger episode reveals some tension even between Boyce and Broadus on how much latitude is allowable on the issue of inspiration before one should be excluded from an influential position. Broadus had no difference with Boyce on the doctrine itself, but manifested broader toleration for those who differed from his view.

Jaeger had made a grand entrance into the awareness of Southern Baptists at the annual meeting of the convention in 1873, the second year that Boyce presided over the convention. Jaeger had been a Jewish rabbi, but in 1873 was a member of the St. Francis Street Baptist Church in Mobile, Alabama. E. T. Winkler moved that Jaeger be invited to speak before the convention on the morning of May 10. His subject was "The Conversion of the Jews to Christianity." After his address, J. M. Wood of Georgia, at the request of Boyce, led the convention in prayer for the conversion of the Jews. Overwhelmed with the importance of the subject and the apparent aptness of Jaeger for such a mission, M. B. Wharton offered a resolution: "That we have heard with great pleasure the address of Rev. A. Jaeger, on Missions to the Jews, and the relation of his Christian experience, and that we recommend his appointment, through the Board of Domestic Missions, as a missionary to the Jews in this country." This call to action took the brethren off guard, and an immediate feverish scramble ensued, including a substitute motion and remarks by four other brethren for more moderation on this issue. A special committee of five was appointed, including Broadus, to bring to the convention a resolution:

> *Resolved*, That we have heard with profound interest and sympathy the narration of the experience of Bro. Jaeger, and his address upon the subject of missions to the Jews.
>
> *Resolved*, That this Convention recognizes the comprehensiveness of the Great Commission, and the obligation to provide for the preaching of Christ to the Jews as well as to the Gentiles.
>
> *Resolved*, That should Bro. Jaeger now, or at a future time, be impressed with a sense of duty to preach Christ to his Jewish brethren, that this Convention pledges its sympathy, its prayers, and its active co-operation.
>
> *Resolved*, That we commend Br. Jaeger to the fraternal regard of the brethren everywhere, and ask for him such Christian courtesies as may facilitate his labors in the cause of our Divine Master.[11]

Jaeger was ordained to the gospel ministry in Greenville, South Carolina, on 21 April 1874. The examining presbytery consisted of J. C. Furman, president of Furman University, J. A. Broadus, C. H. Toy, and J. E. L. Reynolds. This council found him holding generally "such views of Scripture doctrine as prevail in our churches," including strict views of baptism and the Lord's Supper. A subtle caveat stated that the presbytery was persuaded "that certain speculative theories which he states and which do not command the assent of the Presbytery, will not materially affect his practical teachings as a minister of the gospel."[12]

Broadus, however, gave more than mild approval in recommending Jaeger to the churches. Five days before the ordination, on April 16, Broadus penned a letter for the Baptist press. He found something charming, attractive, and useful in Jaeger. Broadus recommended him to Baptist churches as a "remarkably attractive and impressive preacher." In his every thought resided "something very fresh and striking." His words were "exceedingly well chosen"; he had a "vivid imagination, and intense earnestness." One soon learns to overlook his German accent and discovers that "he preaches the *real Gospel*, in a singularly interesting way."[13]

Boyce did not concur with Broadus's enthusiasm about Jaeger. Apparently, due to Broadus's influence, Jaeger taught Church History on a limited contract for the 1875–76 school year. Broadus wrote Boyce that he believed Jaeger "would make it interesting, that being his favorite study." At the same time he acknowledged that "Williams dislikes Jaeger pretty heartily, and would not be satisfied to put his work in his hands."[14] Boyce responded from Louisville, "But I earnestly protest against putting Jaeger in charge of any of these. If he were a regular professor, and did I not suppose that his instruction would terminate this year, I should feel very much worried." Then with a tone of incredulity concerning Broadus's theological perception, "Do you not feel that his sentiments are not accordant with our abstract of principles upon inspiration if on nothing else?"[15]

In a later correspondence about Jaeger, Boyce confided to Broadus, "My impression is that the best thing Jaeger could do would be to live in some large city" where he could lecture on history in a private or public school and do missionary work among his own people. "His loose views," as Boyce called his theology, "will ruin him as soon as he gets out preaching in our English speaking churches."[16]

For some reason, Jaeger continued to be considered by the Greenville seminary as a possible candidate for a teaching position. Even the students became restless and proposed the establishing of a fund to support a missionary labor of Jaeger. Boyce wrote one letter for the eyes of the faculty, the students, and Jaeger. Another he sent discreetly to Broadus for him and the faculty only. Boyce most steadily and clearly opposed creating any kind of connection with Jaeger. Jaeger would hurt the seminary through his imprudence and would upset the harmony on the faculty and be a "constant source of discord." But most importantly, "We must be very circumspect as to the position of influence which we give to a man not thoroughly sound." Ignorant orthodoxy is to be preferred to gifted unsoundness, and "in Jaeger's case his unsoundness comes in the most serious direction for scholarship to dread, that of inspiration."[17] Why could Jaeger not consent to preach for the sake of Christ and thus "overcome repugnance to low life as great as his"? "That is all stuff," Boyce fumed; "A man ought to rise above such childish ideas."

Even the proposal to raise money for Jaeger's support in a mission endeavor, Boyce saw as perilous.

> This movement among the students shows the inconsiderateness and lack of judgment among young men. What would the world be if young men had its rule upon their mere impulses? I do not know any measure that could do us more harm. It is perhaps natural for young men to be stirred with sympathy and then to become enthusiastic. But it would be folly on our part to yield to it. Where would that $10,000 come from? It could not be raised, and Jaeger would only become more disgusted with Baptists and fly off to the Episcopalians. If we had it, how curious a fund. We to hold it for Jaeger's benefit while he remained with us, and it to go to Jewish missions afterwards. Better give it to him at once. We would be held responsible for its preservation. He would stay only as long as he pleased. Our board could not dismiss him without an outcry. If his disbeliefs were mooted ahead, we should be blamed for allowing a fund of this kind to be collected.[18]

Boyce was sorry to object to "anything the rest of you wish, but even if you are unanimous about it you must pardon me for saying I must say 'nay.'" The Jaeger connection clearly disturbed and irritated Boyce. Not only did he find him a potential threat to good feeling in the faculty, but his views of inspiration would cause trouble. Broadus felt the need to assuage Boyce just a bit and wrote, "Jaeger is mistaken in the idea that I would like to have him as instructor. I do not know what I said that produced that impression, but I did not mean to convey any such idea."[19]

Jaeger could be held at bay. The school had made no ongoing commitment to him. Toy was a different story. No later than June of 1876, Boyce and Broadus were seeking to warn Toy about his developing views on inspiration. Broadus wrote, "In a postscript to a letter to Toy I broke into a gentle remonstrance and earnest entreaty on inspiration."[20] One year later, 15 June 1877, Boyce referred Broadus to articles in the *Working Christian* under the pseudonym of Senex. These five articles related to issues of biblical inspiration. Though none knew it when the articles appeared, the articles came from W. C. Lindsay, a full graduate of the seminary (1866–70). The articles argued that spiritual and theological ideas must be distilled from their historical and "scientific" setting. Boyce read the first three articles and suggested to Broadus that this was "some of [the] fruits of Toy's teaching."

How much influence Toy might have had on Senex is debatable, for he was present only the first year of Toy's tenure in Greenville. In addition, Senex (Lindsay) claimed originality in his conclusions on theological matters though he derived them from a voracious reading of the books in Toy's library.[21] Boyce thought, however, that the theology of Senex had such strong similarities to Toy's developing position that the influence had to be direct and substantial.

When the fog cleared later, the linguistic and conceptual similarities between Toy and the pseudonymous Senex justify Boyce's inference of some interdependent theological relationship. In Toy's resignation letter of 1879, he claimed that on the subject of inspiration, he consulted only the facts in the books of the Bible. "Against facts no theory can stand, and I prefer therefore to have no theory, but to submit myself to the guidance of the actual words of Holy Scripture."[22] In reading that, Boyce surely heard echoes of Senex's insistence that "all theories of inspiration are made by men and designed to account for the facts, and if therefore they do not accord with the facts, so much the worse for the theories—the facts remain the same."[23]

Senex, in a five-part series entitled "Letters to My Friend," discussed the Bible, not as a book, but as a collection of Hebrew literature. It must be treated like any other literature as far as its history, poetry, science, and even religion are concerned. Some religious truth enters into each type of literature but to claim that it enters in everywhere is "nonsense." Inspiration, therefore, "is concerned only with the *religious element* of this literature."[24]

In its history, the Hebrew literature "extends back to the outer verge of the historic period, on into the deepening mists and shadows, and still on, through the crevasse made by historic tradition, into the fields of myth and legend." Its assertions reach beyond any possibility of confirmation and "strike the mind as conjectural." Not until the Abrahamic period does it bear the "stamp of probability," and even

325

then its "obscurities and inaccuracies" are so many and so important as to justify a high degree of historical skepticism.[25] Later it became clear that Toy concurred and had reservations in the same areas. Toy disliked admitting "discrepancies and inaccuracies" in the historical narrative, but they certainly occurred, just as surely as they occurred in other genres; but he demurred, "I can no more demand historical science in the Scripture than geological science; I regard them both being outside the domain of religion."[26]

Senex observed that Hebrew poetry had no prescribed canons that would hinder the "free play of fancy." It is intensely human, "semi-barbarous," wild, and exuberant, bearing the marks of a vividness "born of the peerless Oriental imagination." Though some of it is "unfit for our daughters to read," in no literature of the world has poetry reached a "height so giddy, so dizzy a deep." Its songs, its passions, its oratory, its law still search for peers in the world.[27]

As for science, the Hebrews' views, the same as those of their contemporaries, are "frequently erroneous." In fact, some of their contemporaries far exceeded the Hebrews in correctness. Scores of mistakes could be cited to show that in physical science the Hebrews "were crude and erroneous—just as crude and childish as many of ours will appear ten centuries hence." It is simply a mistake to seek to give ingenious interpretations of Scripture to make the Hebrews right in their science, to seek to make the Old Testament author's "puerile utterances square with facts about which he was as ignorant as a Digger Indian." Darwin, so Senex believed, is a better guide than Solomon in science. One example of a palpable error, therefore, that cannot be hidden by interpretation is the creation narrative. "They believed that the creation was accomplished as we find it," Senex observed, "in six days of twenty-four hours each (the foremost Shemitic [*sic*] scholars reject any other interpretation of their language as a perversion) and that plants were made before the sun."[28]

In religion, however, one finds firmer ground. "I believe," Senex wrote, "they were divinely guided in their deliverances of *religious* truth, and *only* of such truth." Again, Toy's resignation letter averred that the incorrectness of the "geography, astronomy, and other physical science" of the Hebrew writers has "nothing to do with their message of religious truth from God." But where does this truth enter, in the view of Senex? Since it is sprinkled throughout and "does not enter everywhere," one finds a development even within the religious thought. "It was not given him fully developed and perfect," but it had its "infancy, its youth, and its manhood." It comes to maturity in "the person of Christ" or, as Toy later would say, "The centre of the New Testament is Christ himself. Salvation is in him, and a historical error cannot affect the fact of his existence and his teaching." An a priori conclusion, however, absolutely mortifies the true spirit of dealing with the biblical text as it is. "I cannot accept *a priori* reasoning," Toy warned; Senex said the same thing with a bit more dash: "Creed it and you kill it. It is beautiful in life, but hideous in its creed coffin." We think of the coffin only when the life is gone.[29]

For Senex, the "Christian Consciousness" served to distinguish the spiritual truth from its fallible cultural constrictions.[30] The Bible yields its spiritual message to spiritual people, to those who search and investigate in the "child spirit." Truth accords with Christian consciousness and awakens "an echo, a vibration, a response there." Susceptibility to error in individual perception may be greatly reduced through subjecting our views to the Christian community and to the religious world at large. Though difficulties of application are present, "we are shut up to it."

The other alternative, "that the writers of this literature were infallibly guided in *all* their utterances, both religious and non-religious, and that therefore no religious consciousness is needed to detect what is inspired—flatly contradicts the facts." Senex viewed the theory of verbal inspiration and consequent inerrancy as an enemy of Christianity, making it susceptible to "ridicule and scorn."[31] Toy reflected this thinking when he asserted that his view would "bring aid and firm standing-ground to many a perplexed mind."[32] That dogma of infallibility has made Christians cling to unsustainable positions and beat a path from one retreat to another, giving greater confusion to the Christian world and allowing its enemies to press on "confident, exultant, insulting." The one impregnable fortress into which we can enter and thereby sustain our position is religious consciousness which

God "doth evermore create in his chosen" to enable them to "discover and appropriate that truth."[33]

Toy evidently knew that Boyce attributed the views of Senex to Toy's influence, for soon after the appearance of article 2, Toy wrote Boyce. He laid before him some of the leading ideas of his understanding of inspiration. Boyce then wrote Broadus:

> I have a letter from Bro. Toy setting forth his theory, in itself well enough. In so doing, I do not know that he goes beyond the statements of others. The trouble is when he enters, as he did in Virginia, into the details and begins to knock away one part and another. I think however that the ice being broken we shall be able to keep all right. His letter to me was very kind, if anything too flatteringly so. I do hope we can keep all right for I prize Toy more than all. I love him very much. He is a noble fellow and adds greatly to the glory of our institution.[34]

One can only imagine what Boyce was really thinking at this point. With Jaeger and Senex already under his scorn, he somehow found sympathy for Toy, though he recognized that Toy's view allowed him "to knock away one part and another." Perhaps the sparkling intellect and Southern charm of Toy made him transcendently valuable. Such appears to have been the settled opinion of Boyce. When considering the possibility in April 1876 of uniting Southern with Crozer for the sake of gaining a large and immediate endowment, he mused to Broadus, "I should gladly accept such a proposition if the Crozers would come into the South. . . . If they would but come to Louisville, that would be the very thing. They may have the name and the glory and all they wish that we could grant. We must have half the professors. You and Toy they would want and they must have. As to myself, I should gladly give way."[35]

Perhaps Boyce believed that between himself and Broadus they could exert sufficient administrative pressure to keep Toy's statements within the bounds of the "Abstract." Later, in fact, when Toy's position began to become more pronounced in Louisville, Boyce sought to produce a change in Toy through the influence of Broadus. As Broadus recalled, "Anxious to avoid anything that might look like an official inquisition, he laid these convictions before Dr. Toy through a colleague who had been the latter's intimate friend from his youth." Broadus sought to explain the severe difficulties, both theologically and pragmatically, that would result from the permission of such teaching and asked Toy to "leave those theoretical questions alone, and teach the students what they needed." They hoped that in executing this kind of teaching "he might ultimately break away from the dominion of destructive theories."[36]

Toy's views soon made their way into the popular press by way of the *Sunday School Times*. As the newly acquired writer of "Critical Notes" for the *Times*, Toy suggested that the "book of the Law of Jehovah" taught by the Levites to all Judah during the reign of Jehoshaphat was "not the Pentateuch as we have it." That, he theorized, "was not completed in its present form till a later period, probably in the time of Ezra and Nehemiah."[37] *The Independent* took note of this statement and said that the conviction that "Deuteronomy was a late compilation" constituted the "very offense for which Professor Robertson Smith is on trial in Scotland." H. Clay Trumbull, the editor of the *Sunday School Times*, professed the "sound orthodoxy" of his paper and dismissed the remarks in *The Independent* as a mere impertinence. Trumbull's remarks sidestepped the issue nicely by avoiding the reality that Toy indeed had taken the higher critical conclusions on the completion of the Pentateuch. "We insist," he closed, "that no bill of particulars can be made out from our columns on this charge of heresy."[38]

The newspaper dialogue that followed the articles of Senex proved ambivalent. C. C. Brown and John Stout both wrote articles critical of Senex. Although Stout later adopted the loose view and became the center of contention in another short controversy, he produced a brief point-by-point challenge to Senex. He closed with the challenge and promise, "These should have more careful and thorough treatment than could be given within the limits the reader's patience would now allow me, but if another pen does not attempt a serious refutation of these views, then mine shall, for I rejoice in a firm persuasion, which Bishop Ellicott has well expressed, 'that every separate portion of the Holy Book is inspired,' and that it furnishes a complete and correct standard for conscience and for faith."[39]

C. C. Brown shared that same persuasion, having worked through earlier struggles with the doctrine of inspiration. He isolated the influence of Renan and Colenso on Senex, and rejected the credibility of their arguments. He wrote, "I believe my positions are correct, and doubtless the best way to remove the harm by those 'Letters to a Friend,' will be to set the subject before your readers from an orthodox standpoint."[40] His article consisted of a sermon that he preached on "The Inspiration of the Scriptures." Brown wrote a second article in response to a criticism of his article by J. C. Hiden.[41]

J. L. Reynolds, though not mentioning the articles of Senex, wrote a highly pertinent remark about the element of Christian consciousness. Taking an indirect approach by talking about a book of German theology he recently had read, Reynolds wrote:

> There is not much said in the book about Christian consciousness, and I am glad of it, for I cannot comprehend it. My Masters in metaphysics have taught me that consciousness is simply the general condition of knowledge, "the illuminated field" (as Sir William Hamilton has it) in which all the phenomena of cognition appear. It is neither a criterion nor a source of truth, but simply apprehends the truth when conveyed to it by the various faculties of the mind. Christian consciousness can be nothing more than the means by which we apprehend divine truth when revealed to us. It can not sit in judgment on the matter revealed. To make man's consciousness the judge of divine revelation is to make him supreme, and to put revelation wherever he may, in his fancy or his ignorance, choose to place it. Besides, if revealed truth makes a man a Christian, and yet a consciousness already Christian is to decide what is revealed truth, then a man must be a Christian in order to become a Christian. This is not exactly "putting the cart before the horse," but it is putting both before each other at the same time. But a German theologian cares nothing about that. For my part I am not equal to such high things, and shall continue to put the horse before the cart and travel along the stony road of theology, after the manner of my fathers.[42]

A spirited defense of Senex, however, also appeared. J. C. Hiden, a graduate of the seminary, a trustee (awkwardly along with J. L.

Reynolds), and an assistant instructor of homiletics during the spring of 1877, felt the critics of Senex did not address the issue. Boyce wrote Broadus in May 1877, "Never had no use for Hiden." Surprisingly, at Broadus's request and unknown to Boyce, Hiden was to represent the seminary at the meeting of the Virginia Association. Boyce wanted Broadus to rectify the situation and explain to Hiden. In his defense of Senex, Hiden made it clear that he would not be a desirable representative of the seminary.

In article 1 Hiden expressed his personal doubts about "some of the current popular teachings about inspiration." A thoughtful man, he asserted, "cannot consent to accept a ticketed and labelled sett [*sic*] of formulated theological catch words." He defended Senex's claim that one cannot point to 2 Timothy 3:16 to assert that all Scripture is inspired of God; no, every inspired Scripture is also profitable for righteousness, and according to Ellicott, while not free from "trifling, historical inaccuracies," is, nevertheless, "pervaded by God's Spirit."[43] Brown responded to Hiden's reference to Ellicott by saying that he had consulted him and been bold enough to disagree with him, and then he quoted Broadus's evaluation of him: "He is profound, suggestive, devout, but very objectionable as to inspiration."[44]

The historical and scientific errors pointed out by Senex obviously make it irrational for anyone to continue to "believe that the writers of the Bible were so controlled that they wrote the truth without any error."[45] Mr. Brown, though obviously a nice fellow and true Christian, has done a poor job of proving otherwise. Hiden took exception to several points of Brown's arguments, not because they had significant bearing on the question of inspiration, but simply because they "were extremely loose and inaccurate."

Early and Deliberate Wholeness

Could all this turmoil over inspiration, particularly as it related to Toy and his position at the seminary, have been avoided? Did obvious hints exist that Boyce should have perceived? Broadus made the unsolicited and candid evaluation in March 1860 that "Toy is among the foremost scholars I have ever known of his years, and an uncommonly conscientious and devoted man."[46] In spite of some spells of insecurity, sometimes distress, and doubt that characterized Toy's spiritual pilgrimage, he seemed secure in his confidence in Christ at the time of the first annual commencement in May.[47] He had decided to go to Japan as a missionary, and less than one week after graduation he spoke at the General Association of Virginia, testifying about his desire to be useful in kingdom work. A. H. Sands, a layman, heard Toy speak and was deeply moved "while listening to the noble remarks of bro. Crawford H. Toy, an accepted Missionary to Japan. . . . He endorsed the experience of bro. Toy, who stated that he felt a new and indescribable joy, so soon as he had made up his mind to relinquish every hope of worldly honor, and devote himself to positive and unremitting labors for the extension of Christ's Kingdom amongst the heathen."[48]

A year later, Toy's commendation of some of the German theologians alarmed some of his elder brothers in the Baptist ministry,[49] but his correspondence seemed to show that he was able to distinguish the helpful ideas from the destructive ideas. His letters to Broadus contained theological and academic observations that had no tendency to alarm. His solicitations for the well-being of the seminary and his concern for the faculty give a picture of one who was of one heart with them.

Toy against Tübingen

On his return from Germany, Toy accepted an appointment to teach at Furman College in Greenville. In 1869, his first and only year of teaching at Furman, Toy wrote a twenty-five-page article for the April number of the *Baptist Quarterly* entitled "The Tübingen School."[50] Toy proposed that knowledge of this school of biblical criticism was essential for Baptists since "Germany guides the theological thought of the world, and our literary intercourse with that country is too extensive, and the impressions made there by the Tübingen school too great to permit us to look on as unconcerned spectators."[51] Toy did not attempt a "detailed refutation" but simply a "clear statement of its positions" mainly from the works of Ferdinand Baur himself. Toy chronicled the development of Baur's thought into religious relativism ("one religion differs from another only in degree of truth"), his break with Schleiermacher's understanding of Christianity, and his full submission to the principles of historical criticism. These he applied to biblical studies and the history of dogma. Though not a new method of scholarly study, Toy pointed out that "the ability with which he has applied it to the New Testament, his general uncompromising consistency, and the destructive nature of his results, give his movement a claim to be considered a new one."[52]

Toy summarized in scintillating brevity the intellectual background of Baur's brand of historical criticism by showing how a rabid rationalism had led to a rebellion by Schleiermacher whose theology dealt a "death-blow to Rationalism" but sowed seeds of pantheism and "bequeathed good and evil together to the following generation."[53] Baur's Hegelianism meant "a development of history according to unchangeably fixed laws, the impossibility of miracles, and the impossibility of a special incarnation of God in one man."[54] When Baur declares that his approach is purely historical, he means that every event must be explained in terms of immanent historical causation.

In addition to a vigorous Hegelianism, Toy detected Hume's arguments against miracles as fundamental to Baur's views of "pure objectivity" and "scientific investigation." Toy showed no fear of a historical investigation of Christianity—he rather welcomed it—but knew that Baur smuggled unjustified assumptions into the process when he called for "the right to regard the supernatural as natural" in order to approach history through "scientific investigation," that is, seeing all of its elements as "the necessary result of preceding causes."[55] Toy responded:

> With respect to which we remark that the alleged indisposition or opposition of orthodox writers to a scientific examination of the records of primitive Christianity, and to the conception of Christianity itself as a purely historical phenomenon, if it has sometimes been manifested, is totally unnecessary. By "the historical" is meant simply "what has actually happened," and we can have no faith in Christianity save as it is demonstrated to be, as it professes, a series of facts. We are not frightened, therefore, at the oft-recurring

emphatic presentation of the "historical conception," "historical development," "pure objectivity." We hold a historical conception to be one founded on actual fact, a historical development to be a progress from the actual to the actual, and pure objectivity to contain nothing different from these. But in the emphasis given to the "pure" lies the intimation that the real facts have been colored and distorted, that the historical narrative has been made a mere vehicle for the opinions of the writer, that a subjective (and therefore untrue) form has been impressed on the objective material. In truth, the real question thus comes to be, what is historical, what are we justified in believing to have actually happened, and the sophistical assumption that the historical excludes the supernatural is contained in Baur's approval of the quotation given above, in which right to regard the supernatural as appearing in historical connection is held to be the necessary condition of scientific research. For historical connection is tacitly assumed to be causal connection, every fact depending upon a preceding one, without which it were impossible; and the causes and facts are assumed to be such as we are now familiar with, and have reduced to scientific shape.[56]

In order to make his point of antithesis and synthesis more secure, Baur, so Toy summarized, sees Christianity only in terms of pure monotheism, universality, and moral consciousness. These certainly are present, Toy concurred, but do not constitute the most essential ideas. Instead, Toy looked to those facts of the redemptive work of Christ as more distinctive of Christianity:

the expiatory death of its founder, the Son of God, by which infinite justice and love are reconciled, and which procures for the believer a new spiritual life; and this life of loving obedience develops profound moral consciousness and universal sympathy. The death and resurrection of Christ form the historical beginning of Christianity, and are pure historical facts standing alongside of, yet distinct from, the religious development of the world up to that time.[57]

Toy continued an astute, energetic, and disciplined interaction with the leading ideas of Baur, showing their weaknesses, inconsistencies, gratuitous assertions, conclusions drawn in absence of evidence, and severe misrepresentations of the content of the actual biblical text. "Hegelianism, which is Baurism," wrote Toy, "seems to us weak and inconsistent."[58] The exigencies of Baur's theory "lead him to arbitrary assumptions and violent distortions."[59] When Baur opted for Matthew as the most genuine and credible source for early Christianity, Toy responded that he would be willing to rest his argument for primitive Christianity on this "scanty admission" but contended Baur's rejection of the others is "unsupported by proof."[60] Baur falls into the error, characteristic of his school, of "generalizing too widely."[61] When Baur dismissed Matthew's resurrection account as having no value as historical narrative but as being a mere statement of belief, Toy rose to the occasion with clear and deserved sarcasm.

> This, then, is what is meant by the "objectivity" on which so much stress is laid; we are to determine what is necessary in order to explain succeeding events, and the rest may be excluded from historical investigation. . . . It is sufficient that the disciples believed that Christ arose; whether he did or not is a matter of indifference. Its reality seemed to them necessary; and so it acquired a subjective reality. In this case, therefore, historical objectivity proves to be pure subjectivity. This is the way in which a method which plumes itself on its conscientious adherence to fact, disposes of a fundamental fact of Christianity. The real "historical" argument of Baur here is: the resurrection is a miracle; miracles are impossible; therefore the resurrection did not take place.[62]

Having interacted with the difficulties of verification and the gratuitous assumptions inherent in a Hegelian approach, Toy moved to concentrate on one specific controlling fact of Baur's approach—the conflict between Pauline and Petrine Christianity that clashed and struggled but finally through mutual concessions settled "into the form of belief which constitutes our Christianity."[63] Toy found Baur's treatment of the book of Acts in light of this controlling thesis simply unconscionable. His description of the difficulties at this point fairly characterized Toy's analysis of Baur throughout.

We feel ourselves embarrassed as to the treatment of Baur's criticism of the first five chapters of the Acts. It is a skilfully constructed cumulative argument, in which holding his theory steadily in view, he makes everything bear on it, and clipping and expanding, asserting, suggesting, insinuating, by quibbles, conjectures, and distortions, accomplishes what an expert advocate does before a jury, he makes out a case; and one is wearied out with stopping at every sentence to define its fallacy, to detect the exact degree of error, to determine just where a false coloring begins, to drag forth the hidden assumptions which lead to conclusions, and in general to sift and examine what is not always worth examining.[64]

As Baur discussed the martyrdom of Stephen as the pivotal event that led to the eventual Paulinization of the church and set up the contest between the Pauline and Petrine parties, Toy commented as to the flimsiness of his considerations. Toy gave a clear and succinct examination of the major points that Baur brought forth as evidence. Toy mentioned seven points of defense from Baur and his own determination to "give a candid examination to the proofs" adduced by Baur for his position: the conference in Jerusalem in Acts 15, Paul's reference to the apostles "who seemed to be somewhat" (Gal. 2:6), Paul's rebuke of Peter (Gal. 2:11), the "hostile relation of Paul's Christianity to the law," Baur's identification of Simon Magus in Acts as a mythologized allusion to Paul and his conflict with Peter, the Pauline character of Luke and its supposed presentation of Christ as a non-Jewish-Saviour-of-the-world Messiah, and the strong anti-Pauline flavor of the Apocalypse.[65]

Toy's analysis of each of these arguments compels admiration and shows a profound knowledge of Scripture as well as the current critical literature. Isolated sentences extracted from the carefully woven critique narrative show Toy's decided orientation to orthodoxy: "Whether, then, we consider the fundamental character of this error, or its plausibility and power for mischief, or the eminently clear and logical character of Paul's mind, it was very natural for him to act with decision on this occasion."[66] "He chooses to distinguish them thus, by position and not by name, both because his interview with them was more especially to his credit, and because he is driven to the necessity of asserting himself by the utterly groundless charge of inferiority and subordination brought against him by the Galatian Judaizers."[67] "It is to be observed that the same charge of dissembling is brought against Barnabas, who is therefore doctrinally to be put alongside Peter, and whose complete agreement with Paul is not questioned."[68] "We rely, however, on the Second [Epistle] of Peter as genuine in accordance with the decision of the Latin and Greek Churches of the fourth century, and the internal evidence, in which there is nothing opposed to the authorship of Peter."[69]

Toy's most lengthy description and refutation centers on Baur's attempt to establish Paul as hostile to the law and as representing Judaism on a par with the heathen religions of nature. Part of Toy's answer contains a concise summary.

> The fallacy in the argument from Paul's supposed hostility to Judaism has already been pointed out. In the first place, it is not the system, but the abuse of it, which he opposes, Jewish particularism, as Baur properly says. Jews and Gentiles stand equally condemned before God and in need of the free salvation of Christ, and any religion which denies the all-sufficiency of Christ is a lie. But, the law is holy, was given to sharpen the conscience and lead to Christ; the Jew has a great advantage over the heathen in the possession of a higher, purer religion; and Judaism itself is swallowed up in Christianity; which last assertion the apostle certainly nowhere makes of any form of heathenism.[70]

"We confess," Toy declared about the Simon Magus myth, "that we do not see the necessity for this absurd explanation of the narrative in Acts, which seems to us to give a good sense if taken literally."[71] As to the Gospel of Luke and its supposed anti-Jewish character, Toy noted, "But we can, against Baur, establish Luke's Pauline relation to the Old Testament by the incident (Luke iv.16–21) where Christ declares an Old Testament Messianic prophecy fulfilled in himself, by the endorsement of the divine character of the writings of Moses and the Prophets (xxiv. 27, 44), and especially by the definite declaration (xvi.17), 'it is easier for heaven and earth to pass, than one tittle of the law to fail.'"[72] Later after referring to and investigating critically several evidences cited by Baur in his view of Luke, Toy concluded, "These citations therefore fail completely to prove Luke's hostility to the Law and to the Twelve."[73]

Concerning the supposed antagonism of the Apocalypse to Pauline thought, Toy pointed out a consistent pattern of error and misunderstanding on the part of Baur.

> In asserting so strongly the Jewish exclusivism of the Apocalypse, Baur seems to forget first, that it is symbolical, and second, . . . that its symbols are taken from the Old Testament. Not only is the universality of its view apparent from such passages as ch. v. 13, and ch. vii. 9, but the Judaism throughout is merely external; under the Old Testament dress and body is seen the New Testament spirit. No circumcision, no appeal to a national covenant, no legal meritoriousness, but salvation through Christ, a life of tribulation followed by glory, cleansing in the blood of the Lamb, a relation to the Redeemer which is based on the individual consciousness and on his bearing towards the individual soul. If heathenism is crushed, it is only as inimical to Jesus, (so Paul, I Corinthians xv. 25; II Corinthians iv. 3; v. 10, 11; vi. 14–18); and the absolute freeness and universality of the gospel is set forth with unsurpassed clearness and beauty in the last chapter: "whosoever will, let him take the water of life freely."[74]

In conclusion, Toy expressed his conviction that "so redoubted an attack has issued in strengthening our defences." He called on Baptists to "gather up our strength and go deeper into the mysteries of the gospel of Christ, that we may unveil its beauties, evolve its power, and be filled with its spirit."[75]

A Baptist for the Bible

With Toy's strong, informed, and erudite interaction with the chief assaulters of the Christian faith, uncompromised affirmation of central Christian truths, and confidence in the simple factual truthfulness of biblical revelation, Boyce and colleagues felt confident in issuing an invitation to Toy to join the faculty at the seminary. As shown earlier, the need for an additional instructor pressed relentlessly in every circumstance of the school, and the faculty sent an urgent appeal to the trustees for a faculty addition. A. T. Robertson stated simply, "By May, 1869, Doctor Broadus's health was still much impaired. A new professor, Dr. C. H. Toy, was added at this meeting by the trustees, so that Doctor Broadus could be relieved of homiletics, Doctor Manly taking homiletics and Doctor Toy Old Testament interpretation."[76] Sectional pride, denominational impression, the needs of the churches, the taxing work on the professors, an expanding student population, incentive for expanded financial support of the school, and sufficient maintenance of the stated academic objectives all entered into the faculty's appeal to the trustees.

In order to fulfill this need, could any conceive of a more apt hire, symbolic of the partial success in one of the more ambitious goals in establishing the seminary—the preparation of scholars for training the Baptist ministry—than the brilliant young man from Norfolk, Virginia? Who could be better qualified to join in this noble and worthy endeavor than one of their own graduates who had returned unscathed from a time of intense study in Europe? His inaugural address in the fall of 1869, "The Claims of Biblical Interpretation on Baptists," would give them further assurance that a Southern Baptist star had arisen. With understandable eagerness to show that neither Boyce nor he himself had reason at that time to hold reservations about Toy, Broadus included a brief but pointedly relevant synopsis of Toy's address in the *Memoir*.[77] In particular, Broadus cited Toy's words, "A fundamental principle of our hermeneutics must be that the Bible, its real assertions being known, is in every iota of its substance absolutely and infallibly true." The printed version of Toy's speech amounts to sixty-one pages.

Toy began by arguing that upon Baptists in particular, a sense of stewardship of the Bible and its proper interpretation rested. More than any other group of Christians, Baptists must embrace the full meaning of the biblical text. The Baptists' "complete dependence on the Bible" as "alone, our religion," the fact that they "look to it alone for instruction" and nothing avails with a Baptist "one iota, except as according with the inspired Record," means that they have no choice but to know it "throughout, in its whole extent." All of its truths are connected, none is unimportant.[78]

One may wonder if Boyce felt some discomfort when Toy asserted, "We are not under the dominion of Articles of Faith, which settle beforehand principles of interpretation." He could have wondered also at Toy's understanding of the relation of individual freedom to corporate confessions when he averred, we "suffer no man's individuality to be swallowed up in the impersonal mass of the body to which he belongs."[79] On the same principle he criticized the early patristic use of the rule of faith in their contest with heretics. He called their appeal to the *regula fidei* a "dangerous principle," the "beginning of a great evil," and the "nucleus of a curse."[80] Later Toy took a similarly dismissive swipe at the early creeds of orthodoxy. Lutherans and Anglicans proved untrue to their own principles, so Toy believed, "by setting up, as standards of faith, the decisions of the General Councils of the first four centuries, or the Apostolic, Nicene, and Athanasian creeds."[81] Boyce's firm commitment to conciliar orthodoxy could hardly have approved the apparent dichotomy Toy implied between biblical faithfulness and the ecumenical creeds.

That Toy made this point, however, only to emphasize the folly of "putting man in place of God,"[82] the necessity to "bring all our intellectual and spiritual strength to bear immediately on the truth, instead of expending it on a *tertium quid*,"[83] and the pursuit of the formal principle of the Protestant Reformation that "the Scriptures were the infallible guide of the Christian in matters of faith and doctrine"[84] probably satisfied Boyce with regard to Toy's intent. Indeed, Toy rubbed the same gall into his comments about commentaries when he reminded his hearers that "commentaries are not of equal authority with the Bible, and that he who neglects the fountain of living waters for these more or less broken cisterns, suffers loss." Any Baptist who "elevates any human utterance into the position of infallible guide" violates his own principles.[85]

That Baptists may not rest with the authority of predigested formulae throws a significant weight of responsibility on the task of biblical interpretation. They must pay constant attention to the factors that increase the likelihood of correct understanding. The two categories that must be meshed in the right way Toy designated by the simple terms "external" and "internal."[86] The *external* includes "the grammatical and logical significance of its sentences" along with knowledge of the social, cultural, and historical setting of the Bible. The *internal* naturally flows from the reality that since the Bible is a "revelation by the Spirit of God given through men filled with a divinely engendered love for God, it is necessary to have the inspiration and guidance of the Holy Spirit."[87] Later, in his comments on Origen, Toy reiterated, "Spiritual sympathy, we repeat, is an essential element of sound interpretation. Only the Christian can properly understand the Bible, and expound it in the pulpit, in the Sunday-school, or in the printed book."[88] These two elements of exegesis must be present in every reader of the Bible; the relationship between them, "the history of their conflicts and union," constitutes the history of biblical interpretation in the church.[89]

Paul House has argued strongly that Toy's colleagues did not grasp "his hermeneutical frailty" at this point of relating the internal to the external principle.[90] He points to an image used by Toy that seems clearly to imply a dichotomy between faith and history: "The gems of truth are indeed divine, but the casket in which they are given us is of human workmanship, and its key made and applied by human skill. To this human side of interpretation, we may hold fast without weakening our grasp on the spirituality, which is its divine side."[91] House interpreted Toy as already committed to a Kantian dualism in which history and empirical methods provide a body of facts, but spiritual life must somehow be sequestered to a "realm of psychology, or emotion and will" so that it is unaffected by scientific fact. Faith, therefore, in this scheme, cannot be based on any palpably historical event and must have no dependence on the findings of empirical study and investigation.[92] Though it was not clear to Toy or his older colleagues at this point, a fundamental difference in approach existed even then. Over time, given Toy's temperament and relentless pursuit of consistency, a fissure was inevitable.

House's analysis, given the outcome of Toy's struggle with the data of interpretation, has merit and may prove true. He also suggested correctly, if his interpretation is true, that Toy had no idea how strong a hold his veiled presuppositions had on him and that it was easy for his colleagues "to assume that he was one with them on the doctrines they held dear."[93] House wrote, "Toy stresses the need for both the internal and external principles, but it is clear that he divides the two, assigning each separate tasks, yet without stating how they are to be integrated or what the interpreter should do if the data seems not to cohere. Toy seems to think that the external principle may inform and shape the internal principle, but the opposite is not true."[94]

Another interpretation of the historical events, however, is possible. While House believed that no fundamental change occurred in Toy's understanding of the relation of the external to the internal principles, it is possible to view Toy's struggle as precisely the opposite. Toy sought, in fact, to develop an interpretive scheme that would assume perfect coherence between the external and internal principles. In the imperfect state of biblical interpretation in the past, it has often been true, given the internal witness of the Spirit, that overall spiritual impressions were more accurate than individual biblical interpretations. Here Toy labored to warn against the illusion of establishing religious convictions built on impressions formed in absence of biblical data. This is consistent with his earlier criticism of Baur for assuming that the New Testament writers constructed theological ideas without historical facts. Toy was wary that Satan presents his suggestions "as the promptings of the Divine Spirit," apparent divine guidance "counterfeited by human fancies."[95]

Toy's designation of an internal principle of hermeneutics would have sounded no alarm since he described it in historic Reformed concepts. It did not seem Kantian but Calvinistic. Only an experimental acquaintance with the truths of Scripture finally embeds within the believer's conscience that the Bible is indeed the Word of God. Toy remarked, "In respect to Biblical interpretation, the fundamental fact is that the interpreter of the Word of God must be spiritually in sympathy with it, and that not merely in the way of a general recognition of its truth and excellence, but in consequence of a supernatural change wrought in him by the Spirit of God."[96] He defined spirituality as an "experimental acquaintance with truths of Scripture."[97]

Though he used the vocabulary of "Christian consciousness" in a positive way and as a synonym for his internal principle of hermeneutics,[98] Toy warned against the abuses of Scripture that have arisen from a false appeal to Christian consciousness. Much of the history of hermeneutics displays the havoc wrought in biblical understanding when the internal principle, falsely applied or falsely perceived, dominates the external principle. Such abuses go back as far as Origen and appeared boldly in Augustine. Most profitable are Augustine's meditations on individual passages of Scripture and their relation to the power of the doctrines of grace developed in opposition to Pelagius. But in spite of his "profound insight into the spirit of the Word," his exegetical errors make him a "loser, and his influence was bad, by reason of this individualness of his expositions."[99] Calling Augustine the "least satisfactory of commentators" and lamenting that many "suffered his eloquence to seduce them into admiration of his perfectly false exegesis," Toy cautioned against perverting the "doctrine of the illumination of the Holy Spirit into a plea for fanaticism" and pointed to Montanus, Swedenborg, and Schleiermacher as examples as well as "some modern preachers guiltless of the arts of reading and writing."[100] Particularly had Schleiermacher and Neander made Christian consciousness "the instrument of destructive error" in believing they "had the faculty of deciding unerringly on the authenticity of all writings pretending to be the Word of God, and pared and rejected as their feeling dictated."[101] At this point, Toy stands at a mighty distance from the position of Senex eight years later.

An apparent intensity of spirituality does not establish permission to pervert the meaning of the text, but must be brought into conformity with it. Had Toy desired to build a case for separation of the heart's grasp of truth from the mere formalities of language, Augustine provided him with the perfect opportunity in his treatment of creation in *Confessions*. After quoting a notable passage in which Augustine focused on the internal operations of divine truth under the prompting of the divine Spirit, convincing one of truth beyond the mere use of Greek, Hebrew, Latin, or barbarian language, Toy remarked, "In this beautiful passage, penetrated with the devout conviction that God is His own interpreter, there is nevertheless a certain tone of carelessness in respect to outward appliances and aids for the understanding of the Scripture, and a dependence on the inner light which may be and has been perverted."[102] Toy urged his audience to seek the spiritual-mindedness and devotion of Augustine, looking to God himself for enlightenment, but reminded them that "God vouchsafes His illumination to those who obey and honour Him by careful use of all means for learning the significance of His words."[103]

Again, Toy displayed the uncertainty of Augustine's treatment of the words of Genesis, "In the beginning God created the heavens and the earth," with the reprimand that Augustine inserted a fatal "doubtfulness in the words of the Inspired Records" by the possibility of their meaning simultaneously two different things. This position is "unworthy of the Divine Author and fatal to exactness of interpretation." Authors of sentences have definite meanings in their constructions, and "it is impossible to suppose that the inspired writer had no distinct idea in his mind when he penned any given sentence."[104] More important than that, it is absurd to suppose that the "Spirit of God meant to convey different ideas by the same form of words, or having one idea in mind, was unable to express it unambiguously."[105] Though language is the casket containing the spiritual jewel, it is of such a nature as to be perfectly congruent with the truth God intends by its use. The Spirit intended to teach precisely what the laws of human language convey.

Toy's purpose in this extended treatment of Augustine is clear. Even the most spiritual and orthodox of writers cannot be excused from building theology on the exact meaning of the biblical text. A robust inner life combined with impeccable theological perceptions does not give us freedom to roam at will in the biblical text. A theological conviction free of textual fetters is a matter of mere opinion and not faith.

Baptists especially must see themselves as "guardians of the Sacred Oracles" and use proper linguistic and exegetical tools as a means of "testing all theories." Some might have legitimate reason for omitting the study of Greek and Hebrew and thus "pass by the original utterances of the Holy Spirit," but, since it is an "undeniable and unchangeable fact that God has spoken specifically in two particular languages," the path to a more "correct knowledge of the truth" as well as efficiency as an instructor and "realness in the possession of the truth" is to establish a foundation of knowledge of Greek and

Hebrew.[106] Every Christian should rejoice in any study that enhances our grasp of "the original expression of the words of God." And, in a sentence that shows that Toy, at this time, harbored no hesitancy as to whether the human element, languages, could be proper vehicles for the divine element, he wrote, "What man is there who does not feel that a very uncommon interest attaches to the words which express exactly the thoughts which the Divine Spirit thought fit to make the embodiment of eternal truth?"[107]

These two elements, therefore, the internal and the external, both play a part in one's understanding of inspiration. One may not engage in seeking definition and expression of the internal conviction, the experience of God in his redemptive work, apart from its being expressed in human language. "The gems of truth are indeed divine, but the casket in which they are given us is of human workmanship."[108] That analogy cannot be interpreted to demean the accuracy and usefulness of the words and even the determinative prerogative they have in the construction of doctrine, for even the human language is of such a nature that the words express exactly the thoughts of the Divine Spirit. All of this means that "under the absolutely perfect guiding influence of the Holy Spirit, the writers of the Bible have preserved each his personality of character and intellect and surroundings." Because, therefore, of this perfect confluence of the external and the internal, "a fundamental principle of our Hermeneutics must be that the Bible, its real assertions being known, is in every iota of its substance absolutely and infallibly true."[109] In this context, the "real assertion" underscores the most probable meaning of the language considering both etymology and contextual argument. Only later after much struggle would Toy make a division between the "real assertion" of the language and the spiritual truth of the text.

Because of this absolute respect for the truthfulness of the text, Toy gave special attention to the relation between science and the Bible. He listed examples of apparent conflict between science and the biblical text with the warning for both scientists and biblical interpreters not to declare the other in error. Biblical scholars must learn to await the results of science, for it certainly will "illustrate rather than denude the Scriptures." Scripture uses the language of appearance—"phenomenal observation"—in such a way that its relevance will last for all time. We must not stake the truthfulness of the text on any scientific theory. He conceded that science had proved the world more than six thousand years old, it did not come into its present form in six twenty-four-hour days, and man has a history of at least more than one hundred thousand years. That poses no problems, however, for "Moses did not necessarily mean days of twenty-four hours each; he might mean long periods; and this view was seen to be perfectly in accordance with the laws of interpretation, and to give a much grander character to the first chapter of Genesis than had before been perceived in it." In short, let any science do what it will and give a true interpretation of the data, and "we may rest in the assured conviction that it will not be in conflict with the inspired record."[110]

Even these points of hermeneutical capitulation would not worry Toy's faculty colleagues. They too had struggled with the issue of biblical authority and interpretation in light of the rapid advances in science that seemed to challenge the biblical text. Boyce, in the antebellum years of the seminary's existence, had included a major discussion of this in the recitation section on creation in his systematic theology course. After dealing with pagan theories of creation, Boyce began a series of questions about the biblical narrative of creation. Much attention has been drawn to the narrative in recent years because "Modern Geology has added new interest to this account. Timid Christians first objected to this science as conflicting with scripture, but it has been shown that true science is always consonant with scripture." Astronomy brought about similar protests but these now seem laid to rest. "Of course," Boyce taught, "our theories are not to be constructed upon a few facts but we must be thoroughly acquainted with all the facts of the case." When conflict appears to arise between science and Scripture, "we must demand of science the most exact proof of the truth of its propositions. If its propositions be proved true," we must not conclude that Scripture therefore is wrong, but only that "our interpretation of scripture is wrong."[111]

But what geological facts have made this reevaluation of biblical interpretation so urgent? Several points of irrefutable evidence indicate that the age of the earth is vastly more than six thousand years. Among these are the time necessary to deposit the fossil remains found in the earth's crust, the existence of animals which must have perished more than six thousand years ago, the alteration of the earth to its present form by eruptions and other forces, fossil remains in coal that show luxuriant growth to which there is nothing analogous in nature now, thousands of species of extinct animals dug from earth in fossil remains, and the perpendicular strata of material several thousand times what would have accumulated in six thousand years. "It is certain that no less than four or five races of plants and animals have passed away." In short these facts show "that creation is to be dated millions of years ago instead of 6,000; that since creation there has been a series of changes; that a few thousand years ago another such change took place; that races of animals now exist which did not exist before this time, and that man had no existence prior to this change; as shown by the fact that no human remains have been found in any of the fossils dug up which belong to an age before 6,000 years ago."

Basil Manly Jr. also had drawn this conclusion. In a course on the Bible and Science, Manly investigated the implications of astronomy, geology, ethnology, and biology for Christian faith. In his discussion of geology, Manly concluded, "It is obvious that if this gradual succession of animal and plant life be recognized, requiring an enormous period of years, and all prior to the introduction of man on the globe, all ideas of limiting existence of the earth to a few thousand years— whether 6 or 8 or 10 thousand—must at once be abandoned."[112] This conclusion represented a change for Manly also, for in 1867 in *Little Lessons for Little People* he had posed the question, "How long did God wait before he destroyed the world for its wickedness?" and penned the response, "1656 years."[113]

Boyce pointed to seven explanations developed in light of these facts of science in relation to the biblical text. He denied the plausibility of the straightforward literal reading of the text, for it "denies the facts of geology" and thus sets up for itself an impossible task in explaining all the data satisfactorily. Boyce found the theory of "Lengthened Periods" most congenial to all the relevant factors. This explanation "represents the 6 days spoken of by Moses as long periods of time which ended at the Creation of Man; . . . the present

time is the seventh day & is a time of rest." He mentioned Taylor
Lewis of Union College in Schenectady, New York, as a proponent
and able defender of this view. Lewis contended that his view "is
deducible from Scripture & is the result of philological and exegetical
knowledge of Moses' writings." Several points in Taylor's argument
that the days are actually long periods, an argument attractive to
Boyce, included, "It is the base language the Hebrew could furnish
for time," the idea of a cyclical and periodic character makes the
language suitable, and this period "marked by two contrasted states"
was most easily stated "by what the Eastern tongues call evening &
morning." Also the nature of the narrative supports, in fact forces on
us, Lewis's view, "especially of the first four days." Literal days, measured by the earth's relation to the sun, seem impossible "because the
sun was not made until the 4th day." The manner in which Scripture
speaks of these four days shows that the "first night was indefinite
& the first morning was unlike our mornings." The period of three
days "before the creation of the sun shows that they were days of
peculiar character & this peculiar character must be determined by
the nature of operations performed in them." Boyce recommended
Six Days of Creation by Lewis, believing that this theory was the
most plausible of all theories, given the intersection of scientific data
and biblical language.

Toy's Capitulation to Religion

The crisis in the interpretation of Genesis thus affected all. Toy's
treatment did not reveal an abiding insidious principle of destruction
always present in his hermeneutic. Instead, his continued attention to
this issue created a fundamental shift in his conception of the necessity
of harmony between the external principle and the internal principle.
Before, he sought to discipline the internal principle by the assumption
of the infallibility of the text. One must not allow his experience to alter
his attention to or conformity with the languages in which God has
spoken. But after consenting to the truthfulness of geological science
and concluding that Genesis definitely taught that creation occurred in
six twenty-four-hour days, he capitulated to the dominance, not of the

external, but of the internal principle. It determined all; the external principle could easily be shoved aside. It becomes a mere testimony to the cultural captivity of the users of the words.

The meaning of the text from a linguistic standpoint was not infallible, and its religious message is easily distinguishable from it. The internal principle, which earlier he sought to discipline by the text, now was given free reign, and he endorsed its dominance. Whereas before he sought harmony between the external and the internal, he came to view such unity as unnecessary. His resignation letter made the new emphasis plain: "And it may be that in some cases my principles of exegesis lead me to a different interpretation of an Old Testament passage from that which I find given by some New Testament writer; . . . but this again I look on as an incidental thing, of which the true religious teaching is independent."[114]

On 22 May 1879, the *Religious Herald* summarized the meeting of the seminary's trustees at the Southern Baptist Convention. The article handled the subject of Toy's resignation in typically congenial fashion.

Another matter claimed the anxious consideration of the Trustees. Reports had for some time been in circulation, and had found their way into the newspapers, that Prof. Toy had adopted views on the subject of Divine inspiration at variance with those held generally by the denomination. Dr. Toy addressed to the Trustees a document setting forth his views on the subject, and also tendering his resignation, that the Board might act without embarrassment. The communication was referred to a committee of his warm personal friends, who after consultation with him, and an anxious consideration of the subject, unanimously reported in favor of the acceptance of his resignation. The report was adopted by the Board, after earnest discussion, with only two dissentients, who deemed the action hasty. It was in no sense a trial of Dr. Toy. He was held in the highest estimation for his scholarship and piety by all the Trustees. There was, however, a conceded divergence in his views from those generally held by the supporters of the Seminary; and the Trustees deemed it inexpedient to subject it to the disadvantages which would inevitably arise from a protracted controversy on an important theological subject, especially while efforts are being made to obtain an endowment.[115]

Broadus wrote his wife after the resignation was accepted by the trustees. "The mournful deed is done," he lamented, and Toy is "no longer professor in the Seminary." The members of the board were all in tears, Broadus recorded, as well they might be since "we have lost our jewel of learning, our beloved and noble brother, the pride of the Seminary."[116]

J. R. Graves did not manifest that kind of lamentation over the dismissal of Toy when he reported his "manifest defection . . . from the standard of orthodoxy in the interpretation of the Messianic Psalms and Prophecies of the Old Testament." Graves commended the trustees on their prompt and just action, noting that "only two members of the Board of Trustees, and they the two youngest, and formerly students of the Seminary, favored his continuance." Graves felt that "the prompt action of the Trustees should inspire the denomination with increased confidence in the Seminary." The entire affair, however, should warn against the appointment of professors "who have been finished off in the rationalistic schools of Germany." The less of German culture, the better. Young ministers should not be encouraged to get a "finishing touch" in Germany, and the churches "had better bid slow for" those that do. Why should they desire to go there unless "it is to bring back some of the advanced thoughts of its great scholars, which are quite as little in accord with inspiration as the views recently put forth by Prof. Toy?"[117]

These views of Toy would soon be placed before the larger public. Toy's letter of resignation to the trustees appeared in the *Religious Herald* on 11 December 1879, after it had begun to appear in other venues. The editor, J. B. Jeter, began a series of articles on the subject of inspiration in the column immediately beneath the close of Toy's letter. In the first, Jeter attempted a twofold task—to defend the actions of the trustees and to point out the inconsistency and danger of dividing the historical from the theological in Scripture. "If the history of the New Testament may be false, where is the certainty that its doctrine is true?" Jeter asked.[118] Jeter reported that the "remaining members of the Faculty," who "embodied their views in the article," opposed "irreconcilably" Toy's divergent view. This fact in itself made Toy's contention impossible that his views were consistent with the "Abstract." The trustees stood ready to defend both their action and their views, "believing that these are in accord with the common faith of evangelical Christendom."[119]

Jeter wrote three articles: one defended the plenary inspiration of the Old Testament, the second the plenary inspiration of the New Testament, and the third answered objections to plenary inspiration.[120] "That God can inspire men to reveal his truth infallibly to the world, it is atheistic to deny," were the words that established his theme throughout the series. The prophets claimed a thorough inspiration even in the very words they used, while Jesus and the apostles never doubted but confirmed those claims. "We think it an error to say that the Scriptures do not teach the manner of inspiration," Jeter contended, and in such a manner "as to preclude the possibility of error in the Scriptures."[121] At Pentecost, the apostles received the promise of the Spirit so that they spoke not just ideas and thoughts from God, but words given them for this purpose. Paul claimed the same revelation for his spoken as well as his written word.[122] In the final article, Jeter wrote, "We should seek to harmonize these apparent contradictions of the Scriptures, not by denying their inspiration, or that of any portion of them: but by subjecting them to a fair and faithful application of the laws of exegesis." Jeter addressed the very examples of internal inconsistencies raised by Toy as well as the supposed conflicts between Scripture and the certain conclusions of physical science with models of how these difficulties could be settled. He closed his articles with a call to belief:

> On the whole, the more carefully the Scriptures are examined, the more obviously their entire inspiration appears. It is really wonderful to notice how, amid the conflicting systems of science, philosophy, and politics, the inspired writers steered their course, without falling into errors, which would have discredited their inspiration. . . . Let us, then, reverently receive the Scriptures as an authentic and perfect revelation from God, interpret them by the law which common sense and careful study supply, and live according to their directions, and we shall not fail to secure a blessed immortality.[123]

Toy was given the opportunity to respond. The *Religious Herald* printed his articles. These articles, "explaining more fully and enforcing with additional arguments the views outlined in his letter," were published "without note or comment" in an attempt "to hear him fully" before mounting a reply.[124]

In treating the "outward form of revelation" Toy asserted that spiritual truth does not depend on verbal exactness or true geography. Textual criticism shows that God has not seen fit to preserve the exact text with no uncertainties, but "the divine thought has been preserved." In addition, we find that the geography of the writers, though truncated and primitive, did not affect their ability to be inspired with spiritual truth.[125] The biblical writers also shared the same tendencies in writing history as other nations and cultures. They borrowed legends and made them their own, they embellished and exaggerated, and sometimes manufactured details. Such facts may alter our "theory of inspiration, but it need not affect our belief in the fact of inspiration." So what if our study uncovers "discrepancies and embellishments"? We may yet "truthfully say that the historical peculiarities of the biblical writers do not affect the message they have for us from God."[126]

Toy recounted his early acquaintance with geology and convictions about its certainty. Alongside that he tried a variety of interpretations of the creation narrative in Genesis in an attempt to "maintain the literal accuracy of the narrative." Along with each new relief he found an intensified fear as each interpretation generated equal difficulties with the geological record and interposed ideas about the text that simply were not there. "As soon as I recovered from the glamour of my delight at my supposed relief from geological and exegetical difficulties, I saw that such a construction of the chapter was impossible." Every ingenious attempt at making the text say something consistent with the geological record failed, and the simple narrative that affirmed six twenty-four days prevailed as the meaning of the text, a fact that brought Toy "extreme apprehension and dismay." He came now to a point of radical shift in his expectations of the text and in his attempt at fusing unity between the internal and external of biblical content. "Can it be possible, I thought, that this chapter, after all, gives us no real history of things, but only the crude cosmogonic ideas of the Israelites and of the Babylonians, from whom the Israelites seem to have got them? What then, becomes of the Bible, its truthfulness, its helpfulness? I confess that I was for a time very unhappy."[127]

Now he must alter his view and engage in a theological method that would "take the kernel of truth from its outer covering of myth." Now he could "distinguish between form and spirit."[128] For Toy this meant that the former way of looking at the relation between the text and spiritual truth must be destroyed, and a new way must be constructed.[129] Toy had already posed the question, "Why jostle the beliefs of the people? Why not let them rest in the traditional opinions which have been inwrought into their religious life? Is there not danger in pulling the whole structure of faith to the ground?"[130] Toy believed this destruction to be his duty; necessity was laid on him to prove all things and hold fast only to that which was good. Refusal to take this approach would be unfaithfulness to God, the Bible, and the religious well-being of men. "In searching for the truth, the result is not our affair; we may safely leave that to the Divine Author and Guardian of truth."[131]

Jesus' confrontation with the viewpoint of the religious leaders of his day proves that it is possible that a prevailing doctrine of the pious and religious may be wrong. Jesus, according to Toy, did not use the Old Testament as an "infallible authority" but as an "inspired but fallible body of religious and ethical truth." Jesus corrected Moses and Paul corrected Peter, and "our moral sense endorses Christ against Moses . . . and Paul against Peter." True disciples would not care if all the "non-spiritual part should be thrown away," including Esther and Song of Solomon, for Christians, having the promise of the Spirit, have a "light in themselves, revering and loving the Scripture, but loving it for the spiritual truth it teaches, which they should perceive and comprehend by their own spiritual instinct."[132] Toy embraced the position that earlier he had viewed as "the instrument of destructive error."

Because of this, one must not conclude that scientific errors mean the Bible is untrue. It is unimportant to its true purpose that it really does teach that creation occurred in six twenty-four-hour days. "The true divinity of the Scripture does not depend on its scientific accuracy."[133]

While Toy believed that his views would give new life and spiritual health to the study of Scripture and to genuine piety in the people of God, many others felt differently and found his views destructive. As Broadus reminisced in 1893 concerning these lamentable and heart-wrenching events, he recalled that Toy simply was unable to appreciate the implications either for himself or others.

> It was hard for Dr. Toy to realize that such teaching was quite out of the question in this institution. He was satisfied that his views would promote truth and piety. He thought strange of the prediction made in conversation that within twenty years he would utterly discard all belief in the supernatural as an element of Scripture,—a prediction founded upon knowledge of his logical consistency and boldness, and already in a much shorter time fulfilled, to judge from his latest works.[134]

Other observers saw the fruit of Toy's position ripening much more rapidly. By 1883, S. H. Henderson of Alabama had seen a notice of Toy's Old Testament primer for Sunday school entitled *The History of the Religion of Israel*, and published by the Unitarian Sunday School Society. The notice was written by W. E. Hatcher, pastor of Grace Street Baptist Church in Richmond and editor of the *Religious Herald*. Henderson referred to the resignation of Toy four years before and to a censure he and some other brothers had received when they dared to predict a swift rather than slow decline in the theological convictions of Toy. He bore the censure "in comparative silence calmly awaiting results." And sure enough, it happened. Henderson expressed an energetic aggravation at the spirit in which Toy handled the Old Testament, the cavalier attitude, the condescending diction, the critical detachment, the condemning implications of faint praise. "To what amazing heights of intellectual grandeur have the 'leaders of advanced thought' attained," Henderson exclaimed, "which enable them to look down with such complaisant dignity upon such men as Moses and the prophets, and Christ and his apostles, and deal out to them such compliments as an Eastern despot would likely do to his courtiers." Henderson was sorry that Toy had come to such a position but "sorrier still that he still retains membership, as we learn, in a Baptist church."[135]

Broadus probably had recently seen Toy's 1891 work when he spoke of "his latest works." Toy concluded, from the citadel of his critical studies, that Jesus "laid no claim, in thought or in word, to other than human nature and power." He had "profound sympathy with the divine mind," despised mere formality in religion, assumed a prophetic role, and relished his union with God that gave him a sense of sonship, but never claimed to cross the "unspeakable distance between God and man." Jesus' thought was clear and he did not suffer under the delusion of equality with the divine.[136] A. H. Newman, who in 1876 had studied Syriac and Arabic with Toy at the seminary in Greenville, recorded that Toy rejected the title "Christian" and preferred to be called a "Theist."[137]

Boyce had not only hoped for the best but had worked for it. He feared the worst, however, and knew that Toy had reached a point from which he would not be recovered. Broadus wrote of "Dr. Boyce's personal grief at the loss" through an impressive anecdote.

> When Dr. Toy returned to Louisville, and had made his preparations to leave, his two colleagues who were here went to the railway station. The three happened to stand for a little while alone in a waiting-room; and throwing his left arm around Toy's neck, Dr. Boyce lifted the right arm before him, and said, in a passion of grief, "Oh Toy, I would freely give that arm to be cut off if you could be where you were five years ago, and stay there."[138]

This event and the tensions leading up to it showed that even the greatest vigilance and most determined confessional commitment could not hold back the pressure toward embracing modernity. At the same time, it demonstrated the clear meaning of the confessional stance of the school and gave Boyce a clear resolution to encourage orthodoxy and cut off error wherever he found it.

10

Securing the Seminary, 1879–86

At graduation on 8 May 1879, J. P. Boyce began to deal with the crisis of identity created by the upcoming resignation of C. H. Toy. The anonymous writer, E. T. R., had put question marks around the safety of the seminary by fingering "at least two Professors in Baptist theological institutes" as unsound in doctrine. She (Broadus had learned the writer was a woman) had implicated Toy, without naming him, and emphasized that "the object of Baptists in establishing theological institutes, is to have the young ministers thoroughly trained in what Baptists believe." She gave a sober admonition for watchfulness to the churches. "In these days of general dishonesty of all kinds, when honor seems to be a forgotten term, it behooves the churches to guard with special care their theological institutes. Don't let the stream be poisoned at the source, or wide-spread death will follow."[1]

A Crisis in Baptist Theology

J. M. Pendleton chastised the *Religious Herald* for publishing an anonymous charge "the tendency of which is to excite injurious suspicions concerning the orthodoxy of our Theological Seminaries."[2] He noted that he could vouch for orthodoxy at Crozer, and in a subsequent letter E. T. R. agreed with him. Her manner of affirmation implied an even stronger difficulty with another seminary—who could help but know she looked toward Louisville?—and its way of dealing with an errant professor.

> Let me assure Bro. Pendleton of one thing. If there is any Professor in Crozer who does not believe in the plenary inspiration of Scripture, . . . such Professor has kept his views very carefully from Dr. Weston. My acquaintance with Dr. Weston is slight, but I think I know the man and if he knew of any heresy in his Faculty, I think he is brave enough to report such Professor's errors to . . . whatever body has an oversight of Crozer. And no love he might have for the Professor, and no admiring he might feel for his talents and learning, would prevent his withstanding him thus to the face, and guarding the young men under his charge from all danger of false teaching.[3]

It would be difficult to imagine a clearer reference to the internal struggles at Southern Seminary concerning the future of Professor Toy. Their admiration of Toy both as a friend and as a scholar was unbounded. Toy was the star; he had been anointed to carry the hopes of the credibility of the seminary into the larger academic world.

The great irony of E. T. R.'s observations is that H. G. Weston at the beginning of 1878 had remarked on the value of Toy as a scholar, showing that he shared the high estimation of Toy's seminary colleagues. Toy began the year 1878 as the author of "Critical Notes" on the Bible lesson discussed in the *Sunday School Times*. Weston expressed his "very great gratification" with that development and noted that Toy was a "master of Hebrew and cognate languages" as well as scientifically acquainted with English, a combination sure to produce reliable and accurate scholarship "expressed in clear, simple vigorous English." He called attention to Toy's excellent formal education, his

357

personal intellectual vigor in making himself "well acquainted with the physical sciences," and his experience as a pastor, giving him valuable knowledge of what is "needed by men in the walks of outdoor life, as well as in the study and lecture-room." He referred to "those private qualities which endear him to his friends, his kindness and generous feeling," and added that the readers of the *Sunday School Times* would find him "a man of varied and excellent scholarship, of extraordinary attainments in many directions, of ready sympathy, and of sound judgment."[4]

When the *Religious Herald* reported on the trustees' acceptance of Toy's resignation, in the forefront was their confidence in his scholarship and piety. The editor noted, however, that the trustees "deemed it inexpedient to subject it [the seminary] to the disadvantages which would inevitably arise from a protracted controversy on an important theological subject, especially while efforts are being made to obtain an endowment."[5] Those issues, the theological integrity of the school and its financial viability, reached crisis proportions at the same time. One was not the cause of the other, but the time of their maturity coordinated ironically well.

A School for the Churches

The same number of the *Religious Herald*, May 22, that recorded the acceptance of Toy's resignation reported on the commencement exercises of the seminary that had been held on May 5 at 2:00 P.M. in Louisville. The article began, "The Seminary has just closed a prosperous session—prosperous not only in the number of students in attendance, but also in the amount of earnest, successful work done."[6] H. H. Tucker, a close friend of Boyce and the editor of the *Christian Index*, preached the Sunday afternoon sermon for one and a quarter hours and "had the undivided attention of a miscellaneous audience." At the graduation proper, three of the five who achieved the status of full graduate gave their speeches. J. H. Eager from Mississippi spoke on "Conditions of the Discovery of Truth." J. P. Greene spoke on "Christian Manhood." H. A. Tupper Jr. gave a "racy and sparkling" address entitled "Bows and Arrows."[7]

Finally came the address of J. P. Boyce. The *Western Recorder* for May 8 printed it. If Boyce had in mind at all the sting of the implied rebuke given by E. T. R., he had to do something that showed a redeeming relationship between the seminary, its graduates, and the churches that would be beneficiary for their ministries. Boyce took the theme of ministerial success for the discourse. Though not discounting the gift of pulpit oratory when done appropriately, Boyce warned against it as one of the "popular fallacies of the day." He contended that "those who have carefully studied its effects have found that its tendencies are really destructive rather than edifying, leading to sinful admiration of and attachment to the person of the preacher instead of his Master." Indeed, one often values the opinions of an orator "above those of the Word of God." The men must guard themselves and their hearers against the many evils that sometimes accompany the use of oratory.[8]

Boyce also warned against identifying success in ministry with the ability to attract huge numbers to church membership. To the degree that the numbers represent true conversions, all genuine Christians will rejoice. Too often, however, this simply represents shallow concepts of conversion on the one hand and little attention to the necessity of church discipline on the other. Boyce mentioned that Baptists had reported 102,738 baptisms and 30,266 exclusions from membership in the past year. "Were the churches more particular in the reception and more faithful in the exclusion of members, these figures would be greatly changed." It is difficult to know precisely what Boyce meant by this. Apparently he meant that, in the present condition of the churches, the baptisms should be fewer and the exclusions more. If greater care were taken, however, he implied that the baptism statistics would diminish but the exclusions also would eventually diminish. "The fact stares us in the face," he continued, "that three out of every ten of those received are thus excluded." Ministers take too little care in their calling beyond the procuring of a profession of faith and baptism.

> Whence is it otherwise that we have so large a membership and so few effective churches? Whence too that so many of our so-called strong churches are utterly inefficient? Why is it that in many not

one-seventh to one-fourth make any contribution at all for work abroad, or even for the expense of their church work at home? Why is it that so often the roll of the membership has to be reviewed and names cut off because no one, not even the deacons, yea, not even the pastor knows what has become of them?[9]

Boyce believed many other evils could be pointed out in the success-by-numbers game, but he pointed to this difficulty only to show the graduates that "in wishing you a successful pastorate we do not mean one which shall be chiefly marked by the numbers which you baptize."

Nor did Boyce identify success with gaining immediate fame through obtaining a large city pastorate. One should not be judged successful by the size and location of his church but by the "manner in which their occupant has discharged their duties." These duties are twofold. One concerns the preparation and delivery of sermons. Some have held important positions by "constantly changing from one to another, never staying in one place longer than two or three years." They arrive with a stock of sermons and have soon "exhausted the whole round of pulpit preparations possessed before they came" because they are so pressured from other work that they cannot make new ones. They escape, then, before "their insufficiency [becomes] too plainly apparent."[10]

The second concern has to do with the development and execution of a strategy by which the people might grow in holiness and in serious work for the cause of Christ. "It is the lack of it which causes all our denominational work to languish and our churches to be feeble instead of strong and mighty in their faith and works." Pastors must be proven in smaller places where corrections can be made more easily and maturity can come at a pace where its gains are more readily conserved. "And when time shall have proved to him and others that he has either naturally or by acquisition the power necessary for the more important field, it will then be soon enough for him to enter upon it."[11]

Boyce described six characteristics of a successful pastorate. One, the pastor must win souls. Always there will be those in the church and the town who are dependent "upon his ministry for the acceptance of Christ through the offer of the gospel." Two, he will instruct his people in the "doctrines and duties of God's word" so they will be able to digest strong spiritual meat. Three, under God he is responsible for the increase of holiness, Christlikeness, in the congregation. Christianity consists not of mere profession and opinion but of divine life infused into sinners so that they become like their elder brother. If not the most important, this aspect of ministry is "one of the most important tests" of a successful ministry. Four, a successful pastor will aid each member in finding what work of the kingdom he is fit to do, and exhort him to do it "faithfully and efficiently."

Five, Boyce believed that the pastor should know the "pecuniary ability of each one and the extent of his contributions." If a member falls short of his potential for giving, the pastor must urge, exhort, instruct, and warn against "the sin of covetousness" and show him "the great blessedness to be experienced in giving." Among the promissionary and proeffort Baptists of the South, the "sin of covetousness" arose frequently as a particularly onerous vice to be opposed and exposed.[12] In part, Boyce inherited these convictions but also had them impressed indelibly on his conscience by his innumerable attempts at fund-raising as well as his knowledge of the work of Broadus in doing the same. Boyce knew well that for work to be supported, pastors needed to encourage the giving and should instruct their people in biblical truth concerning issues of stewardship and the reality of storing up treasures in heaven through the use of unrighteous mammon here on earth.

Six, a successful pastor will "develop the power of prayer among his members." He will instruct them in the duty and joy of private as well as family prayer while encouraging them to unite in the prayer meetings of the church. "Go forth, then, this day," Boyce concluded, "with the earnest desire and purpose by the help of God to become successful pastors of the churches to which you may minister." With a benediction consisting of an impressive catena of scriptural quotations concerning Christian ministry, Boyce closed the sermon emphasizing the biblical foundation of his concerns and the accountability hovering over the ministry of every graduate.

Intended primarily for the encouragement of the graduates, the sermon placed the concerns of the faculty in the middle of the church life of the denomination. The intense earnestness shown in developing a true and substantial denominational strength through faithful God-centered, truth-centered ministers would not be lost in the crisis immediately ahead.

A School for the Truth

Not to lose any momentum in the faculty due to the loss of Toy, and to save face in the most credible way possible, Boyce had arranged for the hiring of Basil Manly Jr., known and trusted by all Baptists in the South and beloved as one of the original four faculty members. Just below the announcement of Toy's resignation, the *Religious Herald* said, "The trustees and the denomination were exceedingly fortunate in securing the services of Rev. B. Manly, D. D., for the chair rendered vacant by the resignation of Dr. Toy." Manly was "universally known and loved." More importantly, "there was no risk in his appointment."[13]

The *Christian Index* wrote that Manly was returning to his old position "with riper learning and increased experience." The *Index* was glad "that we are not obliged to experiment with a new man, but that Providence has vouchsafed to us one whom we have long tried and long trusted, and whom we know to be sound in the faith and of sound learning, of pure piety and of unquestioned ability." Manly knew that his coming would be watched closely by a wide spectrum of people:

> In some respects my position will be one of special delicacy, and difficulty, not only as coming after a man of unusual scholarship, power and attractiveness, but as having to meet doubtless in his students and attached friends the very questions and discussions, the difficulties, which have been brought up by him to them and which in fact lie on the very front of the subjects I will have to teach. . . . If I agree with him, I shall be censured for unsoundness, if I differ, I shall be thought to be actuated by prejudice or narrow views, clinging to orthodoxy rather than the truth. . . . There is nothing for it but just to go ahead and try to do right, for folks will talk.[14]

Manly had the task of reclaiming fully faithed biblical interpretation as the purposeful and self-conscious task of the seminary professor as well as the students that he taught. In his original handwritten inaugural speech Manly had begun with the sentence, "It is with mingled emotions that I stand here to day, to resume the Professorship to which I was chosen, in the foundation of this Seminary, twenty years ago, and which I relinquished ten years ago, taking of my own accord other branches of instruction in order that our honored brother, Crawford H. Toy, might be associated with the institution, in his chosen sphere of Oriental Literature."[15] The reference to Toy was later omitted so that the sentence read, "It is with mingled emotions that I stand here to-day, to resume the Professorship to which I was chosen in the foundation of this Seminary twenty years ago, at Greenville, S. C. in 1859."[16] It was necessary for the seminary in its public pronouncements to distance itself as far as possible from Toy and his defection on Scripture.

Aptly entitled "Why and How to Study the Bible," Manly's exposition was brim full of confidence in the Scripture as fully embodying the revelation of God, God's own utterances, "the divine original, which 'holy men of God spake as they were moved by the Holy Ghost.'"[17] He also restated in its most fundamental form the original purpose of the seminary in providing an abundant ministry for Baptists of the South panoplied in full for the tasks of biblical proclamation and defense. He recalled the determination of the first four faculty members after four years of possible growth in usefulness and financial stability had been "blasted by the east wind of desolating war," and stated in subdued terms the drama involved in their commitment that the seminary would not come to nothing. "I shall never forget," he recounted, "the prayerful, tearful, solemn conference in which the four original Professors met to consult as to whether the Seminary should live or die, and the firm yet humble and unanimous resolve that by God's blessing it should live, and not die." Now, after an eight-year sojourn as president of Georgetown College in Kentucky, he was returning to join his original colleagues, minus the beloved Williams, with the addition of Whitsitt, with the knowledge that though the years "have tinged our locks with gray" they have not diminished mutual affection or confidence "for the cause in which we labor."[18]

Manly asserted in confident images his conviction that the cause of the seminary embraced the cause of God, particularly in its "central object," one that should be connected with any theological seminary, *"a practical knowledge of Scripture."* Without that, a seminary might do much and yet do nothing. He spoke immediately to the students gathered for this commencement: "The great point for us, and for you, honored young brethren whom your churches have sent hither, is that we may be 'mighty in the Scriptures.'"[19] Every department in the seminary must be aimed at that end. "Elucidation of the word of God" including the practical application of its teachings was the intended focus of every aspect of the education, even at the risk of "being charged with Bibliolatry in giving the Bible its central, dominant place in our system and in our affections." Doubt or denial of God's book leads to a denial of God and eventually to an intellectual abyss "where all knowledge is not only lost, but scoffed at, except that which the brute might enjoy as well."[20] Manly originally had included a brief illustration of this point, alluding to "the dog at the express office that had eaten up his tag. He don't know where he is from, or where he is going."[21] Perhaps he omitted this because the illustration evoked an image too ridiculous for the sober point or trivialized the depth of feeling involved in the loss, both theologically and institutionally, of the scholarly C. H. Toy.

Laying aside the perfunctory manner in which many might read the Scripture,[22] Manly established three principal objects for which the Bible might be studied by one who has learned to love the "blessed book": devotional purposes, interpretation, and doctrinal instruction. The first is the great medium of sanctification. The second places us as "near as possible in the position of the first hearers and readers of the Word." The doctrinal object concentrates on the discovery of "truths which are there, but may seem latent, to harmonize apparently conflicting views and statements into that blessed unity in variety, wherein consists its true beauty." (Originally Manly had written "variety in unity" but replaced it with "unity in variety.")

Manly believed that a peculiar danger existed in the study of "learned philology" without the inclusion of devotional and practical exercises in Scripture. In ungodly hands it would lead to "self-sufficient skepticism" as it had in "New England as well as Old, in Protestant Germany as well as Catholic France." Also, microscopic minuteness in biblical studies would yield nothing of benefit apart from the application of the "analogy of faith" to doctrinal truth. One misses the beauty if he ignores the whole for the sake of the parts. Foundational to these types of study is the "direct and careful interpretation of the Bible." Neither piety nor tradition nor the last dicta of the new learning of vaunted scholarship can substitute for truth in interpretation.

> That is no true, no soul-strengthening devotion which is built upon false views of the meaning of the Word. That is no just inference of a doctrinal system which is based on palpable misinterpretations. The doctrine may be true, the devotion may be sincere, though in connection with erroneous exegesis. But a true exegesis would promote both elevated devotion and sound doctrine, for as there is not natural affinity between truth and error, so there is none between mistaken views and correct conduct. Truth is always best for man.[23]

Manly proceeded to delineate "three grades of study of the Bible." He gave a major proportion of space to the "faithful perusal of the word of God" by the "plain unlettered laborer." While God grants transforming infusions of grace to such study and has blessed Baptist life with a large number of self-taught preachers with fire in their bones for God's glory, these observations must not blind one to the pressing stewardship of the greater advantages presently available. "With what scorn would those worthies of a by-gone age regard these praises of themselves, when urged as excuses for modern indolence, and apologies for voluntary ignorance."[24]

The second grade of study takes advantage of "all the helps which are now accessible to the English reader." Manly moved through a variety of these quickly, pointing to commentaries, dictionaries, and critically superior translations as immediately available for use. Though some work is empty and erroneous, "It is still a fact that to the work of making the Scripture plain to English readers some of the noblest intellects, some of the brightest scholarship, and some of the most earnest labor of this age have been consecrated."[25]

The third grade of Bible study and the one that most directly concerned the seminary focused on the ability to become thoroughly independent in the examination and explanation of the biblical text. Those who have such a talent and opportunity and fail to pursue them "sin against themselves, their churches, and their God." This desired skill incorporates the study and mastery of the original tongues, Greek and Hebrew. "It is our indispensable duty, as a body of churches," Manly spoke in the well-worn path of seminary defense, "to see to it that the best arrangements are made to this end, and that encouragement is given to all whose circumstances permit of their pursuing this more thorough course."[26] Only such action will relieve the embarrassing dependence and inconvenience of reliance on others for denominational progress in knowledge of Scripture. Yet the denomination will never restrict the work of the ministry to the technically learned or establish "some human standard of literary attainment," but will continue to value the spiritually qualified man as central to the "very genius of our churches." Given the present opportunities and admitting the caveats, Manly urged the critical importance of his theme.

> But let it never be forgotten that the minister of Jesus Christ is by virtue of his office a teacher; that he is not the vehicle of mysterious sacramental efficacies nor the appointed performer of gorgeous and impressive ceremonies, but the teacher of God's truth, and as such his office is sublimely intellectual as well as spiritual. The sword of the Spirit is the Word of God. And that Word we should strive to be able to understand for ourselves, as God from Heaven gave it to us.[27]

Manly continued with admonitions to let nothing supplant the "divine original" immediately inspired of God. The peculiarities of both Greek and Hebrew were designed by God for the communication "into the tongues of men the themes of angelic meditation and study." He then preserved the documents through historical events that swept away many other records of human culture and at the same time provided "evidences so abounding of their authenticity and divinity" that we must not "content ourselves indolently with some cheap substitute for God's own revelation."[28]

This address, an expression of sincere and conscientious conviction, would also serve the purpose of confirming and giving a "general feeling of satisfaction and confidence" in what Broadus called "the known soundness of Dr. Manly's doctrinal convictions, with his admirable character and abilities."[29]

The solidification of the meaning of the "Abstract of Principles" was no minor matter. An ongoing discussion of the issue in Southern Baptist periodicals gave Manly, the author of the "Abstract," an opportunity to seize the moment. No doubt could exist as to the meaning of the first and foundational article of the "Abstract." If any doubt had existed on that matter prior to Toy's challenge, it would be impossible to mistake what Manly and Boyce meant by it after the publication of *The Bible Doctrine of Inspiration*.

Toy had presented his challenge as a matter of understanding the facts of the Bible itself. No theory, Toy asserted, must challenge the actual biblical material on that subject. Manly agreed that the issue was one of fact. Manly, however, shifted the discussion to a different ground in order to broaden the definition of facts. He wrote, "The Bible statements and the Bible phenomena are the decisive considerations in the case." Toy had given attention only to the apparent discrepancies as the field of facts and had not given room to the facts of the biblical claims about its own inspiration. Given that challenge, Manly proposed to give a "frank and thorough discussion of the Bible Doctrine of Inspiration."[30] Phenomena must be seen in light, not of mere human theories, but of an exegetically constructed Bible doctrine.

W. O. Carver, who viewed Manly as a man of "extraordinary saintliness of character, purity of life, and of gentle strength," called this work a "rather skillful summarizing of the traditional positions and of the arguments in their support in behalf of a rather rigid and literal theory of verbal inspiration." The distinction Manly drew between inspiration and revelation Carver considered superficial. He characterized Manly's entire course on biblical introduction "for thoughtful students, not very comprehensive nor very profound."[31] Carver's reflections embodied changes that began subsequent to the death of Broadus in 1895 and increased, largely under Carver's direction, in intensity and boldness for eighty years. Carver had been enrolled as a student during the final two years of Manly's tenure of teaching and heard him deliver the commencement address for 1891, "The Old Testament in the Twentieth Century," in which he affirmed the same truths of inspiration and revelation.[32]

Before Carver and others began doing their deconstruction, however, the edifice they had to tear apart received a deep footing that could not easily be extracted from the soil of Southern Seminary. Boyce wrote in his *Abstract of Systematic Theology* released in 1887, the year before Manly's work appeared, "By revelation, we mean the knowledge which God conveys by direct supernatural instruction, pre-eminently that given in the book known as the Bible."[33] Boyce, contrary to Toy's contentions, believed that some a priori expectations of revelation were legitimate. Among the five a priori expectations was that "it must be secured from all possibility of error, so that its teachings may be relied on with equal, if not greater, confidence than those of reason."[34] Also like Manly, Boyce established his view of revelation as a doctrine taught in the Bible. In a brief survey of differing opinions about revelation, Boyce wrote, "From no other source can we better obtain it than from the revelation itself, the teaching of which will be seen to be fully corroborated otherwise."[35] An analysis of Boyce's theology and its place in securing the seminary will be found in the next two chapters.

Manly's view confirmed in every particular the view that Boyce had expressed. In Part One he sought a clear definition of the doctrine of inspiration. Manly distinguished his view from several options including that of Thomas Fenner Curtis, an erstwhile Southern Baptist who had advocated a view of inspiration similar to Toy's twenty years prior to Toy. Whereas Curtis had maintained it was unnecessary "to faith in Christ and Christianity, that we should esteem every part of the New Testament to have been so dictated by an unerring Spirit, as to be infallible itself,"[36] Manly opted for plenary inspiration, which states that "the Bible as a whole is the Word of God, so that in every part of Scripture there is both infallible truth and divine authority."[37] Like Boyce he distinguished between inspiration and revelation, defining revelation as "that direct divine influence that imparts truth to the mind." Inspiration is "that divine influence that secures the accurate transference of truth into human language by a speaker or writer, so as to be communicated to other men."[38] Manly gave nine caveats concerning possible misconceptions so as to clarify what is not claimed of the fact of inspiration. We do not know its mode, it is not "mechanical," it does not destroy self-conscious individuality, it is not a mere elevation of faculties, it does not imply omniscience, it does not eliminate errors in human conduct or imply superior spiritual attainments, it does not guarantee mistake-free copying of the originally inspired documents, it does not imply that every recorded speech of Scripture has divine sanction as true, and it does not mean every action recorded is therefore approved.

Second, Manly developed proofs of inspiration. Assuming the presence of divine revelation, he contended that "it is not incredible, not impossible, but likely, that God, in giving a real revelation to man, would inspire it; that is, control, protect from error, and authorize its utterances and its record."[39] Without this controlling inspiration, one is left with the incongruity of a supernatural act in giving a revelation, the intervention of miracle in verifying the presence of revelation, but the omission of any supernatural activity by which the full truthfulness of the revelation and its content is reported to others who personally are without the revelation. If entrusted only to oral tradition or to unaided human record, "it would have neither unerring truth nor absolute divine authority at the very first."[40]

This "assumption" along with its consequences is synonymous with one of the a priori arguments of Boyce. After explaining several "presumptive arguments for inspiration," Manly delineated what direct proofs should be expected and then gave detailed attention to the biblical witness to its own inspiration. He concluded by drawing from Butler's *Analogy of Religion* an argument about the cumulative nature of the evidence for the truth of Christianity and applied it to the argument for inspiration.

> It has been shown that there is a reasonable presumption that God in giving a revelation, as it is agreed He has done, would inspire it; that the proper source and kind of evidence to prove that He has actually inspired the Bible is in its own statements and phenomena; that this conclusion is established,—(1) By the general manner

of quoting Scripture in Scripture; (2) by passages which affirm or imply the inspiration of the Scriptures as a whole; (3) by declarations affirming the inspiration of particular persons or passages; (4) by promises of inspiration to the sacred writers; (5) by assertions of inspiration by the sacred writers; (6) by passages in which that union of the human and the divine authorship which we have seen to be implied, is expressly recognized. Thus the Bible statements on the subject have been considered, in general and in detail, as classified and part by part.[41]

In February 1888, in the very first publication of *The Seminary Magazine*, Manly contributed an article entitled "Alleged Disclaimers of Inspiration."[42] Excerpting from his upcoming book *The Bible Doctrine of Inspiration*, Manly treated several passages that seemed to exempt themselves from the status of inspired utterances. To interpret them so, Manly contended, quoting a number of evangelical authorities on his side, would be a severe misreading of the intent of the passages. In summary Manly claimed that all such passages, seen in proper context, really affirm the position that "all they say is accurate, and is uttered under divine direction and authority."[43]

John A. Broadus also played his part in solidifying the commitment to biblical inspiration. In 1883, Broadus was assigned the sermon at the Southern Baptist Convention meeting in Waco, Texas. Immediately following the convention, Broadus sought a publisher for the sermon. He finally landed on the American Baptist Publication Society, having received an earlier rejection from Harper. He wrote Boyce in June 1883 that "Harper's man declines" and that he had "written him to express the manuscript to me." In light of the manuscript's contents he saw nothing "so good as American Baptist Publication Society. It will confine circulation to Baptists, but the Baptist allusions would be unacceptable to most folks, anyhow." Publishers tolerate "denominationalism from Episcopalians or Presbyterians, but Baptist denominationalism is sectarianism." As the South has no publishing house and the North has no private Baptist publisher, Broadus settled on the Philadelphia publisher. "I think, I can make him pay me something this time," especially since the sermon "would be very appropriate to their new Bible movement."[44] On June 18 he wrote Boyce, "I have today sent Dr. Griffith the sermon."[45] Later he let Boyce know, "Dr. Griffith is printing my sermon, and will send me a proof, and agrees to my proposition about pay."[46]

These efforts to publish came from the obvious success of the message when preached at the convention. "It was evident that the Convention sermon by Dr. John A. Broadus would attract an overflowing congregation," so reported the *Baptist Courier* of Greenville, South Carolina, "as every one manifested an eager desire to be present, and for sometime before the hour for services, it was apparent that the dense throng could not be accommodated."[47] Several hundred persons went away to other churches because they could not find standing room in the Baptist church that B. H. Carroll served as pastor. Broadus took as his text 2 Timothy 3:15, "And from a child thou hast known the Holy Scriptures, which are able to make thee wise unto salvation through faith which is in Christ Jesus." In its reporting of the sermon the *Courier* deferred to a report given in the *Waco Examiner*.

The sermon appeared as a book entitled *Three Questions as to the Bible*. The issue of inspiration took a front and center position in the message as Broadus took aim directly at the problem that had confronted the seminary in the Toy controversy. Broadus outlined the spread of "German infidelity" in its treatment of the whole Bible, including the life of Christ, and summarized, "Involved in all these attacks upon the Bible history, as well as in the older controversies about doctrine and morals, is a denial of the full inspiration of Scripture."[48] Broadus made a point about the seriousness of this denial and how threatening and pervasive was its influence, even in some sectors of evangelical Christianity. "Twenty-five years ago, I myself predicted," Broadus noted, "in a public discourse, that within twenty-five years there would be sharp controversies all over the country in regard to Inspiration."[49]

The reporter for the *Examiner* made positive observations about the appearance, delivery, and tight logic of the speaker and described his topic as "a vindication of the inspiration of the Holy Scriptures." Broadus began by enumerating the "assaults to which the New Testament has been the subject from the days of Celsus to the present, and the failure of those assaults to make a breach in the wall of Christian

371

belief." He then chronicled a similar attack in recent years on the Old Testament's credibility "for which he predicted an equal and disastrous failure." Broadus clearly distanced himself and the seminary from any sympathy with Toy's implementation of the conclusions of higher criticism. In his first point, Broadus affirmed and gave a credible defense of accepting the canon of Scripture as traditionally received among the Protestant churches. Second, he sought an answer to the question of the extent of inspiration. Third, he discussed the question as to how the Scriptures were to be treated.

On the second point, according to the report, "the eminent preacher made some fine and telling arguments in a dissertation on the humanity side of the Bible." The Bible is human throughout, and yet inspired. A variety of objections were "handsomely met and very prettily swept away," including the false syllogism: Man is fallible; the Bible is human; therefore the Bible is fallible. Instead, one must conclude, "Therefore the Bible may be fallible." To this, however, Broadus added another determining factor, "that the inspiration of the Bible made what might be fallible infallible." In fact, Broadus likened the inspiration to the incarnation. Just as Christ was fully human but "free from error," so "the Scriptures do not, because human, necessarily contain error."[50]

Broadus constructed his argument carefully. He designed to remove any hesitation to the belief in the full inspiration and infallibility of Scripture that a variety of objections might have introduced. The Waco writer, in obvious admiration of Broadus's command of his subject and his audience, remarked, "The argument under this head exhibited throughout some very fine logic and the skillful application of a close and accurate thinker." Other phrases used by the reporter show the thoroughness of the impact of Broadus's oration. The discourse was "replete with fine, pointed and clear discussions," "replete with very admirable arguments in defense of the Christian religion and worthy of profound attention from the skill displayed," "treated [its subject] at some length and with pleasing force and clearness, and some excellent logic, which seems to be the strong forte of Dr. Broadus," and "a Baptist sermon addressed to Baptists, but . . . marked by a broad, generous spirit, as pleasing as the finely applied logic was admirable."[51]

The reporter also heard Broadus give warnings against embracing the supposed scientific conclusions of the "noisy and clamorous" unbelieving scientists. Set aside the *ipse dixit* of such scientists, "the special pets of the press," that imply, or assert in an unvarnished manner, that the credibility of Scripture must be relinquished. Wait for more sane and measured conclusions, as well as for more light on biblical interpretation, for then it will be known that there is no conflict between them.

On this particular point, however, the writer noticed a startling and potentially destructive comment. In the swell of a riveting discourse "one part could not fail to command the especial attention and not improbably the astonishment of many persons in the audience." The Waco writer pointed to the "admission" that archaeology creates some uncertainty as to "whether the traditions of heathen nations in regard to the creation of man and the Bible account of the same may not eventually be traced to a common origin." The writer felt that Broadus left open the optional conclusion, unstated by Broadus, that "the Bible account be only second hand." What Broadus actually said, after a carefully constructed description of the state of objections and affirmations about accounts of creation and the flood, was, "In all such cases, the statements given to us are stamped with the authority of inspiration. If the Babylonian narratives in question should prove to be older than Genesis, it will then be a natural supposition that both were drawn from patriarchal tradition, in the one case corrected, in the other corrupted." Believers in the Bible "can wait without apprehension."[52]

Though the post-Toy emphasis gave no uncertain sound in its affirmation of plenary inspiration and the consequent infallibility of the Scripture, the hermeneutical quicksand of Genesis 1 and 2 lingered as dangerous terrain and full of possibility for misunderstanding. In 1885, Broadus published an article entitled "The Value of the English Bible in Secular and Religious Education." He cautioned that one should not seek much information about the physical and material world around us in Scripture, for "in that respect the Bible teaches us very little, and that little is taught only incidentally. The Bible was not given to teach physical science." The Bible speaks of physical phenomena "only in phenomenal language, and only in an incidental way." Concerning the opening chapters of Genesis and evolution, Broadus said that "instead of being so desperately impatient," Christians should wait (assumingly "without apprehension") "until evolution has evolved itself."[53] T. F. Curtis's warning had been absorbed cautiously and discreetly into the literature: "What already appears certain, must render any theory of Inspiration, which suspends our whole faith in Christianity upon the literal and infallible accuracy of Genesis increasingly mischievous."[54]

In order to define more carefully the sphere of authority Baptists claim for the Bible in light of the increasing complexity of challenges to that authority, Broadus went to the well once more on the issue of the Bible. In 1887 he published *The Paramount and Permanent Authority of the Bible.* He explained the phenomenon of general unity among Baptists as a result of "emphasizing downright conformity to the Bible itself. . . . It causes them to exist and keeps them united."[55] But the Bible must be understood in terms of its real meaning. The Bible is the highest authority for "religious truth." It does not assume authority on all subjects but "uses popular language, which must be interpreted accordingly."[56] But, given that caveat, whatever it teaches is paramount in authority.

Broadus discussed the challenges of reason, the Christian conscious-ness, the tendency of the times, the culture, the "Church," individual inspiration, and placed them in proper context, asserting that we do not "make them a ground for setting Scripture aside."[57] Many factors in the providential arrangements of history might cause Christians to look at passages in a different light or shed new light on the cultural and geographical background of certain passages, but resultant changes come not from rejection of authority but more insightful interpreta-tion. Advances in syntax, in fact, have served to make many passages clear so that "those who dislike orthodoxy cannot now be so loose in their exegesis" and consequently have simply become "loose as to the authority of the Bible."[58] He believed that rapidly shifting scientific theories and the explosion of one after the other should help affirm that science, properly evaluated, does not teach "anything contrary to the Bible."[59] Such an experience should help one evaluate evolution. "I do not know how much to believe about it," Broadus wrote, and affirmed what he had stated earlier, "I am waiting for evolution to evolve itself. Let us not be over hasty to reconcile the Bible with the present theories of evolution."[60]

Divine providence has often forced Christians into new ways of seeing certain scriptural emphases, but the key in all of these is that the Bible not be forced into the prejudices of any special interest group.[61] Alterations that might appear slight and harmless at the time can have radical and devastating results, such as Ignatius's viewpoint on the position of the bishop, the Didache's allowance of an alteration in the practice of baptism, and Justin's imprecise expressions concerning the bread and wine in the Lord's Supper. The slightest departure from the teaching of God's Word proves destructive. A fissure in the system of authority, no matter how seemingly insignificant, develops a rupture allowing a massive cataract of cascading error destructive of Christianity. "Let us stop the beginnings of departure from the teachings of God's word," he pleaded.[62]

A School Committed to Orthodoxy

Public impressions and faculty procurement came under a highly selective criterion of scrutiny. Negotiations with D. G. Lyon in 1880 and 1881 show how carefully the issue of inspiration had to be addressed since the disappointing, and alarming, engagement of the modern slipperiness on the subject with Toy. Still needing further help with the teaching of Greek and Hebrew, Boyce asked Broadus to feel out Lyon for the position. Lyon had attended the seminary from 1876 to 1879 and had gone to the University of Leipzig to study. In the spring of 1880, Broadus contacted Lyon with an invitation to return to the seminary as a tutor in Greek and Hebrew contingent upon his being able satisfactorily to answer a question concerning inspiration. Lyon responded with the kind of answer that surely gave pause to Boyce.

Broadus wrote on April 6 but when the letter arrived in Leipzig, Lyon was in Dresden, and the consul forgot to forward Lyon's mail as requested. On May 22, Lyon answered, apologized for the delay but wrote "as if no delay had intervened." He thanked Boyce and Broadus for the interest they showed him. He protested his unfitness for the offer but acquiesced to their judgment in the matter of his qualifications for the tutorship. "I love the Seminary," he affirmed, "and should be willing to do anything reasonable for its prosperity." Accepting the position, however, would greatly interrupt his plans for study of German and the "Shemetic languages," yet "if, for the present, the Seminary must have my services, I should consider it a duty to respond to the appeal."

On the second matter, that is, the requirement to "teach, as to inspiration, in accordance with and not contrary to the opinions which prevail among intelligent American Baptists" gave him difficulty. He acknowledged that he did not know "what the prevalent opinions on this subject are." Though he had been studying inspiration "somewhat," he felt unprepared to answer the question. "In general terms," he affirmed, "I can say that I view the Bible as the inspired Word of God, but in the details of the subject my opinions are not well enough matured for me to write anything definite." The tutorship, however, "would be such as to require no detailed teaching on the subject."[63]

Boyce would never consent to a contract to teach under such circumstances. Broadus continued his correspondence with Lyon, who by July suggested that his view on inspiration was changing and he was beginning to see difficulty in the infallibilist position. Broadus pointed out to him a variety of difficulties implicit in this shift. Evidently Lyon agreed to consider these remonstrances seriously.[64] When this news came to Boyce, he set in place a protocol on dealing with Lyon, leaving the possibility open but with agreed-upon cautions about the issue. On 15 July 1880, Boyce wrote Broadus that he had heard nothing further from Lyon, and then queried, "Did you get a request I wrote in postal or letter to send me the form of telegram agreed on for the reply to D. G. Lyon?" He had not received Broadus's response, and further noted, "I write to ask you to send it at once to Manly so that when he gets the telegram he will know how to reply."[65] With the insufficiency of Lyon's answer, Broadus advised waiting another year. Boyce responded, "Am sorry about our friend abroad, but we can do nothing now. Your reply to him was what must have gone."[66]

By March 1881, Boyce, through Broadus, renewed the invitation to Lyon, but under the same stipulation. Lyon wrote Boyce and declined on the basis that "our divergence of views as to inspiration hinders my accepting a position in the Seminary. If on this one point we could agree, if such views as I hold were not in the South so generally regarded as destructive there is no position which I should more joyfully accept than the one offered."[67] His answer must have been distressing for Boyce, for the reasoning sounded precisely like Toy's.

In sixteen handwritten pages in a subsequent letter to Broadus, Lyon explained and defended his change on the doctrine of inspiration. Though nothing could be more satisfying than to teach alongside the seminary faculty, he lamented, "The tears fill my eyes and sincere grief my heart as I reflect that the demand is an impossibility, for you wish a man who can assert the absolute infallibility of the biblical writers, and that I cannot do."[68]

Lyon pointed to several German theologians, including Tholuck and Delitzsch, who did much spiritual good though they did not receive everything "found between the lids of the Bible" as the Word of God. So had it been through the history of the church and most compellingly in his own experience. "The divine so pervades the Scriptures as to make them the imperishable storehouse of saving truth," Lyon testified. "That mysterious something which draws the mind of the believing reader heavenward is the Spirit of God living and breathing in the Word." One who has felt this "stands on a foundation which cannot be shaken," sensing that "the message loses none of its value or preciousness because penned by hands which were not infallible." Though his own view had changed, he still knew that "there is a God, who leads and saves us through Jesus Christ." In preaching he still felt the importance of the message as much as before the change, and "If on my return my work shall be in the pastorate, I think that my zeal will be the same as if my views of inspiration had never undergone change."[69]

Lyon believed that a general change among the preachers of the South would produce only a temporary shock. The fear of spiritual decline shows a lack of faith in the work of the Holy Spirit. They must learn that "in God's abounding love in Christ they have something infinitely deeper and firmer than any theory on the subject of inspiration." The fear shows a limited knowledge of God: "When brethren say that their theory can be the only possible correct one and that a surrender of that theory would result in spiritual bankruptcy, I am afraid that they either have a very limited knowledge of God's dealings with the soul, or have not seriously reflected on the nature of their utterance."[70] Boyce and Broadus must have winced at this observation from their former student and could hardly have done other than take it personally.

The religious dearth in Germany, according to Lyon's observation, had nothing to do with "loose" views on inspiration. Instead he pointed to "an unconverted ministry, acting in connections with a church fettered by state restrictions." If as much emphasis were laid on faith and godliness "as is laid on infant baptism and confirmation, we should see a very different state of affairs."

Lyon reported the alarming fact that "a goodly number of our American students who spend a year or two in Germany make the same step." Though they are pious, intelligent, and conservative, when released from a constricting environment, they look the "subject squarely in the face, and the issue is generally the same." Though he did not know precisely where the "stopping place" would be, Lyon assured his mentors that there was one. In his view of inspiration "Jesus becomes no less divine, remains as imperative and necessary as ever." In fact, Lyon did not "know of a single doctrine nor of one important fact which could be affected by the admission that a Bible writer has fallen here or there into some insignificant error." The Christian consciousness would rescue these most sublime and necessary doctrines so that "the Christian system remains intact after the admission of inaccuracy has been made."[71]

As to the initial question, "whether I have grown more conservative," Lyon gave the straightforward and obvious answer; "this letter shows that I am not more conservative than I was a year ago." At the same time, Lyon reiterated, "I occupy precisely the same ground held by the recognized leader of German conservatism and orthodoxy, prof. Franz Delitzsch." Small consolation! Lyon knew that the board of trustees would be unanimously against employing one who held Delitzsch's views. Even if Lyon did not have to deal with the subject in class, "popular pressure will require that the new man who takes his place at your sides, should speak out on this subject; while the public utterance of anything which I could now say, if coming from a teacher in the Seminary, could only lead to controversy and perhaps alienation." Even given that reality, Lyon reaffirmed, "I am neither afraid nor ashamed to be known as holding these views, but I should be in no wise willing to involve or endanger the Seminary."[72]

Though removed from his teachers on the doctrine of inspiration, Lyon seemed to have lost no affection for his former instructors or the success of the seminary. In fact he held out hope that sooner rather than later that point of theological strictness would vanish. "What a joy and an inspiration it would be to me," he mused, "if I could dare to hope that after a half a year in Beyrout and another half year in Athens, I might be permitted to give my active services to the Seminary!"[73]

After the first round of letters with Lyon, Broadus, on a trip to New York, decided to ask the recently departed Toy to recommend his best students in those subjects. He could not find Toy and wrote him to express his regret at missing him and gave him "friendly regard." Upon informing him that the faculty "may find it necessary, to appoint a Tutor in Hebrew and Greek," he requested him to "tell me of several of his former students who were good in Hebrew, and exactly what he thought of each." Broadus was careful to give this as his personal request and in no sense an official inquiry from the faculty. Toy responded and Broadus sent Boyce the letter.[74]

Boyce responded, "As to Toy's list of men, so far as I know none would do at all except Dargan or Smith. I am in favor of getting some older man for some other place, and leaving Manly there unless we are sure of the right young man." He proposed other alternatives for covering the courses needed.[75] He delayed until 1883 before investigating some of the names submitted by Toy, when he asked Broadus, "Let me ask you quietly (I have spoken to no one) to find out about the inspiration views of W. R. Smith, E. C. Dargan, and J. E. Holmes. Also, do you think Kerfoot moveable, and if so would he suit us? Would it be wise?"[76]

Both Kerfoot (1887) and Dargan (1892) eventually came to teach; the immediate need, however, was met by selecting George W. Riggan as assistant instructor of Hebrew, Greek, and Homiletics. The trustees advanced Riggan to assistant professor. He had graduated as a master of arts from Richmond College and as a full graduate from the seminary in the spring of 1881. Broadus described his inaugural address, entitled "The Preacher's Adaptation to His Intellectual Environment," as "vigorous and suggestive." Riggan worked himself to an early death in April 1885, maintaining an overly ambitious schedule while becoming increasingly weakened by malaria, or as Broadus stated with striking imagery, "while the subtle something we call malaria was fastening its deadly grasp upon him more and more firmly."[77] Much of the extra load he endured came from a pledge made early in life to provide for his mother. In his funeral sermon for Riggan, Broadus remarked, "We know not whether amid the fancies of a disordered brain our brother had any consciousness that he was drawing near to death."[78] Broadus described him as a man of acute and powerful intellect, while at the same time, though "fully in sympathy with the spirit of progress, . . . unwaveringly convinced of the truth of those opinions which are established among Baptists concerning the authority of Scripture and the Theology which Scripture exhibits."[79]

Riggan's death immediately increased the workload for Broadus and Manly as they assumed his tasks in languages and homiletics. W. W. Landrum from Richmond wrote that "all Richmond deplores his loss," and wondered "where in all the South his successor is to be found." While recognizing the difficulty of replacing such talent, Landrum was assured that "the Seminary is of God and for God, I have no fear as to its ever-increasing influence and power." While he regretted the loss of Riggan, Landrum expressed great admiration for the influence of Broadus with the pledge, "I will seek to reproduce in my life and labors the example, as to creed and conduct, set me by yourself while I was a student there."[80] In May 1885, John R. Sampey was elected to replace Riggan.

Boyce's great caution toward those who seemed close to Toy affected the Foreign Mission Board also. In 1881, T. P. Bell and John Stout, two students of Toy and graduates of the seminary, were appointed as missionaries to China. When Boyce learned of it, he wrote his brother-in-law H. A. Tupper, the corresponding secretary of the Foreign Mission Board, asking if the men had been questioned on their views of inspiration. When Tupper informed him that the usual questions had been dispensed with in their case, Boyce sounded an urgent note to him that they held the views of Toy. Tupper retraced his steps and asked for a statement from both on their views of the inspiration of Scripture. Stout aligned himself solidly with Toy's views, an understanding that he had only recently come to through correspondence with "Senex," W. C. Lindsay. The board heard these views and took action.

> Whereas Rev. John Stout has candidly and courteously presented to the Board of Foreign Missions his views on Inspiration; and whereas his views do not seem to the Board to be in accord with the views commonly held by the constituency of the Southern Baptist Convention; and whereas Bro. Stout reduces the question between himself and the Board to the simple point whether the Board will give their consent to teach or print, if thought advisable by him, these views as a missionary of our Board; therefore,
>
> Resolved, That, while the Board distinctly and emphatically disclaim the least right over the conscience or Christian liberty of any man, they have not right to consent to any missionary teaching or printing anything regarded by them as contrary to the commonly received doctrinal views of the constituency of the Southern Baptist Convention.[81]

Bell aligned himself with the position of Stout. The appointments of these two missionaries, one to Shanghai and one to Tengchow, were rescinded. Lottie Moon, long-time missionary to China who had been converted to Christ in Charlottesville under the ministry of John A. Broadus, threatened to resign as a missionary when she heard this news. Men were needed and these two had great promise. Tupper had to use all his skills as a diplomat and administrator to assuage the feelings of his star missionary, even assuring her of his personal affection for Toy.[82] Not only were two missionaries lost, but the possibility of Toy's joining her on the mission field withered. Boyce, however, was unrepentant. The seminary could not be responsible for importing the new theology to the mission field and sabotaging the work of the gospel from its inception.

Boyce continued to feel responsibility for having introduced Toy's progressivism into Southern Baptist thought and worked to rid Southern Baptists of his influence. He seemed to shoulder the burden of protecting the students from the kind of destructive intellectual provocation represented by Toy's style and the entire school of thought that he had introduced into the academic atmosphere of the seminary. Lindsay, Hiden, Stout, Bell, and Lyon—all gifted young men whose zeal and preparation should have counted toward fulfilling the vision of a sound and scholarly self-sufficiency for Southern Baptists went awry led by one attractive teacher and intriguing books proposing new approaches to biblical studies.

In the summer of 1883, Boyce sent a catalogue to Broadus with specific instructions concerning its use. "I enclose to you the list sent by Scribner. Mark on it the books you need for your own department and I will order them. I see several which seem to me to be of a rationalistic character. I am opposed to the purchase of such for our library when they come into the hands of untrained persons, especially at present with recent tendencies." He explained why he felt certain books fit that category and why others were not needed in the library immediately. He concluded with the reiteration, "My idea is that we should confine our seminary orders to the books requisite for department instruction, that we should omit books which we should merely like to read, and that books of dangerous doctrine should only be purchased by each professor for himself, and not for the library."[83]

Broadus responded that he shared the concern of his friend and worked to select books under the same principle. "I have marked in the enclosed the books which I should be particularly glad to have for my studies in Homiletics or New Testament," he wrote, and soon assured Boyce, "As to the Old Testament books, I fully agree with you about the kind of books we ought to get." He then explained something of his process of investigating a book and how he considered whether it might or might not be useful for the seminary. "Of course, I might misjudge in so hurried an examination," he admitted; but even then, "I am only anxious you should understand that my principle of selection was exactly that which you indicate as proper."[84]

Boyce kept circumspect watch on the impressions given by any activity of the faculty concerning the theological witness of the seminary. On 6 August 1886, Broadus received from Harvard University President Francis Peabody an invitation to preach "on one Sunday during the winter." He suggested the evening of January 30.[85] Broadus sent the note to Boyce and asked his opinion, at the same time expressing his doubt about it. "I very much doubt," he wrote across the top of the handwritten letter, and added, "Toy writes that they pay $50, which would not cover expense of trip from Louisville, but I could perhaps work it some way if really advisable." Boyce, though always deferential to the judgment of Broadus, gave a decisive opinion: "but were I you I should not plan to do so. There is great danger in any encouragement we give to Drs. Toy and Lyon." We should not give any impression that our differences are inconsequential, and, "Besides, I do not like to see the Unitarians helped by favors from others, and especially by sermons from which the 'gospel' must be left out so as not to say what would be unacceptable to Unitarians."[86]

A School in Need of a Settled Security

As late as 1879, the financial stability of the seminary still was precarious. John Stout wrote to Broadus in January, "I sincerely hope that you and dear Doctor Boyce may live to see the Seminary really endowed—and your best expectations of its widespread usefulness fulfilled."[87] One year later E. S. Allen wrote Broadus, "I deeply sympathize with you in your efforts to place the Seminary on a permanent and useful footing. The Baptists of the South cannot afford to let it fail." He went on to observe that if the ministers trained at the seminary were extracted from South Carolina, "what a sad condition we would have to deplore."[88] The letters exchanged between Boyce and Broadus regularly contain the low-grade chronic fever of alarm at the perpetual struggle for finances, which seemed ever and ever to be declining. "May God spare us, if it be possible, and preserve our struggling enterprise," Broadus closed one letter.[89]

In December 1878, Broadus had been on a fund-raising trip to Baltimore, having arranged to meet certain prosperous businessmen regarding support of the seminary. He described his movements, his preaching appointments; and finally the critical meeting that was designed to secure pledges:

It rained all day yesterday. But 7th Church was ¾ filled, including galleries, last night. The rich men all failed us. None went but Dr. Tyler and his son Charles, and they started it out and gave not a cent. I had seen Sryock, Biving, Gunther and Tyler. The two former refused point blank. I happen to know (privately) that Biving went to see Sryock beforehand, and they agreed to refuse. F. Wilson and Henry Taylor did not come.

We raised $10,760 besides the $8,000. I was strongly advised to manage the pledging myself and did it. I feared Williams would be put out, but he seemed in a good humor. His Miss Eliza Wilson gave $500, and Mrs. Patterson $250. I had laid vigorous siege to them in private. There were 9 that gave $500. . . . Then 10 gave $250, including old Mrs. Levering and I believe all the remaining children. Then we came to $125, getting 10 I think. Then 15 gave $100, and 15 $50, and some more on cards. . . . It took 1¼ hours to get the pledges, closing at 10:30. Leaving out the rich men, the people did *nobly*. The chief work has been done by E. Levering and Kerfoot, who gave me suggestions and went about with me last week and stiffened my back bone. Brantly is as friendly as possible, and nobody unfriendly. I must get the bonds signed. E. Levering gives me his carriage for tomorrow. Today at 12 o'clock I have called a committee of laymen (1 for each church) to meet me, and arrange committees for the several churches, to see others not present. And by the advice of E. L. I am going to see the rich men again, at any rate those who have not *refused*, show them what was done, and try hard. Possible something from Gunther and Henry Taylor.

This is not success, my friend, but it is far from being failure. Few people imagined we should do so well. There was joy and gratitude when we closed. As a popular effort, with very great generosity on the part of many, it is encouraging. But that other $6000. We cannot do without it. I shall strain every nerve and shall stay till the very end of the week if I can make it tell, though I want to get home Friday if possible.[90]

Broadus summarized the implications of such enduring financial distress:

> So it came to pass that in the third session at Louisville, when Dr. Manly had returned, and Dr. Boyce had been formally reappointed Professor of Systematic Theology, and the way seemed open for happy work and growing prosperity, it became apparent to his business eye that financially the Seminary was going to ruin. The salaries were inadequate, and could not possibly be lowered. The Faculty had been cut down to four professors again after the death of Dr. Williams, and some of them were gravely burdened with their work. The agents were indispensable, and so much of the money coming in had to be used for expenses that there seemed no reasonable hope of investing an adequate endowment. About the end of the year 1879 Dr. Boyce explained this situation to his colleagues. The Seminary could struggle on in that fashion for several years, but the generous donors would assuredly have a right to complain if their gifts were used up for current expenses. He saw no hope of effecting a permanent endowment unless some person could be found to give a new impetus to the whole movement by personally contributing $50,000. At a meeting of the Missionary Society, which includes all the students, he asked them to join in this special prayer for what he represented as in his judgment the only thing that could provide for the Seminary's permanent existence and large usefulness. He spoke with deep feeling: his heart was evidently set on the idea, and on the particular sum named. He sent a few lines to two or three Baptist papers, expressing the hope and prayer that God would put it into somebody's heart to make this gift.[91]

An ardent friend of the seminary and ex-governor of Georgia, Joseph E. Brown, responded to the call with a gift of $50,000. Broadus recalled Boyce's "radiant and yet tearful face" when he came to his study with the note from Governor Brown asking Boyce to come to Georgia to present the case for the seminary. Boyce's trip convinced Brown that it would be "safe and wise to invest in its endowment," and the gift was made on 11 February 1880.[92] From Petersburgh, Virginia, T. T. Eaton wrote on 25 March 1880, "My Dear Doctor,

A thousand congratulations on the princely gift of Gov. Brown to the Seminary. Amen & Amen!!!"

Very soon the seminary trustees established the policy of securing all money given for endowment as "sacred and inviolate" so that only the interest could be used for operating expenses of the seminary. A financial board of five Louisville businessmen was to be elected for the investment of the principal and for transferring the earnings to the treasurer of the seminary. George and William Norton made further gifts, and Broadus collected $40,000 in New York. Though the goal of a $500,000 endowment still was far off, within two years a sum of nearly $200,000 was collected and removed the seminary from the danger of yearly consideration of the need of closing.

Boyce took advantage of the new life given by Brown's gift to assert the seminary's claims on the hearts of Baptists in the South more vigorously and expectantly. An article he wrote for the state papers entitled "New Hope for the Seminary" began, "Our well-known Baptist brother, Gov. Joseph E. Brown of Georgia, has paid me in cash and in bonds worth over par fifty thousand dollars for the endowment of a professorship in the Southern Baptist Theological Seminary." This became the Joseph Emerson Brown Chair of Systematic Theology held initially by Boyce. He explained that the gift assumed that "the denomination will sustain the Seminary by annual contributions and by a rapid completion of the endowment." Failing that, Brown retained the right to ask for reimbursement of the gift.

Boyce made four specific requests from Baptists of the South to respond to this generosity as well as this challenge. First, surely three or four other wealthy and generous men could give $5,000 or $10,000 or even endow the "school which the Board has fixed at $300,000." Second, all holders of subscriptions or bonds should pay as much as they could at once. "I ask this," Boyce wrote, "of those whose obligations are past due as a matter of justice to us and in fulfillment of their promises." Third, he appealed to churches to make immediate collections "for our annual expenses of the past year." The seminary had barely met its ongoing expenses, leaving nothing for professors' salaries. Boyce had advanced these salaries in January and would have to do the same in April if increased money for annual expenses did not come. Fourth, he asked churches that already had taken collections to forward them immediately rather than send them by delegate to the meeting of the convention in May.[93]

In pursuit of his second request, Boyce sent cards to each individual holding bonds. Broadus records that "a good many outstanding five-year bonds for annual support" still were unpaid and were "hard to collect."[94] He learned, again, that talk of money did not tend to endear the public to the seminary. His attempts yielded some positive fruit, but also provoked response from many who felt that money pledged for benevolent work had no obligation to pay attached to it.

From Mayfield, Georgia, Boyce received a curt and somewhat indignant response from a bond holder.[95] "I received from you the other day an other solicitation, or dun, for money," the letter began, "of which, and by which, I must say I am worried. I have been threatened with interest if I did not pay up. I now have the very favorable promise of being released from the interest, if I will pay the principal by such a time." M. B. Wharton, the agent from Georgia, had recorded this pledge, and Mr. Allen, the letter writer, recalled the event clearly: "If you do not get the money Dr. Wharton noted down in his book, of course you want to know the reason why," he continued. Through his adept use of Scripture, Wharton had prodded many individuals to pledge "(to get rid of him on the subject) regardless of their ability, and perhaps, duty." Many would never be able to pay, and, "just here," Mr. Allen wrote, "I must say, I fear I belong to that class." All he had was land from which he sought to squeeze out a living, but of cash he had none that he felt disposed to give to the seminary. He objected to the note system as unbiblical for the support of God's work and had no desire to expose his capital to the possibility of suit at law. When Wharton assured him that no such contingency existed, he "agreed to give the cause four dollars a year, for five years <u>Provided I felt able</u>, not provided somebody thought I was able." He did not feel able, and, though aware of the necessity of doing his duty before God, did not think it his duty to explain why he so felt. He concluded by referring to the gift of Governor Brown.

There are plenty of as able men as ex Gov Joseph E. Brown of Georgia that has thousands of dollars they have no use for, who could deposit it in your institution, the interest of which would run your whole machine, through ages and they never feel it; great good could be accomplished in the theological department, and let poor people keep what few dollars they can raise, to send their dear children to a little country school somewhere, in their reach, for ought you or I know, the four dollars, I have already given, is as big as Joe Browns 50000, in a certain sense, May the Lord give you comfort and much good come through the Seminary.

Yours Truly, Wm M. Allen[96]

As in attempts immediately after the Civil War, Boyce still found many cases of deep hardship that interrupted the efforts to obtain payment of pledges. Eliza Jane Peddicord wrote, "I received the postal card asking me to send you $5.00. When you came to my house and got me to subscribe you said that if I was not able to pay it I need not pay it." Sickness and old age had overwhelmed the family, and she had a "large doctor bill to pay." She reminded Boyce that her husband "was an old man he has become so badly crippled that he is not able to work any; there is only one boy in the family that is able to work." Calling him "Dear Brother," Mrs. Peddicord affirmed that she was "a true Baptist and wish I was able to help you all I could but I am not able to pay any thing and I ask you in the name of our master to release me of the obligation."[97]

Sometimes the follow-up method of collecting hit the nerve of a supporter in just the wrong way. M. H. Justice explained that though he had paid on time for each note due, "This is not the first time I have been called upon to pay money on this account after it had been paid." Though he felt a deep interest in the seminary, he believed that "if your agents who collect the money in other parts of the country are as derelict as those to whom the subscriptions in this section have been paid the course is well calculated to do injury." Had he known the process would be so disagreeable, he would have "paid what [he] could at the time and made no future promises."[98]

Boyce wrote postcards to various states calling on the pledgers to "pay up." He reminded them that "much of the subscription is now due and not paid." He believed they should feel a "high duty to pay at once"; the "solemn promises ought to have been met at the time" they were due. One responded that he could not address Boyce as "Brother" since he had denounced him as "a delinquent to a cause which above all others I feel most deeply interested, Baptist Education." He had paid and considered the card "very unbecoming to say the least of it, especially when you were trying to collect the money (a gratuitous gift), out of me twice." Later he decided to complete all payments at once "in order that I may get a leave of being annoyed by you."[99]

This attempt not only irritated many people, it failed to produce the necessary flow of income for annual expenses, and, with the endowment now protected from any use for the sake of daily cash flow, the day to day operations came to be even more restrained. The faculty in particular felt this pressure. Broadus wrote from Richmond in June 1883 about a collection he had made of over $4,500. Breaking from his usual policy, Broadus suggested, "I don't know but the Seminary ought to pay me a small commission for this work, which has cost me much exertion and some care. When I could make money by preaching and writing, I was not willing to receive anything for collections. Now I am straitened, and trying to rest for the Seminary's sake as well as my own, and should not refuse it."[100] A year later, money still was tight, and Broadus wrote a negative prognostication about the flow of funds over the next year: "It is clear that we ought to economize rigorously. Unless there are decidedly good crops this season and prices above the average, money will be *very* hard to collect next winter—indeed it will be hard anyhow."[101]

Broadus was spending the summer preaching in Brooklyn and seeking to regain his health. He had fainted while preaching recently and discovered that it was fatigue, an empty stomach, fever, dyspepsia, and malaria. He was improving by riding horseback about two hours a day "over fine roads about a beautiful country and that is for me the finest exercise in the world." He also lectured one and one half hours per day, expected five more Sundays in Brooklyn, but was resting in between. "So I am hopeful about my health," and he confidently expected to be ready for the beginning of the session. But the real difficulty was the balance between work and healthful rest. He saw no way to cure that dilemma for, wrote he, "I cannot live on my salary, I know it cannot possibly be enlarged, and in one way or another I am compelled to do extra work for which I lack strength."[102]

So tight was the money that Boyce warned Broadus against the purchase of any books for the seminary while he was in New York. Boyce had purchased twelve copies of Turretin for his Latin Theology class, but that happened "when I had no idea of any trouble." The concerns even gave him caution about the commitments to rent property for student housing.

Boyce himself felt keenly the tension produced by the constant barrage of appeals for money for a variety of Christian causes. He wanted to put the seminary beyond all necessity for such continued calls for help, but in the meantime felt some degree of embarrassment about his being a part of the constant ring-a-ling for money.

> Last night at Broadway the committee on repairs announced that the outside wood work and steeple and roof must be painted at once. . . . Help for Georgetown College will be pressed this winter. Weaver will still need help and amid all I have not only to pay for the lot, but also to beg for the mission work of the Seminary Society. I tell you I fear the people will begin to feel that the preachers and their projects are nuisances. I assure you that what with schemes of the ladies for Indian Missions, privies for Sunday School, church entertainment, flowers for the pulpit and other fancies of this kind together without regular work scarcely two weeks have passed over my head this past twelve months without having to give something. I have just paid $22 for the Sunday School Convention and got off cheap at that. And others are equally burdened who are willing to do for anything and everything that comes about.[103]

A School in Search of a Place

Necessity, however, not only is invention's mother, but has put many a beggar on the street and many an administrator in the offices of the prosperous. Boyce negotiated constantly and with great shrewdness, and sometimes in undesirable circumstances, for property on which to build a permanent dwelling for the seminary. He confided the unpalatableness of all this to Broadus.

> Newcomb asks $80,000 for his house, any terms we wish. I have told him it is impossible to give over fifty. He says he will not listen to that. But I think he will. He wishes me to talk with Meddis. He says his lot is 320 feet deep x 280 wide. If so the latter allows for 280 x 200 instead of 320 and would be worth $56,000, and $200 per foot, or $42,000 and $150, and we get the extra depth. I pressed him and he did not seem willing that we should stop the negotiation but said we could trade through Meddis. I do not like to trade through that man, but still I do not think he can cheat us.[104]

One year later, persons interested in the progress of the seminary began to ask why it had not yet established a permanent site in Louisville, especially since "about a year ago the Baptists of the State were gratified to learn that a large committee had, by the direction of the Board of Trustees, bought a very eligible location." Materials are "cheap at present" and "the quarters of the Seminary are very insufficient." "Economy," the writer of the article, had in fact heard Boyce in a lamentation over the sad conditions of the physical facilities refer to the "great danger to which the large and valuable library is exposed" and the consequent extravagant insurance payment needed to secure it. The Waverly Hotel no longer had sufficient room for the students, and even the "largest and most desirable" recitation room left much to be desired. Though Economy had only respect for the "wisdom and the prudence" of the seminary's managers, it appeared that in this matter they were "penny wise and pound foolish" and showed a lack of enterprise. Could they not trust the brethren and God in this matter? Would not the Baptists of the South rise to the occasion and "respond to any call necessary to the welfare of the Seminary?"[105]

Economy's challenge provided just the provocation needed for Boyce to give notice of the sadly delinquent state of promises made and the fervency of his feeling about this nonchalant attitude toward pledges. In two successive issues of the *Western Recorder*, Boyce pressed his claims on the Baptists of Kentucky. "The endowment," Boyce reminded the readers, "and establishment of the institution in this State has been projected since 1872, nearly thirteen years." So far this has not been accomplished, and the money that has been gathered has been used to rent buildings, pay professors, and help indigent students, and "even this part of our work has not yet been completed." The endowment must grow significantly before it "will produce a sufficient annual interest to meet current expenditures." In addition, the issue of "putting up the necessary buildings" has not been ignored, but has met with a significant obstacle.[106]

What is the obstacle? "It is that we have not the money necessary." When asked to put faith in the brethren, Boyce replied that such was the very reason the seminary moved to Louisville before the nominal subscription was completed. Boyce reported that over $100,000 had been lost in interest alone that would have been the seminary's had the promised funds been paid on time. Boyce had made public pleas for the payment of the notes, had sent out cards asking for payment, and had sent agents to seek to collect promises. The agents he was compelled to recall "because the amounts collected would so little exceed the expenses of the agency that the Seminary could not afford to employ agents at such heavy proportion of expenses to the collections." Though many believe that they have good reason to be tardy in their payment, the net effect represses the seminary in its ability to function and expand its ministry. A lawyer responsible for some collecting said that if people knew he had the authority to sue, all would be paid at once. "Now to the extent that this is true," Boyce scolded, "it is to the shame of those that owe." In promising to the seminary they have promised to the Lord and to other brethren, and thus the ground they occupy, even unwittingly, is dangerous. "If every one who reads this and owes," Boyce reasoned, "would resolve to send the money at once, I should be able to report at the meeting of the Board at Augusta, . . . enough to warrant us in commencing at once the erection of buildings."[107]

Months passed, the trustee meeting passed, and the same treadmill of beg, wait, expect disappointment, lament, and retain hope was in operation. In July 1885 Boyce wrote, "I did not get a chance to take up my collection at Broadway yesterday as neither Hale nor Cowan were there. I have tramped this morning, saw Wm. Norton and got

promise of $500 which with G. W. Norton's $500 is all." He knew
of others that would not "give a cent this year." Should he go to see
Caldwell? Should Broadus go? Or perhaps together—but they went
together last year. "John McFerrar says I might see his father but he
did not encourage," and Boyce had no time to see Arthur Peter. Smaller
subscriptions might amount to $500 "but that will be very hard to get."
Boyce then added, "I confess I get sick at heart when I see brethren so
perfectly indifferent to the position in which they leave me. I am like
a man sinking in a quagmire or quicksand and seeing others to whom
he cries for help walking off quietly to eat their supper."[108]

In the meantime, visits to the city by Edward Judson, son of
Adoniram Judson, and J. A. Bostwick, a wealthy New York businessman who was a Baptist, began to invite interest in the advancement of the school.[109] When Boyce learned of this, he quickly stirred
Broadus to go to New York and work the brethren for the needed
contributions. In March, Broadus wrote with a sense of great encouragement and impending success, noting, "The turning point thus
far was Mr. Bostwick's interest, which was developed by his visit to
Louisville." George Norton "did much to strengthen his confidence
and deepen his interest." Broadus then told Boyce that getting the
money depended on some assurance that the lot still needed would
be paid for soon and with moneys in hand or available elsewhere,
and immediately. Getting money from two of the potential donors
would be exceedingly difficult without that assurance. "Suppose I
ask you to telegraph me here that you have paid, or have the money
to pay, all that remains due on the lot—can't you do it? You mustn't
change *my* scheme now." Broadus then exhorted, "And you must
strike while the iron is hot, for it might cool."[110]

Louisville weather was miserable and Boyce struggled with a new
attack of gout, but he went to the Nortons and to Theodore Harris,
president of the Louisville Banking Company, with the conditions communicated from New York. That evening he telegraphed Broadus that
the money for the lots had been secured—$30,000 in fact—but on the
condition that the remaining $20,000 for the buildings be forthcoming
from New York. Basil Manly wrote Broadus, "I made urgent appeals . . .
but I did not get a dollar. . . . However, Boyce worked it through, as he

has telegraphed you. But he is in bed still, lame with his exertions, but cheerful and bright."[111] Three weeks more of negotiating finalized the necessary $60,000. On March 16, Broadus wrote his twenty-six-year-old son, Samuel Sinclair Broadus, "I wanted to see whether anything could be done here for our needed building, and have the promise of a good sum, but the remaining third of the requisite amount will be very, very hard to get."[112] Upon learning of Boyce's success, J. A. Bostwick wrote him expressing his pleasure that he was "successful in securing the sixty thousand dollars" and expressing hope that he would be "spared to see the building and the good work continue for many years to come."[113]

When Governor Brown heard that the money had been collected, he sent a check for $5,000 to help with possible overruns in construction. "He especially asks," Boyce informed Broadus, "that this shall not get into the newspapers and therefore I conclude to tell no one but you, not even Manly."[114] In summarizing the impact of the flurry of activity and emotion involved in bringing to culmination this strategic aspect of the seminary's security, Broadus remarked, "Let no one think it easy to obtain large contributions in the great cities. Many applications must necessarily be rejected, wise and conscientious givers must know what they are doing."[115] But when they are satisfied that the enterprise is promising and well managed, they will give and often rally others to do so.

Boyce began negotiations for beginning the new construction. When the bids came in at $73,000, Boyce insisted that he would not do it. He would pay no more than $60,000 excluding the architect's commission. Further negotiations meant a change of plans. "After talking over the matter," Boyce informed, "the only way seemed to be to take off the wing towards Broadway with the lecture rooms and Gymnasium, which will save $8,000, and Macdonald said he could get lower contracts, say for the brick, to save $5,000. This would make $60,000." The architect was to draw up plans and submit them. He added, "When I wrote as to secrecy I did not mean to omit Rockefeller and Bostwick, etc., only they must be told with earnest enjoinder as to secrecy. I told Dr. Manly I had $5,000 from a brother to help extra cost. But I did not tell from whom, and I warned him not to let the architect or the others of the committee know."[116]

The building, named New York Hall, began to be constructed in September 1886, and was completed in March 1888 at Fifth and Broadway in downtown Louisville. Broadus described it:

> New York Hall, as it was named, really cost nearly eighty thousand dollars. It furnishes dormitories for about two hundred students (two in a room), with a beautiful dining-room and an ample culinary department, and also professors' offices and lecture-rooms, so arranged that they could in future be converted into dormitories whenever other buildings should be erected. There is also an admirable gymnasium. Dr. Manly and some honored Baptist laymen gave much time and thought to the duties of a building committee. May New York Hall long continue to remind the successive generations of students that the Seminary was greatly aided in its early days by generous gifts from the great metropolis.[117]

The students felt the importance of this accomplishment not only from a facilities standpoint, but as a confirming spiritual moment. In March 1888, *The Seminary Magazine* observed, "The first prayer meeting in our new building partook largely of the nature of thanksgiving. The brethren were very ardent in thanking the Lord for His rich blessings upon the Seminary. It was a warm and enjoyable meeting."[118] The building had an organ in the new dining hall, and the students appointed two of the brethren to alternate as organists for evening devotions.

While each of the issues developed here tended toward securing the seminary, its lasting security rested in the deep and dynamic theological convictions of the Joseph Emerson Brown Professor of Systematic Theology, James Petigru Boyce. To the formulations of this Gentleman Theologian we now turn.

11

Boyce's Theology

The sources of Boyce's theology are invariably Reformed. From his earliest exposure to preaching in a Baptist pulpit from Basil Manly Sr., to his formal theological education at Princeton, he imbibed doctrine from thinkers saturated with the Reformed tradition. All of his writings reflect this perspective. His own witness to the influence of Manly combined with Broadus's narrative of the impact of the teachers at Princeton and his own analysis of the necessity for creating a school for theological education among Baptists show how aggressively intentional, how consciously active, was his pursuit of Reformed theology as true Baptist theology.

The texts Boyce used in teaching theology show his propensity for the confessional Reformed stream of thought. His first text, used for several years, was by the Southern Baptist John L. Dagg, *A Manual of Theology*.[1] Soon an accompanying text was the Scots Presbyterian John Dick's *Lectures on Theology*.[2] In his Latin Theology Boyce regularly used Frances Turretin's *Institutes of Elenctic Theology*.[3] Other texts that he used only briefly in his Systematic Theology were Johannes Jacobus

Van Oosterzee's *Christian Dogmatics*,[4] Alvah Hovey's *A Manual of Systematic Theology*,[5] A. A. Hodge's *Outlines of Theology*,[6] and finally his own text printed only for his class.

Instructional Method

His study with Charles Hodge had made an indelible impression on Boyce from the standpoint of both method and content. He quoted both Charles and A. A. Hodge frequently in his Systematic Theology course, often employing paragraphs and outlines of lengthy arguments, but at other times differing from these respected mentors. Sometimes Boyce quotes what he labels as "manuscript lecture" from Charles Hodge, probably referring to his own notes taken in theology class. He consulted Turretin, James Buchanan, Robert Dabney, John Dick, John Gill, J. Pye Smith, James H. Thornwell, John Dagg, J. P. Lange, G. C. Knapp, Moses Stuart, and Jonathan Edwards along with a number of linguistic dictionaries (e.g., Gesenius) and theological encyclopedias (e.g., Kitto). He formulated theological positions as foils from a variety of proponents, and stated the views of philosophers on issues where it seemed appropriate.

Boyce enjoyed the recitation method of instruction that he had experienced under Francis Wayland. He believed that this method yielded the most thorough and longest lasting results in instruction; it was "the most effective method of study for the mastery of any subject." He required the student to "prepare a brief but accurate analysis of each lesson." This outline is then memorized so that each paragraph of text can be presented in such a way as naturally proceeds in an attempt "to state all the thoughts of the lesson." Though difficult at first, Boyce claimed, the method soon may be mastered. When it is combined with regular "back review" of each lesson, the student will so "fully have mastered all its contents as to be perfectly familiar with every portion of it, and to be able to recall any part of it at all." This method, Boyce believed, would enable the conscientious student to master any subject and help him cultivate the memory "to a marvellous degree" and also aid immensely in "cultivating readiness of extemporaneous speech."[7]

Theological Method

Boyce accepted theology as a science "eminently worthy of that name." Chapter 1 of his systematic theology carries the title "The Science of Theology." Brooks Holifield mentions Boyce in a section of his *Theology in America* which discusses theologians of "The Baconian Style." This points to the renewed interest in Christian evidences, their "claim of superior rationality," the defense of a "natural religion," and the "Christian defense of a natural theology linked to the biblical revelation."[8] All these traits mark Boyce to some degree. They show that he imbibed the confidence of a broad spectrum of American evangelicals, not limited to Calvinists, and that the Christian faith did not require gullibility or mere credulity. Cut it anywhere and it bleeds truth. Its authority structure can withstand the most withering empirical investigation and remain unscathed.

Along with this style of Baconian induction from established facts, Boyce accepted the Protestant confidence in the perspicuity of Scripture. Often Boyce listed a large number of Scripture passages, sometimes quoting portions, sometimes only giving references, and at the end, or at the beginning, of the catena summarized their meaning by stating an inductive synthesis of the biblical teaching on that subject. For example, when Boyce taught that the penalty of sin "was actually borne by Christ," he proclaimed the proposition and then listed thirteen Scripture texts, quoting the pertinent phrase in each text as conclusive of the doctrinal statement.

At other times he unfolded theological ideas on a particular subject, distinguishing fine points within the discussion through logic acting upon an assumed knowledge of Scripture and would briefly mention a biblical text by way of illustration. His discussion of love as a moral attribute of God covers five pages, divided into five types of love (complacency, benevolence, compassion, mercy, and affection), and mentions only four texts in the entire discussion.

In his discussion of the divine attribute of justice Boyce proceeds for six pages with only one Scripture text mentioned, 1 John 1:9, and then in the space of one page mentions seventy passages of Scripture. For the first six pages he outlined the argument of three different views of divine justice and then sealed his argument for the third view, that of retributive justice, by lining up all those passages in support of nine biblical elements of retributive justice.[9] This method has led some critics to view Boyce as more dependent on reason than on revelation.

Boyce studied theology with one of the most prolific theologians within this Baconian framework, his chief mentor, Charles Hodge. Hodge set the stage for Boyce's approach as evidenced by the title to the first section of his introductory chapter to theology, "Theology a Science." Boyce, like Hodge, saw theology as the discovery and "investigation of the facts" of divine revelation. Theology seeks to determine the relations of these facts to each other, "their systematic arrangement, the laws which govern them, and the great principles which are the basis of this existence." Hodge discussed the inductive method as essential for both natural science and theological science. The student of nature, using induction in a rigorous manner, "proceeds to perceive, gather, and combine his facts. These he does not pretend to manufacture, nor presume to modify." Boyce concurred, in that in gathering the individual teachings, or facts of Scripture, the theologian ascertains them, compares them, and is "warned not to omit any of the truth ascertained from any source, nor to add to it anything not properly embraced therein." Discoveries of new facts call for some rearrangement of each aspect of the system. "A full knowledge of all the facts, and perfect generalization of them," Boyce believed, "will constitute theology an exact science."[10]

Because the totality of these teachings constitutes a system of truth, the omission of any, for any reason, not only destroys the symmetry of the system but, in the case of theology, could be dangerous to souls. "We must take the facts of the Bible as they are," Hodge emphasized, "and construct our system so as to embrace them in all their integrity."[11] "The omission of a single fact," Boyce concurred, "however small, must affect the whole universe of doctrine."[12] He agreed entirely with Hodge's dictum that, "principles are to be deduced from facts." "So long, however, as the binding authority of Scripture is acknowledged," Hodge pointed out, "the temptation is very strong to press the facts of the Bible into accordance with our preconceived theories." He went on to give an extended litany of the results of preconception ruling biblical fact:

If a man be persuaded that certainty in acting is inconsistent with liberty of action . . . he will inevitably deny that the Scriptures teach the contrary, and thus be forced to explain away all facts which prove the absolute control of God over the will and volitions of men. If he hold that sinfulness can be predicated only of intelligent, voluntary action in contravention of law, he must deny that men are born in sin, let the Bible teach what it may. If he believe that ability limits obligation, he must believe independently of the Scriptures, or in opposition to them, it matters not which, that men are able to repent, believe, love God perfectly, to live without sin, at any and all times, without the least assistance from the Spirit of God. If he deny that the innocent may justly suffer penal evil for the guilty, he must deny that Christ bore our sins. If he deny that the merit of one man can be the judicial ground of the pardon and salvation of other men, he must reject the Scriptural doctrine of justification. It is plain that complete havoc must be made of the whole system of revealed truth, unless we consent to derive our philosophy from the Bible, instead of explaining the Bible by our philosophy. It is the fundamental principle of all sciences, and of theology among the rest, that theory is to be determined by facts, and not facts by theory. As natural science was a chaos until the principle of induction was admitted and faithfully carried out, so theology is a jumble of human speculations, not worth a straw, when men refuse to apply the same principle to the study of the Word of God.[13]

In the end, the theologian values each doctrine, sees each as true, "revealed that it might be believed." Though far less prolix, Boyce gave a brief synopsis that showed his entire agreement with the approach of Hodge in deducing principle from the unedited compilation of facts. Not one can be omitted because of its "forbidding aspect, or its seeming unimportance, or its mysterious nature, or its demand for personal sacrifice, or its humiliating assertions, or requirements, or the free terms upon which it assures of life and salvation."[14]

Our discussion of Boyce's theology will largely come from his *Abstract of Systematic Theology*. Other sources include notes from his lectures, manuscripts of his sermons, his catechism, and a few other articles and lectures. Several dissertations contain discussions of the theology of Boyce. These will be referenced where appropriate.

Trifold Division

Though one courts danger and brushes close to error when he seeks to reduce a comprehensive theology to a triad of leading ideas, he also might gain the advantage of coming closer to the truth in his presentation. Because Boyce was so purposefully connectional in his theology, the leading ideas that carry forward the argument emerge splendidly in the progress of his narrative. Boyce's first leading idea is that the sphere in which the knowledge of God arises progresses from simple intuitive ideas easily accessible to all through a series of increasingly complex ideas, with each stage of development commended to us by its demonstrable consistency with the previous stage and its verifiability through miraculous signs. Second, we find that God has bound the demonstration of his glory to the necessity of redemption and its consequent dependence on sovereign and effectual grace. Third, the person of Christ is the only sphere within which redemption can occur, that is, within which God's holy justice can be consistent with the freeness of his grace. This third idea will constitute the subject matter of chapter 12.

The Knowledge of the Being of God

The existence of God is the foundation of theology. If there is no God "there can be no science of God." The corollary to the existence of God is that "God can be sufficiently known." These two ideas lead eventually to Boyce's discussion of reason and revelation. Before that discussion, however, Boyce engaged the question of the "Being," that is, the Existence, of God as far as it can be discerned by human reason.

Boyce deftly pushed aside three major objections, showing that each assumes some knowledge of God that is affirmed in Scripture and that leads to an expanded knowledge of him that appropriately results in worship. Boyce pointed to an almost universal belief in God as evidence that the first humans knew God and told their offspring. This knowledge thus passed down appears in every culture so that true atheism is exceedingly rare. This knowledge of God, however, Boyce does not think of as "innate" but as intuitive, that is, certain truths are "self-evident upon an intelligent conception of what is meant by them."[15]

Hodge, whose lead Boyce follows in this, uses the words "innate" and "intuitive" as virtual synonyms.[16] Boyce gives a slightly different nuance to some of the arguments of Hodge, and offers corrections at some points, but finds him worthy of emulation in most of the discussion. Boyce identifies several intuitive concepts that serve as foundations for further suggestions about the being of God:

1. That which is dependent must have its final support in something purely independent;
2. Derived existence must have its ultimate origin in that which is self-existent;
3. Every effect must have its cause, either within, or without itself.[17]

Although these propositions point to a single deity, they sometimes, among the "uncultivated," have led to polytheism. The objections of Hume and Kant to the universal law of causation Boyce met with the simple observation, "This is an objection to the amount of evidence we have of the effects of causation, which truly is measured by experience only, but our knowledge of the universal nature of the law comes not from experience, but from intuitive conceptions based upon the knowledge of its meaning."[18] Boyce identified two other intuitive conceptions a bit more remote but just as strongly asserted by those who perceive them: (1) the distinction of right and wrong must have some absolute standard that is personal, conscious, and unchangeable, and (2) moral perfection cannot be merely ideal, but must have some real embodiment.

Arguing from these intuitive conceptions, Boyce takes the position that proofs of the existence of God are both a posteriori and a priori. These sometimes overlap in argument, and the a posteriori depends implicitly upon the a priori. Boyce hesitated to affirm, as a matter of ministerial practicality, the widespread usefulness of these proofs. "The existence of God is evident without proof from argument," Boyce taught his students, "and hence it is better to present no argument to the masses, who receive it as a self-evident truth." For them, the attempt to prove what no sane person doubts, more often awakens doubts and suspicions than it convinces. Its usefulness comes in meeting the arguments of the atheist.[19] This caveat seems to emerge from Boyce's knowledge of Turretin, who wrote, "Although that there is a God is an indubitable first principle of religion (rather to be taken for granted than proved, so that they who doubt it are to be punished and not disputed with, as Aristotle says), yet the execrable madness of modern atheists . . . renders this question necessary."[20] Boyce would not agree that atheists should be punished, but he accepted Turretin's confidence in the indubitable nature and evidential power of the knowledge of God "implanted in men by nature."[21]

For the overall impact of Boyce's theological narrative, however, these arguments could not be omitted. His scheme of coherent continuity in identifying the source of divine revelation depended on the true reasonableness of these God-proofs that are founded in intuition, both those that reason from cause to effect and those that reason from effect to cause. John Dick, the author of the theological textbook Boyce used in the seminary, and Charles Hodge discussed both of these types of proof, but did not place as much confidence in the a priori proofs as Boyce did. Dick did not think that the a priori is sustainable or comprehensible:

> As it is very abstruse, and I am not sure that I distinctly apprehend it, I shall give you a statement of it, nearly in the words of Bishop Stillingfleet. . . . It not only follows as a necessary conclusion from these preliminaries, but is in itself evident to the reason of any person, that if necessary existence belongs to the nature of God, he exists; for it implies no less than a contradiction, for a being to exist necessarily, and yet that it should be questionable whether he doth exist or not. . . . You do not demonstratively prove that God exists in opposition to the atheist; you merely conclude hypothetically, that if there is a God, his existence is necessary.[22]

Hodge, also, saw no value in the a priori reasoning that compelled assent. "The argument does not show how the ideal implies the real," Hodge concluded concerning Anselm's construction of the argument. That of Descartes differed only formally from Anselm's and had "no

403

power over the generality of men." Samuel Clarke's argument was not a priori but a posteriori (Boyce disagreed with Hodge on this observation), and at the end of the entire discussion, Hodge concluded, "Theism therefore gains nothing from these metaphysical arguments."[23] Even Boyce's colleague, William Williams, when teaching Systematic Theology in 1866, said, "As to the ontological arguments, they are too metaphysical and abstruse to be of any value."

Boyce differed with both of his theological mentors and his valued colleague on this issue. In his antebellum lectures at the seminary through the publication of his own systematic theology, he spent a significant amount of time on the subject and provided questions and answers for the recitation of the students. He insisted that they learn these answers word for word. The value of this in Boyce's estimation was simply, "God!!! A being in whom resides every perfection in the highest degree."

On contemplation it should not be surprising that this argument from ontology was eminently important to Boyce. His desire to establish a method for grasping the true knowledge that moved from the most primitive kind of "revelation," and thus assured knowledge, to the most advanced kind of knowledge utterly dependent on interventional, supernatural revelation depended on knowledge a priori more keenly than knowledge a posteriori. His apologetic for the revelational status of Scripture would be stronger with the security of this first step. He taught, therefore, his students to reason with this Cartesian foundation.

> Q. 14. What is the nature of this argument? Ans. It is based upon the idea of God which we find to exist in the mind of man. That which may be clearly perceived to belong to the nature and essence of a thing may be affirmed of that thing. (A clear and distinct perception of the mind brings the strongest proof.) We have clear perception that necessary existence belongs to his nature; hence he exists.
>
> Q. 15. What is the 1st point of its proof? Ans. The greatest evidence we can have of the truth of a thing is a clear and distinct perception of it to our minds. Otherwise, our rational faculties were useless, if upon a right use of them we are liable to be deceived. The imperfection of the mind is granted, but that arises only from the

proneness of the mind to be influenced by prejudice and interest. But if the mind is not certain that it is not undeceived then [it] cannot [trust] even mathematical demonstration. Now we find in the mind a clear and convincing evidence of some things as soon as suggested—as that a thing cannot not be and yet be at the same time. That while I reason and discourse, I am. These are so clear that no one supposes himself deceived. If, indeed, we have no certainty of judging things, to what purpose is an idea of true and false in our minds? Under the hypothesis, we could not know one from the other. We do not say that in all perceptions we have a certain evidence of truth, but only in such as are clear and distinct. That is when upon the greatest consideration of the nature of a thing there appears no reason or ground to doubt concerning it. This supposes abstraction from the senses, for they may deceive us, and also that men proceed upon evident principles of reason, and have such notions as do agree with the nature of the things we apprehend. If in such things we have no certainty, it is as much as to say our faculties are to no purpose.

Q. 16. State the second point and its proof. Ans. We have a distinct and clear perception that necessary existence does belong to the nature of God. In other beings we may abstract essence and existence from each other, but in the conception of an absolutely perfect Being, bare possibility of existence is directly repugnant to the idea of Him.

Q. 17. What is the only question that arises? Ans. Whether this necessary existence does really belong to the nature of that being of whom we have the idea of necessary existence or is it only a mode of our conceiving Him.

Q. 18. What is our rule for settling this question? Ans. We must conceive by what rule we can know when [the] connection of things in understanding depends upon [the] operation of the mind or belongs to [the] nature of things and their immutable nature. Those things depending upon an action of the mind, understanding can separate them entirely from each other, but those things which the understanding can not separate without destroying the essence of the thing they belong to belong to the constitution of that thing.

Q. 19. Apply the rule to the case in point. Ans. Now as to all other bodies we can conceive of all perfection without necessary existence for it may be a body still though it have not its existence from itself. But when we conceive of a being absolutely perfect it is impossible to imagine it to have its being from any other. Hence we conclude that necessary existence does belong to God.

Q. 20. What is the 3rd point or conclusion and proof? Ans. That if necessary existence does belong to the nature of God it unavoidably follows that he does exist.

Q. 21. What objection has been made to this argument by Kant? Ans. Mere supposableness of logical possibility of a perfect being is no proof of real or objective possibility of such a being and existence cannot be affirmed from the idea.

To Kant's objection that existence cannot be inferred from a mere ideal, or logical possibility, Boyce responded, "The argument against which it is leveled does not prove mere logical possibility but logical certainty of existence of such a being, and it is not contended that every subjective conception must have objective reality but only that certain ones may have such reality and this one must from the very idea of a God."[24] He gave virtually this same response in his 1887 *Abstract of Systematic Theology*. He added "or necessity" after "certainty" and omitted "of existence." The phrase "this one must from the very idea of God" gave way to the more emphatic "this one, the idea of God, which itself involves the idea of necessary existence, must in consequence of the idea thus involved, possess that reality."[25]

Boyce gave summaries of the views of Anselm, Descartes, Bishop Stillingfleet, Moses Lowman, and Samuel Clarke. In summarizing Lowman's argument Boyce stated, "Therefore, there is one necessarily existent being, the cause of all contingent existence, that is, of all other existences besides himself; and this being is eternal, infinite, possessed of all possible perfections, and is an intelligent free agent,—that is, this being is God."[26] The distillation of Clarke's conclusion runs thus—"But, now, if something has existed from all eternity, either there must always have been some unchangeable and infinite being, or else an infinite succession of changeable and dependent beings, without any original cause, which is absurd."[27] Boyce then gave his summary as to why an infinite regress of causes is absurd, lending further strength to the intuitive a priori acceptance of one infinite necessary being, than which nothing greater can be thought.

In spite of the less than enthusiastic observations about the a priori, or ontological, argument for the existence of God on the part of Dick,

Hodge, even A. H. Strong and others, Boyce seemed fully convinced of its beauty and power personally. Before moving to the arguments a posteriori, which are "more simple, and better adapted to force conviction upon the minds of the masses of mankind," he summarized his satisfaction with the a priori perceptions:

> To these, they have appeared to be clothed with the authority of God himself speaking through the constitution he has given to the mind, and its capacity for the intuitive conception of underlying principles. To those who perceive these principles, the proofs are as conclusive as the consciousness of their own existence, and as authoritative as the dictates of conscience. These principles are accepted, and arguments are formed upon them in the same way as in mathematical demonstrations, and afford those who perceive the truth of them actual demonstrations of the fact that God exists.[28]

Boyce's treatment of the a posteriori proofs focuses on three recurring issues: (1) induction—the gathering of all pertinent data demands its organization and the proposal of a theory that adequately explains those facts; (2) causation—the proposed theory is in the form of a cause, some adequate explanation either within or without the collected data that gives the reason why they exist; (3) the impossibility of an infinite regress of causes.

Boyce spends the largest amount of space on the cosmological argument, for in that context the "law of causality" emerges handily. It drives on to affirm a "Great First Cause" whose cause of existence is within himself. "If there is not such a self-existent and self-contained cause," Boyce reiterated, "we are driven to adopt the idea of an infinite series of finite causes, or an infinite succession of such series, each of which is both impossible and absurd." Within the cosmos, motion, form and life, mind, and conscience each appear with no adequate explanation for their existence either in themselves or in the universe. These effects demand, therefore, that an adequate cause be found outside the universe that is supreme and the cause of all things.

These same principles Boyce then applies to teleology (both in design and adaptation), providence (or evidence of design in the events of the world), miracles (that show a power superior to and in control of, and therefore the creator of, nature), the Bible (its prophecies and its coherent historical account of all events since the beginning of the world that show how they all lead to the necessity of the coming of Christ as well as its strong testimony to God through the character and teachings of Christ himself), recorded history (that shows that man has a relatively short duration on the earth), and geology (everything has had a beginning). The accumulation of data in each area with the accompanying conclusion that only God accounts for the demands of each separate source of data leads ineluctably to the conclusion that a self-existent, omnipotent, self-conscious, perfectly moral, unchangeable deity made and controls the universe with purposes of his own. "Scientific proof is only inductive proof, and no induction of science is more certainly true than that God exists. . . . The theory that God exists [has] been confirmed . . . by the fact that without it there is no explanation of the innumerable facts around us, while with it there is nothing lacking to account for the cause and origin of all things."[29]

The discussion of these proofs leads necessarily to an analysis of reason in its relation to revelation. Boyce defined reason as "that power in man, which enables him to have mental perceptions, to exercise thought, and reflection, to know facts, to inquire into their mutual relations, and to deduce, logically the conclusions which may be drawn from them." In his recitations Boyce defined reason as "that power in man by which he discovers the existence, relations, and properties of himself, & other beings and the world around him & by which he forms conclusions from such knowledge." This may be applied both to the natural and to the supernatural means of knowledge "conferred by God." By revelation Boyce meant "the knowledge which God conveys by direct supernatural instruction, pre-eminently that given in the book known as the Bible."[30] Five a priori expectations surround any view of revelation:

1. It must come from God; as he is the source of all authority, so of this.
2. The information must be suited to our present condition; confirm the truth we have already known and communicate new

truth. Giving knowledge suitable to our condition as sinners, making known any means of hope there may be.

3. It must be secured from all possibility of error, so that we may know that it is absolute truth. This makes us cling to verbal inspiration of Scripture.
4. It must come with authority accompanied by such means that the will of man will submit to it and his passions will be subdued.
5. It would also be accompanied by difficulties i.e. truths which we cannot comprehend. The nearer we get to such a mysterious being as God the more we are filled with incomprehensibility of his nature and ways.[31]

These same five traits, taken from the recitation notebook of 1861, were repeated with little change in Boyce's *Abstract* in 1887. This leads to the question as to how such a revelation would come so that it could be recognized as such. Does it come to each individual with accompanying evidences or merely by personal intuition? Does it come to a few to be given to the entire race of humanity through these few? If so, how attested? Boyce argued that the "Scripture theory," properly understood, removes all reason for insecurity or doubt. It is conclusive and takes into account its necessary relation to reason. "In any new revelation," Boyce proposed, "the prophet of God must present a doctrine perfectly consistent with every past revelation and with the knowledge conveyed by nature." Though new truths might clarify and add content to established truths, they have no higher authority than old truths and cannot contradict them. "What with God is truth is eternal truth." When God has given a truth, it must "remain so forever, as changeless as his own life." In addition, the prophet must "confirm by miracles his authority as a teacher from God." Apart from the miracle for confirmation, the proposition might well be a simple deduction of human reason or imagination. Both miracle and concurrent doctrine are essential in the reception of any new revelation.[32]

Since Boyce believed that "reason is the first revelation," it stands to reason that "the facts of reason cannot be denied by any subsequent revelation." But this judgment takes into account, not only those doctrines deduced by unaided reason, but also those that reason has approved in other previous revelations. Boyce set forth four aspects of the relation of reason to revelation both in his lecture notes and in his *Abstract*. He posed the question, "What now are the offices of reason in reference to Revelation?" The answer: "1. To examine the evidence of miracles upon which revelation rests. 2. To compare the doctrine taught with those previously given [and added in the *Abstract*, 'and recognize their correspondence with or opposition to that teaching']. 3. To adopt or reject according to the evidence that it is God's truth. 4. To interpret its contents by the best lights learning affords."[33]

Another aspect of Boyce's view of reason and revelation must also be borne in mind. Those truths discernible by reason gain their clearest and most distinct form only when they are purged by the pure truth of revelation. Left without such supernatural revelation, the truths of reason tend to be corrupted, and moreover can provide no means of going into the issues of redemption. As he dictated in his recitations, we must affirm

> that Reason gives light enough to teach us our duty to God, ourselves and our fellowmen, yet its teachings are very imperfect, its light very dim. If man in his present enlightened condition were freed from past guilt, and then deprived of the gospel and left to the light of reason alone he would soon be again deeply involved in guilt because of the imperfection of his guide. [In addition, reason] says nothing of how a sinner may be rescued, how God may overlook sin, or that he does overlook sin; tells only of wrath.[34]

Biblical revelation begins therefore with a confirmation of those things that, once suggested, intuitively commend themselves to human reason. "Hence the truths taught were, for the most part, only those that come within the compass of discovery by reason, or acceptance by it upon due suggestion, namely,—the existence of one God, the fact of creation, the law of moral obligation to God and man, the punishment of sinners, the duty of repentance, the pardoning mercy of God, and the law of sacrifices, with substitution and satisfaction."[35] Later, when those elements of reason and revelation have become well settled, truths are revealed that are known only by supernatural revelation. Because they are consistent with what has gone before, and develop the old truth in a way that shows its glory and expands the richness of its meaning, and are confirmed by miracles, such revelation must be received as from God. Of such a nature are doctrines like the vicarious atonement of Christ, the Trinity of the Godhead, the eternal generation of the Son, the duality of natures in the one person of Christ.[36]

Boyce's discussion of the soul's immortality provides an excellent example of the congruence of reason with pure revelation. Boyce recognizes that "reason alone has been supposed by many to furnish adequate arguments in proof of its truth." But after a cogent discussion of five arguments provided by reason, Boyce concludes, "It appears, therefore, that, from reason alone all that can be attained, even as to a merely future state, is expectation." Many palpable hopes, fears, and problems of divine government remain shrouded in mystery through reason alone. "The Scriptures, however, teach plainly the continued existence of all men after death." Scripture everywhere assumes the continued existence of all men, gives narratives built upon that assumption, confirms both the hopes and fears of humanity in its clear doctrine of eternal rewards built on grace and retribution built on human guilt and divine justice. "The Scriptures are thus seen to teach conclusively the doctrine of an unending future life of all men. This, as has been stated, is what is commonly referred to as the immortality of the soul."[37]

Boyce ordered his discussion from revelational doctrines that confirm, as well as clarify and expand, those of reason to those that depend wholly on divine revelation. The point is, as revelation continues to expand, the body of verified revealed truth increases and the revelatory assertions within that sustained body of revelation possess self-sustaining authority. This body of verified doctrine is deduced from a narrative contained in a book, the Bible, the origin of which constitutes a doctrine in itself. Under the first doctrines discussed in the *Abstract of Systematic Theology*, the unity of God and the spirituality of God, Boyce showed that the biblical doctrine of unity and spirituality answers fully the most closely reasoned expectations presented in the rational proofs for God. "The proofs we have thus far presented from nature for the unity of God," Boyce would affirm with as much method as confidence, "are abundantly confirmed by the statements of Scripture." Likewise he showed the fullness of the biblical teaching

411

about the spirituality of God, a truth deducible from careful reasoning from natural evidence, emphasizing that even the anthropomorphic and anthropopathic language is a mere accommodation to highlight the genuine personhood of his spirituality. His unity and spirituality are not attributes of his nature but constitute a "simple declaration of what his nature is."[38]

On the other hand, when Boyce discussed the Trinity and relations within the Trinity, he had surpassed the need to show Scripture consistent with what may be deduced from mere reason. Now a sufficiently large body of revelation has been proven by the tests mentioned earlier, and the consequent acceptance of Scripture as the singular location of propositional revelation. Scripture alone now rules the construction of doctrine. "The nature of these relations," Boyce acknowledged in his discussion of inner trinitarian relations, "can be indicated in no other forms than those set forth in Scripture. They are matters of pure revelation. The fact of their existence is beyond the attainment of reason."[39] In fact, none of the assertions can be strengthened by philosophical speculation, none of the difficulties removed by argument, or explained by human analogies. "We are constrained to fall back upon the simple Scripture statement," and seek to make our expressions of these truths in such ways as not to diminish any, but fully express every, Scripture idea connected with the doctrine. "The Scripture teachings must be accepted with unquestioning belief that relations corresponding to these titles [Father and Son and Spirit] exist in God, and that they, and the causes assigned for them, are duly expressed by the language of his word."[40]

Boyce sought to construct an impregnable fortress of revelation for the knowledge of God, fully verified in the progressive manner by which revelation has entered human experience. "We know that Scripture cannot contradict itself, when rightly interpreted," Boyce assumed in dealing with a difficult interpretive issue; "All its parts, therefore, must be carefully compared to see in what interpretation they agree."[41] The commonsense confidence in the human faculties of perception, understanding, and reason had to be assumed as foundational to any confidence at all in the ability to receive and organize communication from another source. This confidence led then from the most primal source of information as set forth in the a priori argument, through the a posteriori arguments, into revelation concerning the divine nature and attributes, human obligations to God and to one another, relations within the Trinity, and finally the entire scheme of redemption that gives the fullest display of humanity's sinful debasement and intrinsic glory as well as the most excellent manifestation of the attributes of God as governed by his inscrutable wisdom. Flowing through Scripture with ever-increasing power, a self-sustaining system of authority draws the reader more and more into the necessity of unquestioned obedience to the Bible's every utterance as sufficient confirmation in itself of divine truth. "Men spoke from God."

This tightly woven matrix of revelation that materializes in a concept of the absolute perfection of Scripture, its errorless character, and its unwavering sufficiency for all God's purposes in his communication to his fallen image-bearers, served as a foundation for Boyce's convictions about the task of the minister. Though every minister should strive to be familiar with, if not master, the philosophical and rational connections within a full-orbed doctrine of Scripture, his task in the pulpit is not to display those foundational materials, but the Word of God alone.

In an ordination sermon entitled "Thus Saith the Lord" based on Ezekiel 2:4, Boyce made this point strongly. He developed this idea from that text in four assertions about preaching, "the great work of the ministers of Jesus."[42] Preaching should be authoritative, declarative, scriptural, and uncompromising. After all due allowance is made for misinterpretation, erroneous theology, and the warnings against false teachers, when a message is brought to the "touchstone of the Scriptures" and found in accord, "the messenger must be received as would be God Himself." Boyce insisted, "It is not man only that tells of sin and offers a Savior; not man only that presents promises of acceptance through Christ; not man only that calls his fellows to repentance and trust in Jesus; not man only that invites to a life of full consecration to God, and gives assurances to help in the attempt to lead that life." When one hears the plain truthful exposition of Scripture, one hears "the voice of God—of the living God. It is the invitation of Christ—the ever present Christ. It is the Holy Ghost whose sword is thus unsheathed to convict of sin, of righteousness and of a judgment to come."[43]

413

The point concerning the sermon's "declarative" nature empha-sized Boyce's conviction about the surpassing authority of the facts of Scripture. The preachers must "assert and declare what God has revealed and demand its acceptance as such." Biblical truths set forth only on the basis of scriptural authority are not to be "questioned or caviled at or reasoned about." God must not be put into the position of one who must explain the "why" of his declarations, nor must any preacher think that a message gains greater authority if he constructs a philosophical or metaphysical rationale for the assertion of Scripture. Ezekiel was sent to say to the people, "Thus saith the Lord God." Such is especially true for all the "important and fundamental truths of the Bible."[44]

> How otherwise could we know of man's present condition, but for the fact of sin and its beginnings which are revealed? How could we explain the delay of God's punishment of sin, but for the purposes of merciful probation which He has made known? How could we know of the possibility of pardon, but for the statement of that fact: How could we learn of Christ, but from revelation: How could we explain the universal rejection of His salvation anterior to God's compelling grace, but for the Word of God? How shall we know God's future purposes, but for His revelation of that future?[45]

These facts are unknown otherwise and have no higher authority than that God has spoken. "Let the word of God then be simply declared, made known, spoken forth and such, and men called upon to receive it as such, and the most effective preaching must be attained."

In that context Boyce made the point that preaching must be "scriptural." Both the doctrines taught and the practices enjoined "should be those set forth by God in His Holy Word." We go no further than inspired truth. Many have sought to make present sci-ence a touchstone and manipulate Scripture to say the same as science or have used unwarranted inferences to contradict a fact of science. This is a mistaken policy. "What warnings have we not had in con-nection with what is known as science? How frequently have men planted themselves in the past upon positions inferred from the Word of God from which the advancing light of science has driven them, and which have then been seen to have been mere human inferences from very insufficient facts?"[46]

The uneasiness of the seminary community on the subject of science in the nineteenth century has already been noted. Boyce's biblicistic fixation, however, almost drove him to contradict his own calling to teach systematic theology—the discipline that requires the most careful and discreet skill of inferential theology. His zeal for this idea makes him sound like Alexander Campbell:

> And that which makes this especially a practical point is that almost all the differences in the phases of Christian belief and practice have arisen from the admixture of conjecture and inferences, and additions, to the Word of God. If today all men could sincerely agree to take this simple word as the rule of faith and practice, the days of denominational divisions would be over; the people of God would see eye to eye, and all would dwell together in unity, rejoicing in the simplicity which is in Christ.[47]

Such pure clarity of biblical vision, however, does not come easily in a fallen world dominated by sinful prejudices. The discipline of theology arises in order, not to add to Scripture, but to organize its teachings in such a way as to illuminate and protect the fullness of the biblical revelation. A commitment to coherence and synthesis based on the unity of truth, therefore, Boyce demonstrated throughout his career. This clarity, heightened consciousness of the necessity of plenary articulation, and internal unity must be present in each individual doctrine as well as the entire corpus of Christian truth. Boyce referred to this development of doctrine as the process by which the truth becomes "harmoniously stated."[48] In an article entitled "The Doctrine of the Suffering of Christ," he began by asserting, "there is a vast difference between the belief of the prominent truths involved in a doctrine of God's word and the belief of the doctrine itself with the power to state it accurately." Giving further explanation of this difference Boyce wrote:

> The former may often be accompanied by a distortion of the truth, resulting either from pressing some point of it to an extreme, or

restricting it within too narrow limits. The latter necessarily involves
its reception in all the fullness and exactness with which it is revealed,
and such an accurate definition of it as displays the harmony of its
parts and its completeness as a whole. Every student of the history
of doctrine is aware of this. The leading truths involved in every
prominent doctrine of the word of God were held and maintained
long before the doctrine itself became the subject of definition and
the common faith of the Christian world relative to it was distinctly
declared. Such definition has by some been erroneously supposed to
be the assertion of new truth or the foisting in of additional matter.
If this were so, it would be blameworthy, inasmuch as it would be
adding to God's word that which it has not taught. Any doctrine
thus established ought certainly to be rejected. But when all that has
been done has been to gather together all the teachings of the word
of God, to weigh them separately and unitedly, to give to each of
them the place in the doctrine which the Scripture assigns to it, and
to set forth a statement which excludes nothing and comprehends
everything, it is manifest that thus only have we the whole truth
which God has revealed in such a form as to exclude erroneous
statements of its parts.[49]

Under the personal commitment to such unity, therefore, and with
a personal knowledge of correct method and the guiding advantage
of doctrinal orthodoxy, Boyce wanted sermons filled with Scripture
artfully but honestly arranged so as to give the hearers Bible teachings
in their most unblemished form. He urged his students, therefore, to
memorize as much Scripture as possible and use it profusely in their
sermons. He pointed to the examples of the Puritans and Bunyan for
this practice that many consider a fault but that Boyce said was a "good
fault . . . and a very rare one."[50]

The finality and absolute truthfulness of divine revelation means
that its messenger must be "uncompromising." In an age "peculiarly
latitudinarian" in which a misunderstanding of religious liberty has
developed, Baptists have the peculiar obligation to say that "true liberty
of conscience is not affected because one preaches in its proper place the
truths which constitute the difference between him and others." These
differences sometimes mean that "if a church member has departed

irreclaimably from the faith he must be cut off." Though unity is pleasant, sometimes truth demands a separation into denominations.

At times this uncompromising spirit means that the preacher will separate from the prevailing temper of evangelical approval, for "some have learned to believe it best always to speak of a Savior's love, and many regular attendants upon the sanctuary have begun to despise, as rude and unpolished and impolite, and low, and vulgar, and unfashionable, and nauseous, and disgusting, and still others as unwise, and fitted to drive men from the house of God, mere allusions to the hell to which the thousands around us are daily hastening." God says that, without warning, he will require the blood of such at the hands of those that should warn. Under such a threat who would dare compromise God's teaching on hell or on "any point whatever, when God has taught him the truth and made him his witness of its behalf?" One need not be identified with a bitter and sectarian spirit to maintain the right posture, the posture of our Lord and his apostles, on truth and love. "The real love of the truth and desire to see it triumph is inconsistent with bitterness, but is perfectly consistent with the firm maintenance of it upon all proper occasions."[51]

The heavy practicality of Boyce's doctrine of the knowledge of God leads naturally to his second major sphere of theological concern. That is, that God has decreed to show the fullness of his glory through redemption of sinners, and peculiarly in the manner by which he performs this redemption. This is seen in Boyce's emphasis on the doctrines of grace.

Redemption and Grace

In 1880, Boyce delivered an address at Southwestern Baptist University in Jackson, Tennessee, on "The Christian Ethical System: Its Nature, Its Basis, Its Exemplar, and the Motives to Its Obedience."[52] In this sermon more than in his systematic theology he reveals the connective links between his view of the necessary attributes of God, such as holiness, justice, and righteousness, and God's actions of mercy and grace in the pardon of sin. The basis on which these blessings come, Boyce calls the "voluntary character of God." The moral law is based upon the everlasting and immutable distinctions of right and wrong, and the "necessary character of God has the same basis. God is not just, nor holy, nor truthful because he chooses to be so—but because the all perfect being must have this character—just as he also must be wise and powerful, and self-existent and eternal." Without these characteristics, he would not be God. The traits are "immutable and eternal."

Hence "the law of right and wrong proceeds" not from the mere will of God, though it is "fully accordant with His will," but as expressions of an eternal endemic character necessary for God, which cannot be changed any more than God himself can be changed. By this law, justice is demanded for lawbreakers with no possible mitigation of penalty on the basis of the pure, natural, necessary law. Yet the existence of positive law, a "precept being based upon no eternal principle" but "entirely due to and dependent upon the will of God," may be established and then abrogated. The laws of Christian ethics that reflect the principles from which the gospel itself emerges transcend mere natural law; they are not built on positive law. Even angels, who have no categories or experience to grasp this truth, long to look into these things.

The attributes by which salvation comes, and upon which the Christian ethic is based, tap into aspects of God's nature that could not have been revealed apart from the necessity of a gospel of redemption. "Had our God been no more than such an one as natural law would indicate," Boyce surmised, "there could have been no foundation for Christian ethics as well as none for human salvation, . . . but to His glory and praise be it spoken our God is greater than what the mere eternal principles of right and wrong demand in God."

Now, one must know for certain that this higher principle does not contradict any of the "natural" and "necessary" principles. God's nature "meets all these requirements of these eternal principles," but is "better and nobler than natural law could teach." Since such a voluntary character "can be known only by the declarations and the actions of the one willing," a self-revelation of such character was essential. To these attributes of God the Scripture refers when it says that "no man hath seen God at any time; the only begotten Son, which is in the bosom of the Father, he hath declared him" (John 1:18).

This scheme fits perfectly with "the gradual revelation of God and of the relation of the Old and the New Testaments." God had to be shown as a God of creation, providence, and law before the contours of redemption could be revealed. The progress of revelation made it necessary that the God of redemption reveal his character in the earliest stages as consistent with "the attributes of the God of nature." Yet we should not be surprised "to find indications in the old of what is plainly taught in the new." According to Boyce, "The most remarkable exhibition of this was most mercifully made upon the occasion of God's giving to Moses the second time the tables of stone of the law." On that occasion, the Lord descended in the cloud, passed by before him, and proclaimed, "The Lord, the Lord God, merciful and gracious, longsuffering and abundant in goodness and truth, keeping mercy for thousands, forgiving iniquity and transgression and sin, and that will by no means clear the guilty; visiting the iniquity of the fathers upon the children, and upon the children's children, unto the third and to the fourth generation" (Ex. 34:6–7). These immensely tantalizing hints of mercy coexisting with inscrutable justice underwent more and more development, "the true knowledge of which was perceived only in the person and work of Christ. Here was exhibited at once the sacred regard which God has for the moral law and the unchangeable holiness and purity of His nature."[53]

These aspects of the "voluntary nature of God" must therefore be exhibited in a context of redemption. Boyce viewed God's providence as fully involved in the fall of humanity. In light of his entire discussion of creation, providence, the fall, and redemption, Boyce makes an evaluative statement that seems out of harmony with his overall development of thought: "But with all this, with our present knowledge of his will, we are compelled to confess that we cannot tell why he saw that it was better to admit than to exclude it [sin]."[54] Boyce previously had shown that some probation of man was necessary, and that an opportunity for man to exert his "power of contrary choice" would be the only manner to provide this probation.[55] Boyce did not accept the idea that the "power of contrary choice" amounted to the absence of a prevailing disposition or that a person could choose in opposition to a prevailing disposition of heart. Instead, Boyce contended, "He

419

has that power of contrary choice which constitutes him a free agent, although controlled in that choice by the prevailing motive,—by which is meant the motive which most pleases him and which is therefore, that to which his own nature gives prevalence."[56]

Boyce had shown also that God was perfectly within his rights, and it constituted no contradiction to his holiness, nor did it involve compulsion to such on God's part, to act providentially in "accordance only with our nature" in those events that led humanity into sin. Thus, "sin exists only in accordance with the purpose of God," and had he not seen "fit" it never would have occurred "at any time nor in any form." The end that it attains is designed by God; sin and its effects "cannot go any farther than the limits he has assigned." Through the appearance of sin, God "works out his own righteous purposes," and may concur in acts of sin, evilly motivated by the human per-petrator, "from motives, with ends, and in the use of means which are altogether most holy."[57] When Boyce completes his exposition of grace—the motives, ends, and means by which God overcomes sin—it is hard to see why he confessed perplexity as to God's decree to admit rather than to exclude sin. This appears even more clearly in Boyce's discussion of the final judgment, referred to later.

After a discussion of the factors that brought about the fall of man, and again expressing the difficulty of such a discussion,[58] Boyce discussed the effects of the sin of Adam. Besides those uttered imme-diately upon the woman, the man, and Satan in the garden, "we shall find them in connection with the evil condition of his posterity." This evil condition may be described by one word, "death." This includes natural death, spiritual death, and eternal death. Spiritual death includes the death of the soul, that is, aggravated alienation from God, and a corrupt nature. The corrupt nature is universal, appears very early in each individual, is thorough, extending to every affection and thought of heart and mind, is unequally developed in every individual, and thus is capable of virtually infinite development into greater and more vicious sin.

This innate propensity toward sin does not create any mitigation of blame, punishment, or accountability. Free will as the power of con-trary choice, as Boyce has defined it, remains. "This is the ground," he reminds the reader, "upon which men are held responsible by God and by human law and conscience." Again, the sinner "cannot not sin," but only because his nature "loves sin and hates holiness" and "prefers self to God."[59] Without a radical redemption, therefore, eternal death is inevitable. The condemnation inevitably incident upon guilt calls for justification; the corruption of spirit calls for renewal and cleansing. Short of these man's continuance in a punitive condition cannot be reversed but only intensified. At death the state will be irreversible and untempered by any patience or common mercies.

The judgment of condemnation comes on the sons of Adam through their connection with him. Their connection is twofold, by covenant and by nature, that is, Adam is both federal head as well as natural head of humanity.[60] Concerning Adam's natural headship and humanity's consequent corruption from the time of conception, Boyce confirmed, "The Scriptures plainly assume and declare that God righteously punishes all men, not only for what they do, but for what they are. Men are indeed represented as more guilty and sinful than they know themselves to be." Only the restraints of common mercy inhibit their natures from full development into the sin toward which they tend, but in themselves, being born with sinful natures, they must, "therefore, be corrupt and guilty, eternally destitute of God's complacent love, and liable to natural death." It follows, therefore, "that a corrupt nature makes a condition as truly sinful, and guilty, and liable to punishment, as actual transgressions." At the very moment of birth, in fact, "the presence and possession of such a nature shows that even the infant sons of Adam are born under all the penalties which befell their ancestor in the day of his sin. Actual transgression subsequently adds new guilt to guilt already existing, but does not substitute a state of guilt for one of innocence."[61]

As covenant, or federal, head, Adam has bequeathed to all those whom he represented a just condemnation as if they had personally consciously disobeyed the probationary command. Boyce, ever conscious of those divine attributes of holiness, righteousness, and infinite wisdom, defended the way of God in this arrangement, "the Scriptural theory," and concluded that "the federal headship of Adam was just and right, because duly constituted by

421

God, and that too in the fittest person of the whole race."[62] Boyce noted analogies of covenant responsibility in all human society but particularly showed how it dominates the scriptural accounts of man's relation with God.

He accepted the covenant relationship as prior to the natural relationship. Corruption of nature, therefore, followed Adam's disobedience as a punitive consequence of that sin. Our covenant relation to Adam, moreover, establishes a state of condemnation for Adam's posterity that stands prior to the infliction of corruption, the initial punitive consequence of our federal standing under condemnation. "The corrupted nature," Boyce wrote later in his discussion of justification, "is one of the natural consequences of that sin, and is a punishment of it."[63]

Federal headship also prepares for the acceptance of the terms of the gospel. Covenant representation involves imputation, a concept ineradicable from the gospel and therefore necessary as the dominant theme of Adam's relation to his posterity. "By it," Boyce wrote in regard to imputation, "the sin of Adam is transferred to us, or in other words so reckoned to us or put to our account that we are treated as though it were ours. In like manner the sin of man was transferred to Christ, who bore it, though he knew no sin personally." Then, by the same principle "the righteousness of Christ is also imputed to man, who though personally sinful, is treated as though he were righteous." Boyce believed Romans 5 affirms this in no uncertain terms. The parallel between Christ and Adam in that passage "could be drawn only on the ground of federal representation." First Corinthians 15 does the same thing. "These two chapters," Boyce claimed, "show this representative relation of Adam, and that because of it all men have sinned in him and are justly treated as sinners."[64]

The representative character of Adam naturally brought Christ into the discussion. Every grace by which God saves condemned and corrupted sinners originates in the person and work of Christ, according to Boyce. The discussion of Boyce's understanding of this will be dealt with in the next chapter. Elements of that discussion, however, necessarily adhere to every other point concerning God's grace, and for that reason will be anticipated for each distinct doctrine that follows.

Because the fall of Adam and his posterity proceeded fundamentally from the purpose and providence of God, God's determination concerning how salvation would issue in the demonstration of his holy purposes also must be eternal. The fountain of this salvific purpose constitutes the doctrine of election. After dismissing many inadequate definitions such as the election of certain nations to church privileges, election to service, and the Arminian notion of "perseverance in foreseen faith," Boyce entered into a vigorous defense of the traditional Calvinist understanding of eternal, unconditional election of specific individuals unto salvation. He defined his doctrine carefully with appropriate affirmations and denials and caveats inserted parenthetically into the definition.

> The latter theory is that God (who and not man is the one who chooses or elects), of his own purpose (in accordance with his will, and not from any obligation to man, not because of any will of man), has from Eternity (the period of God's action, not in time in which man acts), determined to save (not has actually saved, but simply determined so to do) [and to save (not to confer gospel or church privileges upon)], a definite number of mankind (not the whole race, nor indefinitely merely some of them, not indefinitely a certain proportionate part; but a definite number), as individuals (not the whole or a part of the race, nor of a nation, nor of a church, nor of a class, as of believers or the pious; but individuals), not for or because of any merit or work of theirs, nor of any value to him of them (not for their good works, nor their holiness, nor excellence, nor their faith, nor their spiritual sanctification, although the choice is to a salvation attained through faith and sanctification; nor their value to him, though their salvation tends greatly to the manifested glory of his grace); but of his own good pleasure (simply because he was pleased so to choose).[65]

The definition distilled from all the clarifications runs thus: "God, of his own purpose, has from Eternity determined to save a definite number of mankind, as individuals, not for or because of any merit or work of theirs, nor of any value to him of them, but of his own good pleasure." As is typical in Boyce's method in regard to doctrines utterly dependent on divine revelation, his proof amounts to the citation of large numbers of Scriptures verifying each point of the definition. "To the Scriptures alone," as asserted in the discussion of other such doctrines, "must we look for the truth upon this subject."[66] He offered brief remarks on some passages but for the most part believed that their clarity is such that the meaning self-evidently demonstrates the point.

Boyce discussed the doctrine under six points. After the first four—"Election is an act of God, and not the result of the choice of the Elect"; "the choice is one of individuals and not of classes"; "it was made without respect to the action of the persons elected"; election is made "through the mere good pleasure of God"—Boyce commented concerning the fourth point. He argued the fourth point through passages "such as simply assert sovereign will" (e.g., John 3:3–8; 6:37, 39, 44, 64–65; 17:2; Eph. 1:5; James 1:18), others that "deny merit in the persons elected as well as assert the sovereign choice of God" (e.g., Ezek. 36:32; Rom. 9:11–16), and those that "so describe the persons chosen as to imply this" (e.g., Matt. 11:25–26; 1 Cor. 1:26–30). He interrupted his demonstration of the last two points to emphasize the pervasive weightiness of this teaching throughout Scripture in tones that showed the spiritual depth of his conviction on this doctrine.

> The texts thus exhibited under these three classes prove conclusively that not on account of their own merits, but because of the good pleasure of God, does he choose men. They have been presented at some length, because this is after all the point upon which all that is important in this controversy turns. For, although other matters are equally essential to the doctrine, the whole opposition arises from an unwillingness on the part of man to recognize the sovereignty of God, and to ascribe salvation entirely to grace. This proof, however, has been by no means exhausted, the attempt having been to select some only of the numerous passages, and mainly such as from their conciseness allow of presentation in full. Let the Scriptures be read with reference to this doctrine and every passage marked which indicates God's dealing with men as an absolute sovereign, and also every declaration which ascribes Election or the fruits of it to his choice and not to the will or acts of men, and every illustration afforded

that this is God's usual method, and it will appear that scarcely any book of Scripture will fail to furnish testimony to the fact that in the acts of grace, no less than those of providence, God "doeth according to his will in the army of heaven and among the inhabitants of the earth" (Dan. 4:35).[67]

Point five affirmed the eternity of election from numerous passages, and point six showed that this election "is one to salvation, and not to mere external privileges."[68]

The sovereignty of election is heightened by the doctrine of reprobation. Boyce showed that the doctrine of reprobation did not depend on sublapsarian or supralapsarian order of decrees, for both accepted the reality that election implied nonelection and thus nonbestowal of saving graces. Both accepted the truth that in the bypassing of grace, condemnation comes justly for sins committed and that in some manner God works to harden the nonelect against every influence to repentance and thus to confirm them in their sin. Though Boyce gave several highly plausible arguments that positive reprobation, that is, God's acting as an efficient cause of a person's resistance to gracious overtures, could be accepted without violation of biblical truth or proper theological connection, he saw no final reason to affirm that God exerted "efficient and causal action" in the hardening incident to reprobation. "It can hardly be supposed that, when the work to be done could thus be effected [that is, through the sinful depravity of the heart and the wiles of Satan], God would not leave it to be thus done." "God does not teach us," Boyce concluded when all the relevant passages were seen in their overall context, "that he directly hardens the heart of any." Just as surely, however, the Bible teaches unequivocally that all gracious influences designed finally for salvation "belong, in the purpose of God, to the elect only." These are not rights of creation, but sovereign graces of redemption.[69]

Such operations of sovereign grace in human experience constitute the effectual calling. The external call of the preached, or otherwise proclaimed, gospel goes to mankind promiscuously, because "the Gospel is commanded to be preached to all." The call is sincere and "has all the elements which should secure its acceptance," and as such its failure comes not from any deficiency in the gospel itself, but "because of the willful sinfulness of man."[70] Boyce listed thirty-one evidences that the word is rejected universally apart from effectual calling. This is true of all, even the elect whom God purposes to save in Christ, and thus the gospel word can be successful in its intrinsic tendency only when accompanied by such a work of the Holy Spirit as overcomes the "moral condition of man as 'blind' and 'dead in trespasses and sins.'"[71] Most of Boyce's discussion is given to the intrinsic worthiness of the gospel call and God's sincerity in issuing it even to those for whom he has no purpose of redemption.

Does God's invincible sovereignty established through immutable decrees render his universal call to repentance and consequent forgiveness insincere? This kind of question is the same as that which emerges about prayer in the context of creation and providence. In the context of redemption the urgency of the dilemma intensifies, for one realizes that individual personal destiny is at stake, while the implications of creation and meticulous providence seem, somehow, more remote. The same principle is operative, however, in both.

Boyce attacked the issue concerning prayer and providence in a sermon entitled "The Place and Power of Prayer" based on 1 John 5:14–15. After outlining clearly that true prayer conforms to certain scriptural expectations, he gave examples of promises accruing to earnest prayer and examples of answered prayer, and referred to the prayers of Jesus as paradigmatic in our expectations for God's intervention. "Here is the testimony of one who knows," Boyce reminded his congregation, "and who by his [acts] has told us that prayer has its power." Are the purposes of God and the destiny of man so fixed that there is no place for prayer? But Christ's "most earnest cries unto God are made *and heard*." These prayers in particular had reference to "that hour unto which He had come by the determinate counsel and foreknowledge [of] God."

By the same token one may ask, "Are the laws of creation so unchangeable that God cannot or will not answer prayer?" All Christians, of course, have experienced answered prayer, and this fact in itself cannot be disputed, nor can the fact of miracles be successfully contradicted. But divine intervention and answered prayer do not always, or perhaps even often, depend on what we call miraculous. God has created the world in such a way that the necessary interactions of the physical world accomplish the purposes of intelligence. Intelligent beings design and introduce new elements into the condition of the world, things that would never occur through unaided natural processes but yet depend on the uniformity and traceableness of those processes. Do we deny to God the use of his world in the same way that we use it?

His immutable purposes in the moral world, in the same way, take into account all the means by which those purposes shall be consummated. Prayer is one of the means foreknown. "The doctrine of the eternal purpose of God is one of pure revelation," and thus to be received without equivocation, "and the Scriptures which thus teach are thoroughly committed, as we have before seen, to the fact that there is a place for prayer." Every action, every creative idea, every whimsical desire forgotten or acted upon—every volition "has been known by God from the beginning, and either as decreed or permitted, has constituted a part of His eternal purpose fully as much as His own will." And yet each thought and determination of our will is free but constituted as a means by which God works all things according to the counsel of his will.

Both the natural determinists and the theological determinists who think their philosophy, or theology, renders prayer an irrelevancy are in error. "The fallacy in both the difficulties we have been discussing is the supposition that there must be a change in the acts or the will of God before prayer can be answered," Boyce reasoned. No change is necessary in either because God's hearing and responding to the earnest, spiritual, God-honoring desires of his people were contemplated eternally as means through which he would operate to his own glory. "In each there is not a change in the divine purpose but only the admission of secondary means, contemplated from the beginning as truly as the result, without which that result cannot be attained, and with which it is distinctly associated."[72]

Preaching and effectual calling operate in a similar manner. Boyce did not profess to be able to explain these two bits of data with absolute coherence, but he did believe that the principle established earlier, the progressive and self-sustaining character of divine revelation, rendered both biblical realities consistent, similar to prayer and providence. If the Bible calls on us to believe and act in response to both, then we must. God's sincerity, even in the bare outward call, cannot be questioned precisely because of the biblical portrait of his character. Additionally, however, an absolute determination to save on the one hand does not contradict the earnestness of the invitation on the other. If those invited are left to do just as they please, none can question the sincerity of the call. An accusation of insincerity would never have crossed one's mind if efficient grace had not been introduced to guarantee the salvation of some. Had only an external proclamation existed with no special grace, but all alike were left to the consequences of their own corrupted affections and will, the charge of insincerity could not have arisen, for the urgency of the message itself and its call for repentance and trust with the promise of salvation have all the marks of utter truth and, thus, sincerity. Beyond that, God assures sinners of his sincerity by the nature of his pleading with them as in Ezekiel 33:11: "Turn ye, turn ye from your evil ways; for why will ye die, O house of Israel?"

In his preaching, therefore, Boyce urged on his hearers the transparent sincerity of God in seeking sinners, all sinners, through the message of the gospel. In a sermon entitled "Christ Receiving and Eating with Sinners," based on Luke 15:2, Boyce discussed the accusation brought against Jesus, "This man receiveth sinners, and eateth with them." Since Jesus came to seek and save the lost, he quite naturally would seek opportunities to "consort with those He came to save." But the accusation had greater intensity; they "accused him of waiting, watching, looking out for, hoping to receive." Boyce replied that the accusation does not go far enough, for Jesus manifested a "deep yearning which He feels that every sinner, a single sinner though but one, any sinner the more vile he be the more is it true, should find in Him salvation and restoration to the failed relationship of God."[73] He emphasized this in increasing intensity by showing how Jesus presented himself in three parables.

In the parable of the lost sheep we find that "Jesus thus yearns over every lost sinner and thus longs to find and to bring him back into his fold." Jesus was an "expectant looker-out for sinners" and eagerly desired to "receive and entertain them." And as Jesus brings a sinner home, "he shouts out His triumph throughout the realms of heaven, and the angelic hosts rejoice at the salvation of a single man."[74]

In parable two, Jesus showed his "earnest desire to regain a lost possession." Jesus is the woman with ten pieces of silver and he says, "I have lost my property, which I would regain for my happiness and joy, and I am searching for it." Boyce affirmed that Jesus seeks those that the Father gave him before the foundation of the world and will not fail to find them. That truth Boyce indicated implicitly in preaching this series of parables, but explicitly he affirmed that "it is every sinner. It is any sinner. It is the sinner that is most utterly lost. It is the sinner who cannot even move to come unto Him but upon whom He will throw the light of His candle, and by the reflection of His light from the lost one will recover His own, and replace him in His treasury."[75]

The third parable involved not a sheep or a coin, but an infinitely ungrateful and rebellious son, a true "example of genuine sinfulness" as well as a "real provocation to anger." This gave even greater offense to Jesus' accusers as he pictured the justly offended father yearning for the return of the son, and acting in the most outrageously undignified and incalculably gratuitous manner in receiving him back. "The more they have strayed, the more do I yearn," Boyce pictured the Father as saying. "The greater the sinner, the more anxious my heart. My love has never failed. I have never forgotten one. And I stand as did the father of the prodigal looking out even into the far distance that I may see the penitent return."[76]

The close Boyce handled masterfully, showing that God is the initiator and consummator of the salvation event, but at the same time pressing the divine earnestness in going after all sinners. Boyce believed that in these parables Christ taught "I do not only wait, I go and seek the lost, I am filled with anxiety to find my sheep. I search for my treasure as with lighted candle and sweeping broom. My heart yearns for the wanderer, I look eagerly for him, my spirit within cries out in weariness at his delay, I am ready to welcome him with unequalled honors." And at the return of such, Boyce pictured Jesus as affirming, "It is not pleasure only that I take in the society of these sinners. My soul cries out with joy. I cannot contain my feelings. To all my servants around as each returns I impart my rapture, and the heavens ring with joyful exclamation as a single sinner comes back to God."[77]

To make sure that none could miss his universal intent in setting forth Christ as the willing savior of sinners, Boyce continued, "Do you believe Jesus, my hearers? Has he spoken here the truth concerning Himself? Is it, can it be, true that Jesus thus yearns over each one here? That He thus earnestly desires the salvation of each soul?" He sought to inject the call indelibly into the conscience—"Hearken today to the message of His yearning love by which he would win you. It tells of sinners waited for, longed for with deep desire. . . . Can you resist these pleadings? Can you reject such love? Can you disappoint such earnest longings and desires?"[78]

Left to themselves, none of those thus implored would come, none would be found. The effectual call must issue in a changed heart in order to elicit the proper willing response of repentance toward God and faith in the Lord Jesus Christ. In bondage to sin, spiritually blind, under the power of darkness, incapable of self-change, and spiritually dead the sinner will not give in to the word. "Without regeneration," Boyce noted, "the sinfulness of man keeps him away from God, causes him to set his affections upon self and his own pleasure, and to find gratification in things which are opposed to God and holiness." Regeneration, also known as quickening, the new birth, and creation, precedes conversion, which is the active turning on the part of man toward "God and holiness." Only a regenerated heart, having been given new affections and desires, is "fitted to seek after God and holiness."[79] The relation of regeneration to conversion, therefore, is invariably one of "antecedence," and in some cases there is "an appreciable interval."[80]

Repentance and faith constitute conversion and thus depend upon the spiritual change of regeneration. Repentance involves "a heartfelt change in the inward soul towards God and holiness, which is lasting and effective, and which may be associated with peace and joy in believing . . . [and] is also accompanied by deep regret because of the sins committed in the past, and by determination with God's help to avoid sin and live in holiness hereafter."[81] Faith involves "personal reliance upon Christ for salvation because of belief of God's testimony as to our sinful and ruined condition, and as to what Christ has assuredly done to save us." Although the object of faith in one sense is the entire Trinity, in another sense it is Christ alone, which explains why sometimes the New Testament formula for baptism is summarized as "baptized in the name of the Lord Jesus." This christocentric focus emerges more clearly when Boyce, using a passage from Gill's *Body of Divinity*, describes saving faith as "looking to Christ, . . . as coming to him, . . . as fleeing to him and laying hold upon him, . . . as eating and drinking him, . . . as receiving him."[82]

This kind of faith must be distinguished from the Roman Catholic view of implicit faith that minimizes, or eliminates, intelligent comprehension of what is to be believed. Our salvation does not rest in a mere capitulation to the church's doctrine upon the church's authority, nor does it rest in the belief that the books of the Bible teach the truth, but "in belief of the things which they teach." Nor is saving faith reducible to a "mere intellectual belief of the truths taught in the Scriptures as historical fact," that is, historical faith.

Boyce also distinguished saving faith from "assurance of personal interest in Christ's salvation." Assurance comes on the basis of a distinctly different kind of evidence and operation of the Spirit of God. Nor is faith temporary or delusive, but continues in trusting Christ, usefulness in the work of Christ, love of prayer and the Word of God, love of the children of God "as such," increased knowledge of self as sinful and Christ as Savior. True faith achieves vital union with Christ, thus depositing into our experience the legal and meritorious covenant work done for his people as well as the spiritual revitalization that comes from his giving us his Spirit.

By faith, the elect of God enter into the relationship of justification. Boyce made an extravagant claim for the importance of justification. "No doctrine," he began, "is more important than that of justification. . . . It involves," he continued, "the whole method of the salvation of sinners. It is vitally connected with all other fundamental doctrines." So interwoven is it with the whole fabric of biblical truth that "a correct conception of it cannot exist when other truths are ignored, or only partially received." He stated the definition of justification and discussed it by giving proofs of the several parts of the definition: "Justification is a judicial act of God, by which, on account of the meritorious work of Christ, imputed to a sinner and received by him through that faith which vitally unites him to his substitute and Saviour, God declares that sinner to be free from the demands of the law, and entitled to the rewards due to the obedience of that substitute."[83]

By "judicial act," Boyce means that its necessity arises from the fact that the law has been broken, and a declaration of righteousness, in absence of personal righteousness, is necessary. It is of God, for God alone can make such a declaration. It is not an act of pure sovereignty arising from God's good pleasure, like election, but takes place because the demands of the law have actually been met. Though not arising from mere pleasure, justification nonetheless manifests absolute grace because "it is of his own choice that he accepts a substitute, and because Christ and his meritorious work have been graciously secured and given by God himself."[84]

This justification involves no infusion of holiness but a purely legal declaration of righteousness, a "forensic act." The ground of this forensic act is the meritorious work of Christ. This meritorious work is twofold. "Not his sufferings and death only, but his obedience to, and conformity with the divine law are involved in the justification, which is attained by the believer."[85] In harmony with a long line of Reformed thinkers, Boyce referred to this dual action of merit as active obedience and passive obedience. This forensic act, based on Christ's full obedience, terminates on the sinner by imputation. As in the discussion concerning Adam's connection with the human race, Boyce saw Christ's relationship to the race in terms of imputation. "Adam as the representative of man sinned, and his sin has been imputed to all of his descendants, and they are treated as though personally sinners." By the same kind of divine logic, "Christ stood also as the representative of his people and their sins were imputed to him and he was treated as though personally a sinner." To complete the triangle, "Likewise his righteousness is imputed to them, and they are treated as though personally righteous."[86] Boyce emphasized that faith itself does not constitute righteousness before God. Faith merely appropriates

432

the work of Christ; it has no merit in itself, but "seizes upon the merit in another."[87]

Sanctification, on the other hand, "another of the privileges bestowed upon the people of God," occurs not by imputation or forensic declaration, but on the basis of a true advancement in holiness.[88] Regeneration and justification both precede sanctification, but, unlike justification, regeneration has a natural connection with sanctification as an operation of the Spirit in altering character. The initial change of nature from which faith and repentance flow is regeneration; such a change in nature establishes a desire for continued progress in holiness and a dissatisfaction with anything but perfect freedom from sin so that Christ in the fullness of his glory may be enjoyed. Justification precedes sanctification as the meritorious ground by which all other spiritual blessings are granted the believer, including the gift of the Spirit of adoption and holiness, and gives motivation to be well pleasing to God the Savior. Sanctification never matures absolutely in this life but will become perfect at death, in the spirit, and will include the body at the resurrection. Sanctification immediately flows from the work of the Spirit of God on the soul of man. Here the Word of God is used mediately but most powerfully and aptly by the Spirit. Boyce gives thirteen classes of Scripture that affirm this use of the Word. Secondary means include providence, prayer, the Lord's day, church fellowship and worship (that includes as a matter of biblical mandate a heavy presence of the Word of God), and the ordinances of baptism and the Lord's Supper.[89]

The usefulness of baptism and the Lord's Supper in sanctification, however, has nothing to do with anything intrinsic to the elements or even the act, but only with the truth remembered and contemplated at the time of their enactment. Boyce criticized the Roman Catholic views of the efficacy of the sacraments as propounded at Trent and expounded by Bellarmine. He also took issue with his Protestant brethren in regard to their continued use of the word "sacrament" as well as their interpretation of the "sacraments" as "signs" and "seals." "No man can put marks upon the elect of God which shall authoritatively certify that they are his," Boyce contended, and the "sign" involved, that is, their significance, concerns what "Christ did and suffered, and not . . . what is done to his people."[90] He believed that Charles Hodge imbibed an error of distressing proportions when he taught, "And so when a believer adopts the covenant of grace, he brings his children within that covenant in the sense that God promises to give them, in his own good time, all the benefits of redemption, provided they do not willingly renounce their baptismal engagements."[91]

Boyce summarized what he called "the true statement of the sanctifying power of these ordinances" in four brief propositions: (1) he denied all inherent power in them as means of grace; (2) he recognized that they convey truth by symbolical instruction; (3) that they are partaken because of the command of Christ also makes the act of obedience to him a means of grace to the recipient; (4) only as truth is, in some way or other, brought by them to an accepting heart and mind, can they have sanctifying power. "It is thus seen," Boyce closed the discussion of sanctification, "that all the means of sanctification are connected with the truth, and are secondary to it. They only become such, as they convey the truth, or as they suggest truth, or as they are employed in the recognition of some truth."[92]

In the believer's earthly experience the final demonstration of utter dependence on grace shows itself in the doctrine of the perseverance of the saints. Those that are "effectually called of God to the exercise of genuine faith in Christ will certainly persevere unto final salvation."[93] This perseverance, though it necessarily involves the moral energies of the believer, is to be attributed to the "purpose and power of God and the grace which he bestows, and not to any excellence or power in the believer."[94] So closely connected is this teaching with the other doctrines of grace that they "are universally accepted, or rejected together."

Boyce investigated seven categories that demonstrated that only God's purpose, power, and grace bring the believer's salvation to consummation in perseverance to the end. The Bible teaches the final salvation of all believers (John 10:27–29; 1 Peter 1:3–5), that such is due to the purpose of God (John 6:39), and to the power of God (1 Peter 1:5), and to the grace of God (Rom. 4:16; 1 Thess. 5:23–24). The Bible shows that human sin and weakness are such that any would infallibly fall if left to his own spiritual resources (1 John 1:8–2:1; 1 Cor. 10:13). This fact obtains not only for new or weak Christians, but for the most mature, advanced, and apparently strong. No less are such Christians dependent moment by moment on the sustaining power, purpose, and grace of God. When left to their strength, they find the deceitfulness of indwelling sin too much. Boyce used the illustrations of Peter, the contention between Paul and Barnabas, and Old Testament believers such as Abraham, Moses, Eli, David, and Hezekiah.[95] Only God's grace gives such strength that, of each and every one of the elect, "no one will finally apostatize or be lost; but each will assuredly persevere and be saved."[96]

Boyce made it abundantly clear, as stated above, that the moral energies of the elect person necessarily find expression, for the preservation of God operates effectually in ways appropriate to such an end, that is, perseverance in faith and holiness. He gave expression to this kind of true synergism in his lecture on Christian ethics when he said, "Happy is he whose life is one of such daily emptying of himself and what he loves most for the sake of his dear Lord. They are not many to whom this is granted, but as to many more than have it, it could be theirs if they would but daily stand in waiting willing service to be used as the Lord may demand. Happy those whom by his grace he makes willing thus to give up all for him."[97] The Christian, therefore, pursues faith, actively consecrates himself to the service of Christ, purifies himself from sin, and humbly concedes that biblical warnings about falling away could be true in his own experience apart from such careful circumspectness and consecration. Boyce believed that Hebrews 6:4–6 pictures true Christians in danger of falling irremediably from a saving relationship with Christ; the warning itself, so perceived, acted as the means to stop such a thing from ever happening in any instance.[98]

The subjects of death, the soul's immortality, final judgment, and final destinies culminate Boyce's demonstration that divine decree and providence established an order in creation for the full manifestation of the creature's absolute and utter dependence on his creator with an awesomely pleasing, or threatening, display of the perfections of all God's attributes. "It will furnish a worthy arena for the display of the attributes of God. A continuous purpose of God, in connection with his intelligent creatures, has been to make known to them the glory of his character." None of his attributes will fail to be "signally displayed" in the judgment day. Boyce rises to great heights of literary power and spiritual affection in his description as to how all of God's purposes will be vindicated and displayed then.

> Yet, how signally will then also, appear the wisdom of his purpose, the truth and faithfulness of his promises, his power to accomplish his will, his universal benevolence, his sacrificing love, his unbounded mercy, his delivering power, his conquering grace, and, not to attempt to enumerate further, everything that can be imagined as constituting that holiness which, in one word, embraces all moral perfection.
>
> The wisdom and equity of God, in his providential and gracious dealings with men, will then, also be apparent. These often give rise to perplexity, even in those who most firmly believe in God as one who does all things justly, and well. In this life men are called to exercise faith in God in all these matters. That faith will be vindicated by the manifestations at that time both of his character and acts. The inequalities of this life, and the prosperity of the wicked, and the adversity of the righteous, will then be not only equalized, but all will clearly see the wisdom, justice, and goodness of God, in giving them a place here in his providential government. It is more probable that, in the full exhibition of all his purposes in Creation and Grace, that insoluble problem of this life,—the presence of sin in a world created, and governed by an Almighty, and Holy God,—will become a manifestation of unspeakable glory in God. Then, too, will appear, even more plainly than now, the righteousness of his choice of some to salvation, and condemnation of others for sin; and, also, the full responsibility of men for every sin, even when their circumstances and previous action have rendered certain the things which they will do. Then, too, will be seen such sufficiency, in each man, of the light possessed, if he had walked therein, and of his power for good, if he had exercised it, as makes him guilty in the sight of God, and worthy of the punishment which he will inflict.[99]

All of these attributes find their fullest expression in Christ—God in Christ. To this prominent aspect of Boyce's theology we now turn.

12

In Christ Alone

*T*he knowledge of God, the glory of God, and the scheme of redemption all radiate from the person and work of Jesus Christ, so taught Boyce. Not only so, but the true meaning and exemplar of our worship, our prayer, our ethic, our self-denial, our being in the world but not of the world are bound up in a robust grasp of the incarnation, that is, the true humanity of Christ. Biblical revelation culminates, and finds its most potent verification, in its explication of how Christ makes God known to us through his tabernacling among us for the purpose of redemption.

In Boyce's 1870 *Baptist Quarterly* article entitled "The Doctrine of the Suffering Christ," he makes the claim, "The Scripture doctrine of the Triune God lies at the foundation of that of Christ's sufferings."[1] In an unusual but revealing use of this sentence in the *Abstract of Systematic Theology*, Boyce wrote, "The doctrine of the Trinity lies at the foundation of that of Christ's Person."[2] He saw Christ's person as having become a historical phenomenon in the incarnation solely because of the necessity of redemptive suffering. In Christ one sees the glory of God in all its fullness; in him one sees the wisdom and power of God; in him, all the attributes are present, the fullness of divinity not only in bodily form, but in the redemptive act on the cross. The Father's character as well as his "voluntary" acts of mercy, grace, and loving-kindness find expression through the entire Christ event. The Spirit's peculiar operations of holy love and communication expressed naturally in eternity find economic expression in time through the work of Christ. An understanding, therefore, of Christ must begin with the biblical doctrine of the Trinity.

Trinity

Boyce begins the section on the Trinity by quoting the "Abstract of Principles": "God is revealed to us as Father, Son and Holy Spirit, each with distinct personal attributes, but without division of nature, essence or being." He defends the straightforward propositions that "The Father is God," "This Son is God," "The Holy Spirit is a Person," and "The Holy Spirit is God." Each of these declarations summarizes a conclusion derived from a synthesis of a large number of biblical passages spread widely through Scripture. Woven into the discussion, the consistent reality of the unity, as well as the simplicity, of God permeates every affirmation of separate personality for each person within the deity.

In his catechism, Boyce summarizes the doctrine for children with the question, "Does this imply that there is more than one God?" "No," so begins the answer, "the Bible teaches that the Father is God, that the Son is God, and that the Spirit is God, and yet that there is but one God."[3] His theology contains the more extended summary, "The divine nature is so possessed, by each of the persons in the Trinity, that neither has his own separate divine nature, but each subsists in one divine nature, common to the three." Neither is the divine nature divided "in its relation through the nature to the person," for that would admit parts into the divine nature and contradict its simplicity and the biblical teaching that "there is but one God."[4]

The Scriptures teach everywhere the unity of God explicitly and emphatically. There can be no doubt that they reveal a God that

438

is exclusively one. But their other statements, which we have been examining, should assure us that they also teach that there are three divine persons. It is this peculiar twofold teaching, which is expressed by the word "trinity." The revelation to us, is not that of tritheism or three Gods; not of triplicity, which is threefoldness, and would involve composition, and be contrary to the simplicity of God; nor of mere manifestation of one person in three forms, which is opposed to the revealed individuality of the persons; but it is well expressed by the word trinity, which is declarative, not simply of threeness, but of three-oneness. That this word is not found in Scripture is no objection to it, when the doctrine, expressed by it, is so clearly set forth.[5]

The affirmation of tri-personality begs for some manner of distinguishing the respective persons in their eternal internal relations. Boyce responded in the framework of historic orthodoxy with an extended defense of the eternal generation of the Son and the eternal procession of the Spirit from the Father and the Son. These are particularly important for the coherence of Boyce's argument concerning the character of redemption. The Redeemer must fully represent all the interests of the Godhead in his redemptive work; the Holy Spirit must know exhaustively the inner nature and eternal purpose of God and take delight in his communication of love and truth flowing from the Father to the Son and reciprocally. Redemption would not be worthy of God, and, therefore, there would be no redemption apart from the trinitarian reality of eternal generation and eternal procession. In one sense, for Boyce, the entire doctrine of the Trinity, as well as the covenant of redemption, rested on the reality of eternal generation. Some ground rules, or "general statements," therefore, must be presupposed in this discussion.

First, one must discuss this phenomenon in terms provided by the Bible. The biblical language must be seen as expressive of real relations divested of all that "belongs to human conditions, and imperfections," but consistent with that "eternity, and unity, of the nature of God, which exist even in his purposes towards all things which are without."[6]

Second, these relations exist in the nature of God, that is, necessarily, and not contingently. They are positive revelations of what he is.

Third, the relations must be eternal, though the words "begotten" and "proceed" indicate temporal relations in human connections. And so it is with every word that tells us something about God even in his external relation to the world. But for correct understanding we seek to divest these of their connections to time, space, and partition. In the same way, this divestment of time and succession characterizes the attempt to perceive correctly God's internal personal relations.

Fourth, the words must not be perceived so as to indicate any inferiority of essence from one person to the other. Of the one undivided divine essence three distinguishable personalities partake, whose personalities are defined and eternally exist in terms of relationships denominated by the words Father, Begotten Son, and Proceeding Holy Spirit.

Eternal Generation

In his early lectures as well as his later published text, Boyce gave both space and tightly reasoned theological energy to defending the doctrine of eternal generation. Earlier he had established the scriptural truth that the Son is God. He is expressly called "God"; he is called "Lord." Though these titles sometime appear when their object clearly is not divine, "the manner in which they are applied to Christ, and the frequency of that application, become, along with the other evidences presented, an incontestable proof, that he, as well as the Father, is true God."[7] Jesus is an object of worship; he is equally honored with the Father, and knows the Father as no one else knows him. Boyce listed fourteen proofs of the deity of the Son including the biblical ascription to him of "all the incommunicable attributes of God." Since the Son is God even as the Father is God, what is their relationship that preserves a single essence of deity but eternally distinguished persons? The answer is eternal generation.

Boyce's attention to this issue had precedence in the history of Baptist theology. Notably, both Benjamin Keach and John Gill made strong defenses of the doctrine. They viewed it as a necessary corollary to both the doctrine of the Trinity and the eternal covenant of grace. Keach is particularly insistent on the analogy between the Father's eternal generation of the Son and the arrangement within the eternal covenant by which the Father sends the Son.[8] Gill concurred and also tied belief in the doctrine of the Trinity to the doctrine of eternal generation. "For my own part," he preached, "could I be prevailed upon to part with this article of faith, I would at once give up the doctrine of the trinity, as quite indefensible." Paternity, filiation, and spiration as eternal, natural, and necessary distinctions within the Trinity all depend on the eternal generation of the Son, so insisted Gill.[9]

Likewise, the Philadelphia Association, the confessional mother of the Charleston theological tradition from which came the "Abstract of Principles," took seriously the doctrine of eternal generation. In 1743 the association received recantations from two men, members of associated churches, who had "departed from the literal sense and meaning of that fundamental article in our Confession of faith, concerning the eternal generation and Sonship of Jesus Christ our Lord." After reporting their recantations, an explanation of the means to be used for their recovery and the importance of this action was placed in the minutes. We "are glad," they stated, "that God hath blessed means to convict the said parties of their sin and error; and herein we were *nemine contra dicente*, fully united to repel, and put a stop, as far as we may, unto the Arian, Socinian, and Antitrinitarian systems." They had stiffened their resolve to give a clear testimony to the world of "our joint belief of, and our resolution to maintain, the eternal and inconceivable generation of the second Person in the ever adorable Trinity."[10]

John L. Dagg, who wrote one of the first texts used by Boyce, did not discuss the idea directly but introduced virtually every consideration surrounding the concept that Boyce used in his discussion. In contemplating some of Christ's titles as they relate to his state of "Original Glory," Dagg set the table for profitable development of the doctrine:

> Why he is called the Son of God, is a question on which divines have differed. His miraculous conception, his mediatorial office, his resurrection from the dead, and his investiture with supreme dominion, have been severally assigned, as the reason of the title;

441

but these appear rather to declare him to be the Son of God, or to belong to him because of that relation, than to constitute it. The phrases first-born, first-begotten, only-begotten, seem to refer to the true ground of the name, Son of God: but what these signify, it is probably impossible to understand. The ideas of peculiar endearment, dignity, and heirship, which are attached to these terms, as used among men, may be supposed to belong to them, as applied to the Son of God; but all gross conceptions of their import, as if they were designed to convey to our minds the idea of derived existence, and the mode of that derivation, ought to be discarded as inconsistent with the perfection of Godhead. Some have considered the titles Christ, and Son of God, as equal and convertible; but the distinction in the use of them, as pointed out in our examination of the charges brought against the Redeemer, shows the error of this opinion. . . . Christ, or Messiah, is a title of office: but the phrase "Son of God," denotes, not the mere office, but the exalted nature which qualified for it.[11]

In addition, Boyce's more immediate theological mentors gave the doctrine a high priority in their discussion of the Trinity and Christology. Turretin discusses it in question 29 and devotes thirty-one paragraphs to its defense. One can see with little difficulty the impact that Turretin's discussion had on Boyce's wording, ordering, and arguing. Out of numerous bits and pieces of such evidence, Turretin's brief discussion of the Son's generation being complete explained, "The generation may well be said to be terminated by a termination of perfection, not by a termination of duration."[12] Boyce worded it, "Such an act must be ever continuing, and completed only in the sense of its being always perfect, though not ended."[13]

Also, Boyce adopted a concept of Turretin on the connection between the nature and the will of the Father in his relation to the Son. Whereas Hodge says quite starkly, "It is by necessity of nature, and not by the will of the Father," Turretin preferred a more nuanced statement:

Necessary and voluntary may in a measure be distinguished in God as to our manner of conception, yet they are not really opposed. Hence the Father is said to have begotten the Son necessarily and voluntarily; necessarily because he begat by nature, as he is God by nature, but voluntarily because he begat not by coaction, but freely; not by an antecedent will, which denotes an act of willing (free outwardly), but by a concomitant, which denotes the natural faculty of willing in God; not by the liberty of indifference, but of spontaneity.[14]

Boyce, like Hodge, focused on the nature of God but also acknowledged that the relations of Father and Son are not in the absence of "will." In a way similar to Turretin, while staying close to Hodge, Boyce argued,

> Though it is true that the Father wills to beget the Son, and the Father and Son will to send forth the Spirit; yet the will thus exercised, is not at mere good pleasure, but it results necessarily from the nature of God, that the Father should thus will the begetting, and the Father and the Son the sending forth. The will, thus exercised, is not like that of his purposes, in which God acts of free pleasure, . . . but like that by which he necessarily wills his own existence.[15]

As in many cases Charles Hodge is given the largest amount of space in Boyce's quotations. On three separate issues, Boyce included quotes from Hodge of at least one paragraph.[16]

Even with these powerful precedents and theological influences, Boyce gave original and fresh expression to many of the ideas and organized the discussion on the basis of his own peculiar emphasis. He continued to drive toward a vision of compelling coherence in regard to both revelation and redemption.

Boyce did not share Dagg's shyness on speaking clearly about this issue. In his *Abstract of Systematic Theology* Boyce gave ten pages to it under the title "The Eternal Sonship of Christ." In his 1861 recitation lecture, Boyce included forty-three responses on the doctrine of eternal generation following twenty on the Trinity. His second question on the Trinity set the stage for both discussions. "In what sense is God revealed to us as Father?" Boyce asked. The answer he provided is in words virtually the same as a paragraph in the *Abstract*: "Not merely in the general way in which he is the Father of all created beings &

443

they his sons, nor in that in which he is the father of those who are his sons by adoption in Christ Jesus; but he is the Father as indicative of a relation between himself and another person whom the Scriptures call the 'only begotten Son.'"[17]

His recitation further explored the Father/Son nomenclature in some detail with the purpose of showing its unique and eternal significance. He pointed to four different classes of Scriptures "which speak of God as the Father." Those in which "Christ addresses God as Father," those in which "Christ speaks of the Father as co-working with him," those that represent the "Father, knowing and loving the Son," and "that class in which He is spoken of as the Father giving and sending the Son." He listed many Scriptures under each category. Only once, Boyce claimed, does Jesus use the address "Our Father," but nearly fifty times he uses "My Father." Apostolic language such as Paul's in Ephesians 3:14 assumes uniqueness in the Father/Son dynamic within the Godhead: "For this cause I bow my knees unto the Father of our Lord Jesus Christ." Passages that speak of God calling Jesus his beloved Son, that speak of his being begotten, and that indicate preexistence by saying that the Son was in the bosom of the Father, or that the Father sent the Son, or gave the Son, or that the Father gave certain people to the Son before the foundation of the world give further weight to the idea of an eternal Father/Son relationship. On that basis, he summarized the nature of eternal generation as follows:

> The scriptures make known to us the fact of the sonship of Christ, the fact that that sonship expresses the relation between the first and second person of the Trinity, that this sonship is expressive of nature, consequently it cannot be separated from the relations of the persons in the Godhead. The whole Godhead is possessed by the Father, the whole Godhead is possessed by the Son, consequently the generation is not one of the Godhead but one of the persons in the Godhead. The explanation thus given of this doctrine is, that the Father begets the Son not as God but as a person communicating to him the whole Godhead, so that the Son is God equally as much as the Father is God, that this begetting is consistent with or in accordance with but is not the result of the will of the Father, else would the existence of the Son be a dependent existence, but as the result

444

of a necessity arising out of the very nature of the Godhead, which necessity like God himself, having no beginning nor end, neither has the generation to which it gives rise beginning nor end; consequently the generation is eternal.[18]

In the *Abstract of Systematic Theology* Boyce summarized the evidence that Scripture affords for the relation of Father and Son to be both natural and eternal. Both paternity and filiation in God are not "mere names for something that does not exist, nor for some relation, different from that of father and son, to which these titles were first applied in connection with Christ's creation, or birth, or resurrection, or exaltation."[19] Boyce argued with conviction, taking the same position as Dagg, against those that see the title "Son of God" as being given in light of his offices assumed as mediator. Given either at birth or at resurrection or at his ascension, the title is synonymous with the offices he holds as the Christ, so some objectors contend. Boyce believed that such an assertion had no evidence in the biblical text, but arose only negatively from resistance to the idea of eternal generation. The opposers commandeered Scriptures such as Romans 1:4, Luke 1:35, and Acts 13:32–33 to give biblical support to the view of sonship being an official status, but Boyce believed their exegesis to be contorted. When seen in their overall contextual thrust, such passages actually support natural and eternal sonship rather than official sonship.[20]

Christ's sonship is the fountain of his deity just as the begetting is the foundation of his continuing humanity. A human son, like his father, partakes, alike and equally, of the whole of human nature. Though the father bestows and the son partakes of the nature thus bestowed, nonetheless, the son possesses the nature as an undiminished substance. Even in created things, however, paternity and filiation are coexistent, for one cannot be a father when there is no son, nor a son in absence of a father. So with God; though the Father begets, his begetting is of the undiminished essence of deity and, therefore, eternal. If God is Father by nature, then the Son has always coexisted in the same nature. For this reason the Bible assigns to the Son as Son all the incommunicable attributes of deity (e.g., John 5:17–18, 23, 26).

Priority and succession of events characterize the reality of begetting in temporal, created things. But in God neither beginning nor end, antecedent nor consequent, nor "succession of any kind" characterizes his immanent operations. Generation, therefore, ever continues, did not originate and will not end, does not come in a single act or "at a definite moment in the divine nature," but ever is.[21]

Boyce believed, "The tendency of not maintaining this doctrine is to a denial of the divinity of Christ & of the Trinity & leads to Unitarianism. We may not be thus far led away but those who follow us will if we do not hold to the doctrine."[22]

Completing his view of personal relations within the Trinity, Boyce affirmed the doctrine of the procession of the Holy Spirit from the Father and the Son. Both the Son and the Spirit proceed from the Father's eternal and necessary will in some manner. The Son's manner of proceeding, or coming from, has abundant biblical witness designated as generation. The Spirit's proceeding remains more "difficult to interpret, and the nature of the relation thus indicated even more incomprehensible than that of the generation of the Son." Boyce believed that the term "procession" is especially appropriate for the Spirit, for the idea of outbreathing serves as an image of the relation between the Spirit and both the Father and the Son. He did not insist nearly as stringently on the procession of the Spirit from the Son as he did on the eternal generation of the Son. In fact, the Scripture leaves it so as "to forbid any positive statement about it." He did affirm, however, that "the preponderance of evidence is in favour of a procession from both Father and Son."[23]

This double procession becomes a bit more important when the economy of salvation comes into view. Boyce believed that though Father, Son, and Spirit are equal in essence, in personal relations within the Trinity eternally, subordination of mode of subsistence exists. The Father is of none, neither generated nor proceeding, the Son is generated by the Father, and the Holy Spirit proceeds. If the Spirit is subordinated to the Father and the Son, and the Spirit proceeds, it stands to reason that he proceeds from the Father and the Son. This seems especially consistent with those Scriptures that speak of the Spirit as the Spirit of Jesus, or the Spirit of the Son, or Jesus' promise to send the Spirit. "In God," Boyce surmised, "it is probable that the official subordination is based upon that of the personal relations. It corresponds exactly with the relations of the persons, from which has probably resulted their official subordination in works without, and especially in the work of redemption."[24]

For this reason, the Father sent the Son as the one representing the Father's glory in the interest of salvation. The Spirit, sent by the Father and the Son, effects in the elect those things purchased by the Son in his meritorious redemptive operations. The Spirit, who is the Spirit of the Father and of the Son, takes the things of Christ, which he did in full obedience to the Father, and makes us new creations that we might cry to the Father and trust in the Son even as we are transformed, by the Lord the Spirit, from one degree of glory to another, into the image of Christ, who in his incarnation is the example of the true godliness to which we should aspire.[25]

The Person of Christ

The incarnation of the Son of God constitutes the central event of revelation as well as redemption. The truthfulness of Scripture finds its most sublime and irrefutable point of coherence in this event and its centrality to all of Scripture. Also one finds the incarnate Son of God as the unique, and thus exclusive and necessary, person in whom redemption could occur. "It is well," Boyce remarked, "to see that the true doctrine as to the Saviour of man is not that of the New Testament only, but of the whole Bible." By proceeding from the Old to the New, "the unity of divine revelation will thus appear." The internal self-authentication of Scripture finds ultimate expression in its witness to redemption through the Christ. When the testimony of prophecy combines with the witness of the miracles in the ministry of Jesus, the authority "of the later revelation will be seen to rest, not upon these miracles alone, but also upon the concurrence of its teachings with the inspired truth already accepted by the Jews."[26]

Fulfilled Old Testament

Without the consistency of the Christ event with the Old Testament, no valid claim either to revelation or to the credibility of the redemptive mission of Christ could be affirmed. Boyce set forth in broad strokes, therefore, "Christ in the Old Testament." He is the promised seed of the woman. The strictest grammatical interpretation of Genesis 3 and 4, Boyce argued, shows that not only did Eve "believe that Jehovah was to be the Messiah, but that she expected his appearance in human form."[27] Christ also is the patriarchal seed promised to Abraham, Isaac, and Jacob to which Abraham gave witness in his confidence that "the Lord will provide." The Messiah would be the seed of David, a status that involved a multitude of expectations summarized by Boyce:

> These references will suffice to show that David expected not only the perpetuity of the merely earthly kingdom, with its succession of monarchs of his family, but that he also looked in the same line of descent for a true appearance of Jehovah, whose reign in this human person would thus be universal, whose flesh would never see corruption, of whose kingdom there would be no end, whose power would be terrible and his wisdom and righteousness superhuman, to whom as his Lord, David would himself be subservient, who is already the begotten Son of God and can justly be called God, whose government would be especially spiritual, who, with the kingly, would combine a priestly office of peculiar character and origin, and yet whose sufferings would be intense, and these sufferings the foundation of the blessings of his people and of their devotion to God. Are not these the characteristics of the Christian idea of the Messiah as set forth in the New Testament? In whom, except in Jesus Christ, have these expectations been fulfilled? In what respect has he not met them fully?[28]

The prophetical material promotes expectations of a Messiah born from a virgin, known as Immanuel, born in Bethlehem, the desire of nations, a special king, bearing a relation to God that warrants the attribution to him of divine names and functions, whose sufferings will be substitutionary, unmerited but meritorious, and invincibly effectual, in whose work the Gentiles also will participate. Descriptions of the Old Testament "Angel of the Covenant" raise expectations even higher, for in this one there appeared in true human flesh, even before his birth in Bethlehem, the promised redeemer. He was given divine names, identified with Jehovah, had divine attributes and authority ascribed to him, and received, willingly, divine worship. Glowingly and confidently Boyce summarized the Old Testament witness to Jesus the Christ, the Savior of men:

> As the seed of the woman, he has utterly destroyed the power of the serpent, the great enemy of man. In him the day has come which Abraham foresaw and was glad. In him the Lion of Judah, the seed of David, appears as the King of kings, the Lord of lords, whose reign is universal, not over those living on earth only at any one time, but over all the living and the dead of this world, and indeed, of the whole universe. His untold sufferings have secured the happiness of his people and their devotion to God. His kingdom is an everlasting kingdom. His priesthood has neither beginning nor end. He is the Lamb of God that taketh away the sin of the world, he ever liveth to make intercession for us. He hath made us kings and priests unto God. At his name every knee shall bow and every tongue confess that Jesus Christ is Lord to the glory of God the Father. His flesh is indeed the tabernacle which is filled with the glory of Jehovah, in whom the ancient prophecy to Israel is fulfilled: "Behold your God!"[29]

The increasing detail of the picture given by the Old Testament combined with the actual description of Jesus in the New Testament, his life, his teachings, his actions, his claims, and his miracles fits perfectly the pattern of authentication of revelation and truth established early and carried out consistently throughout Scripture. Though not understood clearly at the time of its being given in the Old Testament, its unfolding in Christ stamps it with clarity. This establishes "the unity of the doctrines of both Testaments" and gives "evidence of the inspiration of each in their testimony in common" to the doctrines foreshadowed in the former and "distinctly declared in the latter revelation."[30]

Jesus, the Son of God

The prophecies distinctly lead to the expectation of a divine Messiah. Jesus, the Son of Mary, is God the Son. The following six responses appear as numbers 11–16 in Boyce's recitation:

11. What first proof of the divinity of this person? That class which ascribes to him divine attributes, powers, and wisdom.
12. What are the divine attributes thus ascribed? (a) self-existence Jo v.26. (b) Eternity Jo 1.3. Jo v.24. Hebrews i.10–12 (from 102 Psalm). (c) Omnipotence Mt. xxviii.18. Lk xxi.15. (d) Omniscience Jo ii.24, 25. Jo xvi.30. Jo xxi.17. (e) Omnipresence Mt. xviii.20. xxviii.20. Jo 3.13.
13. What of Divine worship paid him? John v.23. Philippians 2.10. Hebrews 1.6. Mt. 2.2. Mt. 9.18. Mt. xv.25. Mt. xx.20. Lk xxiv.52. In Revelation the "Lamb of God" is spoken of as the object of worship in various ways.
14. What similarity of nature? Ans. His nature said to be equally incomprehensible with that of the Father. Mt xi.27. Lk x.22.
15. What peculiar knowledge has the Son? He is said to know the Father as he is known by the Father. Jo x.15.
16. What class of passages is last mentioned? That class in which Christ has the titles of the Father and in which equality and identity with the Father are ascribed to Him. (Lord) I Cor ii.8. Rev. xvii.14. (God) John 1.1; John 20.28. Acts xx.28. Romans ix.5. I Tim iii.16 (this passage thought probably to be interpolated). Titus 1.3. Heb. 1.8. I John v.20. Positive equality asserted between Father & son. Jo 5.18. Jo 10.32. Phil 2.6. Col 2.9. Col 1.15. Heb. 1.3.[31]

In his catechism Boyce gave emphasis to the same points. "Was Christ merely a man? No; He was God also," is the first question and answer. "By what name is He called as such? The only Begotten son of God." "How is He described in Hebrews? As the brightness of the Father's glory and the express image of His person." Boyce points out that the Father addresses the Son in terms of deity: "Unto the Son He says, 'Thy throne, O God, is forever and ever.'" Is he called God in any other place, and does he allow himself to be addressed as such? "Yes," Boyce teaches the catechumen, "in the first Epistle of John, speaking of Him, it says, 'This is the true God'"; and Thomas said to him, "My Lord and my God." "In what other ways does the Bible teach the Divinity of Christ? It ascribes to Him the possession of every perfection ascribed to God" such as "omniscience, omnipresence and eternity of existence." "Is the work of creation ever ascribed to Him?" Boyce asked in the final question; "Yes; the Bible says all things were made by Him."[32] Surely such a being is God.

His *Baptist Quarterly* article asserted, "Another important fact taught in the word of God, is that in this incarnation and work the Son of God maintains his essential relations to the divine nature unchanged. He was therefore as truly God during his incarnation as before that event."[33] His subordination came in his official capacity as mediator. This was a subordination, not of essence, but of one divine person to another divine person. For the sake of the necessity of living in obedience, he yielded all his prerogatives of rule and authority "exclusively into the hands of the Father." Even with this voluntarily accepted position, the Scriptures teach so fully that he was God in his incarnation "that we have no evidence at all of Christ's divinity which is not presented with equal force of him while on earth."[34]

While Boyce earlier had stated that Christ yielded his prerogatives of power and authority, here he modified that. "The constant workings of his divine power and energy, by which he is essentially, as God, always working with the Father, were indeed concealed." At times, however, both before the people and more often before his disciples, "the divinity shone through the veil which ordinarily concealed it." He allowed himself to be addressed in terms of divinity and claimed the prerogatives of divinity because "though a servant, he was still the Lord, having his relations to his divine nature unimpaired, and entitled to the names, as he was also able to perform the acts and display the attributes of God."[35] That Jesus maintained his deity unimpaired fit with the demands of his redemptive work.

> It was not sufficient for us to know that the person who died for us was divine before he came into the world. The Scriptures assure us, and we need to comfort ourselves with the assurance, that he was equally divine when a babe in Bethlehem, when suffering upon the cross, when ascending from Olivet, and even now, while in human nature, he rules as Mediatorial King, or makes intercession with the Father as our great High Priest. We must even go beyond the idea of some kind of divinity, and recognize him as the unchangeable God,

who was, and is, and ever shall be, the Almighty, the well-beloved Son of the Father who always hears, and to whom all things have been entrusted, in order that the consummation of his glorious kingdom may be fully attained.[36]

Jesus, the Son of Man

The Redeemer must be not only God, but man. The true humanity of Christ probably astounded Boyce more than any other single idea in Scripture. The Son of God truly became incarnate, that is, he took to himself all that humanity is in its flesh. He possessed a true human body, not just the phantom appearance of one, and a true human soul. That omnipotence took on weakness, that omniscience submitted to ignorance and the necessity of increase of knowledge by instruction, investigation, and deduction, and that omnipresence contracted itself to measurability, all for the sake of sinners, engaged the highest of Boyce's intellect and affections.

Christ's incarnation occurred in such a way "that he became man." This is no mere indwelling of a human person but such a transaction that the Son of God, the Second Person of the Trinity, while retaining the divine nature unchanged, so assumed human nature that "Christ also becomes truly man." Boyce considered the historical heresies on this point, docetism, Nestorianism, and monophysitism, and rejected them, decisively flooding his discussion with a deluge of scriptural evidences for the conclusions that Jesus had a true human body, Jesus had a true human soul.

All the essential elements he taught simply in his catechism under the title "Jesus Christ—A Man." By the answers that Boyce developed we learn that Christ was "a man in every respect; but he was without sin." Also we find out that "He had a human body and soul and could not only suffer, but was also liable to temptation." Satan did in fact tempt him and "tried in every way to make Him sin, but could not." As a man Christ was subject to the law of God "and rendered perfect obedience to it." He had bodily appetites and therefore "felt hunger and thirst, and was liable to all sinless infirmities." Not only could he suffer in body as all humans, but his soul was liable to suffer. In his soul, in fact, he "suffered most severely in fulfilling the work which He came to do." Not only did his humanity allow him to die for us "but also to sympathize with us in our trials and temptations."[37]

Boyce's lecture on Christian ethics set forth the humanity of Christ as the perfect exemplar of the ethical demands of the Christian faith. Considering that Christ has revealed God to us and has taught us that we are to be perfect, even as our heavenly Father is perfect, "we are able to take one step further forward in our discussion and show that the moral ethics of Christianity have been embodied in a perfect human example." Just as Jesus possessed full divinity, "he has also perfect humanity so that in his human nature he can set forth a perfect human example to us." Apollinarianism, or Eutychianism, "the too intimate blending of his two natures" robs him of the character assigned him by Scripture as one "that can suffer, that can be tempted, that can have and does have human emotions, that is a man of sorrows and acquainted with grief." His real humanity also qualified him to "make sacrifices in like manner as we do" and to submit to the "influence of the Holy Spirit for guidance and wisdom." He needed to "grow in favor with God and man" and draw "his replies to temptation from the same storehouse of God's truth" and gain "strength in praying to God," and exercise "faith and trust in Him."[38]

On these particular points of prayer from the Son of God, as well as his obvious faith and trust in the Father, Boyce concentrated in his sermon on "The Prayers of Christ." The twofold nature of Christ gives assurance that Christ neither was ignorant of what he did nor did he intend to deceive in any of his actions. The fact of his divine Sonship makes the prayer of his humanity much more startling and informative.

> But here is the Son of God to whom the Scriptures ascribe the fullness of the nature of God, and even those attributes of self-existence and eternity which cannot be given to a creature, as well as the omnipresence, omniscience, and omnipotence which render impossible any need of aid or protection or of bestowing of blessing. The petitioner is here petitioning God, yet Himself is God. He earnestly prays as man, yet His prayer is to God and He is God. . . . Here it is the Son in his human nature that prays to the Father.[39]

453

Even given the mysterious reality of communication, petition, agreement, and other aspects of interpersonal relationship within the Trinity, Boyce found the prayer of Jesus not to partake of that kind of discourse. Instead, "these have all the marks of human prayer, and these marks enter into their essential elements." His recorded prayers "are just such prayer as might be offered by a sinless perfect man, convinced of His dependence, conscious of His weakness, overwhelmed with His afflictions, resisting His temptations, and looking upward with earnest solicitude to One believed to be a very present help in time of trouble." These prayers of Jesus have no other explanation apart from "the plain teaching of Scripture of the full humanity of our Lord."[40]

Boyce would say emphatically, in resisting any tendencies toward monophysitism, that whatever was "the character of the mysterious union of the human and divine natures in the person of the Son of God, His human nature was still left so unaffected by His divine relations that He was in all respects a man, though He was a sinless and perfect one." Even at that he was "liable to all the sinless weakness and infirmities of human nature and to all the conditions of creaturely existence"; for one must not doubt that though eternally Son of God he had assumed "a mere creation of God, . . . a mere creature . . . subject to the infirmities and conditions of creature existence" who depended on his "constant prayers to the Father for gracious aid and support that He might finish the work which it was His meat to do."[41]

Not only do we observe him dependent upon prayer as a man, but we find all other relations to be developed as a man, a perfect man, would. In his twofold nature, we find that he "no more truly reveals the perfect God than He does the perfect man." He endures the contradictions of sinners. He submits to obloquy and scorn. He gives "his back to the smiters and his cheeks to them that pluck off the hair." In oppression and affliction he opens not his mouth but is brought as "a lamb to the slaughter and as a sheep before her shearers is dumb so he opens not his mouth." We find someone in our nature who is "the author and finisher of our faith, who for the joy that was set before him endured the cross, despising the shame, and is set down at the right hand of God." For the best example of endurance as a human we are to "consider him lest we be wearied and faint," and in his train we must resist "unto blood, striving against sin." In every respect he is the model to us of "obedience to the law of Christian ethics."

Boyce continued to expand his applications of this idea by a massive recalling of biblical material that he considered clearly demonstrable of the perfect human exemplar of Christian ethics. In order to demonstrate the superiority of Jesus in his humanity to any other human, Boyce delved into the study of comparative religions. "The newest form of infidelity," Boyce noted, "is to attempt to show that other religions do present systems which thus compare with Christianity." Among the latest of these Boyce found "a subtle objection" to his position in the "recent poem of Edwin Arnold called the Light of Asia of the great renunciation. It is intended to set forth the life and teachings of Gautama Prince of India and founder of Buddhism." After pointing to the deeds of Gautama, the frivolous account of the nature of his knowledge, his social life, his attempts at coming to terms with the complexity of his culture, and his father's attempt to shield him from it, Boyce compared this to Jesus. Jesus was "no selfwrapt, inward looking, world forgetting, pain despising, or piteously whining dried up, sanctimonious, secluded separatist from his fellow men." He was neither ignorant of human life, detached from it, nor mystified by it, but "He lived in them and with them, as he lived for them, that they also might not only live for him, but in him and with him." Boyce considered this "the highest conception possible of the divine teacher coming among men."

While humanity yearns for God, nevertheless, "it fears him as such." Unlike heathenism, "Christianity presents not a god turned into a man, and that a sinful one, but the Son of God, remaining unchangeably God, yet becoming as truly man also, and in that manhood exhibiting the excellence of that character of God himself." This space-time manifestation "is the basis of the ethical duties Jesus has revealed both in the divine and human natures, and set forth to mankind for their imitation."[42]

Jesus' Two Natures Inhere in One Person

Jesus lived as a being with two distinct natures in one person. He affirmed that the foundation of his personhood was the person of the divine Son of God; given that, nevertheless, he could be called a human person and a divine person as long as one retains the reality that he is one person. Jesus expressed both natures, deity and humanity, in personal relations through the eternal singular personhood of the Son of God because "the characteristics of personality . . . allow a most vital union of the two natures in his one person."[43]

This mysterious union of two natures in one person must be believed solely on the basis of the authority of Scripture and the necessity that Scripture never contradicts itself. "So intimate is the union of the one person with two such distinct natures," Boyce reasoned, "that we cannot always separate what Christ says of himself as God, from what is said of himself as man." While this may puzzle us in interpreting the Word of God, it is vital for "harmonizing its statements." Apart from this doctrine "the word of God cannot be made to agree with itself." When one remembers, however, that though truly divine, Jesus also is human, and "that because of the one person, all that he does in either nature may be as fully said to be done by him as though he had no other, we see the Scripture statements fall beautifully and regularly into their respective ranks, and in that two-fold unity, each receives its full force."[44]

This astounding union of two natures in one person called forth from Boyce some of his most admirable passages of literary passion.

> It is indeed the Son of God, who thus, in human soul, and body, is doing the work. But it is his human soul, not his divine nature, that thus pleads, and shrinks, and fears, and which still willingly submits, resolves to press on, is strengthened by God's messenger, and again, confident in God, goes forward with sublime self-devotion to the cross. The distance, between this and God is infinite; this soul, the creature, the finite, the fearful, the mutable, the suffering, the trusting, the dying; and him, the creator, the infinite, the support of those who trust, the immutable, who cannot suffer, who cannot die. The acts due to the divine nature are marked, and characteristic, and so also are those of the human nature. While we look at the former, we must say, this is God; none but he can perform such acts, can possess such attributes, can be called such names. Equally, while we look at

the latter, we must say, this is man. None but man can thus suffer, can thus be limited, can thus pray.[45]

At the end of his lecture on ethics, Boyce could not let the occasion pass without pressing his hearers to draw the right conclusion for their eternal welfare. "In view of the truth presented to day let me in conclusion ask—what think ye of Christ?" Boyce challenged. "If his wisdom be mere human wisdom, is it not worthy of your acceptance?" he continued; "If his example be merely human, does it not demand your imitation? If his conception of God be mere philosophy is it not the noblest man has ever known?" But as glorious as Christ would be were he merely human, that is not the whole story. He cannot be merely human; he must be divine. As Nicodemus noted, "We know that thou art a teacher come from God, for no man can do these miracles except God be with him." The same must be true of these teachings, Boyce reasoned. "If so, seek him first in that salvation which though so simple is most important. And be not satisfied until it works out in you the full salvation of the ethical system."[46]

The Designated, Covenantal Blood Work of Christ

The Atonement and the Person of Christ

Boyce summarized the teachings about Christ's person in twelve statements that included the following two: "This human nature was assumed because necessary to the work of salvation, it being impossible that a being only divine could undergo the experience necessary to redeem man." "There was here, therefore, no participation of the divine nature in the suffering." In a second summary of nine points, Boyce stated:

> This one person was, therefore, able to suffer and bear the penalty of man's transgressions, because, being of man's nature, he could become man's representative, and could also endure such suffering as could be inflicted upon man; yet, being God, he could give a value to such suffering, which would make it an equivalent, not to one man's penalty, but to that of the whole race.[47]

457

Boyce's catechism dealt with all the essential elements of how Christ's person fits the demands of salvation. After affirming Christ's voluntary offering of himself as a substitute, Boyce asked, "Did He suffer in both natures?" The answer? "No; in the human nature only. The Divine nature cannot suffer." The union of the divine and human was necessary, however, for "otherwise the human nature could not have sustained the sufferings it endured." In addition this union gave "value and efficacy to sufferings which, but for that union, would have been those of a mere creature." That could not have sufficed, for "every creature is bound, as his own duty, to do and suffer all that God wills, and therefore can do nothing to secure merit or pardon for others." The value of the death of Christ, however, is that it delivers "those for whom he died . . . from the guilt and punishment of all their sins."[48]

The Atonement and the Offices of Christ

In the work of redemption, Christ served in and fulfilled the offices of prophet, priest, and king. Boyce gave only four pages to this subject in his theology but stated clearly what is at stake in each of these offices. As prophet he revealed God, even before his incarnation, through various means that resulted in the Old Testament Scriptures, but supremely in his incarnation through his actions that manifest the divine attributes, his instruction on all subjects, and his holy living. As priest Christ made one offering, once for all, of himself, from which it gains its value, actually and effectively procuring forgiveness for "all for whom he died." He continues his priesthood through his present intercession. He is qualified for this by his sinless humanity conjoined with undiminished deity in one person who is in federal union with his people in order to be their substitute. As king he rules as a "Mediatorial king," that is, one that rules not only with the manifestation of justice and power but of mercy and compassion. He rules in the church, over the world, over the universe, and has all angels, men, and demons subject to him.

In his catechism, Boyce covered all these ideas under the subject "The Mediator." A mediator, Boyce taught, is "one who leads persons who are at enmity to become friends, or to be reconciled to each other." Christ serves in this capacity because "He comes between man and

God, and reconciles them to each other." He does this in the offices of "Prophet, Priest and King." Christ is prophet in that he "speaks for God, and Christ is the Great Teacher of Divine Truth." The priest had the duty "to offer sacrifice for sin, and to pray to God to pardon the sinner. Christ is in both these respects the High Priest of His people." As king, Christ "reigns in the hearts of saints and angels," is "King of the Universe" because he is called "King of kings and Lord of lords," a position to be acknowledged by all at the judgment day.

The Atonement, Covenant Blessings, and a Misrepresentation

Boyce's chapter on the atonement covers forty-six pages, the longest chapter in the *Abstract of Systematic Theology*. It precedes chapters on election, reprobation, outward and effectual calling, regeneration and conversion, repentance, faith, justification, adoption, sanctification, final perseverance of the saints, and four chapters concerning the last things. Failure to see all these manifestations of grace in their relation to the atonement has led to puzzling misapprehensions of Boyce's view.

Walter Draughon's treatment of Boyce's view of the atonement isolated five problems. First, he viewed it as a rationalistic presentation that makes God captive to his decrees and hinders his freedom in working on behalf of the world. "His sovereignty is separated from his grace."[49] It is hard to understand this objection as other than an intrinsic resistance to the necessity of penal substitution for the procurement of forgiveness. Grace flows abundantly from Christ's reconciling work and rather than inhibit God's freedom constitutes the most profound manifestation of the freeness of grace.

Second, Draughon maintained that "Boyce neglects the subjective aspect of faith in favor of the objective work of Christ on the cross." He depicted Boyce's view of faith as "an appendage to Christian experience, not an integral part of it."[50] What justifies this dichotomy and depiction in Draughon's perception is a mystery. For Boyce clearly discussed faith both as an acceptance of the facts of the gospel and as trust in the person of Christ. Far removed from Draughon's criticism, Boyce wrote that faith is based on the "knowledge of this testimony as given by our consciences and the word of God." It is truth apprehended by the mind, but as a spiritual truth "so it is apprehended spiritually by the heart." Since this faith occurs in the heart, "it must be the act of a regenerated heart which alone is inclined to such belief as constitutes trust."[51]

Three, Draughon concluded that Boyce's "emphasis on God's justice and law" led "to the neglect of mercy and love." Boyce, he said, failed to appreciate that God is both holy love and holy righteousness.[52] This conclusion tells more about Draughon's views than Boyce's. Boyce maintains the right integration of love and justice throughout his theology and particularly in his discussion of the atonement. Because of the atonement God's "electing love flows out freely" to his elect. "Christ did not die to make the Father love the Elect, but was given to die because of that love," and "Christ made full satisfaction to divine justice in order to render the exercise of love consistent with justice."[53] Boyce's five categories of love in God include a discussion of mercy, which "can be exercised only toward sinners." Then, arguing that one cannot emphasize one attribute at the expense of another, Boyce articulated, "When we say that this mercy must be exercised in accordance with the truth and justice of God, we say no more than is true of every attribute of God. No one can be exercised in such a way as to destroy another. Every one must be in harmony with the others."[54] Draughon has strangely mischaracterized Boyce.

Draughon's fourth objection has no more warrant than his first three: "Boyce's rational and objective atonement results in . . . the omission of the positive outcome of the atonement. . . . Man's fellowship with God suffers in his treatment."[55] But the positive outcome of the atonement includes not just forgiveness of sin, but positive justification, our adoption as sons, all the operations of the Spirit by which sinners are regenerated, and sanctified, or as Boyce stated, "the new covenant made in Christ, is one which includes not only the promise of the blessings, but of the establishment in his people of the conditions upon which these blessings depend."[56]

Draughon's fifth objection is too hackneyed, as well as demonstrably false, to be taken seriously. Boyce's view of "the sovereign will of God, the passivity of man, the objectivity of the atonement, and particular election produces an inadequate platform for missions and evangelism." In Boyce's view, then, "the Great Commission has no reasonable basis."[57] But Boyce's own preaching, his life, and his stated reasons for the founding of the seminary are sufficient refutation of this misrepresentation.

Boyce's Argument for Particular Redemption

Boyce began his discussion of Christ's death as he did several other chapters. He discussed alternate viewpoints that, in his estimation, fell short of the full biblical presentation. He rejected the Socinian theory, the moral influence theory, the Andover Seminary view, the Lutheran view, the Arminian view, and the view proposed by Andrew Fuller among others that the atonement is general in its nature but "limited in its application." To each of these Boyce gave a brief description and a point-by-point catena of objections. The Andover theology and the view of Fuller drew the most attention of these views. The Andover view was making rapid progress in American Christianity at the very time Boyce wrote, and he believed that "it is opposed by Scripture in every particular involved in it."[58] He gave space to Fuller's view because it was the closest to his, yet distinct in important particulars, and was held by many Baptists in the South in the nineteenth century.

The view Boyce intended to defend he described as "that of Calvin and the churches which he established. It is the theory of the Regular Baptists of the past. No other prevailed among those who have held distinctively Calvinistic Baptist sentiments until the days of Andrew Fuller."[59] He defined it by writing, "In the sufferings and death of Christ, he incurred the penalty of the sins of those whose substitute he was, so that he made a real satisfaction to the justice of God for the law which they had broken." Because of such a death, God now pardons all their sins, and being fully reconciled to them, "his electing love flows out freely towards them."[60]

Boyce divided his discussion of this definition into five affirmations. The first stated that "the sufferings and death of Christ were a real atonement." By this he meant that it was truly a sacrifice, not just symbolic, that procured the actual remission of sins. It secured salvation, not just the means of salvation. Drawing his conclusion from Scriptures quoted from the Old Testament as well as the New, Boyce reaffirmed that Christ, by his blood, "procured pardon, peace, redemption and remission of sins for those whom he represented."

Boyce's second point declared that "in order to make this atonement Christ became the substitute of those whom he came to save." He demonstrated that the theme of substitution permeated the Scripture account of God's making a way to accept his people. He particularly concentrated on those passages that speak specifically of Christ's substitute in his people's stead, for example, "Having become a curse for us"; "who gave himself for our sins"; "gave himself up for us"; "made to be sin on our behalf." Such substitution was possible and morally acceptable only because of the Christology discussed earlier. Christ possessed a human nature and a divine nature. He could, therefore, legitimately represent man and naturally infuse infinite value into his sacrifice. He came in just such a mysterious union of nature because he was designated by the Father to "be the legal representative of his people and their covenant head."[61]

Boyce's third assertion stated, "In so offering himself, Christ actually bore the penalty of the transgression of those for whom he was substituted." The first two assertions naturally involve this point by inference, but the idea of such a direct bearing of a penalty is affirmed by numerous Scriptures, Boyce showed. Those that speak of bearing iniquity mean "bear the penalty of iniquity." Passages throughout the Old Testament demonstrate this. The New Testament references to Christ's bearing sin, or iniquities, confirm it. Since Christ represented his people federally, their guilt was considered his and thus their punishment fell on him. "Thus," Boyce concluded, "it became fit that upon him God should inflict the penalty."[62]

These three points taken together lead ineluctably to the fourth point, "he made ample satisfaction to the demands of the law, and to the justice of God." Since Christ substituted himself for sinners, and bore their penalty, the satisfaction made was necessarily ample; "Christ could have made none that was not." Its ampleness is seen from the fact that the demands of the law have been fulfilled both negatively and positively, mercy and justice are reconciled, in the approval that the Father gave to Christ's work as verified in the resurrection, and in the statements made by "the sacred writers of the certainty of the salvation that is based upon it." The confidence with which sinners are urged to come before God, "with boldness unto the throne of grace," argues the ampleness of Christ's atonement. This ample atonement based on a satisfaction of the demands of the law, however, still operates as a purely gratuitous transaction from God to the sinner because it is founded in a premundane electing love and is made to render such love consistent with the demands of justice.

Fifth, Christ's atoning act constituted an actual reconciliation. It did not bring into being merely a way of reconciliation but enacted reconciliation. The Scripture presents Christ's death as the actual time in which redemption, reconciliation, and the deliverance from wrath took place. It did not merely make a way if we would comply, but was done while we were still enemies and guaranteed our compliance.[63]

What does all this mean about the extent of the atonement? How can such certainty for a particular group of sinners be made consistent with the universal offer of the gospel and the Scriptures that speak of Christ's death for the world? One answer to this dilemma is to assert pure universalism. An effectual atonement made for the world results in the salvation of all men. Boyce listed seven objections to that answer including "The descriptions of the judgment day deny universal salvation," and "The Scripture doctrine of Hell prepared for the punishment of the wicked shows it to be untrue."[64]

Boyce similarly listed five objections to the second answer, which makes the atonement itself general but limited only by the belief or unbelief of persons. Boyce's objections included "It does not accord with justice that any should suffer for whom a substitute has actually borne the penalty and made full satisfaction."[65]

The third answer is that the limitation of the atonement comes from divine purpose. God specifically intended it for the salvation of some and not of others. This view answers all the passages that indicate the limitation of the atonement's effects to a specified group of people. It does not, however, seem to satisfy the phenomenon of a universal offer nor the Scriptures that speak of Christ's death as for the world "and in such a way as to contrast the world at large with those who believe."[66]

Boyce followed A. A. Hodge in providing an answer to this apparent difficulty. Hodge said that the sufficiency of the atonement is such that it could "accomplish the salvation of all men, however vast the number." What would save one man would save another, for the "relations of all to the demands of the law are identical" and Christ's death has "removed all legal obstacles from the salvation of any and every man." He added that an incidental effect of the atonement is "to remove the legal impediments out of the way of all men, and render the salvation of every hearer of the gospel objectively possible." At the same time, the specific design in the death of Christ was to impetrate "the actual salvation of his own people, in all the means, conditions, and stages of it, and render it infallibly certain."[67]

Boyce added his own comments and affirmed that "Christ did actually die for the salvation of all, so that he might be called the Saviour of all; because his work is abundantly sufficient to secure the salvation of all who will put their faith in him." In this way the death of Christ opens the way for a sincere offer of the gospel to all who will accept the conditions he has laid down. In his chapter on final judgment Boyce asserted, "While the value of Christ's work is indeed ample for all, we are taught that its benefits are not bestowed upon all."[68] For the elect, however, Christ made, not a possible, but an actual salvation, for he has "obtained for them those gracious influences by which they will be led to comply with those conditions."[69]

Boyce believed his final formulation conformed to the nature of the atonement as described earlier and made room for the elements of the universal provision and offer indicated by many Scriptures.

A Final Observation

The reader may be excused if he is somewhat puzzled by Boyce's closing part of the discussion on atonement. It takes a turn that has every appearance of inconsistency with his earlier argument. He was insistent that the atonement did not render salvation possible, but absolutely procured it. Christ made a real sacrifice, was a real substitute, actually bore the penalty of sin so that nothing legal stands in the way of salvation, accomplished reconciliation of God to man, and thus procured all the means for the elect to be brought to forgiveness and justification. Nothing about his description made any gesture of congeniality toward a theoretical atonement, a mere pathway to be taken at the discretion of the sinner. That work of Christ which guarantees salvation, according to Boyce, and opens the floodgates of grace, including the effectuality of all means, was Christ's becoming a curse for us, his obedience to take on himself the demands of the law against us and thus remove its just penalty of condemnation.

The reader might well ask, then, how is it possible under Boyce's discussion of the nature of the atonement for him to write finally of a "means of reconciliation for all men, which removed every legal obstacle to their salvation" without its being effectual? They did not comply with the conditions, he answered. Ah, but compliance with the conditions is a blessing procured in a real reconciliation; forgiveness must come to all those for whom the legal obstacles have been removed. To conclude otherwise radically changes the nature of the atonement into something other than what Boyce described earlier. The reader might conclude, and this writer would concur, that Boyce has equivocated severely on his definition of atonement. It would have been much better to have found a consistent hermeneutic for the passages that speak of universal provision and offer, than to have become confusingly inconsistent on the doctrine upon which he desired the utmost clarity.

In spite of that unfortunate inconsistency, one can still ponder with pleasure the exhilarating magnitude of his description of the Savior, the Lord Jesus Christ, Son of God and Son of Man who alone can save us.

13

The Dying of James Petigru Boyce

Seminary Magazine (May 1888)
A quite remarkable session in the history of the Seminary has closed. A brief resume will not be out of place. To begin with, a larger number of students has been in attendance than ever before. Our present list, 158, is just a little more than that of any seminary of the country. This token of success is cause for thankfulness and renewed effort for the future. As will be seen from the catalogue, the patronage stretches over the entire country.

The session has also been signalized from the fact that in it we entered our new building, our future home. This alone will mark it off from the rest. In connection with this might be mentioned Dr. Boyce's special effort for an increased endowment. As a result of this we have seen little of him, which of itself is a loss to the boys. Other contingencies were Dr. Manly's accident, and Dr. Broadus' illness. With this session Dr. Kerfoot and Sampey became Assistant Professors.

Boyce's last year of teaching was 1886–87. H. H. Tucker, a trustee, editor of the *Christian Index*, and longtime friend, wrote after Boyce's death,

"This event of overwhelming sadness has been casting its dark shadow before it for two or three years. We all knew that our dear brother's health was failing and that a fatal result might be expected." The May 1887 meeting of the trustees produced a resolution of appreciation for Boyce that at once recognized the mammoth contribution that he had made and tacitly expressed concern that his work might soon be over:

> That the eminent ability with which Dr. Boyce has discharged the laborious & difficult duties of Treasurer of the Seminary for so many years, the many sacrifices he has made in behalf of the institution, & his continued untiring zeal in efforts to place it upon a solid foundation, as to endowment, buildings, & all appurtenances of a thoroughly equipped school for the education of our ministry, entitle him to the thanks of the Board of Trustees & of our whole denomination and we pray that God may spare him to prosecute to a successful issue the great work to which his life has been devoted & that he may live to see his fondest hopes realized.[1]

Later in that same meeting the trustees appointed a committee "to consider what can be done to relieve Dr. Boyce of care till his health can be fully restored. Dr. Pritchard, Hatcher, & Peter were appointed."[2] On hearing of this action, Boyce wrote the trustees that no amount of rest would restore him, but that he should resign outright from the positions he held as treasurer and professor. "I do not think that any rest would give restoration," he informed the board. "The disease under which I suffer is incurable. I can only secure relief from the attacks under which I suffer as each one comes."[3] Boyce requested, therefore, if he were to be relieved of teaching, that the trustees appoint F. H. Kerfoot as co-professor of theology.[4]

T. H. Pritchard recalled, after Boyce's death, what a difficult time the trustees had in finalizing plans to relieve Boyce of the fatal pressures on him. "The truth is," Pritchard remarked, "Dr. Boyce sacrificed his life for the Seminary." When the trustees saw how rapidly he declined and took action to vote him a year or two years away in Europe, "some of us had to go privately to his physician to prevail on him to persuade Dr. Boyce to take a rest." Even after he had consented, he delayed more than a year to finalize his work on finances.[5] The appointment of Kerfoot, however, gave a solid footing to the plan that Boyce finally could take his long-desired trip to Europe with his family.

Ten years earlier, in 1877, Kerfoot had been a candidate for a faculty position, but had instead gone to Eutaw Place Baptist Church in Baltimore. He had divided his theological education between Southern in Greenville, 1869–70, and Crozer for the final year of work. In 1872, he was in Kentucky when Boyce first moved there and encouraged Boyce in the work of raising an endowment, assuring him that in southern Kentucky "they that be for us are more than they that be against us."[6] He also had studied at Leipzig and traveled in Palestine and taught German at Georgetown College. Having returned to Kentucky to serve as pastor at Midway, he took an extra year of theological training at the seminary in Louisville during the year 1886–87 and then taught Systematic Theology in Boyce's stead during the year 1887–88.

When it became clear that Boyce would not return to the classroom, Broadus, Manly, and Whitsitt wondered who could fill the position permanently vacated in the classroom and curriculum by Boyce. They wrote to him in Europe to ask. Though he tried to show deference to his colleagues in this decision, Boyce had no thought of anyone but Kerfoot in that position. He responded that he had "thought over the matter." According to the bylaws he could express himself only as a member of the executive committee that made such nominations. The filling of that position would affect the present faculty personally much more than it would affect Boyce. Given those reservations, Boyce affirmed, "It is otherwise sufficient, I think, that it is understood that I favor the election of Dr. Kerfoot and think of no one who would better fill this place. I have no objection that it should be quietly known and understood that I should put him there if the appointment were solely in my hands."[7] Though he now had turned the future of the seminary over to other minds and hearts, he sought to perpetuate his own as much as providence and the bylaws would allow.

Some of his insistence might have been influenced by the glowing report on the effectiveness of Kerfoot that Broadus had put in the *Religious Herald* on September 13 and had included in a subsequent letter to Boyce. "He showed himself last year to be an excellent teacher," Broadus informed the readers of the *Herald*. He had used Boyce's brand-new text and, though he introduced the students to other books, he continued "that patient and repeated drill in the text book which has always characterized the teaching of Dr. Boyce, and which is so valuable for grounding the student in theological thought." Kerfoot also had striking talent for combing the metaphysical and logical with the practical, and loved "to pursue a thought to its utmost limits," engaging the students in "eager argument," while at the same time he never failed "to recognize gladly the paramount and final authority of Scripture." Kerfoot handled both Hebrew and Greek well, was apt in German, had significant pastoral experience and held a "village pastorate" while he taught.[8] All of these traits and practices fit well into Boyce's desire for the future and would have the effect of elongating his shadow into the future instruction and theology of the seminary.

The pure ardor of the work over the years had challenged Boyce's energy and strength, but its wearisome nature had been multiplied by the growing challenge of pain and a decaying constitution.

Joined by an Unwelcome Companion

Though battling intermittently with difficulties as early as 1871,[9] in 1870 Boyce enjoyed unintermitted vigor and had no thought of ever being anything other than robust. He wrote to an infirm Broadus in London that he was sorry that "the first news was one of bad health." He playfully encouraged Broadus to exercise by threatening to come over and "put myself in the post of physician extraordinary" and "prove most unmerciful in my exactions." That would involve walking with baggage on the back for "one, or two, or even five miles at first, then a gradual increase until you do your twenty to thirty miles a day. I can walk twenty now myself." Boyce thought, if he ever got the chance, it might be worth a try to "pretend to be sick" to enjoy female attention. "I am sure, however," he conceded, "that it is better to pretend than to be really sick."[10]

By 1872, Boyce had begun his fight with the pains of gout that in increasing measures would sculpt his schedule for the rest of his life. Just before moving to Louisville to prepare the way for the move of the seminary, Boyce wrote Broadus from New York, where he attended the American Baptist Educational Convention and the Crozer commencement. "My foot is improving fast," he noted, "and I hope in a few days to be well enough." He had seen his doctor about this problem, and he diagnosed the difficulty as "rheumatic and recommended Sulphur Springs."[11]

After less than a year's labor in Louisville, filled with struggle, humiliation, opposition, apparent failure, Boyce apologized to Broadus for the infrequency of his correspondence. He was "getting quite watchful of my health." His head was affected by "overwork," so he must limit his activities. "I feel that I must reserve all my strength for this work. When that is done I shall be satisfied if I can do no more." He sensed that his growing infirmities called for a purposeful concentration of labor. He told Warren Randolph "something of my health as an excuse for refusing extra work with them." Randolph appealed to Boyce "to stop everything at once and take a year's rest." It would make as much sense, Boyce jested, to "tell a poor man that he must live on dissolved pearls" as to tell Boyce to take off a year. Only two things could occupy his strength now. First, complete the endowment and settle the seminary in Louisville. Second, having done that, "do my professorial work." Should he in the future lose the opportunity of teaching theology, "I am willing to be laid aside." He could afford personally "to sit under the shade of the tree I have planted if I can no longer work."[12]

Letters to Broadus from Boyce as he labored in Louisville were frequently peppered with the difficulties that his unpredictable health caused. When the panic of 1873 severely diminished the hopes of financial success, Boyce increased the intensity of his labors. He wrote Broadus on 14 March 1874, "I have worked myself utterly down two or three times until I feared sickness, if not death. Then I have rested. My arm at times I can hardly move." Broadus wrote back a note of encouragement with advice to rest and a warning that "by living for the seminary you will, I am right confident, save it; by dying for it you inevitably kill it—buried in your grave."[13]

On 3 March 1875, Boyce mentioned a prolonged bout with pain and illness that had prohibited him from answering a request from Broadus for two gallons of whiskey. "I have been sick in bed for a week past," he explained; "out of bed yesterday for first day." Later he passed along the annoying diagnosis. "My sickness was not biliousness, but something worse, gravel. I fear that I may become a martyr to it. I have been pale from it for a long time. Had one attack fifteen years ago, but one of my family has suffered fearfully from it and I dread it." In January 1876, Boyce answered an urgent inquiry of Broadus a few days late because "I have been sick in bed. I have had two attacks since my return home. . . . From the latter I am out of bed today for the first time." In December he confided in Broadus that he had taken absolute rest for two days, even missing church on Sunday. The rest made him feel "quite well"; the main problem had been in his head "which seems to be fatigued by a particular kind of drudgery work, viz., writing names, numbers, or anything over and over again."[14]

Broadus reported the details of his preaching and attempts at raising funds in Baltimore during December of 1878. After describing the curious and intricate web of feelings and traditions and personal prejudices that he constantly had to take into account, he said, "People inquire anxiously after your health, having noted that you seemed unwell. I reply that you are about as well as common again." And then the telling phrase that recognized the intensifying problem, "My dear friend, we are both struggling with ill health, and carrying heavy burdens. May God sustain us, and help us through, and grant that we may live to rest a little while under the shadow of our completed work—if it please him."[15]

This trend of "struggling with ill health" continued and was mentioned by Boyce in a short note to Broadus six months later, June 1879. He had delayed a trip to Chattanooga because he was "still so bad off that I put off one day my departure." In light of his health he requested that Broadus not "make out too much work for me next Sunday. If I preach once, even that may be too much for me. I am excessively weak. Indeed, I should not like to preach at all next Sunday if that can be arranged." He had been doing well, but "on Friday last I had an attack of gout in the left knee joint, which put me back in my bed. I tried to rest, hoping that would do and that it was temporary pain." He took medicine, hoping for relief, which failed, and would have to take another dose the next day. Then he noted with irony: "The tables are turned. It was you who used to apologize for want of strength to do work, but

471

now it is I." Always finding God's will instructive, he closed, "Nevertheless, God knows what is best. I have no complaints. I love to be in His hands. And I feel this when He shows me that He can take away all strength and make even my best natural abilities worthless."[16]

The periods of difficulty increased both in frequency and intensity after 1881. Broadus recalled "increasing evidence of other disorder." On 21 October 1882, Boyce wrote Broadus, "My old enemy has me laid up in bed today. Can you teach my Bible class for me tomorrow at 9 ½ in the church in the pews just in front of the baptistery, simply talking to them about the lesson until 10:20 and then have a collection taken up and Deacon Woodruff will call the roll." Boyce would let him know if he began to feel better by 8:30, but he really had no hope of it. "I am already nauseated," he continued, "and shall be so tomorrow in all probability."[17] His labor in producing the classroom version of the *Abstract of Systematic Theology*, as well as work on new sermons for Broadway Baptist Church, added to his teaching and financial work, brought him to a physical crisis. "He began to suffer seriously."[18] On one occasion after preaching he "complained of a bewildered feeling in the head, and asked if he had said anything unsuitable." He could not remember what he had said for the last few minutes of the sermon.[19] In May of 1885 he informed Broadus that on his return from a trip he was "quite lame, too much so to wear my shoe (gout)."[20]

On 25 March 1886, Boyce received a cane of ebony and gold from his theology class. Presenting it for the class was David M. Ramsey, who thirty-eight years later, in 1924, delivered the Founders' Day address; it was entitled "James Petigru Boyce—God's Gentleman." Ramsey recalled the event, using it as an example of "the beautiful reciprocal affection existing between the student body and Dr. Boyce."[21] Boyce wrote Broadus about the gift, "My systematic class yesterday surprised me by the gift through Mr. Ramsey of a gold headed cane, a very handsome one." The gesture so completely surprised him that he could say only a few brief remarks of appreciation. He did not enjoy being virtually speechless and thus only later realized how by relating "cane" to "Canaan" and "canine" and similar words he could have made a humorous concatenation of ideas. Boyce saw the gift as a gesture of sympathy toward his increasing weakness. "I have been such a sufferer from gout for the past two weeks," Boyce informed Broadus, "that they evidently felt that I needed a good support in my declining years. God bless the boys. We do not know sometimes how kindly they think of us, in our consciousness of our shortcomings in many ways."[22]

A student in that class, C. H. Nash, referred to the incident in a letter to Broadus after the death of Boyce. The letter noted Boyce's response as well as the mutual affection that existed between Boyce and his classes.

> The Grand Old Man was taken completely by surprise, and was evidently much affected by the slight token of appreciation coming so unexpectedly. I never saw him so moved. His voice was partly choked by his emotion, as he replied somewhat brokenly. He said in substance that he appreciated the token of affection all the more highly because he had felt at times that he was not understood by his classes. His English and Latin Theology he knew must be hard and dry to many, while the method of reciting he required, and his examinations, were difficult. He said he knew that other subjects and teachers were more interesting, and he felt sometimes that his efforts were not appreciated, but that in his love and interest in his students and their success he yielded the palm to none. We were all touched, and tears glistened in many eyes.[23]

Ramsey saw the gift in light of another trial that Boyce suffered at this time. John R. Sampey, a full graduate of the seminary in 1885, was elected as an assistant instructor by the board in May 1885.[24] His graduation from seminary and his election as a teacher so nearly coinciding, it was arranged that he would be ordained to the gospel ministry. Ramsey narrates:

> When young Sampey was to be ordained at the Forks of Elk Horn Church in Central Kentucky, it transpired when the people had assembled for the ordination, that the candidate's church letter had not arrived from Alabama [Sampey was from Lowndes County, Alabama]. Dr. Boyce was in the ordination council. He advised that the church go forward with the ordination, which was done. This was

contrary to Baptist custom. At least certain brethren said so, and as a consequence a hot controversy followed in the *Western Recorder* which was very painful and embarrassing to Dr. Boyce. Doubtless some were honest in their contentions, but it was thought at the time others took opportunity of the incident to show bitterness to the Seminary and its great leader. To prove their sympathy, the class in Theology purchased a handsome walking cane and one day at the end of the class I was asked to present the cane. I did so in a few feeble remarks, referring to the unfortunate incident and the newspaper controversy, assuring the Doctor that the boys thought it all folly and that they were indignant. With that I reached under the desk and brought out the cane of ebony and gold, remarking that whatever other people might do, your boys are going to *stick* to you; and the stick was passed over the heads of the boys to the professor. He arose with every feature quivering with emotion and big tears chasing each other down his cheek. He said some very beautiful and appropriate things, but about all the boys could remember after it was over was that we all cried like babies. Leigh West said that he wanted to start a protracted meeting on the spot.[25]

This anecdote reveals a relationship between Boyce and the students that was mutually affectionate and respectful. Ramsey made much of the nickname the students gave Boyce, "Jim Peter," noting that they would never call him this to his face. They did not assume an easy familiarity with Boyce but "they counted him their unfaltering friend" and used the nickname as a term of endearment.

A Puzzling Opinion

Ramsey saw Boyce in a light startlingly different from the image given by William Heth Whitsitt in his diary.[26] Whitsitt presents an unsympathetic Boyce in his regard for student welfare. "Boyce," Whitsitt confided to his diary in November 1886, "was very unwilling to accept an additional burden of fifty dollars a month for the advantage of the sick students." The professors, according to Whitsitt, had to appeal to his vanity to convince him that his policy was "heartless and unfeeling." Ramsey recalled, however, his taking food to sick students from his own home, his loaning needy students money (and asking if they needed more), and his personal pastoral attention to them. Ramsey also recalled the faculty's support of Ernest Cook during a bout with typhoid fever. "Dr. Whitsitt sat around like a family cat but talked like a philosopher," while "the conversation of Dr. Broadus was so brilliant that it sometimes caused a rise of fever," not too high a price for such a pleasing privilege. But above all, Cook claimed he would "never forget to his dying day the sympathy, rest and peace 'Jim Peter' would bring with his visits."[27]

Whitsitt represented Boyce also as a Thanksgiving Scrooge, picturing him as opposing the celebration as a violation of the Baptist principle of separation of church and state. He mused:

> Nov. 20, Saturday, 1886. Manly has brought Boyce to the point of submitting to Thanksgiving Day and the Seminary will adjourn for the 25th inst. He opposes the union of church and state in that particular; but he is eager for a union of Church and State in the far more important business of getting quit of taxes on the Seminary property. This tax amounts to as much as fifteen hundred a year. After a man has stood up for that item of the union of church and state and enacted a lawsuit or injunction of some kind to prevent the city of Louisville from collecting taxes it would be preposterous to stickle for a separation of church and state in any particular; to say nothing at all of declining to observe the President's and the Governor's proclamation enjoining a day of Thanksgiving in the year.

Ramsey's recollections, again, give a different impression entirely. Stating that he wished to "relate an incident that illustrates the generosity of Dr. Boyce to the students," Ramsey recalled an event that probably happened the very Thanksgiving to which Whitsitt referred. When Ramsey managed the student living facility in the Waverly Hotel, a few days before Thanksgiving he received a note from Dr. Boyce instructing him to make arrangements for a Thanksgiving dinner for the resident students. "Let the turkeys be fat and let there be abundance of cranberry, celery, fruits, and nuts, and be kind enough to send me the bill," he wrote. Ramsey recalled that he followed his instructions "without stint," piled up quite an expense for the meal, and presented it hesitatingly to Boyce. Boyce adjusted his glasses, examined the bill, and said, with genuine paternal interest, "Why, Brother Ramsey, this bill is entirely too small, I fear you did not get enough for a good dinner."[28]

If Boyce suspected Whitsitt of holding a condescending and disrespectful attitude toward him, it does not appear in the correspondence. His references to Whitsitt were friendly and positive. He had confidence in Whitsitt as a scholar and enjoyed the energy he put into managing the student fund. In fact, it appears that Whitsitt held his attitude in such privacy that none suspected that his respect for the chairman of the faculty was low. Whitsitt brushed closely against the borders of hypocrisy in his external and public deference for Boyce while festering with judgmental evaluations in private. One might wonder if Boyce's struggle with his health contributed to Whitsitt's startling secret disdain for Boyce.

Whitsitt believed that Broadus had "studied all the weaknesses of Boyce," who would "do nothing unless he has the honor to initiate it." When Broadus made a suggestion in November 1886 for improvement of the living conditions for the students, it was placed, according to Whitsitt, in the entirely plausible context that Boyce himself had initiated and effected it and should receive all the credit for it; "this view of the case tickled Boyce's vanity." Having opposed the measure before, with this happy shift of perception "Boyce was now more enthusiastic than any of us; he was at the head of the enterprise and his vanity was content." Whitsitt believed this vice to be useful in many ways, for it guaranteed Boyce's concentration on projects for the seminary's good. "He is very weak indeed in any other department, and often very weak in that department," Whitsitt wrote, "but he is truly industrious there."

Three months later on 1 February 1887 Whitsitt noted: "Missionary Day. A heavy sleet fell during the night. The annual scare regarding an overflow of the river is now on. Boyce is down with another attack of the gout, since Sunday. I called on him as I went to church at night." Near the end of the teaching year, 1887, Whitsitt recorded his perceptions of a faculty meeting in the home of Basil Manly:

In the evening [11 April 1887] I attended a Faculty meeting at Dr. Manly's. Many topics were discussed. Among other things it was given out that Mr. Bostwick had given the Seminary the sum of Twenty-five Thousand dollars. He has imposed the condition that the sum must be shortly raised to $100,000 and Broadus is hoping to accomplish that addition when he visits New York next Sunday. He is the most powerful influence among the Baptists of America, going a thousand miles ahead of any of his colleagues. Boyce does not relish this condition of affairs very well; therefore Broadus is compelled to walk a trifle circumspectly after achieving a great success. It was he who induced Bostwick to give this money. He is the head and front of the concern.

A year earlier, Broadus had made a major triumph in New York for the financial security of the seminary, but at that time lacked the participation of Mr. Bostwick. Boyce sent earnest and joyful congratulations to Broadus for this accomplishment. "Dear Brother," he wrote, "I am much disappointed that I have to leave just as you are about to make your triumphal entry into the city. Yet I rejoice not only in your success, but also in your having accomplished before I leave home."

Now with the Bostwick participation, other springs for financial success began to flow. In 1887, the trustees expressed their thanks to Bostwick and informed him of their purpose "to make immediate efforts to meet those conditions." There is little if any evidence that Boyce felt chagrined at the success of Broadus in any of his various accomplishments or that he was unwilling for Broadus to be publicly and universally applauded for the profundity of his gifts. Boyce knew that Broadus would accomplish more in some situations than he could accomplish and did not hesitate to send him for that purpose. The judgments of Whitsitt must surely have been colored by the increasing weakness of Boyce physically and the accompanying distress this caused Boyce at his inability to shoulder the load as he had in the past. The smallness of character in Boyce suggested by Whitsitt's comments cannot be inferred from the abundance of evidence and must reflect an interpretation arising from a narrow and self-concerned field of personal experience.

Strategy to Stay the Tide

Prior to the fall term of 1886, Boyce went with his family to the mountains of North Carolina. He had worked himself into a low state of health. "My health not very good. Rest will be all I need, and I shall take three weeks of it."[29] On his return, in an effort to get his theology text ready for publication, Boyce began to spend long hours from 5 A.M. until 11 P.M. of unbroken work with little exercise. His daughter reported that "he would frequently become so exhausted that he could scarcely hold himself erect in his chair."[30] His family urged his physician, Dr. Holloway, to "use his authority and put a stop" to Boyce's intense work on the book. Holloway agreed and warned Boyce that no one could endure such strain without shortening his life. One evening at midnight, Boyce had what his daughter called a "heart attack" that made him gasp for breath and turned his complexion "so ashy that he presented a most alarming appearance." He recovered, but could endure little exertion without a painful shortness of breath.[31]

Lizzie made observations about the sickness that she hoped would dispel some misconceptions as to its origin. "Father, being a man of rather large size," she noted, "was always annoyed by hints that this trouble was caused by high living. He was really a small eater and could diet more severely than anyone I have ever known." She called the source of his chronic difficulty with rheumatism "poverty of the blood." When attacks of gout first began, they "were at long intervals," but eventually "they began to be more frequent." For the final two years, "he was laid up every two weeks." Patience and industry characterized his times of physical inactivity due to an attack. He consoled himself with his books, having them piled beside him on the table and on his bed. "He would write letters by the quantity," Lizzie revealed, "and seemed to us to accomplish as much in a certain way as when well."[32]

Following his birthday in January 1887, he wrote his sister, "I feel very young, indeed, except when the gout seizes upon me and fills me with despair." The moments of unhealthy and painful adversity had increased and brought about longer periods of inability to accomplish anything. To his publishers he lamented, "I find the progress of my book very much impeded by my health, or rather want of health. I shall be forced to do one of two things,—proceed as best I may, and leave out much new matter I wish to introduce, or delay as long as necessary to complete what I wish." As he came nearer to publication, he wrote Joseph E. Brown in June requesting permission to dedicate the book to him as "the only way I have ever had of testifying to my high esteem and affection for you, or of showing my gratitude for your many kindnesses to my work, the Seminary."[33]

On April 2, Boyce cleared up some financial issues with Broadus, letting him know that he would pay the cost "for the whole repairs" involved in painting and other improvements to his home. In addition, he enclosed the agent's fee for portions of the contribution of John D. Rockefeller. In 1883, Broadus had requested that he receive a commission for the work done in raising money. "I don't know but the Seminary ought to pay me a small commission for this work, which has cost me much exertion and some care," he wrote. When he could earn money by preaching and writing, he was unwilling to receive anything from collections, but now "I am straitened, and trying to rest for the Seminary's sake as well as my own, and should not refuse it."[34] Boyce concurred and faithfully sent Broadus his commission on this occasion: "I enclose your draft for one hundred dollars, being for last two payments of John D. Rockefeller, one received this week and one last week, each $2000. Total, $4000. 2 ½%, $100. Subscriptions sent March 23rd and March 29th." Then the reminder of the evil companion that clung to him with only brief periods of relief during these years: "I have managed to get up today but shall have to go back to bed. I am far from well and am threatened with another attack. Have had worst attack I have had in two months."[35]

In May, a nomenclature change in regard to Boyce's relation to the school was proposed in the faculty report to the trustees. Whitsitt recorded on 2 May 1887, "Broadus approached me at the meeting of the Missionary Society this morning to mention the fact that Boyce is solicitous to have his title altered. Ever since the year 1859 he has been called Chairman of the Faculty, but he now desires to be called President of the Southern Baptist Theological Seminary." Broadus asked Whitsitt to sign a petition to the board of trustees requesting the change. Broadus composed the petition.

From the interesting, but often biased and somewhat unreliable, realm of anecdotal history comes a story of conflict between Boyce and Broadus on this issue. Broadus honored the tradition of the University of Virginia's commitment to the faculty method of administration. Boyce, as a business entrepreneur and estate executor, felt that more decisive authority was needed in a single head. The change had been discussed for two years in the faculty with strong points of disagreement left unresolved. Forty years later, the wife of E. Y. Mullins told W. O. Carver "that there was some jealousy and rivalry between Dr. Boyce and Dr. Broadus on this point." Supposedly the fragility of Boyce's health made Broadus generously yield and bring the faculty to issue a unanimous request to the trustees.[36]

Boyce had a high view of the benefits of any institution having a president. He had observed its influence, for good or ill, in the business world with the many positions held by his father on boards including the presidency of a bank. Beyond that, he had observed its beneficial effects in educational institutions. In relation to businessmen who were possible donors, they understood much more clearly the title "President" than the title "Chairman of the Faculty." Moreover, in the matter of vision and practical impact, a president held the authority to create immediate action. The charmed fellowship that had worked and cooperated so felicitously as a faculty could be upset quickly by the addition of one or two who did not share the same fellow-feeling or the fullness of vision about the purpose of the theological institution. Boyce had observed and learned about educational presidencies from Francis Wayland and Basil Manly Sr. In his funeral sermons for Manly, Boyce gave insight into his positive feeling about the influence of the presidential position.

> As a College President, Dr. Manly was undoubtedly one of the most successful. In this respect he will bear full comparison with his beloved friend, the lamented Wayland. Differing in many particulars, both intellectually and physically, located under different influences, entirely unlike in the character of their pulpit efforts; they were re-

markably similar in their administrative capacity, and in the impress they left upon the educational interests in their respective sections. They were both, in the fullest sense, the Presidents, the controlling spirits of their respective Universities. The students, the faculty, the very Board of Trustees looked up to them as to the heads, by which all was to be governed. Neither of them could have brooked any other position. The responsibilities of their office were felt, and in bearing its responsibility they felt that they must exercise its authority.[37]

Why should the same not be true of a seminary? The controlling spirit, viewed by all concerned as the head, the governor, would leave a definite impression on the educational interests of an institution. If one feels the responsibilities of the office, why should he not exercise its authority? Besides, it would not be so much for Boyce himself that this nomenclature change would be effected. He was near death, the time of his departure had come. But for the future, considering the changes that were imminent in faculty relationships, the age and experience differences that soon would become manifest, such a rearrangement seemed most healthy for the school's future.

The faculty report containing this petition came before the full body of trustees by way of committee on 6 May 1887: "We would also advise the changing of the name of the presiding officer of the Seminary from Chairman to President."[38] This item was referred to a special committee with instructions to report at the trustee meeting the next year. At the meeting in 1888, the special committee reported:

> That they have maturely considered the questions submitted to them, and inasmuch as it does not appear that the name of the presiding officer is an essential part of the plan of organization of the Seminary and as it is not now proposed to enlarge the powers, or to increase the responsibilities of the Officer, but to leave the administration and government of the Seminary as heretofore in the hands of the Faculty with equality of rank and position: Your com. Therefore recommend that the request of the Faculty be complied with and that the name of their presiding officer be changed from Chairman to President.[39]

481

If one concedes the disunity within the faculty with regard to the administrative implications connected with this change, that explains both the delay of one year for a committee to study it and the strong caveats within the proposal that this change leave the "administration and government of the Seminary as heretofore in the hands of the Faculty with equality of rank and position." The change of title, however, eventually would alter the nature of the position.

A "generous friend and benefactor" of the seminary, Nimrod Long, died in April, and the trustees in May voted that a memorial notice of his generosity be preserved in the records of the seminary. Boyce wrote his widow a letter expressing his deep sympathy as well as his appreciation for the Christian witness of her husband's life. This death served as a sobering reminder of Boyce's own teetering mortality as well as the unchanging hope of redemptive immortality. He reminded the family of Long's "zeal for God, and love for his brethren and his faith." Though Boyce esteemed him highly and felt the honor of his friendship, he knew that the loss brought a real anguish to those who knew his "intimate fellowship and strongest affections." None that knew him well, however, can grieve as those that have no hope, for "we shall see him again where there will be no parting forever." As he has gone into the "blessed state of the righteous who die in the Lord," so too must we all "soon follow." "May we be as well prepared," Boyce proposed, "May it be to us as great a joy as is his!"[40]

In June, Boyce planned two trips. First he wanted to go to Russellville, Kentucky, to visit Mrs. Long. His life interrupter appeared again, however, and made him change his plans. "An attack of gout yesterday kept me from Russellville," Boyce wrote on June 8. The second still seemed possible, a trip to Providence, leaving at 2 P.M. on Friday to attend the fortieth anniversary of his Brown graduating class.[41] An unexpected delay in departure for that trip, however, meant that he would have to travel on Sunday, so he canceled it. In his absence, the university awarded to Boyce the honorary degree LL.D. Though Boyce had received the same honor earlier from Union University in Jackson, Tennessee, he expressed his deep gratitude to E. G. Robinson, Brown's president. "There is no institution which could give me a degree," he wrote, "that would be as highly prized as one from Brown."[42]

Among Baptists in the South, the physical condition of Boyce drew wide attention, particularly since he had appeared so feeble at the convention meeting. Broadus wrote a newspaper article explaining the ongoing context of his chronic struggles and suggesting that the future held hope for increased vigor.

> So much concern has lately been expressed in the newspapers as to the health of Dr. James P. Boyce, that there is a danger of misapprehension. Some four years ago he was seriously run down while preparing and printing (for the class only) his Abstract of Theology; but when the task was completed he rapidly regained his strength. During the past session he has been carefully rewriting and enlarging this work, which is to be published shortly by H. M. Wharton & Co. . . . This heavy labor has made more frequent Dr. Boyce's attacks of a chronic and not fatal disease, and when the Convention met, he was looking quite badly. But the book is now (June 15) finished, and nearly all printed, and he already looks much better. With the relief he will get from the appointment of Dr. Kerfoot as co-professor, if he can carry through, before the end of this year, his present efforts to increase the endowment, and can next year gratify a long-cherished desire to take his family to Europe, there is every reason to believe that Dr. Boyce's health will again be quite vigorous.[43]

In reality, very few reasons existed to make anyone confident about the future health of Boyce. Boyce had his own doubts. Broadus wrote Boyce on July 19 about getting a permit to drive in Cave Hill Cemetery, for Boyce had recently arranged for the seminary to have a lot there. "They are willing to give this [a permit to drive] to one person representing an institution," Broadus reminded Boyce, "but must have written authority from the person holding the title to the lot." Boyce evidently was preparing for what he felt could be in the near future.

In July, he composed his last will and testament. Having been oppressed all his adult life with the administration of his father's will, having to manage a dizzying variety of investments with specific instruction given concerning their disposal, Boyce made his as simple as possible. He had no inventory made of his estate, but simply left everything to his wife and three daughters with the four of them serving as executors with absolutely full power. After any debts were paid, his wife would receive one-third of the estate and the daughters would each receive two-ninths. He made it clear, "my intention being to leave my executors with as absolute authority to disperse of and divide out my estate to the parties herein named as heirs or legatees as I myself would have."[44] This was signed on 25 July 1887 and witnessed by John A. Broadus and S. B. Richardson.

Later that month, Boyce left with his family for a trip to the Northwest. His oldest daughter, Lizzie, provided notes on the trip, at the request of John A. Broadus. In the flow of effusive descriptions of the beauty of the land and the wonder of natural phenomena, she remarked frequently about the physical condition of Boyce. Lizzie wrote, "We all look back upon this trip as most satisfactory in many respects. He had begun to show signs of his health breaking down completely." Lizzie saw him as "overburdened" and "overworked." The relief from "papers and the daily tasks of finances, teaching administration, and public relations eventually had an excellent effect on him," and he soon "commenced to look like a different man." Her opinion was that the trip "prolonged his life."[45] At one point in the trip, Boyce's perception of his progress differed from the observations of Lizzie. On August 28 he wrote Broadus from Tacoma in the Washington Territory:

> I thank you for the two letters sent me at Chicago. I have not yet seen Louisville papers later than Aug. 15th. . . . I am getting along very well in travelling but find no improvement in health except that my attacks of gout are slighter. But I have had catarrhal cold continuously since leaving home which however is much better now. It has been getting better for past week. Yesterday I bought at Portland some woolen flannel for my Alaska trip, so that I may not be cold. Our boat leaves Port Townsend for Alaska Tuesday the 30th at 12 M. The trip will take us two weeks or a day or two more than that. We shall not therefore be at Louisville before the 25th of September or thereabouts, and if we go to Yellowstone Park we shall be at least ten days from this point back to Louisville.[46]

Boyce also commented on the reception he received from different ministers along the way. He heard "a very excellent sermon" from

Rev. Mr. Mal Lafferty from Tacoma and was treated kindly by him as well as by "brothers at San Francisco, and Portland." In San Francisco he visited with Jesse Hartwell, a missionary who had served in China since 1858 and would spend thirty-five years there. Boyce found himself "much interested in his work." In Los Angeles the Boyces met some old friends from Furman University. He had been asked to preach on several occasions but noted, "I have refused persistently to preach though I was so strongly tempted to do so this morning and might have yielded but for the entreaties of my wife and Lizzie, who thought I should not risk my throat with the present catarrh."[47]

The cruise to Alaska was exhilarating, and Boyce returned quite encouraged. "I think I have been somewhat improved by my trip," he wrote to Broadus, and included several items of evidence for his positive view. "I have had no attack of gout over a month past," though he had felt tendencies to it, and had not been prevented from eating by his medicine. He had in fact gained more than seven pounds from 165 to 172½. His spirits were lifted by the magnificent beauty of Alaska, as beautiful as the most scenic vistas he had seen in the Northeast.[48]

Overall, the trip had a positive effect on Boyce's health so that upon his return, though he did not reenter the classroom, he did some work to continue raising the endowment. This brief brush with renewed health, however, could not shut out the reminders that his physical spiral continued down. In November, he wrote Broadus with information about the endowment work and his health:

> I have been delayed from time to time hoping to send a better report. But this morning I leave Richmond for South Carolina Convention at Sumter so I state for your eyes only what I have done. Including what was done at the general association at Virginia not quite $6000 of which $3217 is from Richmond. I have canvassed all Richmond except Grace Church, and a very few others. Hatcher delayed giving me his list, by accident, until Saturday at which time I was sick and since which I have done nothing, an attack of my old enemy, my slight horror."

From Virginia, Maryland, Tennessee, North Carolina, and Missouri Boyce had obtained in cash and promises over $14,000 for the endowment along with confidence that the final account from the South would amount to $25,000 or $30,000.[49]

Boyce's sister Mary C. Lane wrote him in December expressing concern over a report she had heard that he showed signs of great weakness in Richmond. He wrote to assure her that his health was better than it had been in two years. The trip to the Pacific Coast, he was convinced, had been a genuine boon to his vitality. He appeared to be weak in Richmond only because he took such good care of himself, refusing to work more than five hours a day. She would soon see that he speaks the truth when he comes to New York unless he experiences a relapse, of course. Should that happen, Boyce would be content, for his work "for the Seminary is almost done. I can leave it," he continued, "very soon beyond all ordinary risk." He believed that he had put the Boyce estate in such a condition "as will give little trouble to any of you, should I die." He had just a bit to do to finalize the orderliness of his own financial affairs, but that alone, apart from love for family and friends, made him care to live any longer.[50]

From January 8 to February 12 a protracted meeting under the leadership of Dwight L. Moody continued in Louisville. The meeting facility was built at a cost of $12,000 on seminary property between Fifth and Sixth Streets. The large facility overflowed so that two churches had to be used for overflow meetings. Students worked in the campaign and "derived great good . . . from the experiences gathered by personal work in and out of the inquiry room."[51] A student, J. F. Williams, noted that "the presence of Mr. Moody in Louisville has been a rare opportunity for the Seminary students in instruction in that branch of duty in which many ministers are so deficient—how to talk intelligently and effectively to the unconverted."[52]

The Tide, Nevertheless, Rises

The onset of winter brought a new decline of health for Boyce as well as a stark reminder as to how fragile one's safety is on a daily basis. His longtime friend and colleague Basil Manly Jr. received a blow to the head from thieves who attacked him as he walked from the railway station to his house in the suburbs of Louisville. This blow seriously compromised the health of Manly and eventually resulted in his death four years later. Whitsitt recorded in his diary for 21 February 1888: "The faculty had a meeting at 10 A.M. in Room 102 the first they ever held in the new building [New York Hall]. Boyce was not able to attend; his health appears to be declining gradually." At the May trustee meeting Boyce was granted "leave to be absent till Dec. 1890."[53]

This decline continued throughout the spring and early summer. P. H. Mell, a Southern Baptist statesman, perennial convention officer, preacher, theologian, and educator had died earlier in 1888, so Boyce again received the vote of his brethren to take the gavel at the May meeting of the Southern Baptist Convention. "The name of J. P. Boyce, having been placed in nomination," the minutes recorded, "on motion of J. D. Stewart, Ga., it was resolved to elect a President by a rising vote." And on doing so, they "did unanimously elect JAMES P. BOYCE, KY., President of the body."[54] Broadus recalled, "He presided in manifest bodily weakness, but with all the high courtesy and cordiality of former years."[55] Lansing Burrows, also at that meeting, remembered an event of peculiar poignancy. The attempt of some to have the convention express itself with "unusual emphasis" on the issue of temperance was ruled out of order by Boyce since the constitution did "not provide for discussion of the subject."

> Then arose a contention that was exceedingly painful to the friends and lovers of the old hero, who with his face drawn by the tortures of the disease that within the year was to lay him low, with his characteristic courtesy and courage maintained himself against a veritable onslaught. It was again the man with the rapier contending with the man with the bludgeon. There were men who claimed to have within their veins the blood of the cavaliers who stung with an assumed courteousness and poisoned with a pseudo-gentle demeanor. With their boasted powers of elegant Addisonian English they aspersed the sincerity of their president. The lapse of twenty years has not effaced my recollection of that strong, sad, wan face, immovable in determination, but plainly smitten with an unutterable grief at the animadversions of wild and intemperate men. The Convention sustained the chair in the point of order.[56]

487

By the summer, Boyce's family and doctor had prevailed on him to plan a trip to Europe. They viewed this as the only possibility for extending his life beyond six months. His sister Mary Lane died in July. Boyce could not arrange to be at the funeral. This sadness and personal disappointment coupled with his preparations for leaving took a malignant toll on his strength, put him into a "most alarming condition," and almost brought about a cancellation of the trip. Once they had begun, however, he, along with his wife and daughters, made the trip across with little trouble but with no evident improvement in health. He wrote his sister Mrs. C. L. Burckmeyer from the ship, "The feeling of sadness natural to our starting off to be absent for so long a time has naturally been increased by the condition of my wife's health and my own, and by the death of our dear sister." Nevertheless, Boyce determined to rest himself "entirely upon the care and protection of our Heavenly Father, knowing that he not only knows what is best, but will assuredly will what is best." To Dr. and Mrs. Peter, dear Louisville friends with whom Boyce had lived for a year, he confessed, "I am very weak, and can hardly crawl up on the deck. Walking even a short distance, with the uncertain footing one has on the boat, is very fatiguing."[57]

Once in Liverpool, Boyce took a quick trip to London to arrange money matters for their stay. While there, his horse fell and his coach tipped over, throwing him to the ground. Since he was unhurt, he looked on this as great fun and enjoyed regaling his family with a point-by-point reenactment of the event, even the gathered crowd's enthusiastic response to his generous throwing of pennies in gratitude for their lifting him back to his coach. Doctors who examined him later said that it was a miracle that he did not die on the spot.

The family traveled to Glasgow and attended various events at an exposition opened by Queen Victoria, a "haughty-looking woman" in Lizzie's opinion. Edinburgh, Stirling, Abbotsford, the Highlands, and the English lake country were on their itinerary. During all this Boyce only rarely saw any of the sights but "sat patiently in the carriage . . . and only occasionally venturing to move about a little when feeling particularly bright and well."[58]

In London, Boyce did manage to visit the National Gallery and attend the Metropolitan Tabernacle. According to Lizzie's record of the trip, these events gave genuine pleasure and spiritual excitement to Boyce. She recalled how Boyce consistently cultivated his taste in art by frequent visits to art exhibitions. "On his visits to New York," she remembered, "no matter how busy he might be, he always found time to go to the galleries and taking a catalogue he would walk from picture to picture carefully studying them and making constant notes." Boyce collected "engravings and autographs of many famous works of art," and in studying them would say, "Well some of these days when our ship comes in we will go and see the pictures themselves." In London he did just that. Lizzie observed, "He went from room to room as in a dream lost in admiration of the great masterpieces. He finally sat down in front of a picture by Landseer" and expressed his perfect enjoyment of an abundantly fulfilled anticipation. The paintings excelled his expectation, and "there was nothing to mar his pleasure."[59]

He found Spurgeon having to give a partial surrender to the ravages of gout as he sat during the delivery of his sermon. Spurgeon received Boyce warmly and asked him to speak at the Pastor's College. Boyce told Spurgeon that he was there, in part, to see a Dr. Garrod, a world authority on "gout and kindred diseases." Spurgeon, just on the heels of the Downgrade Controversy, had found no help in his fight with the malady but hoped that Boyce might find it to be different. During the visit, Boyce "was so much excited by this interview with the great preacher that he became pale and exhausted, and began to pant for breath; so we had to cut short our stay, and leave for the hotel." Boyce commented on leaving, "How little I have accomplished, compared with that man! If I can only get well and live a few years longer, I'll make greater efforts."

A telegraph on October 19 from his brother-in-law and longtime friend, H. Allen Tupper, informed him of the death of Tupper's wife and Boyce's sister Nancy, called Nannie. He had prepared himself for the death of Mrs. Lane but this news "was like thunder at noonday from a cloudless sky." Two deaths in three months made him ask, "How soon may we not look for others?" Nevertheless he felt deep gratitude for the decades of sweet happiness they had enjoyed as a family and the evidence of grace that so pervaded each of the homes of those who had died.[60]

From Louisville, Boyce heard news from his dear friend Broadus. Writing on September 19, he included not only points of interest about the seminary but a report on a review of Boyce's newly published *Abstract of Systematic Theology*. Broadus called the review "very gratifying" as it came from a man who obviously was a man of some ability. The high commendation the reviewer gave was only accentuated by "his objections to your Calvinism," and the attention he gave to Boyce's treatment of recent views of the atonement showed that he had examined the argument carefully.[61] Broadus included an article he had written for the *Religious Herald* in which he quoted the *Independent* review and then commented: "Dr. Boyce's *Abstract of Systematic Theology* has received a most remarkable commendation from one of the leading American papers, *The Independent*." In addition to quoting the writer's objections to Boyce's Calvinism, Broadus quoted the reviewer's overall verdict: "The whole is done in a clear, strong and manly way, with no evasion of difficulties, no sentimental coloring or softening, but everywhere bold, honest thinking, expressed in plain, vigorous and excellent English." Though the reviewer believed that readers subsequently might modify the theological system learned from it, those that take seriously the discipline of the method "will have here a robust and fundamental schooling that must invigorate their philosophy."[62]

Broadus's article also informed the public how the seminary would care for the instruction of the increasing number of students. This served as an antidote to the report that the seminary now had "too many students." "Former students," Broadus wrote, "and those who are coming may like to know that special plans are laid for next session to handle some of the larger classes by frequent division into sections." He explained how this would affect the method of instruction, provide more individual time for instruction, allow the homiletics grading to have the intense attention necessary, and provide an encouraging opportunity to form "inspiring special friendships, and become pleasantly acquainted with large numbers of those who are to be among their most useful contemporaries in all parts of the country." In addition, Dr. A. T. Robertson had been added as an instructor in Greek. He and Dr. John R. Sampey would greatly aid in assimilating the large number of students into a challenging academic experience.[63]

Broadus's letter to Boyce gave bits of information about each of the faculty members and how they were carrying on with the special assignments they had. Whitsitt in particular had a challenging task in front of him with his responsibility for the student fund. They expected up to 190 students to enroll. Manly had some work to do to finish his part of managing the student fund if Whitsitt was to begin with a clean slate. "Manly is a noble man," Broadus conceded, "but this weak health simply aggravates his tendency to delay." In addition, Whitsitt was working hard "to have all the State Conventions of importance attended." "I am urging that the trips away must be managed with the least possible loss to the instruction," Broadus stated, knowing that Boyce would agree wholeheartedly, "for I think the Seminary stands on trial, as to whether we can really handle so many students." The Sampeys were well again, Whitsitt's children had passed beyond the crisis stage of whooping cough, A. T. Robertson was revitalized by the Virginia Springs, and "My own health is much improved and I am trying to make out 3 weeks of entire rest." Boyce Broadus, Broadus's son, had been sick but was much improved and also was pleased with Latin. His wife and girls liked Chautauqua "much better than they had imagined, and of course enjoyed the New England trip."

Boyce responded. He appreciated all the news items sent by Broadus, particularly the review of the *Abstract* in *The Independent*. He gave copies of his book to Joseph Angus and also to Charles Spurgeon, hoping to receive some word from them concerning its usefulness. Angus responded with a complimentary note about the book and invited his family on a London tour with himself as guide. Boyce declined. He asked Spurgeon to give mention to the book in the *Sword and Trowel*. "Be on the look out for it," Boyce requested. Spurgeon would give a critical assessment "according to its merits without favor or disfavor. I am therefore the more anxious to see what he will say about it."[64]

News from the seminary greatly pleased Boyce, particularly its prospects for advancing enrollment. He felt perfectly free to offer his advice on all issues that Broadus mentioned. He was "anxious to find out that Manly has raised the money for the deficiency in the student's fund and to hear how Whitsitt gets on with the heavy task he has assumed and especially to know that Kerfoot is succeeding in

lifting the burden which I took from my shoulders and laid upon his."
Certainly faculty members should remain at their posts at all times
and not omit recitations.[65] He showed some anxiety that the student
fund be handled promptly. On October 31 he again expressed concern
about it. "I am glad to hear of the increase of students," he remarked,
but such increase added to the urgency of Manly finishing his business
with the student fund. "I am anxiously awaiting the result of Manly's
appeal," but he feared for its success. The general public "too often
look with indifference on one who had thus sacrificed. The only way
is to keep it ignorant of how much is the need and get the money as
it becomes practicable."[66]

Students must receive far more than financial sustenance. They
should not think that they can be graduated without doing all requirements in a timely fashion. A student named Goldsmith sought to come
to graduation without having written his commencement paper, and
for some reason, he thought Broadus complied with his request. "I
think it will be wise to let the candidates for graduation understand
the preparation of a commencement piece, at least in some degree
acceptable, must have been accomplished and the piece in the hand of
the professor of Homiletics by mid-day of March 13th," Boyce commented. He added that the faculty should see "the doing of this as a
'sine qua non' to graduation and that positively no diploma of full
graduate will be given to anyone who had not so done."[67] In a subsequent letter Broadus concurred, with a mild caveat, "I shall bear in
mind what you say about greater strictness in maintaining rules. I do
not remember any conversation with Peter Goldsmith, but he certainly
managed to misunderstand me seriously. I determined while arranging
with Dr. Whitsitt last spring, to begin about the graduating addresses
much earlier another session, and it will be very well to have the
faculty fix a definite time from which I shall not feel at all liberty to
vary."[68] Boyce knew of course that the fault lay with Goldsmith, not
with Broadus: "The Goldsmith matter is about as I feared. I did not
state it too strongly. He said that he had to be absent preaching and
had examinations, etc., and that you agreed on that account he might
take time until these were over." Boyce loved all his "boys" but he did
not want to encourage any kind of irresponsible behavior.[69]

Though Boyce expressed his views concerning all matters of the seminary with strong conviction, he saw more clearly than ever "the impossibility of my ever again laboring personally in the instruction of the Seminary. It is as well also that my colleagues should begin to know that this is true without any possible contingency." The seminary should begin to work with that reality in mind. "I shall positively resign my positions next May," he reiterated with the additional notice that "someone will also have to take charge of the finances, and upon this point I will communicate with the financial board."[70] Broadus wrote back, "I have communicated to such of our colleagues as I have met the sorrowful intelligence that you feel sure you will never be able to teach again, and must resign next May. I trust that it may please our Heavenly Father to spare you for yet many years of varied usefulness."[71]

This theme persevered as a matter of urgent importance. In a later correspondence, when requesting Boyce's opinion on the issue of his successor in Systematic Theology, Broadus commented, "We earnestly hope and pray that your health may become at least so far better that you may continue a general oversight as President. But it is of course right to remember and act upon your assurance that you cannot retain the professorship."[72] Kerfoot was the man to replace him in theology, so Boyce believed, and the matter of his continuance in any capacity must be dropped absolutely. "As to my future presidency," Boyce lamented, "you would not think it wise should you see the enfeebled condition of my health. No, my dear brother, no more work of that kind for me. All that I can do will be to use what strength I have left to see others entrusted with my work with which, if God grant, I shall be content."[73] When he comes home, he will have strength only to set up all his affairs, enjoy whatever leisure may be afforded him, and "then await my final account."[74]

All of this certitude about the limited scope of his future was not simply intuition and self-diagnosis, but came from the alarm at his condition from Dr. Garrod. He believed that Boyce could die at any moment and must be confined to bed immediately, in a quiet place, and should not attempt even to write a letter.[75] William E. Hatcher visited him in this condition and wrote Broadus about the seriousness of his condition. It bore all the marks of imminent death if he should

attempt any further exertions on the trip, especially if he sought to go
to the Continent as contemplated.

> I hope you are not ignorant of the sickness of Doctor Boyce, and yet
> I feel impelled, in a quiet way to write you some facts concerning
> him. Only last evening while at tea with Doctor Angus, I learned that
> the doctor was in London and quite sick. I went to him at once and
> found him in a condition which gave me much anxiety and alarm.
> From his appearance, as well as from the decision of his physicians,
> as given me by the family, I am led to feel that his case is very serious,
> though not beyond hope. One thing is fixed and that is, he is not
> fit for travel. To-night I called again and while he brightened at my
> coming, I was not encouraged. He looked sadly broken and languid,
> and I felt constrained to join his children in their attempts to dissuade
> him from his purpose to go to the Continent. This he is set on—not
> for himself but for his daughters' sake.[76]

This prompted Broadus to urge Boyce to come back to America.
"My dear Brother," he began, "there is a little circle of us here who
communicate to each other any tidings from you. Having anxiously
considered all the information . . . it is our opinion, and I beg pardon
for obtruding our opinion upon you, that you ought to abandon your
trip and if you are well enough ought to come home." Having stated
how universal this opinion was among all his dearest friends, he noted
the rationality of the proposal. "It seems clear that you cannot soon be
strong enough to enjoy for yourself, or to make very pleasant to your
wife and daughters, the journeying on the Continent which otherwise
you would have all appreciated and delighted as few people can."
Think of how distressing such a venture would be if you should die,
or your mental and physical capacities decline further, and of how
virtually impossible it would be for your wife and girls to cope in such
a situation. "I apologize again, my dear friend—the dearest friend I
have—for speaking about this contingency and its probable effects,"
Broadus continued, but "I want to bring the matter before your mind
with palpable distinctness." Boyce would fare better in the States and his
family certainly would be more secure. "Now of course it is very hard
for a man of your strong will," Broadus frankly contended, "who has

overcome so many mountains of difficulty, to give up a long cherished plan." The daughters would not enjoy the south of Europe constantly being under anxiety at the thought ("the horror of great darkness") that you might die there. It is not too late to "hope for a fairly good voyage across the Atlantic," and he should find no difficulty in finding some young American male willing to promenade the young ladies on the deck of a ship. Delay, and the danger of a voyage increases.[77]

When Broadus's letter of concern arrived, Boyce already had made the trip to France on smooth seas, with a bright sky, and in better health. Since that low point in London, he had revived remarkably, he assured his friend, and firmly believed that staying put in France would be best for any restoration of health. A restoration of some degree of health, however, would not mean a return to work at the seminary.

> I hope to attain this [restoration] this winter and to return home next spring or summer, and finish up there the business of my life which has not yet been completed. I have determined to give myself up to that, which is the final settlement of my father's estate, and on that account also, as I shall not have strength for more, am resolved to cut loose from the seminary and other duties.[78]

The correspondence reveals another important concern that Boyce knew he needed to finalize—the transfer of his theological library to the seminary library. Boyce first broached the subject officially at the May 1887 meeting of the trustees when he offered these books to the seminary on certain conditions. The minutes record:

> That we accept the offer of the chairman of the Faculty in regard to all the theological portion of his library & that Dr. John A. Broadus be requested to prosecute measures for securing the means to meet the conditions of said offer, viz. "If the friends of the Seminary will raise as a part of this hundred thousand dollars or in addition thereto for the library of the Seminary, the sum of fifty thousand dollars, exclusive of a building for that purpose, all the theological portion of the library of the Chairman of the Faculty will be donated at ten thousand dollars as a part of the fifty thousand provided that the money is subscribed & collected by the 1st of July, 1888."[79]

Throughout his life Boyce had carefully collected books—classic theological works as well as recent titles—and had purchased them in most noble and attractive bindings. He loved his books and saw them as a large part of his estate as well as his Christian legacy. He kept them around him as his companions and piled them up within reaching distance when he had to stay in bed for a period of convalescence. He had deep affection for them and wanted them to be used well and appreciated appropriately. The trustee reaction to his offer did not seem commensurate with its magnitude in Boyce's estimation. In later correspondence he confessed this to Broadus as an ad hoc illustration concerning another gift.

With this major matter still unsettled in Boyce's mind and death more and more clouding his horizon, he wrote Broadus, by dictation, from London, "Since my sickness I have been more anxious than ever for the completion of the conditions upon which I offered the larger part of my theological library to the Seminary. It is important that that matter should be completed while I am alive. I have no provision for its transfer after my death."[80]

A few weeks later Boyce returned to the subject. "So also I have felt about my library," he told Broadus. "It is not simply that the Seminary should have so many books of such and such a value, but that this should be my books which I have selected, and bought, and owned, and hoped at some time to be able to bestow on our beloved seminary."

At one point he felt remorse that he might not be able to execute his purpose. "In the days of my seminary troubles and apparent inability to give them because my family would need the money they would bring in the event of my death, the prospect that my wish could not be carried out gave me great pain." This contemplated gift seemed so personal in Boyce's estimation that he confessed to Broadus that "when the Board took so cavalierly in its thoughtlessness the offer I made I was made to feel some sore." That was past, however, and now the transfer must be made, with no reservations or other conditions to be met. Boyce determined to "take immediate steps so to arrange the transfer of my library as to make it all safe to the seminary at once." His wife and daughters understood the plan. All the theological books would go to the seminary library. Others his family would retain. Perhaps others of a "general literary and historical or artistic character" would be given to "some other library or institution." His wife and daughters expressed their desire to retain "all the illustrated books, including even the Roberts books on Palestine, Syria, Egypt, etc." Boyce recommended that Broadus keep the letter for their guidance at the time such a division of the library became necessary. Over five thousand volumes came in this initial gift from Boyce.[81]

Boyce was glad to hear that people asked about him and wondered if Mrs. Peter had received his letter, which was among the first that he wrote. It did indeed arrive, but only after some straying, which led her to speak with "characteristic enthusiasm of the value she set upon it."[82] Just three days later Broadus wrote Boyce and included the tidbit of jovial encouragement that "Mrs. Arthur Peter said yesterday, when I met her, that if Dr. Boyce does not get better in health it will weaken her poor faith in prayer."[83] Boyce took the whole matter of prayer and the divine wisdom too seriously to let such a remark go without some sober reflection on it. "I am sorry to hear of Mrs. Peter's remark about her faith in prayer being dependent upon my restoration to health," he remarked. "What am I, and what are my friends and their prayers, to be weighed against the will and wisdom of our Heavenly Father?" Going still further with his musing, he stated resolutely, "Had I the power today to say what I wish for myself except as consonant with and subservient to his wish supremely, I should dread to decide. Nay, let me ever be in his hands. Pray all my friends to leave me there, I am safe with him and safe only thus."[84]

In the middle of October, Broadus wrote Boyce with news that seemed to satisfy his mind that the seminary indeed was sealed as a matter of divine providence, in the affections of the people of Louisville, and as a viable physical plant. Mrs. J. Lawrence Smith, member of a prominent Louisville family, informed John A. Broadus of her intention to give $50,000 for the erection of a library building. She told Broadus, "You must write to Dr. Boyce about it. He is sick and suffering abroad, and it may give him pleasure to know that the work of his life is making some progress."[85] Accordingly, Broadus wrote his friend in Paris at the Hotel des Deux Mondes to give him this startling and tantalizing, but "highly confidential," bit of news.

497

Although Boyce had earlier promised his theological collection to the library dependent on library endowment, Broadus still felt the load of raising endowment money for the ongoing support of the seminary. He went to ask Mrs. Smith about the propriety of asking Mrs. Caperton for some memorial for her daughters, the nieces of Mrs. Smith, who recently had died. Mrs. Smith said the timing was not right, but at that moment she was thinking about property that could be sold for $50,000 for the purpose of a library for the seminary. She would give this as a memorial for her nieces as well as two nephews, William and Lawrence Caldwell. Broadus suggested that perhaps it "would suffice to spend part on the building and make the rest an endowment of the library." She replied it would be just as they preferred. Though selling the property would cost some trouble, it could be done. "God be thanked, my dear friend," Boyce wrote in closing, "for every new encouragement in the work at which we have toiled so long."[86]

Boyce received the news with a profound sense of debt and gratitude. He had long desired to develop a deeper faith and confidence "in the working of the Lord for our seminary." At each point of despair and fear "God has found us ways of which we have never dreamed." The gift of Governor Brown demonstrated that in a time of deep difficulty eight years before. Now it has happened again and proves, not the merit of the recipients, but the deep generosity of the donor. That this gift had the potential of sealing the security and efficiency of the seminary work as Boyce had originally perceived it comes through clearly in a transparent and powerful ejaculation of appreciation. "God be with you and help you my dear friend. No one knows how much I owe you for your help and your influence in that matter of the establishment of what you call my life work, but which ought to be called 'our life work.'"[87]

Boyce considered several options as to how the money might be used, but stopped writing halfway through his response and carefully read the letter again. "I am deeply impressed," he wrote, "upon its second perusal that the idea that was in her mind was a library building." The seminary must therefore do all in its power "to return the kindness and affection shown in their conception of what they would like to do." For the giver, much more is involved in a gift than money value. He illustrated this by anecdotes of a ring given to his wife, which she traded for another, and the offer of his theological library to the seminary, which was treated "cavalierly" by the trustees. "Now I do not wish to intimate that our friend could be sensitive like myself about a trifle," he urged, "but I am anxious that she should not have her ideas put aside in order to carry out any of ours."

Though his own wishes had been expressed in forceful terms that he desired an endowment for the library separate from the money for a building, a desire Broadus was trying to honor in his suggestion to Mrs. Smith, Boyce evaluated the gift according to the initial impulse of Mrs. Smith. He was therefore for using all the money for a library, "with such arrangements as will permit an increase in its size at any time that may be necessary and for the purpose of such alteration and improvement. I should favor the putting aside in a fund of whatever remainder there might be, to be increased by the annual addition of the interest on such remainder." The entire scheme, in fact, "should be under her supervision."[88] As indicated above, Boyce secured the gift of his library to the seminary apart from his original requirement.

On October 24, before Boyce had received the first letter from Broadus announcing this marvelous providence, Broadus wrote again. "Mrs. J. Lawrence Smith put in my hands this afternoon a list of unimproved lots, tax listed at about thirty thousand, and which Priest (at my request with her approval) estimated at about the same and . . . quite saleable lots." She encouraged the sale of those lots as quickly as possible so she could complete the remainder of the $50,000 with bank stocks. Out of that amount she wanted "as much as necessary to be used for a library building and the rest to be invested for a library fund." In light of Boyce's health and the "uncertainty of [his] movements" a trustee would handle the liquidating of all this and turn over the cash to the seminary. Broadus would insure that no early publicity would be given this gift and that the lots would be sold at the optimum advantage to Mrs. Smith.[89]

On November 7, Broadus gave a report on the progress of completing the Smith library transaction. "On Friday last, Mrs. Smith signed the deeds. On Monday, at the regular meeting of the financial board, the faculty were invited to be present, and also Dr. W. B. Caldwell and Junius Caldwell, Jr. Acting under the authority given by the trust deed, the Board appointed as a building committee the faculty and Dr. Caldwell." Broadus asked members of the faculty to obtain relevant surveys of probable locations for the library and to correspond with other educational institutions to gather data about the most useful ideas for libraries.

One piece of property that the seminary wanted was owned by Mrs. Rupert. Her price exceeded the fair value, and neither Broadus nor Boyce indicated a willingness to compromise for the sake of getting it. Mrs. Rupert wanted income for life from the property and would be willing to take no less than $15,000. Financial advisers "had said eight thousand was enough for the house and ten would be very high and that the Seminary could never think of paying fifteen for it."[90] Boyce returned the comment, "I neglected to say that I am not willing that more than twelve thousand dollars be paid to Mrs. Rupert for her lot."[91]

That comment came close to the end of a letter in which Boyce had written many paragraphs of financial, procedural, and legal information concerning the Smith property, the city's responsibility for the paving of sidewalks, and several other items incumbent on him as treasurer of the seminary. Near the end he breathed the words of relinquishment, "Do not think that I do not feel deep interest in this matter because I wish to settle the whole burden upon someone else." He had begun the entire letter with a paragraph that prophesied the events of the next month.

> [Yours received] over a week ago. It demanded an immediate answer, and I should have written then, but I was anxious to write the reply myself and expected to do so from day to day. I have, however, been sick again and although not confined to my bed, I am so nervous that I cannot control my hand sufficiently to write legibly and with force. I am thus compelled to dictate a letter to you rather than keep you waiting any longer.[92]

As indicated by that note, Boyce's health began to decline rapidly in Paris. An inefficient doctor and ineffective medicine perhaps failed to halt the rate of his decline, but even the greatest efficiency and effectiveness could do little to prolong his life. He wrote F. H. Kerfoot, toward whom he had consistently manifested great interest, "I think the days of such service are nearly over, and that there is not much to live for when one is really rusted out. . . . He often uses us for nothing as well as for something. I wish only to be His and to serve Him, He helping me to do so in humility and faith."[93]

Boyce's declining condition, loss of mental energy, incessant drowsiness combined with nocturnal insomnia made a move from Paris necessary. The move had to be done with great care and without making him walk at all. Lizzie recounted the move and the last days.

> Dr. Garrod had recommended that he should go to Pau, in the south of France, and we found it possible to get a *coupe a lit* from Paris to Pau without change of cars. We left the city at night, Father being taken in his chair to a carriage, and lifted into the train. Our night was fearful, as we were in great anguish of mind for fear he might die at any moment. He seemed much exhausted, and for hours before we got to Pau he was asking if we were not nearly there. We arrived at Pau on time, but there was much delay in securing the physician whom Garrod had recommended. But in a few days Father began to improve. This, however, did not last long, and we soon realized that the end was near. Only once did he rally sufficiently to talk with me on business, and then it was only a few words. He was out of his head a great deal, and in his wanderings his talk was nearly always of the Seminary. We would constantly catch the names of the different professors, and perhaps the last words we distinctly heard were something about Seminary and students. The day before he died he was conscious for several hours, but could not talk, as his tongue was much swollen. He recognized us, and pressed our hands or returned our kisses, but did not attempt to speak. An English clergyman, whom we asked to visit him, saw him for a few moments that morning, and prayed and talked with him. Father tried to say a good deal to him, but it was impossible to understand what he was saying. He soon became unconscious, and remained so until the end. This was on Friday, Dec. 28, 1888.[94]

501

An Unlikely Eulogist

When Whitsitt heard in October of the gravity of Boyce's illness, he recorded, "I feel a thrill of regret in view of the early departure of my old enemy. He has been for nearly ten years sternly opposed to me and has done me a deal of damage, but he has many good qualities, and I cannot avoid respecting him."[95] When news of Boyce's death arrived, Whitsitt wrote in his diary for Friday, 28 December 1888, "Boyce died this morning at Pau, France. . . . There was a faculty meeting at 10 A. M. in which it was decided that the remains should be brought to Louisville instead of Charleston, S. C. for interment. It is about arranged that a Seminary lot will be purchased at Cave Hill for the interment of members of the Faculty and their families. Boyce was a great man in several respects."

That afternoon an impromptu memorial meeting was held in the main chapel at the seminary. Students, friends of the seminary, the faculty and their families, and a few others attended. Broadus took the chair and led the congregation in singing "My Hope Is Built on Nothing Less than Jesus' Blood and Righteousness." No one had been asked to speak, but several gave unprepared addresses concerning Boyce and his impact on Baptists. Apparently the first to rise to the occasion was William Heth Whitsitt. The substance of his remarks was reported by T. T. Eaton.

Boyce was chiefly responsible for the greatest accomplishment of Southern Baptists, in Whitsitt's estimation, the establishing of the Southern Baptist Theological Seminary. Boyce, whose "character was greater than his work," had a rare combination of qualities. Born and trained in the most pristine location in the "golden age of Southern nobility," Boyce embraced the highest traits of that character and gave it an elevation worthy of emulation. Added to these gracious Southern virtues were the traits of "great simplicity" and "vigorous sturdiness." Though he had strong convictions, Boyce, so Whitsitt testified, was "gentle and accessible" and "thoroughly reasonable" in his conservatism. "Nature made him great and grace made him greater," and his character and accomplishment will "be one of the landmarks of our denominational history." Boyce was a born leader, and the many serious crises of the seminary brought out and developed his great powers. He was permitted to die "in the sunshine of the Seminary's prosperity."[96]

The faculty met in the office of Broadus on 2 January 1889. Broadus had requested Whitsitt to compose a resolution of appreciation and sympathy connected with the death of Boyce. The document passed the faculty unanimously.

> The faculty of the Southern Baptist Theological Seminary having heard with profound sorrow of the decease of Rev. James P. Boyce, D. D., LL. D., the honored President of the Institution, at Pau, in France on the morning of December 28, 1888, be it
>
> Resolved, That we admired our departed brother as a man whom nature had cast in the largest mold, and rejoiced in his elevated character, his conspicuous abilities, and his remarkable achievements. The fact that his powers were early sanctified by the Spirit of God, and throughout his career were consecrated to the highest uses will always render his memory a precious heritage.
>
> Resolved, That we gratefully recognize his merits as the foremost leader in the enterprise of establishing our seminary for the higher education of the Christian ministry, to whose interests he gave many years of thought and exertion, and for which he made many sacrifices.
>
> Resolved, That in the loss which has fallen most directly upon us and our Institution, Southern Baptists have likewise been deprived of one of their safest and most efficient leaders, and society has been deprived of the public-spirited and influential citizen.
>
> Resolved, That while we shall always cherish the memory of his deeds and virtues, we beg to assure the stricken family of our warmest sympathy in their irreparable bereavement, and we humbly commend them to the consolations of divine grace.
>
> Resolved, That these resolutions be spread upon our minutes and that the Secretary be directed to forward a copy to the family.
>
> John A. Broadus, Chairman
> Wm. H. Whitsitt, Secretary

Whitsitt also wrote the biographical sketch of Boyce that appeared in two successive numbers of *The Seminary Magazine*.[97] He summarized succinctly the biographical highlights of Boyce and punctuated the narrative with a variety of superlatives along the way. Concerning his name, Whitsitt remarked, "It was one of the worthiest names on the annals of recent Carolina history, and it has been worthily borne by the namesake through all these three-score years."[98] Pointing to his election as a young man to the post of editor, Whitsitt gushed, "His powers were so highly esteemed that the next year he was appointed to be editor of the *Southern Baptist*."[99] Furman University had a worthy record of professors, but Whitsitt averred that in electing Boyce "it has never had a name connected with it that sheds more lustre upon it."[100] His inaugural address became a "famous performance." Boyce endured the press of "anxieties, trials, and labors" during days when the seminary's future appeared bleak and exerted "herculean toils" to surmount these seemingly invincible difficulties. Baptists "were always delighted to show their appreciation" of Boyce and bestowed on him their highest offices.[101] He died in possession of the titles president of the Southern Baptist Convention as well as president of the Southern Baptist Theological Seminary. Whitsitt concluded, "One of the noblest leaders of Southern Baptists has fallen. He easily takes a place in the galaxy where shine Furman, Fuller, Manly, Poindexter, Jeter and Taylor. A sturdy, honest, godly man; and elevated and wise counselor; who can tell all we have lost in our departed friend and President!"[102]

Unlike Antony's evaluation of Caesar, for Whitsitt, the evil that Boyce did was interred with his bones, and the good lived after him. Evaluations and testing of the contributions and character of Boyce would build layer by layer in the following decades.

14

Their Works Do Follow Them

⟡

*T*hough the impact of Boyce's death most keenly affected the Baptists of the South, thoughtful persons in the culture at large knew that a prominent voice for good had now been silenced.

A Good Report of Them Which Are Without

"His life was full of useful work the results of which remain after him to bless every community with which he was associated, his church and the general cause of Christianity. He will never be forgotten; the fruits of his labors will never cease from ripening and multiplying." The residents of Greenville, South Carolina, read that estimate of Boyce with interest and confirmation according to the *Greenville Daily News*. Though he had not lived there in the latter part of his life, he remained a potent force in the memories of the people who felt that he belonged there. "The community generally will feel a sense of loss," the paper claimed, "and will share the sincere grief of the Baptists of the entire country and many thousands outside the denomination of which Dr. Boyce was at once a conspicuous ornament and a powerful active force."[1]

From Chattanooga, Tennessee, a newspaper noted his death with a historical sketch of the financial and commercial advance of the city. "His life has been identified with the history of Chattanooga," the article stated, and noted the real estate interests developed by Ker Boyce, which were "under the active management and control of Rev. J. P. Boyce since about 1853." The writer considered him a "man of brain, a financier of the highest order of ability," and pointed out that "no one in this city of 'wonderful surprises' has been more successful in the management of real estate than he." When Boyce conceived of the idea of moving the seminary from Greenville, he made a proposal in 1868 to Chattanooga and in response the four thousand people of the town "subscribed nearly $150,000 as a donation." Though Louisville, stronger and richer, got the seminary, due to Boyce's influence "Chattanooga then realized the power of co-operation, and from that date we began the development" of the last twenty years. His work for theological education succeeded to such a degree that "no theological seminary in the United States is its superior." The writer saw Boyce as "one of the ablest of the 'mighty men' of the Baptist church in America." He was a man of "courtly manners," and of the highest "culture, polish, and refinement."[2]

Another Southern paper, the *Augusta Chronicle*, feted Boyce with a long series of encomiums. He "measured fully up to the best standards" in whatever position he was called to fill, whether preacher, theological educator, scholar, or a savant in the "ways of the world." Not only did he manifest a "sterling manhood and a rounded character," but his life was spent in the "even discharge of the noblest duties." Though steadfast in his own faith, Boyce was free from the "taint of intolerance." His "manly exterior," his "inherent dignity, . . . noble breeding, . . . and elegant culture" presented to the world an air of "aristocratic grandeur." Though the mean, ignoble, self-seeking, and vain were not drawn to him, his "largeness of heart" drew him to them. He was fit for positions that the world would have applauded and rewarded with honor and remuneration, but his "tenderness of nature" drew him to the obscurity of ministerial life. Even there, however, the "clear bright light of a pure life, shining in companionship with the achievement of scholarship," made it impossible for him to remain obscure in any calling. "He was great. He was good. What better can be said of man?"[3]

Immediate Memorials

A student from Mississippi, P. I. Lipsey, who served as an editor of *The Seminary Magazine*, told of the events connected with the news of Boyce's serious sickness and then death. At the first cablegram that communicated that Boyce was dying, Lipsey said the school exercises were canceled. At prayer meeting at Walnut Street Baptist Church on the evening before they learned of Boyce's death, T. T. Eaton spoke on "Help Lord, for the godly man ceaseth," giving tribute to Dr. Boyce. Dr. Manly also "spoke feelingly of his friend and co-laborer."[4] On the morning of December 28, the cable came announcing the death of James Petigru Boyce.

The students of the seminary were among the first to respond with a resolution as an expression of love and respect for Boyce.

Dr. Boyce is dead! The news fills our hearts with deepest sadness. It is a personal grief to every one, for we had all learned to love him. Inestimable are the blessings which his life has secured for us. In the institution whose success has so largely resulted from his labors and generosity, in the wisdom and learning which he has left us in his writings, in the sterling integrity and exalted worth of his character and life, truly we have a noble heritage. But in being deprived of his further personal instructions, and of his superior skill in directing the affairs of the Seminary, we feel that our loss is irreparable.

Be it resolved, 1. That we tender to his bereaved relatives our sincere sympathy and commend them to the tender mercies of our loving heavenly Father.

2. That we cherish grateful recollections of his noble life and strive to emulate his virtues.

3. That we consecrate our lives more fully to the cause for which his life was spent, and pray the Lord of the harvest to send forth more laborers into the harvest.

4. That a copy of these resolutions be furnished the family of the deceased, and that they be published in our denominational papers.

For the entire student body the resolutions were signed by J. B. Pruitt, E. B. Pollard, and B. D. Ragsdale, and dated 28 December 1888.

The impromptu memorial service on the day of Boyce's death, in addition to the speech of W. H. Whitsitt, included the words of many others. T. T. Eaton summarized the meeting for the *Western Recorder* of Kentucky, J. A. Baunson wrote a description for the *Baptist Courier* of South Carolina, and P. I. Lipsey reported it to the *Southern Baptist Record* of Mississippi. The variety of recollections and testimonies to Boyce's usefulness and personal inspiration provided a summary of his life. Broadus called these "brief and loving addresses."[5] George W. Norton, a continual and generous benefactor of the seminary, indicated that in all the relations he had had with Boyce regarding his most intimate views and extensive desires for the seminary he had grown to admire his "great ability and nobleness." Dr. J. W. Warder expressed joy and gratitude for the benefits that all had received from the life of Boyce from its beginning to the end. Warder, corresponding secretary of the Kentucky State Mission Board, had served as pastor of Walnut Street from 1875 till 1881 and had observed Boyce during the last years of seeking to bring the school to Louisville and during the days of his serving the convention as president. Boyce was a master at such leadership, even as everywhere. To contemplate his life "gave him a feeling of exaltation."[6]

The pastor of the Chestnut Street Baptist Church, Dr. Weaver, recounted a moving anecdote about the weakness and greatness of Boyce. "Eight months ago, Dr. Boyce was in my pulpit seated in the large chair. When he arose to go to the desk he staggered. I saw his feebleness and could scarcely refrain from tears." Weaver said good-bye to Boyce before he left for Europe and thought that he "should never see him again on this earth." Though expecting his death, he was unprepared for it when the news came. "He was my friend," Weaver said. "I knew no man who had the deep spirituality of Dr. Boyce. In this was the great strength of his character. When in his presence one instinctively felt as if he was in the presence of a man who loved God."[7]

F. D. Hale attended the seminary in 1884–85 and was an English graduate. He served as pastor of the 22nd and Walnut Street Baptist Church in Louisville. He remembered Boyce's influence over him as a student. "When he began Dr. Boyce's Systematic Theology it threw him into great perplexity as to doctrines." The experience edified him greatly, however, as he learned the "old doctrines of grace as he never had before by studying under Dr. Boyce." In addition he learned to "sympathize with lost souls."

Hale's testimony to Boyce's influence on his theology has particular pertinence in demonstration of the theme of this chapter. In 1887, a Missouri pastor, W. W. Carter, a convert to Baptists from the Campbellites, accused Hale of preaching Campbellite doctrine. The phrase on which he based his judgment was "To be a Christian means: To do what Christ says, as he says it, when he says it, and simply because he says it." Hale's close relation with Boyce and the other professors at the seminary meant, in Carter's estimation, that Campbellism and Baptist theology differed in no essentials and the only barrier between them was the "ugly feeling of prejudice." Hale wanted to clear his name as well as that of the seminary and of Baptists on the whole.[8]

Hale, as Boyce himself would say, contended that at root Campbellism maintains the "essential elements of Arminianism." Unlike Baptists, the knowledgeable Campbellite "rejects unconditional, eternal election of individuals to salvation." He also "rejects the total depravity of human nature, and says that the Holy Spirit does not regenerate the dead sinner's heart by direct and personal influence, before that sinner has repented, believed, or been baptized." Faith is the simple crediting of the historical record of Jesus and his saving work and submission to baptism. In this, remission of sins is granted. Following that, if one does not obey the commands of Christ, "he will fall from grace and be eternally lost." Hale repudiated that entire theological structure.[9]

On the other hand, as Hale had learned so clearly from Boyce, for Baptist theology "the essential elements are Calvinistic." God elects the individuals that are to receive eternal life, his Son makes atonement for their sins, "because of which God can be just and forgive," and the Holy Spirit "quickens them from a state of death in sin and gives them the power and will to repent toward God and trust in his Son as their personal savior—taking him as their Lord." This operation of the Spirit creates the desire for obedience from the first moment of repentance from sin, recognition of "God's method of saving through the meritorious work of His Son," so that by the Spirit one accepts these realities and trusts in Christ alone for salvation. Because regenerated by a sovereign operation of the Spirit of God, the Christian continues in a course of humble obedience manifesting the reality that he is a Christian doing "what Christ says, as he says it, when he says it, and simply because he says it." His life of obedience includes baptism, regular partaking of the Lord's Supper with the gospel church of which he is a member, and letting his light shine "enduring to the end."[10]

In short, Hale taught "what is God's part and what is man's part." On that basis he taught a person to examine his heart for proper evidences of regeneration, producing confidence "that he is chosen to salvation hereafter and to a life of good works here." The concern of Boyce for the challenge of both Arminianism and Campbellism had taken deep root in F. D. Hale, and many others.

In his brief words at the impromptu memorial service, Dr. Peter voiced his deep affection for Boyce and professed that he "cherished as a precious treasure, his acquaintance with Dr. Boyce." He was sure that Boyce's heavy labors and great exertions and under stressful conditions in the removal of the seminary from Greenville to Louisville "undoubtedly hastened his death." These stresses not only taxed him physically, but weighed on his mind and heart.

T. T. Eaton, editor of the *Western Recorder* and current pastor of Walnut Street Baptist Church, spoke of the great accomplishments of Boyce in several important areas, but especially of how he had given his life and energy for the seminary.[11] Baunson reported that Eaton said, "He lived his full time, did his full work. He lived to see the Seminary established." Now others must be challenged by Boyce's death to pick up the work and complete it.[12]

M. D. Jeffries remembered Boyce as a ceaseless worker to whom heaven is a "sweet, sweet rest." Jeffries's student tenure included the days of Toy's theological departure, and as he recalled, "There were then doubts and discussions among the students on doctrines, which he [Boyce] could most happily allay. To him is largely due the vigorous adherence to the old doctrines on the part of the Baptist ministry." Theodore Harris, a gifted Louisville businessman, felt he could hardly speak, for Dr. Boyce had been to him the brother his natural ties had never provided. He respected him greatly for his business gifts, but more importantly, "he was a great man: the most perfectly rounded character Mr. Harris had ever seen."[13]

Dr. Kerfoot, for several years a colaborer, "had never learned to feel toward Dr. Boyce other than as a student." From the beginning Kerfoot had been impressed with Boyce's greatness, "and that impression has deepened through the years." He knew him as tender and kind in times of sickness and sorrow, and saw the greatness of his wisdom in his work of raising money. Since entering the ministry, Kerfoot had never taken an important step apart from consulting with Dr. Boyce and valued his friendship and counsel as "among his chief treasures." He cast an imaginary picture of Boyce returning home from Brown University, inspired by Francis Wayland, with a vision of ministerial education and determined to seize upon the first opportunity to define and promote it. Kerfoot speculated that God would grant Boyce to see "from the skies" a view of his completed work that he could not see "with his natural eyes."[14]

Broadus closed the testimonies with the reminder of how Boyce had encouraged a concert of prayer from students, faculty, and friends to "raise up some friends to save the work." Soon, "the letter came, telling of Governor Brown's magnificent contribution." The deepest concern of Boyce was that "the men trained here should love and preach the old, dead-in-earnest Gospel."[15] Manly offered a prayer, the congregation sang "Praise God from Whom All Blessings Flow," and Dr. Sampey dismissed the assembly with a benediction.[16]

P. I. Lipsey provides a few details and observations that give more texture to the meeting. He recorded that Broadus was "almost overcome with the loss." As others who reported this meeting, Lipsey summarized the remarks made by all who participated. He reported some of Broadus's words slightly differently than did Eaton. Instead of "dead-in-earnest gospel" Lipsey put in quotes "dead in earnest truths of the Bible." He also gave space to the testimony of F. D. Hale of how Boyce had led him "out of difficulties in theology," and in the process how he was "settled on rock foundation in theology," and had learned a greater love for souls. Lipsey included words from Harris not noted by others. Harris not only greatly admired Boyce's great business sense, but spoke of him as "clear-headed, far-sighted, ever ready with an opinion and ever an opinion that was a good one, and withal as modest as a girl." To the remarks of Weaver, Lipsey added the twist that he worked hard for the seminary "when it was very painful to put his foot to the ground." To Weaver's comments about Boyce's spirituality, Lipsey added, "He was not a cold man but delighted to talk of experimental religion."[17]

The Eulogy of the Papers

News that Boyce had died spread throughout the Baptist world. First a cablegram on Wednesday that he was dying and then the news on Friday, December 28, that he had died. A Baptist paper wrote, "The news of the death of this eminent man of God will bring sorrow to the entire American Baptist family. He stood officially at the head of our Southern Baptist host, being at the time of his departure, the president of the Southern Baptist Convention, and also the president of our Theological Seminary." The article, written by William E. Hatcher, called the seminary Boyce's "monumental work" and noted that to him "we are largely indebted for its existence." Hatcher, who mentions visiting Boyce in England and finding him "fearfully broken and weak," inserted a personal word about his impressions of Boyce. Boyce's strong and emphatic nature gave the impression that he was "severe and overbearing." This trustee, in former years, did Boyce "the injustice" to have such an opinion of him. He admitted frankly, however, "We were mistaken." Though the deceased brother was "firm and determined," he also was "courteous, forbearing, and full of affectionate respect for his brethren." He found Boyce a "pleasant man to work with," demonstrating "no unlovely points of character which frequent contact would bring to light." As a thoroughly Christian gentleman, fearless and with intense conviction, Boyce nevertheless could "warmly respect an opponent, and knew how to bear with grace his defeats."[18]

From Shelbyville, Kentucky, J. A. French wrote the *Western Recorder* with an evaluation of Boyce. The editor prefaced the letter with the comment, "Every word in it is so just and true and well chosen. Nothing which shall be said or spoken of Dr. Boyce can say more in a little space, or say it in truer and more forceful words than these."

All our people in this vicinity who knew Dr. Boyce's great worth and work are pained to hear of his death. In him we lose a kingly man. It has been said some men are great on account of what they are and others on account of what they do. Dr. Boyce was both. As a man, he was noble and true; as a friend, he was unsurpassed; as a scholar, pains-taking and thorough; as a preacher, eminently instructive; as a teacher, helpful and kind. He was a princely parliamentarian, and will be sadly missed as President of the Southern Baptist Convention. But his loss to the denomination will be most sorely felt in the work of our noble Seminary, which is his enduring monument.[19]

Eaton, in addition to giving a summary of the impromptu memorial service, surveyed in an editorial the traits of greatness that he observed in Boyce. Though born into wealth and luxury, he grew to a "pure and noble manhood." He stood in the front rank as a preacher, and had he given himself wholly to pulpit ministry would certainly have "attained the highest eminence." He was "clear and profound" as a theologian, and his recently published *Abstract of Systematic Theology* never will be obsolete. He possessed coveted talents in his financial ability. Eaton felt that the most demanding job in the world of finance would not have overstretched Boyce's abilities. The founding of the seminary demonstrated Boyce's wisdom in developing a place of elevated instruction precisely adapted to the demands of the Baptist ministry. "The Seminary is his monument," Eaton reminded the reader; "It was for that he lived and wrought." And what a capacity for work Boyce had: he has done "the work of three men and done it well." His impressions on people always were positive, and he wore well and grew in the estimation of his friends. He exhibited persevering energy all aimed at the "glory of God." Contrary to Whitsitt's impression, Eaton believed that "he cared not who received the credit."

As others had done, Eaton pointed to the theological influence of Boyce, calling him a man of "strong and clear convictions." Everyone knew where Boyce stood on the "questions of the day." In particular, "his firm adherence to the old doctrines of grace and redemption, his simple faith in the full inspiration of the Bible, and his unshakeable confidence in God, have had much to do with keeping our Southern Baptist pulpits free from the new theology and other noxious isms."

Eaton had great hopes that the seminary would stand as a "great bulwark against the tides of false doctrine that ever and anon sweep over the earth."

Boyce never exhibited cowardice, but always urged what he believed to be right and best, no matter who opposed. This contributed to his "most distinctive quality," that is, his "freedom from all policy." Boyce's decisions seemed free of being affected by their impact on a person's opinion about him. "He never seemed to think of his reputation at all; and considerations of policy, he never regarded." Add to these traits that he was a "man of deep piety . . . strong faith . . . a bright and indomitable hope." The discouragements he confronted of such an intense and extenuated nature "would have crushed a weaker man."

Eaton asked in closing, "Who will take Dr. Boyce's place? Nobody." Boyce filled his own place well and now stands among the redeemed in glory. Each person must fill his own place "all the more worthily" because of Boyce's example. In particular, "we can best honor him by rallying around the Seminary and by carrying forward the great work for which he gave his life—training men whom God calls and whom the churches send forth to preach 'the unsearchable riches of Christ.' "[20]

James C. Furman, writing in the *Baptist Courier*, called Boyce a man of "masterly endowments, and in the command of such work as would tempt most men to luxurious self-indulgence," who yet by God's grace made his life "a noble self-sacrifice for the good of others and the glory of Christ." Furman spoke in superlatives of Boyce's far-reaching vision and his strength to carry through without being threatened or defeated by discouraging details. In unison with many others, Furman noted Boyce's intuitive financial wisdom and business acumen and recognized that a career in that area "would have placed him among the commercial magnates who handle millions." Furman also recognized the mighty talents and contribution of the "true yokefellow," John A. Broadus, but still averred of Boyce that "no other man could have accomplished what he has done." The two stable pillars of Boyce's legacy, his enduring monuments, were "the erected Seminary and its precious appliances for the highest Christian education, and his work on Systematic Theology."[21]

An article in the *Religious Herald* announced the details concerning the death of Boyce and gave a brief biographical sketch. At his close the writer summarized his view of Boyce's virtues.

> We shall not attempt here any extended description of his great abilities. He had a great intellect. He thought widely and profoundly, and spoke and wrote with clearness, precision and force. His character was remarkable for its simplicity. Trustful as a child, free from every form of affectation and false pride, he had the affectionate and reverent esteem of all who knew him.[22]

Following the article the editor inserted a P. S. describing a memorial service held in North Danville, Virginia, in honor of Boyce. J. R. Moffett, pastor in North Danville and husband of Boyce's cousin, related Boyce's kindness to him as a student in his Latin Theology class, offering him and another student special sessions in Boyce's own home. G. B. Eager spoke of the first time that he met Boyce. The occasion was in Greenville as Boyce provided a sumptuous Christmas meal for the students. The last came at the Southern Baptist Convention in Louisville in 1887. Eager asked Boyce about his health. He answered, "I am really no better, nor do I ever expect to be any better. What I am praying for is to be spared long enough to finish this work I now have on hand, and then I shall be ready to be offered up." Eager remarked, "If I were to attempt to express the profound sorrow of my heart, utterance would fail me. I would have to turn away and in silence weep."[23] The person reporting the meeting observed that "no allusion was made to Dr. Boyce's having been President of the Southern Baptist Convention." The speakers were so absorbed with "the magnitude of the work Dr. Boyce had done on his own chosen line that they forgot to refer to the honors his brethren had put upon him."

H. H. Tucker had known Boyce since they both lived in Charleston. When Tucker was twenty, Boyce was twelve and a pupil in Tucker's Sunday school class. Tucker's respect for Boyce was profound and transparent and his love for him deeply rooted. "The event has been a revelation to us," Tucker wrote; "We never knew before how dreadful a loss the loss of Boyce would be. We never knew before how much we loved him. We have now a view of our own hearts that we never had before."[24] Tucker could not contain himself in speaking of the uniqueness of Boyce in his generation, calling him "great, . . . strong, . . . so pure and so true!" A later generation could possibly see another like Boyce, but Tucker did not expect ever again to write words "on an occasion of like character and equal moment." It would take a long time, Tucker predicted, for Boyce's mantle to "fall from the skies." He, like virtually all others, called the seminary Boyce's "monument," an institution that "could not have survived its trials and troubles but for the immense force of character which Boyce brought to bear upon its interests." Tucker characterized as "beautiful to see" the financial abilities Boyce devoted to the work of the Lord rather than personal enrichment. From his mother, Boyce inherited a spirit of meekness; "where was there ever a gentler spirit than his?" Tucker could not refrain himself from an incredible list of superlatives about Boyce.

> We have had men, and have them now, superior to him in one particular or in another, but where is there another such combination of forces intellectual, moral, and social, that completely round out the character of a perfect man? There are some (not so many) who excel him in learning, some (a considerable number) who are more brilliant, none of better balanced mind, or of better balanced character, none of more trustworthy judgment, none more soundly orthodox, none of profounder convictions, none truer to their convictions, none more industrious, none more generous, none more self-sacrificing, none more genial or magnetic in personal intercourse, and not one who combines all these qualities in a character so full of power. It was his Washingtonian evenness of development, his perfect poise, and his huge motive force that made him great.[25]

The *Biblical Recorder* from North Carolina carried the statement by T. H. Pritchard on Boyce's death. Pritchard, serving as pastor of First Baptist Church of Wilmington, North Carolina, knew the personalities and institutions of Baptists in the South as well as any living person. Writing on the night that the news was received from France of Boyce's death, Pritchard noted, "For twenty years I have been a trustee of the Seminary over which he presided and for a time I sustained most intimate and confidential relations to him as his pastor." This pastorate occurred at Broadway Baptist Church in Louisville in 1882, immediately after he had served as president of Wake Forest College from 1879 to 1882. Pritchard had served on the committee of seven that recommended the removal of the seminary from Greenville to Louisville, was an associate editor of the *Biblical Recorder*, and wrote the sketches of North Carolina Baptists for their inclusion in William Cathcart's *Baptist Encyclopedia*.

Pritchard honored Boyce for his "great intellect, his strong faith, his tireless energy, his indomitable courage, his extraordinary executive ability and the stupendous work he was enabled to accomplish." Beyond all this, however, Pritchard knew Boyce as a great heart, unselfish, kind, true, and the most generous man he ever knew, with the exception of "the sainted Wingate." Pritchard was referring to W. M. Wingate, who had served as president of Wake Forest College for twenty-five years before his death in 1879. Pritchard called Wingate "an admirable college president, the ablest preacher the Baptists of North Carolina have yet had, and the sweetest saint that the writer has ever known."[26] It was no faint praise, then, when he wrote, "No person ever had a more faithful friend and supporter than he [Boyce] was to me, and I feel tonight as I pay this humble tribute to his memory that henceforth there will be less of sunshine in this world to me now that this great and good man has left it."[27]

Pritchard knew of the great obstacles encountered in the removal of the seminary to Louisville and was privy to much inside information from Boyce as well as John A. Broadus. Pritchard did not know "another man in the world who could have over come [sic] all these obstacles and have so successfully achieved this great victory but Dr. J. P. Boyce." He believed fully that Boyce's fellow faculty members would say amen to this evaluation. He issued a call for John A. Broadus, for "no one knew him better" and "no one loved him more tenderly," to provide a biography that would "tell to future generations how a great heroic soul lived and labored in our day."[28] Pritchard also held a memorial service for Boyce in the church in Wilmington on the first Sunday in January.[29]

Pritchard closed with a poem composed for his deceased friend.

My brother, not for thee we mourn,
For thou hast fallen asleep in Christ,
Blessed! For God hath called thee blest.
High lifted gates admit thee into rest:
But for ourselves, alas! Bereft,
Of thy prevailing prayers, thy heart warm,
Thy goodly spirit and thy valiant arm.

The Funeral

After preparation of the body, the voyage of Boyce's body across the Atlantic started on January 5 from France. Several representatives from the seminary met the body as well as Boyce's wife and three daughters on their arrival in New York and accompanied the family to Louisville. The body arrived in Louisville on January 15 and was taken to the seminary the next day, Wednesday, January 16. The students immediately organized a guard of honor to be present with the body every hour until the funeral scheduled for Sunday afternoon, January 20. One student, E. V. Baldy, reported that "a quietude pervaded the building, and throughout the long nights the lights burned in New York Hall, while the students by turns kept sad vigil over the remains of their much loved professor."[30] L. O. Dawson recounted the event as one who stood watch: "The writer will ever count it one of the greatest privileges of his life, the honor of watching by the side of our President, Jas. P. Boyce, for one short hour."[31] On Sunday—"a gloomy day, no sunshine, but dark, cloudy and rainy"—the hearse arrived soon after two o'clock with the pallbearers.[32] The procession from the seminary to Broadway Baptist Church included the hearse, carriages with the family, other relations, friends, and professors and students marching in a long double file line beside the hearse. All this was done through a cold drizzle.

People from every sector of Louisville society and every religious persuasion—Protestant, Catholic, Jew—filled the ample auditorium. Baldy reported that "many of Main Street's leading business men, many lawyers, judges, and doctors were there also." Dawson described the scene at the church with all the pathos of a deeply involved mourner.

> The funeral service began at 3 o'clock. We have never witnessed such a scene. Since a sorrowing people laid Robert E. Lee in his tomb there has not been such an occasion in the South. It was cold and raining, but every seat and all standing room back to the very doors was taken, while immediately around their President were the boys in chairs and on pulpit steps. In the great throng sat and stood people from all parts of the country. Canada and Florida, Virginia and California, all jammed and crowded together lifted their sad, tear-stained faces to the speakers who tried, but failed, to tell what a man he was.[33]

Flowers virtually hid the pulpit from view. "Ordinary boquets [*sic*], crown, crosses, pillars, pyramids, harps, anchors, all fashioned out of the choicest flowers lay in rich profusion about the altar, while rising above them all was the design of the students bearing the significant words, 'Your boys will ever love you.'"[34] Another conspicuous offering consisted of white camellias in the shape of a harp with the word, in purple letters, "Victory" at its foot. This was sent by First Baptist Church of Augusta, Georgia, the church in which the Southern Baptist Convention received its birth. The casket was placed in front of this vast array of floral tributes from across the nation.

The pulpit personnel consisted of representatives of every segment of Baptist life, auspicious for their long list of credentials. These included W. H. Williams, editor of the *Central Baptist* from St. Louis; Judge Alexander P. Humphrey of Louisville; J. L. M. Curry, a former trustee at the seminary, former president of the Foreign Mission Board in Richmond, former teacher at Howard College and Richmond College, and most recently (1885–88) U.S. ambassador to Spain; Rev. Kirtley, the moderator of the General Baptist Association of Kentucky; James M. Pendleton, pastor at Bowling Green for twenty years, professor of theology at Union University, Jackson, Tennessee, for four years, writer of several volumes including *An Old Landmark Reset* and *Christian Doctrines*, and a leading force in the founding of Crozer Theological Seminary; Lansing Burrows, recording secretary of the

Southern Baptist Convention (for thirty-three years total) and pastor of First Baptist Church, Augusta; John A. Broadus, intimate friend of Boyce and presently serving as chair of the seminary faculty; I. T. Tichenor, secretary of the Home Mission Board, whose work in that position had salvaged the viability of the Southern Baptist Convention; S. H. Ford, editor of *Christian Repository* in St. Louis; R. M. Dudley, president of Georgetown College in Frankfort; and three Louisville ministers, T. T. Eaton, J. M. Weaver, and J. W. Warder.[35]

Another account made mention of C. C. Bitting of the American Baptist Publication Society; H. A. Tupper, corresponding secretary of the Foreign Mission Board and Boyce's brother-in-law; Ker Boyce, postmaster of Augusta and Boyce's younger brother; and Mrs. Burckmeyer of Charleston, Boyce's sister. Honorary pallbearers consisted of representatives of the Confederate Association of Kentucky: Rev. T. D. Witherspoon, Rev. M. M. Benton, Judge William M. Jackson, General J. B. Castleman, Judge R. H. Thompson, and General Basil W. Duke.[36]

The opening prayer was led by I. T. Tichenor, and Eaton served as facilitator of the entire service. "It was an occasion of such solemnity," according to Dawson, "that it will be long before its impression will be removed from the minds of those who witnessed it."[37] Speeches were to be given by Basil Manly Jr., Broadus, Curry, and Judge Humphrey. Manly was sick and unable to participate. His difficulty, brought on by the attack on him some months earlier, was described as "complication of heart trouble, with pleurisy."[38] Broadus said, "He was sick with pneumonia."[39] Before anyone spoke, a hymn written by Marcus B. Allmond, Boyce's secretary, specifically for this occasion was sung by the entire congregation.

> Deal gently, Lord! Our souls are bowed
> In grief; our hearts are fraught with tears;
> Shed sunlight on the passing cloud,
> And chase away our rising fears.
>
> Deal gently, Lord! Thy mighty ways
> Are not as ours: O Blessed Name,
> Teach us in sorrow still to praise
> Thy goodness, and Thy love proclaim.

Deal gently, Lord! For we are weak;
The archer, Death, has smitten low
Our leader, and we pray Thee speak,
And cheer us in this hour of woe.

Deal gently, Lord! In darkness let
Thy fiery pillar lead the way;
Bring us, though foes within beset,
Unto the bright and better day.

Deal gently, Lord! Our dead shall be
New cause to fill our hearts with love;
New peace and joy in man and Thee;
New hope and faith in Heaven above.

After the hymn, Lansing Burrows read three passages of Scripture, followed by a prayer by Weaver. Broadus and Humphrey spoke, Katie Elliott Upperman sang "One Sweetly Solemn Thought," and J. L. M. Curry finished the formal presentation. Dawson said that "the traces of keen suffering were so clearly seen" in Broadus's face that people felt "here was a man called upon to preach his own brother's funeral, and who instead of comforting, himself needed all the consolation he could get." Observers noted with what powerful restraint he held his feelings in check but still often uttered sentences in broken bits. The language of Judge Humphrey was "chaste, scholarly and elegant."[40] The address of Dr. Curry "was rendered in the style of a great Christian statesman."[41]

The congregation sang "Nearer, My God, to Thee," and J. M. Pendleton prayed after which T. T. Eaton announced that the service would be concluded at the graveside. A long procession accompanied the body to Cave Hill Cemetery where Kerfoot concluded the service with prayer. "Darkness settled around the weeping crowd as they lowered him into the resting place of all mankind," Dawson recounted, and "the clouds had changed their tears to crystal snow, as if anxious to fill the grave with a covering as pure as his life had been."[42]

The three addresses given that day were published in the February number of *The Seminary Magazine*. In addition, the publication included a tribute to Boyce given by Rabbi Moses of Louisville to a large audience of Jews and Christians. The speech was delivered on January 4, "the eve of the Sabbath." The editors of *The Seminary Magazine* sought a full manuscript from the rabbi, but "having spoken without writing" he could not reproduce the speech. An abstract written by a reporter appeared in the *Louisville Commercial* on January 5 and was reprinted in the *Baptist Courier* on 17 January 1889.

Rabbi Moses posed the question as to why he should honor in the synagogue a "Gentile of the Gentiles, a Christian of the Christians" who was of the "purest Anglo-American blood." He answered, "Because I have loved him as one of the purest and best of mortals." He knew Boyce to be "a righteous and upright man," with a profound sympathy for humanity, who "in his whole life never did, consciously, a wrong to any being." He was a great encourager of individuals, generous to a fault, "a golden vessel full to the brim of the milk of human kindness" that overflowed in every direction at the slightest touch. He was of the "noblest of his race," a natural leader of men who wanted to leave a legacy of knowledge, intellectual attainments, and a community of righteousness and loving-kindness.

Rabbi Moses said that Boyce's *Abstract of Systematic Theology* was a masterpiece. "Concede his premises," he acknowledged, "and you are carried by his logic irresistibly to his conclusions." Boyce could have been a financier, a senator, a president! Before coming to Louisville, Moses had known Christianity only in books, but in Boyce he found it to be a living force and in him he learned to "respect and reverence the spiritual force called Christianity." He could see in Boyce that Old Israel and Christian Israel were united in seeking to make all men more God-like. He prayed, therefore, that God would grant "that Christianity may long continue to produce such men as he, for such men as Dr. Boyce bring heart to heart, and draw us all toward that goal of which we have only glimpses—that is God and the Kingdom of Righteousness forever."[43] The editors prefaced the article with the caveat "that the radical difference between the theology of the two men made it impossible for the speaker to recognize the real fountain of Dr. Boyce's greatness."[44]

Broadus spoke with as much reserve as he could, preferring to err "by defect rather than excess." Boyce's father received several minutes of discussion in order for Broadus to clinch the point of J. P.

Boyce's early development of trustworthiness and mature judgment. He became executor of a sizable fortune at twenty-five years of age. Broadus continued for some time with biographical points: Boyce's education, his conversion, his surprising decision to enter the gospel ministry, his theological education, his marriage, his work as an editor, a pastor, and a college theological professor. He spoke of the pivotal and formative impact of Boyce's address "Three Changes in Theological Institutions," and emphasized the absolute dependence, from a human standpoint, that the seminary had on the leadership, energy, devotion, and sacrifice of Boyce. "I speak not of the plans of an idle dreamer," Broadus summarized, "but of a great projecting mind who knew whereof he thought and hoped."[45]

His final section emphasized the "leading traits of character of our dear friend." Broadus believed that Boyce was "made out of good timber all the way through," thoroughly genuine in every part of his makeup. He had extraordinarily good judgment, like his father, and was a man of "very strong convictions and very decided opinions" combined with an "immense tenacity of purpose." With all of this, however, while it was not easy, "it was never impossible to convince him he was wrong." In addition, Boyce disregarded personal considerations but moved unrelentingly to what he thought was right, and at the same time highly regarded "other people's wishes and opinions." Boyce was generous both in material munificence and in praise of friends. "If he was ever extravagant in language," Broadus noted, "it was when he praised his friends." Boyce was a man of honor, a thoroughgoing "South Carolina gentleman," and in the most exalted sense a "Christian gentleman."

Broadus viewed Boyce as a "very deep and strong thinker." He tied this trait to his Calvinist theological convictions.

> The Scotch-Irish seem to have Calvinism running in the blood. The very make of their minds seems to suit that style of belief. And Calvinism compels men to think. James P. Boyce from profound conviction and life long study was led to believe that the Bible teaches that which men call for praise or blame by the name of Calvinism. If you want to see old-fashioned straight-forward Calvinism drawn right out of the Bible with full sincerity of conviction and with infinite painstaking, you will read it in his Abstract of Systematic Theology. It was prepared as a text

book for students, but any lawyer or intellectual business man who wants to grapple with the great question of Christian truth may derive the highest advantage and profit from this treaties [*sic*].[46]

Broadus called Boyce a "marvelous teacher" who exacted honest and patient work from the students. If they were "worth much," they rejoiced that they were taught "to deal with christian [*sic*] truth in so thorough a fashion." He illustrated by referring to an opinion of C. H. Toy. "One of the first students of the Seminary who was afterwards our colleague and now a Professor at Harvard told me many times that Dr. Boyce grounded him in the truth of the Bible so that it all hung together in his mind, and must stand together or fall together."

He was a man of "remarkable general attainments," loving art and poetry, and widely read in politics. Had he given his life to it, Boyce would have been a great preacher; yet even as overwhelmed with other duties as Boyce constantly was, he could sometimes preach with great strength and at other times be very melting and delightful. Boyce's final days were filled with thoughts of the goodness of God as evidenced in securing the future usefulness of the seminary. His final words were about the students and the school. Broadus ended with an emotional appeal and exhortation.

> Oh, if our people had known James P. Boyce as I knew him, the thought of that as his last feeble effort would stir the souls of our brethren in Louisville and all the land, and the desire of his heart would be more than fulfilled in what would be done for the enterprise to which he gave his life, and that while yet the early grass is green upon his grave. In the long years to come may the men who teach and the men who learn in the Seminary which he beyond all other persons put together built up, feel still the impress of that high character, that noble simplicity, that genuineness, that love of God, that faith in prayer, that simple, humble hope of Heaven, that willingness to turn from the highest earthly inducements and live a life of sacrifice to accomplish something for the good of man and the glory of God.[47]

When Judge Humphrey spoke, he remembered not only Boyce's impressions on him but on his father. "I have not the vantage ground of a personal intimacy, nor have I enjoyed the long association which has been so much enjoyed by others here," Humphrey began, but his veneration for Boyce came from "lips that are silent." Humphrey's father had been an eminent minister in the Presbyterian Church and a good friend of Boyce.[48] In spite of denominational differences, very little separated these "two good soldiers, both in the Army of the one living God under the one Great Captain of our salvation." Humphrey discerned Boyce's character from the singleness of mind he demonstrated about the work to which God called him; he observed the "devotion and the virility of the Christian minister, a single mind, single purpose, one constant allegiance, a putting of the hand to the plow and not looking back, a giving of every force and strength of mind, health, character and estate in dedication to the God who made him."[49] When Boyce became a minister, he did not cease to be a man; he demonstrated at once both manliness and devotion, and regarded as irrelevant and foolish the kind of "patronizing respect which is akin to contempt" often conferred sneeringly by worldlings.

Like Broadus, Humphrey had deep respect for the doctrinal strength of Boyce. A Calvinist must have a clear and courageous mind, and Boyce served as a "remarkable example of what is the power of control of pure Calvinism." His theology had fitted him for just the kind of service he was to offer—"He believed that before the foundation of the world had been laid God had fixed what part he should take in the great drama of the universe, that his calling and election was sure and that he must live worthy of the high vocation wherewith he was called."[50] The crowning labor of his life was the foundation of the Southern Baptist Theological Seminary. One must never doubt the courage as well as the personal sacrifice involved, not only in founding the school, but in removing it from South Carolina to Louisville. With that stroke Boyce did more for Louisville's honor, prosperity, and glory than "if he had belted the world with a girder of iron, or transferred at one stroke to our borders all the looms of Manchester." Boyce had made Louisville a city that "sits upon a hill."[51]

Curry compared Boyce to great leaders of the past, not only comprehensive in abilities but superior, "not a follower, not a mere floater on the surface and current of thought and affairs, but a leader, a seer, a thinker, a born ruler." Subduing the temptation to use his many talents for more spectacular undertakings, Boyce took the noble and long-sighted course of investing himself in education—education of the most exalted kind, the Southern Baptist Theological Seminary. Curry believed that what Boyce and his coworkers did "will live on through the centuries, reproducing itself in men who shall glorify Christ and exalt the Bible, rightly preaching and interpreting God's truths."

Curry also commended Boyce for his work with the Slater fund. This fund, endowed for the education of the "lately enslaved Negro," engaged a controversial and volatile issue for those loyal to the Lost Cause. Boyce, however, though every inch a Southerner, "brought wide and varied experience, vigorous intellect, moral elevation, courageous conviction and strong adherence to duty to the discharge of his duties as trustee of that fund, and what that fund is doing grandly for the negro race is largely due to his influence and his character."[52] In light of the possibility of what Curry described as "vulgar prejudice, much Bourbonism, much antichristian prejudice" in reference to "that most difficult problem of civilization, the negro problem," Curry addressed those mourners that represented the Confederate heritage. He had confidence that they were not there to "revive bitter memories, but to express deepest sympathy for this loss" in recognition of all that is noble and true in the "fellowship of common humanity." Boyce had won in the conflict against sin and Satan, had struck a blow for "humanity, for truth, for liberty, for God," for he marched under the banner of "the great Captain of our Salvation, who brought life, liberty and immortality to light through the Gospel."[53]

A Convention Memorial

The Southern Baptist Convention meeting in Memphis in 1889 held a memorial service for Boyce in the Court Street Presbyterian Church on Sunday at 3:30 P.M. The service opened with devotional exercises by J. Lansing Burrows of Virginia. Following were speeches by H. H. Tucker of Georgia (who died the following September), J. H. Luther of Texas, E. C. Dargan of South Carolina, and W. E. Hatcher of Virginia.[54] Dargan, only thirty-six years of age, had graduated from the seminary in 1877 in the last Greenville session and then served as pastor of several churches throughout the country. In 1892 he would come to teach homiletics at the seminary for fifteen years, giving aid to John A. Broadus in the gathering of material for a second edition of *On the Preparation and Delivery of Sermons*.[55] Dargan also would write *A History of Preaching* and *Doctrines of Our Faith*. William E. Hatcher served as president of the Baptist General Association of Virginia and had just published (1887) a biography of J. B. Jeter,[56] later published (1908) a biography of John Jasper, a famous and beloved black preacher in Richmond, and would compose a genial autobiography entitled *Along the Trail of the Friendly Years*. Broadus recorded that both Tucker and Dargan spoke of Boyce's meekness. He reported lengthy portions of their remarks at this memorial service.

Dargan regarded Boyce's "strong character" as the product of "a clear mind, a pure heart, and a powerful will," neither an accident nor ephemeral, but the achievement of a lifetime of consistent application of thought. "His powers of mind," Dargan observed, "were perhaps not naturally greater than those of many others; but he trained and used them well." Everything he pursued in word and deed had "honest, hard thinking back of them."[57]

Tucker's speech at the convention memorial service blended large portions of his earlier newspaper article about Boyce with seasoned observations and striking images. As before, Tucker highlighted the variety of gifts blended in Boyce's personality and activity. Having inherited the strong no-nonsense business talent of his father, its integration in a beautiful symmetry with the meekness of his mother gave Boyce an impressive and striking presence in any situation. "He was as tender as a woman," Tucker reiterated; "his artlessness and simplicity of nature were like a little child." At the same time Boyce was brave and wise, and when a time of "great emergency called for a man, there was Boyce!" In this maturely balanced man one could see the lion and the lamb lying together, making Boyce always "just what the occasion demanded." As Tucker repeated from his earlier article the impressive list of peerless qualities he had observed in Boyce, he added the qualifying phrase "all sanctified by grace."[58]

The speech of J. H. Luther, president of Baylor Female College in Belton, Texas, appeared in a Texas paper. Luther, who had known Boyce for forty-five years, reminisced about the powerful personalities that had made the Southern Baptist Convention, to that point, successful. In addition, he recalled their time at Brown University, the aspirations that possibly filled their young minds, and the last years of the Triennial Convention. Luther "sat in the gallery of the Old Church during the last session of the Triennial Convention" and recalled "the unyielding, truth-loving Cone, the impressive presence of the great orator Welch, the massive Wayland." He referred to others who "had no peers." He remembered the visit of Adoniram Judson to the United States in 1846, the year after the formation of the Southern Baptist Convention, and how it brought a sense of enthusiasm, prayer, unity of purpose, and "throbbings of pious hearts." He spoke of the departure of "life-long companions to meet at Augusta" in forming the convention—"the scholarly Johnson; the lion hearted Howell; Mell with the bearing of a Prince; Poindexter, our Stonewall; Manly our magnetic St. John; Fuller with all the graces of oratory."

Returning to Boyce, Luther said that their meetings subsequent to college—always joyous—pulsated with such intense interest in the "teeming present that 'old time' talk soon gave place to the all absorbing theme which taxed every faculty and gave his mother-heart an object of fondness for a life-time—a theological seminary which in some of its features should have no rival." In their college group—"a happier set of fellows I have never met since," Luther remarked—Boyce was "the leading spirit." He demonstrated a "magnetism in his humor, a nobility in his presence and a manly expression in his language, which made him attractive to all." Even in college, Boyce showed on many occasions his insatiable generosity.

Luther recalled Boyce's conversion, his first pastorate, his teaching at Furman, and his famous address on theological education. Luther added in a handwritten note, "And I remember too with what dignity and self possession he presided over the Southern Convention. He felt at home. He had the courage unawed by popular clamor or the generous impulses of the unreflecting to make his rulings the echoes of the letter and spirit of the constitution." He also knew of the series of difficulties that "environed him": "The loss of a part of his fortune, the terrors of the civil war, the want of faith shown by men of ample means in the enterprise, and the loss of doctrinal fellowship in a beloved colleague." None of these things made him falter but only "strengthened a character in which a childlike faith, a humility born of suffering, and a purpose with ribs of steel, had been for years the ruling elements."

Boyce needs no monument, Luther believed. The seminary will perpetuate his name, and the *Abstract of Systematic Theology*, a book that "deserves a place by the side of Andrew Fuller and Charles Hodge, will give to many an earnest student in the years to come the good old Pauline theology free from vagaries and wild speculations." Like many others, Luther viewed Boyce's character as "complete, . . . solid, symmetrical." Boyce's common sense and quick perceptive powers made him trustworthy as a guide, not only in theology, but in the matters of his estate and the affairs of the seminary. Luther, as many others, saw the almost feminine tenderness of Boyce's spirit of benevolence and compared his conscientiousness to that of Adoniram Judson. "He moved in an atmosphere higher than his critics could reach. His prayers ascended to heaven amid the incense of daily sacrifices." Luther closed with an emotional "Farewell" to his "companion of youth, co-worker in our Zion." He saw his generation rapidly passing away, but living with the hope that "we shall soon be together again at a reunion where the watchmen shall see eye to eye, and best of all when we shall know even as we are known." He closed with a hymn written for the occasion:

Falling asleep—the day's work o'er
Soon to behold the golden shore;
Sinking to rest while angels keep
Watch o'er the loved one's quiet sleep.

Falling asleep—the shadows grow deep;
The stout hearted bow—the loving must weep;
But morning is near—the night will soon break—
The day-star arise—the hero awake.

Falling asleep, the victory won;
Life's offering made, life's suffering done;

And soon the Paradise above
Will greet the spirit born to love.

Falling asleep—forgotten be
The burdens of life's mystery;
Remember last of all below
The blood that makes us white as snow.

Farewell, dear soul—we soon shall meet;
Together walk the golden street;
Together view the great white throne,
And know the Lord as we are known.

The Broadus *Memoir*

The 7 February 1889 issue of the *Christian Index* carried the announcement, "A memoir of the late Rev. James P. Boyce, D. D., is to be prepared by Dr. John A. Broadus. Friends in any part of the country who have letters from him, or can furnish newspaper articles or any matters of personal recollection, great or small, are requested to send them at once to Dr. Broadus" at his address.[59] None could have been more apt to write such a memoir. Their friendship had been deep and imperturbable since their first acquaintance with each other in 1855. In 1870, when Boyce wrote an extended and peculiarly clever letter to Broadus, he interjected a telling paragraph. "But I must address myself to some news or you will think me a brute thus to inflict on you the nonsense of my brain." An explanation for such candor Boyce believed was in order: "You are, unfortunately, one of those upon whom I fear no disastrous effects, and therefore I dam up my little Catskill the most of the time and let it forth—a petty stream at best, but somewhat swollen by its usual pent up state."[60] He could tell Broadus anything, and unburden both his distress and his exhilaration to him.

Broadus closed the memoir of his beloved friend with a chapter entitled "General Estimates of Character." He included many of the personal memories sent him including more material from the lengthy narrative provided by Lizzie Boyce. He utilized material also from

530

his funeral oration about Boyce. Broadus synthesized from a number of sources and the various anecdotes a profile of Boyce's personality. Illustrated with strong firsthand observations were the traits that made Boyce an excellent man of business—good judgment, strong conviction, decided opinions, impeccable habits of organization. The penchant for systematic arrangement reflected from every facet of Boyce's life. Letters, pamphlets, books, and furniture all came under his eye for logical as well as aesthetic arrangement. Once Boyce remarked in a speech before a historical society that a man that would throw away a pamphlet should be hung.

Boyce's understanding of the value of arrangement flowed over into his understanding of time. He demanded punctuality of himself and lamented its failure in others. Lizzie reported that "in his anxiety to be always on time, he would start say fifteen minutes earlier than necessary for a city engagement, to allow for any interruption or other detention on the way; and he never failed to be at an appointment some minutes before the time, watch in hand, ready to pounce upon the tardy comer." She pinpointed this trait as the "only drawback to our pleasure when travelling with Father." He would have them at the train station sometimes an hour before departure, a feature that was "exhausting" to his traveling companions.[61]

Broadus characterized Boyce as a "deep thinker" with the observation "very rarely do you find a man so widely acquainted and actively occupied with practical affairs, yet so delighting in the profoundest thought." His ability to focus on a single thought and carry it out in a finely spun analysis or refutation or vindication did not inhibit his love for general reading in a wide variety of subjects and genre. Merchandising, banking, politics, law, history, poetry, fiction (both American and French novelists), and a wide variety of newspapers and other periodicals fascinated his intellectual curiosity. He achieved a substantial knowledge in this dizzying array of special interests. On one occasion he hired a tutor in French for his entire family and enjoyed greatly these lessons, exchanging jokes and laughter with the family over mistakes made by each, including himself.

531

His daughter wrote at length of Boyce's love for books and the numerous gifts he made of finely bound and richly illustrated editions. The largest part of his library was purchased before the war; his subsequent purchases more specifically related to his necessary studies. His daughter considered this "one of the greatest trials that loss of fortune brought upon him."[62]

Broadus considered Boyce a man of exquisite taste, "in all the high senses of the term." He loved flowers and delighted spending winter evenings looking at catalogues, deciding what to order for the coming spring planting. When his purchases arrived, he laid aside his books and pen and took up trowel and water pail to give aid under his wife's leadership in planting the garden. Despite extravagant efforts, he had no success in growing Kentucky bluegrass in Greenville. But his wife had over four hundred potted plants when the Boyces left Greenville for Kentucky.

Broadus gave significant space to a discussion of Boyce's love of art and fashion. He maintained entrée to every private collection in Charleston and knew well the leading pieces in the museums of Philadelphia and New York. He outfitted his wife with jewelry and the finest of fashion, saw to the furnishing and decoration of their homes in Columbia, Greenville, and Louisville to the finest details. He was impeccable in his courtesies to women including those of his family. Boyce engaged in humor on many occasions, particularly when in friendly company, and had no scruples against a pun. He was "entirely free" from any attempt "to raise a laugh by irreverence, indecency, or sarcastic severity." He loved the Christmas season, entering into it with "all the delight of the children," and took great pleasure in purchasing personally all the presents for his children, each one aptly chosen.

Broadus portrayed Boyce as a man of honor and honesty and somewhat incredulous at the ease with which many people ignored the truth. He was a man of humility and modesty and genuine meekness. He loved to praise and encourage and took advantage of any opportunity to catapult a student or a friend to success with praise. He found ways of prompting them to press on toward excellence. If sternness had greater promise of accomplishing the goal, he could be stern. His correspondence was massive, mostly concerning financial matters, but quite often complex and lengthy on doctrinal, moral, and ecclesiological issues. He wrote letters to family members and would not allow the press of other correspondence make him neglect his family. Lizzie remembered the profound impression made by these letters.

> His letters written to us are filled with expressions of love, and sweet assurances of his perfect confidence that we would always do what would be pleasing to him. These letters were charmingly adapted to our childish years. He had the rare power of entering into the little things that please and interest a child. Sometimes his letters were quite merry, abounding in all kinds of pleasantry; others were full of serious talk in reference to our characters and aims in life. He sometimes wrote to his small namesakes when babies, with comical messages for the baby to tell Mamma, etc. When it is remembered that these form a part of an enormous daily correspondence of a man who often wrote late into the night, not daring to postpone to another day the answering of letters, which if allowed to accumulate would have become an insurmountable task, one cannot but wonder at his never neglecting these little things, as many might have felt justified in doing under similar pressure.[63]

Another trait mentioned frequently by Broadus was Boyce's great generosity. Numberless testimonies of gifts bestowed for godly causes at all levels of society could have been garnered, but Broadus contended that the full extent of Boyce's generosity could never be measured. Much of it was hidden, and even his closest associates were unaware of many of the people and causes to which he gave. His brother-in-law, H. A. Tupper, knew that he had given away more than he had spent on himself and his family, and that the amount would be in the hundreds of thousands of dollars. He delighted not only in responding to applications for help but in anticipating points at which he might meet needs before being asked. Even in his last illness he continued to give, so Tupper said, but in ways "too sacred for the page of history."[64]

In summary, Boyce was characterized by the marvelous roundedness of his personality and Christian grace. Arthur Peter spoke of "the well-rounded development and perfect balance of all his powers." G. W. Samson wrote some months after Boyce's death, "Dr. Boyce was in every respect the noblest spirit that I ever met."[65]

Broadus's final words erupted as an apostrophe to his dear friend whose memory he sought to elongate and whose character and contribution, in his estimation, deserved naught but sincere eulogy. Intended or not, its words are poetry.

> O Brother beloved,
> True yokefellow through years of toil,
> best and dearest friend,
>
> Sweet shall be thy memory
> Till we meet again.
>
> And may the men be always ready,
> As the years come and go,
> To carry on, with widening reach and power,
> The work we sought to do,
>
> And did begin![66]

The Aftermath

Boyce has occasionally been the subject for Founders' Day addresses at Southern Baptist Theological Seminary. On 11 January 1907, eighty years after the birth of Boyce, Lansing Burrows delivered an address focusing on Boyce. Burrows, pastor of First Baptist Church, Nashville, emphasized "the genius and mastery of James P. Boyce in the domain of theological education." Entering the Christian ministry from a patrician family was unusual in the mid-nineteenth century, Burrows averred, but such an unusual circumstance was needed for the changing culture; "If ever God raised up a man to meet the conditions of an altering age, he raised up James P. Boyce." Boyce's tenacity after the Civil War brought about both the renaissance of the seminary and the rehabilitation of Southern Baptists. Boyce's singular vision of the purpose of any organization, including the seminary as well as the Southern Baptist Convention itself, often led him into a storm of opposition in which he always maintained his nobility. The keynote of Boyce's life, Burrows propounded, was courage.[67]

Fifteen years later, 11 January 1922, A. J. Holt delivered a message entitled "Christ the Builder: Boyce the Builder." After establishing several traits of Christ as the builder of his church, Holt, the first student from Texas to attend the seminary, pointed to the astounding things that Boyce attempted in the building of the seminary. His drawing Baptists, especially the Baptists of South Carolina, to embrace the idea even when it meant the "disestablishment of the theological department at Furman University" embodied in clearest perspective a "lesson in the magic art of management." His attempt to raise an endowment when Baptists were "neither willing nor able to assume great things" was the stroke of a master builder. So it was with establishing the initial location in Greenville "where the singing, sighing pines made music with the swish of Reedy River hard by," but then eighteen years later Boyce's character shone with even greater luster "during the settlement of the difficult and delicate question of the removal of the Seminary from Greenville."

Noting that this generation calls for a visionary and noble builder like Boyce, Holt composed a poem in celebration of Boyce's immense accomplishment.

> All honor to the man, God's man,
> That wrought the winning plan, God's plan,
> Who with deep discretion rare,
> With persistence and with prayer,
> Put his hand unto the plow,
> And his heart unto the vow
> That built this glorious now,
> Out of Nothing.
>
> All honor to the men, God's men:
> With penetrating ken, God's ken;
> Labored long against the wrong,
> Wrought with might to win the right,
> Marched through darkness into light,
> Making all the future bright,
> Turning all of faith to sight,
> Out of Nothing.

All honor to the school, God's school;
That has taught full many a fool, God's fool;
Till his folly did depart,
Leaving him an humble heart,
Showing him the way to win,
Against ignorance and sin,
Until wisdom entered in—
Out of Nothing.

All honor to this day, God's day;
That celebrates the way, God's way,
That the victory was gained,
The might of right maintained,
Just as had been ordained
Thro' the sacrificial test
That brought Boyce unto his best,
Given neither pause nor rest—
Out of Nothing.[68]

    David M. Ramsey delivered the Founders' Day address in 1924, entitled "James Petigru Boyce—God's Gentleman." Ramsey used the occasion to demonstrate "the beautiful reciprocal affection existing between the student body and Dr. Boyce."[69] He concentrated on anecdotes that pictured Boyce as intimately concerned for the personal lives of the students, and in doing so winning their deep and sincere affection.

    Such affection developed slowly, according to Z. T. Cody. On 11 January 1927, on the one hundredth birthday of Boyce, Cody presented the Founders' Day address. Cody was an 1887 graduate of the seminary. In 1927 he was editor of the *Baptist Courier* located in Greenville, South Carolina. Cody introduced his speech with a narrative of the impression Boyce made on new students.

> To a new student he had the appearance of sternness. There was hardly anything of the open cordiality and personal charm that instinctively invites to familiarity. In his presence always you were one person, he another. Familiarity was out of the question. He was as naturally an aristocrat as Mr. Bryan . . . was a democrat. The first impression he

made on a student was not pleasant. I can never forget my own first utterly erroneous opinion of him. This soon changed. But there was one impression he made on all new students that never changed. It was of respect. He might not be loved at first. But who ever failed to stand in awe of him? In my day only one student ever uttered a disrespectful word to him, and this he expressed in an insulting note. It created consternation among the student body; and no one was surprised when, a few months later, this student became so deranged that he had to be sent to the asylum for lunatics.[70]

Cody presented a biographical summary of Boyce's life and isolated three contributions of Boyce to Southern Baptists: he was the founder of the seminary; he gave Southern Baptists his *Abstract of Systematic Theology*; he gave Southern Baptists "his own character." In the first section Cody showed the mammoth energy and sacrifice involved in settling the seminary securely during the trials of decades. In the second he pointed out that Boyce was a "whole-hearted Calvinist" who accepted totally "the solutions of that system of theology, . . . not reluctantly as if driven to it by irresistible logic, against will and heart. Nay he loved it. He found in it satisfaction, repose and freedom." Though some do not see this as the best solution to religious problems of the day, for Boyce it flowed naturally from his delight in the "greatness and holiness of God," but also from the fact that "he loved God." Cody insisted that Boyce loved God "supremely with all his heart," with a "mind that fearlessly, and regardless of man, carried his thoughts of the holy God to the limits of every conclusion," and with "a might that would crown God absolutely over all things." Cody believed Boyce was a theologian of high order.[71]

Cody also called Boyce's character "one of the greatest treasures in our history." It contained the right proportions of "righteousness and love, humility and strength, gentleness and power, meekness and will, prayer and self-reliance." His business was so high that people trusted him too completely and failed to do their part. He was honest in his opinions without being obstinate. Though not an orator, he "could support a proposition with power." "He was too genuine to be a great orator," Cody noted, "for he could not improvise feelings, nor was there in him a touch of the histrionic. He paid his debts to the cent, kept his appointments to the minute, and answered his correspondence with promptness. He was simple, generous, and intent on self-sacrifice. These aspects of character may be explained only by his encounter with the forgiving grace of the cross of Christ."[72]

On 2 February 1988, Timothy George presented a Founders' Day address entitled "Soli Deo Gloria! The Life and Legacy of James Petigru Boyce." George sought to dust off the obscurity into which Boyce had fallen in the sixty-one years since Cody spoke.[73] "I present him to you not as an artifact from the past," George informed his audience, "but as a living dynamic Christian, theologian, denominational leader, seminary founder, a forebearer in the faith, whom I too have learned to love." He gave a historical synopsis of Boyce's life emphasizing his entire devotion to the seminary's well-being, and that to the glory of God. Summarizing his theology, George characterized Boyce as "fundamental without being Fundamentalist," "a Reformed Baptist without being a hyper-Calvinist," and "an ecumenical churchman without being a denominational relativist." Seeing Boyce as a key in the "theological revitalization" of the Baptist tradition, George said, "Boyce calls us back to a vision of the true and living God, not the unblinking God of a Byzantine dome, distant and aloof, but the God who meets us in mercy and judgment, the God whose favor we can never earn, but who in His sheer mercy and grace has come very close to every one of us, in a Baby in a manger, and in a Man on a cross."[74]

Considering the widespread approbation of Boyce's vision for theological education, including its confessional and Calvinist orientation, one could be quite surprised to find how quickly those traits became irrelevant in the governing of the school. The form remained constant, but the conscience gave way. Broadus's presidency from 1889 to 1895 saw growth of the physical plant in downtown Louisville, increase in students, the awarding of the first doctorates in theology, and the addition of two faculty members, E. C. Dargan and William J. McGlothlin.

William H. Whitsitt was elected president in 1895. During his presidency, a shift began in the attitude of the faculty toward the vision cast by Boyce. This shift was most notable in William O. Carver, who began his professorial career in 1896 teaching New Testament and homiletics. Soon he shifted his focus to missions and continued in that field of study and activity until his retirement in 1943. In a review of F. H. Kerfoot's revision of Boyce's theology text, *Abstract of Systematic Theology*, Carver found an opportunity to becloud Boyce's influence. "But while Boyce's text with Boyce's teaching is said to have caused little trouble in comprehending it," Carver related, "it is abundantly testified that the text without the author to explain, amplify and enforce it was far from being lucid."[75] Carver objected to more in Boyce than his alleged lack of lucidity. Though Carver had never studied with Boyce, he learned from others the distinguishing characteristic of his style and was less than enthusiastic about his method as well as his intended outcome. "His method was purely didactic," Carver wrote, "not creative or stimulating to original thought or research. He was training a ministry to pass on a theological tradition, not to independent experience and thought."[76] For Carver this was not a compliment but the notation of a fault.

Carver's intent in teaching demonstrated just as much starch as Boyce in seeking to mold students according to his perceptions of Christian ministry. His antipathy toward Calvinism matched Boyce's love for it. Election, in Carver's exposition, was instrumental and conditional. For example, Abraham was chosen, not for salvation, but for service— entirely conditioned on Abraham's willingness to respond. "This was a new idea to many who brought with them to the seminary a rigid Calvinistic concept of Election," Cornell Goerner commented, but Carver convinced them of his viewpoint through his approach to the Bible. "It may be that some rejected this modified Calvinism," Goerner speculated, "but I never heard a student who was able to debate it successfully with his professor."[76] One may be sure that Carver could overwhelm his students in debating the issue, but no amount of subtlety could put him in alignment with the institution's governing confession of faith, the "Abstract of Principles."

In his exposition of Ephesians, Carver argued consistently for this instrumental concept of election. The nature of foreordination, predestination, and election is God's choice "of all the means and all the instruments that enter into the process."[78] Election does not involve the purposeful setting aside of particular individuals for salvation while others are passed over. "God who knows, cares, has power, and has purpose must have plan and plans. He chooses means and instruments. This is election."[79] By his power and wisdom and grace, God produces "a spiritual and ethical realm out of the human material which we are." He chooses "men, nations, institutions, religious groups to participate in or to be used in his purpose and his plans."[80] While salvation "usually" coincides with the condition of being an elect person, the main point is that one is "chosen and called to participate in the plan of salvation which God is working through Jesus Christ to save the world, to found and perfect his kingdom, to glorify himself in human history." The church is "chosen for service, for stewardship, saved to serve in the plan of saving the world."[81]

Carver rejected particular atonement, obviously, but beyond that presented an atonement that was not even propitiatory or truly substitutionary. While, in his confessional context, he was savvy enough not to attack the doctrine of penal substitutionary atonement, he does treat it as a dogma somehow foreign to the real life of Christian witness. In one marvelously long sentence Carver disarmed the historic commitment to an objective atonement and questioned the church's confessional Christology:

> The church succeeded in making the doctrine of the Cross central in its theology, the symbol of the Cross central in its cult and liturgy, the dogma of deity central in its own controversies, and the rock of offense and a stone of stumbling to scientists and philosophers, and all too often deity and Cross a word of magic for masses of unthinking men who desire the gift of security for heaven without the experience of ethical achievement in a kingdom in which the will of God must be done on earth.[82]

For Carver, giving doctrinal status to redemptive actions enervates Christian life, compromises its witness, makes it sterile and oppressive.

Hundreds of students formed their view of election in relation to missions under the enchanting, and dogmatic, tutelage of W. O. Carver. Dale Moody, the last graduate student to major under his supervision in Philosophy of Christianity, wrote, "As one deeply in debt, in both intellectual and personal ways, I wish to give thanks to God for the teacher who set the course of my theological pilgrimage more than any other."[83] This was a pilgrimage going the opposite direction from that inculcated by Boyce.

This clear confessional divergence on the part of Carver established a practice at Southern Baptist Theological Seminary that teachers were allowed to sign the "Abstract" and given as much interpretive latitude as they needed in order to fit within it. Frank Stagg said, "Through most of Southern Seminary's years, professors were permitted to sign the *Abstract of Principles* as they interpreted it, contrary to Boyce's demand."[84] This same principle was enunciated by Duke McCall in 1980 in his discussions with Dale Moody over his public disagreement with the "Abstract." He wrote Moody reminding him of "the freedom given to faculty members across the years in their interpretation of the document." He encouraged him to find a way to fit his understanding of the Bible into his understanding of the article on perseverance. "If you are absolutely convinced," McCall reasoned, "that there is only one way to understand Article XIII of the *Abstract of Principles* and that way contradicts the clear meaning and message of the Bible, I hope you will take the initiative in activating your normal retirement."[85] Moody did not initiate his normal retirement and taught by contract for two more years. He expressed his attitude clearly in an interview with Walter Draughon in exclaiming, "Well, I just simply think that Baptists need to shift away from confessionalism to biblical theology, and forget about their Calvinism."[86]

Frank Stagg felt keenly the difficulty posed by Boyce's confessional shadow cast across the faculty conscience. He argued that Boyce "built into Southern Seminary a major flaw which has plagued the seminary from its founding." He did this by establishing the school on a non-negotiable confessional basis. This requirement was "explicit" and "no mere formality." "No professor was to have his private interpretation of the abstract." Boyce erred in at least two ways. One was his belief that a confessional document could "insure the truth of the gospel." Boyce failed, according to Stagg, to reckon with his own finitude and fallibility and to realize that "an abstract can protect error as well as truth." Second, the specific strand of theology Boyce placed in the confession was Calvinism, long ago displaced by more critically and philosophically aware methods of searching for Christian truth. "If we now return to Boyce and the Abstract of Principles," Stagg warned, "it will be bondage to a mixture of truth and error, frustrating honest and competent search for truth."[87]

Resistance to the Calvinism of Boyce reached the depth of insult. W. R. Estep proposed in the state paper for Baptists in Texas that current devotees of Calvinistic theology had "only slight knowledge of Calvin or his system" and "simply borrow that which they assume to be both biblical and baptistic without adequate research." He asserted that "this is essentially what James P. Boyce did, as reflected in his Abstract of Systematic Theology."[88] The editor of that same paper had included an unsubstantiated and highly anachronistic misrepresentation of Boyce earlier. In defending a "whosoever will" kind of gospel, Presnall Wood wrote, "Boyce endorsed all five points of Calvin's teachings. His commitment to limited atonement and irresistible grace was so complete that he refused to issue invitations at the conclusion of sermons for fear he might tempt some poor soul to salvation whom God had not chosen to save."[89] He could not be speaking of the Boyce who saw the first element of successful theological education as that which "exalts first of all, the feelings and devotion of the heart—not only piety—but a piety that longs to speak of Jesus, and to win souls to Him."[90]

Systematic theology took a turn away from Dagg and Boyce, culminating in the direct assault on Boyce's theology in *The Word of Truth* by Dale Moody. E. Y. Mullins dedicated his volume *The Christian Religion in Its Doctrinal Expression* to Boyce, but never quoted him throughout the volume. Instead he determined that he would steer a theological course between Calvinism and Arminianism, creating a system more biblical than both.[91]

W. T. Conner quoted Boyce three times, each time to demonstrate the viewpoint of someone with whom he disagreed. "One theologian has said that the atoning work of Christ 'was only Godward, and only removed all the obstacles in the way of God's pardoning the sinner.' This is the meaning usually given this term. But it is doubtful if this adequately represents the view of what Christ accomplished for us on the cross."[92] Again he quoted Boyce, presenting his view through an impersonal citation: "One theologian has said that mercy and justice are represented (in the Scriptures) 'as antagonistic; mercy pleading for the sinner, and justice demanding his punishment.' According to this way of viewing the matter, the cross of Christ is a manifestation of righteousness, because on the cross Christ met the demands of justice in paying the penalty of our sins."[93] The other occasion came in the same discussion: "This making of justice supreme tends to make our salvation something that God owed to Christ as a matter of debt. It also tends to take away the element of grace in God's dealing with us. In that case, Christ would be gracious; God would be just."[94] Dale Moody, a professor of Systematic Theology at the school founded by Boyce, did not mention Boyce's theology or Boyce by name. Instead, he made an aggressive attempt to refute every distinguishing aspect of Calvinistic theology, while in his denominational presence he called for the alteration of the "Abstract of Principles."[95]

H. H. Tucker's words at the close of his address at the memorial service in Memphis in 1889 drew attention to the possibility of surprise in the future but with confidence in the purpose of God:

> When we need another Boyce, God will give him to us. . . . The past is safe, we can look back and see it; the present is safe, we can look around and see it; the future is hidden from us, but still we are just as certain that it too is safe, for
>
> > Behind the dim unknown
> > Standeth God within the darkness,
> > Keeping watch above his own.

Tucker would never suspect that the contribution of Boyce could be so mangled and his distinctive convictions so maligned. He would be vindicated, however, in his confidence in divine providence, for a staunch defender of the Boyce tradition did arise in the very position in which Boyce had died. In 1993 R. Albert Mohler Jr. came to the presidency of Southern Baptist Theological Seminary. In his opening convocation address, "Don't Just Do Something, Stand There," he gave a hearty exposition and defense of Boyce's purpose in establishing the seminary on a confessional basis. He gave an exposition of the "Abstract" and assurance of his intention to follow its prescriptive intent.

> Let those who would understand Southern Seminary understand this: That our faith is not in the *Abstract of Principles*, but in the God to whom it testifies; that the revealed text we seek rightly to divide is not the *Abstract of Principles*, but the Holy Scripture, but that this Abstract is a sacred contract and confession for those who teach here—who willingly and willfully affix their signatures to its text and their conscience to its intention. They pledge to teach "in accordance with and not contrary to its precepts."[96]

He further explained, "For faculty, the *Abstract* is the charter to teach and the standard of confessional judgment. Southern Seminary is a confessional institution, a pre-committed institution."[97] When Frank Stagg two years later mounted his shrill protest against this policy, Mohler responded with a firm determination to maintain faithfulness to the original intent of the "Abstract." He expressed dismay at Stagg's cavalier willingness to ignore the intent of Boyce and the seminary's founders. Mohler called this a "dishonest perversion of a contractual pledge" and "an act of consummate arrogance." In fact, Stagg provided a straightforward example of the kind of confessional prevarication that Mohler had rejected and Boyce had warned against. "He discarded the classical orthodox doctrine of the Trinity . . . dismissed Christ's substitutionary atonement as cruel and bloody," while the "very notion of unconditional election was dismissed out of hand." Mohler called the "Abstract" a "Reformed statement of Baptist conviction" that testifies clearly "to the sovereignty of God and his saving purpose. It truthfully reflects the doctrinal convictions of those who founded the Southern Baptist Convention."[98]

Molly Marshall, a teacher of theology at Southern until dismissed by Mohler in 1995 for teaching in opposition to the "Abstract," demonstrated something of the confusion and hostility generated by Mohler's return to Boyce. She spoke of the softening influence of E. Y. Mullins, "a clear move away from the arid rationalism of Boyce, Dagg, and others, which presumed to understand the decrees of God before the foundation of the world." Before Mullins, Marshall contended, "no one seriously challenged the predominance of Calvinist theology." Those analyses showed her understanding that Mohler had resorted to the pre-Mullins context of the "Abstract" and acted in accordance with it. They also revealed the inconsistency of the opposition to Mohler's return to Boyce, for later Marshall said that Mohler "read our confessional statement not as a Baptist document, but as a Calvinist creed, something the author did not intend."[99] If Calvinism dominated prior to the softening influences of Mullins, Mohler might well wonder how his interpretation of the document as a Calvinist creed was not intended by its authors.

In his inaugural address, Mohler again stated his intent to be true to the original intent of Boyce. He said that the confession "presents a contractual and covenantal outline" of the theology that built, sustains, and preserves the seminary. It "constitutes and codifies the parameters within which each professor in this institution will teach." Publicly and clearly, every professor makes it his intent to teach "in accordance with and not contrary to" the statement of faith. He viewed the "Abstract" as a "confessional safeguard and a public witness."[100]

Mohler also produced a pamphlet summarizing the life and contribution of J. P. Boyce and entitled "To Train the Minister Whom God Has Called." He surveyed the biography of Boyce, giving special attention to the theological influences on his life. He pointed to the influence of Charles Hodge in theology. He looked also with interest on the impact of Samuel Miller and his defense of creeds and confessions on Boyce. In light of that Mohler discussed Boyce's "Three Changes in Theological Institutions." He noted the impact of each respective point on the history of Southern Seminary and theological education in general. Again, he highlighted the impact and the necessity of reinstituting the seriousness of the confessional charter of the school. "This *Abstract of Principles* constitutes an unbreakable bond and covenant between the seminary and its churches through the denomination," Mohler reiterated. Such a covenant does not compromise any legitimate freedom of a professor but establishes the boundaries and parameters within which he is fully free to teach. "The professor is not free to violate that covenant either through implicit or explicit disavowal."[101]

Mohler reasserted also the theological position of Boyce and of the "Abstract." The great truths of the sovereignty of God and the doctrines of grace expressed and molded the theological commitments of the first faculty. "Here was to be found no lack of doctrinal clarity and no ambiguity on the great doctrines which had united Baptists to this date." Any who wish to understand the "true substance of our theological heritage," Mohler informed his readers, "need look no further than the *Abstract of Principles* for a clear outline of the doctrines once most certainly held among us." He pledged that Southern Seminary would be "unashamedly and unhesitatingly committed to these same doctrinal convictions as set forth in this incomparable document."[101]

In a closing section on the legacy of James Petigru Boyce, Mohler focused on "this giant of our heritage, who gave birth by heart and calling" to the seminary and awakened Southern Baptists to the need for theological education and the means to guard its integrity for the sake of the churches. In an era that experienced "moral and doctrinal decline beyond James Boyce's most dreadful imagination" his vision of theological accountability must be restated with clarity, insistently, and consistently. The present generation, Mohler wrote, suffers from "theological and historical amnesia concerning the Baptist heritage," a reality demonstrated all around him by many who were self-declared enemies of Boyce and, thus, Mohler.

Southern Seminary came from the loins of Boyce and his brethren as a school to train ministers for the faithful exercise of Christian calling in preaching the glorious gospel of the Lord Jesus Christ. "This was the passion of James Petigru Boyce," Mohler asserted. "May Southern Baptists of this generation give our proper respect to that legacy, and leave for generations which will follow the same deposit of truth, and an equal commitment to its perpetuation."

Boyce felt such conviction in his generation and would view this reassertion of his views, not as a personal vindication, but as a triumph of divine grace.

Notes

Introduction

1. Brooks Holifield, *The Gentlemen Theologians: American Theology in Southern Culture, 1795–1860* (Durham, NC: Duke University Press, 1978), 218.

2. Quotations in the preceding paragraphs are from Lizzie Boyce, "Stray Recollections," a handwritten notebook that will be referred to in various places throughout the text.

3. John A. Broadus, *Memoir of James Petigru Boyce* (New York: A. C. Armstrong and Son, 1893), 209f.

4. Jon Butler, "Slavery and the African Spiritual Holocaust," in *Awash in a Sea of Faith* (Cambridge: Harvard University Press, 1990), 129–63.

5. Lizzie Boyce, "Stray Recollections."

Chapter 1: The First Two Decades

1. 1 Corinthians 4:2.

2. Robert A. Baker, Paul John Craven Jr., and Robert Marshall Blalock, *History of the First Baptist Church, Charleston, South Carolina, 1682–2007* (Springfield, MO: Particular Baptist Press, 2007), 60. This book cites Nathan E. Wood, *The History of the First Baptist Church of Boston* (Philadelphia: American Baptist Publication Society, 1899), 180. As my use of this source will come from the Charleston history and from the part written by Robert A. Baker, I will note all references as "Baker."

3. Ibid., 60–61.

4. Ibid., 68–70. In the absence of clear documentary evidence explaining this move, Baker shows the plausibility of each of these factors in influencing it.

5. Ibid., 78. Baker discusses all the documentary evidence, and lack of it, on the relation of the Kittery Baptists to the South Carolina Baptists and their union in the

one church initially formed in Kittery, Maine in 1682. Some of the South Carolina Baptists were General, or Arminian, Baptists and for a while worshiped amicably in the largely Calvinistic congregation. Eventually, however, they desired a pastor of their own theological persuasion and after creating some tension within the congregation, separated and formed their own congregation in the mid-1730s.

6. Letter from Screven recorded in Isaac Backus, *A History of New England with Particular Reference to the Baptists*, 3 vols. (New York: Arno Press and the New York Times, 1969 [reprint of Newton, MA: Backus Historical Society, 1871]), 1:467–68. Baker, 90–94, examined several different types of records and approximated the ninety to which Screven referred.

7. David Benedict, *A General History of the Baptist Denomination in America*, 2 vols. (Boston, 1813), 2:123.

8. Baker, 20. Baker gives five very tightly written pages in describing the intersections of vision, political maneuvering, exploration, and settlement procedures that led to the eventual establishment of Charles Town in 1670.

9. Erskine Clarke, *Our Southern Zion: A History of Calvinism in the South Carolina Low Country, 1690–1990* (Tuscaloosa: University of Alabama Press, 1996), 32–34. Clarke derived his summary of information from consulting a variety of sources including Robert M. Weir, *Colonial South Carolina: A History* (Millwood, NY: KTO Press, 1983); Peter H. Wood, *Black Majority: Negroes in Colonial South Carolina from 1670 through the Stono Rebellion* (New York: W. W. Norton, 1974); David Brion Davis, *Slavery and Human Progress* (New York: Oxford University Press, 1984); Frank J. Klingberg, *An Appraisal of the Negro in Colonial South Carolina: A Study in Americanization* (Philadelphia: Porcupine, 1975); Geoffrey Barraclough, ed., *The Times Atlas of World History: The Revolutionary Era, 1760–1790* (Princeton: Princeton University Press, 1976); W. Robert Higgins, "The Geographical Origins of Negro Slaves in Colonial South Carolina," *South Atlantic Quarterly* 70 (Winter 1971): 34–47.

10. Charles Wesley, *Journal* (London: Mason, 1849), 1:36, cited in S. T. Kimbrough, *Lost in Wonder: Charles Wesley, The Meaning of His Hymns Today* (Nashville: Upper Room, 1987), 54.

11. Ibid.

12. E. T. Winkler, "Southern Baptist and Mrs. Stowe," *Southern Baptist*, 10 November 1852, 2. Winkler had been the editor for just over six months and had dealt carefully and judiciously with abolitionist literature, especially that of the Beecher family and the newly minted *Uncle Tom's Cabin* from Harriet Beecher Stowe. He had to remind his readers that his views of slavery and its legitimacy as a biblical institution were well known and published widely. "As a Baptist, and a slaveholder," he reiterated, "we have never repudiated them, nor do we suppose that they are obnoxious to the censure of those who, with us, not only maintain these relations, but defend them from the armory of God's word."

13. John A. Broadus, *Memoir of James Petigru Boyce* (New York: A. C. Armstrong and Son, 1893), 185. This work will be referred to throughout as Broadus, *Memoir*.

It is a rich source of biographical information about every phase of Boyce's life from one who knew him intimately from the mid-1850s until Boyce's death. Broadus had a knowledge of Boyce's actions and activities, including many of the most trying aspects of Boyce's ministry, that was available to no other person. He also had access to first-hand accounts of Boyce's life from many persons who knew him from childhood and others from every other stage of his professional and personal development.

14. Clarke, *Our Southern Zion*, 29.

15. Ibid. Clarke cites Weir, *Colonial South Carolina*, 61. He also cites Alexander Hewat who wrote *An Historical Account of the Rise and Progress of the Colonies of South Carolina and Georgia* (London, 1799) reprinted in R. B. Carroll, comp., *Historical Collections of South Carolina*, 2 vols. (New York: Harper and Brothers, 1836).

16. Clarke, *Our Southern Zion*, 32.

17. Broadus, *Memoir*, 2.

18. Ibid., 4. Broadus gathered his information about John Boyce from a document entitled *Annals of Newberry* written by a chief justice of South Carolina named John Belton O'Neall.

19. *South Carolina Historical and Genealogical Magazine* 49 (1948): 81.

20. Broadus, *Memoir*, 7–8; Samuel Gaillard Stoney, *The Story of South Carolina's Senior Bank* (Columbia, SC: R. L. Bryan, 1955), 14. This 75-page book gives the history of the Bank of Charleston, mother of the South Carolina National Bank of Charleston.

21. Broadus, *Memoir*, 8. The biographical summary of Ker Boyce came from the preceding four pages.

22. Ibid., 14. Broadus mentioned a "Biographical Sketch of J. L. Petigru by W. J. Grayson. New York: Harpers, 1866." Petigru outlived Ker Boyce by nine years, dying in 1863.

23. Basil Manly Sr., *Diary*, November 4, 6, 1830.

24. Basil Manly, *Mercy and Judgment: A Discourse Containing Some Fragments of the History of the Baptist Church in Charleston, South Carolina, Delivered at the Request of the Corporation of Said Church, September 23rd and 30th, A.D. 1832* (Charleston: Knowles, Vose, 1837). The social, political, and religious context of this sermon/history is discussed by A. James Fuller, *Chaplain to the Confederacy: Basil Manly and Baptist Life in the Old South* (Baton Rouge: Louisiana State University Press, 2000), 89–105.

25. Fuller, *Chaplain*, 104.

26. Ibid., 103.

27. Manly, *Diary*, June 9, 1831 (168); July 5, July 6, 1831.

28. Fuller, *Chaplain*, 123. Fuller discussed Manly's view of slavery in a chapter entitled "A Parable of the Ants," a title taken from a paper Manly delivered in July 1836 before a literary society in Charleston.

29. Manly, *Diary*, September 17, 1831 (178).

30. H. A. Tupper, "Biographical and Historical Sketches, 1826–1883," in H. A. Tupper, ed., *Two Centuries of the First Baptist Church of South Carolina* (Baltimore: R. H. Woodward, 1889), 158f.

31. James P. Boyce, *Life and Death the Christian's Portion* (New York: Sheldon & Co.; Richmond: Starke & Ryland; Tuscaloosa: Manly and Co., 1869), 44–46.

32. Ibid., 67f.

33. Tom J. Nettles, *The Baptists*, 3 vols. (Fearn, Ross-shire, Scotland: Christian Focus, 2005–7), 2:264–82.

34. Boyce, *Life and Death*, 68f. Boyce's testimony about the impact of Manly makes one pause before affirming wholeheartedly the assertion of Wiley Richards that the pastors of Boyce's childhood in Charleston did not have much theological influence on him. See W. W. Richards, "A Study of the Influence of the Princeton Theology upon the Theology of James Petigru Boyce and His Followers with Special Reference to the Work of Charles Hodge," Th.D. diss., New Orleans Baptist Theological Seminary, 1964, 109–20. Walter Draughon's concurred with this opinion: "His [Boyce's] rigid Calvinism is not to be found in any of the preaching which he heard there, save that of N. M. Crawford, who served the church from 1845 to 1847." See Walter Draughon, "A Critical Evaluation of the Diminishing Influence of Calvinism on the Doctrine of Atonement in Representative Southern Baptist Theologians: James Petigru Boyce, Edgar Young Mullins, Walter Thomas Conner, and Dale Moody," Ph.D. diss., Southwestern Baptist Theological Seminary, 1987, 15.

35. H. A. Tupper to John A. Broadus, 24 May 1889 (box 12, folder 69).

36. Broadus, *Memoir*, 17f., 21.

37. Carol Jones of the Charleston Library Society copied for me the certificate of Ker Boyce on file at the Library Society Building in Charleston. It is certificate number 51 issued on 19 March 1836.

38. Broadus, *Memoir*, 18–19.

39. *A Catalogue of the Books of the Charleston Library Society, Purchased since 1826*, vol. 2 (Charleston: Miller & Browne, 1845).

40. Broadus, *Memoir*, 22.

41. Ibid., 24.

42. For a brief biography but full discussion of the theological contribution of Tucker, see Jeff Robinson, "The Pastoral Intent in the Writing of Henry Holcomb Tucker," Ph.D. diss., Southern Baptist Theological Seminary, 2008.

43. Baker, 259. Baker has an excellent summary of the ministerial gifts and shortcomings of Brantly and the impact that his ministry had on First Baptist Church of Charleston. Ibid., 259–66.

44. Daniel Walker Howe, "Protestantism, Voluntarism, and Personal Identity in Antebellum America," in *New Directions in American Historiography*, ed. Harry S. Stout and D. G. Hart (New York: Oxford University Press, 1997), 219. See also the unpublished dissertation, Robert Arthur Snyder, "William T. Brantly (1787–1845): A Southern Unionist and the Breakup of the Triennial Convention," Ph.D. diss.,

Southern Baptist Theological Seminary, 2005, 6–9. Snyder's work is the most comprehensive discussion of Brantly available. He shows the validity of this insider status in his demonstration that "Brantly's longtime mission of uniting Christians in useful effort for a moral revolution exemplified the early vision of the Triennial Convention" (ibid., 2).

45. Baker, 261.

46. William B. Sprague, *Annals of the American Pulpit: Baptist*, vol. 6 (New York: Robert Carter & Brothers, 1865), 497–507.

47. Basil Manly, in Sprague, *Annals*, 501. This was written in March 1848, three years after Brantly had died.

48. Ibid., 501–2.

49. Richard Fuller, in Sprague, *Annals*, 505f. Fuller also used some phrases that indicate that Brantly charted his own course theologically and sometimes went beyond the language and conceptions contained in confessional Calvinism. "I never knew a man whose mind had worked itself more free from all those prejudices and formal systems, . . . which cause many Christians to welcome the Sacred Oracles, only so far as they concur with the creeds of a sect, or the old hereditary sanctities and shibboleths of a church" (505). "His divinity . . . embodied the Bible in its fullness; in all that ampleness which the schools have so fettered and abridged, in order to accommodate the Inspired Oracles to their narrow dogmas, and at the same time in all its harmony. . . . It was this that caused his mind to cast off the wrinkled and withered skin of an obsolete Theology, to put on the freshness of Gospel light, and to flourish in the strength and beauty of that Word which liveth and abideth forever" (506). This, however, probably reflects only his willingness to find common ground on the atonement between "Gillites" and "Fullerites" and his insistence on a universal offer of the gospel because he embraced the Edwardsean distinction between natural ability and moral ability. These traits probably led Wiley Richards to say that Brantly was one of the men that helped "break up the rigid Calvinism," and also to characterize Brantly's writing as in "conflict with the Calvinistic doctrine of total depravity." See Wiley Richards, *Winds of Doctrine* (Lanham, MD: University Press of America, 1991), 51.

For balanced and accurate appraisal see Snyder, "William T. Brantly," 11–49. Snyder entitled this chapter "Evangelistic Calvinism." Snyder focused his attention on total depravity and atonement in showing Brantly's integration of evangelistic preaching with both those Calvinist expressions of doctrine. Snyder concluded, "William T. Brantly fit well within the Calvinistic tradition of Andrew Fuller. Though moving slightly beyond Fuller on the atonement, Brantly in general remained within the acceptable boundaries of Baptist orthodoxy, epitomized by Gill and Fuller. Brantly's strong adherence to total depravity and divine sovereignty in salvation kept his indefinite doctrine of atonement from straying into Arminianism. Like many of his contemporaries, he maintained that the result of Christ's redemption is certain for all the elect" (148–49).

50. Ibid.

51. Tupper, *Two Centuries*, 163–67.

52. Broadus, *Memoir*, 27.

53. Ibid., 28.

54. Ibid., 29.

55. For the most thorough discussion of Brantly and his contribution to the theory of denominational benevolence, see Snyder, "William T. Brantly."

56. Richard Fuller, *Intrepid Faith. A Sermon on the Death of the Rev. William Tomlinson Brantly, D.D.; with a Sketch of His Life and Character; Delivered at the Request of the First Baptist Church of Charleston, S.C.* (Charleston: Published by the Church, 1845), 32.

57. J. B. Taylor, "An Examination of the Review of the Minutes of the Southern Baptist Convention," *Christian Review*, May 1846, 129.

58. Robert A. Baker, *A Baptist Sourcebook* (Nashville: Broadman, 1966), 94.

59. Basil Manly Sr. to E. B. Teague, 15 March 1845. In this letter, Manly summarized for Teague the history of his own perceptions about the Baptists in the North and South concerning the recent call for a consultative convention in Augusta, Georgia, that led to the formation of the Southern Baptist Convention. He explained how his perceptions eventually led to queries presented at associational meetings and finally to his participation on the committee that sent resolutions to the acting board in Boston for the General Missionary Convention.

60. Basil Manly Sr. to Basil Manly Jr., 22 November 1844.

61. William Williams, "Historical Sketch," *Proceedings of the Seventeenth Meeting of the Southern Baptist Convention* (Baltimore: John F. Weishampfel Jr., 1872), 2.

62. Baker, *Sourcebook*, 107, 109, 113.

63. This information was taken from *The Baptist Encyclopedia*, ed. William Cathcart (Philadelphia: Louis Everts, 1881), s.v. Brown, Nicholas.

64. Francis Wayland and H. L. Wayland, *A Memoir of the Life and Labors of Francis Wayland, D.D., LL.D., Late President of Brown University*, 2 vols. (New York: Sheldon, 1867), 1:13.

65. Ibid., 1:35.

66. Francis Wayland, *The Moral Dignity of the Missionary Enterprise* (London: Thomas Ward and Co., n.d.).

67. Francis Wayland, *Memoir of the Life and Labors of the Rev. Adoniram Judson*, 2 vols. (Boston: Phillips, Sampson, 1853).

68. Francis Wayland, *Notes on the Principles and Practices of Baptist Churches* (New York: Sheldon, Blakeman, 1857).

69. Broadus, *Memoir*, 34.

70. Frances Wayland, *The Elements of Intellectual Philosophy* (New York: Sheldon, 1865; originally published Boston: Philips, Sampson, 1854), 195–99.

71. Boyce, *Life and Death*, 56f.

72. Broadus, *Memoir*, 34f.

73. A. J. Holt, "Christ the Builder: Boyce the Builder" (photocopy of typescript delivered before the Southern Baptist Theological Seminary, 11 January 1922), 7.

74. Wayland, *Moral Dignity*, 8, 13.

75. Ibid., 13–17.

76. Ibid., 20.

77. Broadus, *Memoir*, 43.

78. Reuben A. Guild, "Revivals in Brown University," *The Watchman*, 2 May 1889, 1. This series began on 14 February and continued through 30 May 1889 incorporating ten articles in all, all of them appearing on the first page of the paper.

79. Guild, "Revivals" (no. 7), 9 May 1889, 1. This point by Guild is inconsistent with the statement in Cathcart's *Baptist Encyclopedia* that Brantly "in 1834, was baptized into the fellowship of the First [Baptist] Church of Philadelphia, the baptism being in the Delaware River; and in 1838 he was licensed by the same church to preach." The explanation probably is that Brantly felt called to gospel ministry during the revival at Brown in 1838, and Guild did not remember accurately.

80. Ibid.

81. Ibid.

82. Broadus, *Memoir*, 45.

83. J. H. Cuthbert, *Life of Richard Fuller* (New York: Sheldon, 1879), 132–34.

84. Broadus, *Memoir*, 47.

85. Ibid., 50–51.

Chapter 2: A Time of Theological and Denominational Refinement

1. John A. Broadus, *Memoir of James Petigru Boyce* (New York: A. C. Armstrong and Son, 1893), 53–54.

2. Ibid., 58.

3. Ibid., 57.

4. *Southern Baptist*, 27 December 1848.

5. J. P. Boyce, "I Blot Out a Day," *Southern Baptist*, 20 December 1840, 2.

6. J. P. Boyce, "Our Present Number," *Southern Baptist*, 27 December 1848, 2.

7. "Editorial Change," *Southern Baptist*, 22 November 1848, 2.

8. "Amicus," "Mr. Editor," *Southern Baptist*, 6 December 1848, 3.

9. James P. Boyce, "Our Salutatory," *Southern Baptist*, 22 November 1848, 2.

10. James P. Boyce, "Missions among the Slaves," *Southern Baptist*, 28 February 1849, 2. This article will be discussed briefly in chapter 5 on Southern Baptist views toward slavery.

11. J. R. Kendrick, "Practicability of the Missionary Work," *Southern Baptist*, 3 January 1849, 2.

12. J. P. Boyce, "Spring Collections," *Southern Baptist*, 28 March 1849.

13. James P. Boyce, "Purity of Heart," *Southern Baptist*, 29 November 1848, 2.

14. James P. Boyce, "The Blessedness of Affliction," *Southern Baptist*, 31 January 1849, 2.

15. James P. Boyce, "The Love of the Spirit," *Southern Baptist*, 18 April 1849, 2.

16. James P. Boyce, "Our Book Table," *Southern Baptist*, 31 January 1849, 2.

17. James P. Boyce, "Our Book Table," *Southern Baptist*, 29 November 1848, 2.

18. Cathcart's *Baptist Encyclopedia* recorded, "As a preacher, Dr. Poindexter was deservedly held in every high regard, especially with large out-door assemblies, such as convene at Associational meetings. . . . As an extemporaneous debater he stood almost alone among disputants. . . . As an agent for the Columbian and Richmond Colleges he was greatly successful, while as secretary of the Southern Baptist Publication Society, and afterwards as co-secretary of the Foreign Mission Board of the Southern Baptist Convention, he won a noble reputation for energy and executive ability."

19. James P. Boyce, "Pamphlets and Reviews," *Southern Baptist*, 2 May 1849, 2.

20. Broadus, *Memoir*, 53.

21. James S. Mims, *Orthodoxy. An Address Delivered before the Board of Trustees of the Furman Theological Institution, on the Day of the Annual Commencement, June 19, 1848* (Columbia, SC: I. C. Morgan, 1848), 21.

22. James P. Boyce, "Our Correspondents," *Southern Baptist*, 21 February 1849.

23. Greg A. Wills, *The First Baptist Church of Columbia, South Carolina, 1809–2002* (Nashville: Baptist History and Heritage Society, 2003), 44–51. See especially p. 51, where Wills begins, "Reynolds was undoubtedly the author of a series of unsigned scholarly articles that appeared in the South Carolina newspaper in defense of the doctrine of imputation." Reynolds served as pastor at Columbia from 1837 to 1839 and taught at Furman College from 1839 to 1844. He was very active in seeking to sensitize Baptists to the dangers of the New Divinity, and even though out of the state from 1845 to 1851, had deep concerns about the influence of J. S. Mims at Furman College.

24. Mims, *Orthodoxy*, 19.

25. J. L. Reynolds, *Inaugural Discourse Delivered before the Board of Trustees of the Furman Institution* (Columbia, SC: I. C. Morgan, 1842).

26. Benjamin Beddome, *A Scriptural Exposition of the Baptist Catechism*, introduction by J. L. Reynolds (Richmond: Harrold & Murray, 1849).

27. Ibid., 26–27.

28. Boyce, "Purity of Heart," 2.

29. W. B. Johnson, "Imputation," *Southern Baptist*, 11 April 1849, 2–3.

30. Johnson, *Southern Baptist*, 21 March 1849, 3.

31. Johnson, *Southern Baptist*, 14 Mark 1849, 3.

32. J. L. Reynolds, "On Imputation," *Southern Baptist*, 14 March 1849, 2.

33. Reynolds, *Southern Baptist*, 21 March 1849, 2–3.

34. Reynolds, *Southern Baptist*, 21 February 1849, 2.

35. J. P. Boyce, *Abstract of Systematic Theology* (Philadelphia: American Baptist Publication Society, 1887), 394–95, 402–3.

36. Samuel Stillman (1737–1807) was born in Philadelphia and moved to Charleston with his parents when almost eleven years of age. He was converted under the ministry of Oliver in the First Baptist Church and called to the ministry there. Eventually he served as pastor of First Baptist Church in Boston for forty-two years, 1765–1807. Stillman was a strong experiential Calvinist, unafraid to defend the distinctive doctrines of that position, whose sermons have been described as "stirring, eloquent, pathetic, impassioned, graceful." See William Cathcart, *Baptist Encyclopedia*, s.v. "Stillman, Samuel, D. D." Also, William B. Sprague, *Annals of the American Pulpit* (New York: Robert Carter & Brothers, 1865), 6:71–79. A volume of his sermons published in 1808 included a biographical memoir.

37. James P. Boyce, "Injustice," *Southern Baptist*, 11 April 1849, 2.

38. James P. Boyce, "Strictures of the Christian Index," "Our Correspondent 'Countryman,'" *Southern Baptist*, 11 April 1849, 2.

39. James P. Boyce, "Central Theological Institution," *Southern Baptist*, 28 March 1849, 2.

40. Broadus, *Memoir*, 64–65.

41. Basil Manly Jr., "The Beginnings of the History of the Seminary," *The Seminary Magazine*, December 1891, 114.

42. David B. Calhoun, *Princeton Seminary*, 2 vols. (Edinburgh: Banner of Truth Trust, 1994), 1:336.

43. Ibid., 1:28–30.

44. Ibid., 31.

45. Broadus, *Memoir*, 78.

46. Calhoun, *Princeton Seminary*, 1:105; Calhoun cited *Life of Charles Hodge*, 47.

47. Ibid., 1:90f.

48. Francis Wayland and H. L. Wayland, *A Memoir of the Life and Labors of Francis Wayland*, 2 vols. (New York: Sheldon, 1867), 2:174–75.

49. Calhoun, *Princeton Seminary*, 1:427–28.

50. Samuel Miller, *Letters on Clerical Manners and Habits, Addressed to a Student in the Theological Seminary at Princeton, N. J.*, 3d edition (Princeton: Moore Baker, 1835), 206, 208–9.

51. Samuel Miller, *The Utility and Importance of Creeds and Confessions* (Philadelphia: Russell & Martien, 1833), 306, 311–12, 317, found in Samuel Miller, *Spruce Street Lectures* (Philadelphia: Presbyterian Board of Publications, 1840).

52. Calhoun, *Princeton Seminary*, 1:369–71, 377–79; Broadus, *Memoir*, 69–70.

53. Broadus, *Memoir*, 70.

54. Ibid., 71.

55. Charles Hodge, *Princeton Sermons* (London: Thomas Nelson and Sons, 1879), 362.

56. Calhoun, *Princeton Seminary*, 1:382.

57. Ibid., 1:118–22.

58. Charles Hodge, *Systematic Theology* (London and Edinburgh: Thomas Nelson and Sons; New York: Charles Scribner and Co., 1872), 2:440.

59. Ibid., 2:591. For other passages of the same sort see 2:250, 524–27, and 1:17. "This universal faith of the church is not to be sought so much in the decisions of ecclesiastical councils, as in the formulas of devotion which have prevailed among the people," Hodge claimed. "It is, as often remarked, in the prayers, in the hymnology, in the devotional writings which true believers make the channel of their communion with God, and the medium through which they express their most intimate religious convictions, that we must look for the universal faith" (2:250).

60. Broadus, *Memoir*, 73.

61. Calhoun, *Princeton Seminary*, 1:335.

62. Broadus, *Memoir*, 76.

63. Ibid., 77f.

64. Hodge, *Princeton Sermons*, 219–21.

65. Broadus, *Memoir*, 80–81.

66. Ibid.

67. Ibid., 82.

68. Calhoun, *Princeton Seminary*, 1:424.

69. "Doings in Columbia," *Southern Baptist*, 10 December 1851, 2.

70. Broadus, *Memoir*, 88.

Chapter 3: From Preacher to Professor

1. Greg Wills, *The First Baptist Church of Columbia, South Carolina, 1809 to 2002* (Brentwood, TN: Fields, 2003), 1.

2. J. R. Kendrick, *Southern Baptist*, 10 December 1851, 2.

3. John A. Broadus, *Memoir of James Petigru Boyce* (New York: A. C. Armstrong and Son, 1893), 84.

4. Wills, *First Baptist Church*, 54.

5. James V. Lyles, "Extra Meeting of the Church," *Southern Baptist*, 19 March 1851, 2.

6. Ibid.

7. W. C. Lindsay to John A. Broadus, 30 May 1889. Lindsay, pastor of the church from 1877 to 1910, at Broadus's request scoured the church minutes for information related to Boyce's time as pastor. He sent his somewhat meager findings to Broadus in a letter.

8. Ibid.

9. Kendrick, *Southern Baptists*, 10 December 1851.

10. Lindsay to Broadus.

11. Broadus, *Memoir*, 88.

12. Wills, *First Baptist Church*, 55. Wills cites the statistical tables in the 1850–55 Minutes of the Charleston Baptist Association.

13. Lindsay to Broadus.

14. Broadus, *Memoir*, 92.

15. James P. Boyce, "For the Southern Baptist," *Southern Baptist* 10 March 1852, 2.

16. Lindsay to Broadus.

17. For a discussion of Winkler's life and his theological contributions see Tom J. Nettles, *The Baptists*, 3 vols. (Fearn, Ross-shire, Scotland: Christian Focus, 2005, 2007), 3:323–61.

18. James P. Boyce, "Church Discipline—Its importance," *Southern Baptist*, 18 February 1852, 2.

19. James P. Boyce, "Preaching Plain Truths," *Southern Baptist*, 25 February 1852, 2.

20. Lindsay to Broadus.

21. "South Carolina Baptist State Convention," *Southern Baptist*, 5 August 1856, 2.

22. Wills, *First Baptist Church*, 56–57.

23. J. P. Boyce, "The Uses and Doctrine of the Sanctuary," in *James Petigru Boyce: Selected Writings*, ed. Timothy George (Nashville: Broadman, 1989), 111–23. A description of the service will be given in the next chapter. Some of the contents of this sermon will be used in the chapters on Boyce's theology.

24. *The Courier*, 21 March 1854, 2.

25. Broadus, *Memoir*, 93.

26. "The Last Will and Testament of Ker Boyce," in Southern Baptist Library and Archives in Nashville, Tennessee.

27. Broadus, *Memoir*, 97.

28. For a brief discussion of the difficulty with Roberts see W. R. Estep, *Whole Gospel, Whole World* (Nashville: B&H, 1994), 90–91. For the Foreign Mission Board's account of this conflict see *Proceedings of the Southern Baptist Convention, 1855*, 75–89.

29. Basil Manly Jr., "The Beginnings of the History of the Seminary," *The Seminary Magazine*, December 1891, 118–19; see also J. P. Boyce, *History of the Establishment and Organization of the Southern Baptist Theological Seminary, Greenville, South-Carolina to which is appended the First Annual Catalogue* (Greenville, SC: G. E. Elford, 1860), 4.

30. James S. Mims, *Orthodoxy. An Address Delivered before the Board of Trustees of the Furman Theological Institution, on the Day of the Annual Commencement, June 19, 1848* (Columbia, SC: I. C. Morgan, 1848).

31. "Professor James P. Boyce," *Southern Baptist*, 22 August 1855, 2.

32. J. P. Boyce, *Life and Death the Christian's Portion: A Discourse Occasioned by the Funeral Services of the Rev. Basil Manly, D.D. at Greenville, S.C., December 22, 1868* (New York: Sheldon & Co.; Richmond: Starke & Ryland; Tuscaloosa: Manly & Co., 1869), 51.

33. Broadus, *Memoir*, 106.

34. Boyce, *History of the Establishment*, 6.

35. Broadus, *Memoir*, 119.

36. Basil Manly Sr. (as chair of the committee), "Southern Central Theological Institution," *Southern Baptist*, 17 June 1856, 2.

37. J. P. Justin, "South Carolina Baptist State Convention," *Southern Baptist*, 5 August 1856, 2.

38. J. P. Justin, "South Carolina Baptist State Convention," *Southern Baptist*, 12 August 1856, 2. Also see Boyce, *History of the Establishment*, 10. A footnote said, "The above resolutions were accompanied by another, which was not a part of the original report of the Committee appointed, but was offered as an amendment. This resolution pledged South Carolina for her quota, provided the Institution was located in some other State. Unfortunately, the slip of paper upon which the amendment was written was lost, and hence the additional resolution was not inserted in the Minutes, although it was passed by the Convention. The Secretary was ignorant of the omission until his attention was called to it after the distribution of the Minutes. The brethren present at the South Carolina Convention, however, have a vivid recollection of the fact, inasmuch as many declared that they would not vote for the resolutions at all unless so amended. The fact that this resolution was passed was stated at Louisville, Ky., before the decision of the Committee was arrived at."

39. J. P. Boyce, *Three Changes in Theological Institutions* (Greenville, SC: C. J. Elford's Book and Job Press, 1856).

40. J. P. Justin, "Prof. Boyce's Address," *Southern Baptist*, 12 August 1856, 2–3.

41. A. D. Gillette, ed., *Minutes of the Philadelphia Baptist Association from A. D. 1707, to A. D. 1807* (Philadelphia: American Baptist Publication Society, 1851), 27. "Mr. Hollis" refers to Thomas Hollis of England who financed much education for the ministry. Though he was a Baptist, he gave large amounts of money to Harvard, endowed a theological chair (the Hollis Chair of Divinity), endowed scholarships that were to include four Baptists each year. Cathcart wrote, "We know nothing of the way by which these funds for Baptist students have been appropriated; for the honor of old Harvard we trust that the requisite number of Baptist students have regularly received the ten [pounds] per annum which Mr. Hollis left them. But we fear if the godly Calvinist, Thomas Hollis, heard the divinity taught in Harvard now he would bitterly regret his well-meant generosity." Perhaps the perversion of the intent of this endowment influenced Boyce's view of the relation between an endowment and a confessional standard.

42. G. William Foster, comp. and ed., *Life and Works of Dr. Richard Furman, D. D.* (Harrisonburg, VA: Sprinkle, 2004), 166.

43. Ibid., 505–8.

44. Ibid., 515.

45. Richard Furman, "Address of the Convention," *American Baptist Magazine*, September 1817, 175–78. The two young men ready to go west were John Mason Peck and James Welch. This work in the West is chronicled in a fascinating account by Peck in *Memoir of John Mason Peck*, ed. Rufus Babcock (Carbondale, IL: Southern Illinois University Press, 1965).

46. Furman, "Address," 179–80.

47. Charles D. Johnson, *Higher Education of Southern Baptists* (Waco: Baylor University Press, 1955), 5–15; *Encyclopedia of Southern Baptists* (Nashville: Broadman Press, 1958).

48. Jesse Mercer, *Knowledge Indispensable to a Minister of God* (Washington, GA: Christian Index, 1834).

49. Ibid., 6–11.

50. Ibid., 12–14.

51. Ibid., 15–16.

52. Ibid., 16–17.

53. Ibid., 17–18.

54. Basil Manly, "Theological Education in the Southern States," *Southern Baptist and General Intelligencer*, 13 March 1835, 170–72.

55. Basil Manly Sr. to J. L. Reynolds, 10 January 1844.

56. Basil Manly Jr., "The Beginnings of the History of the Seminary," *The Seminary Magazine*, December 1891, 116–18.

57. Justin, "Prof. Boyce's Address," 3.

58. Boyce, *Three Changes*, 9.

59. Ibid., 11.

60. Ibid., 12–13.

61. Ibid., 13.

62. Ibid., 14.

63. Ibid., 17.

64. Ibid., 18–19.

65. Ibid., 20.

66. Ibid., 22.

67. Ibid., 25.

68. Ibid., 28–29.

69. Ibid., 29–30.

70. Ibid., 31–33.

71. Mims, *Orthodoxy*.

72. Boyce, *Three Changes*, 33–34.

73. Mims, *Orthodoxy*, 7.

74. Boyce, *Three Changes*, 35–36.

75. Mims, *Orthodoxy*, 7.

76. Boyce, *Three Changes*, 36.

77. Ibid., 35.

78. Ibid., 37–38.

79. Mims, *Orthodoxy*, 18.

80. Ibid., 11.

81. Boyce, *Three Changes*, 39.

82. Mims, *Orthodoxy*, 10.

83. Boyce, *Three Changes*, 44.
84. Mims, *Orthodoxy*, 25.
85. Boyce, *Three Changes*, 44.
86. Ibid., 46–48.

Chapter 4: The Dream Fulfilled

1. "Theological Convention," *Western Recorder*, 20 May 1857, 1.
2. Ibid.
3. Ibid.
4. Basil Manly Jr., "The Beginnings of the History of the Seminary," *The Seminary Magazine*, December 1891, 120.
5. Basil Manly Jr., "The Beginnings of the History of the Seminary," *The Seminary Magazine*, January 1892, 208.
6. "Theological Convention," 1.
7. J. P. Boyce, *Life and Death the Christian's Portion* (New York: Sheldon & Co.; Richmond: Starke & Ryland; Tuscaloosa: Manly & Co., 1869), 52.
8. John A. Broadus, *Memoir of James Petigru Boyce* (New York: A. C. Armstrong and Son, 1893), 108.
9. "Rev. J. P. Boyce," *Western Recorder*, September 1857.
10. A. C. Dayton to James P. Boyce, 22 August 1857, Boyce Papers.
11. Broadus, *Memoir*, 150.
12. J. L. Reynolds to J. P. Boyce, 22 June 1857; C. M. Reynolds to J. P. Boyce, 24 August 1857.
13. Greg Wills, *The First Baptist Church of Columbia, South Carolina, 1809–2002* (Nashville: Fields Publishing; Brentwood, TN: Baptist History and Heritage Society, 2003), 45.
14. Boyce to Broadus, 9 April 1858; 12 April 1858. See Sean Michael Lucas with Jason Fowler, eds., "'Our Life Work': The Correspondence of James P. Boyce and John A. Broadus, Founders of the Southern Baptist Theological Seminary, 1857–1888" (unpublished volume in the archives of Southern Baptist Theological Seminary, 2004), 2–3. This work contains a transcript of most of the correspondence between Boyce and Broadus from the beginning of their friendship to its end at the time of Boyce's death. The editors used the Boyce files and the Broadus files in the Archives and Special Collections of the James P. Boyce Centennial Library at the Southern Baptist Theological Seminary. A few letters they found in other files, such as the Robertson files. I will refer to this correspondence by date and, when it is an item in this volume, by the abbreviation "L&F" along with the page number.
15. Cathcart's *Baptist Encyclopedia*, s.v. "Buck, William Calmes."
16. Manly, *Seminary Magazine*, 1892, 209.
17. John Landrum to Boyce, 19 October 1857.
18. Elias Dodson to Boyce, 20 April 1858.
19. George Dargan to Boyce, 22 April 1858.

20. Sam C. Cross to Boyce, 26 April 1858.

21. J. P. Tustin, "Southern Theological Convention," *Southern Baptist*, 11 May 1858, 2. Most of the details of this meeting will be taken from this source. Some details are taken from J. P. Boyce, *History of the Establishment and Organization of the Southern Baptist Theological Seminary, Greenville, South-Carolina* (Greenville, S.C.: G. E. Elford, 1860). Boyce compiled the various committee reports and newspaper accounts from 1855 to 1858 as well as very brief personal summaries of events in this historical chronicle included at the beginning of the first catalogue of the seminary.

22. Jeter preached the sermon, Poindexter gave a charge to the twenty-three-year-old Hartwell, Manly gave the "right hand of fellowship," and Richard Furman gave the benediction. Hartwell sailed for China in November and spent thirty-five years as a missionary there. He also did home mission work with Chinese in San Francisco for several years. His criticism of T. P. Crawford's missiology led eventually to Crawford's resignation from the board and the establishment of the Gospel Mission Movement. Hartwell was still in China in 1907 when R. J. Willingham, corresponding secretary of the Foreign Mission Board, visited.

23. Broadus, *Memoir*, 151–52.

24. Manly, *Seminary Magazine*, 1892, 209.

25. J. P. Tustin, "Abstract of Principles," *Southern Baptist*, 11 May 1853, 3.

26. G. W. Samson to Boyce, 10 May 1858.

27. Manly to Broadus, 14 and 17 May 1858; A. T. Robertson, *Life and Letters of John Albert Broadus* (Philadelphia: American Baptist Publication Society, 1909), 149–52. This compilation by Robertson provides a rich source for letters between Broadus and a wide variety of correspondents. In addition it gives special comments, insights, and opinions by Broadus's son-in-law, A. T. Robertson, who studied at the seminary from 1885 to 1888, receiving his Th. M.

28. Broadus, *Memoir*, 154.

29. Broadus to Boyce, 15 May 1858, L&F, 4f.

30. E. T. Winkler to Broadus, 26 May 1858; Robertson, *Life and Letters*, 153.

31. Boyce to Broadus, 17 June 1858, L&F, 5.

32. J. P. Boyce, "Address of Rev. J. P. Boyce, at Hampton," *Religious Herald*, 1 July 1858, 2.

33. Ibid.

34. Ibid.

35. Boyce to Broadus, 29 March 1859, L&F, 6.

36. Broadus to Boyce, 4 April 1859, L&F, 6.

37. Boyce to Broadus, 11 April 1859 (Robertson Papers), L&F, 7.

38. Ibid., 7–8.

39. Broadus to Manly, 21 April 1859; Robertson, *Life and Letters*, 159.

40. Boyce to Broadus, 26 April 1859; Robertson, *Life and Letters*, 160.

41. "Proceedings of the Board of Trustees of the Southern Baptist Theological Seminary," *Western Recorder*, 4 July 1859, 1.

42. Ibid.

43. Broadus to Boyce, 16 July 1859, L&F, 11.

44. Broadus, *Memoir*, 168.

45. Broadus to Boyce, 29 July 1859, L&F, 14.

46. "Southern Baptist Theological Seminary," *Western Recorder*, 18 July 1859, 1.

47. George Boardman Eager, *William Williams* (Louisville: Baptist World, 1909), 16.

48. J. P. Boyce, "Southern Baptist Theological Seminary," *Religious Herald*, 18 August 1859, 3.

49. John S. Gilliam to Boyce, 24 August 1860.

50. Boyce, *Religious Herald*, 18 August 1859, 3.

51. John A. Broadus, "Southern Baptist Theological Seminary," *Religious Herald*, 18 August 1859, 2.

52. John A. Broadus, "Southern Baptist Theological Seminary," *Religious Herald*, 25 August 1859, 2.

53. Robertson, *Life and Letters*, 169.

54. John A. Broadus, "Southern Baptist Theological Seminary," *Religious Herald*, 25 August 1859, 2.

55. John A. Broadus, "Southern Baptist Theological Seminary," *Religious Herald*, 8 September 1859, 2.

56. Ibid.

57. Broadus to Boyce, 23 July 1859, L&F, 13.

58. J. R. Graves, *Old Landmarkism: What Is It?* 2d ed. (Memphis: Baptist Book House, 1880), xi.

59. Basil Manly Jr., *The Seminary Magazine*, December 1891, 115.

60. Graves, *Old Landmarkism*, xi.

61. J. M. Pendleton, *An Old Landmark Re-set* (Fulton, KY and St. Louis, MO: National Baptist, 1899), 9–14.

62. Broadus, *Memoir*, 99.

63. Homer Grice and Paul Caudill, "Graves-Howell Controversy," *Encyclopedia of Southern Baptists*; James E. Tull, *Shapers of Baptist Thought* (Valley Forge, PA: Judson, 1972), 129–52.

64. Basil Manly Sr. to Boyce, 2 December 1858.

65. J. H. De Votie to Boyce, 20 July 1858.

66. "Education," *Religious Herald*, 25 August 1859, 2. Eight men went from Virginia the first year, ten the second year.

67. W. F. Broaddus to Boyce, 11 August 1858; 14 December 1858; 4 January 1859; 17 January 1859; 1 April 1859; 12 April 1859; 17 May 1859; 16 December 1859.

68. I. T. Tichenor to Boyce, 20 December 1860.

69. J. F. B. Mays to Boyce, December 1857; 22 September 1858; 30 July 1859; 15, 27, 29 August 1859; 15 September 1859; 3, 7, 17 November 1859.

70. R. B. C. Howell and J. R. Graves led two factions in Nashville. Howell's First Baptist Church had disfellowshiped Graves (fall 1858) on charges of slander and

abusive actions toward their pastor. A sizable contingent had followed Graves out of the church. At the Southern Baptist Convention in 1859 Graves had challenged Howell's bid for reelection as convention president, but failed to unseat Howell. Dagg had defended the actions of the First Baptist Church of Nashville in their right of discipline. Earlier in 1858 his *Manual of Church Order*, which took issue with several central Landmark emphases, had been published.

71. Pettigrew served a number of churches in Mississippi and wrote for the denominational papers. L. S. Foster described him as a "laborious and zealous pastor, looking after the development of his churches along all the lines of church efficiency and benevolence." See L. S. Foster, *Mississippi Baptist Preachers* (St. Louis: National Baptist, 1895), 539f.

72. J. F. B. Mays to Boyce, 12 January 1860; 21, 24 August 1860; 26, 28 September 1860; 21 October 1860; 8, 19, 23 November 1860; 17 December 1860; 14 March 1861; 19 June 1861.

73. J. P. Boyce, (no title), *Southern Baptist*, 11 October 1859, 1; Broadus, relying on a faulty memory at this point, wrote, "About the end of the session Dr. Boyce preached at the dedication of the new Baptist Church in Columbia" (*Memoir*, 175).

74. Boyce, *Southern Baptist*, 11 October 1859, 1.

75. Ibid.

76. "Opening of the Baptist Theological Seminary at Greenville," *Southern Baptist*, 25 October 1859, 1; *Western Recorder*, 7 November 1859, 1.

77. J. P. Boyce, *History of the Establishment and Organization of the Southern Baptist Theological Seminary, Greenville, South-Carolina* (Greenville, S.C.: G. E. Elford, 1860), 36–37. Contained in this work is the catalogue for the first year at the seminary (hereafter referred to as "Catalogue"). See also Broadus, *Memoir*, 169. Broadus gave information about the background and the subsequent ministry of several of these students as evidence that from the very first session the ideal envisioned in the variety of students that could benefit from the training and could coexist in the same classes with reciprocal advantages had borne sweet fruit.

78. Boyce, "Catalogue," 46.

79. Ibid.

80. Ibid., 47–48.

81. J. B. Taylor, "Greenville Theological School," *Religious Herald*, 19 April 1860, 1.

82. Robertson, *Life and Letters*, 171.

83. Broadus, *Memoir*, 172–73. Broadus gives several anecdotes concerning Boyce's generosity and kindness during the first session as well as how deeply he was loved and appreciated by the plain people in the church that he served as pastor on a quarter-time basis.

84. Ibid.

85. Observer, "Southern Baptist Theological Seminary," *Religious Herald*, 14 June 1860, 2.

Chapter 5: The Devastation of War

1. A. T. Robertson, *Life and Letters of John Albert Broadus* (Philadelphia: American Baptist Publication Society, 1909), 174.

2. Broadus to Boyce, 20 June 1860, in Sean Michael Lucas with Jason Fowler, eds., "'Our Life Work': The Correspondence of James P. Boyce and John A. Broadus, Founders of the Southern Baptist Theological Seminary, 1857–1888" (unpublished volume in the archives of Southern Baptist Theological Seminary, 2004), 16 (hereafter L&F).

3. James Petigru Boyce, "Valedictory Address," 27 June 1861, *Southwestern Baptist*, 1.

4. Boyce to Broadus, 16 July 1860, L&F, 18ff.

5. Broadus to Boyce, 23 July 1860, L&F, 22.

6. Broadus to Boyce, 31 August 1860, L&F, 24–26.

7. Boyce to Broadus, 10 October 1860, L&F, 26–27.

8. Thirty-six is the number given in John A. Broadus, *Memoir of James Petigru Boyce* (New York: A. C. Armstrong and Son, 1893), 176. On 25 October 1860 he had written Cornelia Taliaferro, "We now number thirty-one students." To the same correspondent on 22 January 1861 he wrote, "The Seminary numbers thirty-eight students, though four or five of them have left, from sickness at home, etc., etc."; see Robertson, *Life and Letters*, 176, 182. The seminary catalogue list the names of thirty-six students for commencement that year.

9. Robertson, *Life and Letters*, 178.

10. Boyce to H. A. Tupper, 15 December 1860; Boyce to Mrs. H. A. Tupper, 10 January 1861, both cited in Broadus, *Memoir*, 184–85.

11. "Controversy Ended," *Southern Baptist*, 25 May 1858, 1, 4.

12. [J. M. Pendleton], "The Letter of A. W. Chambliss," *The Baptist*, 29 May 1858, 2.

13. P. H. Mell, *Slavery: A Treatise, Showing That Slavery Is Neither a Moral, Political, nor Social Evil* (Penfield, GA: Benj. Brantly, 1844).

14. J. B. Taylor, "An Examination of the Review of the Minutes of the Southern Baptist Convention," *Christian Review*, May 1846, 134f.

15. Richard Furman, "Exposition of the Views of Baptists Relative to the Coloured Population of the United States," in James A. Rogers, *Richard Furman: Life and Legacy* (Macon: Mercer University Press, 1985), 274–86.

16. Furman, "Exposition," 278f., 282.

17. Mell, *Slavery*, 7.

18. Ibid., 10–22. Furman, "Exposition," 279, concluded his survey of the biblical material with the statement, "In proving this subject justifiable by Scriptural authority, its morality is also proved; for the divine Law never sanctions immoral actions."

19. Francis Wayland, *Elements of Moral Science* (London: Religious Tract Society, 1835). See the sections on personal liberty beginning ca. 200.

20. Mell, *Slavery*, 28f. Furman, "Exposition," 281, discussed various abuses of legitimate social and political relationships but reminded the reader, "This does not prove, that magistracy, the husband's right to govern, and parental authority, are unlawful and wicked."

21. Wayland, *Elements*, 206ff.

22. Mell, *Slavery*, 33.

23. Ibid., 35ff.

24. Ibid., 36.

25. Ibid., 39–40. Furman, "Exposition," 281, argued similarly, "If, also by their own confession, which has been made in manifold instances, their condition, when they have come into the hands of humane masters, here, has been greatly bettered by the change; if it is, ordinarily, really better, as many assert, than that of thousands of the poorer classes in countries reputed civilized and free; and, if, in addition to all other considerations, the translation from their native country to this has been the means of their mental and religious improvement, and so of obtaining salvation, as many of themselves have joyfully and thankfully confessed—then may the humane master, who rules his slaves and provides for them, according to Christian principles, rest satisfied, that he is not in holding them, chargeable with moral evil, nor with acting, in this respect, contrary to the genius of Christianity."

26. E. T. Winkler, "Southern Baptists and Mrs. Stowe," *Southern Baptist*, 10 November 1852, 2.

27. "South Side View of Slavery," *Southern Baptist*, 10 January 1855, 2.

28. Ibid.

29. Ibid.

30. Mell, *Slavery*, 9.

31. Lizzie Boyce, "Stray Recollections of Dr. Boyce," 7–9. After Boyce's death, Broadus asked his oldest daughter to handwrite a collection of events and character traits that she could recall. He gave her a blank notebook and wrote on the outside cover, "Stray Recollections of Dr. Boyce." Broadus wrote, in pencil, the following instructions on the inside cover: "Do not be too solicitous to put everything under the right head; jot things down as they occur to you. Give even trivial incidents or slight sayings, if they may throw any light upon character. If you doubt, put it down, & let me judge. Do not stop for pen & ink, but write away with pencil. Not necessary to write in full; broken sentences, any way." Broadus divided the book into several categories, seeking to prime the pump of Lizzie's memory. On some of these subjects she wrote significant amounts, on others she wrote nothing. The notebook includes the following topics:

Punctuality	1 1/2 pages
System in affairs (dislike of waste)	blank
Charities (public, private, secret)	blank
Delicate consideration for others	3 pages

Devotion to his wife	blank
Treatment of his children	4 pages
Friendships	blank
Hospitality	blank
Delight in travel	7+ pages
Humor and witty jests (puns), favorite anecdotes	blank
Love of pictures	2 pages
Love of flowers, trees, &c	2 pages
Taste, as to dress (ladies' dress), furniture &c	2 pages
Scorn of everything base and mean	blank
Wide reading—history, poetry fiction, periodicals, reading aloud	3 1/2 pages
Love of his books	2 1/2 pages
Love of music	1 1/2 pages
Miscellaneous	blank
Trip to Europe	18 pages

32. John L. Dagg, *The Elements of Moral Science* (Charleston: Southern Baptist Publication Society, 1859), 345.

33. John A. Broadus, "Religious Instruction of the Colored People," *Christian Index*, 30 October 1856, 1.

34. James P. Boyce, "Missions among the Slaves," *Southern Baptist*, 28 February 1849, 2.

35. Broadus, *Memoir*, 177.

36. Robertson, *Life and Letters*, 182.

37. Ibid., 184.

38. Broadus, *Memoir*, 179.

39. *Proceedings of the Southern Baptist Convention, 1861*, 11.

40. Robert A. Baker, *The Southern Baptist Convention and Its People* (Nashville: Broadman, 1974), 227.

41. *Proceedings of the Southern Baptist Convention, 1861*, 62–64.

42. Broadus, *Memoir*, 179.

43. I infer Boyce's reasons for resistance to this action of the convention from his sermon at the dedication of the new building in Columbia. See the *Southern Baptist*, 11 October 1859, 1.

44. J. William Jones to Boyce, 23 May 1861.

45. James Petigru Boyce, "Valedictory Address."

46. Andrew Broaddus to Boyce, 30 May 1861.

47. Boyce to trustees, 25 November 1861; W. B. Johnson to Boyce, December 1861.

48. Iveson L. Brookes to Boyce, 4 December 1861.

49. Boyce to Broadus, 23 December 1861; Robertson, *Life and Letters*, 188–89, L&F, 31–32.

50. Boyce to Broadus, 4, 16, 30 January 1862; 27 November 1862, L&F, 32–36. Another was dated 24 December 1862 in L&F, but this could not be correct as the material follows immediately upon requests made in the letter of 16 January 1862.

51. Broadus to Boyce, 14 March 1862, L&F, 39.

52. Boyce to Broadus, 16 March 1862, L&F, 39f.

53. Broadus, *Memoir*, 188f.

54. Robertson, *Life and Letters*, 194, 196.

55. J. P. Boyce, *Remarks of Mr. Boyce, of Greenville, in the House of Representatives of South Carolina, on the 9th December, 1862* (Columbia, S.C.: R. W. Gibbes, 1862), 3–5.

56. J. P. Boyce to Elizabeth Boyce, 15 December 1862.

57. Printed text of the bill in the Boyce file at the Southern Baptist Library and Archives in Nashville, Tennessee. The bracketed portion is an addition Boyce inserted in his own hand. He also stated at the top, "I got Col. Ware to introduce it in the Senate. It is the bill I introduced into the House."

58. J. P. Boyce to Elizabeth Boyce, 15 December 1862.

59. Broadus to Boyce, 15 December 1862.

60. *Proceedings of the Southern Baptist Convention, 1863*, 54–55.

61. Baker, *Southern Baptist Convention*, 231. Also see *Proceedings of the Southern Baptist Convention, 1863*, 45.

62. *Proceedings of the Southern Baptist Convention, 1863*, 47.

63. Robertson, *Life and Letters*, 198–209; J. William Jones, *Christ in the Camp* (Richmond: B. F. Johnson & Co., 1887; reprint Harrisonburg, VA: Sprinkle, 1986), 312–15.

64. The contents of this catechism included chapters on the Bible, God, providence, the original and present condition of man, Jesus Christ as a man, Jesus Christ as God, the Trinity, the Mediator, the sacrifice of Christ, the offer of salvation, election, regeneration and sanctification, repentance and faith, justification, good works, assurance and perseverance, the future life, baptism, the Lord's Supper and the Sabbath. Some of the content of these subjects will be treated in the chapters on Boyce's theology.

65. C. C. Memminger to J. P. Boyce, 8 January 1863. At the beginning of a speech to the Georgia legislature, "Mr. Boyce stated that a little over two weeks ago he received a communication from the Secretary of the Treasury, asking him to act as agent of that department to present to the different Legislatures the subject of State endorsement of Confederate bonds." See "Speech of Rev. J. P. Boyce on the Endorsement of Confederate Bonds," *Patriot and Mountaineer*, 23 April 1863, 1.

66. Broadus, *Memoir*, 193f., commented, "It was precisely this that reduced General Lee's army, during the winter of 1864–1865, to such small numbers that he was

compelled to evacuate the Petersburg defences, and presently to surrender at Appomattox. When the soldier's monthly pay would buy scarcely half a bushel of corn, when word came from many a home that they were already suffering from lack of food, and hopeless as to raising a crop for the coming year, then many a husband and father did that which nothing else on earth could have induced him to do,—left his place in the ranks, and went home."

67. Boyce, "Speech," 1.

68. Memminger to Boyce, 7, 15 April 1863.

69. Memminger to Boyce, 31 March 1864.

70. Broadus to Boyce, 6 August 1863; Boyce to Broadus, 16 August 1863, L&F, 49–54.

71. Broadus, *Memoir*, 196.

72. Ibid., 197.

73. Walt Whitman, "O Captain! My Captain!" *Civil War Poetry and Prose* (New York: Dover, 1995), 34.

Chapter 6: The Struggles of a Phoenix

1. Broadus to Basil Manly, 3 July 1865; Manly to Broadus, 6 July 1865. See A. T. Robertson, *Life and Letters of John Albert Broadus* (Philadelphia: American Baptist Publication Society, 1909), 212–14.

2. John A. Broadus, *Memoir of James Petigru Boyce* (New York: A. C. Armstrong and Son, 1893), 200.

3. J. B. Richardson to Boyce, 2 November 1864.

4. Broadus, *Memoir*, 201; also Robertson, *Life and Letters*, 216.

5. George Hyde to Boyce, 4 December 1865.

6. James P. Boyce, "Letter from Washington," *Christian Index*, 29 March 1866, 1. See also the letter labeled "Letter from Washington City," *Christian Index*, 5 April 1866, for extended observations by Boyce on the political developments of early 1866.

7. James Petigru Boyce, "From South Carolina," *Christian Index*, 3 May 1866, 1. For other comments on the situation in the South, especially its efforts to adjust to the policies of the first stages of Reconstruction and the new relation with the former slaves, see "From South Carolina," *Christian Index*, 10 May 1866.

8. Boyce to Broadus, 4 November 1867, in Sean Michael Lucas with Jason Fowler, eds., " 'Our Life Work': The Correspondence of James P. Boyce and John A. Broadus, Founders of the Southern Baptist Theological Seminary, 1857–1888" (unpublished volume in the archives of Southern Baptist Theological Seminary, 2004) (hereafter L&F).

9. Broadus, *Memoir*, 203.

10. James P. Boyce, "Letter from South Carolina," *Christian Index*, 21 June 1866, 1.

11. Robertson, *Life and Letters*, 217.

12. James P. Boyce, "Letter from South Carolina."

13. Broadus, *Memoir*, 205; Robertson, *Life and Letters*, 218.

14. J. P. Boyce, "Southern Baptist Theological Seminary," *Biblical Recorder*, 28 June 1866, 2.

15. Ibid.

16. J. D. Hufham to Boyce, 29 June 1866.

17. J. D. Hufham and J. P. Boyce, "Dr. Boyce's Disclaimer" and "The Unduly Exalted Seminary—A Disclaimer," *Biblical Recorder*, 5 July 1866, 2–3.

18. J. P. Boyce, "The Southern Baptist Theological Seminary," *Western Recorder*, 30 June 1866, 2.

19. J. P. Boyce, "The Southern Baptist Theological Seminary," *Western Recorder*, 14 July 1866, 2.

20. R. C. Burleson to Boyce, 2 October 1866. Burleson (1823–1901) was converted in 1840 in Nashville, Tennessee, under the ministry of R. B. C. Howell, began preaching at seventeen years of age, studied theology at Western Baptist Literary and Theological Institute in Kentucky, graduating in 1847, and began serving as pastor of First Baptist Church in Houston, Texas, in 1848. In 1851 he became president of Baylor University in Independence, Texas. Friction between Burleson and Horace Clark, head of the independent female department of the school, led to a break and Burleson's move to Waco in 1861 along with his faculty and the entire senior class of the male department of the school to establish Waco University. Baylor University at Independence gradually declined and in 1886 merged with Waco University in Waco, with Burleson as president, now reclaiming the name of Baylor University for the merged schools. Burleson remained as president until 1897.

21. W. M. Lea to Boyce, 3 October 1866.

22. J. W. Jones to Boyce, 20 June 1866.

23. A. M. Poindexter to Boyce, December 1866. Also see Cathcart's *Baptist Encyclopedia*, s.v. Poindexter, Abram Maer.

24. J. F. B. Mays to Boyce, 18 December 1865; 25 September 1866.

25. J. F. B. Mays to Boyce, 1 November 1866.

26. George Lorimer to Boyce, 14 January 1867.

27. G. W. Samson to Boyce, 1 March 1867.

28. J. F. B. Mays to Boyce, 4 March 1967.

29. J. F. B. Mays to Boyce, 16 April 1867. Mays eventually rose to some degree of prominence. He served as pastor in Knoxville, Tennessee, and for a brief time (December 1878 through August 1879) served as corresponding secretary of the Tennessee Baptist Convention, called at that time the Board of Missions. He served so shortly because the corresponding secretary was expected to raise his own salary, which he found it difficult to do. In 1873 he was called on to give a speech on education before the Educational Convention sponsored by the Baptists of East Tennessee. Typical of the outlook and language of Mays, he closed that speech with the challenge, "And may I humbly say, give to me the measures I have advocated to-day, and I will have a school in every neighborhood, an academy in every association, a

Sunday-school in every church, a newspaper in every family, and one grand university for all Tennessee, yes, for all the South, whose graduates shall be missionaries and teachers through earth's remotest bounds, on account of the splendor of their erudition and the severity of their mental and moral discipline." See J. F. B. Mays, *The Necessity of Denominational Education* (Knoxville: Chronicle Steam Job Printing Office, 1873), 12.

30. W. D. Thomas, "For the Western Recorder," *Western Recorder*, 11 May 1867, 2.

31. George Hunt, "The Claims of the Southern Baptist Theological Seminary," *Western Recorder*, 8 June 1867, 2.

32. Ibid.

33. Copy of letter in Boyce file, box 1, folder 7.

34. Copy of letter in Boyce file, box 1, folder 7.

35. J. R. Kendrick to Boyce, 1 August 1867.

36. Thomas Porter to Boyce, 1 August 1867.

37. D. B. Deland to Boyce, 2 August 1867.

38. J. William Jones to Boyce, 12 August 1867.

39. Adiel Sherwood to Boyce, 18 August 1867. The "highly extolled speech" probably was the baccalaureate sermon delivered before the graduates and faculty, including Robert E. Lee, at Washington College in June. It was a rainy day, but the Presbyterian church was almost overflowing including four hundred college students and cadets. See Robertson, *Life and Letters*, 224–26.

40. Joseph S. Baker to Boyce, 26 August 1867.

41. Cordelia Mansfield to Boyce, 13 August 1867.

42. D. Bartley to Boyce, 26 August 1867.

43. J. G. Councill to Boyce, 13 August 1867.

44. Thomas J. Truman to Boyce, 20 August 1867.

45. Broadus to Boyce, 23 April 1868, L&F, 67f.

46. Robertson, *Life and Letters*, 228.

47. *Proceedings of the Southern Baptist Convention, 1868*, 24.

48. Ibid.

49. Ibid., 24–25.

50. J. P. Boyce, *Life and Death the Christian's Portion* (New York: Sheldon & Co.; Richmond: Starke & Ryland; Tuscaloosa: Manly & Co., 1869), 8.

51. Ibid., 14–18.

52. Ibid., 34f.

53. Ibid., 52f.

54. Lizzie Boyce, "Stray Recollections of Dr. Boyce," 41, 18, 13–14.

55. Ibid., 35f.

56. Ibid., 35.

57. Ibid., 33f.

58. Broadus to Boyce, L&F, 88.

59. Broadus to Boyce, 30 August 1870, L&F, 88–91.

60. Boyce to Broadus, 24 September 1870, L&F, 95–96.

61. J. P. Boyce, "Book Notice," *The World*, 5 November 1870. Reviews of Broadus's *Treatise* are collected in the archives of the Boyce Memorial Library at the Southern Baptist Theological Seminary, the Broadus Collection, box 22, folders 7–9. The bibliographical information on all these reviews is incomplete.

62. J. P. Boyce, *Courier* (Charleston, 1870).

63. Letter of 7 February 1871, printed in two columns in the Boyce file.

64. Broadus to Manly, 11 August 1871, Robertson, *Life and Letters*, 280f.

Chapter 7: The Move to Louisville

1. *Proceedings of the Seventeenth Meeting of the Southern Baptist Convention* (Baltimore: John F. Weishampel Jr., 1872), 12.

2. A. T. Robertson, *Life and Letters of John Albert Broadus* (Philadelphia: American Baptist Publication Society, 1909), 284.

3. John A. Broadus, *Memoir of James Petigru Boyce* (New York: A. C. Armstrong and Son, 1893), 228.

4. Ibid., 223.

5. Boyce to Broadus, 1 June 1872, in Sean Michael Lucas with Jason Fowler, eds., "'Our Life Work': The Correspondence of James P. Boyce and John A. Broadus, Founders of the Southern Baptist Theological Seminary, 1857–1888" (unpublished volume in the archives of Southern Baptist Theological Seminary, 2004), 116 (hereafter L&F).

6. Robertson, *Life and Letters*, 285.

7. W. H. Whitsitt, "The Position of Baptists in the History of American Culture," Inaugural address, 2 September 1872, 8.

8. Ibid., 13.

9. Ibid., 20.

10. Boyce to Broadus, 12 October 1872, L&F, 117f.

11. Boyce to Broadus, 22 October 1872, L&F, 119.

12. *Minutes of the South Carolina Baptist Convention, 1872*, 14.

13. Broadus to Boyce, 15 November 1872, L&F, 121.

14. Boyce to Broadus, 18 November 1872, L&F, 122ff.

15. Boyce to Broadus, 10 December 1872, L&F, 126.

16. Boyce to Broadus, 6 March 1873, L&F, 131f.

17. Boyce to Broadus, 10 March 1873, L&F, 133f.

18. Broadus to Boyce, 14 March 1873, L&F, 134ff.

19. Ibid.

20. Boyce to Broadus, 17 April 1873, L&F, 139.

21. Ibid.

22. Boyce to Broadus, 21 April 1873, L&F, 142.

23. *Proceedings of the Southern Baptist Convention, 1873*, 19.

24. Broadus, *Memoir*, 238.

25. Boyce to Broadus, 2 October, 1873, L&F, 142–44.

26. Broadus to Boyce, 11 October 1873, L&F, 144f.

27. Boyce to Broadus, 23 December 1873, L&F, 146–47.

28. Broadus to Boyce, 29 December 1873, L&F, 148.

29. A. T. Robertson, *New Testament Interpretation: Notes on Lectures*, prepared and printed by William Fouts and Alice M. Fouts, taken originally by W. E. Davidson (Louisville, 1921), 139.

30. Boyce to Broadus, 4 February 1874, L&F, 151–52.

31. J. R. Graves, "The Influence of Unsound Theological Professors," *The Baptist*, 14 February 1874, 4.

32. J. R. Graves, "English Baptists," *The Baptist*, 28 February 1874.

33. M. P. Lowery, "The Southern Baptist Theological Seminary—A Misunderstanding," *The Baptist*, 28 February 1874, 8.

34. Ibid.

35. Ibid.

36. Boyce to Broadus, 24 March 1874, L&F, 158f.

37. Boyce to Broadus, 28 March 1874.

38. J. P. Boyce, "To the Baptists of Kentucky," *Western Recorder* 4 April 1874, 2.

39. J. P. Boyce, "A Question for Every Baptist to Consider," *Western Recorder*, 4 April 1874, 2.

40. Ibid.

41. J. R. Graves, "Dr. Boardman Fallen!!" *The Baptist*, 28 March 1874, 4.

42. J. R. Graves, "George Dana Boardman," *The Baptist*, 4 April 1874, 4.

43. J. R. Graves, *Old Landmarkism: What Is It?* (Memphis: Baptist Book House, 1880), 140. Graves himself uses the terms "Landmarker" and "Landmarkism."

44. Boyce to Broadus, 7 April 1874, L&F, 161–62.

45. Boyce, "The Two Objections to the Seminary, I," *Western Recorder*, 11 April 1874, 2.

46. Ibid.

47. Ibid.

48. Boyce, "The Two Objections to the Seminary, II," *Western Recorder*, 18 April 1874, 2.

49. Boyce, "The Two Objections to the Seminary, III," *Western Recorder*, 25 April 1874, 2.

50. Ibid.

51. Broadus to Boyce, 21 April 1874, L&F, 169–170.

52. "Southern Baptist Theological Seminary," *Western Recorder*, 16 May 1874.

53. Boyce to Broadus, 14 April 1874, L&F, 164–65.

54. Ibid. "As to our summer's work, I am yet in perplexity. But for the emergencies in Kentucky I should say all work elsewhere to make up the other money. Divide it out among us. In that event I should wish you to work Maryland and Virginia—

Williams, North and South Carolina, unless he prefers to continue in Texas. If so then Toy in North and South Carolina. But if Williams takes NC and SC, then Toy in Alabama and Mississippi, and Whitsitt in Tennessee and Georgia, and let me keep on in Kentucky, or dividing out so that I work with you. Let me take either SC or GA or MS. I have a half fancy for the latter, particularly after I have said what I have said and shall yet say in the articles. I just state the above sketch in the rough. We must in working those states, get others to work at the associations we cannot attend."

55. Ibid., 166.

56. William Carey Crane and Rufus Burleson both were giants among Texas Baptists, both presidents of universities. Crane presided over Baylor University in Independence and Burleson over Waco University in Waco. In 1886 the schools merged under a new charter as Baylor University in Waco.

57. Boyce to Broadus, 14 April 1874, L&F, 167.

58. J. P. Boyce, "The Two Objections to the Seminary, IV," *Western Recorder*, 9 May 1874, 2.

59. "L.", "Convention Sabbath in Jefferson," *Christian Index and Southwest Baptist*, 21 May 1874, 5.

60. Broadus, *Memoir*, 240.

61. J. P. Boyce, "Two Objections to the Seminary, V," *Western Recorder*, 20 June 1874, 2.

62. Ibid.

63. Ibid.

64. Ibid.

65. Ibid. Boyce quoted A. C. Dayton, *Pedobaptist and Campbellite Immersions* (Nashville: Southwestern Publishing; New York: Sheldon, Blakeman & Co., 1858), 125.

66. Broadus to Boyce, 26 May 1874, L&F, 171.

67. Ibid.

68. Robertson, *Life and Letters*, 296.

69. Broadus to Boyce, 26 May 1874, L&F, 171.

70. Robertson, *Life and Letters*, 296.

71. Broadus, *Memoir*, 241.

72. Ibid., 244.

73. Broadus to Boyce, 26 June 1876, L&F, 238.

74. Broadus, *Memoir*, 244.

75. Boyce to Broadus, 6 October 1874, L&F, 176–77.

76. Boyce to Broadus, 5 December 1874, L&F, 182–83.

77. Boyce to Broadus, 6 October 1874, L&F, 176.

78. Boyce to Broadus, 30 November 1874, L&F, 180.

79. Broadus to Boyce, 3 December 1874, L&F, 181.

80. Boyce to Broadus, 9 March 1875, L&F, 195.

81. Boyce to Broadus, 31 December 1874 and 1 January 1875, L&F, 183–84.

82. Boyce to Broadus, 23 August 1875, L&F, 204.

83. Z. A. Owens, "From the Southern Baptist Theological Seminary," *Western Recorder*, 21 November 1874, 2.

Chapter 8: Finalizing the Move to Louisville

1. John A. Broadus, *Memoir of James Petigru Boyce* (New York: A. C. Armstrong and Son, 1893), 244–45.

2. Boyce to Broadus, 20 September 1875, in Sean Michael Lucas with Jason Fowler, eds., "'Our Life Work': The Correspondence of James P. Boyce and John A. Broadus, Founders of the Southern Baptist Theological Seminary, 1857–1888" (unpublished volume in the archives of Southern Baptist Theological Seminary, 2004), 208 (hereafter L&F).

3. A Dollar Roll certificate in the possession of the author. This was issued to E. O. Taylor of Cleburne, Texas, and countersigned by the collector, R. W. Whitehead.

4. Boyce to Broadus, 14 January 1875, L&F, 187f.

5. Boyce to Broadus, 13 January 1875; 10 February 1875, L&F, 186, 191. Daniel Webster Whittle had begun his evangelistic career in 1873 at the instigation of D. L. Moody. He continued in this work until his death in 1901, spending some of his last years among the soldiers in the camps in the Spanish American War. Philip P. Bliss joined him in his campaigns in 1874, but at the age of thirty-eight in 1876 died in a train wreck trying to save his wife. Both Whittle and Bliss were prolific gospel hymn writers.

6. Broadus to Boyce, 16 February 1875, L&F, 192.

7. Broadus to Boyce, 18 July 1876, L&F, 246.

8. Lottie Broadus to John A. Broadus, 12 June 1872 (Broadus Papers, box 4); Annie Broadus to John A. Broadus, 10 July 1876 (Broadus Papers, box 7). I am indebted to my colleague Greg Wills for some insight on this issue as well as these references. He also pointed out several medical books of the period that recommended whiskey and brandy in a variety of strengths and solutions for numerous ailments, including pulmonary tuberculosis, flatulent colic, indigestion, vomiting, fainting, and some fevers.

9. Broadus to Boyce, 26 June 1876, L&F, 239.

10. Morrell (1803–83) moved to Texas in 1835 after highly effective ministries in Tennessee and Mississippi. He strongly supported benevolent organizations and missionary labors. In 1872, three years prior to Boyce's visit, Morrell had published a history of Texas Baptists entitled *Flowers and Fruits in the Wilderness; or Forty-six Years in Texas and Two Winters in Honduras.*

11. Boyce to Broadus, 5 July 1875, L&F, 199ff. For information on Hackett and Pettigrew see L. S. Foster, *Mississippi Baptist Preachers* (St. Louis: National Baptist Publishing, 1895), 323ff., 539f. Pettigrew attended the seminary for one session immediately prior to the Civil War.

12. Broadus to Boyce, 16 September 1875, L&F, 205.

13. Boyce to Broadus, 20 September 1875, L&F, 208.

14. Broadus to Boyce, 9 February 1876, L&F, 220.

15. Boyce to Broadus, 23 March 1876; Broadus to Boyce, 27 March 1876, L&F, 224f.

16. Boyce to Broadus, 10 April 1876; Broadus to Boyce, 15 April 1876, L&F, 228ff.

17. Boyce to Broadus, 17 April 1876, L&F, 230–34.

18. Ibid.

19. Ibid.

20. J. B. Jeter, "A Singular Dream," *Religious Herald*, 22 June 1876, 1.

21. "That Singular Dream," *Western Recorder*, 29 June 1876, 4.

22. J. P. Boyce, "Dr. Jeter's Dream," *Western Recorder*, 29 June 1876, 5.

23. Boyce to Broadus, 24 October 1876, L&F, 259.

24. Pike, "A Dangerous Doctrine," *Religious Herald*, 22 June 1876, 1.

25. Pike, "Concerning the Landmark Doctrine," *Religious Herald*, 17 August 1876, 1.

26. J. M. Pendleton, "The Last Article of 'Pike,'" *Religious Herald*, 31 August 1876, 1.

27. J. R. Graves, "Pendleton, 'The Last Article of "Pike,"'" *The Baptist*, 23 September 1876, 1.

28. R. C. Buckner, "The Last Article of 'Pike,'" *Texas Baptist*, 5 October 1876, 1.

29. Ibid.

30. Their names were T. N. Rhymes and Eustace Eugene King. Both became successful and effective pastors in Mississippi and also served churches in Louisiana. King became pastor of First Baptist Church in San Antonio, Texas (1890), and led the church to be a center for church planting.

31. Broadus to Boyce, 15 July 1876.

32. Broadus to Boyce, 18 July 1876, L&F, 246.

33. Boyce to Broadus, 14 September 1876, L&F, 250.

34. Broadus to Boyce, 19 September 1876, L&F, 252.

35. Boyce to Broadus, 5 October 1876, L&F, 255.

36. Boyce to Broadus, 7 October 1876, L&F, 256–57.

37. James P. Boyce, untitled article, *Texas Baptist*, 19 October 1876, 4.

38. R. C. Buckner, "'Pike' and the Seminary," *Texas Baptist*, 19 October 1876, 6.

39. Boyce to Broadus, 21 October 1876, L&F, 258.

40. Boyce to Broadus, 24 October 1876.

41. Broadus to Boyce, 25 October 1876, L&F, 264.

42. Boyce to Broadus, 6 December 1876.

43. Broadus to Boyce, 6 December 1876, L&F, 267ff.

44. Boyce to Broadus, 11 December 1876, L&F, 269.

45. A. T. Robertson, *Life and Letters of John Albert Broadus* (Philadelphia: American Baptist Publication Society, 1909), 303.

46. Ibid., 192. Robertson cites a letter from Boyce to Broadus, 16 March 1862.

47. Broadus to Boyce, 16 February 1876, L&F, 222.

48. Broadus to Boyce, 5 August 1876, L&F, 248.

49. Broadus to Boyce, 27 September 1876, L&F, 253f.; Boyce to Broadus, 5 October 1876, L&F, 255.

50. Boyce to Broadus, 29 January 1877, L&F, 273.

51. Boyce to Broadus, 9 February 1877, L&F, 275.

52. Ibid.

53. Robertson, *Life and Letters*, 304.

54. Ibid. Some of the remarks interspersed in this paragraph come from the note immediately below.

55. D. F. H., "Lectures on Preaching," *Western Recorder*, 1 March 1877, 1. Some of this student's observations are interspersed in the preceding paragraph.

56. William A. Mueller, *A History of Southern Baptist Theological Seminary* (Nashville: Broadman, 1959), 106.

57. Broadus, *Memoir*, 247.

58. Mueller, *History*, 110. Mueller cites *Faculty Minutes*, book 1, 57–59. See also "Rev. William Williams," *Western Recorder*, 1 March 1877, 5.

59. Boyce to Broadus, 29 January 1877; 9 February 1877, L&F, 273ff.

60. Boyce to Broadus, 23 March 1877, L&F, 276.

61. Broadus to Boyce, 27 March 1877, L&F, 277f.

62. Boyce to Broadus, 4 April 1877, L&F, 279f.

63. —— Anderson, "Southern Baptist Convention," *Working Christian*, 17 May 1877, 2.

64. Boyce to Broadus, 26 May 1877, L&F, 285.

65. Robertson, *Memoir*, 307.

66. M.G.H., "The Theological Seminary," *Working Christian*, 21 June 1877, 2.

67. Boyce to Broadus, 15 June 1877, L&F, 287. Obviously Broadus's notice had come out in other places prior to its appearance in the *Working Christian* on June 21.

68. Boyce seemed pleased at the prospect of the young Kerfoot coming. He related to Broadus that Jeter had asked him if he could get a Kentucky man to fill the vacancy. Boyce responded that he had one and then leaned forward and said in a confidential tone, "Kerfoot" (Boyce to Broadus, 15 June 1877). Later he wrote Broadus, "Kerfoot was with me yesterday. He will accept, and as he evidently prefers History and Homiletics, I think we had best let that stand" (Boyce to Broadus, 19 June 1877, L&F, 289f.).

69. "I told Kerfoot all about the Baltimore matter when I first saw him about the Seminary so that in deciding there might be no such clash. . . . The church will call if he will accept. He never gave me his formal acceptance, but all that he said, with his preparations at Midway for you and him to preach, was based upon acceptance. I fear it will throw us out of gear, but I shall give no advice" (Boyce to Broadus, 11 August 1877, L&F, 322).

70. Boyce to Broadus, 18 June 1877, L&F, 289.

71. Broadus to Boyce, 2 July 1877, L&F, 297.

72. Broadus to Boyce, 16 July 1877, L&F, 312.

73. Boyce to Broadus, 15 July 1877, L&F, 307.

74. Broadus to Boyce, 16 July 1877, L&F, 313.

75. Boyce to Broadus, 16 July 1877, L&F, 310.

76. Boyce to Broadus, 23 July 1877, L&F, 316.

77. Boyce to Broadus, 11 July 1877, L&F, 303.

78. Broadus to Boyce, 14 July 1877, L&F, 306.

79. James P. Boyce, "Seminary Opening," *Western Recorder*, 23 August 1877.

80. J. P. Boyce, "Introductory Lecture," *Western Recorder*, 6 September 1877, 2.

81. Ibid.

82. Ibid., 3.

83. Ibid.

Chapter 9: The Toy Affair

1. C. H. Toy, "Resignation Letter" (May 1879). The most complete study of Toy is Billy Grey Hurt, "Crawford Howell Toy: Interpreter of the Old Testament," Th.D. diss., Southern Baptist Theological Seminary, 1965. He includes a discussion of Toy as a scholar in general but focuses his major attention on the controversy at the seminary.

2. John A. Broadus, *Memoir of James Petigru Boyce* (New York: A. C. Armstrong and Son, 1893), 261.

3. James P. Boyce, "Three Changes in Theological Institutions," in *James Petigru Boyce: Selected Writings*, ed. Timothy George (Nashville: Broadman, 1989), 32.

4. Ibid., 50.

5. Toy, "Resignation Letter."

6. John A. Broadus, *Memoir*, 260–61.

7. Ibid., 261.

8. E. T. R., "E. T. R. Again! Honesty—False Teaching, &c.," *Religious Herald*, December 1878, 2.

9. Broadus to Boyce, 12 December 1878.

10. E. T. R., "The Objective Side of Justification by Faith," *Religious Herald*, January 1879, 1.

11. SBC Convention Annual, 1873, 19–20, 35–36.

12. "Baptist Items," *Christian Index and Southwestern Baptist*, 21 May 1874, 5.

13. John A. Broadus, "Rev. A. Jaeger," *Christian Index and Southwestern Baptist*, 7 May 1874, 5.

14. Broadus to Boyce, 9 February 1876.

15. Boyce to Broadus, 11 February 1876.

16. Boyce to Broadus, 23 March 1876.

17. Boyce to Broadus, 6 December 1876.

18. Boyce to Broadus, 6 December 1876, in Sean Michael Lucas with Jason Fowler, eds., "'Our Life Work': The Correspondence of James P. Boyce and John A. Broadus, Founders of the Southern Baptist Theological Seminary, 1857–1888" (unpublished volume in the archives of Southern Baptist Theological Seminary, 2004), 265–66 (hereafter L&F).

19. Broadus to Boyce, 29 January 1877.

20. Broadus to Boyce, 20 June 1876.

21. Greg Wills, *The First Baptist Church of Columbia, South Carolina, 1809–2002* (Brentwood, TN: Baptist History and Heritage Society, 2003), 156. Wills identifies Senex as Lindsay, who had just gone to serve as pastor of First Baptist Church in Columbia, South Carolina. John A. Broadus had recommended him to the position.

22. Toy, "Resignation Letter."

23. Senex, "Letters to My Friend—No. 1: The Bible a Literature—Not a Book," *Working Christian*, 24 March 1877, 2.

24. Senex, "Letters to My Friend—No. 2: The Bible a Literature—Not a Book," *Working Christian*, 31 May 1877, 2.

25. Ibid.

26. Toy, "Resignation Letter."

27. Senex, "Letters to My Friend—No. 1," 2.

28. Senex, "Letters to My Friend—No. 2," 2.

29. Ibid.; Toy, "Resignation Letter."

30. Senex, "Letters to My Friend—No. 3: The Christian Consciousness a Source of Truth," *Working Christian*, 21 June 1877, 2.

31. Ibid.

32. Toy, "Resignation Letter."

33. Senex, "Letters to My Friend—No. 3."

34. Boyce to Broadus, 22 June 1877.

35. Boyce to Broadus, 17 April 1876.

36. Broadus, *Memoir*, 262.

37. C. H. Toy, "Critical Notes," *Sunday School Times*, 12 January 1878, 23.

38. H. Clay Trumbull, editorial remarks, *Sunday School Times*, 26 January 1878, 49.

39. John Stout, "The Senex Letters," *Working Christian*, 21 June 1877, 2. Stout eventually came to the views of Lindsay and Toy.

40. C. C. Brown, "The Bible the Word of God," *Working Christian*, 28 June 1877, 1.

41. C. C. Brown, "Dr. Hiden and 'Senex,'" *Working Christian*, 26 July 1877, 1. Brown identifies himself as a former student of John A. Broadus.

42. J. L. Reynolds, in a letter to the editor entitled "Flat Rock, N. C.," *Working Christian*, 21 June 1877, 2.

43. J. C. Hiden, "Senex and His Critics—No. I," *Working Christian*, 19 July 1877, 1.

44. C. C. Brown, "Dr. Hiden and Senex," *Working Christian*, 26 July 1877, 1.

45. J. C. Hiden, "Senex and His Critics—No. II," *Working Christian*, 26 July 1877, 2.

46. A. T. Robertson, *Life and Letters of John Albert Broadus* (Philadelphia: American Baptist Publication Society, 1909), 173.

47. Handwritten copy of "Sketch of My Religious Life" in the T. T. Eaton Collection in the archives of the J. P. Boyce Memorial Library at the Southern Baptist Theological Seminary. Toy describes lengthy periods of "alternating doubt and hope" and much "trembling, sometimes almost in despair, but never for a long time unable to look to Christ as my salvation." In 1861 he wrote Broadus that he came to begrudge "every moment of time that's not spent on what I consider profitable employment." Though he had rapidly cultivated unrelenting habits of using time for measurable ends, he pondered whether this urgency to act out of duty might not disguise "the absence of Christian emotion." "It is a difficult question to decide," Toy wrote as he reasoned about himself, "how far it is just treadmill work and how far the genuine outspeaking of earnest feeling." His spirit was deeply exercised about this issue and sincerely troubled. "It makes me doubt now sometimes," Toy continued confiding to Broadus, "whether my heart has ever been changed. I can only pray God to deepen my Christian feeling and strengthen the internal evidence of my calling."

48. "Meeting of the Private Members of Baptist Churches in Staunton," *Religious Herald*, 14 June 1860, 2.

49. See R. H. Bagby in *Religious Herald*, 8 November 1861, 1: "It may be well for our young men to visit Germany in search of learning; but it is to be hoped that they will look elsewhere for their theology; and that we of the South shall be spared any communication of the least taint of the heretical doctrines with which that country abounds."

50. C. H. Toy, "The Tübingen School," *Baptist Quarterly* 3 (1869): 210–35.

51. Ibid., 210.

52. Ibid., 212.

53. Ibid., 214.

54. Ibid., 215.

55. Ibid., 216–17. Toy quotes from the preface and first section of the second edition of Baur's *History of the Christian Church in the First Three Centuries*.

56. Ibid., 216.

57. Ibid., 217.

58. Ibid., 218.

59. Ibid.

60. Ibid., 219.

61. Ibid., 220.

62. Ibid., 222.

63. Ibid.

64. Ibid., 223.

65. Ibid., 226–34.

66. Ibid., 226.
67. Ibid., 227.
68. Ibid.
69. Ibid., 228.
70. Ibid., 229–30.
71. Ibid., 231.
72. Ibid., 231–32.
73. Ibid., 233.
74. Ibid., 233–34.
75. Ibid., 234.
76. Robertson, *Life and Letters*, 232.
77. Broadus, *Memoir*, 211.
78. C. H. Toy, *The Claims of Biblical Interpretation on Baptists* (New York: Lange & Hillman, 1869), 5.
79. Ibid., 6.
80. Ibid., 15–16.
81. Ibid., 53.
82. Ibid., 16.
83. Ibid., 6.
84. Ibid., 53.
85. Ibid., 54.
86. Ibid., 8.
87. Ibid., 9.
88. Ibid., 24.
89. Ibid., 9.
90. Paul House, *Crawford Howell Toy and the Weight of Hermeneutics: A Founder's Day Address* (Louisville: n.p., 1997), 11.
91. Ibid., 5; citation from Toy, *Claims of Biblical Interpretation*, 42.
92. House, *Toy*, 8.
93. Ibid., 11.
94. Ibid., 4.
95. Toy, *Claims of Biblical Interpretation*, 55.
96. Ibid., 8.
97. Ibid., 54.
98. Ibid., 43.
99. Ibid., 30.
100. Ibid., 29, 55.
101. Ibid., 43.
102. Ibid., 31.
103. Ibid., 31.
104. Ibid., 32.
105. Ibid., 33.

106. Ibid., 56–57.

107. Ibid., 45–46.

108. Ibid., 42.

109. Ibid., 44.

110. Ibid., 49.

111. J. P. Boyce, series of questions for recitation in a notebook by William Harrison Williams, October 1861. The notebook is located in the archives of the James P. Boyce Library, Southern Baptist Theological Seminary. The material in this and the following paragraphs comes from this 1861 notebook.

112. Basil Manly Jr., "The Bible and Science," located in the archives of the James P. Boyce Library, Southern Baptist Theological Seminary.

113. Basil Manly Jr., *Little Lessons for Little People* (Nashville: Sunday School Board, 1867), 11.

114. Toy, "Resignation Letter."

115. J. B. Jeter, "The Southern Baptist Convention," *Religious Herald*, 22 May 1879, 2.

116. A. T. Robertson, *Life and Letters of John A. Broadus* (Philadelphia: American Baptist Publication Society, 1901), 313.

117. J. R. Graves, "The Convention: 'The Seminary,'" *The Baptist*, May 1879, 229.

118. J. B. Jeter, "Dr. Toy's Address," *Religious Herald*, 11 December 1879, 1.

119. Ibid.

120. J. B. Jeter, "Inspiration," *Religious Herald*, 18 December 1879, 1; "Inspiration," *Religious Herald*, 25 December 1879, 1; "Objections to Plenary Inspiration," *Religious Herald*, 1 January 1880, 1. These articles appeared together as "The Inspiration of the Scriptures," in C. A. Jenkens, ed., *Baptist Doctrines* (St. Louis: Chancy R. Barns, 1882), 49–69. An early account of the life and contributions of Jeter is found in W. E. Hatcher, *Life of J. B. Jeter, D. D.* (Baltimore: H. M. Wharton and Company, 1887).

121. Jeter, "Inspiration," 18 December 1879, 1.

122. Jeter, "Inspiration," 25 December 1879, 1.

123. Jeter, "Objections to Plenary Inspiration," 1.

124. (Acting Editor, A. E. Dickinson?), "Inspiration," *Religious Herald*, 15 April 1880, 2. J. B. Jeter died in February, having spent his last months giving feverish attention to the issue of inspiration.

125. C. H. Toy, "The Outward Form of Revelation," *Religious Herald*, 22 January 1880, 1.

126. C. H. Toy, "The Historical Books of the Bible," *Religious Herald*, 11 March 1880, 1.

127. C. H. Toy, "A Bit of Personal Experience," *Religious Herald*, 1 April 1880, 1.

128. Ibid.

129. C. H. Toy, "Destruction for Reconstruction," *Religious Herald*, 15 April 1880, 1.

130. Toy, "Historical Books."

131. Ibid.

132. Ibid.

133. C. H Toy, "Genesis and Geology," *Religious Herald*, 6 May 1880, 1.

134. Broadus, *Memoir*, 262–63.

135. S. H. Henderson, "Dr. Toy's Sunday-school 'Primer,'" *Christian Index*, 12 April 1883, 6.

136. Crawford H. Toy, "Relation of Jesus to Christianity," *Christian Register*, 12 March 1891, 168.

137. A. H. Newman, *A History of the Baptist Churches in the United States*, 6th ed. (Philadelphia: American Baptist Publication Society, 1915), 519.

138. Broadus, *Memoir*, 263–64.

Chapter 10: Securing the Seminary, 1879–86

1. E. T. R., "E. T. R. Again! Honesty, False Teaching, &c.," *Religious Herald*, 12 December 1878, 2.

2. J. M. Pendleton, "Bro. Campbell and 'E. T. R.'—'E. T. R.' and the Seminaries—Editorial Fallibility, &c," *Religious Herald*, 16 January 1879, 2.

3. E. T. R., "E. T. R. Again! A Word to E. T. R.'s Critics—The Seminaries—Dr. Pendleton—Dr. Weston and G. Washington Jones," *Religious Herald*, 6 February 1879, 2.

4. H. G. Weston, "Professor Toy as a Critical Scholar," *Sunday School Times*, 5 January 1878, 3.

5. J. B. Jeter, "The Southern Baptist Convention," *Religious Herald*, 22 May 1879, 8.

6. G. W. R., "Southern Baptist Theological Seminary," *Religious Herald*, 22 May 1879, 1.

7. Ibid.

8. J. P. Boyce, "S. B. Theological Seminary—Address," *Western Recorder*, 8 May 1879, 1.

9. Ibid.

10. Ibid.

11. Ibid.

12. R. B. C. Howell, "Editorial," *The Baptist*, February 1835, 1. As seen before, Howell had been a friend of the effort to found the seminary and served conscientiously as a trustee of the school.

13. *Religious Herald*, 22 May 1879, 8.

14. William A. Mueller, *A History of Southern Baptist Theological Seminary* (Nashville: Broadman, 1959), 96–97.

15. Basil Manly Jr., "Why and How to Study the Bible," handwritten manuscript in the Manly collection in the archives of the J. P. Boyce Memorial Library at Southern Baptist Theological Seminary.

16. Basil Manly Jr., *Why and How to Study the Bible* (Louisville: Hull & Brothers, 1883), 3.

17. Ibid., 13.

18. Ibid.

19. Ibid., 4.

20. Ibid.

21. Manly, handwritten manuscript.

22. Manly gave a picture of what Sundays in the South were like when he wrote, "I do not pause, however, to describe for your avoidance that formal or careless reading, which as children we used to give them, because it was Sunday, and that was the most convenient book, and possibly with a sort of impression that we were acquiring a stock of merit, which would redound to our account" (*Study the Bible*, 4–5). An unpublished comment in the handwritten text adds, "Can we not remember how, in the intervals between church and meals, we would let our eyes move over its blessed pages with a sleep provoking languor?"

23. Manly, *Study the Bible*, 7.

24. Ibid., 7–10.

25. Ibid., 10.

26. Ibid., 11.

27. Ibid., 12.

28. Ibid., 14.

29. John A. Broadus, *Memoir of James Petigru Boyce* (New York: A. C. Armstrong and Son, 1893), 264.

30. Basil Manly Jr., *The Bible Doctrine of Inspiration* (New York: A. C. Armstrong and Son, 1888), v.

31. W. O. Carver, "Unpublished Notes," 22, cited in Mueller, *History*, 98, 101.

32. Basil Manly, "The Old Testament in the Twentieth Century," *The Seminary Magazine*, October 1891, 1–12.

33. J. P. Boyce, *Abstract of Systematic Theology* (Philadelphia: American Baptist Publication Society, 1887), 47.

34. Ibid., 48.

35. Ibid., 50.

36. Thomas Fenner Curtis, *The Human Element in the Inspiration of the Sacred Scriptures* (New York: D. Appleton & Company, 1867), 207. Basil Manly Jr. had a copy of this book that had been given to him by the author in 1867, the year of its publication. Curtis had been a member of the same church as Basil Manly Sr. and John L. Dagg in Tuscaloosa, Alabama. He had been at the organizational meeting of the Southern Baptist Convention in 1845 and had coauthored the address to the public. He maintained the traditional views of inspiration while he taught at Howard College, but while teaching at Bucknell came under the influence of the writings of Horace Bushnell and found himself unable to maintain the idea of infallibility.

37. Manly, *Inspiration*, 59.

38. Ibid., 37.
39. Ibid., 93.
40. Ibid., 96.
41. Ibid., 175.
42. Basil Manly, "Alleged Disclaimers of Inspiration," *The Seminary Magazine*, February 1888, 3–9.
43. Ibid., 9. The authors Manly quotes in support of his position are Ladd, DeWette, Alford, Hodge. The Scriptures that he treats are Luke 1:3; 1 Corinthians 7:6–25; Romans 6:18–19; 2 Corinthians 11:17; 2 Corinthians 12:2–3; 1 Corinthians 1:16. The list of Scriptures to which he is responding appears in Curtis's *The Human Element*, 207–32.
44. Broadus to Boyce, 8 June 1883, in Sean Michael Lucas with Jason Fowler, eds., "'Our Life Work': The Correspondence of James P. Boyce and John A. Broadus, Founders of the Southern Baptist Theological Seminary, 1857–1888" (unpublished volume in the archives of Southern Baptist Theological Seminary, 2004), 350 (hereafter L&F).
45. Broadus to Boyce, 18 June 1883.
46. Broadus to Boyce, 14 July 1883, L&F, 353.
47. "Southern Baptist Convention," *Baptist Courier*, 24 May 1883, 1.
48. John A. Broadus, *Three Questions as to the Bible* (Philadelphia: American Baptist Publication Society, 1883), 9.
49. Ibid., 10.
50. Ibid., 27.
51. *Baptist Courier*, 24 May 1883, 1.
52. Broadus, *Three Questions*, 37.
53. John A. Broadus, "The Value of the English Bible in Secular and Religious Education," *Western Recorder*, 26 March 1885, 1.
54. Curtis, *Human Element*, 165.
55. John A. Broadus, *The Paramount and Permanent Authority of the Bible* (Philadelphia: American Baptist Publication Society, 1887), 3.
56. Ibid., 4.
57. Ibid., 7.
58. Ibid., 9.
59. Ibid. Broadus wrote specifically of astronomy when he made that statement, but applied the principle in general to all the sciences.
60. Ibid.
61. Ibid., 12–14.
62. Ibid., 15–16.
63. Lyon to Broadus, 24 May 1880.
64. This correspondence is not available, but Lyon summarized it in a letter on 28 March 1881: "I have naturally thought more or less on the subject for the past year but have not seen sufficient ground for changing the views expressed in my letter of last July. The practical difficulties which you suggest have often occurred to me: if

one admits mistakes in the Scriptures what must be the consequences, and where is the stopping place? If the step involves an 'overthrow of everything,' then it would be impossible for me to make it, for I have something which is so positive as to be a part of my very being, something which seems to me as enduring as my existence. But I cannot see that such consequences legitimately follow."

65. Boyce to Broadus, 15 July 1880.

66. Boyce to Broadus, 29 July 1880; L&F, 341.

67. Lyon to Broadus, 28 March 1881.

68. Ibid.

69. Ibid.

70. Ibid.

71. Ibid.

72. Ibid.

73. Ibid.

74. Broadus to Boyce, 19 August 1880, L&F, 343.

75. Boyce to Broadus, 23 August 1880, L&F, 345.

76. Boyce to Broadus, 25 August 1883, L&F, 361.

77. John A. Broadus, "Funeral Sermon for G. W. Riggan," *Sermons and Addresses* (New York: Hodder and Stoughton, 1886), 364.

78. Ibid., 354.

79. Ibid., 360.

80. A. T. Robertson, *Life and Letters of John Albert Broadus* (Philadelphia: American Baptist Publication Society, 1909), 345.

81. "Minutes," Foreign Mission Board of the Southern Baptist Convention, June 1881, 434–35, as cited in William R. Estep, *Whole Gospel, Whole World* (Nashville: Broadman & Holman, 1994), 138.

82. Tupper to Lottie Moon, 12(?) August 1881.

83. Boyce to Broadus, 31 July 1883, L&F, 357f.

84. Broadus to Boyce, 7 August 1883, L&F, 358ff.

85. Francis G. Peabody to Broadus, 6 August 1886.

86. Boyce to Broadus, 14 August 1886, L&F, 389.

87. Robertson, *Life and Letters*, 312.

88. Ibid.

89. Broadus to Boyce, 18 July 1879, L&F, 335.

90. Broadus to Boyce, 16 December 1878, L&F, 331f.

91. Broadus, *Memoir*, 272–73.

92. Ibid., 274.

93. J. P. Boyce, "New Hope for the Seminary," *Alabama Baptist*, 1 April 1880. This news notice was sent to many, if not all, of the state Baptist papers.

94. Broadus, *Memoir*, 271.

95. William Allen to J. P. Boyce, 12 April 1880.

96. Ibid.

97. Eliza Peddicord to J. P. Boyce, 18 April 1880.

98. M. H. Justice to J. P. Boyce, 20 April 1880.

99. David J. Corbett to J. P. Boyce, 23 March and 20 April 1880.

100. Broadus to Boyce, 5 June 1883, L&F, 349f.

101. Broadus to Boyce, 24 June 1884.

102. Broadus to Boyce, 14 August 1884, L&F, 372f.

103. Boyce to Broadus, 19 June 1884, L&F, 367f.

104. Boyce to Broadus, 29 March 1884, L&F, 364f.

105. Economy, "The Seminary—Why Not Build?" *Western Recorder*, 5 March 1885, 8.

106. J. P. Boyce, "Why Does Not the Seminary Build?" *Western Recorder*, 19 March 1885, 5.

107. J. P. Boyce, "The Seminary—The Obstacles to Building," *Western Recorder*, 26 March 1885, 5.

108. Boyce to Broadus, 25 July 1885, L&F, 376, for the last two sentences. Also, Robertson, *Life and Letters*, 348.

109. Broadus, *Memoir*, 280–82.

110. Broadus to Boyce, 15 March 1886, L&F, 378–79.

111. Robertson, *Life and Letters*, 349.

112. Ibid., 348.

113. Ibid., 349.

114. Boyce to Broadus, 12 August 1886, L&F, 388.

115. Broadus, *Memoir*, 282.

116. Boyce to Broadus, 14 August 1886, L&F, 389f.

117. Broadus, *Memoir*, 282–83.

118. *The Seminary Magazine*, March 1888, 77.

Chapter 11: Boyce's Theology

1. John L. Dagg, *A Manual of Theology* (Charleston: Southern Baptist Publication Society, 1858).

2. John Dick, *Lectures on Theology*, 2 vols. (New York: R. Carter and Bros, 1854–55).

3. Francis Turretin, *Opera*, 4 vols. (Edinburgh: J. D. Lowe, 1847–48). This is the edition listed in the "Authors" volume of the catalogue of Boyce's library.

4. J. J. Van Oosterzee, *Christian Dogmatics*, trans. John W. Watson and Maurice J. Evans (New York: Scribner, Armstrong and Co., 1874). Boyce dropped this text after a brief trial because it was too cumbersome and its views of the nature of biblical inspiration differed from Boyce's.

5. Alvah Hovey, *A Manual of Systematic Theology* (Philadelphia: American Baptist Publication Society, 1877).

6. A. A. Hodge, *Outlines of Theology* (New York: Robert Carter and Bros, 1872).

7. J. P. Boyce, *Abstract of Systematic Theology* (Philadelphia: American Baptist Publication Society, 1887), vi, viii.

8. Brooks Holifield, *Theology in America* (New Haven: Yale University Press, 2003), 159.

9. Boyce, *Abstract*, 92–98 and 99–106.

10. Ibid., 3–4; compare with Charles Hodge, *Systematic Theology*, 3 vols. (New York: Charles Scribner and Company, 1872), 1:1–17.

11. Hodge, *Systematic Theology*, 1:13.

12. Boyce, *Abstract*, 4.

13. Hodge, *Systematic Theology*, 1:14.

14. Boyce, *Abstract*, 7.

15. Ibid., 16.

16. Hodge, *Systematic Theology*, 1:191ff.

17. Boyce, *Abstract*, 16–18.

18. Ibid., 19.

19. J. P. Boyce, "Questions for Recitation" in a theological notebook by William Harrison Williams at the Southern Baptist Theological Seminary, October 1861.

20. Francis Turretin, *Institutes of Elenctic Theology*, trans. George Musgrave Giger, ed. James T. Dennison Jr., 3 vols. (Phillipsburg, NJ: P&R, 1992–97), 1:169 (1.3.1).

21. Ibid., 1:169 (3.1.4).

22. Dick, *Lectures*, 1:160–62.

23. Hodge, *Systematic Theology*, 1:204–7.

24. Boyce, "Questions."

25. Boyce, *Abstract*, 22.

26. Ibid,. 23.

27. Ibid.

28. Ibid., 24.

29. Ibid., 46.

30. Ibid., 46–47.

31. Boyce, "Questions."

32. Boyce, *Abstract*, 50.

33. Boyce, "Questions."

34. Ibid.

35. Boyce, *Abstract*, 52.

36. Mark Matheson, "Religious Knowledge in the Theologies of John Leadley Dagg and James Petigru Boyce: With Special Reference to the Influence of Common Sense Realism," Ph.D. diss., Southwestern Baptist Theological Seminary, 1984, discusses Boyce's theory of religious knowledge. He views Boyce's dominant philosophical context as commonsense realism. This probably is largely true. He draws conclusions from this observation, however, that, while interesting and worthy of consideration, finally fall short of adequate demonstration. For example,

Matheson wrote, "Great confidence was placed in the conclusions of man's reasoning and natural theology, a confidence that did not take seriously the fall of man" (203). He concluded that Boyce's method gave him an "anthropocentric starting point" that compromised his commitment to divine revelation in favor of reason (203, 208). Concerning both Dagg and Boyce Matheson wrote, "While they both asserted that the Scriptures carried authority in religious matters and were a source of knowledge concerning God, they elevated the authority of man's reason to a status equal to that of the Scriptures" (208). Matheson criticized Boyce for preferring a "more objective, rational authority over a subjective, emotional authority" (208). Boyce believed that, even in the fallen state, the mind of man still was suited for the reception of information from a variety of sources and for devising schemes by which it might discern the truth or falsity of any number of claims and propositions. As the discussion has shown, and will show, Boyce gave full sway to the doctrine of depravity and the utter dependence sinners have on special revelation, contained in Scripture, for all knowledge of the saving work of Christ. The bulk of Boyce's theology is absolutely dependent on special revelation, with reason being used only to discern the meaning of words, sentences, arguments, and propositions and to discern the congruity of any proposed new revelation with past verified revelation.

37. Boyce, *Abstract*, 443–44.

38. Ibid., 54–65.

39. Ibid., 137.

40. Ibid.

41. Ibid., 459.

42. James P. Boyce, "Thus Saith the Lord," in *James Petigru Boyce: Selected Writings*, ed. Timothy George (Nashville: Broadman, 1989), 67.

43. Ibid., 70.

44. In addition to the evidence given above, this statement serves to show that Matheson's dissertation missed a substantial, in fact dominant, idea of Boyce's view of the relation of reason to revelation when he stated that Boyce elevated "the authority of man's reason to a status equal to that of the Scripture." See Matheson, "Religious Knowledge," 208.

45. Boyce, "Thus Saith the Lord," 71.

46. Ibid., 73.

47. Ibid.

48. J. P. Boyce, "The Doctrine of the Suffering of Christ," *Baptist Quarterly*, October 1870, 386.

49. Ibid., 385–86.

50. Boyce, "Thus Saith the Lord," 74.

51. Ibid., 74–76.

52. J. P. Boyce, "The Christian Ethical System: Its Nature, Its Basis, Its Exemplar, and the Motives to Its Obedience," handwritten manuscript bound with handwritten

sermons in the archives of Boyce Memorial Library, Southern Baptist Theological Seminary, Louisville, Kentucky.

53. Ibid.

54. Boyce, *Abstract*, 225.

55. Ibid., 214, 216, 224, 227, 231.

56. Ibid., 214.

57. Ibid., 226.

58. Ibid., 230–39.

59. Ibid., 244–45.

60. For an excellent discussion of how Boyce fits within the framework of Reformed thinkers on the issue of immediate and mediate imputation and other aspects of his doctrine of original sin see David Aaron Depp, "A Critical Evaluation of the Developments in the Doctrine of Original Sin as Taught at the Southern Baptist Theological Seminary," Ph.D. diss., Southeastern Baptist Theological Seminary, 2002, 30–78, esp. 44–52.

61. Boyce, *Abstract*, 249–51.

62. Ibid., 252.

63. Ibid., 400.

64. Ibid., 256–57. Mark Gstohl, "A Critical Analysis of the Doctrine of Original Sin in the Writings of Selected Southern Baptist Theologians," Ph.D. diss., New Orleans Baptist Theological Seminary, 2001, 26–57, claims that Boyce did not demonstrate from exegesis that Adam in any sense represented humanity covenantally. There is no covenant language and there is no explicit promise, and no evidence that Adam consented to a formal agreement of any kind. Gstohl criticizes Boyce's use of Galatians 4 in this context, because Paul described there a Mosaic covenant, not a covenant with Adam. Gstohl bases his analysis in part on the "Index of Allusions and Verbal Parallels" in the Greek text of the United Bible Society (42–45). Boyce, however, does not say Galatians 4 speaks of Adam, but sees it as a paradigm for discussing the biblical issues of law, covenant, curse, and death, especially if the context of Galatians 3 is taken into account. Life is promised in return for perfect obedience under the Mosaic covenant, this typifying the "covenant of works"; the law given to Moses does not differ from the law written on the heart of Adam, and so the assumption is that perfect obedience brings life (235–38).

Gstohl wanted Boyce to exegete "the passage in great detail" (46). For Boyce, however, the theological reflections drawn from all over Scripture brought to bear on the leading idea of Galatians 4:22–31 were exegesis, at least in the discussion of a point in systematic theology. Gstohl also criticizes Boyce's discussion of Romans 5 and 1 Corinthians 15, believing that he had assumed a theological construct as true before his exegesis of the pivotal passages (48–52). Gstohl strangely characterizes Boyce as believing that "persons who died between the time of Adam and Moses did not commit personal sin" (52). Boyce's point, however, was not that persons did not commit personal sin, but that death did not come because of personal sin, but because of Adam's representative position. Otherwise, why would infants die (257)?

Gstohl also criticizes Boyce's appeal to "the natural and common nature of the principle of representation" as the first element of his defense of covenant headship. On this last point, Gstohl shows his misunderstanding of, or perhaps lack of sympathy for, Boyce's theological method. Immediately subsequent to the statement of the natural acceptance of representation, Boyce gave numerous scriptural examples of the point. Gstohl also approves Matheson's criticism that Boyce focused on reason more than Scripture in his argument and had a "tendency toward overconfidence in the use of reason in his argumentation" (47). That misjudgment should be amply refuted by the discussion herein.

65. Boyce, *Abstract*, 347–48.

66. Ibid., 348.

67. Ibid., 353.

68. Ibid., 354.

69. Ibid., 364–65.

70. Ibid., 367.

71. Ibid., 372.

72. Boyce, "The Place and Power of Prayer," in *Selected Writings*, 85–95.

73. Boyce, "Christ Receiving and Eating with Sinners," in *Selected Writings*, 77–80.

74. Ibid., 81.

75. Ibid., 82.

76. Ibid., 83.

77. Ibid., 84.

78. Ibid.

79. Boyce, *Abstract*, 379.

80. Ibid., 381.

81. Ibid., 383–84.

82. Ibid., 388–89.

83. Ibid., 395.

84. Ibid. Boyce's presentation of the aggressive nature of God's providing such certainty in salvation, combined with his concept of the "voluntary character of God," shows the inadequacy of Walter Draughon's criticism that Boyce presents a God whose "sovereignty is separated from his grace" and that Boyce's view of atonement "involves, therefore a denial of God's freedom to respond to the needs of his creation." Draughon understood the concept of the necessity of the atonement as bringing about a division in the Godhead, with Christ, as our substitute, moving toward God, but God having no freedom to move. See Walter Draughon, "A Critical Evaluation of the Diminishing Influence of Calvinism on the Doctrine of Atonement in Representative Southern Baptist Theologians: James Petigru Boyce, Edgar Young Mullins, Walter Thomas Conner, and Dale Moody," Ph.D. diss., Southwestern Baptist Theological Seminary, 1987, 237–38.

85. Boyce, *Abstract*, 399.
86. Ibid., 400.
87. Ibid., 401.
88. Ibid., 409.
89. Ibid., 411–21.
90. Ibid., 423–24.
91. Ibid., 425, quoting Hodge, *Systematic Theology*, 3:555.
92. Ibid., 425.
93. Ibid.
94. Ibid., 426.
95. Ibid., 426–31.
96. Ibid., 426.
97. Boyce, "The Christian Ethical System," 20–21.
98. Boyce, *Abstract*, 433.
99. Ibid., 466–67.

Chapter 12: In Christ Alone

1. J. P. Boyce, "The Doctrine of the Suffering Christ," *Baptist Quarterly* 4, October 1870, 386.

2. J. P. Boyce, *Abstract of Systematic Theology* (Philadelphia: American Baptist Publication Society, 1887), 272.

3. J. P. Boyce, "A Brief Catechism of Bible Doctrine," in *Teaching Truth, Training Hearts*, ed. Tom J. Nettles (Amityville, NY: Calvary Press, 1998), 170.

4. Boyce, *Abstract*, 135–36.

5. Ibid., 136.

6. Ibid., 137.

7. Ibid., 127.

8. Benjamin Keach, *The Everlasting Covenant, A Sweet Cordial for a Drooping Soul* (London, 1693), 24.

9. John Gill, *A Collection of Sermons and Tracts*, 2 vols. (London: George Keith, 1773), 2:56–57. See also John Gill, *The Doctrine of the Trinity Stated and Vindicated* (London: George Keith, 1752), 150, and the entire chapter entitled "A Dissertation on the Eternal Sonship of Christ," in *Collection*, 2:534–64.

10. *Minutes of the Philadelphia Baptist Association* (Philadelphia: American Baptist Publication Society, 1851), 47–48.

11. John L. Dagg, *Manual of Theology* (Charleston: Southern Baptist Publication Society, 1857), 203–4.

12. Francis Turretin, *Institutes of Elenctic Theology*, trans. George Musgrave Giger, ed. James T. Dennison Jr., 3 vols. (Phillipsburg, NJ: P&R, 1992–97), 1:294.

13. Boyce, *Abstract*, 144.

14. Turretin, *Institutes*, 1:301.

15. Boyce, *Abstract*, 138.

16. Ibid., 144–45, 147f. Boyce quotes from Hodge, *Systematic Theology*, 1:474–76. Hodge's discussion covers pages 468–77.

17. James P. Boyce, "Questions for Recitation" in a theological notebook by William Harrison Williams at the Southern Baptist Theological Seminary, October 1861; *Abstract*, 125.

18. Boyce, "Questions," 105–6.

19. Boyce, *Abstract*, 142.

20. Ibid., 144–49.

21. Ibid., 143.

22. Boyce, "Questions," 112.

23. Boyce, *Abstract*, 152.

24. Ibid., 154–55.

25. Ibid., 162–66.

26. Ibid., 258.

27. Ibid., 261.

28. Ibid., 264.

29. Ibid., 271.

30. Ibid.

31. Boyce, "Questions," 90–91.

32. Boyce, "Catechism," 169–70.

33. Boyce, "Doctrine of the Suffering Christ," 389.

34. Boyce, *Abstract*, 274.

35. Ibid., 275.

36. Ibid., 275.

37. Boyce, "Catechism," 168–69.

38. J. P. Boyce, "The Christian Ethical System," handwritten manuscript in the archives of the J. P. Boyce Memorial Library at Southern Baptist Theological Seminary.

39. Boyce, *Selected Writings*, ed. Timothy George (Nashville: Broadman, 1989), 99.

40. Ibid.

41. Ibid., 100.

42. Boyce, "Ethical System."

43. Boyce, *Abstract*, 289.

44. Ibid., 288.

45. Ibid., 284.

46. Boyce, "Ethical System."

47. Boyce, *Abstract*, 289, 291.

48. Boyce, "Catechism," 172f.

49. Walter Draughon, "A Critical Evaluation of the Diminishing Influence of Calvinism on the Doctrine of Atonement in Representative Southern Baptist Theologians," Ph.D. diss., Southwestern Baptist Theological Seminary, 1987, 237.

50. Ibid., 238.

51. Boyce, *Abstract*, 386.
52. Draughon, "Critical Evaluation," 238f.
53. Boyce, *Abstract*, 317, 332f.
54. Ibid., 96.
55. Draughon, "Critical Evaluation," 239.
56. Boyce, *Abstract*, 435.
57. Draughon, "Critical Evaluation," 239.
58. Boyce, *Abstract*, 310.
59. Ibid., 317.
60. Ibid.
61. Ibid., 325.
62. Ibid., 328.
63. Ibid., 333f.
64. Ibid., 336.
65. Ibid., 337.
66. Ibid.
67. Ibid., 338f. Boyce quotes from A. A. Hodge, *Outlines of Theology*, 2d ed. (New York: Robert Carter and Bros, 1878), 416–17.
68. Ibid., 485.
69. Ibid., 340.

Chapter 13: The Dying of James Petigru Boyce

1. "Minutes of the Board of Trustees," Southern Baptist Theological Seminary, May 1887, 123.
2. Ibid., 125.
3. Ibid., 129.
4. Ibid., 131.
5. T. H. Pritchard, "Death of Dr. J. P. Boyce," *Biblical Recorder*, 4 January 1889, 3.
6. Boyce to Broadus, 12 October 1872, in Sean Michael Lucas with Jason Fowler, eds., "'Our Life Work': The Correspondence of James P. Boyce and John A. Broadus, Founders of the Southern Baptist Theological Seminary, 1857–1888" (unpublished volume in the archives of Southern Baptist Theological Seminary, 2004), 118 (hereafter L&F).
7. Boyce to Broadus, 4 November 1888, L&F, 120.
8. John A. Broadus, "Southern Baptist Theological Seminary," *Religious Herald*, 13 September 1888, 2.
9. John A. Broadus, *Memoir of James Petigru Boyce* (New York: A. C. Armstrong and Son, 1893), 314.
10. Boyce to Broadus, 24 September 1870, L&F, 92.
11. Boyce to Broadus, 1 June 1872, L&F, 116.
12. Boyce to Broadus, 17 April 1873, L&F, 141.
13. Broadus to Boyce, 19 March 1874, L&F, 157.

14. Boyce to Broadus, 3 March 1875; 9 March 1875; 24 January 1876; 11 December 1876, L&F, 194–95, 217, 269.

15. Broadus to Boyce, 9 December 1878, L&F, 326f.

16. Boyce to Broadus, 1 June 1879, L&F, 333.

17. Boyce to Broadus, 21 October 1882, L&F, 348.

18. Broadus, *Memoir*, 314.

19. Ibid.

20. Boyce to Broadus, 9 May 1885, L&F, 374.

21. David M. Ramsey, *James Petigru Boyce—God's Gentleman* (Nashville: Sunday School Board of the Southern Baptist Convention, n.d.), 8.

22. Boyce to Broadus, 26 March 1886, L&F, 382.

23. Broadus, *Memoir*, 367.

24. Telegram from Boyce to Broadus, 7 May 1885.

25. Ramsey, *James Petigru Boyce*, 9.

26. These quotations from Whitsitt's diary are taken from notes made by W. O. Carver. He had special permission and limited access to the 16-volume diary that, at Whitsitt's stipulation, was sealed for one hundred years, that is until January 2011. One historian, James H. Slatton was permitted access to the entire 16 volumes and has produced a biography of Whitsitt built largely on the diary: *W. H. Whitsitt: The Man and the Controversy* (Macon: Mercer University Press, 2009). On Whitsitt's antipathy to Boyce, and others, see chapter 7, pp. 103–22. Slatton's book was published shortly before this volume went to press.

27. Ramsey, *James Petigru Boyce*, 6.

28. Ibid., 8.

29. Boyce to Broadus, 12 August 1886, L&F, 389.

30. Broadus, *Memoir*, 328; Lizzie Boyce, "Stray Recollections of Dr. Boyce," 77.

31. Broadus, *Memoir*, 329; Lizzie Boyce, "Stray Recollections," 78.

32. Lizzie Boyce, "Stray Recollections," 75–76.

33. Broadus, *Memoir*, 318–19.

34. Broadus to Boyce, 5 June 1883, L&F, 349.

35. Boyce to Broadus, 2 April 1887, L&F, 397.

36. William A. Mueller, *A History of Southern Baptist Theological Seminary* (Nashville: Broadman, 1959), 50.

37. James P. Boyce, *Life and Death the Christian's Portion* (New York: Sheldon & Co; Richmond: Starke & Ryland; Tuscaloosa: Manly & Co., 1869), 55.

38. "Minutes of the Board of Trustees," May 1887, 126.

39. "Minutes of the Trustees," Southern Baptist Theological Seminary, May 1888, 136.

40. Broadus, *Memoir*, 319.

41. Boyce to Broadus, 8 June 1887, L&F, 398; Broadus, *Memoir*, 319.

42. Broadus, *Memoir*, 320.

43. John A. Broadus, "As to Dr. Boyce's Health," *Religious Herald*, 30 June 1887, 2.

44. "Boyce Will," Probate Court, Louisville, Kentucky.

45. Lizzie Boyce, "Stray Recollections," 25.

46. Boyce to Broadus, 28 August 1887, L&F, 399.

47. Ibid.

48. Boyce to Broadus, 18 September 1887, L&F, 401.

49. Boyce to Broadus, 30 November 1887.

50. Broadus, *Memoir*, 325.

51. P. V. Bomar, "The Moody Meetings," *The Seminary Magazine*, February 1888, 31.

52. J. F. Williams, "Local and Personal," *The Seminary Magazine*, February 1888, 37.

53. "Minutes of the Trustees," May 1888, 135.

54. *Proceedings of the Annual Meeting of the Southern Baptist Convention, 1888*, 7.

55. Broadus, *Memoir*, 327.

56. Lansing Burrows, "James Petigru Boyce," *Review and Expositor*, April 1907, 186–87.

57. Broadus, *Memoir*, 331.

58. Ibid., 333.

59. Lizzie Boyce, "Stray Recollections," 30.

60. Broadus, *Memoir*, 337.

61. Broadus to Boyce, 19 September 1888.

62. John A. Broadus, "Southern Baptist Theological Seminary," *Religious Herald*, 13 September 1888, 2.

63. Ibid.

64. Boyce to Broadus, 5 October 1888. *The Sword and Trowel* did not carry a review of the book in 1888 or 1889.

65. Boyce to Broadus, 5 October 1888, L&F, 410ff.

66. Boyce to Broadus, 31 October 1888, L&F, 421–26.

67. Boyce to Broadus, 5 October 1888, L&F, 410ff.

68. Broadus to Boyce, 17 October 1888, L&F, 414ff.

69. Boyce to Broadus, 31 October 1888, L&F, 421–26.

70. Boyce to Broadus, 5 October 1888, L&F, 410ff.

71. Broadus to Boyce, 17 October 1888, L&F, 414ff.

72. Broadus to Boyce, 20 October 1888, L&F, 417f.

73. Boyce to Broadus, 4 November 1888, L&F, 426.

74. Ibid. Boyce quoted from Virgil's *Eclogues*, "patulae recubans sub tegmine fagi."

75. Broadus, *Memoir*, 337.

76. A. T. Robertson, *Life and Letters of John Albert Broadus* (Philadelphia: American Baptist Publication Society, 1909), 372.

77. Broadus to Boyce, 24 October 1888, L&F, 418ff.

78. Boyce to Broadus, 8 November 1888, L&F, 431f.

79. "Minutes of the Board of Trustees," May 1887, 124.

80. Boyce to Broadus, 5 October 1888, L&F, 413–14.

81. Boyce to Broadus, 31 October 1888, L&F, 423–24. Broadus gives details. "It is proper to state that his wishes in this regard were of course very carefully carried out. The following year his daughters selected all the properly theological works, to the number of some five-thousand, and took great pains to complete the collection and classification of the immense mass of pamphlets and periodicals which he had gathered with loving care through life, and which are a treasure to the Seminary collection" (*Memoir*, 340). Two folio volumes in the archives of the Boyce Memorial Library at Southern Baptist Theological Seminary contain a list of all the works in Boyce's library. One volume contains the works listed by title and the second by author. Each contains close to 350 pages.

82. Broadus to Boyce, 17 October 1888, L&F, 414ff.

83. Broadus to Boyce, 20 October 1888, L&F, 417f.

84. Boyce to Broadus, 4 November 1888, L&F, 427.

85. Broadus, *Memoir*, 338.

86. Broadus to Boyce, 17 October 1888, L&F, 416.

87. Boyce to Broadus, 31 October 1888, L&F, 421–26.

88. Boyce to Broadus, 31 October 1888, L&F, 421–26. Broadus wrote, "The Memorial Library building was opened in May, 1890. It was carefully planned according to the best recent ideas and examples, and is one of the most beautiful, convenient, and every way satisfactory library buildings in existence. Its 'book-room' will hold sixty thousand volumes, and can be easily enlarged to more than double that space when necessary hereafter" (*Memoir*, 339).

89. Broadus to Boyce, 24 October 1888, L&F, 418–21.

90. Broadus to Boyce, 7 November 1888, L&F, 428.

91. Boyce to Broadus, 20 November 1888, L&F, 436.

92. Boyce to Broadus, 20 November 1888, L&F, 433–38.

93. Broadus, *Memoir*, 341.

94. Lizzie Boyce, "Stray Recollections," 90; Broadus, *Memoir*, 342.

95. Slatton, *W. H. Whitsitt*, 141.

96. "Theological Seminary," *Western Recorder*, 3 January 1889, 5.

97. W. H. Whitsitt, "Biographical Sketch of James P. Boyce, D. D., LL. D.", *The Seminary Magazine*, February, 1889, 38–42.

98. Ibid., 38.

99. Ibid., 39.

100. Ibid.

101. Ibid., 41.

102. Ibid., 42.

Chapter 14: Their Works Do Follow Them

1. *Greenville Daily News* as copied in *Baptist Courier*, 3 January 1889, 2.

2. Fragment of a newspaper from Chattanooga, dated Sunday, 30 December 1888, found in the J. P. Boyce file in the Southern Baptist Historical Library and Archives in Nashville, Tennessee.

3. *Augusta Chronicle*, as copied in *Baptist Courier*, 3 January 1889, 2.

4. P. I. Lipsey, "The Seminary in Mourning," *Southern Baptist Record*, 3 January 1889, 2.

5. John A. Broadus, *Memoir of James Petigru Boyce* (New York: A. C. Armstrong and Son, 1893), 342.

6. *Western Recorder*, 3 January 1889, 5.

7. J. A. Baunson, "A Great Man in Israel has Fallen," *Baptist Courier*, 3 January 1889, 2.

8. Fred D. Hale, "Fred D. Hale Not a Campbellite," *Western Recorder*, 7 July 1887, 5.

9. Ibid.

10. Ibid.

11. *Western Recorder*, 3 January 1889, 5.

12. Baunson, "A Great Man," 2.

13. *Western Recorder*, 3 January 1889, 5.

14. Ibid.

15. Ibid.

16. Ibid.

17. Lipsey, "The Seminary in Mourning."

18. William E. Hatcher, "Death of Dr. J. P. Boyce." Internal evidence determines that Hatcher wrote the article. Hatcher had served as pastor for twenty-six years at Grace Street Church in Richmond, Virginia, at the time and formerly had edited the *Religious Herald* of Virginia. This article, however, was printed in some other paper and discovered in the Boyce file in the Baptist Archives in Nashville. No bibliographical information was attached to the article.

19. J. A. French, "To the Editor," *Western Recorder*, 3 January 1889, 5.

20. T. T. Eaton, "Dr. James Pettigru [*sic*] Boyce," *Western Recorder*, 3 January 1889, 4.

21. James C. Furman, "Rev. James P. Boyce, D.D., LL.D." *Baptist Courier*, 3 January 1889, 2.

22. "Death of James P. Boyce, D. D., LL. D.," *Religious Herald*, 3 January 1889, 2.

23. Ibid.

24. Henry H. Tucker, "Death of Dr. Boyce," *Christian Index*, 3 January 1889, 8.

25. Ibid.

26. *Baptist Encyclopedia*, ed. William Cathcart, s.v. "Wingate, W. M."

27. T. H. Pritchard, "Death of Dr. J. P. Boyce," *Biblical Recorder*, 4 January 1889, 3.

28. Ibid., 10.

29. *Baptist Courier*, 17 January 1889, 2.

30. E. V. Baldy, "Funeral Services of Dr. Boyce," *The Christian Index*, 31 January 1889, 3.

31. L. O. Dawson, "The Shadow of Death," *The Seminary Magazine*, February 1889, 44.

32. Baldy, "Funeral Services."

33. Dawson, "Shadow of Death," 44.

34. Ibid., 44–45.

35. The list of platform personalities was included by Baldy in his report.

36. "Funeral of Dr. Boyce," *Christian Index*, 24 January 1889, 9.

37. Dawson, "Shadow of Death," 45.

38. *Christian Index*, 7 February 1889, 9.

39. Broadus, *Memoir*, 343.

40. Baldy, "Funeral Services."

41. Ibid.

42. Dawson, "Shadow of Death," 45.

43. Rabbi Moses, "An Israelite's Tribute," *The Seminary Magazine*, February 1889, 59–61.

44. Ibid., 59.

45. John A. Broadus, "Address of Dr. John A. Broadus at the Funeral of Jas. P. Boyce," *The Seminary Magazine*, February 1889, 50.

46. Ibid., 51–52.

47. Ibid., 53.

48. Broadus, *Memoir*, 346.

49. Alex P. Humphrey, "Address of Judge Alex P. Humphrey," *The Seminary Magazine*, February 1889, 54.

50. Ibid., 55.

51. Ibid., 56.

52. J. L. M. Curry, "Address of Dr. J. L. M. Curry," *The Seminary Magazine*, February 1889, 56.

53. Ibid., 58–59.

54. *Proceedings of the Southern Baptist Convention, 1889*, 22.

55. John A. Broadus, *A Treatise on the Preparation and Delivery of Sermons*, ed. Edwin Charles Dargan, 2d ed. (New York: Hodder and Stoughton, 1898).

56. William E. Hatcher, *Life of J. B. Jeter, D. D.* (Baltimore: H. M. Wharton, 1887).

57. Broadus, *Memoir*, 369.

58. Ibid., 370.

59. *Christian Index*, 7 February 1889, 9.

60. Boyce to Broadus, 24 September 1870, in Sean Michael Lucas with Jason Fowler, eds., "'Our Life Work': The Correspondence of James P. Boyce and John A. Broadus, Founders of the Southern Baptist Theological Seminary, 1857–1888" (unpublished volume in the archives of Southern Baptist Theological Seminary, 2004), 95.

61. Ibid., 349; Lizzie Boyce, "Stray Recollections," 2.

62. Broadus, *Memoir*, 351.

63. Ibid., 365.

64. Ibid., 362.

65. Ibid. 370.

66. Ibid., 371. The words are written as a prose paragraph. I have taken the liberty to arrange them in verse form.

67. Lansing Burrows, "James Petigru Boyce," *Review and Expositor*, April 1907, 173–89.

68. A. J. Holt, "Christ the Builder: Boyce the Builder," typescript of message delivered before the Southern Baptist Theological Seminary, 11 January 1922.

69. David M. Ramsey, *James Petigru Boyce—God's Gentleman* (Nashville: Sunday School Board of the Southern Baptist Convention, n.d.), 8.

70. Z. T. Cody, "James Petigru Boyce," *Review and Expositor*, April 1927, 145.

71. Ibid., 160–61.

72. Ibid., 163–66.

73. Timothy George, *James Petigru Boyce: Selected Writings* (Nashville: Broadman, 1989), 15. George did not access Cody's address, and thus thought that Ramsey's in 1924 was the last address given on Boyce.

74. Ibid., 19–25.

75. W. O. Carver, "Boyce-Kerfoot Systematic Theology," *Baptist Argus*, 14 September 1899, 588.

76. W. O. Carver, "Unpublished Notes," cited in William A. Mueller, *A History of Southern Baptist Theological Seminary* (Nashville: Broadman 1959), 57.

77. Cornell Goerner, "The Greatest Teacher I Knew," in *God's Glory in Missions: In Appreciation of William Owen Carver*, ed. John H. Johnson (private publication, 1985), 16.

78. W. O. Carver, *The Glory of God in the Christian Calling* (Nashville: Broadman, 1949), 36.

79. Ibid., 37.

80. Ibid., 38.

81. Ibid., 40.

82. W. O. Carver, *Christian Missions in Today's World* (Nashville: Broadman, 1942), 81.

83. Dale Moody, "Holding Fast That Which Is Good," in Johnson, ed., *God's Glory*, 94.

84. Frank Stagg, "As the Twig Is Bent . . . Theological Institutions and the J. P. Boyce Legacy," *Baptist Record*, 5 January 1995, 6.

85. Interoffice memo, Duke McCall to Dale Moody, 25 February 1980, in Dale Moody's file on "The Apostasy Controversy" in the archives at the James P. Boyce Memorial Library at Southern Baptist Theological Seminary.

86. Dale Moody, "Dale Moody's Doctrine of the Atonement," appendix to Walter Draughon, "A Critical Evaluation of the Diminishing Influence of Calvinism on the Doctrine of Atonement in Representative Southern Baptist Theologians," Ph.D. diss., Southern Baptist Theological Seminary, 1987, 272.

87. Stagg, "J. P. Boyce Legacy."

88. W. R. Estep, "Doctrines Lead to 'Dunghill,' Prof Warns," *Baptist Standard*, 26 March 1997, 12.

89. Presnall Wood, "Nothing Wrong with 'Whosoever Will,'" *Baptist Standard*, 16 August 1995, 6.

90. J. P. Boyce, "The Southern Baptist Theological Seminary," *Western Recorder*, 14 July 1866, 2.

91. E. Y. Mullins, *The Christian Religion in Its Doctrinal Expression* (Valley Forge, PA: Judson, 1917), vii. Also see Douglas Clyde Walker III, "The Doctrine of Salvation in the Thought of James Petigru Boyce, Edgar Young Mullins, and Dale Moody," Ph.D. diss., Southern Baptist Theological Seminary, 1986. Walker traced the soteriological shifts that took place from Boyce to Mullins and then finally to Moody. Boyce, he observed, was a consistent Calvinist in his views of salvation; Mullins, while maintaining some consistency with Calvinist ideas, made some substantial shifts in his views of the human will, the atonement, election, and the *ordo salutis* (212). Moody made the jump all the way to a self-conscious, aggressive Arminianism filtered through an acceptance of higher critical methods of biblical interpretation and an ongoing dialogue with a variety of twentieth-century theologians.

92. W. T. Conner, *The Gospel of Redemption* (Nashville: Broadman, 1945), 76. Conner quotes Boyce's *Abstract of Systematic Theology*, 297.

93. Ibid., 93; citation of Boyce, 287–88.

94. Ibid., 95; citation of Boyce, 289.

95. Dale Moody, *The Word of Truth* (Grand Rapids: Eerdmans, 1981), 65–67, 322, 328, 343–65, etc.; also Moody, "Seminary Professor Answers Arkansas Critics," *Western Recorder*, 8 December 1982, 10. See also "Moody Defends Apostasy Position," *Baptist Record*, 9 December 1982, 6.

96. R. Albert Mohler Jr., *Don't Just Do Something, Stand There! Southern Seminary and the Abstract of Principles* (Louisville: n.p., 1993), 12.

97. Ibid., 13.

98. R. Albert Mohler Jr., "Abstract of Principles Provides Theological Accountability," *Baptist Record*, 19 January 1995, 6.

99. Molly Marshall, "A Ministry of Dissent," *Baptists Today*, 4 May 1995, 4.

100. R. Albert Mohler Jr., *For Such a Time as This: The Southern Baptist Theological Seminary and the Future of Theological Education* (Louisville: n.p., 1993), 9–10.

101. R. Albert Mohler Jr., *"To Train the Minister Whom God Has Called": James P. Boyce and Southern Baptist Theological Education* (Louisville: n.p., n.d.), 15.

102. Ibid., 17.

Index